HOSPITALITY MANAGEMENT AND ORGANISATIONAL BEHAVIOUR

HOSPITALITY MANAGEMENT AND ORGANISATIONAL BEHAVIOUR

Fourth edition

Laurie J Mullins

Longman

Pearson Education Limited
Edinburgh Gate
Harlow
Essex CM20 2JE, England
and Associated Companies throughout the world

First published (published as *Hospitality Management: A human resources approach*) 1998
Second edition 1995
Reprinted 1996, 1997
Third edition (published as *Managing People in the Hospitality Industry*) 1998
Fourth edition (published as *Hospitality Management and Organisational Behaviour*) 2001

ISBN 0 582 43225 1

British Library Cataloguing-in-Publication Data

A catalogue record for this book is available from the British Library.

Set by 35 in 9.5/12.5pt Garamond
Printed in Malaysia by VVP

Contents

About the author

Laurie Mullins was a principal lecturer in the Department of Business and Management, University of Portsmouth, where he specialised in teaching Managerial and Organisational Behaviour and Managing People at Work to Business and Hospitality Management students. He has been a regular contributor of numerous articles in a variety of professional journals and is also author of the best-selling *Management and Organisational Behaviour*, published by Financial Times Pitman Publishing.

Laurie has undertaken a range of consultancy work and acted as adviser and tutor for a number of professional and educational bodies. He also has considerable experience as an external examiner for university degree and postgraduate courses, and professional organisations.

Laurie completed a year's academic exchange as visiting professor in the Management Department, Univerisity of Wisconsin, USA, and has also given invited lectures to hospitality audiences in Holland and South Africa. Recently, Laurie was invited as a visiting fellow for a semester at the Royal Melbourne Institute of Technology University, Australia.

In acknowledgement and appreciation

A very special tribute is due again to my wife Pamela, children and family for their continuing interest, encouragement and support. I also wish to record my gratitude and thanks to the following for their valuable contribution to this fourth edition:

- Gordon Oliver and colleagues at the Department of Business and Management, University of Portsmouth, with a particular acknowledgement to Derek Adam-Smith, Gary Akehurst, Gerry Banks and Karen Meudell.

- Martin Brunner, Independent Consultant.

- Xiangping Bo, International Business School of Hunan University, China.

- Nigel Maggs-Oosterhagen, Highbury College, Portsmouth.

- Nicky Hayward, Proprietor of The Seaview Hotel and Restaurant, Isle of Wight, for permission to reproduce extracts from the Business Excellence Model in small hotels.

- Sandra Jones, Director Higher Education General Programs, School of Management, RMIT University, Australia

- Hotel and Catering International Management Association.

- British Quality Foundation.

- Those hospitality managers who have kindly given permission to reproduce information from their own organisation, including Linda Astbury, Marilyn Harding-Brown, Tim Chudley, Tim Gates, Andrea McIntyre, Marie Pollock, Chis Kelsall, Janet Richardson, Jane Neil and Pat Perridge.

- Colleagues at Pearson Education – especially Jill Jones, Judith Harvey, Sonia Wilson and Eva Martinez – for their enthusiasm, encouragement and valued support for this fourth edition.

I am also grateful to those who gave permission to reproduce copyright material. Every effort has been made to give references for sources of work by other writers but I apologise to any concerned if acknowledgement has inadvertently not been recorded. Should there be any queries, errors or omissions, please contact the publisher.

LAURIE J. MULLINS

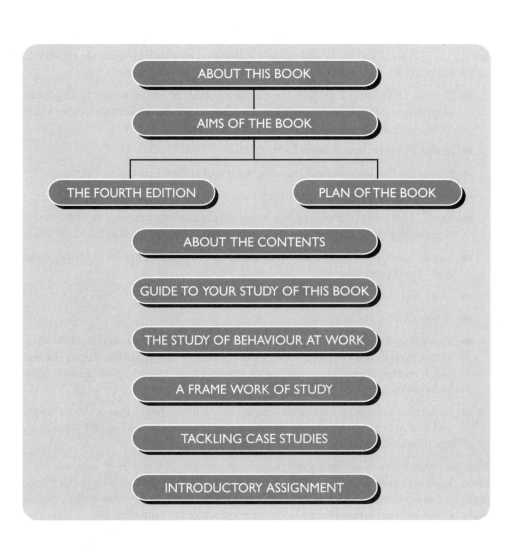

ABOUT THIS BOOK

AIMS OF THE BOOK

THE FOURTH EDITION

PLAN OF THE BOOK

ABOUT THE CONTENTS

GUIDE TO YOUR STUDY OF THIS BOOK

THE STUDY OF BEHAVIOUR AT WORK

A FRAME WORK OF STUDY

TACKLING CASE STUDIES

INTRODUCTORY ASSIGNMENT

Chapter one

Introduction: setting the scene

Introduction

However the nature of the hospitality industry is viewed, it is an inescapable fact that organisational performance is ultimately all about its members of staff. The concepts and ideas presented in this book provide you with a basis for the critical analysis of the structure and management of hospitality organisations, and interactions among people who work in them. This introductory chapter explains the main features of the book, provides a framework of study, and sets the scene to encourage a greater awareness and understanding of hospitality management and organisational behaviour.

About this book

The central theme of this book is improved organisational performance through the effective management of human resources. **This involves an understanding of individual and group behaviour in organisations, and factors influencing the effective management of people.** There is frequent debate about the true nature of management and whether managers are born or made; or whether management is an art or a science. The answer to either question is surely a combination of both. Even if there are certain innate qualities which make for a potentially good manager, these natural talents require encouragement and development. Clearly managers require competence in the fundamental skills and techniques required for effective operational performance. But management must always remain at least something of an art especially insofar as it involves personal judgement and dealing with people.

There are many aspects to management but the one essential ingredient of any successful manager is the ability to handle people effectively. Management is very much a human activity and managerial style can be as important as managerial competence.[1]

In recent years there has been a general movement towards flatter organisation structures, flexible working and greater employee involvement. In the general business world
this has placed increasing emphasis on an integrating/participative style of management
rather than a hierarchical/controlling style. To what extent this applies to hospitality organisations is in part for you, the reader, to judge.

The title of 'hospitality' has become increasingly popular as a generic term to cover
a wide range of different sectors within the hotel and catering industry, and sometimes
associated industries. The use of terminology varies and headings are subject to different
interpretation. But whatever the headings no one book of manageable size could hope to
cover adequately all sectors of the industry or all aspects of such a wide and diverse area
of study. In order to attain a reasonable depth, the book concentrates on selected topics
of particular relevance to the effective organisation of work and an understanding of the
behaviour and management of people. This is supported with specific hospitality contexts,
situations and examples.

Aims of the book

The aims of this book are to:

- indicate ways in which performance may be improved through the better use of
  human resources;
- examine the relevance and applications of general management theory and principles to hospitality organisations;
- present an integrated view embracing both theory and practice;
- balance academic rigour with a pragmatic approach to the subject area.

An important underlying philosophy is that getting work done through the efforts of other
people is an integral part of any managerial activity. The personnel/human resource
management function is part of the generality of management, and all managers and
supervisors have a responsibility for the management of people.

Within the scope of this book it is clearly not possible to provide detailed coverage of
all aspects influencing the effective management of people. Rather, the intention is to enhance
understanding and appreciation of the subject area, and to suggest to the reader an analytical framework in which you may think about what has been read and explore specific
applications within the hospitality industry.

There are many ways of seeing organisations.[2] This book concentrates on the nature
and structure of work organisations, the process of management and styles of managerial
behaviour, and achieving results through the efforts of other people. Certain organisational
processes, for example delegation and recruitment and selection, require managers to give
attention to basic principles and procedures. Accordingly, the objective analysis of hospitality operations is supported, where appropriate, by a more prescriptive stance to the execution of work.

It is intended that this book will appeal to students at undergraduate, professional or
post-experience level who are aspiring to a managerial position. It is also hoped that the
book will appeal to practising managers and supervisors who wish to extend their knowledge of the subject area.

The book provides a basis for the critical appraisal of organisational and managerial processes which influence the behaviour and performance of people in the hospitality industry.

Hopefully this will encourage you to be more aware of, and sensitive to, the importance of the effective management of human resources – that is, the management of people.

The fourth edition

- **A particular feature of this edition is the accompanying website to be found at:www.booksites.net/mullins**

- The change in the title of this edition is intended to reflect more closely the importance of the process of management and applications of organisational behaviour for the better use of human resources and improved performance.

- The book retains the same underlying approach, and carries forward the same overall framework and structure, which has been a successful hallmark of previous editions.

- There are, however, changes to the sequencing of certain chapters. There is a general review and update of material and rationalisation of the contents.

- Building on the strengths of the previous editions, there is additional contemporary material of particular interest to hospitality students and practising managers, including cases, practical commentaries and vignettes, and practical examples.

- There is now a fuller and more detailed list of contents of the book, and each chapter starts with an outline plan of main contents.

- There are over 120 revised, updated or new references.

- A significant addition to the fourth edition is the supporting pack of OHT masters of figures from the text. **Copies of these will also be available on the website.**

- Continuing attention to the overall layout and presentation should further enhance the appeal and user friendliness of this latest edition.

Plan of the book

About the contents

- Chapter 2 considers the nature of the hospitality industry, and its characteristic and distinctive features. Attention is given to ways in which ideas from general management theory and practice could be applied with advantage to the industry.

- Chapter 3 looks at organisational behaviour and people as the central focus of effective management. If managers are to improve their performance they need an understanding of what influences the behaviour and actions of people at work.

- Chapters 4 and 5 study the nature of management as the cornerstone of the people –organisation relationship. Chapter 4 explores the process of management through which the activities of the hospitality organisation are carried out. Management is essentially an integrating activity which permeates every facet of hospitality operations. Chapter 5 explores the nature of the manager–subordinate relationship as a central component of effective hospitality operations. The behaviour of managers and their style of management will influence the effort and performance of members of staff.

● Chapter 6 studies the development of organisation theory which has highlighted the importance of structural design and the management of human resources. It is by means of structure that the work of the hospitality organisation is actually carried out.

● Chapter 7 examines those areas that motivate staff to work well and promote staff satisfaction. Managers achieve results through the efforts of other people, and the ability to motivate staff to work willingly and effectively is an essential ingredient of successful management.

● Chapters 8 and 9 provide an understanding of work groups as a major feature of organisational life, and the meaning and nature of the leadership relationship. Chapter 8 reviews the operation of groups and the need for effective teamwork. Individuals seldom work in isolation from others. Groups are an essential feature of the structure of hospitality operations and improved organisational performance. Chapter 9 explores the nature of managerial leadership. An essential part of the management process lies in coordinating and directing the efforts of members of staff. This entails the process of leadership and choice of an appropriate style of behaviour.

● Chapter 10 studies the personnel/HRM function as an integral part of the process of management and effective use of people. Proper attention to the personnel/HRM function will help to improve the efficiency of the workforce and level of organisational performance.

● Chapter 11 examines arrangements for carrying out organisational processes and the execution of work. In order for the hospitality organisation to function effectively the activities of its members need to be channelled and guided towards corporate goals and objectives.

● Chapter 12 concludes with a review of dimensions of organisational effectiveness and improved work performance. The hospitality organisation is not only a work organisation, it is a also complex social system, and managers need to understand those factors which influence the successful management of people.

Guide to your study of this book

This book adopts an applied approach to the analysis of concepts and theories of organisation and management, and their relevance to hospitality operations. You should not be confused by the use of the word 'theory'. Most rational decisions are based on some form of underlying theory which contains a message on how managers might behave. This will influence attitudes towards management practice and lead to change in actual behaviour. Theory helps in the building of generalised models applicable to a range of different organisational situations. It further provides a conceptual framework and gives a perspective for the practical study of the subject. Theory and practice are inseparable. Together they lead to an improved understanding of patterns of behaviour in organisations and applications of the process of management.[3]

The format of the book is clearly structured and written with a minimum of technical terminology. Each chapter is fully supported with diagrams and contains:

- an outline plan of the chapter and a brief introduction;
- a summary of key points;
- review and discussion questions;
- practical assignments and/or case studies; and
- comprehensive notes and references.

There is a logical flow to the sequence of topic areas with appropriate cross-referencing between chapters. However, each chapter is self-contained, and the selection and order of chapters can be varied to suit personal preferences or the demands of your particular course of study. Main sections are identified clearly with detailed headings and sub-headings.

The use of separate topic areas is a recognised academic means of aiding study and explanation of the subject area. However, in practice the activities of an organisation and the process of management cannot be isolated neatly into discrete categories. The majority of actions are likely to involve a number of simultaneous functions relating to the total process of management. The topic areas in this book should not be regarded therefore as entirely free standing.

A feature of your studies is the invariable difficulty in identifying one right answer to a particular situation or problem area. There is no single truth and this can make study of the subject area potentially frustrating for some people. But it can also be interesting and challenging, and stimulate creative thought and healthy academic debate. For example, the views of the author on the role of the social sciences and the need for vocational relevance (Chapter 3) are in part challenged by Wood.[4] Readers who wish to pursue further this debate are likely to achieve a deeper appreciation of the use of social sciences for hospitality management.[5]

The review and discussion questions provide a basis for revision, and a test of your understanding and knowledge of the chapter contents. The questions, assignments and case studies provide an opportunity to think about the major issues of each chapter, and to discuss and compare views with colleagues.

The notes and references at the end of each chapter should help you to pursue further any issues of particular interest. In order to provide more detailed and specific referencing, and to keep the main text uncluttered, a simple numbering system has been chosen. This system appears to be favoured by most readers. The thoughts and ideas of other people are not always distinguishable clearly from one's own. While I have made every effort to give references to the work of other writers, I apologise to any concerned if acknowledgement has inadvertently not been recorded.

You are encouraged to complement your reading of the book by drawing upon your own practical experience. Search for good and bad strategies and examples of the management of people within the hospitality industry, and consider reasons for their apparent success or failure.

The study of behaviour at work

The systematic study of the behaviour of people at work is a comparatively recent development and terminology is not always consistent. The wording 'organisational behaviour' has, however, become increasingly accepted as a means of referring to the study of the behaviour

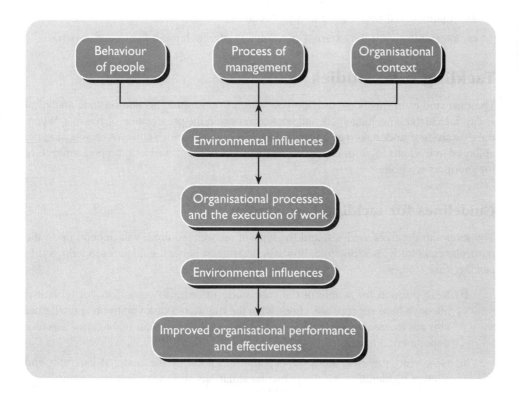

Figure 1.1:
A basic
framework
of study

of people within an organisational setting. It involves the understanding, prediction and control of human behaviour and the factors which influence the performance of people as members of an organisation.[6] It provides a behavioural approach to management.

Strictly, organisational behaviour is a misnomer because rarely do all members of a hotel (or any other work organisation) behave collectively in such a way as to represent the behaviour of the hotel as a whole. In practice we are usually referring to the behaviour and actions of individuals or a small group of people. For example, when we talk about a caring organisation we are usually referring to the philosophy, attitudes and actions of particular managers or even an individual manager. Nevertheless, the wording 'organisational behaviour' has become widely accepted and is found increasingly in literature and textbooks on hospitality management. 'Organisational behaviour' is a convenient form of shorthand to refer to the multiplicity of interrelated influences on the behaviour of people within formal organisations.

A framework of study

The study of organisational behaviour involves consideration of interactions among members of staff, the formal structure, the tasks to be undertaken, the technology employed and methods of carrying out work, the process of management and the external environment. This provides a basic but convenient framework of study (Figure 1.1) which embraces an understanding of:

- the behaviour of people;
- the process of management;
- the organisational context in which the process of management takes place;

- organisational processes and the execution of work; and
- interactions with the external environment of which the organisation is part.

Tackling case studies

The case studies in this book provide you with an opportunity to demonstrate analytical ability, logical thinking, judgement and persuasiveness in the presentation of answers. Where the case study is undertaken as a group exercise, it also provides a means of assessing the ability of individuals to work effectively as members of the group and the performance of the group as a whole.

Guidelines for tackling case studies

The level and depth of analysis, and the type of answer required, will depend upon the particular case study. It is possible, however, to suggest general guidelines to help you in tackling case studies.

(i) Read through the whole of the case study in order to get a 'feel' for what it is about. Where appropriate, check what the question(s) ask you to do and whether you are to assume a specific role, for example the general manager or a senior departmental manager.

(ii) Now read the case study a second time. Look at the material carefully and attempt to identify with the particular situations and the characters involved.

(iii) Approach your analysis of the case study with an open mind. Avoid any pre-dispositions which may influence your perception of the case material. Do not formulate hard opinions until you have collated all the available evidence. And do not jump to hasty or unfounded conclusions.

(iv) Adopt a brainstorming approach and take the case apart by exploring all reasonably possible considerations. You may need to search for hidden meanings and issues which are not at first readily apparent. Remember there may be a number of separate or related matters and a number of alternative courses of action.

(v) A particular feature of case study work is that you are likely to have only limited information. You should, therefore, make a point of studying all the details in order, firstly to make certain of the facts, and secondly to identify what deductions or inferences can be drawn from these facts. It will probably be necessary to make certain assumptions which should follow *reasonably* from the case material and serve to clarify the situation. *Make clear any necessary, reasonable assumptions as part of your answer.*

(vi) The case study may set out deliberately to present a tangle of information, events or situations which need to be unravelled. Attempt to clarify links and relationships, and to distinguish causes from effects. Concentrate on what you see to be the most important matters.

(vii) Where appropriate, relate your analysis of the case material to your studies and reading, general points of principle and relevant practical experience.

(viii) Consider how the use of visual displays such as diagrams, charts or tables may enhance the presentation of your answer. But do not be tempted to use visual displays just for their own sake, and make sure they are meaningful, accurate and clear.

(ix) Draw up a plan of key points as the basis for your answer. Identify clearly existing or potential difficulties or problem areas. Where you have identified a number of possible courses of action, indicate where you see the need for most urgent action and your recommended priorities. Bear in mind practical considerations such as priorities and timing, costs, existing personalities and likely effects on staff.

(x) Where appropriate, include a list of references and/or a bibliography.

General principles and prescriptions relating to the process of management apply equally to all forms of hospitality organisations. However, it is important to bear in mind, for example, the context of the particular organisational setting within which the process of management actually takes place (Chapter 2), and the nature of individual differences and cultural influences (Chapter 3).

Many of the cases in this book are deliberately pragmatic, and based on actual events and situations. Nevertheless, they also provide an opportunity to explore potential links with related theoretical concepts and may be developed to draw out and illustrate particular points of interest as a basis for further discussion.

Introductory assignment

Meet in small self-selecting groups, and discuss and compare:

- what exactly you understand by the term 'organisational behaviour'; and
- the particular difficulties associated with the study of organisational behaviour and managing people at work.

From your own experience, give practical examples of:

- the behaviour of people;
- the process of management;
- the organisational context; and
- environmental influences

which illustrate applications of organisational behaviour and the management of people in the hospitality industry.

Introductory case study I

Winston Chua
South Avenue
Singapore

Dear Laurie

I am a former Hotel and Catering Management degree student who graduated last year. I'm now working for a company that is relatively new. It has just recently taken over a restaurant chain with three outlets and at the moment running just one of them. The second outlet will be taken over in two months' time and the third in another two months. My job is like a trouble-shooter. I will be overseeing the operations of the three outlets and literally report any trouble and try to resolve it. I will be liaising closely with the Board of Directors and the outlet managers. The directors tell me what they ▷

expect of the company. I formulate this in writing and pass it down to the outlet managers. The managers then relay any messages they wish to communicate with the directors through me. In other words, I am very much like an Operations Manager, or a General Manager of sorts.

My problem is this. I am able to get along well with the directors and managers as at the moment we have only one outlet. I spend two-thirds of my time in the restaurant and the remaining time at the office (they are at different places) doing my paperwork such as formulating a standard operating procedure for service and kitchen staffs. I get certain resentment from some of the staff – maybe they think that I should spend more time on the floor, which I cannot commit myself to. In four months' time when I am running the three outlets I can hardly dedicate two-thirds of my time on just one of them. Furthermore, I am a little bit behind on my paperwork. So how do I resolve this staff resentment problem? (And I am the one supposed to be a trouble-shooter!!)

TASKS

Working in small self-selecting groups, draft a suitable letter in reply giving your advice and recommended courses of action.

Introductory case study 2: The King's Restaurant

John Hill is the restaurant manager who has been employed at ABC Hotel for the last three years. He is quite good at his job, even though he only attended one catering course at the beginning of his management career. He has tried to convey an image of an experienced restaurant manager.

Mario Tazzi is an Italian waiter who is working under Hill's guidance. He has been involved with restaurants all his life, being the son of a restaurant owner. Tazzi lives in England with his attractive wife, who also works at the hotel as a silver service waitress.

Mrs Tazzi speaks very little English but she is a very charming person and many customers have told Hill how pleased they were with the way she served them at table.

A few weeks before Mr and Mrs Tazzi were employed in the King's Restaurant, Mr Hill introduced a young woman from his home town to the hotel general manager, Mr Fulbright, and this woman – Susan Green – was employed as a waitress.

Up to the time of the Tazzis' arrival Hill used to see a lot of Miss Green, and as he was in charge of allotting the shifts he always made sure that Susan worked on the same shift as he did so that they could leave the restaurant together.

Mr Fulbright received some complaints from a number of customers eating in the restaurant who said that Hill was stuck up and that Susan did not know her job at all.

Mr Fulbright called Hill to his office and told him that he had some complaints about the service in the restaurant but he did not mention that people had complained about Mr Hill's attitude, nor had Hill ever told Fulbright of the way that some customers praised Mrs Tazzi.

During the meeting they could not pinpoint the cause of the trouble, but they decided that Mrs Tazzi should change her shift with Susan so that Mr and Mrs Tazzi would not be on the same shift.

A week after this change Susan went up to Mario who had been working on her shift and told him that John Hill was having an affair with his wife.

Source: Reproduced, with amendments, from *BACIE Case Studies for Practical Training*, with the permission of the British Association for Commercial and Industrial Education.

Notes and references

1. For a fuller discussion, see Mullins L J, *Management and Organisational Behaviour*, 5th edn, Financial Times Pitman Publishing (1999).
2. See, for example, Guerrier Y, *Organizational Behaviour in Hotels and Restaurants: An International Perspective*, John Wiley & Sons (1999).
3. See, for example, Billsberry J (ed.), 'There's Nothing So Practical As a Good Theory: How Managers Become More Effective', *The Effective Manager: Perspectives and Illustrations*, Sage Publications (1996), pp. 1–27.
4. Wood R C, *Organizational Behaviour for Hospitality Management*, Butterworth Heinemann (1994), p. 184.
5. See, for example, Carmouche R and Kelly N, *Behavioural Studies in Hospitality Management*, Chapman & Hall (1995).
6. Luthans F, *Organizational Behaviour*, 7th edn, McGraw-Hill (1995).

```
                    THE HOSPITALITY INDUSTRY

                 GENERAL MANAGEMENT THEORY

                  THE ORGANISATIONAL SETTING

         ORGANISATIONAL AND STAFFING CHARACTERISTICS

                  SMALL-SIZE ESTABLISHMENTS

                THE NATURE OF SERVICE INDUSTRIES
                                |
            Are service industries different from other industries?

                      SERVICE MANAGEMENT

              THE OPEN SYSTEMS MODEL OF ANALYSIS

       Applications to          |          Environmental
     hospitality management     |            influences

     Analysis of hospitality    |          The socio-technical
          operations            |              approach

                    ORGANISATIONAL GOALS

           ORGANISATIONAL IDEOLOGIES AND PHILOSOPHY

                      THE PROFIT MOTIVE

     Multiple performance       |        Social responsibilities
          objectives            |            of management

                     CORPORATE STRATEGY

                          APPENDIX
```

Chapter two

The nature of the hospitality industry

Introduction

The hospitality industry does have a number of characteristic features, but it also shares important common features with other business industries and faces the same general problems of organisation and management. Attention should be given to ways in which ideas drawn from general management theory and practice can be applied with advantage to the industry.[1]

The hospitality industry

In recent years the term 'hospitality' has become increasingly popular as an all-embracing nomenclature for a larger grouping of organisations including hotels. As a collective term, the hospitality industry may be interpreted in a number of ways. For example according to an HCTC Report it 'includes hotels, restaurants, pubs, clubs, cafes, guest houses, contract catering, public sector, industrial, hospital, education and leisure catering'.[2] The hospitality industry may also be divided into two major sector headings: commercial, and industrial and public services.

Commercial

- accommodation;
- meals;
- licensed trade;
- tourism and travel.

Industrial and Public Services

- industrial;
- public services; and
- hospitals and residential homes.[3]

An alternative way of dividing the industry is suggested by Hornsey and Dann who 'for the sake of convenience' use four headings:

- the hotel sector (hotels, restaurants, pubs and clubs);
- industrial catering;

- institutional catering and domestic services; and
- fast food.[4]

Although there are some common factors among the different divisions, and some movement of staff from one division to another, the hospitality industry comprises separate and distinct sectors. The hotel sector and the catering sector, for example, are in many respects entirely different businesses and each is worthy of separate study.

But what is hospitality?

From a survey of the literature for the historical and sociological bases of hospitality, King describes hospitality in general as having four attributes:

- a relationship between individuals who take the roles of host and guest;
- this relationship may be commercial or private (social);
- the keys to successful hospitality in both the commercial and private spheres include knowledge of what would evoke pleasure in the guest; and
- hospitality as a process that includes arrival, providing comfort and fulfilment of the guest's wishes, and departure.

King suggests that commercial hospitality has several key elements that must be included in a model of hospitality including host-employee and guest-customer who are involved in face-to-face interactions[5] (see Figure 2.1).

Figure 2.1: Hospitality model

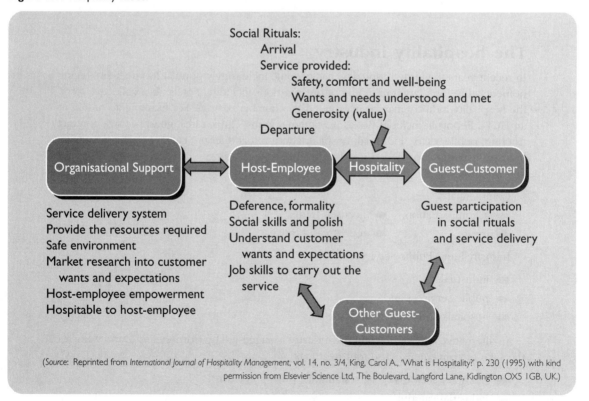

Social Rituals:
  Arrival
  Service provided:
    Safety, comfort and well-being
    Wants and needs understood and met
    Generosity (value)
  Departure

Organisational Support ⟷ **Host-Employee** ◁ Hospitality ▷ **Guest-Customer**

Service delivery system
Provide the resources required
Safe environment
Market research into customer
  wants and expectations
Host-employee empowerment
Hospitable to host-employee

Deference, formality
Social skills and polish
Understand customer
  wants and expectations
Job skills to carry out the
  service

Guest participation
in social rituals
and service delivery

Other Guest-Customers

(*Source:* Reprinted from *International Journal of Hospitality Management*, vol. 14, no. 3/4, King, Carol A., 'What is Hospitality?' p. 230 (1995) with kind permission from Elsevier Science Ltd, The Boulevard, Langford Lane, Kidlington OX5 1GB, UK.)

From insights of the natural processes of hospitality relevant to modern commercial hospitality organisations, Guerrier explains the provision of hospitality as:

- providing basic human needs for food, drink and somewhere to sleep for people who are not regular members of the family;
- rewarding hosts by enhanced prestige in the community if they provide lavish hospitality to guests; and
- an exchange for the mutual benefit of the host and the guest.[6]

General management theory

Managers in hotels and catering tend often to view the industry as unique, to regard it as somehow special and unlike any other industry. But to what extent is such a view justified? According to Fearn, writing in 1971, management in the hotel and catering industry has not developed at the same pace as in other industries:

little progress has been made in terms of management attitudes, knowledge and thinking. When one considers the astounding management progress in industries which have been created during this century it is difficult to account for the lack of progress and change in the hotel and catering industry.[7]

Developments have clearly been made since that time and increasing emphasis is being placed on ways in which ideas drawn from general management theory may be applied to the industry.[8] There is, however, still a long way to go. For example, Medlik makes the point that 'only limited progress has been made in the translation of business and management theory from manufacturing to service industries generally and to hotels in particular'.[9]

What then are the reasons for lack of management progress and change? Is it because the hospitality industry is significantly different from other industries and therefore defies meaningful comparison?

Hospitality education and research

From a review of the present development of hospitality education and research, Jones poses the question: 'Is there such a thing as hospitality research?' to which he suggests the answer is an unequivocal 'Yes'. However, Jones also goes on to argue that hospitality research is not truly discrete and distinctive, and there is little work that does not derive from other disciplines.[10]

Focusing on the nature of academic research within UK hospitality management, Taylor and Edgar take the view that there is some evidence that hospitality research is still somewhat embryonic and although considerable progress may have been made in recent years in terms of both the quantity and quality of research, the field has yet to reach a state of maturity.[11]

From a survey of 156 books and articles on organisational behaviour and human resource management in the hospitality industry, Guerrier and Deery conclude that researches are primarily engaged in applying mainstream ideas to the hospitality industry rather than influencing mainstream research. The industry provides a wonderful environment in which to explore current issues in organisational studies and human resource management. However, although there is a considerable body of knowledge about hospitality management, even here there are gaps and compared with the rhetoric little is known about the real nature of management work.[12]

So is the hospitality industry unique?

A number of writers suggest a strong case for viewing the hospitality industry as 'unique'.[13] However, it can also be argued strongly that every industry is of course unique in the strict sense of the word. The important point is that all industries share common features but they also differ in many important respects.

Accordingly, the questions to be examined are:

(i) What are the common features that the hospitality industry shares with other industries?

(ii) To what extent is the industry different in significant respects from other industries? and

(iii) Are these differences sufficient to mark the hospitality industry as unique, and to restrict the application of general management theory and practice?

In order to examine these questions we need some perspective in which to attempt a meaningful comparison of hospitality operations with those in other industries. We need to consider the nature of the organisational setting.

The organisational setting

The process of management does not take place in a vacuum but within the context of an organisational setting. Organisations are diverse and come in all forms, shapes and sizes. The structure, management and functioning of organisations will vary because of differences in their nature and type, goals and objectives, external environment, goods and/or services supplied, customers, and the behaviour of people who work in them.

By way of an extreme example let us consider just two types of organisation towards the opposite ends of a possible continuum – say a maximum security prison and a university largely concerned with research – as a framework within which to focus our attention. We can appreciate readily that, although both types of organisation will be concerned with the basic activities of management, their actual procedures and methods of operation, structure, systems and styles of management, and orientation and behaviour of members will differ considerably.

We can therefore bear such a comparison in mind when exploring both the general and distinctive features within the organisational setting of the hospitality industry.

Common factors in organisations

Despite the differences among various organisations there are, however, at least four common factors in any work organisation:

- people;
- structure;
- objectives;
- management.

It is the interaction of **people** in order to achieve **objectives** which forms the basis of an organisation. Some form of **structure** is needed by which people's interactions and efforts are channelled and coordinated. It is through the process of **management** that the activities of the organisation and the efforts of its members are directed towards the pursuit of objectives.

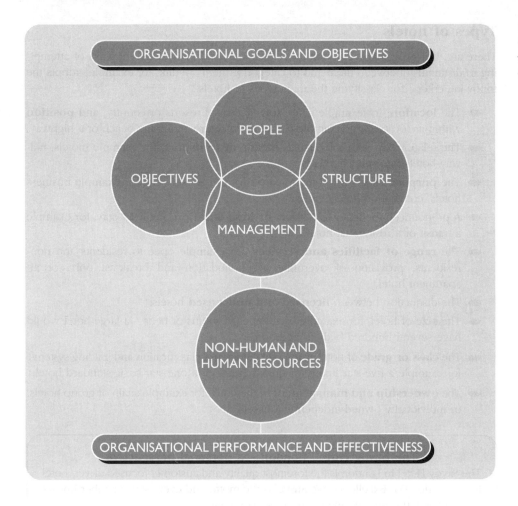

Figure 2.2:
Common
factors in work
organisations

The effectiveness of the organisation will depend upon the quality of its people, its object-ives and structure, and the resources available to it. There are two broad categories of resources:

- **non-human** – physical assets, materials, equipment and facilities; and
- **human** – members' abilities and influence, and their management.

The interrelationship of people, objectives, structure and management, together with the efficient use of resources, will determine the success or failure of the organisation and the extent of its effectiveness (Figure 2.2).

Hotel operations and the hospitality industry

The broad and variable nature of hotel operations means that they can be seen to embrace, to a greater or lesser extent, elements of associated sectors of the hospitality industry such as the licensed trade, catering and leisure activities. **In general terms, then, the hotel sector is also likely to exhibit a wider and more diverse range of organ-isational and staffing characteristics than might necessarily be found in other sectors of the hospitality industry.**

Types of hotels

There are, however, many different types of hotels, and many different ways of attempting to distinguish between them and to categorise them. Medlik, for example, adopts the following criteria for classifying the main types of hotels.[14]

- The **location**, for example cities, towns, coastal resorts or country; and **position** within its location, for example city or town centre, along the beach or a highway.
- The relationship with a particular **means of transport**, for example motels, railway hotels or airport hotels.
- The **purpose of visit** and main reason for the guests' stay, for example business hotels, convention hotels, holiday hotels.
- A pronounced tendency to a **short or long duration** of guests' stay, for example a transit or a residential hotel.
- The **range of facilities and services**, for example open to residents and non-residents, provision of overnight accommodation and breakfast only, or an apartment hotel.
- The distinction between **licensed and unlicensed** hotels.
- The **size** of hotel, for example by number of rooms or beds – a large hotel would have several hundred beds or bedrooms.
- The **class or grade** of hotel as in hotel guides and classification and grading systems, for example a five-star luxury or quality hotel, or a one-star basic standard hotel.
- The **ownership and management** of the hotel, for example chain or group hotels, or individually owned independent hotels.

The Savoy Hotel, London – a personal perspective

The Savoy Hotel in London is the foremost quality and customer focused driven hotel in the world. 'For Excellence We Strive' is the motto and every staff member knows it and lives it throughout every day of employment.

What I remember so vividly is the feeling that I got when I started my very first shift as a commis waiter in the 'River Room' Restaurant. When I served my first guest there was nothing that was going to stop me giving the best service this customer had ever had. I didn't know way, it was something in the atmosphere that spurred me on to do it. I noticed this throughout my whole time there. If it is possible to say it was almost like the staff fed off the teamwork and generated motivation, no matter how busy we were or how tired. The result of this was finishing a shift feeling completely drained but overwhelmingly satisfied with what we had achieved.

The Savoy is a frightening place to work in partly due to the superstition and history that surrounds it and given the fact that few people ever get the chance to go there in their life time. For the staff, however, it is a rare opportunity to be taught the basics by the best in the world. This was the reason, I feel, that the staff gave their all. It is seen as a platform where careers are either launched or destroyed, such is its power. Those who succeed in completing their training there have really accomplished a great deal and something to be rightly proud of.

continued

continued

From my own perspective there were countless times when after a shift starting at 6 am and ending at 11 pm that all I wanted to do was hand in my resignation and say that it was all over. However, this was compensated for when, after a 13-hour day of continuous walking, carrying, cleaning and serving, you had the opportunity to stay in a staff room on the top floor of the hotel if you were on an early the next day. All for free. What more can I say? Sought after days off were cancelled at short notice, double shifts back to back were not uncommon, but you rarely heard anyone complain or argue. It never occurred to me why.

Training was on the job. You looked and listened to everyone and the speed at which you learnt was your own personal task. Most certainly you learned fast. There was no opportunity to slacken off as it was reiterated time and time again that there was always something to do. Someone once told me he had worked out that in a day he would walk nearly 5 miles. So comfortable shoes were an essential.

A typical day at the Savoy started for me at 4.30 am. Arriving at work at 5.50 am, I would then change into black trousers, a clean white waiters jacket ensuring that all buttons were polished and black shoes, also polished. Dirty jackets and/or shoes were not acceptable and failure to have a clean jacket would either mean that you would be sent back to the changing room or kept well out of the way of the guests. I would arrive in the restaurant at around 6 am and begin to prepare the station. Once all the silver cutlery had been cleaned and the bread baskets filled with fresh rolls and danish pastries we would all go for breakfast in the table room at 7 am. Half an hour later we would begin service. As a commis waiter there was nothing else to do except follow orders from the Chef de Rang (head of the station). The commis would run back and forth from the kitchen collecting orders, clearing tables, re-laying tables with fresh linen and getting countless pots of tea and coffee. Taking an order from a guest was a real honour and from a commis point of view it was an experience not to be forgotten.

I remember one instance when I realised how extraordinarily high the standards were at the Savoy when, upon a guest spilling a glass of orange juice over their table, I was asked by the Chef de Rang to re-lay the table while the guest was reseated at another one. There was a knack to changing a table-cloth whereby the guests never saw the green baize of the table. On this occasion, however, I saw it fit to place an old menu underneath the table cloth to stop the dampness on the baize seeping through to the new table cloth. It seemed that one of the guests saw the green baize of the table, for what could have only been seconds. Twenty minutes later I was up in front of the Food and Beverage Manager and had to explain my actions and reassure him that it would not happen again. You could say that this was absurd but it seemed that this was common procedure.

I look back at my training at the Savoy with great pride and honour. There is no place else where such an exceptional level of training could be given. It seemed almost as though no guest had a bad experience there. The Savoy is a time capsule where everyone works to their limits to achieve the ultimate, if that is possible. I have served Princes and Kings, pop stars and politicians and I thank the Savoy, hard though it was, for the opportunity to do so.

(*Source*: The author is grateful to Christian Ternofsky for providing this contribution.)

> **Stress and the airport hotel**
>
> High stress abounds in airport hotels due to a number of factors, which are in some ways unique to these properties.
>
> A high proportion of hotels around an airport means that the labour pool is usually smaller than the area requires, bearing in mind that more money could be earned doing unskilled jobs within the airport than working for a hotel as a chambermaid, for instance. Staff tend to move around the hotels. Staff shortages are common, especially with hourly paid job – workers will follow the highest bidder.
>
> Airport hotels are busy on a 24-hour basis. Food outlets must be operational for up to 18 hours a day. Room service has to be 24-hour. Guests can be ill-tempered due to delays or jet lag. Food requirements can be obscure because international travellers are in the wrong time zone, i.e. an American traveller may demand breakfast during lunch service. Air crews are commonplace and they require early and accurate wake up calls, quiet rooms and low room rates.
>
> Delayed flights cause untold upheaval to catering outlets because of the large number of people descending on coffee shops and bars with very short notice. They are usually issued with a meal voucher; they are often cross with the delay. Children can cause havoc to other guests.
>
> Car parks must be manned to avoid free parking for weeks on end. Security needs to be of a high standard as the high turnover of guests and the international factor adds to the risks.

Organisational and staffing characteristics

Hotels, then, are not an homogeneous grouping. It is, however, possible to summarise a number of important organisational and staffing features which are characteristic of hotels in general, and in which in part at least may be a feature of other sectors of the hospitality industry. For example:

- large numbers of individual units of varying size and many different types are located throughout the whole of the country and internationally;
- many units operate for 24 hours a day, seven days a week;
- there are high fixed costs, a fixed rate of supply but a fluctuating, seasonal and often unpredictable demand;
- it is both a production and service industry;
- production and sales are combined on the same premises;
- there is a diverse range of customers seeking to satisfy a variety of needs and expectations;
- services are supplied direct to the customer on the premises and the customer leaves with no tangible product;
- a wide range of operations are combined, many of which are provided simultaneously;
- a high degree of coordination is required, often measured over very short time scales;

- managers are expected to demonstrate proficiency in technical and craft skills as well as in management areas;
- staff may live on the premises;
- many different skills are required but there are also high numbers of unskilled staff;
- the majority of staff receive low pay;
- staff are often expected to work long and 'unsocial' hours;
- there is a large proportion of young, female, part-time and casual staff;
- there is also a high proportion of staff from other countries; .
- there are many trade unions but generally trade union membership is low;
- there is high mobility of labour within the industry, and a high turnover of staff joining and leaving the industry.

Distinctive nature of the industry

It is these characteristics which collectively determine the distinctive nature of the hotel industry, which shape organisational design and structure, and largely determine managerial policies, procedures and behaviour.[15] It is the combination of these organisational and staffing characteristics which determines the process of management and which has a distinctive effect on the behaviour of staff and on employee relations.[16] As an example of the nature of work in the hospitality industry, Figure 2.3 gives an insight into the job of a room attendant at the Four Seasons Hotel, London as seen through the eyes of her daughter's diary as part of 'Take Your Daughter to Work Day'.

Clearly, however, not all of these characteristics will apply, necessarily, to every hotel. It is important to remind ourselves of the importance of the organisational setting, of the diverse nature of the industry, and to repeat that **hotels are not a homogeneous grouping**. For example, large city-centre hotels are likely to have a wider range of operations, more bureaucratic procedures, narrower and more specialised areas of responsibilities, and a proportionally higher level of mobility and staff turnover than smaller country hotels. And particular types of hotel will exhibit more specific characteristics; for example, retirement hotels will have a narrower range of customer, and provide a range of facilities and services directed specifically to their particular needs and expectations.

The hospitality industry is also very cosmopolitan and hospitality organisations exist in all parts of the world. It is therefore important to recognise the significance of national, cultural and ethnic values, and socio-political influences.[17]

Small-size establishments

Major hotel groups provide a significant number of rooms and much of the 'theory' of hospitality management is grounded in the study of large-scale organisations. However, it is important to remember that a characteristic feature of the industry is the predominant number of small, independent hotels who often may be operated and managed by the proprietors. Such hotels provide an equally important area of study into organisational behaviour and the effective management of people.[18]

Figure 2.3: So this is what Mum does all day

Marjorie Williams, 41, is a chambermaid at the Four Seasons Hotel, Park Lane, London. She works a 40-hour week and is responsible for cleaning and overseeing the standards of rooms.

ALISON'S DIARY

9 am Went to collect my uniform. I enjoyed wearing it – it helped me think my way into the job.

9.30 am Went to the morning meeting to go through the night manager's log and find out what has happened in the hotel the night before. It says if a guest has complained or if anything unusual happened that needs to be looked at. Then department heads went through a list of things happening today which will affect the running of the hotel – things you might not even think of, like a march outside, or famous guests booked in. I hope someone famous comes in today.

11 am I went with Mum to help clean and check the rooms. She has to get everything just right and exactly the same in every room – even the space between the phone and the note pad. Everything has to be done to the hotel's set standard, and you can't overlook anything. I didn't think Mum would have to work so hard or have to remember so many things – it's no wonder she thinks I'm so untidy at home. I cleaned the coffee table – about eight times – and helped make up the bed. Replaced all those little shampoo and bath supplies that guests use – or take home with them!

12 noon Got changed into a different uniform and went to work as a doorman – or door girl. I couldn't carry the cases, but showed people where to check in. Some guests are so nice and smile or chat, and some ignore you completely – you are just someone to wait on them. The trouble is, you can't tell from just looking at them which sort they are. Someone said I looked cute in my hat.

It gets so busy at lunch time. Ernie Wise and Alan Whicker turned up, but I was too shy to speak to them. They seemed so normal, even though they were famous. Perhaps I should have told them I'd like to be an actress – they might have given me my big break.

1 pm Grabbed some lunch – fish and chips – in the canteen with some of the other girls. We swapped stories about the guests we had seen but we were all feeling quite tired already. I think half a day at work might be enough for me.

2 pm It was much quieter in the afternoon, but I still had to look attentive and be on my best behaviour. When you are on show, you can't afford to relax. Thank goodness it wasn't January – I would have frozen to death.

3 pm Did a shift on room service and in the kitchens. It's amazing what guests need brought up to their rooms. The activity never seems to stop; the service runs 24 hours a day. At least at school you get breaks and the chance to gossip with your friends; here, you barely have time to nip to the loo.

3.30 pm Review meeting. I can't decide whether it's better to be at work or at school. When it was really busy I kept wanting to be back at school for a rest but then, when it was quieter, I really enjoyed watching how everyone works in a team. What Mum does is just as important as anyone in the management. The first thing guests judge in a hotel is their room and my mum is responsible for making sure their first impressions are good ones. That makes me really proud of her, and I wish more people would realise that. Some guests really appreciate what she does and leave tips, others ignore her.

Went back after the meeting to 'help' Mum but I wasn't in a fit state to do anything so I just put my feet up until it was time to go home.

> 'I didn't think Mum would have to work so hard or remember so much. No wonder she thinks I'm untidy'

(*Source:* reprinted with permission of Solo Syndication from *YOU Magazine*, 20 April 1997, p. 32.)

A model of excellence

The Seaview Hotel and Restaurant is a small, privately run hotel situated on the Isle of Wight. It offers customers sixteen bedrooms, two restaurants and two bars. It caters for all-comers: smokers, non-smokers, babies, children, pets, and has special ground floor rooms and access facilities for disabled guests. The hotel has achieved national praise from the Department of National Heritage and received a number of accolades for its standards of efficiency and service, customer satisfaction and staff training. In 1998, the hotel won a 'business Oscar' UK Quality Award for Business Excellence from the British Quality Foundation and has been used as a role model for businesses in the leisure, hotel and catering industry.[19]

**EXTRACTS FROM THE HOTEL'S EXCELLENCE MODEL ARE
GIVEN IN VARIOUS CHAPTERS OF THIS BOOK.**

The appendix to this chapter also provides an original commentary on some of the characteristic features associated with the ownership and management of a small, six-bedroom country house hotel.

The nature of service industries

Hotel operations combine both a productive and a service element. However, although hotels are not pure service organisations, they exhibit many of the basic characteristics common to other service industries.[20]

Services may be viewed as displaying seven main characteristic features:

- the consumer as a participant in the process;
- simultaneous production and consumption;
- perishable capacity;
- site selection determined by customer demands;
- labour intensive;
- intangibility; and
- difficulty in measuring performance.[21]

The consumer as a participant in the process

Unlike physical production, where the environment of the 'factory' does not concern the eventual purchaser, the presence of the consumer requires attention to the surroundings and characteristics of the service facility. Customer satisfaction will be influenced by the location, furnishing and decoration of the establishment, and the environment in which the delivery of services takes place. The customer is part of the service process and can influence its operations. For example, hotel guests may make use of tea/coffee facilities in their own rooms and thus reduce the demand for room service.

Simultaneous production and consumption

Services are created and consumed simultaneously. Unlike manufacturing there can be no inventory of the service itself. For example, a receptionist giving assistance to a guest cannot be stored for future use. Services cannot be stockpiled to meet fluctuating demand. For the delivery of services to take place there must be direct, personal interaction with customers. The lack of an inventory can result in customers having to wait for attention or delivery of service.

Perishable capacity

Services cannot be stored and if they are not used they are likely to be wasted. Unlike manufacturing, services are time-perishable. High fixed costs will still occur during periods of low demand. The income lost from a hospitality room unsold on one day cannot be recouped later: it is lost forever. Additional hotel rooms may not be available to satisfy a higher than expected demand, resulting in a lost opportunity to generate additional income.

Site selection determined by customer demands

Unlike manufacturing, services do not move through distinct channels of distribution. The delivery of services and the customer must be brought together. Services cannot be provided at a single, centralised location for different geographical markets and it may not be possible to achieve economies of scale. Experience of hospitality services is dependent upon personal contact. As services are provided direct to the customer this may result in smaller-scale operations and limited geographical locations.

Labour intensive

In service operations work, activity is people-orientated and labour is the important resource in determining organisational effectiveness. The personal nature of hospitality services places emphasis on the importance of direct interaction between employees and customers. The effective delivery of services is dependent upon the attention and attitudes of staff as well as their performance. The increased use of technology and automation may well lead to a demand for a higher level of personal attention and service.

Intangibility

Compared with physical products, the particular features of services are more difficult to explain or communicate. Promotion requires an understanding of consumer behaviour and needs to focus attention on the actual delivery of the service. Benefits derived from services are associated with feelings and emotions. The quality of service in a hotel is usually identified with its general culture and ambience, the disposition and attitudes of staff, and the nature of other customers.

Difficulty in measuring performance

The measurement of output is difficult because there is unlikely to be a single, important criterion on which to evaluate effective performance. For example, profitability or the number of customers staying at a hospitality establishment is not necessarily a measure of the quality of service. The intangible nature of services, coupled with the heterogeneous nature of customers, means that the actual delivery of services will differ widely. It is difficult, therefore, to establish or to monitor objective standards of performance. Even within the same establishment the actual delivery of services to individual customers is likely to vary noticeably according to, for example, the reasons for the customers' presence and their particular requirements, together with the personalities and behaviour of both customers and members of staff.

Lack of ownership

Another feature of service operations is that, unlike manufacturers or suppliers of products, the purchase of services does not bestow ownership upon the customer. All the physical features remain in the ownership of the hotelier, and customers are only hirers of facilities for the duration of their stay.[22]

Are service industries different from other industries?

Hospitality organisations, then, exhibit many of the basic characteristics of service industries and may share many common features such as high fixed costs, labour-intensiveness, low wages and unsocial working hours. But is a service industry any different from other industries? Not according to leading writers such as Levitt:

> *Purveyors of service, for their part, think that they and their problems are fundamentally different from other businesses and their problems. They feel that service is people-intensive, while the rest of the economy is capital-intensive. But these distinctions are largely spurious. There are no such things as service industries. There are only industries whose service components are greater or less than those of other industries. Everybody is in service.*[23]

However, Macdonald claims that there are substantial differences between manufacturing and services, and that service organisations have every right to claim that they are different. Internal contrasts between manufacturing and service include the following.

- *Manufacturing* – production is capital or equipment orientated; technical skills dominate; training will dominate; production results are variable.
- *Service* – production is people orientated; interpersonal skills dominate; education will dominate; service results are subject to even more variation.[24]

The distinction between goods and services products is also demonstrated by Stamatis[25] (Figure 2.4).

The nature of management

In addressing the question 'What is the nature of management in service industries?', Jones suggests that implicit in the question is the fundamental assumption that managers of services face different problems and act differently from other managers. However, Jones acknowledges that this assumption is contentious. And even where there is agreement that services are in some way different, there is no agreement on the cause or importance of this difference.[26]

A major characteristic of the hospitality industry is of course the role of people and the direct contact and interactions between staff and customers. The majority of managers of the author's acquaintance stress the need for a high level of commitment to the job and

Figure 2.4:
Distinction
between goods
and services
products

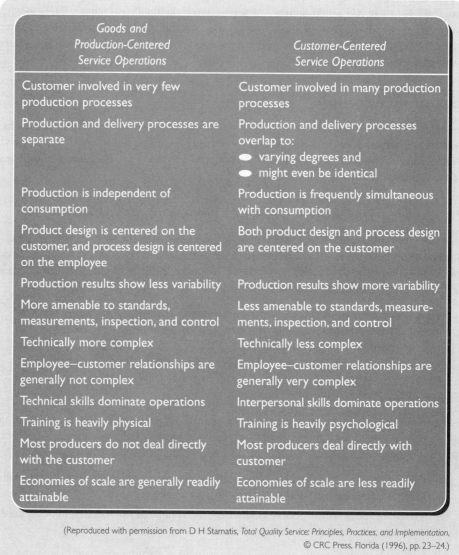

Goods and Production-Centered Service Operations	Customer-Centered Service Operations
Customer involved in very few production processes	Customer involved in many production processes
Production and delivery processes are separate	Production and delivery processes overlap to: ● varying degrees and ● might even be identical
Production is independent of consumption	Production is frequently simultaneous with consumption
Product design is centered on the customer, and process design is centered on the employee	Both product design and process design are centered on the customer
Production results show less variability	Production results show more variability
More amenable to standards, measurements, inspection, and control	Less amenable to standards, measurements, inspection, and control
Technically more complex	Technically less complex
Employee–customer relationships are generally not complex	Employee–customer relationships are generally very complex
Technical skills dominate operations	Interpersonal skills dominate operations
Training is heavily physical	Training is heavily psychological
Most producers do not deal directly with the customer	Most producers deal directly with customer
Economies of scale are generally readily attainable	Economies of scale are less readily attainable

(Reproduced with permission from D H Stamatis, *Total Quality Service: Principles, Practices, and Implementation*, © CRC Press, Florida (1996), pp. 23–24.)

the ability to be all things to all people. (As an example, the attributes of a hotel manager are discussed further in Chapter 5.)

But whatever one's view of service industries, they still have some functions and purpose to fulfil as part of their role within society. Service industries are in need of management in order to operate effectively in the same way as any other industry.

Service management

Hospitality organisations, while created to provide both service and hospitality, have not always effectively managed service. Today, other service organisations as well as the hospitality industry must recognise the need to manage service effectively and deliver high-quality products. Increased emphasis on quality also means an increased focus on customer service. As this refocusing takes place, management strategies referred to as 'service management' are being developed. Service management takes a market-orientated approach to service delivery, with an emphasis on long-term customer relationships. Albrecht defines service management as 'a total organisational approach that makes quality of service, as perceived by the customer, the number one driving force for the operation of the business'.[27]

While traditional management approaches emphasise internal consequences and structure, service management emphasises external consequences and process. This change in focus requires changes in the work culture. The entire organisation needs to understand the emphasis on service and that the organisation can survive only if it meets the needs of the customer. The mission statement, along with company goals and objectives, emphasise the focus on customers. These statements clearly delineate the direction the company is taking. Employee goals are customer orientated and reward systems are based on customer satisfaction.

Service strategy

The service strategy is the formal organisational link that delineates the focus on customer satisfaction. The strategy outlines what will be done for a certain customer segment, how this should be achieved, and with what kinds of resources. The service strategy reinforces the mission strategy of the organisation. Without a clear service strategy, inconsistent behaviour is evident. Strong service strategies not only aid in strengthening customer relationships, but they also aid in retention of employees. Service strategies can be a powerful management tool to sustain a competitive advantage in the marketplace.

For example, Chacko maintains that: 'In an industry that is in the mature stage of its life cycle and where there is tremendous competition, hoteliers have realized that quality of service may be the most important competitive advantage.'[28]

Management focus

The focus of an organisation that utilises service management is different from that of a traditional organisation. The organisation will be structured so that it supports front-line workers and provides the resources that are necessary for them to serve the customers effectively. Decision-making, supervisory focus, reward systems and feedback mechanisms are also different. Decision-making is decentralised so that employees who are involved in the customer interaction are empowered to take action and do what is necessary to satisfy the customer. For example, if guest service representatives have an unhappy guest at the front desk, they have the authority to take care of the problem. Representatives have the authority to give a discount, offer a free meal or make arrangements with outside entities to satisfy the customer. However, long-term strategic decisions remain centralised.

Managers and supervisors focus on the encouragement and support of employees. Services by nature cannot be standardised, therefore the organisation needs to be flexible. Also, for employees to deliver quality service, some flexibility is needed to meet the special needs of every customer. The role of managers changes from that of 'order giver' and controller to 'facilitator', coach and team leader. The role of workers changes from merely being an 'order taker' to becoming an active participant in the creation of guest-satisfying values. Reward systems are based on customer satisfaction. Frequently, managers utilising a service management approach use moments of truth as evaluation points. These moments of truth are the critical points of interaction between the customer and the service provider. Performance is measured against expectations at the critical moments. Customer feedback plays an instrumental role in this type of evaluation.

Service culture

Service management strategies are successful only when they are accompanied by a corporate culture that can be labelled a service culture. The culture can be described as 'a culture where an appreciation for good service exists, and where giving good service to internal as well as ultimate external customers is considered a natural way of life and one of the most important norms by everyone'.[29] Management, top executives and front-line employees all need to live the service culture. A service culture enhances the ability truly to meet the needs of the customers.

The increasing recognition of a service culture, the delivery of high quality products and the overriding importance of the customer (common in the USA) is a growing feature of hospitality organisations. Some examples of attempts to provide a more customer(guest)-orientated environment and the satisfaction of their needs are given in Figure 2.5.

Figure 2.5: Satisfaction of customer needs

Thank you for choosing to stay with us. We hope you have a comfortable and enjoyable visit. We have tried to anticipate all your needs, but if there is anything we have overlooked which can make your stay more pleasurable, please do not hesitate to contact the manager on duty. Every effort will be made to assist you. Our staff is dedicated to making your stay trouble free.

Northwest Lodging Inc. prides itself on offering the best possible accommodations at a reasonable price. I welcome your comments or suggestions. You may drop this comment card in the mail or call me directly. We hope to see you again and again.

Dear Guest,

Just finished cleaning your room and wondered if you have any special needs such as extra linens or supplies during your stay. Let me know what it is that you need on the back side of this note and leave it on the table.

I want to help make your stay a comfortable one!

Your Housekeeper,

WELCOME

Dear Guest,

Hello, I'm Roxanne your room attendant. I cleaned your room today and trust that you will find everything to your satisfaction. If you have additional requests, please dial '0' for the Lodge Operator.

It has been our pleasure serving you and we wish you a most enjoyable stay.

THANK YOU FOR BEING OUR GUEST

Figure 2.6: The open systems model of organisations

(*Source:* Mullins L J, *Management and Organisational Behaviour,* 5th edn, Financial Times Pitman Publishing (1999), p. 100.)

The open systems model of analysis

Earlier in this chapter we raised the debate about whether the hospitality industry is unique. For example, Riley suggests that: 'Looked at solely as a "managerial task", running a hotel, restaurant or institutional establishment can be seen as a set of systems and processes common to managing anything.' The approach of scientific management is greatly under-valued and unused by hospitality managers but this does not really contradict the case for uniqueness.[30]

The important questions, however, are:

● to what extent do the particular characteristics of the hospitality industry distinguish it from other industries? and

● to what extent do general principles of management theory and practice apply to hospitality organisations as work organisations?

The open systems model provides us with a useful basis of analysis.

All business organisations can be seen as open systems which take inputs such as people, finance, materials, and information from the external environment. Through a series of activities these inputs are transformed or converted and returned to the environment in various forms of outputs such as goods produced, services provided and completed processes or procedures. Outputs are intended to achieve certain goals such as profit, market standing, level of sales or consumer satisfaction (Figure 2.6).

The open systems model applies in exactly the same way to hospitality organisations as to any other business organisation. By way of a representative example, Figure 2.7 shows the hotel as an open system. However, the same basis of analysis is equally applicable to other sectors of the hospitality industry.

The customer as the major throughput

Hospitality organisations are 'people-moulding' organisations and they are concerned with human beings as the basis of the nature of work carried out.[31] The major input is the

Figure 2.7: The hotel as an open system

INPUTS →

Raw products
Equipment and materials
Finance
Staff
Management and technical
  expertise
CUSTOMERS

TRANSFORMATION OR CONVERSION PROCESS

Clean, comfortable and secure
  accommodation
Preparation of food and beverages
Conference/leisure facilities
Congenial atmosphere
Social needs of customers
Delivery of services
Upkeep and maintenance
Staff training and welfare
Planning, organising, directing and
  controlling activities

MEASURES OF ACHIEVEMENT

Returned customers
Guest questionnaires and comments
Compliments/complaints received
Occupancy rates
Level of scrap, wastage, breakages
Cash flow and accounting ratios
Staff appraisals, absenteeism and turnover
Recommendations – e.g. 'star' ratings and guide books
Relationships – e.g. with local population, and health
  and fire inspectors

OUTPUTS →

Income
Trained and experienced staff
Goodwill
SATISFIED CUSTOMERS

→ ORGANISATIONAL GOALS

Higher profitability
Greater market share
Increased level of sales
Improved productivity
Good reputation
High standards
Satisfaction of social
  responsibilites

customer seeking satisfaction of certain needs. The desired output is a satisfied customer. In order to achieve this output the transformation or conversion process will entail the customer being suitably rested/refreshed/entertained or undergoing a rewarding experience in a comfortable and safe environment. The customer is therefore also the major throughput of the system. It is the demands of the customer which will have the greatest influence on the series of activities involved in the transformation process.

Compared with most business organisations, the hotel is unusual in that customers as the main throughput are provided with and consume services within the establishment, and leave with no tangible product.[32] However, in terms of the open systems model, the hotel is no different from any other business organisation. It is subject to the same basic processes of:

- organisational aims and objectives;
- inputs;
- series of activities as the transformation or conversion process;
- outputs;
- realisation of goals and measures of achievement.

Applications to hospitality management

Reservations about the application of management practices and techniques developed in other sectors of industry prompted Nailon to propose a model specifically related to elements of hospitality management.[33] This model was criticised heavily by Wood, however. The reasoning behind the attempt to create a model of management specifically suited to hospitality organisations was spurious considering the criticisms levelled at the 'blinkered' approaches of previous management theorists.[34]

Wood argues that Nailon's model could describe adequately the factors affecting the management of any organisation and follows closely the structure of the more general open systems theories which are themselves based on previous studies of manufacturing firms.

> *there is nothing special about either management or hospitality management. A 'theoretical' understanding of 'management' can only be obtained through an appreciation of how management practices are produced within a framework of social and economic constraints, and how such practices interrelate at the societal level in respect of* all *social and economic institutions.*[35]

Comparison with management elsewhere

Viewing the hospitality industry as unique, or as somehow special and different from other industries, will not improve the level of organisational performance. On the other hand, it may help to account for lack of progress and change in the industry. For example, although based on a small and limited study, Dodrill and Riley were unable to find any distinctive attitudes towards work by hotel workers.[36] (This study is discussed further in Chapter 3.) From his practical experience of hotel management, Venison comments on the striking similarity between the hotel industry and the retail industry. Venison believes hotel management students would benefit from a study of retailing.[37] Wood also challenges the myth of uniqueness in the hotel and catering industry which provides:

for employers, managers and some workers a self-serving device for justifying the unjustifiable in terms of inadequate basic rewards, feudal management practices and the maintenance of a culture that discourages intervention in the affairs of the industry by others.[38]

We have seen, then, that the hospitality industry does differ in important respects from other industries. But this should not be seen as a convenient reason for disguising comparison with management procedures and practices elsewhere.

Common point of reference

A series of activities by which inputs are transformed into outputs is a common feature of any industry, and makes possible the application of general principles of organisation and management within the hospitality industry. A suitable form of structure must be designed. Essential administrative functions must be carried out. Legal requirements must be observed (for example, in respect of employment legislation). The common activities of management – clarification of objectives, planning, organising, directing and control – apply to a greater or lesser extent.

It is important to emphasise these common features. There are of course differences in the activities and methods of operation of organisations even of the same type, for example in relation to the nature, size and scale of activities of different establishments. The open systems approach provides not only for the critical analysis of the operations of a particular establishment but also a basis for comparison with other hospitality organisations, for example in highlighting similarities or variations in the nature of inputs, the series of activities in organisational processes and execution of work, environmental influences, organisational goals and measures of achievement.[39]

Such an approach will remind us yet again of the diverse nature of the industry but also that differences in the application and implementation of the common features are largely a matter only of degree and emphasis. Using the open systems model provides a common point of reference and enables us to take a general approach to the study of hospitality organisations, to analyse them, and to review applications of general management theory.[40]

Environmental influences

Hospitality organisations are in continual interaction with the external environment of which they are part. In order to be effective and maintain survival and development, they must respond to the opportunities and challenges, and risks and limitations, presented by changing circumstances. The open systems approach views the organisation within its total environment and emphasises the importance of multiple channels of interaction.

The increasing rate of change in major environmental factors (technical, economic, social and governmental) has highlighted the need to study the establishment as a total organisation and to adopt a systems approach. In addition to these major areas of change, the hotel faces a multiplicity of constantly changing environmental factors which affect its operations and performance (Figure 2.8).

Beyond the control of the manager

Environmental influences are generally beyond the control of the individual manager. Consider how the functioning and operation of a hospitality organisation might be affected by such external environment influences as, for example:

Figure 2.8:
External
environmental
influences

- government actions on the rate of VAT, transport policies, health and safety regulations, drink-driving laws;
- inflation, interest rates, levels of unemployment;
- international situations and foreign exchange rates;
- technological advances;
- activities of competitors;
- local business trade, or tourism or leisure attractions;
- a major trend towards eating organically grown produce;
- increased leisure time for a wider range of the population;
- bankruptcy of, or a major strike at, an important supplier;
- a large increase in trade union activities and membership;
- the opening or closure of a local catering college;
- a long spell of particularly good or inclement weather.

The effectiveness of hospitality operations will be determined not only by internal considerations and choices, but also by the successful management of the opportunities, challenges and risks presented by the external environment. Managers must therefore be readily adaptable to changes in the environment and the demands which are placed upon them.

Importance of environmental scanning

From a review of themes in academic journals in the areas of hospitality, and a comparison with those regarded by practitioners as affecting their companies' performance, Costa *et al.* found it clear that the broader range of issues is addressed by academics. Managers are too concerned with the short term, and the reduced areas of concern identified by practitioners may reflect a somewhat narrow view about the external business environment. The pace of change in competition faced by hospitality organisations means that only a core group of factors can be monitored closely. However, Costa *et al.* conclude that the identification and management of environmental opportunities and threats is fundamental to the competitive position of companies, and suggest the need for a different attitude towards scanning the business environment.[41]

Analysis of hospitality operations

By itself, the open systems model reveals little about the detailed activities undertaken within the hospitality establishment. To benefit from such an approach the system needs to be analysed in such a way that the total operations of the establishment as a unified whole can be reviewed and amended as necessary. Within the hospitality system as a whole each of the main transformation or conversion processes can be seen as separate sub-systems interacting with other sub-systems. For example, the analysis of the system could be based upon the traditional organisation structure with different departments or sections as sub-systems – such as front office, accommodation, food and beverage, conferences, accounting, personnel, security and maintenance. However, this form of analysis could lead to an investigation concentrating on blinkered, sectional interests rather than on the need to adopt a unified, corporate approach.

Interrelationships and interactions

Each department or section of the establishment might perhaps be operating efficiently in its own right. But what is equally important is the interrelationships and interactions with other departments or sections, and the attitudes and behaviour of staff.

For example, food preparation and food service should not be considered separately but as integrated sub-systems. The preparation of food in the kitchen and the equipment used need to be related to the method of service in the restaurant, and the training and skills of the waiting staff.[42] It is the integration of preparation and service, together with other sub-systems, which determines overall effectiveness of the establishment.

It is more beneficial, therefore, to analyse major elements or functions within the system and to recognise the importance of the interdependence of sub-systems in terms of the effectiveness of hospitality operations as an integrated whole.

The socio-technical approach

The interrelationship of different parts of the system raises the question of identification of sub-systems. These may be identified in a number of different ways although there is a degree of similarity among alternative models.[43]

For example, following their study of changing technology in British coal mines, Trist and others drew attention to the importance of the socio-technical system.[43] This is concerned with the transformation or conversion process itself and the importance of the relationships between technical efficiency, social considerations and the effect on people.

The researchers suggested that there are three sub-systems common to any organisation:

- the **technological** sub-system;
- the sub-system of **formal role structure**;
- the sub-system of **individual members' feelings or sentiments**.

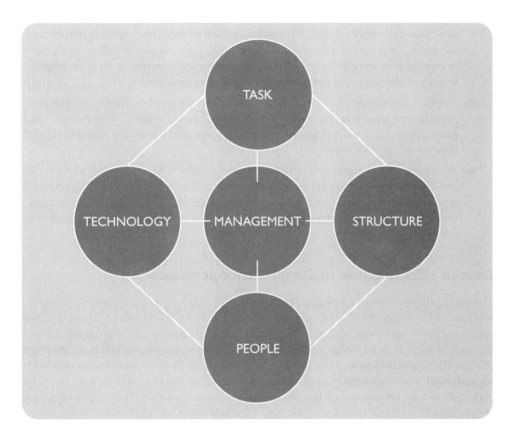

Figure 2.9:
Interrelated
sub-systems
of hospitality
operations

Interrelated sub-systems

However the sub-systems are identified, the task of management is to coordinate them and to ensure that the activities of the organisation as a whole are directed towards the accomplishment of its goals and objectives. Developing the idea of the socio-technical approach, we can therefore analyse hospitality operations in terms of five main interrelated sub-systems – task, technology, structure, people and management (Figure 2.9).

● *Task* – the goals and objectives of the establishment and the work to be carried out. This is the scale and nature of activities, and the range and quality of services provided, for example: the type of customers and their needs; family, conference or leisure facilities; nature of accommodation; speciality menus; standards of meals and service in the restaurant; opening hours of bars; porterage and room service.

● *Technology* – the manner in which the activities are carried out and the nature of work performance. The meaning of 'technology' is interpreted broadly and includes the physical aspects of equipment, machines, materials and work layout, and the methods, systems and procedures used in the transformation or conversion process, for example: the use of computers, microwaves and cook/chill; methods of food preparation; booking and reservation systems; procedures and methods for cleaning bedrooms. The technology of production in the kitchen is related to table d'hôte, à la carte or banquet service.

- *Structure* – patterns of organisation, lines of authority, and channels of communication among members of staff. This is the division of work and coordination of tasks by which the series of activities are carried out, for example: whether mechanistic or organic; the extent of centralisation; management and supervisory roles; the responsibilities of departmental managers; the informal organisation.
- *People* – the nature of the staff undertaking the series of activities, for example, training and qualifications; skills and abilities; loyalty; attitudes and interpersonal relationships; cultural influences; needs and expectations; group functioning and behaviour; styles of leadership.
- *Management* – coordination of task, technology, structure and people, and policies and procedures for the execution of the work of the hospitality establishment as a whole, for example: corporate strategy; decision-making; planning, organisation, direction and control of activities; systems and styles of management; interactions with the external environment; social responsibilities.

Overall effectiveness of hospitality operations

The overall effectiveness of hospitality organisations is dependent not only upon the products, services and facilities offered but very strongly on the social relationships which develop within each establishment. The idea of a socio-technical approach to the operations and methods of work is of particular relevance. **The open systems approach is an attempt to view the organisation as a purposeful, unified whole in continual interaction with its external environment.** Consideration needs to be given to interactions between technical and social aspects of the organisation's operations. The five sub-systems are inextricably linked and changes in any one area will affect all other areas of the organisation's activities.

Organisational goals

All organisations need clear aims and objectives which will determine the nature of inputs, the series of activities to achieve outputs and the realisation of goals. A goal is a future expectation. It is something the organisation is striving to achieve. The goals of an organisation are the reason for its existence.

The meaning of a goal is, however, subject to different interpretations. It can be used in a very broad sense to refer to the overall purpose of a hospitality establishment, for example to make a profit. A goal may also refer to more specific desired achievements, for example to provide a given level of facilities and standard of service to its customers.

Integration of goals

Organisational goals are established by people, either individually or, more usually, by a number of individuals cooperating together. Strictly, organisations do not have goals; only people do.

Members and customers have different and often conflicting goals. Owners may have a particular concern with high profits and the return on their investments, customers with prices and the standard of facilities and services, employees with security of employment, high wages and good working conditions. Members and customers will also have their own perception of the goals of the establishment, and their own personal goals which they expect to fulfil by participating in its activities, for example responsibility to the community, social satisfaction, recognition and status.

If organisational goals and personal goals are pulling in different directions, conflict will arise and performance is likely to suffer. It is the responsibility of management to clarify organisational goals and to reconcile conflicting interests. This demands the formulation of clear lines of direction for the establishment as a whole and its subsequent activities and operations. To be effective, goals should be emphasised, stated clearly and communicated openly to all members of staff.

One important attempt at integrating organisational goals with the needs of individual members of the organisation is the approach of management by objectives, which is discussed in Chapter 5.

Organisational ideologies and philosophy

The goals of the organisation may be pursued in accordance with an underlying ideology or philosophy based on beliefs, values and attitudes. Company philosophy determines the common doctrine or codes of behaviour which guides the establishment in the conduct of its operations and its dealings with others. In recent years it has become increasing popular for organisations to produce a mission statement setting out its overall philosophy and objectives, the general direction for the organisation to follow, and its guiding values and principles.

Certain aspects of an organisation's philosophy may be so dominant that they become the hallmark of the organisation, place constraints on other areas of activity, and determine the culture of the organisation and its overall conduct and management. Examples could include the Walt Disney Company where quality service, and the focus on individual and mutual effort, is embedded deeply within its corporate culture; and the Body Shop with its overriding byword for honesty.[45]

Company philosophy of Forte

To increase profitability and earnings per share each year in order to encourage investment and to improve and expand the business.

To give complete customer satisfaction by efficient and courteous service, with value for money.

To support managers and their staff in using personal initiative to improve the profit and quality of their operations whilst observing the company's policies.

To provide good working conditions and to maintain effective communications at all levels to develop better understanding and assist decision making.

To ensure no discrimination against sex, race, colour or creed and to train, develop and encourage promotion within the company based on merit and ability.

To act with integrity at all times and to maintain a proper sense of responsibility towards the public.

To recognise the importance of each and every employee who contributes towards these aims.

Source: Forte C (Lord), *Forte: The Autobiography of Charles Forte*, Sidgwick & Jackson (1986), p. 191.

Vision, mission and values

The shared vision is to provide:

'The perfect small seaside hotel
run by a happy team
dedicated to
the art of delighting our guests'

The mission is:

'To provide a deluxe hotel experience at a small hotel price'

Key shared values are:

Delighting the guests
Caring for the staff
Supporting the community

THE SEAVIEW HOTEL AND RESTAURANT

Objectives and policy

Goals are translated into objectives and policy in order to provide corporate guidelines for the operations of the establishment. Objectives and policy provide a focus for management decisions and actions. Terminology varies in the literature but objectives can be seen as the 'what', and policies as the 'how', 'where' and 'when', the means that follow the objectives.

● Objectives set out more specifically the goals of the organisation, the aims to be achieved and desired end results.

● Policy is developed within the framework of objectives. It provides the basis for decision-making and courses of action to follow in order to achieve objectives.

Objectives and policy are an essential part of the decision-making process and form a basis for the process of management. Objectives and policy may be formulated within the frame-work of an underlying philosophy of sets of beliefs, attitudes and conventions. These may not always be incorporated into formal policies but still influence the overall conduct of the establishment, and the behaviour and performance of staff.

Ethical and operational foundation

Company philosophy can be based on both an ethical foundation and an operational foundation.[46]

● The **ethical foundation** embodies basic principles which govern the external and internal relations of the establishment and concern standards of behaviour in all dealings with, for example, customers, suppliers, competitors, representatives, health or fire inspectors, educational establishments, staff and union representatives.

● The **operational foundation** relates to the nature, operation and conduct of hospitality activities, for example methods of production, use of equipment, hygiene and cleanliness, dress and appearance, systems and styles of management and supervision.

The underlying philosophy of the establishment will also have a bearing on the nature of the psychological contract which is discussed in the following chapter.

Upchurch suggests that: 'In general, hospitality researchers have determined that management is confronted with ethical issues surrounding guest rights, empowerment, sexual harassment, equal opportunity, departmental relations, vendor relations, yield management, community and public relations, and the balance of personal and organisational values . . . Overall, these studies have reflected on profiling ethical situations and in understanding management's role in resolving ethical situations within a service based setting.'[47]

Objectives may be just implicit but the formal, explicit definition of objectives will help to highlight the activities which the establishment needs to undertake and the comparative importance of its various functions. Objectives should not be stated in such a way that they detract from the recognition of possible new opportunities, potential danger areas, the initiative of staff, or the need for innovation or change. However, a clear, explicit statement of objectives may assist communications, reduce misunderstandings and provide meaningful criteria for evaluating performance.

General and sectional policy

Policy is translated into rules, directives, plans and procedures; it relates to all activities of, and to all levels in, the establishment. General policy is determined by top management (directors, owners or senior managers) and provides broad guidelines for the operations as a whole.

Certain aspects of general policy may be so dominant that they become the overriding image or 'hallmark' of the establishment and place constraints on other policy areas. The desire to create a unique corporate image and experience, such as for instance with all TGI Friday's restaurants wherever you are in the world (discussed in Chapter 3) is an example of a dominant aspect of general policy. Another example could be a country and golf hotel that wants to see itself as a high-class establishment and goes out of its way to show that it is not a family hotel and does not provide for children under five years of age.

Sectional policy flows from general policy and provides, in more specific operational terms, guiding principles for particular aspects and activities of operations. Specific policies have more defined areas of application and time limits.

For example, specific policy relating to **customer relations** could include areas of decision-making and delegation relating to types of customers, facilities provided, pricing and discounts, customer care and standards of service, attitudes and behaviour of staff, and handling of grievances and complaints.

Specific policies may also be formulated for other areas of relationships such as employees and suppliers, for main areas of activity such as accommodation, and food and beverages, and areas of functional support such as accounting and marketing.

The profit motive

The hospitality industry involves an economic activity and its aims and objectives are of a commercial nature. To be successful the primary objectives may be seen as: to survive as a business and continue in existence, to maintain growth and development, and to make a profit. If we accept survival as the ultimate objective of the hospitality establishment, this involves the need for a steady and continuous profit. The establishment must be prepared to accept the possibility of a reduction in short-term profitability in order to provide for future investments.

The importance of profit as a means of business survival has been suggested by Lord Forte.

> *The policy which binds all our business together is the simple axiom that we are in it to make a profit and we base our policies on a strict analysis of the potential in each area we enter. We are convinced that making profit is the surest way of guaranteeing the livelihood of our workforce. It follows from this philosophy of business that there is no room, if growth is to be maintained, for lame ducks.*[48]

Other considerations and motivations

Although the objective of profit maximisation is undoubtedly of great importance it is not, by itself, a sufficient criterion for the effective day-to-day management of hospitality operations. This view is supported by Fearn, who suggests a somewhat different interpretation of the role of profit in the objectives of hospitality management.

> *'Why are we in business?' The favourite answer to this question, and one often thought to be the correct one, is 'to make a profit'. This is indeed important, but it is hardly an adequate basic approach to the administration of a business. To consider profit as the sole reason for the existence of a company is certainly an attractive idea, but it is more logical to consider profit as the reward for serving others well. It is therefore the things that are done to obtain profit which are the subject of objectives.*[49]

In practice, there are many other considerations and motivations which affect the desire for the greatest profit or maximum economic efficiency. Attention needs to be given to multiple areas of objective setting, including the importance of social responsibilities.

Multiple performance objectives

Any business organisation has a number of important areas of performance and results which require the setting of objectives. Drucker has referred to the 'fallacy of the single objective' of a business. The search for the one, right objective is not only unlikely to be productive, but is certain to harm and misdirect the business enterprise.

> *To emphasise only profit, for instance, misdirects managers to the point where they may endanger the survival of the business. To obtain profit today they tend to undermine the future . . . To manage a business is to balance a variety of needs and goals . . . the very nature of business enterprise requires multiple objectives which are needed in every area where performance and results directly and vitally affect the survival and prosperity of the business.*[50]

Drucker lists eight key areas in which objectives should be set in terms of performance and results. This list provides a useful framework in which to review objectives of hospitality organisation.[51]

- ● *Market standing* – for example, type of customers and their requirements as the principal source of business, nature of facilities and services offered, distinctions from main competitors.
- ● *Innovation* – for example, need for flexibility in a dynamic environment, opportunities to reach new customers, developments arising from technological advances, new processes and procedures.

- *Productivity* – higher productivity distinguished from higher production or output, for example, more advanced equipment, optimum use of resources, decision-making techniques, improved methods, systems and procedures.

- *Physical and financial resources* – for example, location, size and nature of premises; equipment and facilities; supply of capital and budgeting; financial planning; provision of supplies.

- *Profitability* – for example, capital investment policy, profitability forecasts and planning, sales objectives such as for accommodation, food and beverages, measurements of profitability such as return on capital employed and food costs to sales.

- *Manager performance and development* – for example, the direction of managers' work, areas of responsibility, results achieved by subordinate staff, achievement of objectives, staff relationships, strengthening the management team, management succession planning.

- *Worker performance and attitudes* – for example, organisation and execution of work, standards of performance, control systems, staff appraisals, customer relations, personnel policies, employee relations, respect for authority, loyalty.

- *Public responsibility* (commonly referred to as social responsibilities) – demands made upon the organisation internally and by the external environment, for example, by customers and staff, by law or public opinion, or by responsibilities to society and the public interest. The importance of the social responsibilities of management is considered more fully in a separate section below.

Constraints and limitations

We can see, therefore, that although the profit objective is clearly of importance it is not, by itself, a sufficient criterion for the effective management of hospitality operations. Individuals in the hotel are not necessarily guided at all times by the profit objective. This is only one of a number of constraints.

> *Profit may not enter directly into the decision-making of most members of a business organisation. Again, this does not mean that it is improper or meaningless to regard profit as a principal goal of a business. It simply means that the decision-making mechanism is a loosely coupled system in which the profit constraint is only one among a number of constraints and enters into most sub-systems only in indirect ways.*[52]

The key areas of performance and results draw attention to the many constraints which may affect the satisfactory attainment of objectives, for example, the failure to innovate, low productivity, lack of physical and financial resources, poor management development or staff training. Other limiting factors may arise as a result of general policy decisions or environmental pressures.

Realistic level of objectives

It is important, therefore, to take account of constraints and to set limitations and objectives at a realistically attainable level. Objectives set at too low a level do not stretch staff, or provide a sufficient challenge or sense of achievement. This can result in a lost opportunity for higher performance and results.

However, if objectives are set at too high a level this will be counter-productive. Staff may feel that undue pressure is put upon them and will again fail to gain a sense of achievement or personal satisfaction. If objectives are not seen to be in reasonable reach this is likely to result in the loss of positive motivation and a lower-than-possible level of performance. (See also the discussion on achievement motivation in Chapter 7.)

Social responsibilities of management

In striving to satisfy their goals and achieve their objectives hospitality organisations cannot operate in isolation from the environment of which they are part. Such organisations require the use of factors of production and other facilities of society. Economic efficiency is affected by governmental, social, technical and cultural variables. In return, society is in need of the products and services supplied by the organisation, including the creation and distribution of wealth.

Economic survival and performance are dependent upon a series of activities between the hospitality organisation and its environment. These exchanges and the continual interaction with the environment give rise to a number of broader obligations to society in general. These broader obligations are both internal and external and are usually referred to as social responsibilities.

Broad range of responsibilities

The potential range of social responsibilities is very broad and concerns different groups of people. Social responsibilities may be considered under a number of different headings such as, for example, employees, shareholders, customers, community, the government, and suppliers, business associates and competitors.

- *Employees* – responsibilities extend beyond formal terms and conditions of employment and include, for example, justice in treatment, consultation and participation, effective personnel and employee relations policies, equal opportunities employment, working conditions and live-in accommodation, training in new skills and technologies, job satisfaction, observance of the psychological contract (discussed in Chapter 3).

- *Shareholders or other providers of capital* – shareholders are drawn from a wide range of the population, including private individuals. Many people also subscribe indirectly as shareholders through pension funds and insurance companies. Responsibilities to shareholders extend beyond a purely financial reward for risk-taking and include the safeguarding of investments, the opportunity to exercise rights as owners, participation in policy decisions, the opportunity to question top management on the affairs of the company, the provision of full information in a clearly understood format.

- *Customers* – responsibilities to customers may arguably be seen as no more than a natural outcome of good business especially in the hospitality industry. There are, however, broader social responsibilities including fair standards of advertising and promotions, good value for money, a positive approach to customer satisfaction, honesty and full information on all costs and charges, prompt and courteous attention to queries or complaints, safety and security.

- *Community* – it is in the area of concern for the community at large that social responsibilities can usually be seen most clearly. The hospitality organisation has a responsibility to society, to respect environmental considerations and take care of amenities. Examples under this heading include: the effects and potential nuisance of the siting and appearance of new buildings, noise, pollution and disposal of waste, the use of biodegradable materials and aerosol sprays which do not contain chlorofluoro-carbons (CFCs), concern for the welfare of the local community. Some larger organ-isations extend the range of social responsibilities further, for example by donations to, or sponsorship of, the arts, educational or sporting organisations, or charities.

● *Government* – hospitality management should, of course, respect and obey the law relating to the conduct of business operations even if it is not regarded as in their best interests. What is debatable is the extent to which top management should also cooperate voluntarily with actions requested by the government, for example, attempts to avoid inflation, acceptance of controls over imports, employment of staff under government training schemes, control of potential social problems such as the sale of tobacco or accidents at work.

● *Suppliers, business associates and competitors* – examples under this heading include: fair standards of trading, honouring terms and conditions of purchase and settlement dates for payment of accounts, assistance to small organisations, engaging in only fair competition and not to disparage competitors.

A question of balance

The distinction between the exercise of social responsibilities for genuine philanthropic reasons and actions taken in pursuit of what is seen as no more than good business practice and enlightened self-interest is not always easy to determine. In practice it is a question of degree and balance, of combining sound economic operations with an appro-priate concern for broader responsibilities to society.

The recognition of social responsibilities should form part of strategic planning, and the formulation of objectives and policy. It is up to top management to determine the extent to which, and the manner in which, the hospitality organisation will attempt to satisfy its social responsibilities.

Corporate strategy

Increased business competitiveness and the dynamic external environment have placed important emphasis on corporate strategy and the competencies of managers. According to Kanter, for example, 'Managing means managing an entire context. If you strip out one element and apply one methodology, it won't work.'[53] Effective management therefore takes place within the total corporate context (see, for example, Figure 2.10), and involves clearly established relationships and coordination among all levels of the organisation.

Objectives and policy are formulated within the framework of a corporate strategy. Some form of corporate strategy is necessary for all organisations but particularly for large ones – and this includes service organisations.[54] Organisational performance is dependent upon the process of matching structure, strategy and the environment.[55]

From research at Swallow Hotels, Webster draws attention to the importance of strategic management in a hospitality context.

In outline, strategic management entails a stream of decisions and actions which lead to the development and implementation of effective strategy. Strategic decisions determine the future direction and competitive position of an or-ganisation and thus have fundamental effects on it. Strategies such as growth,

Figure 2.10: The corporate context

The Corporate Context

Managing a hotel within .... Limited means managing within a corporate organisation.

The role of the general manager is just that – the generalist (expert in his or her own way) who oversees the multi-million pound asset in his/her care.

The assistant management team support the general manager in his/her main tasks.

A corporate organisation can provide a degree of specialism not available to the single operator and so adds value to the management of the business. The philosophy of synergy – the whole being greater than the sum of the individual parts (2 + 2 = 5) – adds this value.

It is important for effective management that there is a clear understanding of the relationship of the general manager and his/her team, and the specialist support departments.

As well as providing a level of professional expertise for their specialist area of the business, each specialist function is responsible for looking forward and assisting the Managing Director in defining the direction which we need to take the business to ensure its success in the future.

We call this *visioning*. Thus each department has a responsibility to 'live' the company's *vision*.

This is done in conjunction with members of our hotel management team to ensure the *vision* is realistic and as close to our customers' wishes as practical.

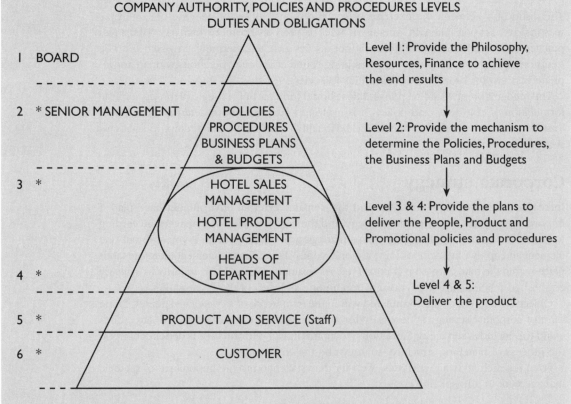

*This diagram clearly illustrates the many levels there are between policy makers and customers. It is, therefore, essential that there is a regular review (to include ongoing customer feedback systems) within all our hotels

(Reproduced with permission)

consolidation and diversification are general programmes of action which have an implied commitment of resources.[56]

A series of stages

Strategic planning can be approached in a number of ways. Keiser, for example, suggests the following seven specific steps to accomplish strategic planning in the hospitality industry.[57]

- *Assess the current position of the organisation* – what are the present strengths and weaknesses, competition and market, challenges and opportunities?

- *Assess the current and future environments* – what is happening in the external and internal environment, what changes will affect present business or create possible new opportunities?

- *Assess the impact of projected changes* – what impact will the changes be likely to have on present operations, will they provide threats or opportunities?

- *Identify possible opportunities and evaluate possible risks* – identify possible opportunities from changes in the environment, and estimate the risks including cost, different markets and effects on present business.

- *Select feasible goals or objectives* – expanding current business or developing into new opportunities.

- *Establish priorities and allocate resources* – decide on selection of objectives and ensure supply of necessary resources.

- *Provide operational guidelines* – implement detailed operational and tactical plans.

SWOT analysis

An important aspect of strategic planning and change is the analysis of the internal strengths and weaknesses of the hospitality organisation following the formulation of objectives, and the opportunities and threats presented by its external environment.[58] SWOT is an acronym for the analysis of these Strengths, Weaknesses, Opportunities and Threats. The use of SWOT analysis can also assist the evaluation of hospitality operations and performance.

- *Strengths* are the distinctive attributes and positive aspects which provide a significant market advantage, or upon which the hospitality organisation can build and develop, for example, present market position, size and structure of operations, physical and financial resources, managerial expertise, staffing, image and reputation.

- *Weaknesses* are those deficiences in the present skills and expertise or resources of the hospitality organisation, or its image or reputation, which need to be corrected and for which action needs to be taken to minimise their effect. Weaknesses may stand in the way of achieving particular goals or objectives. Examples of weaknesses could include a high cost structure compared with competitors or a high level of customer complaints.

- *Opportunities* are favourable situations which arise from the nature of environmental change. The hospitality organisation needs to be responsive to changes which will provide an opportunity to offer new, or develop existing, facilities and services. Opportunities may arise from, for example, improved economic factors, greater leisure time, failure of competitors, new markets or products, or technological advances.

- *Threats* are the converse of opportunities. Threats refer to unfavourable situations which arise from environmental change and which are likely to endanger the operations of the organisation. Examples could include government legislation, new competitors, or demographic changes.

(For other examples of potential opportunities or threats look back at the section on Environmental Influences above.)

Identification of opportunities and risks

Costa *et al.* refer to the pace of change in the business environment, the fierce competition faced by hospitality organisations, and the need for better identification of opportunities and risks. Managers need to understand the importance of formal environmental scanning in order to provide decision-makers with the support information for their managerial activities. Hospitality organisations would explore opportunities and avoid threats better if these could be identified at an early stage.[59]

Summary

- Managers in hotels and catering tend often to view the industry as unique. The hospitality industry does have a number of distinctive features but it also shares important features with other business organisations. Hospitality education and research is in need of further development, and attention should be given to potential applications of general management theory.

- The process of management takes place the context of an organisational setting. The interrelationship of people, objectives, structure and management determine the effectiveness of hospitality operations. The nature of hotel operations, and their organisational and staffing characteristics means they are likely to embrace to a greater or lesser extent elements of associated sectors of the hospitality industry. Hospitality organisations need to give attention to the effective management of services.

- Applying the open systems model provides a common point of reference and a perspective for a meaningful comparison with other industries. The socio-technical approach is of particular relevance to the operations and work of the hospitality industry. We can analyse hospitality operations in terms of five inter-related sub-systems: task, technology, structure, people and management.

- All organisations need clear goals, objectives and policy which provide a focus for management decisions and actions. Organisational goals should be integrated with the needs of individual members. Objectives and policy may be formulated within the framework of an underlying company philosophy which influences the overall conduct of the hospitality organisation, and the behaviour and performance of staff.

- Although undoubtedly of great importance the profit motive is not by itself a sufficient criterion for the effective management of hospitality operations. Attention needs to be given to multiple areas of objective and performance setting including social responsibilities. Organisational performance is dependent upon the process of matching organisational structure, strategy and the environment.

Appendix

The following original commentary has been provided by the owners/managers of a six-bedroom country house hotel.

In the running of a small establishment as opposed to a larger organisation one of the first points to consider is what type of guest you wish to attract. This is not so narrow minded as it might appear. There are many people with like tastes and interests across the population no matter what class or creed and in a small establishment you need an easy mix of characters to create a comfortable atmosphere. This means therefore, giving careful thought as to where and how you will advertise. For instance, we accentuate the aspect of wildlife, and peace and quiet with adults only. Once you have decided to stipulate any limitation, such as, for example, no children or pets, it is essential not to waver for many guests will often choose your establishment because of that stipulation.

Most small hotels are run by the owners who probably do most of the work involved, if not all of it. This means you have to be well organised, able to turn your hands to all tasks and trades, and most importantly of all not panic if things go wrong as they are bound to from time to time. When people choose a small family-run hotel they expect to receive personal attention which means you have to be around and in view for most of the day and evening with a pleasant expression, and prepared to spend time with your guests, not just the passing hello or pleasantry.

The job, which it is really, requires an abnormally high degree of dedication and input but can be most rewarding. If you are successful at putting yourself and your establishment across, your return rate of guests takes a lot of hard work from you because they will usually chat among themselves, therefore setting the stage for a relaxed and happy atmosphere. Small additions to the furnishings and surroundings can add greatly to the well-being of your guests without being costly, for instance small ornaments, pictures or even photographs or personal portraits.

Finance and profitability are of course very important and require a lot of thought. Small establishments are not normally vastly profitable and most owners are happy if they can make a reasonable living from the business. Do not neglect the bookkeeping side of the business. If your accounts are in a mess then very likely your finances will be also. Try to keep on top of your bills and remember to put aside any VAT that will be due. We find it helpful to put this into a separate account and try to forget it is there until payment is due. Always look after and pay the small local traders you deal with. They are probably struggling too and you are more likely to get excellent service if you remember this.

Food is obviously very important and probably a high proportion of your outgoing commitments. We found that we could give a good, varied choice by displaying our menu each morning and asking guests that, if they were dining with us, could they possibly let us know and choose their meal at least an hour before dinner time. It is amazing how obliging people can be and often we know in the morning what to prepare as guests have already made their choice. This method not only cuts down on waste enormously but also ensures the dishes are freshly cooked and appetising.

Another important point is flexibility. If guests would like a slight variation from the menu this should be available and can easily be achieved in a small establishment. While it is understandable that there is the need to be cost effective, do not be meagre in proportioning the meals. For example, a good cheeseboard always receives favourable comment. You will have far happier customers if they leave the table fully satisfied rather than still feeling peckish.

If you are fortunate enough to be able to employ staff make it clear what you require of them and then trust them to get on with the job. Nobody likes to be continually monitored and it can cause bad feeling if you are always looking over their shoulders. This does not mean that you do not check their work. This can be done quite surreptitiously and if found to be lacking then a quiet word is often sufficient to rectify any shortcomings.

Should your staff at any time seem to be struggling with a task (perhaps, for example, they may not feel well) then you should be able to muck in and help. This will gain you respect apart from showing that you can do the job as well as give orders. Often this can work as a bonus as when you are pushed for time the help will be reciprocated. Build up a trust with your staff and be prepared to back them unless you know them to be in the wrong. Contrary to popular belief the customer is not always right and good staff can be hard to get.

Honesty is of the utmost importance. It will only cause dissatisfaction if your establishment is not as advertised. Do not over-embellish or state things that are not accurate. This is the surest way of inviting complaints, and one dissatisfied customer can destroy the atmosphere for all the other guests. Should you still get a guest who is unhappy then it is best to refund the deposit if applicable and let the person find somewhere else. Even if you feel that you are in the right and the complaint is unjustified this is still the best course open to you. As the saying goes 'one bad apple in the barrel . . .'

In conclusion, it is really worthwhile to establish a successful hotel business, however small, and the sense of pride and achievement outweighs the work and worry involved.

Source: The author is grateful to Stella and Paul Silver, for providing the above commentary.

Review and discussion questions

1. Explain what is meant by the organisational setting. What are the common factors that hospitality organisations share with other work organisations?

2. Summarise, with supporting practical examples, the important organisational and staffing characteristics of a hospitality organisation of your choice.

3. Identify clearly the main characteristic features of service industries. To what extent are service industries different from other industries?

4. Hospitality organisations were developed on the basis of service delivery. Does this mean that hospitality organisations by nature utilise service management? Provide examples to justify your answer.

5. Explain a hospitality organisation as an open system. How does the open systems model help in providing a basis for the analysis of hospitality operations?

6. Assess the importance of organisational goals and company philosophy. Identify examples of objectives and policy from a hospitality organisation of your choice and comment on the effectiveness of their implementation.

7. Discuss the extent to which profit maximisation is, by itself, a sufficient criterion for the effective management of hospitality operations. In what other areas should objectives be set in terms of organisational performance and results? ▷

8. Justify the extent to which you accept the concept of the social responsibilities of management. Give practical examples of how a hospitality organisation has attempted to satisfy (and/or has failed to satisfy) its social responsibilities or obligations.

9. Explain the specific steps needed to accomplish strategic planning in the hospitality industry. Assess the practical value of SWOT analysis as part of the process of strategic planning and change.

Assignment 1

According to Venison there is a striking similarity between the hotel industry and the retail industry.

(i) Investigate: (a) a hotel organisation; (b) a retail organisation; and (c) a different type of organisation.

(ii) Develop a comparative profile of the key characteristic features of each of your chosen organisations, together with a description of what is involved in their management.

(iii) Highlight common factors, similarities and significant differences across the three organisations.

(iv) What conclusions do you draw from your analysis?

Assignment 2

With the aid of a diagram, depict an actual hospitality organisation of your choice in terms of the open systems model.

(i) Explain the type and nature of the organisation including its size and location, and main characteristic features.

(ii) Give specific examples of how the functioning and operation of the organisation are affected by external environmental influences. How effective is the organisation in adapting to changes in its external environment?

(iii) Analyse, with supporting examples, the nature of the organisation's operations in terms of main interrelated sub-systems: task, technology, structure, people and management. How effective are the interrelationships and interactions among these sub-systems?

(iv) Discuss critically the effectiveness of management in coordinating the sub-systems and directing the activities of the organisation as a unified whole towards the accomplishment of its goals and objectives.

Assignment 3

The following commentary represents the personal views of the former General Manager of a Golf and Country House Hotel.

Attributes of the hotel manager

I will endeavour to list a few points on what in my opinion are the attributes of being a hotel manager and where we go wrong.

Firstly, degree students expect status but there is not any. Like a war, the best generals lead from the front, not the back. So you always put yourself in the firing line. Customers like to see the manager – not deputy manager, bar manager or restaurant manager. It might be a nod, shake of the hand or a wave, but they want recognition from the top. You should lead by example. Too many managers think that they have done all the hard work getting there, and then stop.

The hotel and leisure industry is too large to bracket. You cannot classify the Savoy or Hilton with a golf and country-house hotel or night-club. So a manager needs different attributes. You need to have the ability to socialise with your customers. It may be a granny, newly-weds, a couple on their first date, a football supporter on a night out – the list is endless. You need to be able to converse with them in their language and put them at ease. So you need an ability to judge people very quickly.

Are we attracting people to the industry and giving them a false impression? It is not an easy way of earning a living. It is very hard work and stressful. You have to work split shifts, be up early, maybe in the middle of the night, and you work late at night. It is not a glamorous career where you just stand around in a dinner suit looking pretty.

It is a people industry, full stop. You have to get on well with staff and customers and put on a smile even if your mother has died. Customers are not interested, in fact they could not give a damn, but the other way round is a totally different ball game.

As a manager you are there for when problems arise. If there are no problems you would not need a manager, so you are busy when there are difficulties. You need an ability to make quick decisions and you may not have the time to correct them so they must be right first time. You will have no social life because of the commitment needed for the job. You have to live, eat and breathe the establishment to be successful.

The hotel industry is unique. It should not be, but it is, in various ways – but then so are most industries. A good hotel manager may not be able to manage a circus or a coal pit. If hotel workers were rude to or ignored customers, as in some shops, I would be out of a job within a week. Very few people would complain when out shopping, but put them in a hotel and they change their character. So you have to have a thick skin and a long fuse. You must therefore have the ability to stay calm and composed when everything around you is burning to the ground.

I think it would be impossible to improve the standard of management without first tackling many major problems. In this country, hotel workers are always looked down upon. In France and Germany, for example, a restaurant waiter is a class job and held in high esteem. In this country, if you cannot get a job you can always work in the hotel and catering industry as a last choice.

We need more of a breakdown of what makes a successful manager. For example, making money, not receiving complaints, keeping staff, improving turnover, etc.? The job varies if it is company or privately owned. If you manage for a company you need no vision whatsoever as you get sent memos on everything from how to answer the telephone the correct way of opening a can of beans, positioning the vegetables on a plate, serving a 2 oz portion of carrots. There is a standard for everything which cannot, and will not, be deviated from in any form.

So the only way to improve turnover is people-orientated again. You have to be nice to people. Large companies do not want managers but clones – they tell you how to do everything, full stop. And when you will not do it their way, you are replaced.

Large companies in their head offices have budget forecasters, company trainers, area managers, sales and marketing departments, planners, design consultants, auditors, stock-brokers, wage departments. In fact they have the lot. They tell you how to run a successful hotel, but they miss out the most important factor – life. When do I stop serving Mr Smith who is about to knife me? Or how do I deal with Mrs Jones who has just collapsed?

▷

In the end it goes back to people. They can manage the whole show from 200 miles away, but they cannot control my tone of voice. You can say the word 'Hallo' in so many different ways – gruff, abrupt, sexy, quiet, pleasant, relaxing – the list is endless.

So you possibly need to define the word 'manager'. A manager of a cafe whose bosses are living in Spain probably has to be more of a 'manager' in some contexts than someone managing a 500-room chain hotel.

Do students who go into the trade know what they want from it? If you want to make decisions, then do not work for a company.

So far I have reached the conclusion that the most important attribute of a manager is the ability to carry out what you are told to do and not question people in authority. Maybe good hotel managers should either be trained in the police or the services because the only times you make decisions, or should make them, concern people again.

We are always given the guidelines or standards. We just have to adhere to them and this is probably the case for 95 per cent of managers. Perhaps you could analyse good managers as all yes-men?

So you need a totally new approach to the whole issue. Technical ability would be extremely high on the agenda while strategic-planning and decision-making skills are low down. If you do not know the technical side very well, you would not know if things were going amiss.

Now if we carry on this train of thought we come across a very big problem. Working for companies the amount of paperwork in triplicate is very high, so you have to spend a lot of time in the office. You have to rely on a second person or a third person, so good managers are only as good as the people around them. They therefore have to have the ability to choose a good team. And we are again back to people.

So when it comes down to the nitty gritty I do not think that you can generalise. Every case is individual. Yes, you have to mix with people. You have to give orders and clear instructions, have no social life, have an eye for detail. You take flak from all directions: from guests, staff, owners or directors. It can be a very lonely life because you are always on your own. You cannot get too close to people. You must never have a relationship with anyone you work with as this will cause you problems. You must try to stay aloof.

You must be cheerful, happy, honest, and above all fair. You must always be seen to look at both points of view and never go into conversation wearing blinkers. If you are a good listener it helps, as the hotel life varies so much. For many live-in workers, it is not a job – it is their life. Everything rolled into one. It is not a job where you clock off and go home on Friday forgetting everything until Monday morning.

At the end of the day you have to *love* the work and you are only as good as the weakest link in the chain. If you cannot stand the heat, get out of the kitchen, hotel, and grounds – because you will never make a successful manager.

Tasks

Meet in self-selecting groups of four to six.

(i) **Discuss critically what you see as the main points and issues which are raised in this commentary.**

(ii) **To what extent do you agree or disagree with the comments? Explain how these are borne out by your own experiences. How much agreement is there among members of your group?**

(iii) **Working as a group, suggest what actions you would propose in order to help overcome problem areas identified from the commentary.**

Case study 1: The New Jamaica Hotel

The New Jamaica is one of the smaller hotels owned by the Pearmain Group. Situated in a well-known South Coast resort the hotel has a 2-star rating which has been given largely on the strength of the cuisine. The chef is an Italian, Alberto Ciccetti, who would be able to choose a more highly paid job in almost any of the group's hotels in Britain or the rest of Europe, but Alberto's daughter has married an Englishman and they are living within a few miles of the New Jamaica, and this accounts for his presence in this particular hotel.

Another distinctive member of the staff is Jane Garner. Jane is the assistant manager. She is the first female appointed by the group to a top management post. They are watching her carefully to see whether the experiment is a success.

Jane was appointed 10 weeks ago and until now she has been understudying the manager, but he has started a fortnight's holiday. During the first week of the holiday Jane is confronted with the following problems:

1. Alberto Ciccetti comes to her office. He is distraught. His daughter has started divorce proceedings against her English husband. He says he has decided to take his daughter and grandchildren (2 boys aged 6 and 10) back to Italy at the earliest possible moment.

2. Jane has discovered that the manager has been charging the hotel more than he has been paying the suppliers, in some instances. In one particular case the invoice presented regularly for poultry and game shows £90, while the cheques paid out each week are for £98. Only two invoices are available (for the most recent payments), but both appear to have been altered from £90 to £98.

3. A young couple on honeymoon have taken possession of Room 29, one of the best rooms in the hotel, with sea views, bath en suite and balcony. No other room in the hotel has all these features. Another guest has now arrived and claims he booked the room two months ago. It becomes obvious that a mistake was made when the receptionist made the booking. Although this guest is shown as having booked Room 30 the amount of the deposit paid obviously relates to Room 29. The guest is very upset.

4. In the course of a few days two different guests have complained of the loss of personal belongings. One has lost a roll of colour film from a bedside table. The other has lost a nearly-full phial of Chanel No. 5. There has been no suggestion of involving the police by either of the parties, but they are in no doubt that these items have been stolen.

5. Passing through the restaurant at lunch-time – it was crowded – she heard one of the customers complaining about an overcooked steak. The harassed waitress retorted, 'Don't blame me. That's the way they cooked it.' Her manner was decidedly off-hand, and the customer and his companion were obviously displeased with her manner.

(Reprinted with permission of the author, Joe Chilver.)

TASKS

(a) Discuss the main issues which are raised by each of these matters.

(b) Explain how you think Jane should deal with each of these situations.

Case study 2

The General Manager has passed to you the following letter recently received from a guest.

PERSONAL
(Name)
General Manager
ABC Hotel, London

22 March xxxx

Dear (Name)

My wife and I have just stayed for two days at ABC Holiday (Room 117). There was no questionnaire form in the room so I am writing to you with my comments.

1. In the bathroom there was a stained washbasin, broken shower rail and rusty showerhead. Although there was a soap container on the wall close to the shower there were no individual tablets of soap – how is one to wash in the bath with the soap container four feet above your head?

2. On the first morning after arrival there was not hot water in the room. This I duly reported to reception only to be received with a less than enthusiastic response or concern, which appeared to border on indifference and a perceived attitude of 'what do you expect me to do about it?'

3. In the bedroom there was a loose fitment between the two beds and a noticeable absence of the bowl of fruit, which is implied from the picture in your promotional leaflet.

4. For breakfast you are advised that coffee/tea/toast would be served at your table by the waiting staff. On both days after a lengthy delay we had to specifically request this service.

5. There seemed very little help with baggage – or if there is, this was not made apparent and there was definitely no rush of staff offering assistance.

6. Although not openly rude, staff at reception do not appear to realise that they are allowed to smile at and exchange if not pleasantries, at least common courtesy, with guests. As an example, when my wife said 'good morning' and enquired please if there was a postal collection service she received only a nod. Upon further enquiry I was pointed to leave our outgoing mail on the reception desk, again without any spoken response.

Charges for bed and breakfast at ABC Hotel are not cheap especially as we were private guests (not conference delegates or business people) paying our own way. I was not at all happy with the overall standard of service which was certainly not in keeping with expectations from experiences elsewhere. I hope you feel able to give consideration to these comments. Thank you.

Yours faithfully

TASK

Draft a suitable reply for the General Manager

Notes and references

1. See, for example, Mullins L J, 'Managerial Behaviour and Development in the Hospitality Industry', *Proceedings of The International Association of Hotel Management Schools Symposium*, Leeds Polytechnic, November 1988.
2. *Training: Who Needs it? Research Report 1995: Executive Summary*, HCTC, 1995.
3. *Statistical Review of the Hotel and Catering Industry*, HCITB and MMD Consultants, May 1984.
4. Hornsey T and Dann D, *Manpower Management in the Hotel and Catering Industry*, Batsford (1984).
5. King C A, 'What is Hospitality?', *International Journal of Hospitality Management*, vol. 14, nos 3/4, 1995, pp. 219–234.
6. Guerrier Y, *Organizational Behaviour in Hotels and Restaurants: An International Perspective*, Wiley (1999).
7. Fearn D A, *The Practice of General Management: Catering Applications*, Macdonald (1971), p. 1.
8. Guerrier Y and Lockwood A, 'Managers in Hospitality: A Review of Current Research', in Cooper C (ed.), *Progress in Tourism, Recreation and Hospitality Management*, vol. 2, Bellhaven Press (May 1990), pp. 151–167.
9. Medlik S, *The Business of Hotels*, 3rd edn, Butterworth-Heinemann (1994) p. xvi.
10. Jones P, 'Hospitality Research – Where Have We Got to?', *International Journal of Hospitality Management*, vol. 15, no. 1, 1996, pp. 5–10.
11. Taylor S and Edgar D, 'Hospitality Research: The Emperor's New Clothes?', *International Journal of Hospitality Management*, vol. 15, no. 3, 1996, pp. 211–227.
12. Guerrier Y and Deery M, 'Research in Hospitality Resource Management and Organizational Behaviour', *International Journal of Hospitality Management*, vol. 17, 1998, pp. 145–160.
13. See, for example, Riley M, *Human Resource Management in the Hospitality and Tourism Industry*, 2nd edn, Butterworth-Heinemann (1996).
14. Medlik S, *The Business of Hotels*, 3rd edn, Butterworth-Heinemann (1994).
15. For example see, Guerrier Y and Lockwood A, 'Core and Peripheral Employees in Hotel Operations', *Personnel Review*, vol. 18, no. 1, 1989, pp. 9–15.
16. See, for example, Mars G, Bryant D and Mitchell P, *Manpower Problems in the Hotel and Catering Industry*, Saxon House (1979).
17. See: For example, Ahmed Z U, Heller V L and Hughes K A, 'South Africa's Hotel Industry', *Cornell HRA Quarterly*, February 1999, pp. 74–85.
18. For a discussion on the small hotel, see for example: Medlik S, *The Business of Hotels*, 3rd edn, Butterworth-Heinemann (1994).
19. Hayward N, *There's a Small Hotel*, Methuen (2000).
20. Jones P (ed.), *Management in Service Industries*, Pitman (1989).
21. Fitzsimmons J A and Sullivan R S, *Service Operations Management*, McGraw-Hill (1982).
22. Jones P and Lockwood A, *The Management of Hotel Operations*, Cassell (1989).
23. Levitt T, 'Production-Line Approach to Service', *Harvard Business Review*, September–October 1972, p. 41.
24. Macdonald J, 'Service Is Different', *The TQM Magazine*, vol. 6, no. 1, 1994, pp. 5–7.
25. Stamatis D H, *Total Quality Service*, St Lucie Press (1996).
26. Jones P (ed.), *Management in Service Industries*, Pitman (1989).
27. Albrecht K, *At America's Service*, Dow Jones-Irwin (1988), p. 20.
28. Chacko H E, 'Designing a seamless hotel organization', *International Journal of Contemporary Hospitality Management*, vol. 10, no. 4, 1998, p. 134.
29. Gronroos C, *Service Management and Marketing*, Lexington Books (1990), p. 244.
30. Riley M, *Human Resource Management in the Hospitality and Tourism Industry*, 2nd edn, Butterworth-Heinemann (1996), p. 1.

31. Katz D and Kahn R L, *The Social Psychology of Organizations*, 2nd edn, Wiley (1978).

32. See, for example, Wachtel J M, 'Marketing or Sales? Some Confusion in the Hospitality Industry', *International Journal of Hospitality Management*, vol. 3, no. 1, 1984, pp. 38–40.

33. Nailon P, 'Theory in Hospitality Management', *International Journal of Hospitality Management*, vol. 1, no. 3, 1982, pp. 135–143.

34. Wood R C, 'Theory, Management and Hospitality: A Response to Philip Nailon', *International Journal of Hospitality Management*, vol. 2, no. 2, 1983, pp. 103–104.

35. *Ibid.*, p. 104.

36. Dodrill K and Riley M, 'Hotel Workers' Orientations to Work: The Question of Autonomy and Scope', *International Journal of Contemporary Hospitality Management*, vol. 4, no. 1, 1992, pp. 23–25.

37. Venison P, *Managing Hotels*, Heinemann (1983).

38. Wood R C, *Working in Hotels and Catering*, 3rd edn, International Thomson Business Press (1997) p. 74.

39. Mullins L J, 'Is the Hotel and Catering Industry Unique?', *Hospitality*, no. 21, September 1981, pp. 30–33.

40. Mullins L J, 'The Hotel and the Open Systems Model of Organisational Analysis', *The Service Industries Journal*, vol. 13, no. 1, January 1993, pp. 1–16.

41. Costa J, Eccles G and Teare R, 'Trends in Hospitality: Academic and Industry Perceptions', *International Journal of Contemporary Hospitality Management*, vol. 9, no. 7, 1997, pp. 285–294.

42. See, for example, Keiser J R, *Principles and Practices of Management in the Hospitality Industry*, 2nd edn, Van Nostrand Reinhold (1989).

43. See, for example, Mullins L J, *Management and Organisational Behaviour*, 5th edn, Financial Times Pitman Publishing (1999).

44. Trist E L *et al.*, *Organizational Choice*, Tavistock (1963).

45. Roddick A, *Body and Soul*, Ebury Press (1991).

46. Brech E F L (ed.), *The Principles and Practice of Management*, 3rd edn, Longman (1975).

47. Upchurch R S, 'Ethics in the Hospitality Industry: An Applied Model', *International Journal of Contemporary Hospitality Management*, vol. 10, no. 6, 1998, p. 227.

48. Forte, Sir Charles, 'Catering for Everyone', *Professional Administration*, vol. 9, no. 9, October 1979, p. 24.

49. Fearn D A, *The Practice of General Management: Catering Applications*, Macdonald (1971), p. 17.

50. Drucker P F, *The Practice of Management*, Pan Books (1968), pp. 82–83.

51. For a more detailed account see Gullen H V and Rhodes G E, *Management in the Hotel and Catering Industry*, Batsford (1983).

52. Simon H A, 'On the Concept of Organisational Goal', *Administrative Science Quarterly*, vol. 10, June 1984, p. 21.

53. Merriden T, 'The Gurus: Rosabeth Moss Kanter', *Management Today*, February 1997, p. 56.

54. Jones P (ed.), *Management in Service Industries*, Pitman (1989).

55. Schaffer J D, 'Structure and Strategy: Two Sides of Success' in Rutherford D G (ed.), *Hotel Management and Operations*, Van Nostrand Reinhold (1990).

56. Webster M W, 'Strategic Management in Context at Swallow Hotels', *International Journal of Contemporary Hospitality Management*, vol. 6, no. 5, 1994, pp. 3–8.

57. Keiser J R, *Principles and Practices of Management in the Hospitality Industry*, 2nd edn, Van Nostrand Reinhold (1989).

58. Ansoff H I, *Corporate Strategy*, rev'd edn, Penguin (1987).

59. Costa J, Eccles G and Teare R, 'Trends in Hospitality: Academic and Industry Percerptions', *International Journal of Contemporary Hospitality Management*, vol. 9, no. 7, 1997, pp. 285–294.

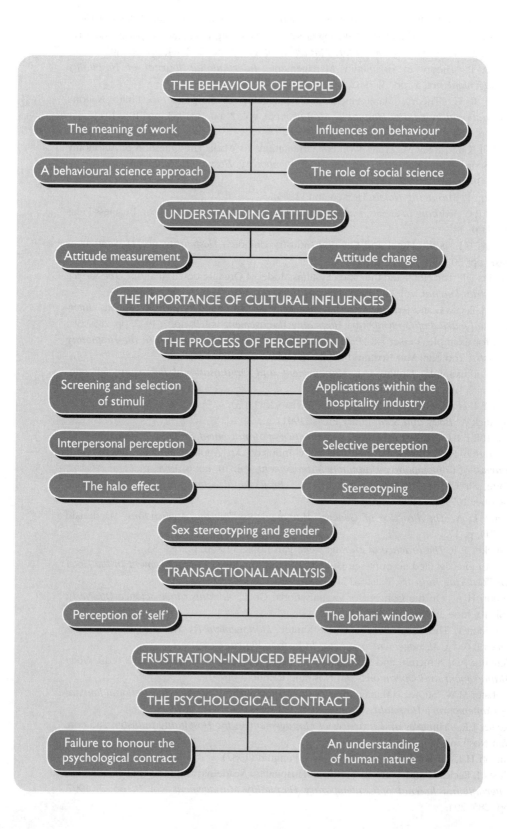

Chapter three

Working with people

Introduction

People are the central focus of effective management. It is the interaction of people in order to achieve objectives which forms the basis of an organisation. Without people the hospitality industry cannot function. If managers are to improve performance, they need a knowledge and understanding of what influences the behaviour of people at work.[1]

The behaviour of people

We saw in Chapter 2 that a major characteristic of the hospitality industry is the role of people. Experience of service delivery is dependent upon personal interaction between staff and customers. Effective management is therefore about working with people. Unlike physical resources, people are not owned by the organisation. And of course people differ as individuals.

> *People are not all made the same way. They are not all rounded. Some are angular, some are difficult, and you have to fit in with them and their personality.*[2]

Members of staff will have their own perceptions of the hospitality organisation as a work organisation, and hold their own views on the systems and style of management. People bring their own feelings and attitudes towards their duties and responsibilities, and the conditions under which they are working.

Human behaviour is capricious and results from a multiplicity of influences which are difficult to identify or explain. Scientific methods or principles of behaviour cannot be applied with reliability. Tensions, conflicts and stress are almost inevitable, as are informal structures of organisation and unofficial working methods.[3]

The day a red-hot chef let his temper boil over

One of Britain's top young chefs has resigned from an exclusive restaurant after allegedly branding a trainee with a hot knife.

continued

continued

Tom Aikens is said to have 'turned on' 19-year-old Marcus Donaldson after he made a minor mistake in the kitchen of Pied a Terre, in London's West End.

The chef, the youngest in the country to be awarded two coveted Michelin stars, is claimed to have picked up a knife and held it under a blowtorch – normally used for putting a crisp top on creme brulee desserts – until it was red hot.

He is then said to have pressed the knife against Mr Donaldson's arm, telling him: 'You don't have enough burns to work in this restaurant.'

Shocked staff in the basement kitchen were apparently told to 'get on with their work' and to 'forget' about the incident.

But yesterday, directors of the restaurant, in Charlotte Street, confirmed that fellow director Mr Aikens, 29, known for his fiery temperament, had been forced to resign as head chef. His wife Laura, who was assistant manager, also quit.

It is understood Mr Aikens faced disciplinary action if he had not agreed to leave immediately.

A source at the restaurant said: 'Aikens's resignation is directly linked to the incident last Friday night. We cannot have things like this going on in the kitchen. Even if it was in the heat of the moment it was a very stupid thing to do and gives Pied à Terre a very bad image.

'Behaviour like this cannot be tolerated, and it was the unanimous decision of the four other directors that he had to go.'

Restaurant senior partner David Moore added: 'Tom is a very talented chef who demands high standards from those around him.

'But in a hot kitchen, what people might accept as being normal is not always regarded as so in the cold light of day.'

He predicted a bright future for Mr Aikens, but added: 'His temperament needs to be worked on.' The incident at the Pied a Terre has not been reported to the police.

Mr Aikens's departure over his alleged behaviour is the latest in a long line of incidents involving leading London chefs in what is a lucrative but increasingly competitive business.

The trend for fiery chefs was set most notably by Marco Pierre White. More recently, former professional footballer Gordon Ramsay – who has a restaurant in Chelsea – has gained a reputation for his 'ranting and raving' in the kitchen. Mr Aikens and Mr Ramsay are themselves said to have become 'fierce rivals'.

'There can be a lot of aggravation'

Last night Mr Ramsay, who said he 'didn't have a problem' with being described as 'fiery or volatile' revealed he had heard about the alleged branding incident at Pied a Terre because one of his apprentices shared a flat with Mr Donaldson. He claimed the teenager's father Malcolm had come to London from the family home in Sheffield 'looking for Tom Aikens'.

Last night neither Mr Aikens nor Mr Donaldson – who was back home in Yorkshire but planned to return to Pied a Terre – was available for comment.

Mr Aikens, from Norwich, was awarded the Michelin stars for his 'brilliant and cutting edge' cuisine. He was 26 when he scooped the award only months after joining Pied a Terre. At the time, he said: 'I can't believe it. It's a dream come true.

continued

continued

'And being the youngest ever gives me an even greater buzz.' Mr Aikens, who has a twin brother, has spoken of 'nurturing' his ambition to become a top chef since the age of 12, and has worked up to 20 hours a day in pursuit of that goal.

He has also talked about 'violence' in restaurant kitchens, saying: 'There can be a lot of aggravation there. We all know the chefs who like to beat their staff up, but there is absolutely no need for it.'

He was 'OK with giving someone a really good shouting at' but 'punching them and hitting them is totally out of order'.

He said of trainee staff: 'Some have talent, some don't. Those ones that don't, you've got to push them a bit more, and sometimes they still can't get it right.'

Reproduced with kind permission from the *Daily mail*, 17 December 1999, p. 8

Cooking up a success

Chefs have a reputation for being quick tempered and constantly shouting at incompetent staff. However, according to Gill Scott, chef and co-owner of the Bistro Montparnasse, Southsea, the chef's job does not have to be like that. She stresses that not all chefs are highly strung prima donnas and would recommend the job to anyone with the ambition to do it.

'If you are organised enough then you don't need to get into a panic. I have worked in places where the head chef would throw a pan along the floor at your ankles if you were talking or doing something you shouldn't. You can go to work in some kitchens and the head chef won't talk to you for two days. I have seen chefs sweep a whole batch of food on the floor because it hasn't been done the way he wants it. But I don't believe that is productive. I try not to lose my temper. It happens maybe once or twice a month. My two second chefs and I get on very well. It's a very happy environment and we enjoy what we do. The hours are long and unsociable. Hotel chefs have to work shifts, either late at night or very early in the morning. Some days you might have to do "back-to-back" shifts finishing at midnight and starting again at 5.30 the next morning. I start work at around 10 am and my two second chefs join me at 2 pm and work until midnight with one break between 6 pm and 6.45 pm. It's a long day and the wages are not very high but both my second chefs have been with me for a long time. They enjoy it. You have got to be determined and have ambition to succeed in cheffing and in catering.'

The meaning of work

Work holds a number of different meanings and values for people, and plays a variety of roles in their lives. Work helps to fulfil a range of diverse needs and expectations relating to, for example, economic rewards, intrinsic satisfaction and social relationships. (These sets of needs and expectations are discussed further in Chapter 7.) People differ, therefore, in the extent and manner of their involvement with work. Goldthorpe, for example, has identified three general sets of attitudes, or orientations, to work.[4]

● Some individuals may have only a calculative or economic involvement with work. This suggests an **instrumental orientation** with an attitude to work not as a central life issue but simply as a means to an end.

● For other individuals work may be seen more as a central life issue. There is a sense of obligation to the work of the organisation and a strong positive involvement in terms of a career structure. This suggests a **bureaucratic orientation**.

● Yet other individuals may view work primarily in terms of group activities and an ego involvement with work groups rather than the work of the organisation itself. This suggests a **solidaristic orientation** with a close link between work-related and social activities.

These different orientations will shape the individuals' attitudes towards work, and have a significant influence on the importance attached to those factors which affect their motivation and job satisfaction. Some people may have a set orientation to work whatever the nature of the work environment, while for other people different work situations may influence their orientation to work. For example, a perceived lack of opportunities for high economic rewards or job security may result in greater emphasis on a solidaristic orientation to work, and a primary concern for teamwork and satisfaction of social expectations.

Orientation towards work

To what extent, then, does the nature of work in service industries and features such as low pay, poor working conditions, and the often routine and mundane nature of tasks give rise to a particular orientation or set of attitudes towards work? For example, Dodrill and Riley undertook a small research project in order to investigate the theme that hotel workers value variety and scope in their work.[5] The questionnaire project was expected to show that hotel workers display a positive attitude towards five characteristic factors – ambition, the desire for scope in the job, mobility, security and autonomy. However, the findings from 88 hotel workers of various ages and occupations, plus the control sample, did not support this contention. Only ambition and scope in the job were found as strong positive attitudes with the control sample following a similar pattern. From this, admittedly small and limited, study Dodrill and Riley conclude that hotel workers do not hold any unique orientation or distinctive attitudes towards work.

Influences on behaviour

The behaviour of people at work cannot be studied in isolation. The hospitality organisation as a work organisation is a constantly changing network of interrelated activities. Using the open systems model discussed in Chapter 2 we can see that effective performance will be dependent upon interactions among people and the nature of the tasks to be undertaken, the technology employed and methods of carrying out work, patterns of organisation structure, the process of management, and the external environment.

These variables provide parameters which enable us to formulate a simple four-fold framework in which to view influences on behaviour: the individual, the group, the organisation and the environment.[6]

● *The individual* – for example, the personality, skills and attributes, values and attitudes, needs and expectations of individual members. The individual is the central feature of organisational behaviour, whether acting in isolation or as part of a group, in response to demands of the organisation or as a result of environmental influences.

● *The group* – for example, the structure and functioning of work groups, the informal organisation, role relationships. Groups are essential to effective working and everyone will be a member of one or more groups. People in groups influence each other in many ways, and groups may develop their own hierarchies and leaders. Group pressures can have a major influence on the behaviour and performance of individual members.

● *The organisation* – for example, objectives and policy, technology and methods of work, styles of leadership, methods of supervision and control. Individuals and groups interact within the formal organisation. The design of structure, patterns of management and organisational processes for the execution of work will impact on the behaviour of people.

● *The environment* – for example, technical and scientific developments, economic activity, social and cultural influences, governmental actions. The hospitality organisation functions as part of the wider environment of which it is part and must be responsive to the external demands placed upon it. Environmental factors are reflected in terms of the management of opportunities and risks, the operations of the organisation and the behaviour of people.

A behavioural science approach

Within the framework of individual, group, organisation and environment we can identify a number of interrelated dimensions which collectively influence the behaviour of people in the work situation. The framework presents a number of alternative approaches to the study of human behaviour which give rise to frequent debate and discussion.

It is possible, for example, to adopt a psychological approach with the main emphasis on the individual, or to adopt a sociological approach with the main emphasis on human behaviour in society. It is also possible to adopt an anthropological approach with emphasis on the study of culture and customs of human behaviour as a whole.

An interdisciplinary approach

All three areas are important, as are other related areas of the social sciences such as economics and political science. But our main concern here is not with finer details of specific academic disciplines, per se, but with the behaviour and management of people as human resources of the hospitality industry.

An understanding of people's behaviour at work cannot be achieved in terms of the study of a single discipline. It is more appropriate therefore to take an interdisciplinary, behavioural science approach by drawing upon relevant aspects of psychology, sociology and anthropology (see Figure 3.1).

● *Psychology* is concerned broadly with the study of human behaviour, with traits of the individual and membership of small social groups. The main focus of attention is on the 'personality system' and individual traits and properties such as perception, attitudes, motives and feelings.

● *Sociology* is concerned more with the study of social behaviour, and relationships among social groups and society. The main focus of attention is the 'social system' and the analysis of social structures and positions, for example the relationships between the behaviour of leaders and followers.

● *Anthropology* is concerned with the science of mankind and the study of human behaviour as a whole. A main focus of attention is on the 'cultural system' and the beliefs, customs, ideas and values within a society which affect the emphasis that individuals place on certain aspects of behaviour.

Figure 3.1: An
interdisciplinary
approach to
the study of
behaviour

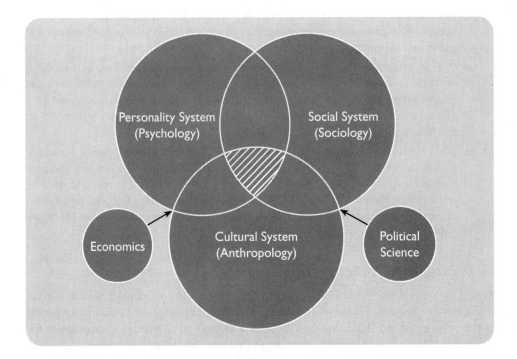

Figure 3.1: An interdisciplinary approach to the study of behaviour

Applications of behavioural science

Once again, terminology is not always consistent and the wording 'behavioural science' has no strict scientific definition. It may be used in a generic sense for all the social sciences concerned with the study of human behaviour. But the term is now frequently applied in a more narrow and selective way to problems of organisation and management in the work environment. Behavioural science attempts to structure organisations in order to secure the optimum working environment. It is concerned with reconciling the needs of the organisation for the contribution of maximum productivity, with the needs of individuals and the realisation of their potential. Some applications of behavioural science to the hospitality industry are given by, for example, Atkinson,[7] Wood,[8] and Carmouche and Kelly.[9]

The role of social science

The nature of the hospitality industry as a people industry and the importance of the study of social science is widely recognised. For example, Slattery argues that the social sciences alone are able to offer theoretically grounded interpretations of people and social events in hospitality. The success of these interpretations depend upon:

- the selection of relevant theories;
- developing hospitality versions of the theories; and
- an evaluation of flaws and limitations, and value to the hospitality industry.[10]

Slattery suggests that although not all of the social sciences are useful or relevant, the range of theories which are useful is still vast. The selection of a theory depends upon the problems or issues in which we are interested. Theories of motivation, commitment and organisation are necessary bases.

The need for vocational relevance

In a critique of the role of social science subjects in hospitality management education, Wood suggests the need for a substantial reappraisal of social science education.[11] He questions the need to ensure vocational relevance and argues that such an approach could lead to dilution of the tenability of the subject matter. An alternative would be the grounding of specific components of social sciences – principally economics and sociology – with a theoretical and empirical base. However, as Wood himself states, 'whilst this approach *may* encourage intellectual integrity, it can promise nothing else'.

Such an approach as suggested by Wood would seem unlikely to gain much favour with either students or practitioners. The use of the social sciences should be seen as part of the tool kit of management, to be drawn upon and used as particular circumstances demand. The overriding objective must surely be how an understanding of the practical application of relevant aspects of social science can improve the people–organisation relationship.

A 'learning to manage organisations' approach

In a study of the teaching of sociological subjects on vocational degree courses in hotel and catering management, Lennon and Wood also report on the claimed intellectual dilution of sociology and social scientific knowledge. Such dilution is seen as a result of a number of institutional pressures including the views of industrialists, and is characterised by a multi-disciplinary approach related to the criteria of relevance to the job of a manager and a 'learning to manage organisations' approach to social studies. Lennon and Wood conclude that 'there seems little danger of contradiction in asserting that (hotel and catering) management and business studies education is, in social scientific terms at least, intellectually weak and of dubious practical value.'[12]

Although one can perhaps understand Lennon and Wood's scepticism about the idea that the social sciences represent a unified body of knowledge, this should not detract from the advantages of an interdisciplinary, behavioural science approach to an understanding of the behaviour of people at work.

Problems of organisation and management

Sociological aspects clearly can be important but much of the argument tends to be presented in the abstract and is lacking in constructive ideas on how, in practical terms, action could be taken to improve organisational performance. A requirement for intellectual rigour is of course a commendable aim. But this should not be allowed to disguise the fact that an integral part of hospitality management and business studies education should rightly involve an emphasis on vocational relevance and attention to learning to manage organisations.

Our knowledge of human behaviour stems from different sources. In attempting to solve problems of organisation and management in the work environment it is necessary to cut across traditional academic disciplines.[13] It is for this reason that behavioural science has developed as a body of knowledge. There is now strong support for the belief that:

> *a knowledge and understanding of behavioural science, and the application of some of the key ideas about behaviour, can help improve both managerial and organisational performance.*[14]

Understanding attitudes

Organisations consist of people working together but individuals offer different attitudes and perceptions towards their working life. Differences between people can be a source of developing creativity or the root of potential conflict, frustration and organisational problems. It is possible to differentiate among individuals in terms of their types/traits, physique, gender, abilities, developmental aspects, attitudes, perception, motivation, and social and cultural environment. In order to help understand the behaviour of people managers need to be aware of, and sensitive to, factors affecting individual differences and their own assumptions and attitudes.

Referring to a person's attitude is a common occurrence within the work situation, and especially within the hospitality industry where members of staff must cooperate closely with other people and may have direct contact with the customer. An understanding of the nature of attitudes and their relationships to behaviour is therefore an important aspect of the effective management of people. *Attitudes can be defined as providing a state of 'readiness' or tendency to respond in a particular way.*[15] Attitudes differ from opinions, beliefs (which are concerned with what is known about the world), and values (which are concerned with what is desirable and 'should be'). Gross suggests that 'to convert a belief into an attitude, a "value" ingredient is needed which, by definition, is to do with an individual's sense of what is desirable, good, valuable, worthwhile and so on'. Whereas adults may have thousands of beliefs, they may have only hundreds of attitudes and a few dozen values.[16]

Attitudes are learned throughout life and embodied within our socialisation process. There is no limit to the attitudes people hold. Some attitudes, such as religious beliefs or other cultural influences (discussed below) may be central to us – a core construct – and may be highly resistant to any change. Other, more peripheral attitudes may be subject to change more easily with new information or personal experiences. Specific events, particularly traumatic ones, for example unexpected redundancy, may have a dramatic effect on our attitudes.

Functions served by attitudes

Attitudes and motives are interlinked and, depending on an individual's motives, Katz has suggested that attitudes can serve four main functions.

- *Knowledge* – a basis for the interpretation and classification of new information. Attitudes provide a knowledge base and framework within which new information can be placed.

- *Expressive* – a means of expression. Attitudes enable individuals to indicate to others the values they hold and to express their self-concept and adopt or internalise the values of the group.

- *Instrumental* – held attitudes maximise rewards and minimise sanctions. Attitudes towards other people, or objects, might be held because of past positive (or negative) experiences. Knowledge or behaviour which has resulted in satisfaction of needs is more likely to result in a favourable attitude.

- *Ego-defensive* – attitudes may be held in order to protect the ego from an undesirable truth or reality.[17]

Important implications for the study of attitudes

It seems that people do not always behave in a way that is true to their beliefs: what they say and what they do may be very different. Attitudes can be revealed not only in behaviour but also by the individual's thoughts (although these may not be revealed in public) and by feelings, the strength of which demonstrates the extent to which the attitude is a core or peripheral construct.

This point is illustrated in a classic study by La Piere. Visiting American hotels and restaurants with a Chinese couple, La Piere found no apparent sign of prejudiced attitudes in face-to-face situations, but in the follow-up attitude survey there were marked racist attitudes. He found complete contradictions between public and private attitudes.[18]

There are two important issues in the study of attitudes for both the psychologist and the manager.

- *Attitudes cannot be seen; they can only be inferred* – heavy reliance is placed therefore on the accuracy of assessment. The attitudes held by members of staff are important for morale and organisational effectiveness so it is important to have confidence in the techniques used to assess the nature and strength of attitudes.

- *Attitudes are often shared within organisations* – they may be embodied in the culture of the organisation. Attitudes are not just formed individually but arise out of interaction with others (although not only just within the organisation but also within the wider community). Sharing the belief system of others can influence either positive or negative feelings about working in an organisation.

Attitude measurement

There are a number of different techniques which could be used to measure attitudes, the two most common being direct observation and self-reporting techniques. Direct observation relies on an informal, unsystematic approach based on assumptions and an understanding of social cues and body language. However, managers may be erroneous in their assumptions and beliefs. These may never have been tested – merely assumed to be correct – and they may be mistaken in their judgements.

Organisations which assess their employees' attitudes by questionnaires (self-reporting techniques) are attempting to systematically gauge and measure these assumptions and beliefs. Attitude questionnaires are used by many organisations as a barometer of attitudinal climate, and to enable managers to be in touch with employees' views and feelings.

However, attitude questionnaires are time consuming to design and administer. The questions asked, their relevance, style and length are all important variables in the validity of the questionnaire. So, too, is the honest completion of questionnaires. Making public people's private attitudes may also have its dangers as expectations of change may be envisaged and if these do not occur, disappointment and low morale may result.[19]

A shared view of the industry

Research by Hicks in the hotel industry revealed that irrespective of personal circumstances (age, gender, education, social class) managers had been exposed to a process which had 'encultured' them to a shared view of the industry, resulting in common attitudes on a range of topics. Attitudes towards their management trainees were found to be significant with regard to the trainees' development; such high expectations ensured broad training opportunities and the use of their own personal network of contacts to ensure their protégés' success. The significance of positive attitudes of managers towards their trainees cannot, therefore, be over-emphasised.[20]

Attitude change

Theories on attitude change stress the importance of balance and consistency in our psyche. For example, Heider suggests that not only would we find it uncomfortable to hold two conflicting attitudes but to do so would motivate us to change one of the attitudes to reach a state of balance.[21] Festinger's theory of cognitive dissonance refers to the psychological discomfort felt when we hold inconsistent beliefs or act in a way that is inconsistent with our true beliefs. The theory suggests that we are motivated to reduce the impact of this discomfort by taking appropriate action and to change a belief.[22]

The process of attitude change is dependent on a number of key factors including: why an attitude is held in the first place; why it should change; what the benefits are and for whom; and the likely outcomes if it does not change. As mentioned previously, peripheral attitudes may be subject to change more easily with new information or personal experiences, whereas central attitudes tied to a core construct may be highly resistant to any change.

The importance of cultural influences

The hospitality industry is very cosmopolitan and it is therefore particularly important to recognise the significance of different cultural and ethnic values, and associated traditions, religious beliefs and customs. Understanding other people's views of the world will not only make for better customer and staff relations, but may also help to prevent possible allegations of discrimination.

Account must clearly be taken of differences in diet, language, touching, gestures and mannerisms. For example the English language is written from left to right but Hebrew is written from right to left, and Chinese is written downwards. There are many instances of different cultural gestures and mannerisms. For example, when the Dutch point a forefinger at their temples this is likely to be a sign of congratulations for a good idea. Elsewhere, the gesture has a less complimentary implication. In many European countries it is customary to give three or four kisses on the cheek and pulling the head away may be taken as a sign of impoliteness. When talking to another person, British people tend to look away spasmodically but Norwegians tend to look people steadily in the eyes without changing their gaze.

A multi-cultural environment is a feature of the hotel industry. An understanding of cultural characteristics, including spiritual and moral persuasions of varying ethnic groups, will help in understanding the behaviour of both staff and customers, and should therefore form an essential part of induction and training programmes. Managers also need to be aware of how cultural differences can influence the attitudes and motivations of staff, and their pace of work. This demands effective systems of communication and attention to interpersonal relationships.[23]

Effects of cultural differences

An example may be found in people who follow the Islamic faith. If they have a large number of Muslim customers some hotels may remove alcoholic beverages from the mini-bars in their bedrooms. During Ramadan, Muslim members of staff may fast through the daylight hours, eat meals only at certain times and not be prepared to work on certain days for religious reasons. The manager may therefore arrange holidays and shift working accordingly.

A number of London hotels now provide special meals for the growing number of Japanese customers and some hotels even provide separate menus and dining facilities. If there is a large number of Jewish customers some restaurant managers will not put pork on the meat trolley. Airport hotels which receive many Jewish customers may even make special arrangements for the preparation and service of kosher food.

Differences in culture may also help to explain the attitude of certain customers. Japanese businessmen who are accompanied by their wives may expect the best seats at the dining table. Americans often have a reputation for being particularly demanding and expecting a high level of personal attention. Such expectations might be better understood if managers and staff are aware of cultural differences and, as the author can testify, the high standards of customer service and concern for individual requirements which is customary in many parts of America.[24] German business people tend to respect formality in relationships at work, which are conducted formally in terms of the organisational hierarchy, and to avoid familiarity in public. Another aspect of cultural values is physical space. All cultures have specific values related to personal space. For example, Arabs tend to stand very close when speaking to another person but most Americans when introduced to a new person will, after shaking hands, move backwards a couple of steps to place a comfortable space between themselves and the person they have met.

Culture will also influence appearance and dress. There are many examples of this: saris worn by Hindu women; long flowing robes worn by Arabs; Sikhs wearing their hair uncut and by tradition carrying a steel comb and bangle. Because of their culture many Muslim women will not wear clothes that show their legs, and will cover their heads and sometimes much of their faces with scarves. A further example is the dreadlocks hair style of Rastafarians.

The process of perception

A particularly significant aspect of individual differences and a major determinant of behaviour within the hospitality industry, is the process of perception. People all 'see' things differently. Owners, managers, staff, union representatives, customers, guests, visitors, suppliers, health inspectors and local residents will all have their own perception of the functioning and operations of the particular establishment. And so will each person as an individual. All people have their own, unique picture or image of how they arbitrarily view what is to them the 'real' world. Consider the following example.

People perceive things differently

The general manager is preparing a human resource plan for the establishment and wishes to gather information which may help to improve future staffing levels. The manager requests section heads to provide details of agency and temporary staff employed within their section during the past six months and projections for the next six months.

● One section head may perceive the request as an unreasonable demand, intended only to enable management to exercise closer supervision and control over the activities of the section.

● Another section head may see the request only as increased bureaucracy and more paperwork, and believe that nothing positive will come of it anyway.

● A further section head may welcome the request and perceive this as a hopeful sign of an increase in permanent staffing levels for the section.

● But yet another section head is concerned that the manager is intending to put pressure on permanent staff to work harder and longer hours.

Figure 3.2:
The process
of perception

Figure 3.3:
An example
of incomplete
stimuli

Stimuli from the environment

Why is it that the same request can provide such mixed reactions and why do people perceive things differently? We are faced constantly with a vast amount of information (stimuli) from the environment such as shapes, colours, movement, taste, sounds, touch, smells, pain, pressures and feelings. *Perception is the process by which stimuli are screened and selected to provide meaning and significance to the individual.* The manner in which stimuli are selected and organised gives rise to individual behavioural responses (Figure 3.2).

Individuals have their own 'mental' view of reality. Despite the fact that a group of people may 'physically' see or hear the same thing, each person has his or her own version of what is seen or heard. A person's pattern of behaviour is shaped in response to how that person perceives a particular situation. The process of perception is essential, therefore, to an understanding of human behaviour. Consider, for example, the shape in Figure 3.3.[25] *Write down exactly what you see.* Do this before reading further. We shall return to this later.

Perceptual ambiguity

A well-known example of what might be termed a perceptual ambiguity is the shape in Figure 3.4.[26] What do *you* see?

Most people will probably see a younger, well-dressed woman looking sideways. But other people will see an older, poor looking woman facing more to the front. And some people will quickly see both. How can people who view the same thing 'see' something so different? This helps to explain the importance of perception.

Can you now see the other picture? If so this should help you to understand why other people have a different perception to your own. Also, once you have seen clearly both pictures your mental image may quickly jump from one to the other, causing some confusion as to what you really do see.

Screening and selection of stimuli

Because there is such a vast amount of stimuli, we cannot cope adequately with all of them so we focus on certain selected stimuli and screen or filter out others. This screening and selection of stimuli is based on a combination of internal and external factors, and the context in which the stimuli occur (see Figure 3.5).

Internal factors

Internal factors relate to the characteristics of the individual such as personality, attitudes, learning, motives, needs and preferences, interests, expectations and previous experiences. People usually perceive stimuli that are likely to satisfy their needs or prove pleasurable. People may also learn to ignore mildly disturbing stimuli but respond to more important ones. For example, a manager may screen out the constant movement of people, ringing telephones and other forms of activity, but respond quickly to a guest complaining to a receptionist.

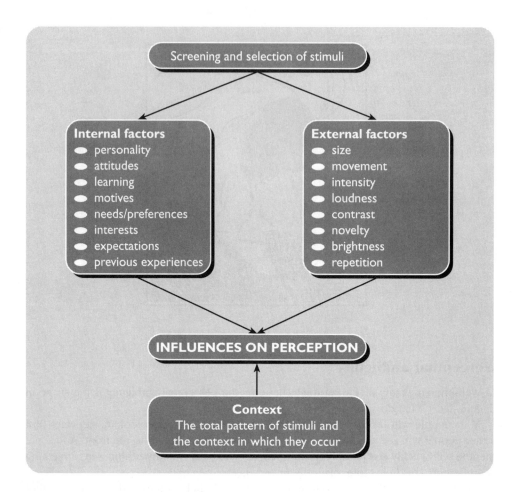

External factors

External factors refer to the nature of the stimuli themselves. People will usually give more attention to stimuli which are, for example, large, moving, intense, loud, contrasted, bright, novel, repeated or standing out from the background. An example is the distinctive red and white 'pie-man' sign of Little Chef Travelodges. As another example, a fire extinguisher should be immediately visible and stand out clearly from its surroundings.

Only certain stimuli enter into an individual's perception. An intended customer entering a hotel reception area sees a member of staff having an angry exchange with a guest and walks away without booking. The customer sees only the argument and disregards the many positive features of the hotel. Another intended customer for a restaurant notices only that it is crowded and noisy and leaves without seeing the empty spaces at the back, and unaware that the food and service are excellent.

The importance of context

Any number of stimuli may be present at a given time or situation. It is, therefore, the total pattern of stimuli and the *context in which they occur* that influence perception. The sight of a rack of muddy wellington boots is likely to be perceived quite differently in the entrance

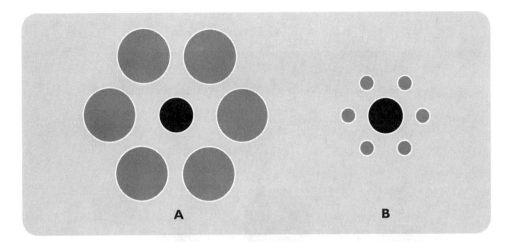

A   B

to a working farm offering bed and breakfast accommodation than in the reception area of a city-centre conference hotel.

Look now at the example in Figure 3.6.[27] Which centre black circle is the larger – A or B?

In fact both circles are the same size and many of you might have guessed this to be the answer. However, because circle B is framed by smaller circles it certainly *appears* larger to the vast majority of people.

Organisation and arrangement of stimuli

Once incoming stimuli have been screened, they are organised and arranged in such a way that provides meaning and significance to the individual. The organisation and arrangement of stimuli can be influenced by continuity, proximity or similarity, that is *the principle of grouping.*

For example, in Figure 3.7(a) guests in a dining room are more likely to be perceived as 16 individuals, or possibly one large group. But in Figure 3.7(b) the guests are more likely to be perceived as four distinct sets or groups of people. And this perception may well influence the manner of the delivery of service.

The principle of closure

When people have incomplete or ambiguous stimuli there is a tendency to 'close' the information in order to complete the mental picture and create a meaningful image. Let us now return to Figure 3.3 (page 68).

It is probable that most people will perceive the shape either as an unconnected letter B or the unconnected number 13. However, some people may see the shape as no more than 11, or a series of, discrete blobs. For other people the shape may be perceived as some different meaningful object, for example a butterfly. Among responses from hotel and catering management degree students are a clown, a dog, a face, a series of letters of the alphabet, or a golf course (Figure 3.8). We may have difficulty in understanding how other people could possibly see such objects *but this is what they perceived the shape to be.*

The principle of closure is important as it applies not only to visual stimuli but to our other senses. We can probably all think of an example when we have 'got hold of the wrong end of the stick' as a result of our perception from overhearing only part of a conversation.

Applications within the hospitality industry

As people are selective in the stimuli which determine their responses and patterns of behaviour, it is important to be aware of those factors most likely to influence perception and create the desired image in the minds of customers. For example, many large hotel and catering groups adopt a standard colour scheme and layout for each of their individual establishments. This helps to influence customer perception through instant recognition and familiarity, and through helping the customer to know what to expect and to feel at home. The aim is to reinforce identification with the group and to generate repeat business.

For example, with TGI Friday's the distinctive wooden floors, tin ceilings, Tiffany lampshades, red striped table cloths, traffic lights by the toilets and collection of badges worn by the waiters, in all restaurants wherever you are, help to create a unique corporate atmosphere.

Visual effects

Perception is influenced strongly by the appropriate use of visual effects which create a feeling of, for example, warmth or cold, intimacy or formality, large or small, cluttered or spacious. The design and layout and the lighting, patterns and colour schemes of premises, accommodation, restaurants and bars have a major impact on ambience and the atmosphere that is created.[28] Perception is also important in terms of how customers respond to the appearance and presentation of food, and to the arrangement, balance of colour and size as well as the aroma, texture and taste.

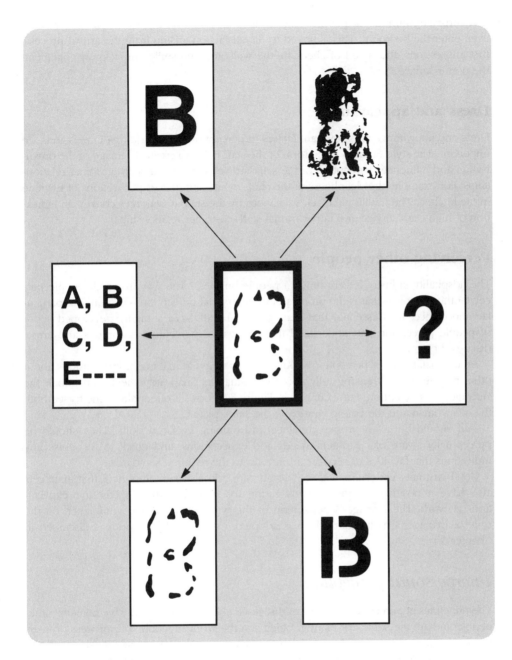

Figure 3.8:
Examples of
responses from
the incomplete
stimuli in
Figure 3.3

Importance of first impressions

First impressions are important. If a telephone enquiry from a potential new customer is received in a friendly, courteous and efficient manner by the receptionist the customer is likely to receive good 'vibes' and form a favourable perception of the establishment as a whole. Equally, the one curt, unhelpful receptionist can create an unfavourable perception of what is, in every other respect, a very friendly, pleasant and well-managed establishment.

A surprising number of people make a decision not to return to a hotel before they even enter the bedroom. This is linked to dissatisfaction arising from the arrival process: first impressions, the speed of check-in, the welcome, the smile, the acknowledgement, the porter service.[29]

Dress and appearance

Dress and appearance are important factors in perception, and again first impressions are important. The style of dress or uniform of the staff helps to create an image of the organisation and influences perception of the standards of service and staff–customer relationships. For example, the cleanliness of the chefs' whites influences perceptions of hygiene in the kitchen. The traditional black suits worn by the staff at Claridges convey an indication of high-class service and rather formal staff–customer relationships.

Perceiving other people

The hospitality industry is very much a people business. The way in which people perceive other people – that is the process of interpersonal perception – is clearly of particular importance. It is essential that managers and staff have a highly developed sense of people perception and understand the reasons for perceptual distortions and errors discussed below.

An understanding of perception should help us to avoid making hasty decisions about other people before thinking fully about the situation. Snap judgements can impair the 'accuracy' of perception. For example, in Figure 3.4 above it often takes time to see both the old woman and the young woman in the same picture.

Staff should be given proper guidance and training in social skills. They should be perceptually aware of customers' needs and expectations, and quick to recognise any indications that facilities or services are not up to the required standards.

Good customer care starts with good staff care.[30] It is equally important that managers also have a positive attitude towards caring for staff, and their needs and expectations at work. The manager's perception of the workforce is a major influence on the style of managerial behaviour which is adopted. (Managerial behaviour is discussed in Chapter 5.)

Interpersonal perception

The principles of perceptual differences discussed above reflect the way we perceive other people and are the source of many problems in the work situation. The process of interpersonal perception can influence both the manager–subordinate relationship and the staff–customer relationship. The perception of other people is a major determinant of behaviour and standards of service delivered.

Judgements about other people

Judgements made about other people can be influenced by perceptions of stimuli such as role or status, occupation, physical factors and appearance, and body language, for example eye contact, facial expression or tone of voice. For instance, the estimated height of a person may vary with that person's perceived status.

In a study with American college students, an unknown visitor from England was introduced briefly to five separate groups. The visitor was described with a different academic position to each group before leaving the room. Students were then asked to estimate the height of the visitor. As ascribed academic status increased, so did the group's estimate of the height of the visitor.[31]

Every person sees things in his or her own way and, as perception becomes a person's reality, this can lead to misunderstandings. There are three main factors which can create particular difficulties with interpersonal perception and cause problems in dealings with other people – selective perception, the halo effect and stereotyping.

Selective perception

Because of their own internal characteristics, people are selective about the information to which they pay particular attention. They see and hear only what they want to see and hear. This selectivity gives rise to perceptual defence. People may tend to select information which is supportive of their point of view and choose not to acknowledge contrary information. Consider the following example.

Selective perception

A manager has on a number of occasions expressed dissatisfaction with the head chef, with whom there have been a number of personality clashes. On leaving the restaurant the manager enquires of a regular guest who was entertaining some business colleagues whether they enjoyed the meal. The guest replies with a smile and pointing at a colleague says: 'Peter would have preferred his steak cooked a little less, he likes it really raw so he can put a piece on his black eye.' Then with a straight face, the guest continues: 'Apart from that it was an excellent meal and we all enjoyed it, thank you.'

The manager 'hears' only the comment that the steak could have been cooked a little less and does not 'see' the accompanying smile or gesture. The manager then reports back to the chef that there has been 'another' complaint and a customer's steak was overcooked.

Another manager who has experienced no difficulties with the chef, and who gets on well with him, could perceive the guest's comments quite differently. The comments about the steak could be seen simply as a joke against Peter. The manager is pleased to hear that it was an excellent and enjoyable meal and reports this back to the chef.

The halo effect

This arises when the judgements made about another person are formulated on the basis of particular characteristics or impressions that are readily available. The halo effect tends to influence perceptions of the rest of that person, either positively or negatively, and results in assumptions and generalisations from limited information.

A well-known example is with selection interviewing. A candidate arrives punctually, is smart in appearance, well-spoken and friendly. All positive characteristics – but these may well influence the perception of selectors of the candidate as a whole person. Because of the halo effect the selectors may tend to assume the candidate will perform well, and as a result place less emphasis on checking experience and technical ability.

The rusty halo effect

The process may also work in reverse (the rusty halo effect). This is where general judgements about a person are formulated from the perception of a negative characteristic. For example, a candidate is seen arriving late for an interview. There may be a very good reason for this and it may be completely out of character. But on the basis of that one particular event the person may be perceived as a poor timekeeper and unreliable.

Significance for managers

The halo effect has particular significance for managers and supervisors who may observe only a limited aspect of the behaviour or activities of staff. A single trait, such as good or bad timekeeping, may become the main, or even the sole, criterion for judging overall performance. A manager observing a member of staff performing a single task particularly well or badly may tend to see this as a judgement of that person's overall level of competence.

A danger associated with the halo effect is that the perceiver may become 'perceptually blind', and screen and shut out subsequent observations or information at variance with the original perception. For example, a manager who has recently refused to promote a member of staff despite the recommendations of the head of department may then tend to ignore favourable information about that member of staff and select only information which supports the decision not to agree to the promotion.

Another danger is that of projection. This is the tendency of people to project their own feelings, motives or characteristics to their perception of other people. A manager may make a more favourable judgement about members of staff who have characteristics largely in common with, and easily recognised by, the manager.

Stereotyping

This is the tendency to ascribe positive or negative characteristics to a person on the basis of a general categorisation and perceived similarities. Stereotyping is a form of typecasting. It is a means of simplifying the process of perception and making collective judgements of other people, rather than the recognition of each person as an individual.

Stereotyping results in the tendency to classify people according to easily recognisable characteristics and perceived common groupings and this may (perhaps subconsciously) influence the manner of the service delivery. For example in a busy inner city four-star hotel the usual Monday to Thursday guest may be typecast as typically male, wearing a dark or grey suit, who prefers to dine alone often reading or makes frequent use of room service, makes little conversation, has a formal relationship with staff and whose company is paying the bills. This form of stereotyping contrasts with any individual Monday to Thursday guests who are private customers paying their own way or with families taking advantage of weekday leisure breaks. Without proper training it is possible that some staff may have difficulty in adjusting to the different patterns of behaviour and expectations of service of individual guests.

Typecasting may also be based on, for example: nationality, gender, age, skin colour, speech, appearance and style of dress. For example, in some hotels male guests are required to wear jackets and ties in the restaurant. Other establishments will not admit people wearing jeans or studded jackets. In each case there is a collective stereotyping of suitable or unsuitable clientele on the basis of their dress.

Perceiving each person as an individual

We all tend to make use of stereotypes. And they *may* be helpful in enabling us to make quick predictions of likely patterns of behaviour, and reducing stress in dealing with people we do not know as individuals. However, although there is likely to be some truth in under-lying stereotypes (this is why they exist) they are simplistic over-generalisations.

People of the same generalised 'grouping' do not necessarily fit into the stereotype. It is important, therefore, to be receptive to personal aspects of attitudes and behaviour. Initial perceptions based on stereotyping may need to be revised in order to perceive each person as an individual in his or her own right.

Sex stereotyping and gender

The (then) HCITB report on the image of hotel and catering work highlighted the import-ance of sex stereotyping which is well established and persistent. Jobs are still perceived as being male or female and the distinction is seen as relevant in making a job choice which must be of the appropriate gender.

> *The jobs which people consider suitable show substantial sex stereotyping, jobs in reception, accommodation services and the job of kitchen counter assistant being mentioned as suitable primarily by women, reception work also clearly being the most popular alternative overall. Men dominate responses concerned with management and portering. It may thus be desirable to counter established sex stereotyping and encourage women into training for management.*[32]

The perception of women

Although the HCITB report demonstrated the existence of sex stereotyping, the image is grounded in reality. It is possible to predict who is most likely to be meeting customers at the reception desk, who will be cleaning their rooms and who will be cooking their meals. Typically, a woman will meet the customers, clean the rooms and serve the meals; and a man will cook the meals, repair any defects and manage the hotel.

> *Statistics show that women dominate the industry, particularly at an operational level in part-time jobs. However, at a management level men outnumber women. Sex segregation can be seen in operation within some hotel departments; kitchens being almost exclusively male and housekeeping departments female.*[33]

Why such distinct roles?

Why is it that men and women have such distinct roles within hotels? Is it that these roles suit their abilities or are there other explanations? Is it the women themselves who lack the ambition to become managers, or do the tradition and beliefs of the industry (the cul-tural milieu) exclude women? Are the ways in which management is perceived and the ways managers are developed the key to understanding the sex stereotyping of women in the industry?

In one respect it could perhaps be perceived that hotels typify the stereotype of 'women's work'. Hotels are temporary homes where staff have to anticipate and care for the physical needs of guests in terms of sleep, food and comfort. In such an environment it might be expected that women should be perceived to hold the necessary abilities, knowledge and understanding to perform well – and to attain managerial positions in large numbers.

Lack of women in management positions

For the past decade, 75 per cent of all students on higher-level hotel management courses have been female. Hence one might reasonably expect a greater proportion of women than men in management positions. However, a (then) HCITB report revealed that women are not well represented in general management positions but tend to opt for specialist career routes. Barriers exist for women, particularly with regard to differences in training opportunities.[34]

The research team also pointed out that barriers can exist 'within' women themselves and felt there was a lack of confidence shown both in their aspirations and in their career planning. However, it would seem that the study exaggerated the differences between men and women, at least in terms of their long-term ambitions, and tended to accept uncritically the 'fast' masculine route as being ideal.

Practical skills and personality

Hotel managers are expected to be multi-skilled and to be available at all times. A recurrent theme of the hotel industry is the 'traditional' style of operations characterised by a high level of activity linked to an emphasis on technical and craft skills.[35] Recent studies also confirm that hotel management is concerned primarily with the demonstration of practical skills and the personality to act as 'mine host'.[36]

If multi-skills are taken to refer to the skills of the kitchen rather than the housekeeping department, then clearly women would be disadvantaged. The food and beverage department has always held a key position in hotels, but women frequently do not receive experience or training in this section.[37] The notion of 'mine host' suggest connotations of a personality which in the past has always been associated with a male image. A number of studies have found personality to be the essential criterion in the selection and promotion of managers.[38]

The assessment of personality, however, is very subjective, it is open to interpretation and can be more concerned with whether the individual fits into the culture of the hotel. Career progression rests not only on the development of skills, or with a set of personality traits, but may be more related to whether the persona of an individual matches the culture of the hotel.

Kanter has shown that in this respect women are disadvantaged because they do not fit the conventional male profile.[39] Hicks in her research demonstrated that women were perceived in non-managerial terms, that management work was interpreted in a masculine framework and that not only was encouragement given predominantly to male trainees but females did not have an easy access to informal networks.[40]

Informal relationships and networks

Building alliances and networks are considered to be key factors in the career development and effectiveness of managers.[41] Career progression in the hotel industry is highly dependent on the managers of hotels assessing promising trainees and ensuring they receive the necessary guidance and experience. Using their own networks hotel managers ensure the progression of trainees and reinforce the significance of the maxim 'it is not what you know, but who you know'. Research has indicated that managers expect their male trainees to be committed to a career in hotel management whereas they suspect that the females are more likely to leave the industry. Thus certain trainees, typically male, are pushed towards new opportunities and advancement.[42]

Action on employment practices

According to Jagger and Maxwell, many current employment practices discriminate covertly against women. Positive action is possible, however, to prevent such discrimination. This requires attention to practices and procedures relating to job evaluation, recruitment and selection, training, management development, career planning, appraisal systems, re-entry policies, tertiary education and childcare responsibilities.[43]

Concern is becoming more widespread about the 'cloning' of organisations and that typically a board of directors consists of white, middle-class, middle-aged males. Recent attention is being given to the idea that diversity is important for the success of organisations and hence women's contributions are regarded as being paramount.[44] Positive action can therefore be seen to lie with senior managers. There is no doubt that sexism is damaging for individuals and organisations. 'Until the more powerful own the responsibility for prejudice, it will continue to cripple us all.'[45]

Transactional analysis

We have seen that the ability to relate effectively to other people is a particularly important feature of work in the hospitality industry. One means of helping to understand interpersonal behaviour at work is the concept of transactional analysis which has been popularised by writers such as Berne[46] and Harris.[47] Transactional analysis is a development of the ideas of Sigmund Freud and basically entails a means of applying sources of personality to provide a simplistic categorisation of social interactions.

Transactional analysis expresses an individual's personality in three patterns of feelings and behaviours, or ego states: parent, adult and child.

- *The parent state* relates to feelings about right and wrong, and how to care for and relate to other people. The parent state results from earlier conditioning and what has been learnt from external sources. It is associated with superiority and authority. For example: 'Why can't you remember to enter telephone bookings for the restaurant straight away like I've told you before. You know what happens if . . .'

- *The adult state* represents the objective, rational, thinking and reasoning aspects of personality and behaviour. Transactions are based on unemotional and calculative behaviour, and factual discussions. For example: 'We seem to have a problem with the recording equipment in the conference room. Do you think we will be able to have it repaired by this evening or should we consider alternative arrangements?'

- *The child state* is characterised by responses developed through childhood experiences. This state may be associated with wanting, having fun, playing, impulsiveness, rebelliousness, spontaneous behaviour and emotional responses. For example: 'I can't get this silly computer to work. Anyway it's not my problem, you're the one supposed to be in charge of the front office.'

An understanding of human behaviour

These states have nothing to do with chronological age but according to Berne represent aspects of psychological positions, or ego, common to everyone. All people are said to behave in each of these states at different times. The three ego states exist simultaneously within each individual although at any particular time any one state may dominate the other two. If the transactions are parallel (that is parent–parent, adult–adult or child–child) they may continue indefinitely.

However, in the adult state a person processes transactions in a reasonable and unemotional manner and responds to the other party as a responsible and sensible person. In the *majority* of work situations, therefore, the most effective form of communication is when each individual perceives the other as an adult and both adopt an adult ego state so that an adult stimulus is followed by an adult response. This form of transaction is more likely to encourage a rational, problem-solving approach and reduce the possibility of emotional conflict. There may, however, be certain situations in which different transactions may be more effective, for example a manager deliberately playing the parent state to help restore the confidence of a new member of staff who has made a mistake and is adopting a child state.

In addition to the analysis of verbal interactions, for example vocabulary and tone of voice, transactional analysis includes the perception of non-verbal communications such as posture, body language and facial expressions. Crossed transactions tend to inhibit effective communication and can lead to conflict situations. By focusing attention on the interactions occurring within a relationship, transactional analysis can aid the understanding of personality states and human behaviour. It can help to improve communication skills by assisting in interpreting a person's ego state and which form of state is likely to be the most appropriate response. This should lead to an improvement in both customer relations and management–subordinate relations.

Perception of 'self'

An important factor of interpersonal behaviour and relationships with other people is perception of self, or self-image. This is how people see and think of themselves, and their evaluation of themselves. People tend to have an ideal image of themselves and how they would like to be. This is the image that is projected in dealings with other people.

The responses of other people, and their approval or disapproval, influences the development of self-image. Approval from other people will serve to reinforce that image and will contribute to an individual's self-esteem. People tend to come to see themselves how other people come to know and expect them to be. Self-esteem is the extent to which people approve of and accept themselves, and their feelings of self-respect.

Role relationships

Self-image is influenced by the different roles that people play both inside and outside the work environment. A role is an expected pattern of behaviour and forms part of the network of activities and relationships with other people. Each individual will have a number of role relationships – a 'role-set' which comprises the range of associations or contacts with whom the individual has meaningful interactions.

The expected pattern of behaviour of a hospitality manager will influence the manager's self-image. And certain characteristic features associated with this self-image will tend to

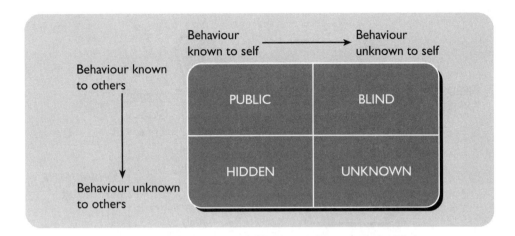

persist outside the work environment, for example smart appearance and courteous behaviour in dealings with other people. (The importance of role relationships is discussed in more detail in Chapter 8.)

The Johari window

In order to achieve effective interactions with other people it is necessary for individuals to be aware of their own personality characteristics and patterns of behaviour. A simple framework for looking at self-insight and the individual's own self-examination is the 'Johari window' (Figure 3.9).[48] This presents four views of personality and classifies behaviour in matrix form between:

● what is known–unknown to self; and

● what is known–unknown to others.

● *Public* is the open area containing things known both to the individual and to other people. This is the part of 'self' shared with others and where there is free disclosure of information and feelings. The larger the public area, the more effective are likely to be interactions with other people.

● *Blind* is the area containing information unknown to the individual but known to other people. This blind spot can be, for example, attitudes, mannerisms, way of speaking, body language, or the way of relating to other people. In the blind area other people may perceive readily modes of behaviour which are not obvious to the individual.

● *Hidden* is the area of behaviour which the individual wishes to conceal from, or not to communicate to, other people. An individual may try to disguise his or her real self, for example by attempting to hide shyness or nervousness behind a façade of confidence.

● *Unknown* is the area containing information unknown to both the individual and other people. Certain things may still be present but are not apparent. For example, an individual may have some 'hidden' ability, talent or past experiences.

Figure 3.10:
Behavioural
responses to
frustration

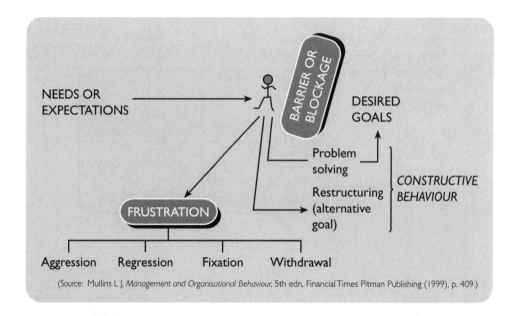

(*Source:* Mullins L J, *Management and Organisational Behaviour,* 5th edn, Financial Times Pitman Publishing (1999), p. 409.)

Changes in behaviour

In order to help individuals to understand themselves better and to improve their inter-actions with other people it is necessary to expand the individual's public area and reduce the hidden and blind areas. To reduce hidden behaviour it is necessary to encourage greater self-disclosure in a non-threatening environment and an atmosphere of confidence and trust. To reduce blind behaviour requires feedback which the individual is prepared to accept on how other people perceive the individual's behaviour.

Frustration-induced behaviour

The behaviour and actions of people at work result from the desire to achieve some goal in order to satisfy certain needs or expectations. This is the basis of a person's motiva-tional driving force and a major influence on the nature of interpersonal relationships. Needs and expectations at work include the satisfaction of economic rewards, for example pay and security; intrinsic satisfaction, for example variety and an interesting job; and social relationships, for example comradeship and a feeling of belonging. (Motivation, and the needs and expectations of people at work, are discussed in Chapter 7.)

When a person's motivational driving force is blocked before reaching a desired goal there are two possible sets of outcomes: constructive behaviour or frustration (Figure 3.10). Even if a person engages in constructive behaviour it could be said that the person was 'frustrated', if only mildly or in the short term. The term 'frustration', however, is usually interpreted as applying to negative behavioural responses to a barrier or blockage which prevents satisfaction of a desired goal and results in a feeling of psychological discomfort.[49]

Constructive behaviour

This is a positive reaction to the blockage of a desired goal and can take two main forms: problem-solving or restructuring. These are not necessarily exclusive forms of reaction, and constructive behaviour may involve a combination of problem-solving and restructuring.

- *Problem solving* entails removal of the barrier, for example: by-passing an unco-operative colleague; repairing broken equipment; undertaking training or gaining a qualification, persuading the manager to grant promotion, finding an alternative method of working.

- *Restructuring* involves the substitution of an alternative goal, although such a goal may be of a lower order or priority. Restructuring may also entail compromise between the satisfaction of conflicting goals, for example: requesting a transfer to another department or to a different shift, taking an additional part-time job, accepting a less interesting job because the hours of work are more convenient.

Frustration

This is a negative response to the blockage of a desired goal and results in a defensive form of behaviour. There are many possible reactions to frustration but these can be summarised under four broad headings: aggression, regression, fixation, and withdrawal.[50] Again, these categories are not mutually exclusive and most forms of frustration-induced behaviour at work are a combination of aggression, regression and fixation.

- *Aggression* is a physical or verbal attack on some person or object, for example: striking a supervisor, damaging equipment, destroying documents, shouting or using abusive language, spreading malicious gossip about a colleague. This form of behaviour may be directed against the person or object perceived as the actual blocking agent and the source of frustration.

- *Regression* is reverting to childish or a more primitive form of behaviour, for example: screaming, tantrums, crying, sulking, refusing to cooperate with colleagues or listen to reasoned arguments, constantly moaning, displaying neurotic behaviour, striking or kicking broken equipment or machinery.

- *Fixation* involves persisting in a form of behaviour which has no adaptive value and continuing to repeat actions which have no positive results, for example: continually trying to operate equipment which obviously will not work, insisting on applying for promotion to a position for which clearly not suited, being excessively critical, refusing to accept change or new ideas.

- *Withdrawal* is apathy, giving up or resignation, for example: losing interest in the job, poor timekeeping, increasing sickness and absenteeism, refusing to accept responsibility, passing work over to colleagues, avoiding decision-making, failing to give support to colleagues, refusing to join in group or social activities, leaving the job altogether.

Displaced aggression

Frustration-induced behaviour may often result in displaced aggression. This may occur when the source of the frustration is not clear or specific or where the source is feared such as a powerful superior. With displaced aggression the person may find an easier or 'safer' person or object as an outlet of frustration, for example: being short-tempered with subordinates, slamming doors, kicking the waste-paper basket, being irritable with friends.

The concept of displaced aggression has particular significance in the hospitality industry. Staff may well be expected to act in accordance with a doctrine of 'the customer is *always* right' and, however trying or demanding the circumstances, should not give vent to their frustration in public view of customers or guests. By the same token, however, managers and colleagues should be understanding when staff need to find some alternative outlet as a scapegoat for their frustration.

Factors influencing frustration

There are many factors which influence the feeling of frustration and an individual's reactions, for example the importance of the desired goal and strength of the need, cultural values, the perceived nature of the barrier or blocking agent, the pressure under which the individual is working, previous experience, the personality characteristics and social skills of the individual.

It must also be remembered that most people do not necessarily separate their working lives from their domestic or social lives; neither is it reasonable to expect them to do so.[51] The behaviour and actions of people are influenced by problems and frustrations outside as well as inside the work organisation. Managers have a social responsibility to recognise that people cannot always leave their personal difficulties behind when they come to work.

The psychological contract

The manager should attempt to mould elements of individual and group behaviour in order to avoid conflict and frustration. An important aspect of the effective management of people is the concept of the psychological contract. This is not a written document but implies a series of mutual expectations and satisfaction of needs between the individual and the hospitality organisation. The psychological contract covers a range of rights, privileges, behaviour, duties and obligations which are not part of a formal agreement but still have an important influence on the behaviour of people.[52]

Expectations of the individual

Expectations of the individual vary widely and may change over time but could include that the organisation will, for example:

- pay overtime rates or allow time off for additional hours worked in excess of the contract of employment;
- adopt equitable personnel policies and procedures;
- provide a reasonable standard of live-in accommodation;
- respect the privacy of staff when not on duty;
- provide reasonable working conditions and staff facilities;
- treat members of staff with consideration and respect;
- show an understanding attitude towards any personal problems;
- provide opportunities for training in new skills and career progression.

Expectations of the hospitality organisation

Expectations of the hospitality organisation arise from the implicit attitudes and behaviour of its members. These expectations may include that members will, for example:

- accept the philosophy of the organisation and uphold its image;
- make every reasonable effort to satisfy customers' requirements;
- be prepared to work additional hours or undertake extra jobs, with appropriate recompense, when the need arises;
- show loyalty and honesty, and not betray positions of trust;
- work diligently in pursuit of objectives and accept the authority of managers;
- not abuse goodwill shown by customers or management;
- accept the approach that the customer is always right.

Bargaining and balancing

The hospitality organisation's side of the psychological contract may place emphasis on expectations, requirements and constraints which often differ from, and conflict with, the expectations of the individual. It is unlikely that all expectations of either side will be met fully. The nature of these expectations is not defined formally and there is a constant process of bargaining and balancing.

Understanding the nature of the psychological contract is an important aspect of the socialisation of members of staff new to the organisation. The informal expectations serve as important determinants of behaviour and may have a major influence on an individual's subsequent attitudes, job satisfaction and work performance, and on the level of staff turnover.

Failure to honour the psychological contract

Unfortunately the hospitality industry in general does not have a good reputation for honouring the psychological contract towards its members. A prime example of this can be seen in respect of students on placement. Although not always the case, the following views expressed by college HND students appear all too typical of their experiences:

> *We go on placements and see staff being treated badly which is why I would not go into the hotel industry, unless things change. It's slave labour.*

> *. . . I was working six days a week for 14 or 15 hours every day, receiving no training . . . When I went for my interview I was given a wonderful presentation about the training I would receive – but I was training others. I signed a contract to work 40 hours a week but when I raised the subject of overtime I was laughed at.*

Situations such as these are clearly one reason why many degree and HND students turn their backs on the industry only to be snapped up by large retailing groups.[53]

Securing the commitment of staff

Hiltrop suggests that the increasing pressure for organisations to change has prompted grow-ing disillusionment with the traditional psychological contract based on lifetime employment and steady promotion from within. Companies must develop new ways to increase the loyalty and commitment of employees. This includes attention to reward strategies based on recognition of contribution rather than status or position, systematic training and devel-opment including the skills for working in cross-functional teams; and the training of man-agers in counselling, coaching and leadership skills.[54]

According to Altman, restructuring and advances in technology mean it is time for a new psychology contract between employers and employees.

> *How can employees continue to believe in any established, if unwritten, psycho-logical contract based on previous secure employment, training and personal development? . . . Reducing layers of middle management is largely a consequence of technology and cutting down on bureaucracy. The more companies down-size, the more they are seen to be breaking the 'psychological contract' with employees. And once individuals perceive this to be the case, they will look after their own careers and their chief loyalty will be to themselves.*[55]

If managers in the hospitality industry are to increase the willing commitment of staff to the aims and goals of the organisation, continual attention must be given to the import-ance of the psychological contract.

An understanding of human nature

At the heart of successful management is the ability to relate well to other people.

> *The fact is that management ultimately depends on an understanding of human nature. I suggest it goes much further than that. In the first place, good management depends on the acceptance of certain basic values. It cannot be achieved without honesty and integrity, or without consideration for the inter-ests of others. Secondly, it is the understanding of human foibles that we all share, such as jealousy, envy, status, prejudice, perception, temperament, motiva-tion and talent, which provides the greatest challenge to managers.*
>
> HRH *The Duke of Edinburgh, Patron Institute of Management.*[56]

Understanding the feelings of staff, and their needs and expectations, together with a genuine concern for their welfare, go a long way in encouraging them to perform well. Attention should be focused, therefore, on improving the people–organisation relationship and cre-ating a climate in which people work willingly and effectively. The people–organisation relationship is discussed further in Chapter 5.

Summary

- Effective management is all about working with people and this is particularly important in the hospitality industry. People differ in their attitudes or orientations to work. The behaviour of people at work is influenced by a combination of factors and cannot be understood in terms of the study of a single discipline. It is more appropriate to adopt an applied, interdisciplinary approach including attention to the importance of cultural influences.

- Individuals offer different attitudes and perceptions towards their working life. An understanding of attitudes and their relationships to behaviour is an important aspect of the management of people. A major determinant of behaviour of particular importance within the hospitality industry is the process of perception. Interpersonal perception influences both the manager–subordinate relationship and the staff–customer relationship.

- One means of helping to understand interpersonal behaviour at work is the concept of transactional analysis. This can help to improve communication skills and reduce emotional conflict. An important factor of interpersonal behaviour and relationships with other people is the perception of 'self' or self-image.

- If a person's motivational driving force is blocked this can result in two possible sets of outcomes: constructive behaviour or negative responses (frustration-induced behaviour). The main reactions to frustration can be summarised as aggression (including displaced aggression), regression, fixation and withdrawal.

- At the heart of successful management is the ability to relate well to other people. A high level of interpersonal skill is important for effective work performance. Managers should focus attention on improving the people–organisation relationship and creating a climate in which staff work willingly and effectively. A major influence on the people–organisation relationship is recognition of the importance of psychological contract.

Review and discussion questions

1. Suggest main headings under which to view influences on behaviour in work organisations. From your own experience, give brief practical examples under each heading.

2. Comment critically on the role of social science within the hospitality industry. Explain your understanding of behavioural science as an interdisciplinary approach to the study of behaviour. Provide your *own examples* of the importance of cultural differences.

3. Why is the study of perception of particular importance within the hospitality industry? Explain what is meant by perceptual illusions, and the screening and selection of perceptual stimuli. ▷

Review and discussion questions continued

4. Discuss the factors which influence the judgements we make of other people. Explain the main sources of distortions and errors in interpersonal perception.

5. Give your views, with supporting examples, on the extent of sex stereotyping and gender in the hospitality industry today. How would you attempt to overcome such stereotyping?

6. Discuss the value to the hospitality manager of an understanding of transactional analysis. Suggest how managers might become more aware of their perception of 'self' and self-image, and bring about changes in their behaviour.

7. Explain what is meant by frustration-induced behaviour. Distinguish between constructive behaviour and frustration. From your own experience, give practical examples of both types of behaviour.

8. Explain what is meant by the psychological contract. Give practical examples of: (a) expectations that might be held by individuals; and (b) expectations that might be held by the hospitality organisation. Give examples of your own expectations that you would hope to see covered by the psychological contract.

Assignment 1

We all tend to be guilty of distortions and errors in interpersonal perception, and of making hasty decisions about the behaviour and actions of other people before thinking fully about the situation.

(i) Consider honestly the biases, prejudices and attitudes that you have about certain people. Explain how you attempt to guard against these biases, prejudices and attitudes in order to make a fair and objective assessment of others.

(ii) Relate examples of judgements you have made about other people on the basis of:
    (a) the halo effect;
    (b) the rusty halo effect; and
    (c) stereotyping.

(iii) Give a brief account of situations when you have:
    (a) made a judgement about another person on the basis of *selective perception*; and
    (b) assumed too much from *limited information* and when there was a reasonable, alternative interpretation which differed from your first reaction.

Be prepared to share and discuss your experiences in self-selecting groups of four to six. Make notes of what you feel has been learnt from undertaking this assignment.

Assignment 2

From your own experience, provide a short account of an actual problem or difficulty you have encountered in working with other people in the hospitality industry. Explain clearly:

(i)   the exact nature of the problem or difficulty;

(ii) the behaviour/actions of the person(s) involved;

(iii) the steps taken to help overcome the situation and with what results, *and/or* the actions you would now propose be taken.

Assignment 3

Is it a woman's perspective?

People often ask the questions:

● What is it like being a female general manager?

● Have you had to work harder to keep up with your male colleagues?

● Have you found it difficult being a woman general manager?

The answer is usually quite simple – how would I know! I've never been a man? I haven't had the opportunity to see the world from male eyes. A rounded view could come from trial and comparison and unfortunately perhaps my one regret could be that I never had the opportunity to make the comparison and therefore, can't imagine and never mind comment.

To me it is not about what life is like as a female – but just simply as a general manager. I'm certainly not going to be the one who tells my male colleagues that I must have worked any harder than they have to get where I am today – I'll leave that to their better judgement. Perhaps I am lucky to have been brought up in an organisation where I have not felt like a female GM – but just simply a GM, a valuable part of the team.

If my colleagues feel that I am any different then they've made a good job out of hiding the fact over the years. Perhaps my shoulders are just broad. I didn't even notice – I was too busy becoming a GM.

I've had the benefit of a solid, logical career that has provided the right opportunities at the right time. I never once considered that my sex may have held me back or interrupted my goals. At the end of the day I am a firm believer – say, do and try as you like, from whatever background or gender you come. It is only 'performance that is reality'. It is that space and opportunity to perform that is key to success though, coupled with personal drive, ambition and experience. That is what has led me to be the hotel general manager that 17 years ago on leaving Tertiary College I dreamed I could one day be. Did my 'femaleness' provide extra drive and determination? Who knows the answer to that?

I am not able to give a woman's perspective of the role of general managers in the effective management of people. As I've said, I am only able to give the perspective of a current general manager in our industry today. Just *some* of the key tricks of the trade are as follows.

People are our single biggest asset. It is only through them that our success will come. Simplistically, look after your people and they in turn will look after our guests and ultimately influence the bottom line. Surely therefore, this asset deserves our time, patience and focus. There are three things I consider to be very important to my success: my people, my guests and the financial status of my business. My people, therefore, deserve one third of my time, focus, energy and commitment – an equal share of my efforts. This is how I plan my day, week, month, year. The three most important areas have ▷

a natural right to my time. If all I work today is the 'untraditional' eight hours then I can spend 2 hours and 40 minutes with my people. Some individuals will need more time than others but collectively the whole team can and should benefit from my being here today.

We all know how to manage by wandering about. That's fine, but I like to add 'with purpose'. Have a plan: what am I going to achieve? The purpose of wandering about can be mistaken. You may wander about smiling, saying hello. Now you see me – but, you're unlikely to see me again for the rest of the day! There is more to it than that. Use 'wandering' for training, coaching, corrective coaching. Catch people doing something right and make your visit to the ground floor a pleasant experience for all concerned, and don't forget the room maid tucked away on the floors. Managing people is affected by the relationship you have with them.

It is important to remove all hierarchical barriers, not to just say it or document it through flat-line management structures, but to actually do it. Let them know you are one of them, take away the formalities, be on first name terms. If you call your associates, Peter, John or Jane, why expect them to address you with a title? Respect comes from what you do and say, not from what you are called (when you are in earshot).

It is important to let your people know that you are 'one of them'. I came from the average social background, like many of them. Time and position has not changed that, so why pretend! We learn to try to get close to our employees. We feel achievement when we not only remember their names, but the names of their partner, children, their hobbies and likes and dislikes, but we forget one thing – don't keep yours a secret; let them know all about you too. If you have a nasty habit or snore from dusk till dawn, tell them about it – they'll feel more comfortable in your presence, they'll open up, give more feedback and, let you know when things are wrong. True relationships are transparent. You don't want them to hide the most recent guest feedback. When the world 'smells of paint' – you're in the wrong one! . . . By being 'one of them', we actually also need to demonstrate it in reality. Eat with them in the canteen, not the guest areas. If there is a staff car park and entrance, use that too. If you make the rules, ensure religiously that you abide by them. There is no surer way of severing relationships than by not practising what you preach.

In this transparent relationship here nothing is hidden – dirty washing appears – that's fine – know about the mistakes and problems – congratulate it, not reprimand. Mistakes are our biggest learning tool. Those who make mistakes are the entrepreneurial risk takers of the future, with past experience and resolutions to draw upon. Squash them early and the next appropriate time when the risk could work – they won't try again for memory is short and recollection of the last reprimand takes over.

If our world does not 'smell of paint', then, neither should theirs. Share the negatives, disappointments and problems with the associates too. Sometimes this can be avoided in the battle for high morale, but, it shouldn't be. Let them help – let them join problem-solving groups. This shows that their contributions and opinions are valued and that they too can make a difference.

If each and every one of our associates believe that this hotel is 'my' hotel, then they have every right to share the problems. As the manager you get to learn a new skill – how to manage disappointment. In 'my' hotel you should also get to share the success – congratulate, celebrate, reward and recognise at every opportunity.

I remember and I don't think anything has changed today, that all too often our teams (particularly middle management) feel as though they work so hard and have a real impact and at the end of the day the boss gets all the credit. We should avoid this at all costs.

▷

I recall a recent experience when my hotel received an annual award at a company ceremony. I telephoned the hotel immediately to let the team know and begin to celebrate our success. On my return the next day with our trophy, many cheers went up and one employee shook my hand and congratulated me on my award. I replied, 'Congratulations to you too. This is not my award this is our award, yours too.' 'No', she said, 'We would never have done it without you.'

A very humbling experience and quietly my proudest moment, even more so than receiving the award at the ceremony. This certainly brought a tear to my eye. (As only a woman's can)?!!

The effective management of people comes from many skills, under the guises of excellent team leadership – but, before you can have a team to lead, you must have a relationship.

I leave you with a question. Is that a woman's perspective?!

Source: The author is grateful to Pam Monks, General Manager of Swindon Marriott Hotel for providing this information.

TASKS

Meet in small groups, preferably containing both men and women.

(i) **Discuss critically what you see as the main points and issues which are raised by this commentary.**

(ii) **To what extent do you agree or disagree with the comments? Explain how these are borne out by your own experiences.**

(iii) **How much agreement is there among members of your group?**

Case study 1: John Adams

John Adams was on duty as a member of the night service staff with ABC Hotel. After an overseas guest clicked her fingers and whistled for service Adams lost his temper. 'You're not the only guest in this hotel.' He then warned the guest that if she did not stop her obnoxious behaviour no one would provide her or anyone else with service. Next day the guest complained to a room attendant. Adams was reprimanded by the personnel manager of the hotel and threatened with dismissal. In his defence Adams admitted that heated words were exchanged with the guest when she left the lounge late that night to go to her room. 'I did not swear at her but I did allow her to rile me. She started causing trouble as soon as she came into the lounge after the bar had closed. The day staff warned me about her when they went off duty. She was clicking her fingers and whistling for service all night. She threw the tray back at me when I took food to her room at 3 o'clock in the morning. I told her it was about time she stopped behaving like that. I just had enough of everything. I told her she would not get any more service if she treated people like that.'

TASKS

(i) **Analyse the main issue(s) of management and organisational behaviour identified in this situation.**

(ii) **Suggest how the issue(s) might best be resolved. Assuming you are the general manager of ABC Hotel what action would you propose to take?**

Case study 2: What happened next?

Richard Jackson is an outgoing person with a keen sense of humour who enjoys talking with other people. He has spent the majority of his working life in the catering trade, largely in public houses. After moving from London, Jackson was pleased to accept the opportunity of a partnership in managing The River View, a public house and restaurant situated on the coast. The other partner, Tony Wheeler, was a younger man with a degree in Business Studies. It was agreed that Jackson would have particular responsibility for the kitchen and food preparation, and assisting with bar work when necessary.

At first all seemed to be going well. After meals had finished being served Jackson would often help behind the bar. He regularly joined customers drinking and laughing with them, and quickly became a very popular figure. The partnership had been in operation for about a year when, much to Jackson's surprise, Tony Wheeler announced his engagement to Belinda Daniels, a divorcee some years older than Wheeler. Jackson could not hide a certain feeling of unease at this development. As Belinda Daniels started to spend a greater amount of time at The River View, Jackson became more and more disillusioned.

Jackson felt that he was increasingly expected to undertake too much of behind-the-scenes work with little involvement in the management decision-making. When a member of the kitchen staff left, Wheeler was reluctant to appoint a replacement, claiming that Jackson could undertake more of the work. Relationships with Wheeler became very strained.

As a result, Jackson applied for, and was both delighted and surprised to obtain, a position of chef at The Hollow, a nearby golf and country club hotel. Jackson immediately informed Wheeler that he was withdrawing from the partnership and left The River View the same week.

The Hollow has 75 bedrooms in a modern building with conference facilities for 180 people. It is set in beautiful countryside and with a high-standard golf course and leisure centre. Well-known local celebrities and sportspeople are frequent customers at the hotel. The Hollow is located in a high-wage area and suffers from a constant shortage of staff, especially during the summer months.

Jackson quickly struck up a friendship with the restaurant manager and gained a reputation for being a more than competent chef, conscientious and uncomplaining at the long hours of work. However, two months after Jackson was appointed, the restaurant manager who had started at The Hollow four months previously, left at short notice. Much to his obvious pleasure Jackson was offered the position. This did not please the assistant restaurant manager, a younger but more highly qualified person than Jackson, who had been in the post for the last 10 months.

Jackson seemed to revel in his new appointment. One of his first actions was to remove the desk from the restaurant entrance where customers would book or confirm their reservations. This was 'to create more open space as a welcome to customers'. Jackson could constantly be seen chatting and laughing with customers. He would greet them at the door of the restaurant and often take their orders personally.

One evening, after finishing the main dish, a regular and well-known customer, accompanied by a number of guests, asked to speak to Jackson. There were obvious signs of merriment from the customer's table.

'I don't like to have to say this but the meat was overcooked, the plates far too hot to touch and service was very slow. And the soup was certainly not up to standard. Last time we were here the meal was not all that great. I didn't want to complain before in case it upset you, but – sorry – this is just not good enough.'

Jackson offered reassuring words and went immediately into the kitchen. Shortly afterwards he returned with a bottle of wine. He pulled up a chair from a nearby table.

'Sorry for the hiccup. Bit of an off-night for the kitchen staff, I'm afraid. Please accept another bottle of house wine with my compliments, and there is a free choice of sweet on the house.'

'Thanks very much' responded the guest. 'We knew you would sort this out for us.'

'That's OK. Now – anything else I can do for you moaning minnies?' said Jackson in a mock-serious tone.

'No, thank you. As we said, we didn't want to upset you.'

'Good. Now you can let me have a glass of that wine I've just brought you.'

'Sure thing,' replied one of the guests, who with a smile poured a glass of wine and handed it to Jackson.

Jackson then happened to look round and to his surprise noticed the hotel manager standing quietly in a corner near the entrance to the restaurant.

The following morning in the hotel manager's office

An apprehensive Jackson is standing in front of the manager, who is sitting behind the desk.

'It seems there have been a number of complaints from the restaurant lately. Also, I am told that because of problems with delivery, on more than one occasion staff have had to go to the off-licence to buy wine for the customers. I believe yesterday was the chef's day off, and the only part of the meal he prepared was the soup of the day before. You know that, however well anyone knows their job, you can't work on your own here but as a member of a group.'

'You mean everything by rules and committee,' responded Jackson.

'No,' replied the manager. 'I mean the need for cooperation and teamwork. Anyway, we need to talk more about that later.'

The manager then left the desk, and beckoned Jackson to sit in a nearby chair. Jackson wasn't sure, but wondered if he detected a change in the expression on the face of the manager, who said, 'Now, about last night . . .'

TASKS

(i) **Analyse the main issues which appear to be raised in this case.**

(ii) **Assuming you are the manager of The Hollow, explain fully what actions you would now propose to take.**

Notes and references

1. See, for example, Arnold J, Cooper C L and Robertson I T, *Work Psychology*, 2nd edn, Pitman (1995).

2. Forte, Charles (Lord), *Forte: The Autobiography of Charles Forte*, Sidgwick & Jackson (1986), p. 123.

3. For example, see Wood R C, *Working in Hotels and Catering*, 2nd edn, International Thomson Business Press (1997)

4. Goldthorpe J H *et al.*, *The Affluent Worker: Industrial Attitudes and Behaviour*, Cambridge University Press (1968).

5. Dodrill K and Riley M, 'Hotel Workers' Orientations to Work: The Question of Autonomy and Scope', *International Journal of Contemporary Hospitality Management*, vol. 4, no. 1, 1992, pp. 23–25.

6. Mullins L J, 'The Organisation and the Individual', *Administrator*, vol. 7, no. 4, April 1987, pp. 11–14.

7. Atkinson P E, 'Applications of the Behavioral Sciences Within the Hospitality Industry', *Hospitality,* September 1980, pp. 7–13.

8. Wood R C, *Organizational Behaviour for Hospitality Management,* Butterworth-Heinemann (1994).

9. Carmouche R and Kelly N, *Behavioural Studies in Hospitality Management,* Chapman & Hall (1995).

10. Slattery P, 'Social Science Methodology and Hospitality Management', *International Journal of Hospitality Management,* vol. 2, no. 1, 1983, pp. 9–14.

11. Wood R C, 'Against Social Science?', *International Journal of Hospitality Management,* vol. 7, no. 3, 1988, pp. 239–250.

12. Lennon J J and Wood R C, 'The Teaching of Industrial and Other Sociologies in Higher Education: The Case of Hotel and Catering Management Studies', *International Journal of Hospitality Management,* vol. 11, no. 3, 1992, pp. 239–253.

13. See, for example, Drake R and Smith P, *Behavioural Science in Industry,* McGraw-Hill (1973).

14. Cowling A G *et al., Behavioural Sciences for Managers,* 2nd edn, Edward Arnold (1988), p. 1.

15. Ribeaux P and Poppleton S E, *Psychology and Work,* Macmillan (1978).

16. Gross R D, *Psychology: The Science of Mind and Behaviour,* Edward Arnold (1987).

17. Katz D, 'The Functional Approach to the Study of Attitudes', *Public Opinion Quarterly,* 21, 1960, pp. 163–204.

18. La Piere R T, 'Attitudes versus Action', *Social Forces,* vol. 13, 1934, pp. 230–237.

19. For a simplified version of attitude measurement see Riley M, *Human Resource Management in the Hospitality and Tourism Industry,* 2nd edn, Butterworth-Heinemann (1996).

20. Hicks L, Gender and Culture: A Study of the Attitudes Displayed by Managers in the Hotel Industry, unpublished doctoral thesis, University of Surrey, 1991.

21. Heider F, 'Attitudes and Cognitive Organization', *Journal of Psychology,* vol. 21, 1946, pp. 107–112.

22. Festinger L A, *A Theory of Cognitive Dissonance,* Row, Peterson and Co (1957).

23. For example, see Hornsey T and Dann D, *Manpower Management in the Hotel and Catering Industry,* Batsford (1984).

24. See, for example, Weaver P A and Oh H C, 'Do American Business Travellers Have Different Hotel Service Requirements?', *International Journal of Contemporary Hospitality Management,* vol. 5, no. 3, 1993, pp. 16–21.

25. Morgan C T and King R A, *Introduction to Psychology,* 3rd edn, McGraw-Hill (1966), p. 343.

26. Hill W E, *Puck,* 6 November 1915.

27. Hellriegel D, Slocum J W and Woodman R W, *Organizational Behavior,* 8th edn, South Western College (1998), p. 76.

28. For example, see: Jones P, *Food Service Operations,* Holt, Rinehart & Winston (1983).

29. Hubrecht J and Teare R, 'A Strategy for Partnership in Total Quality Service', *International Journal of Contemporary Hospitality Management,* vol. 5, no. 3, 1993, p. iii.

30. Klein S, 'Customer Care Needs Staff Care', *Proceeding of The International Association of Hotel Management Schools Symposium,* Leeds Polytechnic, November 1988.

31. Wilson P R, 'Perceptual Distortion of Height as a Function of Ascribed Academic Status', *Journal of Social Psychology,* no. 74, 1968, pp. 97–102.

32. Ellis P, *The Image of Hotel and Catering Work,* HCITB (1981), p. 26.

33. *Women in the Hotel and Catering Industry,* HCITB (1987).

34. *Women's Path to Management in the Hotel and Catering Industry,* HCITB (1984).

35. Guerrier Y and Lockwood A, 'Developing Hotel Managers – A Reappraisal', *International Journal of Hospitality Management*, vol. 8, no. 2, 1989, pp. 82–89.

36. Baum T, 'Toward a New Definition of Hotel Management', *Cornell HRA. Quarterly*, Educators' Forum 1988, pp. 36–39.

37. *Women's Path to Management in the Hotel and Catering Industry*, HCITB (1984).

38. See, for example, Hicks L, 'Excluded Women: How Can This Happen in the Hotel World?', *The Services Industries Journal*, vol. 10, no. 2, April 1990, pp. 348–363.

39. Kanter R B, *Men and Women of the Corporation*, Basic Books (1977).

40. Hicks L, 'Gender and Culture: A study of the attitudes displayed by managers in the hotel industry', Unpublished PhD dissertation, University of Surrey, 1991.

41. Kotter J P, 'What Effective General Managers Really Do', *Harvard Business Review*, vol. 60, no. 6, November–December 1982, pp. 156–167.

42. Hicks L, 'Gender and Culture: A study of the attitudes displayed by manager in the hotel industry', Unpublished PhD dissertation, University of Surrey, 1991.

43. Jagger E and Maxwell G, 'Women in Top Jobs', *Proceedings of the International Association of Hotel Management Schools Symposium*, Leeds Polytechnic, November 1988.

44. Caulkin S, 'Minorities Get The Vote', *The Observer*, Sunday 14 November 1993.

45. Quote by Gloria Steinem in Reardon, K, 'The Memo every woman keeps in her desk', *Harvard Business Review*, March–April 1993, pp. 16–22.

46. Berne E, *Games People Play*, Penguin (1966).

47. Harris T A, *I'm OK – You're OK: A Practical Guide to Transactional Analysis*, Harper & Row (1969).

48. Luft J, *Group Processes: An Introduction to Group Dynamics*, 2nd edn, National Press (1970). (The term 'Johari Window' was derived from a combination of the first names of the original authors, Joseph Luft and Harry Ingham.)

49. See, for example, Riley M, *Managing People: A guide for managers in the hotel and catering industry*, Butterworth-Heinemann (1995).

50. Brown J A C, *The Social Psychology of Industry*, Penguin (1954 and 1986).

51. See, for example, Hornsey T and Dann D, *Manpower Management in the Hotel and Catering Industry*, Batsford (1984).

52. See, for example, Schein E H, *Organizational Pyschology*, 3rd edn, Prentice-Hall (1988).

53. Robinson S, 'The Learning Curve', *Inside Hotels*, April/May 1992, pp. 40–45.

54. Hiltrop J M, 'Managing the Changing Psychological Contract', *Employee Relations*, vol. 18, no. 1, 1996, pp. 36–49.

55. Altman W, Cooper C and Garner A, 'New Deal Needed to Secure Commitment', *Professional Manager*, September 1999, p. 39.

56. 'In Celebration of the Feel-Good Factor', *Professional Manager*, March 1998, p. 6.

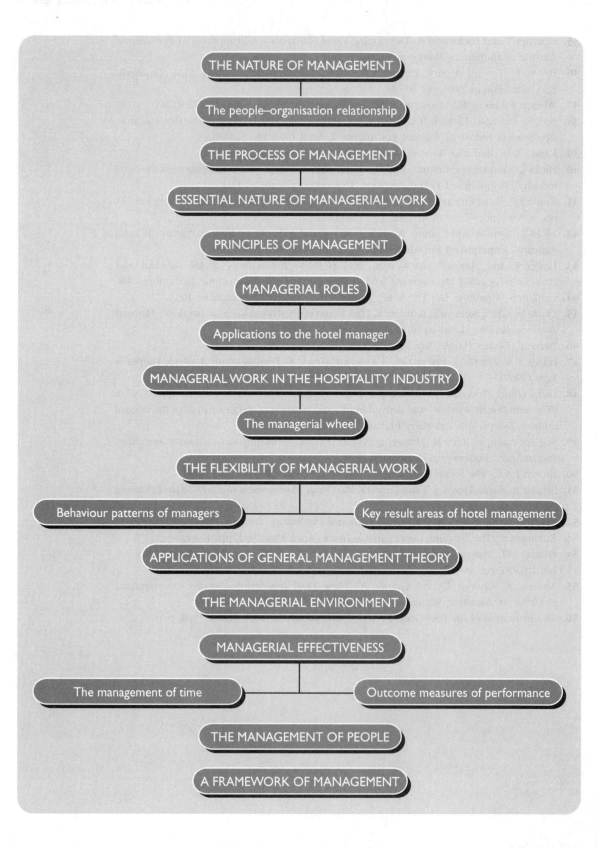

THE NATURE OF MANAGEMENT

The people–organisation relationship

THE PROCESS OF MANAGEMENT

ESSENTIAL NATURE OF MANAGERIAL WORK

PRINCIPLES OF MANAGEMENT

MANAGERIAL ROLES

Applications to the hotel manager

MANAGERIAL WORK IN THE HOSPITALITY INDUSTRY

The managerial wheel

THE FLEXIBILITY OF MANAGERIAL WORK

Behaviour patterns of managers

Key result areas of hotel management

APPLICATIONS OF GENERAL MANAGEMENT THEORY

THE MANAGERIAL ENVIRONMENT

MANAGERIAL EFFECTIVENESS

The management of time

Outcome measures of performance

THE MANAGEMENT OF PEOPLE

A FRAMEWORK OF MANAGEMENT

Chapter four

The nature of managerial work

Introduction

It is through the process of management and the execution of work that the activities of the hospitality organisation are carried out. The task of management is to get work done through other people. It is the cornerstone of the people–organisation relationship. Management is essentially an integrating activity which permeates every facet of hospitality operations.

The nature of management

Management is a generic term and subject to many possible interpretations. It is also frequently the subject of debate and discussion.[1] A number of different ideas are attributed to the meaning of management and to the work of the manager. For our purposes, however, we are concerned with management as:

- taking place within a structured work organisation and with prescribed roles;
- directed towards the attainment of goals and objectives;
- achieved through the efforts of other people; and
- using systems and procedures.

The setting of objectives and formulation of policy take place at different levels in an organisation but as part of the same process. The board of directors, or their equivalent, establish objectives and formulate policy for the organisation as a whole. Management is responsible for the implementation of policy decisions and for the execution of work designed to meet these objectives.

The importance of management

The responsibility and importance of management are widely, and rightly, recognised. Among the leading writers emphasising this is Drucker:

> *The responsibility of management in our society is decisive not only for the enterprise itself but for management's public standing, its success and status, for the very future of our economic and social system and the survival of the enterprise as an autonomous institution.*[2]

The importance of management within the hospitality industry is also widely acknowledged:

> *Effective management is one of the most important factors in the success or failure of any business. This applies to hotel, catering and institutional services as much as any other industry particularly as their managers need a balance of technical and management knowledge and skills acquired through a blend of education and experience.*[3]

Lord Forte has also illustrated the importance of management to effective organisational performance.

> *Success rests first and foremost on the activities of the manager on the spot, whether of a hotel, restaurant, cafe or motorway area. It is his or her ability to run the enterprise effectively and to inspire and guide the staff that is decisive. A hotel or restaurant is only as good as its manager. If the manager is good the staff is good, if the staff is good, the hotel or restaurant is good.*[4]

Management as an integrating activity

Management is not a separate, discrete function. It cannot be departmentalised or centralised. A hospitality organisation cannot have a department of management in the same way as a department for other functions such as, for example, front office, food and beverage, housekeeping, personnel, marketing, reception, conferences. And management is not homogeneous. The nature of management is variable. It relates to all activities of the organisation. It takes place in different ways and is undertaken at all levels of the organisation.[5] For example, Webster draws attention to the importance of strategic management in a hospitality context. Strategic decisions determine the future direction and competitive position of an organisation and the contingent management processes.[6]

It is difficult to think of any aspect of the functioning of a hospitality organisation or the behaviour of people which does not concern, or relate back to, management in some way or another. For example, a personality clash between two members of staff could possibly be traced back to management procedures for recruitment and selection, induction and training, delegation or the level or style of supervision. And personality clashes are likely to have an adverse affect on the work performance of the individuals concerned, the morale of other staff and possibly the standard of customer service.

The people–organisation relationship

We have seen that at the heart of successful management is the ability to relate well to other people. Managers spend much of their time in meeting and talking with other people,[7] and this is especially the case in the hospitality industry.[8] A high level of interpersonal skills is clearly important therefore for effective work performance; and harmonious interpersonal relationships are also likely to enhance job satisfaction and the quality of work.

Attention should be focused, therefore, on improving the people–organisation relationship, and creating a climate in which people work willingly and effectively. Management is the integral and essential part of this relationship. The objective is to create the optimum working

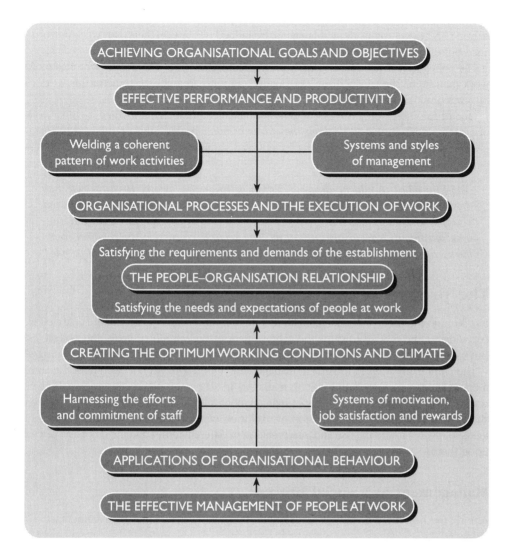

environment and to reconcile the demands of the organisation for effective performance and productivity, with satisfying the needs and expectations of people at work (Figure 4.1).

Management is concerned with arrangements for the carrying out of organisational processes and the execution of work. It is the task of management to weld a coherent pattern of work activities best suited to the environment in which the establishment is operating, to harness the efforts and commitment of staff, and to ensure equitable systems of motivation, job satisfaction and rewards. Consideration should be given to applications of organisational behaviour, and to systems and styles of management.

Authority over other people

Responsibility for the execution of work involves managers looking beyond their own activities, and exercising formal authority over the behaviour and performance of other people.

The manager can be seen as someone who has the power and authority to make things happen and to get things done. Managers are judged not just on their own work performance but on the results achieved by subordinate staff.

The concept of a manager is usually seen therefore in terms of a person who has more work than he or she can perform personally, and who arranges for some of this work to be carried out by others through delegation to subordinate staff.[9]

One of the most popular ways of defining management is that it involves getting work done second-hand, that is *through the efforts of other people*. Stewart attempts to integrate the various definitions of management and summarises the manager's job broadly defined as:

> *deciding what should be done and then getting other people to do it. A longer definition would be concerned with how these tasks are to be accomplished. The first task comprises setting objectives, planning (including decision-making) and setting up formal organization. The second consists of motivation, communication, control (including measurement) and the development of people.*[10]

The process of management

It is through the process of management that the efforts of members of staff are channelled, coordinated and guided towards the achievement of organisational goals and objectives. But what does the process of management involve and what activities does it encompass?

There are many ways of looking at management. One approach is to search for the common activities which are applicable to managers in all organisations. This approach gives rise to many different descriptions of management, although on closer study they often show a basic similarity. The inclusion or exclusion of a particular aspect of management tends to revolve round the use and interpretation of different terms, and the emphasis placed upon them.

Management as a social process

Among the best-known analysis is that given by Brech, who defines management as:

> *A social process entailing responsibility for the effective and economical planning and regulation of the operation of an enterprise, in fulfilment of given purposes or tasks, such responsibility involving:*
>
> *(a) judgement and decision in determining plans, and in using data to control performance and progress against plans;*
> *(b) the guidance, integration, motivation and supervision of the personnel composing the enterprise and carrying out its operations.*[11]

This is a useful definition in that it draws attention to management as a 'social process', to the responsibilities of a manager and to the importance of the people–organisation relationship.

As part of a debate on the need for a framework for the study of hospitality management (discussed in Chapter 2), Wood also draws attention to the recognition of the essentially **social** nature of management. The social and therefore variable nature of management as an activity precludes the evolution of any 'systematic' theory or theories of such activities.[12]

The tasks and contribution of a manager

Another approach to describing management is provided by Drucker, who identifies three tasks, equally important but essentially different, that have to be performed:

- fulfilling the specific purpose and mission of the institution, whether business enterprise, hospital or university (and we can add 'or hospitality organisation');
- making work productive and the worker achieving; and
- managing social impacts and social responsibilities.[13]

The work of the manager requires a combination of analytical ability, synthesising ability, integrity, human perception and insight, and social skill.

Drucker also suggests that managers can be defined by their function and by the contribution they are expected to make:

The function that distinguishes the manager above all others is the function no one but the manager can perform. The one contribution a manager is uniquely expected to make is to give others vision and ability to perform. It is vision and moral responsibility that, in the last analysis, define the manager.[14]

Unlikely managers

Restaurateur: Le Gavroche restaurant, London

Name: Silvano Giraldin

When did you become a manager? In 1973, when Le Gavroche was in Chelsea and I was 26. I was one of the youngest restaurant managers in the country.

What does management mean to you? Full control of Le Gavroche – except the food, which is done by Michel [Roux] – so all the beverages and the front of house. The restaurant has to look nice, the team has to be there and if someone's missing, positions have to be filled without customers noticing. There has to be a good atmosphere – if a restaurant's chefs and waiters are yelling at each other, it's a badly run place. My job is to act as a go-between and ensure these situations never arise – a happy staff means happy customers. It's no secret I also have to deal with difficult customers. We insist on a jacket and tie and one man refused to keep his jacket on. When I said, 'Sir, you have to keep it on,' his wife took her skirt off and asked: 'Now what will you do?' I said: 'Nothing madam, you look very pretty like that, but your husband still has to keep his jacket on.'

What do you love/hate about it? I love the quality of the guests. It brings me into contact with everyone, from pop stars to politicians and from the bottom of society to the top. The only thing I don't like is the long hours.

Reprinted with permission from *Management Today*, October 1999, p. 24.

Essential nature of managerial work

The overall responsibility of management can be seen as the attainment of the given objectives of the establishment. The essential nature of managerial work is not easy to describe, however, because aspects which may be common in many applications might escape us in others. And neither can you necessarily identify a manager by what a person is called or by his or her job title. In some organisations there is a liberal use of the title 'manager' in an apparent attempt to enhance the status and morale of staff. As a result there may be a number of people whose job title includes the term manager but who in reality are not performing the full activities of management. On the other hand, there are many people whose job title does not include the term 'manager' – for example head chef, controller, group accountant and of course *maitre d'* – but who in terms of the activities they undertake and the authority they exercise are very much managers.

'Managing' distinguished from 'doing'

However, if you look at how staff actually spend their time you should be able to see a difference between those whose main occupation is the carrying out of discrete tasks and the actual doing of work themselves; and those who spend proportionally more of their time in deciding what is to be done, determining the work to be undertaken by others, planning and organising their work, issuing them with instructions and giving advice, and checking on their performance.

From a study of 65 Irish hotels, Baum found that managers were actively involved in supervision, and frequently in the operation of such areas as front office, restaurant, bar and kitchen. Time was spent on tasks that craft or semi-skilled employees could perform and this suggested little awareness or concern for cost-effective use of time. However, central to the operational focus of the managers was the 'mine host' concept. More than half the managers defined their job as being essentially concerned with satisfying the needs of guests.[15]

Main activities of management

The particular nature of the hospitality industry, including the frequently perceived need for managers to demonstrate proficiency in technical and craft skills (discussed in Chapter 2), means that certain managers might be seen to be spending somewhat more time 'doing' than managers in other types of organisations. Nevertheless, the basis of the distinction between 'managing' and 'doing' still applies and this enables us to see the main activities of management (Figure 4.2) as:

- the clarification of objectives and policy;
- the planning of work to be carried out;
- organising the distribution of activities and tasks to other people;
- directing and guiding subordinate staff; and
- controlling the performance of other people's work.

Clarification of objectives and policy

Objectives are the aims to be achieved and the desired end results. Policy provides guidelines for the operations of the hospitality organisation and determines the course of action to follow. The clarification of objectives and policy is a prerequisite if the process of management and execution of work is to be effective. If not, the manager has no secure basis for decision-making and the management of subordinate staff.

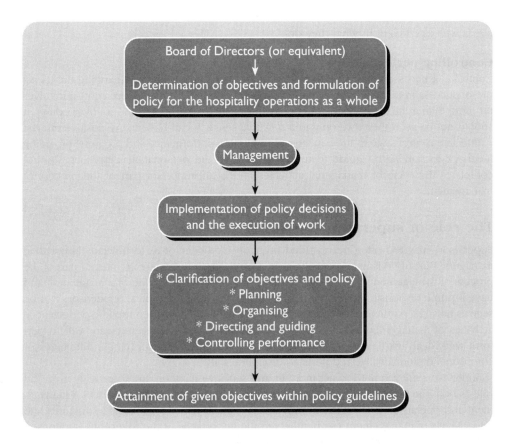

Planning of work

Planning sets out the courses of action to be followed in order to meet objectives and achieve desired end results, for example in relation to occupancy rates, financial measures or sales performance. Good forward planning is essential if staff are to know what to do and what is expected of them, for example the timing and sequencing of operations, methods by which the operations are to be carried out and standards of performance.

Organising

The work of the establishment has to be divided among its members. Organising involves the structuring of related areas of work activities such as reception, accommodation, kitchen and restaurant. Organisation provides the framework within which the process of management takes place. It makes possible the execution of work and involves the allocation of tasks and responsibilities, levels of hierarchical authority, formal relationships and coordination among individuals, groups and departments.

Directing subordinate staff

It is the responsibility of managers to encourage staff to work willingly and effectively. This is often referred to as motivation. It is certainly part of a manager's job to motivate staff and to provide them with job satisfaction, but it involves more than this. Subordinate staff also need development and guidance. They need to be motivated to *perform well in the right areas*. Their efforts should be directed towards the achievement of given objectives within stated policy guidelines. The manager has a responsibility to see that staff are effective as well as efficient in what they do.

Controlling performance

Control is a necessary part of the process of management. It involves gauging the measure of success in achieving objectives and planned targets. Management control involves far more than a means of restricting behaviour or the exercise of authority over others. It should not be seen therefore only in a negative sense; it can have many positive effects.

Effective control systems are a means of monitoring performance and progress, providing feedback to staff and a guide to future operations and personal development. Control completes the cycle of managerial activities and is an important part of the process of management.

The role of supervisors

Supervisors may too often be regarded primarily as 'doers' or as technicians rather than managers. But supervisors, especially in the hospitality industry, are an integral part of the process of management. They are usually very much in the front line of management and have a prime responsibility for seeing that work gets done by others. Supervisors can be seen as having a particular concern with the directing, guiding and controlling performance activities of management. They need to have the required skills to motivate staff to perform well, deal first-hand with problems of production or service, handle difficulties or complaints diplomatically, and perhaps discipline staff.

Supervisors are required to act in a fair and sensitive manner, and to provide a pivotal role as both the link and the buffer between the opposing expectations of senior management and operatives.[16] The general movement towards flatter organisation structures and fewer levels of management has highlighted the importance of the role of the supervisor.

There are also opportunities to recruit high level hospitality managers from the ranks of existing supervisory staff.[17]

Principles of management

Despite the variable nature of management, Fayol has suggested a set of 14 well-established principles to help concentrate discussion on management theory:[18]

(i) *Division of work* – the advantages of specialisation and the division of work. However, there are limits to division of work which experience and a sense of proportion suggest should not be exceeded.

(ii) *Authority and responsibility* – responsibility is the corollary of authority. Wherever authority is exercised, responsibility arises. The application of sanctions is essential to good management, and is needed to encourage useful actions and to discourage their opposite. The best safeguard against abuse of authority is the personal integrity of the manager.

(iii) *Discipline* – this is essential for the efficient operation of an organisation, and is in essence the outward mark of respect for agreements between the organisation and its members. The manager must decide on the most appropriate form of sanctions for offences against discipline.

(iv) *Unity of command* – in any action an employee should receive orders from one superior only; if not, authority is undermined and discipline, order and stability threatened. Dual command is a perpetual source of conflicts.

(v) *Unity of direction* – in order to provide for unity of action, coordination and focusing of effort, there should be one head and one plan for any group of activities with the same objective.

(vi) *Subordination of individual interests to general interest* – the interest of the organisation should dominate individual or group interests.

(vii) *Remuneration of personnel* – remuneration should as far as possible satisfy both employee and employer. Methods of payment can influence organisational performance and the methods should be fair and encourage keenness by rewarding well-directed effort, but should not lead to over-payment.

(viii) *Centralisation* – is always present to some extent in any organisation. The degree of centralisation is a question of proportion and will vary among particular organisations.

(ix) *Scalar chain* – the chain of superiors from the ultimate authority to the lowest ranks. Respect for line authority must be reconciled with activities which require urgent action, and with the need to provide for some measure of initiative at all levels of authority.

(x) *Order* – this includes material order and social order. The objective of material order is avoidance of loss. There should be an appointed place for each thing, and each thing in its appointed place. Social order involves an appointed place for each employee, and each employee in his or her appointed place. Social order requires good organisation and good selection.

(xi) *Equity* – the desire for equity and for equality of treatment are aspirations to be taken into account in dealing with employees at all levels.

(xii) *Stability of tenure of personnel* – generally, prosperous organisations have a stable managerial personnel. But changes of personnel are inevitable and stability of tenure is a question of proportion.

(xiii) *Initiative* – this represents a source of strength for the organisation and should be encouraged and developed. Tact and integrity are required to promote initiative and to retain respect for authority and discipline.

(xiv) *Esprit de corps* – this should be fostered as harmony and unity among members of an organisation is a great strength. The principle of unity of command should be observed. It is necessary to avoid the dangers of 'divide and rule' of one's own team, and the abuse of formal communication. Wherever possible, verbal contacts should be used.

General guidelines for the process of management

These principles provide a helpful framework within which to view organisational processes and the execution of work. They apply as much to hospitality operations as to any other type of work organisation although their applications may vary according to particular situations. For example, the principles of discipline, the scalar chain and *esprit de corps* might be seen to be of particular significance for hospitality management.

The principles must also be flexible and adaptable to changing circumstances, and certain principles are likely to be emphasised more in certain types of operations. For example, decisions on the division of work and the extent of centralisation are likely to be more significant in large establishments. However, as general guidelines for the process of management, the principles are difficult to argue against. They provide a helpful basis against which to review the native of managing in the twenty-first century.[19]

Managerial roles

The classical view of the manager as someone who organises, coordinates, plans and controls is not always easy to relate to what we see of the work of the manager. Mintzberg, for example, believes that the classical view tells us little about what managers actually do. It is more meaningful to describe the manager's job in terms of various 'roles' or organised sets of behaviour identified with a position.[20]

Based on a study of the work of five chief executives in medium-to-large organisations, Mintzberg classifies the essential functions of a top manager's job into ten interrelated roles. These roles are divided into three main groups: (i) interpersonal roles; (ii) informational roles; and (iii) decisional roles.[21]

The manager's formal status and authority give rise to the importance of interpersonal relationships. As a result of the interpersonal roles the manager is the focus for the collection and processing of information. The informational roles provide the basis for decision making (Figure 4.3).

Figure 4.3:
The manager's roles

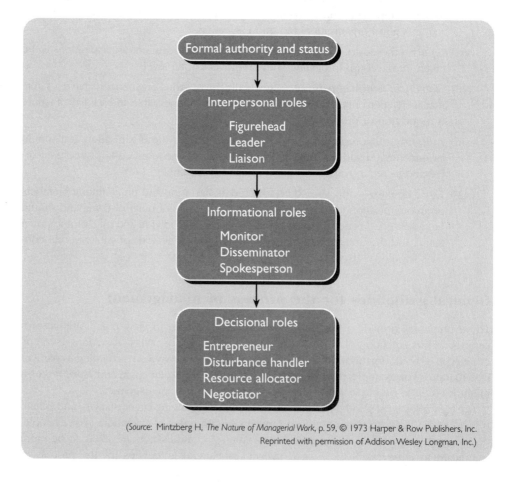

(*Source:* Mintzberg H, *The Nature of Managerial Work*, p. 59, © 1973 Harper & Row Publishers, Inc. Reprinted with permission of Addison Wesley Longman, Inc.)

Interpersonal roles

Interpersonal roles are relations with other people and arise from the manager's status and authority.

(i) *The figurehead role* is the most basic and simple of managerial roles. The manager is a symbol and represents the organisation in formal matters such as signing documents or at important social occasions. The manager is also available for people who insist on access to the 'top', for example a guest with a serious complaint or a member of staff with a major grievance.

(ii) *The leader role* is among the most significant of roles and permeates all activities of a manager. This role involves a responsibility for staffing, and the motivation and guidance of subordinate staff.

(iii) *The liaison role* involves the manager in relationships with individuals and groups outside their own unit, for example other managers, or outside the organisation, for example conference organisers. This role provides a link between the organisation and its environment.

Informational roles

Informational roles relate to the sources and communication of information arising from the manager's interpersonal roles.

(iv) *The monitor role* identifies the manager in seeking and receiving information in order to develop an understanding of the working of the organisation and its environment. This could include, for example, information on occupancy rates, future bookings or levels of staff turnover.

(v) *The disseminator role* involves the manager in the transmission of external and internal information. External information, for example the results of a meeting with another manager, is passed through the liaison role. Internal information, for example a request to comply with new instructions, is passed through the leader role between subordinates.

(vi) *The spokesperson role* involves the manager as formal authority in transmitting information to people outside the unit, for example the board of directors, or to people outside the organisation such as suppliers, guests, government departments or the press.

Decisional roles

Decisional roles involve making strategic organisational decisions on the basis of the manager's status and authority, and access to information.

(vii) *The entrepreneurial role* is the manager's function to initiate and plan controlled change through exploiting opportunities or solving problems, and taking action to improve the existing situation, for example by introducing a wider range of low-season offers or improving productivity.

(viii) *The disturbance handler role* involves the manager in reacting to involuntary situations and unpredictable events. When an unexpected disturbance occurs, for example the sudden and unexplained breakdown of kitchen equipment, the manager must take action to correct the situation.

(ix) *The resource allocator role* involves the manager in using formal authority to decide where effort will be expended, and making choices on the allocation of resources such as money, time, materials and staffing; for example, a choice might be required between enlarging the leisure facilities or improving conference facilities.

(x) *The negotiator role* involves the manager in negotiation activity with other individuals or organisations, for example a new wages agreement with staff representatives or a trade union, or negotiations with a potential new supplier.

An integrated whole

Mintzberg emphasises that the set of ten roles is a somewhat arbitrary division of the manager's activities. It presents one of many possible ways for categorising the view of managerial roles. The ten roles are not easily isolated in practice but form an integrated whole. If any role is removed this affects the effectiveness of the manager's overall performance.

The ten roles suggest that the manager is in fact a specialist required to perform a particular set of specialist roles. Mintzberg argues that empirical evidence supports the contention that this set of roles is common to the work of all managers.

Applications to the hotel manager

Among the studies of the application of Mintzberg's work to the hotel manager are those by Ley, Arnaldo and Shortt.

Head office rating of managerial effectiveness

Ley undertook a detailed observation of general managers in seven medium-sized Holiday Inn hotels in America. The study was concerned with time spent on different managerial roles related to head office ratings of the managers' effectiveness.[22] After classifying the functions of the managers' jobs in terms of Mintzberg's roles, the managers were then rated by their corporate superiors.

- Two managers were rated highly effective,
- Three were rated effective and
- Two were rated less than effective.

Effective managers appeared to allocate their time among the roles in a manner different from less effective managers. Those managers who devoted a high proportion of their time to the **entrepreneurial** role were judged to be more effective. But managers who worked the longest hours were also rated most effective by head offices and this raises doubts about the validity of the rating system. Although all managers saw the **leadership** role as important there appeared to be no direct relationship between time spent on this role and ratings of effectiveness. The two highly effective managers actually allocated less time to the leadership role than the two less effective managers.

Time and importance assigned to roles

Arnaldo surveyed 194 American hotel general managers who were asked to classify their activities in terms of Mintzberg's ten managerial roles, and to indicate the amount of time and importance assigned to each of the roles.[23] The study asked the managers to provide a relative ranking of time and importance to the various functions within each of the three main groupings.

- Of the interpersonal roles that of **leader** clearly absorbed most time (71.7 per cent) and was considered of most importance (86.1 per cent).
- With the informational roles, both **monitoring** and **disseminating** were said to be relatively time-absorbing and important. The spokesperson role took up less time and was considered less important.
- Of the decisional roles, all apart from negotiating absorbed roughly equal time. The **entrepreneurial** role was clearly judged to be the most important (55.2 per cent), although a lesser proportion of time (35.6 per cent) was spent on this role.

From the results of this study Arnaldo suggests that the development of training programmed might emphasise the crucial activities of leader, monitor, disseminator and entrepreneur.

A similar study undertaken by Shortt concerned 62 general managers of inns in Northern Ireland.[24] The most important roles were identified as **disturbance handler**, **leader** and **entrepreneur**. The least important roles were identified as **figurehead**, **disseminator** and **negotiator**.

Managerial work in the hospitality industry

From a review of the literature on the nature of managerial work in the hospitality industry, which has focused primarily on hotel management, Wood summarises six principal characteristics of management work:[25,26]

- People enter hotel management careers via a range of routes including: formal hotel school training, training for management within the industry and late entry after an earlier career in another industry. The last appears most typical of the owner-manager but in general all three routes seem typical of career paths in the industry.
- Hotel management like other occupations and the industry itself is very insular. Students are usually separated from general business studies students and their industrial placement training serves as a means of pre-entry socialisation. There is a perceived need for an emphasis on technical skills and competence particularly in food and beverage management.
- Most senior hotel managers obtain their appointment at a relatively early age. Formal qualifications do not appear to influence either entry position, or career patterns or promotion prospects. Vocational education or time spent gaining experience of the industry are alternatives that make little difference to long-term prospects.
- Hotel management positions are gained as a result of substantial mobility. Hotel and catering managers change their jobs more frequently than managers in other industrial sectors. Experience of both front of house and food and beverage is usually essential to promotion. Experience may be gained from frequent lateral moves between hotels within the same company or from moves involving a change of company. Pay appears to be generally linked to size of hotel and this therefore provides another incentive to mobility.
- The degree of latitude given to individual managers in the running of their units is reflected in the conduct of hotel management work. Particular importance is attached to leadership and entrepreneurial roles. Hotel management is dominated by operational demands and time spent in supervision of staff and contact with customers.

Managers have a preference for active management and, rather than sitting behind a desk, emphasise the 'being there' aspect of the job. The attitudes of management at unit level evidence a unitary outlook as opposed to a pluralistic perspective.

● Managers' basic remuneration, like the rest of the hotel and catering workforce, is relatively poor. Average salaries for hotel and catering managers are below those in other industrial sectors. Although hotel management careers are easier for some, the work is usually hard and the rewards are perceived, to outsiders at least, as somewhat limited.

The managerial wheel

Addressing the issue of the relationship between expected and actual behaviour, Hales and Nightingale studied managers in a wide range of organisations in the hospitality industry.[27] They identified a 'role-set' – that is, the set of people with whom the manager has contacts and the demands made upon the manager from a variety of role senders. In addition to the manager's own perception of his or her role, each member of the role-set was asked to identify the demands, requirements and expectations of the manager under study. These were recorded in a 'managerial wheel', as depicted in Figure 4.4. (The nature of role relationships and the role-set are discussed in more detail in Chapter 8.)

As might be anticipated, the study found that the unit manager's job is subject to a range of competing and conflicting demands from a wide range of sources, both internal and external. The range of expectation of the manager varied between different sectors and different members of the role-set. A main conclusion was that the character of unit management is determined as much by the kind of unit and what is being managed as by the general characteristics of the management process.

The flexibility of managerial work

Based on earlier studies of managerial jobs, Stewart has developed a model for understanding managerial work and behaviour.[28] The model directs attention to the generalisations that can be made about managerial work and differences which exist among managerial jobs. It acknowledges the wide variety among different managers in similar jobs in terms of how they view their jobs and the work they do. The three main categories of the model are demands, constraints and choices. These identify the flexibility in a managerial job.

● *Demands* are what anyone in the job *has* to do. They are not what the manager ought to do, but only what must be done, for example, meeting minimum criteria of performance, work which requires personal involvement, complying with bureaucratic procedures which cannot be avoided, meetings that must be attended.

● *Constraints* are internal or external factors which limit what the manager can do, for example, resource limitations, legal or trade union constraints, the nature of technology, physical location, compliance with company philosophy, attitudes of other people.

● *Choices* are the activities that the manager is free to do, but does not have to do. They are opportunities for one job holder to undertake different work from another job holder, or to do the work in a different way, for example, what work is undertaken within a defined area, to change the area of work, the sharing of work, participation in organisational or public activities.

Figure 4.4: A managerial wheel: expectations of unit manager by regional general manager

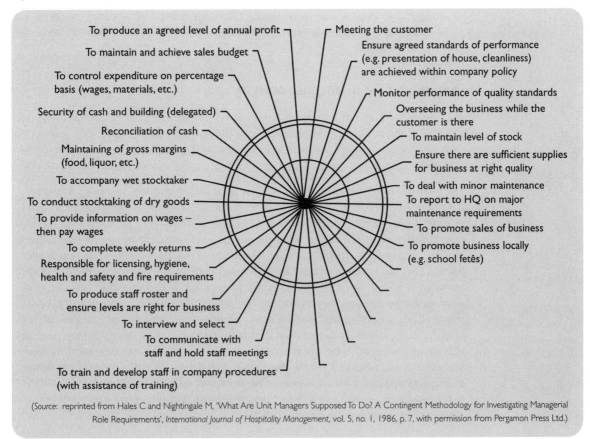

To produce an agreed level of annual profit

To maintain and achieve sales budget

To control expenditure on percentage basis (wages, materials, etc.)

Security of cash and building (delegated)

Reconciliation of cash

Maintaining of gross margins (food, liquor, etc.)

To accompany wet stocktaker

To conduct stocktaking of dry goods

To provide information on wages — then pay wages

To complete weekly returns

Responsible for licensing, hygiene, health and safety and fire requirements

To produce staff roster and ensure levels are right for business

To interview and select

To communicate with staff and hold staff meetings

To train and develop staff in company procedures (with assistance of training)

Meeting the customer

Ensure agreed standards of performance (e.g. presentation of house, cleanliness) are achieved within company policy

Monitor performance of quality standards

Overseeing the business while the customer is there

To maintain level of stock

Ensure there are sufficient supplies for business at right quality

To deal with minor maintenance

To report to HQ on major maintenance requirements

To promote sales of business

To promote business locally (e.g. school fetês)

(*Source*: reprinted from Hales C and Nightingale M, 'What Are Unit Managers Supposed To Do? A Contingent Methodology for Investigating Managerial Role Requirements', *International Journal of Hospitality Management*, vol. 5, no. 1, 1986, p. 7, with permission from Pergamon Press Ltd.)

Stewart suggests that the model provides a framework for thinking about the nature of managerial jobs and about the manner in which managers undertake them. To understand what managerial jobs are really like it is necessary to understand the nature of their flexibility. Account should be taken of variations in behaviour and differences in jobs before attempting to generalise about managerial work.

Behaviour patterns of managers

From a detailed study of 15 successful American general managers involved in a broad range of industries, Kotter found that although their jobs differed and the managers undertook their jobs in a different manner, they all spend most of their time interacting with other people and meetings provided exchanges of information over a wide range of topics in a short period of time. Managers had two significant activities in common: agenda setting and network building.[29]

- *Agenda setting* is a constant activity of managers. This is a set of items, or series of agendas involving aims and objectives, plans, strategies, ideas, decisions to be made and priorities of action in order to bring about desired end results.

- *Network building* involves the managers interacting with other people and establishing a network of cooperative relations. These networks are outside of the formal structure and often included a large number of people, many of whom were in addition to their boss or direct subordinates and also included individuals and groups outside the organisation. A major feature of network building was to establish and maintain contacts that could assist in the successful achievement of agenda items.

Management as a human activity

From a review of research into managerial behaviour, Stewart concludes that the picture built up gives a very different impression from the traditional description of a manager as one who plans, organises, coordinates, motivates, and controls in a logical, ordered process. Management is very much a human activity.

> *The picture that emerges from studies of what managers do is of someone who lives in a whirl of activity, in which attention must be switched every few minutes from one subject, problem, and person to another; of an uncertain world where relevant information includes gossip and speculation about how other people are thinking and what they are likely to do; and where it is necessary, particularly in senior posts, to develop a network of people who can fill one in on what is going on and what is likely to happen. It is a picture, too, not of a manager who sits quietly controlling but who is dependent upon many people, other than subordinates, with whom reciprocating relationships should be created; who needs to learn how to trade, bargain, and compromise; and a picture of managers who, increasingly as they ascend the management ladder, live in a political world where they must learn how to influence people other than subordinates, how to manoeuvre, and how to enlist support for what they want to do. In short, it is a much more human activity than that commonly suggested in management textbooks.*[30]

How restaurant managers spend their time

Using a similar methodology to Kotter, a study of nine restaurant managers was undertaken by Ferguson and Berger. From observation and documentation of the activities of the managers, their time was categorised as being used in the following five ways:

- Desk sessions   17%
- Telephone calls   13%
- Scheduled meetings   29%
- Unscheduled meetings   35%
- Tours   6%

Ferguson and Berger see the two categories of desk sessions and scheduled meetings as suggesting a reasonable level of structure and organisation, and conducive to organising, planning and deciding. However, from their study, the activities of the restaurant managers seemed far removed from textbook descriptions of planner, organiser, coordinator and controller and Ferguson and Berger have similar findings to Stewart.

> *Mintzberg described executives' activities as brief, fragmented and reactive. The restaurant operators' activities in this study seem even further removed from*

the textbook description of a planner, organiser, coordinator and controller than did those in the Mintzberg sample. Planning seems to have been eclipsed by reacting; organizing might be better described as simply carrying on; co-ordination appears more like juggling; and controlling seems reduced to full time watching.[31]

Key result areas of hotel management

Jones and Lockwood suggest a model of hotel management based on key result areas, defined as 'an area of activity that must be successfully managed in order to ensure the continued existence and the ultimate success of the operation'.[32]

Three component key result areas are:

- ensuring customer satisfaction;
- maintaining employee performance; and
- protecting assets from threat.

The three components are not managed in isolation but interact and overlap with each other. This highlights other key result areas that the manager must consider, such as managing customer service, maximising productivity, maximising income and profit contribution, and managing quality (Figure 4.5).

The focus of attention or relative priority of the key result areas will vary according to particular circumstances and requirements of the hotel. The model can also be modified to suit other sectors of the hospitality industry.

Figure 4.5: A model of hotel management

(*Source:* Jones P and Lockwood A, *The Management of Hotel Operations*, Cassell (1989), p. 30. Reproduced with permission of Cassell plc.)

Applications of general management theory

You will recall from the discussion in Chapter 2 that the hospitality industry shares important common features with other business industries and faces the same general problems of management. Particular models of managerial behaviour for the hospitality industry have little relevance and, if anything, provide a constraint on an open and fluid interpretation of managerial development.[33]

In identifying major areas of activity and knowledge needed by students of the hospitality industry, *The Profile of Professional Management* has this to say about the management areas:

> *Management areas cover functions common to management in any situation which have been identified as important to successful performance in hotel, catering and institutional services. Thus these areas reflect management functions which merit special emphasis in this industry and which represent the links between managements in this and other industries.*[34]

Managerial work in the hospitality industry

From a review of recent studies, Dann concludes that managerial work in the hospitality industry can be seen to fit comfortably with the main body of studies in the field. The need now is to integrate the studies of managerial work connected with the hospitality industry into the general body of knowledge of managerial work.[35]

A model for future research studies

Drawing on previous studies, Dann presents a model for the better understanding of the managerial work process and a guide for the direction of further research studies. The model involves three interlinking levels: inputs and demands; conduct and choices; and ends and outputs.

- *Level 1* concerns the inputs to the position and demands that are made on the role incumbent, for example: hierarchical level, size of the role-set, demands and expectations of those in the role-set, company strategy, the inherent nature of the job environment.

- *Level 2* relates to the conduct and choices available to the individual in managing the situation, for example: development of the managerial team, patterns of contact, delegation, usage of time, choice of job functions, and effective behaviour.

- *Level 3* relates to the ends and outputs of the manager. A clear pattern of the ends managers are attempting to achieve is a factor in shaping the nature of managerial work. Managers may wish to be judged not just on quantitative factors but also, for example, on relationships with their staff, and greater account is made of external influences which affect profitability.

The three levels are not intended to be mutually exclusive or divided. They are presented as a continuum rather than as distinct and clearly defined areas, and there is an interaction between each level. According to Dann, the hospitality industry requires much more research at all three levels.

Links with other industries

The common activities of management apply to a greater or lesser extent within the hotel industry. Stewart makes the point that managers' jobs vary and 'the differences are many and important' but 'we need, and with the help of research can make, useful generalisations about managerial work.'[36]

Rather than over-emphasising its uniqueness, attention should be given to ways in which ideas drawn from management theory may be applied with advantage to the industry. This point, which has been made previously by the author, is reinforced by Baum:

> While the business environment in hotels does have very distinct features, there is a danger that the emphasis which the industry places on uniqueness should not be at the cost of the application of the more general principles of good management.[37]

From a review of what hospitality managers do and how they do it, Guerrier and Lockwood conclude that:

> It is encouraging that researchers into hospitality management are increasingly drawing on the general management literature at the same time that researchers in general management are showing more interest in hospitality – clearly a consequence of the greater interest in service industries in general. Perhaps undue attention has been paid to certain theories and theorists. With the richness of management research available to draw upon, it is hoped that hospitality researchers will continue to broaden the scope of their studies.[38]

Stewart has highlighted the variations in behaviour and differences in managerial jobs. Study of managers in similar jobs indicates that their focus of attention differs.[39] This applies as much to hospitality managers as to any other group of similar managers.

We should also recall the discussion on the dangers of viewing the hospitality industry as unique (Chapter 2) and to recall the warning by Wood that perpetuating the myth of uniqueness is:

> for employers, managers and some workers, a self-serving device for justifying the unjustifiable in terms of inadequate basic rewards, feudal management practices and the maintenance of a culture that discourages intervention in the affairs of the industry by others.[40]

The managerial environment

Managers have to manage in the situation in which they find themselves. A major determinant of an individual hospitality manager's job is the environment, both internal and external, in which that manager is working.[41]

> As both an academic discipline and a set of 'real-life' practices, management is essentially a response to the demands of the wider environment and also part of it.[42]

The functioning and operation of a hospitality organisation takes place within the context of the total environmental setting. The actual process of management and execution of work is influenced by a combination of:

(i) the internal environment in which organisational processes take place, and which management is able to influence; and

(ii) the external environment of which the organisation is part, but which is outside the direct control of management.

The environment in which the manager is working will determine both the nature of the managerial roles, and the demands, constraints and choices which identify the flexibility in managerial behaviour.

The internal environment

Despite similarities in the general activities of management, the work of the manager is varied and fragmented. The jobs of individual hospitality managers, for example, will differ widely and be influenced by such interrelated factors as:

- *the nature of the organisation itself* – its culture, philosophy and objectives, size, type of building, location, type and range of services offered, facilities and guests;
- *its structure* – whether mechanistic or organic, division of work, patterns of organisation and formal relationships, channels of communication;
- *the nature of the work and tasks* to be carried out;
- *the 'technology'* – how work is carried out, the materials, equipment and furnishings;
- *its people* – their knowledge, skills, and experience, attitudes and motivations, patterns of behaviour, group functioning and the informal organisation;
- *the level at which the manager is working* – higher-level policies or decisions, the leadership style of the manager's superior.

These differences do not exist only between different hospitality organisations. Many large hospitality organisations may have more in common in their operations and management with other business organisations of the same size, than with very small hospitality establishments.

The external environment

The process of management is not only determined by internal considerations and choices, but is also influenced by a range of external factors. In Chapter 2 we saw that the hotel is an open system and in continual interaction with the external environment of which it is part (see Figure 4.6). All business organisations operate within, and are affected by, their external environment. For hospitality managers the demands of the external environment, for example guests/customers, may be particularly significant.[43]

Also in Chapter 2 we looked at the importance of major external factors including technological innovations, economic activity, social attitudes and government policies. There are a multiplicity of constantly changing environmental factors which are outside the control of management but which affect the operations of the hospitality organisation.

As further examples, consider how the process of management within a hotel might be affected by specific external influences such as:

- a government decision to include VAT on food;
- a total ban on all drinking and driving;

Figure 4.6: The managerial environment

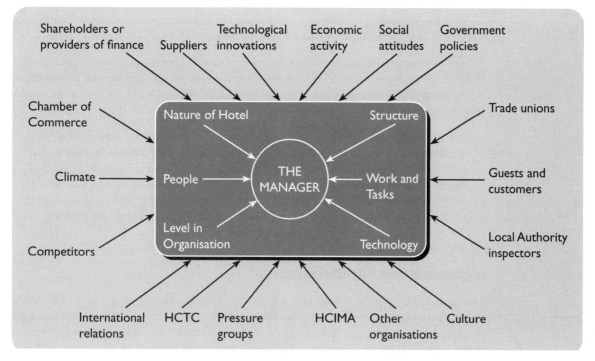

- severe restrictions on the use of water because of prolonged drought conditions;
- the building of a new hotel in close proximity by a major competitor;
- an unexpected and exceptionally high rise in the price of electricity;
- a TUC recommendation for members to boycott hotels paying below certain wage levels;
- a major advance in computer technology;
- a prolonged period of economic recession.

Not always easy to distinguish

It is important to note that, in practice, it is not always easy to distinguish clearly between situations that arise as a result of the internal environment or the external environment. The one tends to impinge upon the other. For example, to what extent might difficulties in recruiting high-calibre staff be due to poor selection procedures, low pay and poor working conditions (and within the control of the management), or due to demographic changes in the population (and outside the control of management)?

Managerial effectiveness

We have seen that if the hospitality organisation is to be successful there is a clear and important need for effective management. Effectiveness should be distinguished from efficiency.

- **Efficiency** is concerned with 'doing things right' and relates to inputs and what the manager does.
- **Effectiveness** is concerned with 'doing the right things' and relates to outputs of the job, and what the manager actually achieves.[44]

Effectiveness should also be distinguished from activity. Rees, for example, distinguishes between those managers who define what has to be done and get on with it, and those who seek to justify their positions by creating a flurry of activity rather than by the results they achieve.

The great danger is that, if managers spend too much time simply justifying themselves, they may fail actually to diagnose what they should be doing and therefore fail to do it. Ultimately managers are much more likely to be judged by results than by anything else. Activity-centred behaviour is in any case much more likely to spring from incompetence and/or insecurity rather than adroit political behaviour. This type of behaviour is likely to aggravate the position of the manager in the long run rather than ameliorate it.[45]

Measurements of effectiveness

Managerial effectiveness should be related to the performance of the process of management and the execution of work, and measured in terms of the results that the manager is expected to achieve and the quality of decision-making.[46] But managerial effectiveness is not easy to measure objectively. Managers are judged not just on their own performance but also on results achieved by subordinate staff. The manager's effectiveness may be assessed in part, therefore, by such criteria as the strength of motivation and morale of staff, the success of their training and development, and the quality of their work performance (Figure 4.7).

However, the difficulty is determining objective measures of such criteria. Some possible indicators might be given by, for example, the level of staff turnover, the incidence of sickness or absenteeism, poor time-keeping, accidents at work, breakages and the amount of scrap.

The added difficulty in applying such measures is that figures are likely to be influenced also by broader organisational or environmental factors outside the control of an individual manager. For example the type, size and location of the establishment, the competitive level of the market, the general economic climate giving a feeling of poor job security, company philosophy or general policy directives.

Outputs of the job

To be effective the manager must give attention to the outputs of the job – to performance – in terms of factors such as obtaining the best possible results in the key areas of operations, optimal use of resources, increasing profitability, and attainment of the aims and objectives of the hotel.

Criteria which *may* give some indication of managerial effectiveness include the efficiency of systems and procedures, the standard of service afforded to other departments, meeting important deadlines, adherence to quality standards, the number of recorded errors or complaints, keeping within agreed budget limits and productivity.

Again, however, there is the question of how to determine objective measurement of such criteria and to what extent they are under the control of the manager.[47]

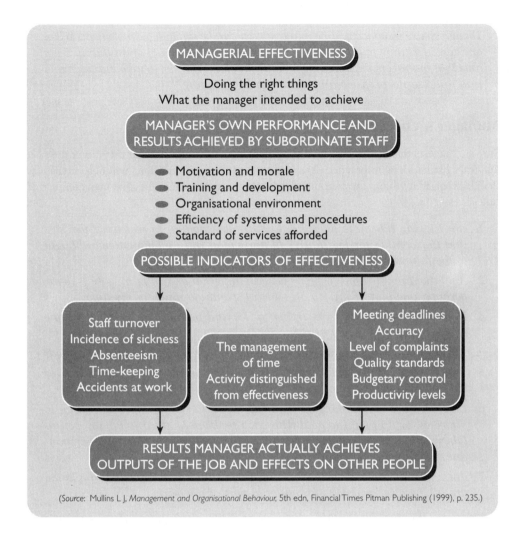

Figure 4.7:
Possible
indicators of
managerial
effectiveness

MANAGERIAL EFFECTIVENESS

Doing the right things
What the manager intended to achieve

MANAGER'S OWN PERFORMANCE AND
RESULTS ACHIEVED BY SUBORDINATE STAFF

- Motivation and morale
- Training and development
- Organisational environment
- Efficiency of systems and procedures
- Standard of services afforded

POSSIBLE INDICATORS OF EFFECTIVENESS

Staff turnover
Incidence of sickness
Absenteeism
Time-keeping
Accidents at work

The management
of time
Activity distinguished
from effectiveness

Meeting deadlines
Accuracy
Level of complaints
Quality standards
Budgetary control
Productivity levels

RESULTS MANAGER ACTUALLY ACHIEVES
OUTPUTS OF THE JOB AND EFFECTS ON OTHER PEOPLE

(*Source*: Mullins L. J, *Management and Organisational Behaviour*, 5th edn, Financial Times Pitman Publishing (1999), p. 235.)

The management of time

Although it is currently a popular topic of attention, the importance of time management has long been recognised as an inherent feature of effective management. For example, Drucker refers to time as the limiting factor. It is a unique resource which you cannot rent, hire, buy or otherwise obtain. The supply of time is totally inelastic; time is totally irreplaceable and everything requires time.[48] According to the Institute of Management, good time management has always been an important skill, but is arguably now more essential than ever.[49]

Whatever the attributes of a successful manager, or the quality of subordinate staff, one essential underlying criterion is the effective use of time. A major characteristic of the hospitality industry is that it involves a wide range of services and operations, and direct interactions between both staff and customers. This places particular demands upon the time of its managers. With many managers who complain that they do not have sufficient time, it may be more a case that they have failed to organise themselves or their work properly. The most important members of staff to be managed are themselves.

Time management involves putting available time to the best possible use. Though simple in concept, time management can be difficult to implement. When one considers time management more deeply, it becomes apparent that it is not time that managers must manage, but themselves. The key to time management is to understand proper planning and priority setting.[50]

Manager's checklist

Stewart suggests that it is often salutary for managers to compare what they think they do against what happens in practice. Answers to the following questions will help managers decide what, if anything, they should check, and to review their effective management of time.[51]

1. Am I giving adequate attention to current activities, to reviewing the past and to planning for the future? In particular, am I giving enough thought to the future?

2. Am I dividing my time correctly between different aspects of my job? Is there, perhaps, one part of my job on which I spend too much of my time?

3. Have I changed what I am trying to do, and how I work to allow for the effects of changes in my work?

4. Am I certain that I am not doing any work that I ought to have delegated?

5. Who are the people that I ought to be seeing? Am I spending too much or too little time with any of them?

6. Do I organise my working day and week, as far as possible, according to priorities, or do I tend to deal with each problem as it turns up, or even as I think of it, without stopping to think whether there is something more important that I should be working on?

7. Am I able to complete a task, or am I constantly interrupted? If the latter, are all these interruptions an essential part of my work?

There are three questions that managers should ask of each of their activities:

- *Should it be done at all?*
- *If so, when should it be done?*
- *Should it be delegated?*

(The nature of delegation is discussed in Chapter 11)

Outcome measures of performance

As part of a study of 63 managers from three different American hotel firms, Umbreit and Eder asked participants to record important outcome measures that a typical hotel manager should have control over, and against which their performance should be evaluated. After discussion among the group, a list of 14 outcome measures was identified:[52]

- *Guest comments* – to staff or on cards.
- *Market share* – percentage of room nights occupied in comparison to the total in the market.

- *Room nights sold* – total of rooms sold in a given period.
- *Reduction of employee turnover* – compared with a previous period.
- *Budget controlled* – sales generated and expenses controlled against budget figures.
- *Food and beverage department profit* – profit figure after deduction of expenses from departmental sales.
- *Rooms department profit* – profit figure after expenses are deducted from departmental sales.
- *Employee complaints* – about job conditions or treatment compared with a previous period.
- *Employee training course completions* – numbers formally completing a training programme during a certain time.
- *Collection of receivables* – outstanding number and amount of receivables during a given period of time.
- *Number of leadership positions held* – by a manager in the community.
- *Hotel rating* – the rating of the hotel by an outside agency.
- *Frequency of employee accidents* – reported to management compared with a previous period.
- *Adherence to productivity standards* – such as number of rooms cleaned per shift.

Behavioural dimensions of evaluation

Umbreit and Eder also suggest seven 'behavioral dimensions' for the evaluation of a hotel manager:

- handling guest complaints and promoting guest relations;
- developing market strategy and monitoring sales programmes;
- communicating with employees;
- motivating and modifying behaviour;
- implementing policy, making decisions and delegating responsibility;
- monitoring operations and maintaining product quality;
- handling personnel responsibilities.

These seven dimensions can be applied as a basis for the performance review of a hotel manager and can provide important feedback on what behaviour is desirable to improve future performance.[53]

What constitutes a successful hospitality manager?

Peacock undertook a study of a sample of 200 hospitality managers who were asked in a telephone survey: 'How do you determine whether you've done a good job?' From the responses a sevenfold classification was derived. (See Figure 4.8.)

Where managers gave more than one response this was categorised according to their initial response.

- The largest group defined success in *financial terms*. Managers were fairly evenly divided among all sectors of the industry.

Figure 4.8:
Hospitality
managers'
perspectives
on success

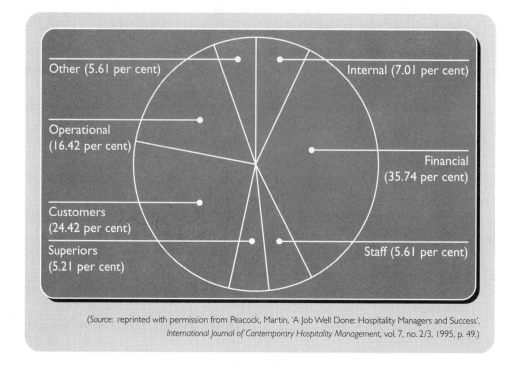

(*Source:* reprinted with permission from Peacock, Martin, 'A Job Well Done: Hospitality Managers and Success',
International Journal of Contemporary Hospitality Management, vol. 7, no. 2/3, 1995, p. 49.)

- The next largest group defined success by *talking about customers*. Managers were more likely to work for smaller establishments.

- The third largest group defined success in relation to '*operational factors*' – basically the smooth running of the establishment. Managers are found in larger establishments but evenly divided between hotels and restaurants, chains and multiples.

- The fourth largest group defined success in terms of *internal factors* or something felt personally – job satisfaction or an intrinsic value. Managers tend to work for smaller establishments, restaurants rather than hotels, and are more likely to work for independent establishments than for chains.

- The fifth group defined achievement in terms of *the staff they supervised* including staff retention, morale and feedback. Managers are more likely to be working in large establishments especially hotels and are unlikely to be working in the independent sector.

- The sixth group took their performance measure *from their superiors* and what their boss thought of them. Managers tend to work in large establishments, are twice as likely to work in hotels and are unlikely to work for independents.

- The final grouping is those minority who did not provide an answer or who gave answers too vague to categorise.[54]

The management of people

Criteria for assessing managerial effectiveness should be considered in terms of measuring the results that the manager is intended to achieve and over which the manager has control. But what is also important is the manner in which the manager achieves results and the effects on other people. This may well influence effectiveness in the longer term.

We have seen that there are many aspects to management in hospitality operations, but the one essential ingredient of any successful manager is the ability to handle people effectively. The manager needs to be conversant with social and human skills, and to have the ability to work with and through people. Without people there can be no organisation and no meaningful activity.[55]

Behind every action or document there are people. The importance of the manage–subordinate relationship and the effective management of people are considered in the following chapter.

A framework of management

We have seen that there are many ways of looking at the nature of management and the work of a hospitality manager. A summary of the main aspects considered in this chapter is given in Figure 4.9. This provides a convenient framework in which to direct study of the subject area.

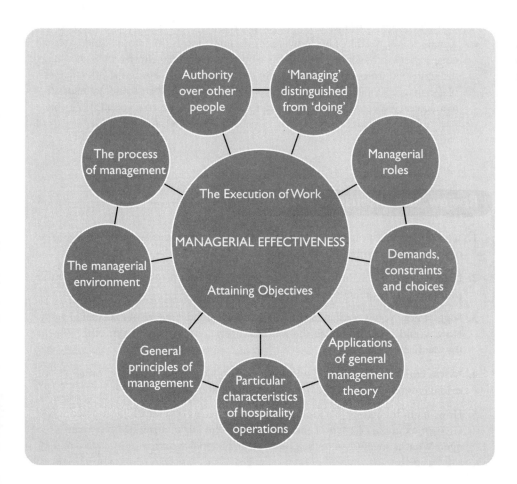

Figure 4.9: A framework for the study of management

Summary

- The importance of management, including that within the hospitality industry, is widely recognised. Management is responsible for the implementation of policy and the execution of work. This involves the exercise of authority over other people. Management is essentially an integrating activity – it is the cornerstone of the people–organisation relationship.

- By distinguishing 'managing' from 'doing' the essential nature of managerial work can be summarised as clarifying objectives and policy, planning, organising, directing and controlling. General principles of management provide helpful guidelines for the process of management.

- The job of a manager can be viewed in a number of ways including as a set of interrelated roles; in terms of a role-set and the managerial wheel; demands, constraints and choices and the flexibility in a managerial job; and key result areas of management.

- The hospitality industry has its own characteristics and features but it also faces the same general problems of management. Rather than over-emphasising its uniqueness, attention should be given to applications of general management theory and to integrating studies of hospitality management with ideas drawn from other industries.

- A major determinant of an individual manager's job is the internal and external environment in which the manager is working. Managerial effectiveness should be distinguished from efficiency and activity. Criteria for assessing the effectiveness of a manager should be related to the output measures of the job and to results the manager is expected to achieve, and to the successful management of people.

Review and discussion questions

1. Why do organisations need managers? Give your own views on the importance of management within the hospitality industry.

2. Discuss what is meant by: (i) the people–organisation relationship and (ii) the process of management.

3. Suggest how you would attempt to analyse the essential nature of managerial work. How would you distinguish the job of a hospitality manager from other jobs in the establishment?

4. Assess critically the practical relevance and applications of common principles of management within a large hospitality organisation.

5. How might the manager's job be described in terms of a set of interrelated roles? Give an example of each of these roles from the job of a senior hotel manager. What is meant by the flexibility of managerial work?

6. Discuss critically the extent to which general management theory can be applied successfully within the hospitality industry. Justify your answer with practical examples.

7. What is meant by the managerial environment? From your own experience, give *specific* examples of both internal *and* external environmental influences within hospitality organisations.

8. How would you attempt to distinguish between an effective and an ineffective manager? Suggest what specific criteria you would use to assess the effectiveness of a particular hospitality manager.

Assignment

Select a particular hospitality managerial job and observe the manager in action, preferably over an extended period of time.

(i) Make notes of how much of the manager's work and time is spent on:
   (a) the carrying out of discrete tasks and the actual 'doing' of work personally; and
   (b) deciding what work is to be done and planning, organising, directing or controlling the work of other people.
(ii) Identify clearly those factors which determine the demands, constraints and choices of the job. Comment critically on how these factors determine the flexibility in the manager's job.
(iii) Analyse particular ways in which features of the internal and external environment influence the job of the manager.
(iv) State clearly what conclusions you draw from your observations.

Case study: What *is* management?

A thing may look specious in theory, and yet be ruinous in practice; a thing may look evil in theory, and yet be in practice excellent.   EDMUND BURKE

Adam Smith sat at his desk and reflected that it was now exactly 12 months since he had been appointed general assistant to Charles Gaynor, managing director of Gaynor Hotels. During this time he had been used as adviser, counsellor, internal consultant and therapist. He had investigated problems, developed concepts, established principles and generally contributed to the decision-taking process which took place in the mind of his employer, Gaynor. His attention had been attracted by an article he had been reading, which said:

In order to maintain its internal dynamic which is essential to progress, a company needs the existence of a rebel group which is primarily concerned with challenging company policy, a group which regards as its main function the generation of sceptical attitudes towards the ▷

company's methods of operation, organisation and policies. Such a group should adopt as a work-ing principle the slogan 'if it works it's obsolescent'. In other words the mere fact that a system is working satisfactorily should in itself be sufficient reason for its re-examination.*

Adam ruminated on this and considered that with Carson, his assistant, they really had created a two-man management services activity since they had concentrated on looking at, and solving, old problems in new ways. A pocket of rational thought in a wilderness of emotionalism – if only that were really true, thought Adam!

He felt depressed. Although he realised that some progress had been made, it seemed infinitesimal when one looked at the company as a whole. Where is the real answer to the achievement of progress?, thought Adam. If only one could put one's finger on it. Particular aspects, methods, solutions and so on were looked at which all seemed part of the answer, but where was the whole answer? Charles Gaynor, although a man inculcated at an early age with the attitudes and ways of traditional hotel-keeping, was most receptive to new ideas; indeed, he could generate them himself and boasted of his preparedness to accept necessary change. But nothing much seemed to have changed in these 12 months; Gaynor Hotels was still making a profit, its managers were still 'managing' but problems continued to abound and there seemed just as many unanswered questions.

Adam leaned forward on his desk with his head in his hands. He wondered if the company was really progressing, if things were any better, and whether he was just deceiving himself. Perhaps the problem was that the company was just 'managing', that it was just getting by, just keeping its head above water. Is it really geared to grow and develop and prosper? Is it really looking ahead and ready to exploit the changing circumstances of a changing world? That's the central question, thought Adam, and I wish I could answer it confidently.

Management! It is all in the management, a handful of men cannot carry a company – it is in the strength and depth of *all* the people who form the firm. His thoughts were interrupted by the door opening and Gaynor appearing with a benevolent smile, and a friendly 'Good afternoon, Adam.'

Gaynor: I thought I would let you know it looks as though I will have to fire a manager, or to put it euphemistically, to ask him to resign.

Adam: Who is it, sir?

Gaynor: Hedges, at the Zephyr. Nasty business and the sort of scandal I deplore. I had a letter from a Mr Coloniki; his wife is secretary to Hedges who, he asserted, has been sleeping with her. I thought there couldn't be anything in it and I referred it to our Mr Hedges never expecting anything other than a denial. Well the damn fool confirmed it as being true, he *has* been sleeping with his secret-ary. Doesn't leave me much alternative, does it? I can't compromise my principles and I will not have my hotel executives entering into this sort of relationship with their staff. My goodness! What sort of an example is it? Oh, the stupid man, and he was doing quite a good job for us.

Adam: Well, sir, there's an old Hungarian proverb which says that when a man's fancy is titillated his brain goes to water.

Gaynor: How very true! But a little control, a little sense of responsibility, a little maturity, that's all I ask. It isn't even as if he was serious about her; as he told me, it was just his 'little indiscretion' and he hoped that I wouldn't find out. By the way, you didn't already know about it, did you?

Adam: No, certainly not, sir. I haven't heard the slightest suggestion.

*Ward, T R, Management Services – The Way ahead, *National O & M Conference*, 1964; published as an Anbar Monograph, Anbar Publications, 1965.

Gaynor: Well, back to the old problem of finding a new manager, as if good managers grew on trees! They are such rare animals – they take such a great deal of finding, such a great deal of raising.

Adam: How about his assistant, Gripple, do you think that he might be ready to take over?

Gaynor: He might . . . I don't know, even if we knew what job we were really picking him for; I mean, what *is* management, what is it *really?* What are we looking for?

Adam: Well, quite honestly, sir, I do not think that he's ready. I think he could develop into a manager, but he needs more time.

Gaynor: All right, we will have to find somebody. I'll tell you what we can do: you take over as manager of the Zephyr for the next month or so. During that time I will find a new manager. This *has* caught us unawares, I can't think of anybody suitable in the company at present.

Adam: But I've never actually managed a hotel!

Gaynor: Well, it will be an excellent experience for you. Anyway, I have no doubt about *your* management abilities. But you still didn't answer my question just now. What actually *is* management – do you know what it is?

Adam: Strange you should ask me that this afternoon. I think that I was going to ask myself the same question just as you walked in.

Gaynor: Fine, but can you answer it?

Adam: Well, it's obviously to do with concern for profits and its equally to do with concern for people and creating a climate where they can grow and develop.

Gaynor: That's rather vague.

Adam: Well, let me go on, sir. If it's to do with concern for profits then it is also to do with knowledge of modern management methods and techniques and how to use them. If it's to do with concern for people, then it's also to do with knowledge of human behaviour and its application.

Gaynor: You're struggling, Adam. I remember we talked about the purpose of business and it must lead on from there. We agreed that this was the satisfaction of the needs, wants and desires of those who control the business and generally, but not always, this involved a certain level of profitability. Now purpose must define or set the aims and objectives. Subsequently the policy indicates the means as to how to accomplish these. Policy acts then as the firm guide in all decision-making at an operational level. Management, therefore, is the implementation of policy to achieve company aims and objectives. Yes, I rather like that – I must remember to use it again.

Adam: I know you won't mind Mr Gaynor, but I can't agree with you.

Gaynor: Go on then, I am not very busy at the moment.

Adam: I don't disagree with what you say, but really I am concerned with the assumptions which are being made. Indeed, the business purpose sets aims or objectives but this implies that the business purpose has been established, is commonly perceived and is accepted. You next assume that policy is rationally formulated and promulgated, that managers are aware of it, and take their decisions within its limitations.

Gaynor: Perhaps that describes the ideal situation, but I would still maintain that what I said – what was it? – management is the implementation of policy to achieve company aims and objectives, is a good description.

Adam: May I ask what policy Mr Hedges offended?

Gaynor: Ah, well, now, there are several. First it is unethical; second, if it became known it would damage our image and create havoc in staff relationships, and there are more besides.

Adam: But Mr Hedges took a decision, presumably with a knowledge of the policies you mention, whose effects could militate against our aims and objectives as well as damage his career.

Gaynor: And a damn fool he was, too!

Adam: Were it a less serious affair, and something which was only a minor departure from Company policy, I can't help wondering how he or we would know that a departure had occurred. For example, if a manager gave 11 per cent commission to travel agents during the winter to obtain some preference from them, would this be stopped if you became aware of it?

Gaynor: I hope that he would have discussed this with me first, but I can appreciate the point. After all we must be flexible enough to deal with special situations.

Adam: Doesn't this, then, highlight the problem of what we mean by policy? Earlier you said that policy acts as a firm guide, but payment of commission is pretty well fixed at 10 per cent, although you would be prepared to consider exceptions. I hope I am not splitting hairs if I suggest that our policy is to pay commissions, and a procedure has been established which fixes this at 10 per cent.

Gaynor: I think, in this case, you are tending to split hairs but I see what you are getting at; a confusion exists between policy and procedures. I must admit that I have confused these at times. Yes, I see the point – policy should act as a guide. But formulating policy in this way must make it so general that it cannot provide much of a guide, a paradox in fact. Another thought that occurs to me is that if the policy is to be an effective guide it should be written out and available for the manager to consult. I must say that this would be an unenviable task!

Adam: Reading textbooks about management I have found the exhortation to have a written policy a common theme. I have never actually seen one so far for a hotel and one can appreciate why this is so. At the same time I would think comparatively easy to spell out some policies; in the financial areas, for example, this would seem a fairly straightforward exercise.

Gaynor: Yes, and I think it could be done in the operating area too. I must admit, though, that I am not sure that I would like to have an exhaustive written policy document. I feel it would be a restriction on me.

Adam: I believe this is a fairly common feeling among senior executives. Glacier Metal Company introduced a written policy and their experience was that flexibility *increased* since, when a change had to be made, everybody could be informed and a written amendment incorporated. This makes sense to me, but I have always had a sneaking feeling that they wrote a procedure manual rather than a policy handbook.

Gaynor: So you are back to your distinction between policy and procedures! Am I to take it, then, that you are advocating that we should try to produce a policy document for the Company?

Adam: No, sir, I may tend to overstate the case, but I would think that the existence of such a document represents a failure of management. At a unit level, and indeed at company level, it is essential to have *procedure* manuals since these provide a means of establishing and maintaining standards as well as a basis for training. I would also say that it is essential for a company to spend a lot of time clarifying its objectives and aims at the top level. The real problem is that many so-called policy documents are little more than a public relations handout. If a company is clear about what it wants to be, surely it should make every effort for everybody to understand and accept these aims and behave in a supportive way towards them.

Gaynor: I would have thought that having a written policy would help to do this, since people could see just what the aims are and act accordingly.

Adam: I am sure that this is partly true, but what I am trying to say is that if, starting at the top, members of an organisation demonstrate by their behaviour what the policy is, this will be reflected downwards. If the senior executives behave as though they believed the customer was important, then other employees will adopt similar behaviour.

Gaynor: In other words, people will learn by example. I am rather intrigued that you should have such a charming old-fashioned idea!

▷

Adam: By example, yes. But it is a little more than this. Put into jargon, I would say that it is minimising corporate discrepancy. That is, reducing the difference between what a company as a collection of people say, and what in fact they do.

Gaynor: Very well, I agree with what you say but I must say there are some grave dangers of misinterpretation. If the conclusion without the supporting argument is adopted it can become an excuse for avoiding the necessary analytical thinking at the top level. We seem to have strayed a long way from my attempt to define management; taking into account all you have said we still have a good description.

Adam: I agree, but the whole problem of vocabulary in management continues to be a stumbling block I always remember a lecturer at college who said at his lecture to us that he had to devise a vocabulary to talk to us which we would automatically adopt, but never to attempt to use it outside. Since there is no generally accepted or defined vocabulary he had to fashion his own to communicate to us. We all forgot, of course, and it took some time to stop using our private language when we went into industry.

Gaynor: You still forget sometimes!

Adam: Sorry! If we do understand that policy and company aims and objectives are in some way related to individual interpretation, depending on the perceptions of the people involved, then I think it is a good *desc*ription. But shouldn't a definition of this sort be a *prescription*? By saying what it is, it gives some indication of how to do it?

Gaynor: Description, prescription, you're chopping words again. I will accept, although I think you are trying to find a philosopher's stone if a definition can tell a manager how to do his job!

Adam: To come back to the definition, sir, suppose the policy is wrong or the aims and objectives are wrong. Is it true to say that an individual is managing if he keeps things going to achieve these and doesn't have the wit or the insight to besiege his superiors for a change of direction?

Gaynor: Ah! Now you are introducing value judgments about 'good' management and 'bad' management!

Adam: No, Mr Gaynor. You will accuse me of sophistry again, but I would say that a person who is a manager is managing effectively. If he is ineffective, then he is not a manager.

Gaynor: Save me from quibblers! But do go on.

Adam: When I was in America I was given an assignment to collect together as many definitions of management as I could find. It really was a fascinating exercise but eventually I found myself in a such a muddle that I could hardly think straight. The things that people have to say about this process, which hundreds of thousands of people go about for five days a week, year in and year out is amazing. The one that I remember, and considered the most banal of a very sad bunch, was 'Management is getting things done through people.'

Gaynor: Oh! I always considered that a truism.

Adam: Well, yes. But it doesn't advance our understanding. Bus conductors, waitresses and supervisors get things done through people – but they are not managers.

Gaynor: Very interesting; so you don't think supervisors are managers?

Adam: No. Managers are tacticians; that is they are people who are once-removed from the actual operators who serve the food or make the beds. Managers are concerned with the deployment of resources. A manager *says* what has to be done, a supervisor frequently *shows* people what has to be done. The supervisor is a technician, the manager is a tactician. In this sense he is *always* 'getting things done through other people' and the other people are his supervisors.

Gaynor: Well, then, why does this 'getting things done through other people' grate on you so much?

Adam: Chiefly because of its lack of prescription. Would you say that a person is an effective manager who spends all his time with his supervisors, guiding, instructing, directing and giving decisions?

Gaynor: No, certainly not. I would expect him to set the guidelines – policy, if you like – and by his selection and development of the supervisors, reach a stage where they got on with the work and left him time to think.

Adam: Exactly. I think it has been sufficiently demonstrated from studies of managers' and supervisors' behaviour that these are very different roles. We must be careful, however, about actual titles that go with a job.

Gaynor: Yes indeed. It was always a source of amusement to me, when I had the title of General Manager, to sit next to people, with the same designation, at conferences who ran a hotel with twenty bedrooms. I would be the first to insist that we belonged to the same industry, but our needs and problems were vastly different! Do we have any common ground, I wonder? The other thing that concerns me is an entrepreneurial aspect. The owner of a twenty-bedroom hotel is an entrepreneur, whereas Kimble at the Diana is a manager employed by the Company. Yet he is responsible for about twenty times the turnover of this entrepreneur!

Adam: I have often pondered about this. In many ways it is a very personal thing. Occasionally I meet people who ask me why I work for Gaynor Hotels when I could be my own boss running a small hotel in the Cotswolds and probably able to take each afternoon off for golf. But it really depends on what you mean by being one's own boss. I am sure there is great satisfaction in being personally involved with the customers in the small business, but the real boss is then the bank manager and there is a very real dependence on suppliers. I think that one can over-emphasise the differences between the entrepreneur and the manager. Probably the owner of a small hotel spends about 5 per cent of his time on entrepreneurial decisions and the rest of the time he is a manager. So Kimble and the proprietor have 95 per cent of common activity if they are running similar establishments.

Gaynor: I suppose I am the professional entrepreneur of this Company, but I have never been able to find any courses which deal with this topic! But we are still groping about. You have the advantage of your research on definitions of management, what are your conclusions? After all, people like me that just manage, what time do we have for all this introspection?

Adam: Now I am in difficulties! On the one hand, I am asked to offer my conclusions against your experience, and on the other hand, I am asked to sit in judgement on the multitude of writers on management!

Gaynor: I thought this is what you did anyway, but please! You know that I want to know about your ideas and that I shall use my experience to challenge you where I think you are wrong. I know that you will produce research findings that I have never heard of, like rabbits from a hat. But I am still interested in your ideas.

Adam: Sorry, Mr Gaynor, but I just realised the enormity of what you asked me to do. It is one thing to make comments about a definition that somebody proposes; it is quite another thing to be asked, from limited experience, to fly in the face of the savants!

Gaynor: I quite understand, but go ahead.

Adam: Well, the early writers about management became heavily involved in trying to define management but I think because they were engineers or technologists, they wanted it cut and dried. They saw the world in mechanical terms and placed all the emphasis on what should be done to create orderliness and an organisation which works like a smoothly oiled machine.

Gaynor: Then the social scientists came along and started to demonstrate that most of the problems were centred round people who did not behave like machines. In fact they were unpredictable.

Adam: Yes, but I think that the success of techniques in advertising show that there are quite a lot of predictable elements in people's behaviour. But the effect of the behavioural scientists' findings tended to tip the balance with a lot of managers from concern for production to concern for ▷

people. In fact I sometimes think this still persists today to a large extent; from the way some people talk, one would think that the Hawthorne experiments were the only studies which have been conducted in this field.

Gaynor: You mean that a manager should be involved in maintaining a balance between his concern for people and for production?

Adam: Yes. This means that management is a process which involves achieving business goals while at the same time providing a means of satisfaction for the individual needs or goals of employees. Now I think that the real danger to maintaining this balance might be described as the return on invested time. A comparatively short time spent in replanning a layout of a kitchen, or the desirability of installing a room state indicator, can quickly produce economies. We can see that more meals can be produced or customers allocated rooms speedily. But to increase people's effectiveness requires a much greater investment in time to establish what goals they are seeking to achieve.

Gaynor: I think most managers would agree with you and that they appreciate the need for developing people, but there is always the pressure of other things to be done and the consequent shortage of time. And what about decision-taking? I would think that this is a basic and fundamental part of managing.

Adam: The problem of time is something I would like to come back to. I must admit that I feel slightly nervous when decision-taking is regarded as some prerogative of managers. After all, everybody is involved in taking decisions every day. A housewife faces a major problem in a supermarket when she has to decide between paying 28p for a family-sized pack of detergent or 32p for a special large size accompanied by a free plastic flower!

Gaynor: I see what you mean, but surely we cannot divorce this business of making decisions from a process of management? I keep reading that use of computers is likely to remove a lot of decision-taking from middle management in the future. But I don't think this will come for a long time and I certainly think that in running hotels there will continue to be a lot of decisions which would defy any computer. We will still need the reception manager who can fit an unexpected regular customer into the hotel which the computer says is full.

Adam: Yes indeed, we cannot ignore that decisions have to be taken in business organisations and it needs some careful thinking to distinguish between normal human decision-taking and the special characteristics of those in business.

Gaynor: That should not be too difficult. I am sometimes very conscious of spending time collecting information in order to make a decision. In a similar way, you or the chief accountant sometimes spend time preparing briefs about the possible alternatives available and the likely results. A lot of this involves figures and projections and so on. With no disrespect to you, most of this could be done better on a computer, but I will still have to make the decision about which line to follow. I would also think that the unit managers will have to continue making similar decisions; perhaps these are less important in that a wrong one will be unlikely to damage the company, whereas mine might! In these decisions, at both levels, we have to use experience and our personal judgement.

Adam: If most of the operating decisions at unit level are to be made by computers in the future, the manager's role becomes one of a human relations mechanic.

Gaynor: I don't see it that way. I hope that they will use information from the computer in reaching operating decisions; I suppose I am agreeing with your balance between people and production. My concern, however, is that this is the only method I can see for developing executives. As you know, we are a fairly decentralised company and I want my managers to feel that they are more than what you call 'human relations mechanics'. This really goes back to what I was thinking earlier when I used the word 'policy'. One would like to feel, as a company, that decisions are made in accordance with the policy and this is the paradox you saw. I am reluctant to start writing everything ▷

down, but I do want decisions made which support what we are trying to be as a company. Perhaps it would be a better way of describing this to say that I would like to create an ethos or spirit that ensures this.

Adam: I would say that creating this environment or ethos is a very important part of the management process. It can probably be compared to the training we have as children, having confidence in social situations because we have a good idea of what is the 'right thing to do' like not putting our elbows on the table.

Gaynor: I thought only great-aunts worried about that nowadays! But I think you have something. Tell me, where does problem-solving come into all this? I certainly seem to spend a significant part of my time dealing with problems and I am sure it is the same with all managers.

Adam: Just before you came in I was thinking about this; after a year I am still involved in solving problems and I find this rather disappointing.

Gaynor: This is what I mean. Surely you can't expect problems to stop requiring solving. I would think that this is almost the core of what management is about.

Adam: This makes me feel uncomfortable. Identifying problems and solving them certainly is a significant part of managing. But I can't help feeling that this is catching hold of the wrong end of the stick. Surely if we concentrated on identifying the causes of problems and removing those we could be much more effective?

Gaynor: I am not sure I understand you.

Adam: Perhaps I can illustrate it with the problem we had at the Apollo. Rather, I should say, problems; no potential managers were being produced, there was a high labour turnover and so on. We could have attempted to solve these by introducing different methods of selection, higher pay and various other means. These might have had some effect but in the long run we hadn't identified and remedied the cause. That was Whitstone, whose autocratic behaviour as a manager was the cause of the problems.

Gaynor: Yes, I see what you mean. It is like worrying about the problem of high labour costs at Head Office when the cause is people wanting to have things in writing as a protection.

Adam: Exactly. But having said that, I am not sure just how this fits in with the management process. Undoubtedly managers are involved in solving problems and now it sounds as though I am saying they shouldn't be.

Gaynor: From what you say, and it is certainly a new slant for me, I would see this as part of the ethos. It involves analysing the cause of problems rather than saying 'we have a problem'. This reminds me of one of the British Institute of Management's luncheons when Peter Drucker spoke. It was very impressive to me when he said something like 'We are concerned with effective management rather than efficient management, because a manager can be very efficient at doing something that does not need to be done.' I remember that I was disturbed for several days afterwards!

Adam: This really typifies how one can see a whole new dimension to the task of managing by taking a step sideways and looking at the words we use. I sometimes think that words and clichés are like old slippers, they are comfortable until you notice the holes in them.

Gaynor: Comfortable, but not presentable! What about communication? I recall that we have said something about this before. It must come in somewhere.

Adam: I think on that occasion you quoted Thoreau and said, 'How can I hear what you say, when what you are keeps drumming in my ears.'

Gaynor: Ah yes! A favourite quote of mine.

Adam: Well, the way I see it is that if your ethos exists, then communication will occur. Most people in talking about communication generally emphasise the skills of writing, speaking and ▷

reading. Sometimes they also include the skill of listening. These are, of course, important, but I would think that the emotional and social context are important. Which is just what Thoreau was saying.

Gaynor: So you don't consider communication is a part of managing?

Adam: Oh, I think it is, but if we mix Drucker with Thoreau and add a dash of your observation on the ethos of the enterprise, we can see that communication is a function of the internal environment. If trust exists and people appreciate the objectives, then communication will occur. If not, then no communication.

Gaynor: In some ways I would describe it as 'good' and 'poor' communication, but I am a little worried that you might take me to task on these words! Look, I have a lunch appointment and must go in a few minutes. This has been a very interesting discussion. What shall I do, sum up what we have been saying or leave it to you to prepare a memo?

Adam: I would rather you summarised, Mr Gaynor. After all, I don't want to land myself with solving a problem of overloaded Head Office typists!

Gaynor: Your motives are suspect, but let me see. The management process seems to be concerned with creating an environment in which a balance between concern for production and concern for people is maintained as well as providing a guide to decision-taking. It is directed towards an analysis of the causes from which problems arise and seeks to provide for achievement of organisational objectives while satisfying individual needs. Is that adequate?

Adam: It really is a concise statement of what we have been talking about.

Gaynor: Does it satisfy your demands for prescription?

Adam: I think it does because it stresses the things that a manager must do. Creating the environment, for example. But I wonder how long this takes to achieve.

Gaynor: You have a chance to find out, Adam. Tell me about it when you come back from the Zephyr! Goodbye for now, and enjoy yourself.

Source: Reprinted with permission of Professor P W Nailon and R Doswell from their book, *Further Case Studies in Hotel Management*, Century Hutchinson (1977).

Notes and references

1. See, for example, Doswell R and Nailon P, 'What is Management?', in *Further Case Studies in Hotel Management*, Century Hutchinson (1977), pp. 15–26.
2. Drucker P F, *The Practice of Management*, Pan Books (1968), p. 455.
3. *The Profile of Professional Management*, Results from Research into the Corpus of Knowledge, HCIMA (1977), p. 20.
4. Forte, Charles (Lord), *Forte: The Autobiography of Charles Forte*, Sidgwick & Jackson (1986), p. 119.
5. Mullins L J, 'Management and Managerial Behaviour', *International Journal of Hospitality Management*, vol. 4, no. 1, 1985, pp. 39–41.
6. Webster M W, 'Strategic Management in Context at Swallow Hotels', *International Journal of Contemporary Hospitality Management*, vol. 6, no. 5, 1994, pp. 3–8.
7. Mintzberg H, 'The Manager's Job: Folklore and Fact', *Harvard Business Review Classic*, March–April 1990, pp. 163–176.
8. See, for example, Ferguson D H and Berger F, 'Restaurant Managers: What Do They Really Do?', *Cornell HRA Quarterly*, vol. 25, no. 1, May 1984, pp. 26–36.
9. See, for example, Brown W, *Organization*, Penguin (1974) and Gullen H V and Rhodes G E, *Management in the Hotel and Catering Industry*, Batsford (1983).
10. Stewart R, *The Reality of Management*, 2nd edn, Pan Books (1986), p. 12.
11. Brech E F L (ed.), *Principles and Practice of Management*, 3rd edn, Longman (1975), p. 19.

12. Wood R C, 'Theory, Management and Hospitality: A Response to Philip Nailon', *International Journal of Hospitality Management*, vol. 2, no. 2, 1983, pp. 103–104.
13. Drucker P F, *People and Performance*, Heinemann (1977), p. 28.
14. *Ibid.*, pp. 59, 28, 29.
15. Baum T, 'Toward a New Definition of Hotel Management', *Cornell HRA Quarterly*, Educators' Forum August 1988, pp. 36–39.
16. See, for example, Wentworth F, 'It's Time We took Supervisors Seriously', *Professional Manager*, January 1993, pp. 15–17.
17. Williams P W, 'Supervisory Hotel Employee Perceptions of Management Careers and Professional Development Requirements', *International Journal of Hospitality Management*, vol. 11, no. 4, 1992, pp. 347–358.
18. Fayol H, *General and Industrial Management*, rev'd edn by Gray I, Pitman (1988).
19. 'Managing in the 21st Century', *Manager, The British Journal of Administrative Management*, January/February 2000, pp. 8–10.
20. Mintzberg H, 'The Manager's Job: Folklore and Fact', *Harvard Business Review Classic*, March–April 1990, pp. 163–175.
21. Mintzberg H, *The Nature of Managerial Work*, Harper & Row (1973).
22. Ley D A, 'The Effective GM: Leader or Entrepreneur?', *Cornell HRA Quarterly*, November 1980, pp. 66–67.
23. Arnaldo M J, 'Hotel General Managers: A Profile', *Cornell HRA Quarterly*, November 1981, pp. 53–56.
24. Shortt G, 'Work Activities of Hotel Managers in Northern Ireland: A Mintzbergian Analysis', *International Journal of Hospitality Management*, vol. 8, no. 2, 1989, pp. 121–130.
25. Wood R C, *Working in Hotels and Catering*, 2nd edn, International Thomson Business Press (1997).
26. See also, Wood R C, *Organizational Behaviour for Hospitality Management*, Butterworth-Heinemann (1994).
27. Hales C and Nightingale M, 'What Are Unit Managers Supposed to do? A Contingent Methodology for Investigating Managerial Role Requirements', *International Journal of Hospitality Management*, vol. 5, no. 1, 1986, pp. 3–11.
28. Stewart R, *Choices for the Manager*, McGraw-Hill (1982).
29. Kotter J P, 'What Effective General Managers Really Do', *Harvard Business Review*, vol. 60, no. 6, November–December 1982, pp. 156–167.
30. Stewart R, 'Managerial Behaviour: How Research Has Changed the Traditional Picture', in Earl M J (ed.), *Perspectives on Management: A Multidisciplinary Analysis*, Oxford University Press (1983) pp. 96–97.
31. Ferguson D H and Berger F, 'Restaurant Managers: What Do They *Really* Do?', *Cornell HRA Quarterly*, May 1984, p. 30.
32. Jones P and Lockwood A, *The Management of Hotel Operations*, Cassell (1989), p. 30.
33. Mullins L J, 'Managerial Behaviour and Development in the Hospitality Industry', *Proceedings of The International Association of Hotel Management Schools Symposium*, Leeds Polytechnic, November 1988.
34. *The Profile of Professional Knowledge*, Results from Research into the Corpus of Knowledge, HCIMA (1977) pp. 16–17.
35. Dann D, 'The Nature of Managerial Work in the Hospitality Industry', *International Journal of Hospitality Management*, vol. 9, no. 4, 1990, pp. 319–334.
36. Stewart R, *The Reality of Management*, 2nd edn, Pan Books (1986), p. 20.
37. Baum T, 'Managing Hotels in Ireland: Research and Development for Change', *International Journal of Hospitality Management*, vol. 8, no. 2, 1989, p. 139.
38. Guerrier Y and Lockwood A, 'Managers in Hospitality: A Review of Current Research', in Cooper C (ed.), *Progress in Tourism, Recreation and Hospitality Management*, vol. 2, Bellhaven Press, May 1990, p. 164.
39. Stewart R, *Choices for the Manager*, McGraw-Hill (1982).
40. Wood R C, *Working in Hotels and Catering*, 2nd edn, International Thomson Business Press (1997), p. 74.
41. See, for example, Gullen H V and Rhodes G E, *Management in the Hotel and Catering Industry*, Batsford (1983).

42. Wood R C, 'Theory, Management and Hospitality: A Response to Philip Nailon', *International Journal of Hospitality Management*, vol. 2, no. 2, 1983, p. 104.

43. For example, see Nailon P, 'Theory in Hospitality Management', *International Journal of Hospitality Management*, vol. 1, no. 3, 1982, pp. 135–143.

44. See, for example, Drucker P F, *People and Performance*, Heinemann (1977).

45. Rees W D, *The Skills of Management*, 4th edn, International Thomson Business Press (1996) p. 26.

46. Gore J, 'Hotel Managers' Decision Making: can psychology help?' *International Journal of Contemporary Hospitality Management*, vol. 7, no. 2/3, 1995, pp. 19–23.

47. See, for example, Morey R C and Dittman D A, 'Evaluating a Hotel GM's Performance', *Cornell HRA Quarterly*, October 1995, pp. 30–35.

48. Drucker P F, *The Effective Executive*, Heinemann Professional (1988).

49. 'Managing Your Time Effectively', *Management Checklist 016*, The Institute of Management (1997).

50. Berger F and Merritt E A, 'No Time Left for You: Time-management Strategies for Restaurateurs', *Cornell HRA Quarterly*, October 1998, p. 33.

51. Stewart R, *Managers and Their Jobs*, 2nd edn, Macmillan (1988) p. 123.

52. Umbreit W T and Eder R W, 'Linking Hotel Manager Behavior with Outcome Measures of Effectiveness', *International Journal of Hospitality Management*, vol. 6, no. 3, 1987, pp. 139–147.

53. Umbreit W T, 'Developing Behaviorally-Anchored Scales for Evaluating Job Performance of Hotel Managers', *International Journal of Hospitality Management*, vol. 5, no. 2, 1986, pp. 55–61.

54. Peacock A, 'A Job Well Done: Hospitality Managers and Success', *International Journal of Contemporary Hospitality Management*, vol. 7, no. 2/3, 1995, pp. 48–51.

55. See, for example, Maher A, 'Accounting for Human Resources in UK Hotels', *Proceedings of CHME Research Conference*, Manchester Metropolitan University, April 1993.

MANAGERIAL BEHAVIOUR

Staff and customer satisfaction

MANAGERS' ATTITUDES TOWARDS PEOPLE

THE MANAGERIAL/LEADERSHIP GRID

Management by walking about

THE INFLUENCE OF MANAGEMENT STYLE

SYSTEMS OF MANAGEMENT

PROFILE OF ORGANISATIONAL CHARACTERISTICS

MANAGEMENT BY OBJECTIVES

APPLICATIONS TO SERVICE OPERATIONS

PERSONALITY PROFILE OF HOSPITALITY MANAGERS

THE ATTRIBUTES OF A HOSPITALITY MANAGER

HARD AND SOFT SKILLS OF MANAGEMENT

THE EFFECTIVE MANAGEMENT OF PEOPLE

Basic managerial philosophies

The manager's use of authority

The human cost of poor mangement

Chapter five

Managerial style and behaviour

Introduction

Managers achieve results through the efforts of other people and this involves the effective management of human resources. The behaviour of managers and their style of management will influence the effort expended and level of performance of subordinate staff. The manager–subordinate relationship is the central component of successful hospitality operations.

Managerial behaviour

The task of management is to make the best use of staff and to ensure that they satisfactorily meet the standards required of them. It is the responsibility of management to manage. But it is people who are being managed and people should be considered in human terms. The efficiency of staff and their commitment to the aims and philosophy of the establishment are fostered by good human relationships and by the nature of managerial behaviour.

> The majority of staff come to work eager to do a good job and with the desire to perform to the best of their abilities. Where actual behaviour fails to match the ideal this is largely the result of the manner in which staff are treated by management and the perception they have of the managerial function. This places a heavy responsibility on managers.[1]

We saw in the previous chapter that attention should be focused on improving the people–organisation relationship and in creating a climate in which members of staff work willingly and effectively. At the heart of successful management is the ability to relate well to other people. The manager's perceptions of the workforce are a major influence on the style of managerial behaviour which is adopted. **Management style can be as important as management competence**. The general movement towards flatter organisation structures, flexible working arrangements and greater employee empowerment places greater emphasis on an integrating rather than a traditional controlling style of management.

Intent and implementation

Understanding the feelings of staff, and their needs and expectations, together with a genuine concern for their welfare, go a long way in encouraging them to perform well. How managers exercise the responsibility for, and duties of, management is important. Many problems at work arise not so much from *what* management does as *the way in which it is done.*

It is not necessarily the intent of management but the manner of implementation that is often the root cause of staff unrest and dissatisfaction. For example, staff may accept, although perhaps reluctantly, that unexpected staff sickness necessitates management introducing a revised duty rota timetable. However, they may feel resentful about the lack of consultation, failure to consider the personal needs of individual members of staff and the manner in which they were told about the new rotas. And staff may feel that management are using 'unexpected contingency' as an easy excuse for lack of adequate planning and consultation.

Staff and customer satisfaction

Good manager–subordinate relationships are the starting point for customer satisfaction. It is important to remember that good customer care starts with goods staff care. Staff are the most important ambassadors for the hospitality organisation and should be treated as its the most important customers. Supportive and harmonious relationships are more likely to create a working environment which results in high levels of both staff *and* customer satisfaction. Managers need to adopt a positive attitude towards staff and develop a spirit of mutual cooperation. Staff should feel they are working *with* the management rather than *for* the manager.

> 'People Satisfaction' is obvious to anyone visiting the hotel. Guests frequently comment on the courteousness and friendliness of staff. The 'atmosphere' feels right. This strongly implies the presence of a contented workforce, without which a high level of customer satisfaction is never sustainable in the service industry. Staff clearly find the hotel a pleasant place to work and feel free to voice their opinions and discuss issues. Like customers, staff are looked after as individuals with their own unique requirements and personal problems. There is variation in salaries based on responsibility and experience and bonus arrangements for team leaders based on achievements; but in all other respects people are treated totally individually. In the same way that customer complaints are all treated individually, issues raised by employees are also individually addressed.
>
> **THE SEAVIEW HOTEL AND RESTAURANT**

From an examinaion of several well-performing firms in America, Waterman draws attention to organisational arrangements as the key, achieved from a humanist rather than a 'business process re-engineering' viewpoint. Successful firms are organised to meet the needs of their people so they attract better people, who are more motivated to do a superior job and better organised to satisfy the needs of their customers. Firms need to manage the intricate interplay between people, strategy, organisational arrangements and customers. The conclusion is 'people first'. Treat your own people and your customers well and good results will follow.[2]

The importance of staff and customer satisfaction in the hospitality industry is emphasised by Klein:

Emphasis on the role of interpersonal skills in customer satisfaction is of great relevance to the hotel and catering industry . . . customer care really does depend on staff care being obtained first.[3]

Managers' attitudes towards people

The way in which managers approach their jobs and the behaviour they display towards subordinate staff is likely to be conditioned by predispositions about people, human nature and work. The style of management adopted is a function of the manager's attitude towards people.

Drawing on Maslow's hierarchy of needs model, McGregor put forward two sets of suppositions based on polar assumptions about the attitudes of managers towards people at work: Theory X and Theory Y.[4]

The Theory X assumptions

Theory X represents the assumptions on which traditional organisations are based and was widely accepted and practised before the development of the human relations approach. The assumptions are that:

● the average person is lazy and has an inherent dislike of work;

● most people must be coerced, controlled, directed and threatened with punishment if the organisation is to achieve its objectives;

● the average person avoids responsibility, prefers to be directed, lacks ambition and values security most of all;

● motivation occurs only at the physiological and security levels.

The central principle of Theory X is direction and control through a centralised system of organisation and the exercise of authority. Assumptions based on a Theory X approach, and the traditional use of rewards and sanctions exercised by the nature of the manager's position and authority, are likely to result in an exploitative or authoritarian style of management.

The Theory Y assumptions

At the other extreme to Theory X is Theory Y, which represents assumptions consistent with more recent approaches to human nature and behaviour. The assumptions are that:

● for most people work is as natural as play or rest;

● people will exercise self-direction and self-control in the service of objectives to which they are committed;

● commitment to objectives is a function of rewards associated with their achievement;

● if given the right conditions, the average worker can learn to accept and to seek responsibility;

● the capacity for creativity in solving organisational problems is distributed widely;

● the intellectual potential of the average person is only partially utilised;

● motivation occurs at the affiliation, esteem and self-actualisation levels as well as the physiological and security levels.

The central principle of Theory Y is the integration of individual and organisational goals. It is the task of management to create the conditions in which individuals may satisfy their motivational needs, and in which they achieve their own goals through meeting the goals of the organisation. McGregor develops an analysis of the implications of accepting Theory Y in regard to performance appraisal, administration of salaries and promotions, participation, staff–line relationships, leadership, management development and the managerial team.

The manager–subordinate relationship

Although based on polar extremes and an over-simplification, Theory X and Theory Y do represent identifiable philosophies which influence the nature of the manager–subordinate relationship. The two views tend to represent extremes of the natural inclination of managers towards a particular style of behaviour.

Assumptions based on the traditional use of rewards and sanctions, close supervision and control, and the nature of the manager's power are likely to result in an exploitative or authoritarian style of management.

Most people, however, have the potential to be self-motivating. They can best achieve their personal goals through self-direction of their efforts towards meeting the goals of the organisation. Broadening educational standards and changing social values mean that people today have wider expectations of the quality of working life, including opportunities for consultation and participation in decisions which affect them.

McGregor implies that a Theory Y approach is the best way to elicit cooperation from members of an organisation. Based on practical experience of hotel management this view is supported by Venison.

> *I have personally always tried to manage more in accordance with the assumptions of Theory Y than those of Theory X and my experience seems to concur with much research which indicates that Theory Y assumptions about people's attitudes are closer to the truth. Theory Y, however, does not involve abdication of management, absence of leadership or the lowering of standards. It is not a 'soft' approach to management. It is, in fact, more difficult to achieve but potentially more successful.*[5]

Demands of the situation

Theory X and Theory Y tend to represent extremes of the natural inclination of managers towards a particular style of behaviour. In practice, however, the actual style of management adopted will be influenced by the demands of the situation. Even when a manager has a basic belief in Theory Y assumptions, and in the self-motivation and self-direction of subordinate staff, there may be occasions when it is necessary or more appropriate to adopt a modified approach.

When the nature of the job itself offers little intrinsic satisfaction or limited opportunities to satisfy higher-level needs, a more authoritative and controlling style of management might work best. Some jobs are designed narrowly, with highly predictable tasks and output measured precisely. With these types of jobs, a Theory X approach may be needed if an adequate level of performance is to be maintained.

Emergency situations, or where there is a shortage of time or other overriding factors, may demand a greater use of management authority and control in directing the tasks in hand. Consider, for example, the hustle, heat and noise of a busy kitchen where a range of fresh meals needs to be prepared for a large banquet. Many tasks must be coordinated over very short timescales and a more forceful and directed style of management may therefore be appropriate. And while such conditions persist, this form of managerial behaviour appears also to be understood by the kitchen staff.

Where both the manager and subordinates share the Theory Y assumptions this style of management is likely to be effective. However, it must be recognised that given the staffing characteristics of the hospitality industry (discussed in Chapter 2) there are many staff who do not wish to exercise self-direction or accept responsibility at work and may have little commitment to organisational objectives. They have an instrumental orientation to work and seem to prefer, and respond better to, a more directed and controlled style of management. There are times, therefore, when the manager may be justified in adopting Theory X assumptions about staff.

The managerial/leadership grid®

One means of identifying and evaluating different styles of management is the Blake and Mouton Grid®, first published as the Managerial Grid®, in 1964, restated in 1978 and 1985, and republished as the Leadership Grid® in 1991.[6] The Grid provides a basis for comparison of managerial styles in terms of two principal dimensions:

(i) concern for production; and

(ii) concern for people.

Concern for production is the amount of emphasis which the manager places on accomplishing the tasks in hand, achieving a high level of production, and getting results or profits. This is represented along the horizontal axis of the Grid. *Concern for people* is the amount of emphasis which the manager gives to colleagues and subordinates as individuals, and to their needs and expectations. This is represented along the vertical axis of the Grid.

Each axis is on a scale of 1–9 indicating varying degrees of concern that the manager has for either production or for people. The manner in which these two concerns are linked together depends upon the use of the hierarchy, the 'boss' aspect, and assumptions that the manager makes about the use of power and how to achieve production.

Five basic combinations

With a nine-point scale on each axis there is a total of 81 different combinations (see Figure 5.1). The four quadrants of the Grid provide five basic combinations of concern for production coupled with concern for people. These five combinations represent the extremes of managerial behaviour.

- *Impoverished managers* (1,1 rating) tend to be remote from their subordinates and believe in the minimum movement from their present position. They do as little as they can with production or with people. Too much attention to one will cause difficulties with the other.

- *Authority-compliance managers* (9,1 rating) are autocratic and tend to rely on a centralised system and the use of authority. Staff are regarded as a means of production. If staff challenge an instruction or standard procedure they are likely to be viewed as uncooperative.

- *Country club managers* (1,9 rating) believe that a contented staff will undertake what is required of them and achieve a reasonable level of output. Production

Figure 5.1: The Leadership Grid® figure

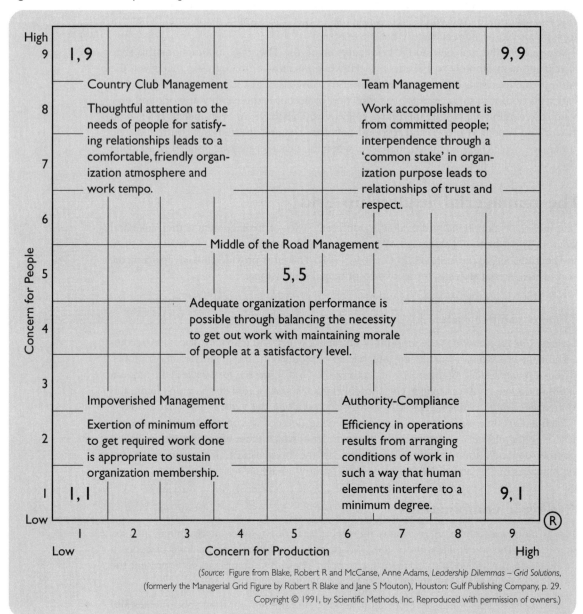

(*Source:* Figure from Blake, Robert R and McCanse, Anne Adams, *Leadership Dilemmas – Grid Solutions*, (formerly the Managerial Grid Figure by Robert R Blake and Jane S Mouton), Houston: Gulf Publishing Company, p. 29. Copyright © 1991, by Scientific Methods, Inc. Reproduced with permission of owners.)

is secondary to the avoidance of conflict and maintaining harmony among the staff. Managers will seek to find compromise solutions acceptable to everyone. Innovation may be encouraged but good ideas tend to be rejected if they are likely to cause difficulties among the staff.

● *Middle of the road managers* (5,5 rating) adopt an approach of 'live and let live' and tend to avoid the real issues. This style of management is the 'dampened pendulum', with managers swinging between concern for production and concern for people. Under pressure this style of management tends to become task management (9,1) but, if this causes resentment from staff, pressure is eased and managers adopt a compromise approach.

● *Team managers* (9,9 rating) believe in the integration of task needs and concern for people. They believe in creating a situation whereby people can satisfy their own needs by commitment to the objectives of the organisation. Managers will discuss problems with staff, seek their ideas and give them freedom of action. Difficulties in working relationships will be handled by confronting staff directly and attempting to work out solutions with them.

Two additional Grid styles

The 1991 edition of the Grid also refers to two additional styles.

● *9+9 paternalistic 'father knows best' management* where reward and approval are granted to people in return for loyalty and obedience, and punishment is threatened for failure to comply.

● *Opportunistic 'what's in it for me' management* in which the style utilised depends on which style the manager feels will return him or her the greatest self-benefit.

The importance of team management

The Managerial Grid provides a framework in which managers can identify and review their patterns of behaviour. Blake and Mouton claim the Managerial Grid illustrates that the manager can gain the benefits of maximising, simultaneously, methods which are both production-orientated and people-orientated. The 9,9 combination of team management, although an ideal, is worth working for.

Effective team management is clearly important in any work organisation, but especially so in the hospitality industry. In hotel operations, for example, it is necessary to combine the 'production' element of speedy and efficient provision of accommodation and food and beverage, with the 'people' element of a high standard of service, and an appropriate attitude and behaviour from staff. This emphasises the need for consultation and teamwork, and for a style of managerial behaviour based on the effective integration of a high concern for production balanced with a high concern for people.

Employee performance is a key result area of management. Poor team management will have serious consequences for the morale of staff, it can prove costly and time-consuming for the manager, and it can have serious consequences for the effective operations of the hotel.[7] It is part of the manager's responsibility to develop and maintain a high level of performance from subordinate staff as members of an effective work team.

Relevance today

According to Newborough:

an organisation's structure, plan and concept are crucial to its effectiveness. Yet beyond these, the most significant single factor is the behaviour of the management team. Its members must act as leaders. They must accomplish their objectives through their ability to guide, motivate and integrate the efforts of others.

The ultimate purpose of studies of managerial style is to aid in the training and development of those who wish to become better leaders, and Newborough maintains that the Managerial/Leadership Grid is as relevant today as when it was first launched.[8]

Management by walking about

A key aspect of effective management is visibility.[9] In the previous chapter we referred to managers reviewing their effective use of time. Managers need to balance time for themselves with their availability for consultation with staff and customers, and ensuring effective processes of communication.[10]

The approach of Management By Walking About (MBWA), together with informal communication processes, is often heralded as a positive management practice – and indeed it may well be. However, it is only likely to be effective if perceived by staff as part of a genuine belief by management in listening to and understanding the actual working conditions, feelings and problems of staff; and not with the suspicion of management snooping.[11]

Administrative or mobile type of manager

The approach of 'management by walking about' has arguably always been a feature of hospitality managers work patterns.[12]

For example, Venison refers to the use of a simple ten-point scale which distinguishes between an excessively administrative type of manager, and an excessively mobile and promotions-orientated manager.[13]

Applicants for hotel management positions are asked to indicate their own management style. The majority place themselves between points 3 and 4 or between points 6 and 7. This suggests that the two distinct ends of the scale are recognised clearly and that most potential hotel managers have a natural leaning towards one direction or the other.

Venison draws attention to the importance of the manager being at the 'front' of the hotel and of '*being there*'. The manager is then in a position to see employees at work and to get to know them, to check standards of service, and quickly to see trouble spots and to take corrective action.

The ideal hotel manager, however, does not sit permanently at any one point of the scale but is able to move freely from one end to the other as particular situations demand. The 'perfect' hotel manager needs to be comfortable at all positions on the scale. Success in extending the range of comfortable behaviour is an important aspect of the manager's personal development.

The influence of management style

From a further examination of several well-performing organisations in America, Waterman draws attention to meeting the needs of their staff so that they attract better people, who are more motivated to do a superior job and satisfy the needs of their customers. The conclusion is 'people first'. Treat your own people and your customers well and good results will follow.[14] From case histories of hospitality organisations, Lockwood *et al.* refer to the importance of management style linked to the subjects of control, corporate culture and motivation.[15]

In the previous chapter we saw that the 'being there' style of management and a directive approach to staff is one of the principal characteristic features of hospitality management.[16] In a study of five seasonal seaside hotels, all privately owned and operated and with between 30 and 65 bedrooms, Lee-Ross investigated the influence of management style on employee job perceptions and job satisfaction.[17]

The investigation contrasted a 'hands-on' style of management (whereby managers worked for most of the time alongside operatives and undertook similar tasks), with a 'coordinative' style of management (where for most of the time managers delegated tasks to operatives). It was suggested that, given the nature of hotel jobs, the hands-on managers who work alongside their staff may be expected to have similar job perceptions, be more aware of operational problems and therefore be more effective in engendering job satisfaction than coordinative managers.

Little effect on employee job perception

In practice, however, the concepts of hands-on and coordinative styles of management were often not clearly definable. Management style appeared to result from the demands of the customers, the employment policy of the hotel and the manager's departmental expertise. Managers occupied both roles and were involved at the operative level in certain departments while leaving other departments unsupervised. The study also indicated that although employees who experience a hands-on management approach are more likely to share the managers' perception of their jobs, management style has little significant effect on the way employees perceive their jobs.

Systems of management

On the basis of extensive research into a wide range of organisations, Likert views the nature of the manager–subordinate relationship in terms of a four-fold model of management systems.[18] The systems are identified by number:

- System 1: Exploitative authoritative;
- System 2: Benevolent authoritative;
- System 3: Consultative;
- System 4: Participative group.

System 1: Exploitative authoritative – Decisions are imposed on subordinates; motivation is based on threats; there is very little teamwork or communications; responsibility is centred at the top of the organisational hierarchy.

System 2: Benevolent authoritative – There is a condescending form of leadership; motivation is based on a system of rewards; there is only limited teamwork or communications;

there is responsibility at managerial levels but not at lower levels of the organisational hierarchy.

System 3: Consultative – Leadership involves some trust in subordinates; motivation is based on rewards but also some involvement; there is a fair degree of teamwork and communications take place vertically and horizontally; responsibility for achieving the goals of the organisation is spread more widely throughout the hierarchy.

System 4: Participative group – Leadership involves trust and confidence in subordinates; motivation is based on rewards for achievement of agreed goals; there is participation and a high degree of teamwork and communication; responsibility for achieving the goals of the organisation is widespread throughout all levels of the hierarchy.

Profile of organisational characteristics

Likert has also established a profile of organisational characteristics describing the nature of the four different systems of management. The profile compares the four systems in terms of a table of organisational variables under the headings of:

  (i) leadership processes;
 (ii) motivational forces;
(iii) communication processes;
(iv) interaction-influence processes;
 (v) decision-making processes;
(vi) goal setting or ordering; and
(vii) control processes.

A shorter and simpler form of the profile of organisational characteristics is provided by Likert and Likert[19] (see Figure 5.2).

The benefits of System 4 management

On the basis of extensive research in many organisations, Likert confirmed that the most productive departments employed management practices within Systems 3 and 4. System 4 management is based on involvement, supportive relationships and participation. Organisational decisions are improved as they are based on more accurate information and there is greater motivation to implement the decisions.

> *In Systems 1 and 2 organisations . . . high performance goals by superiors, coupled with high-pressure supervision using tight budgets and controls, yield high productivity initially because of compliance based on fear.*[20]

However, because of unfavourable attitudes, poor communications, lack of cooperative motivation and restriction of output, the long-term result is high absence and labour turnover, and low productivity and earnings. Likert indicates strongly that the nearer the behavioural characteristics of an organisation approach System 4 the more probably this will lead to long-term improvement in labour turnover and high productivity, low scrap, low costs and high earnings.

Given the typical organisational and staffing characteristics of many hospitality operations, it would seem that managers would have much to gain from adopting a System 4 style of management. But what does System 4 management actually involve?

Figure 5.2: Short-form profile of organisational characteristics

Organisational variables	System 1 Exploitive Authoritative	System 2 Benevolent Authoritative	System 3 Consultative	System 4 Participative Group	Item no.
Leadership					
How much confidence and trust is shown in subordinates?	Virtually none	Some	Substantial amount	A great deal	1
How free do they feel to talk to superiors about job?	Not very free	Somewhat free	Quite free	Very free	2
How often are subordinates' ideas sought and used constructively?	Seldom	Sometimes	Often	Very frequently	3
Motivation					
Is predominant use made of 1 fear, 2 threats, 3 punishment, 4 rewards, 5 involvement?	1, 2, 3 occasionally 4	4, some 3	4, some 3 and 5	5, 4 based on group set goals	4
Where is responsibility felt for achieving organisation's goals?	Mostly at top	Top and middle	Fairly general	At all levels	5
How much co-operative teamwork exists?	Very little	Relatively little	Moderate amount	Great deal	6
Communication					
What is the usual direction of information flow?	Downward	Mostly downward	Down and up	Down, up and sideways	7
How is downward communication accepted?	With suspicion	Possibly with suspicion	With caution	With a receptive mind	8
How accurate is upward communication?	Usually inaccurate	Often inaccurate	Often accurate	Almost always accurate	9
How well do superiors know problems faced by subordinates?	Not very well	Rather well	Quite well	Very well	10
Decisions					
At what level are decisions made?	Mostly at top	Policy at top, some delegation	Broad policy at top, more delegation	Throughout but well integrated	11
Are subordinates involved in decisions related to their work?	Almost never	Occasionally consulted	Generally consulted	Fully involved	12
What does decision-making process contribute to motivation?	Not very much	Relatively little	Some contribution	Substantial contribution	13
Goals					
How are organisational goals established?	Orders issued	Orders, some comments invited	After discussion by orders	By group action (except in crisis)	14
How much covert resistance to goals is present?	Strong resistance	Moderate resistance	Some resistance at times	Little or none	15
Control					
How concentrated are review and control functions?	Very highly at top	Quite highly at top	Moderate delegation to lower levels	Widely shared	16
Is there an informal organisation resisting the formal one?	Yes	Usually	Sometimes	No...same goals as formal	17
What are cost, productivity and other control data used for?	Policing, punishment	Reward, punishment	Reward, some self-guidance	Self-guidance, problem solving	18

(*Source:* Adapted and reproduced from Likert R and Likert J G, *New Ways of Managing Conflict*, McGraw-Hill (1976), p. 75, with permission of McGraw-Hill, Inc.)

Likert sets out three fundamental concepts of System 4 management. These are the use of:

● the principle of supportive relationships among members of the organisation, and in particular between superior and subordinate;

● group decision-making and group methods of organisation and supervision; and

● high performance aspirations for all members of the organisation.

The principle of supportive relationships

Supportive relationships are intended to enhance self-esteem and ego building, contribute to subordinates' sense of personal worth and importance, and maintain their sense of significance and dignity. The manager's behaviour towards subordinates is regarded as supportive when this entails:

- mutual confidence and trust;
- helping to maintain a good income;
- understanding of work problems and help in doing the job;
- genuine interest in personal problems;
- helping with training to assist promotion;
- sharing of information;
- seeking opinions about work problems;
- being friendly and approachable; and
- giving recognition and credit when due.

In System 4 management interaction and decision-making rely heavily on group processes, and discussions focus on the decisions to be made. Managers should have high performance aspirations for themselves and for every member of staff. However, to be effective, high performance goals should not be imposed but they should be set by participation and involve group decision-making.

Management by objectives

One major, participative approach to management, which directly concerns the involvement and motivation of staff, is management by objectives (MBO). The phrase 'management by objectives' appears to have been introduced by Drucker in 1954.[21] The approach was taken up by McGregor who advocated its use as a preferred means of goal setting, appraisal of managerial performance and self-assessment. MBO attempts to relate the achievement of organisational goals to individual performance and development. The basis of MBO is the *involvement and participation* of subordinates through:

- the setting of objectives and targets;
- agreeing results to be achieved and criteria of performance; and
- the regular review and appraisal of performance.

MBO is viewed best as a continuous cycle of activities (Figure 5.3).

Agreement on objectives and targets

The central feature of MBO is that objectives and targets should not be imposed but established and agreed between superior and subordinates. Rather than being told exactly what to do and when to do it, subordinates accept responsibility for definite targets and results to be achieved.

For each job there should be a key result analysis to identify clearly the critical areas of work activities and standards of performance which indicate satisfactory achievement of results. In support of performance improvement plans there should be an effective process

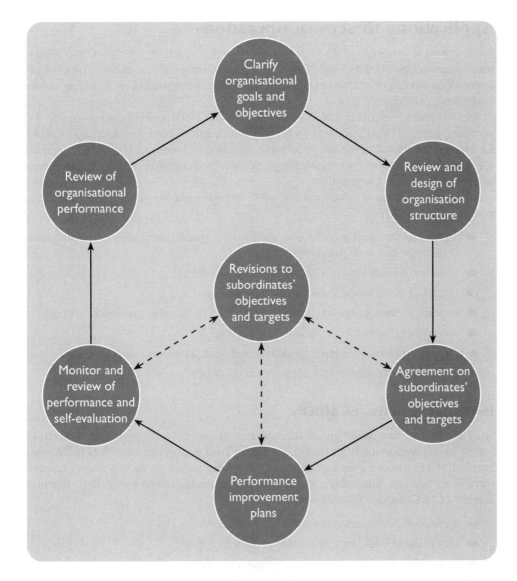

Figure 5.3:
The cycle of
MBO activities

of guidance, training and development for the subordinate together with a related system of rewards.[22]

Measurement of performance is in terms of the subordinates' accomplishment of results rather than the ability to follow detailed instructions on how to undertake their work. Within agreed limits and policies, subordinates are given freedom of action to decide how best to achieve these results. A system of management by objectives can be contrasted, therefore, with a style of management based on authority and control, and the adherence to rules.

MBO is sometimes likened to a system of budgetary control.[23] Although there are some broad similarities, the two systems are distinct. MBO involves agreed objectives and targets for individual members of staff as positive indicators of achievement, and not just a series of financial spending limits. Budgeting may form part of the agreed MBO targets but it is likely to be only one of the main aspects involved.

Applications to service operations

Some writers also refer to MBO as a technique but it is much broader than this. MBO is more correctly described as a style or system of management. It can take a number of different forms and can be adapted to the demands of different organisations, including smaller hospitality organisations.

MBO appears particularly suited to service activities when it is not always easy to discern clear-cut quantified standards. In hospitality operations objectives and targets could, for example, be related to the key result areas identified by Jones and Lockwood: (i) ensuring customer satisfaction; (ii) maintaining employee performance; and (iii) protection of assets[24] (discussed in Chapter 6).

Some obvious areas in which specific MBO targets could be agreed for a stated time period could include:

- an increase in general occupancy rates or in a specific area such as return guests, conference business, restaurant trade;
- reduction in staff turnover or incidence of bad debts;
- control of costs, stock levels, breakages, wastage;
- increase in sales or spend per head in the bars or on other customer services;
- reduction in staff absence, accidents or injuries;
- increase in favourable guest comments/reduction in number of complaints;
- improved profit related to turnover or costs of purchases.

Potential benefits of MBO

MBO is therefore potentially an attractive system. It provides an opportunity for staff to accept greater responsibility and to make a higher level of personal contribution. Properly installed, and as part of a general participative style of management, there is much to recommend it to both the hospitality organisation and individual members of staff. Potential benefits of MBO include the following:

- it concentrates attention on critical areas of activity;
- subordinates know exactly what is expected of them;
- it identifies problem areas in achievement of targets;
- it improves management control information;
- it encourages review of organisation structure and aids the process of delegation;
- it aids management succession planning;
- it identifies training needs and encourages personal growth and development;
- it provides a sound basis for appraisal systems and an equitable procedure for determining rewards and promotion;
- it encourages motivation to improve individual performance.

An effective system of MBO can enhance the feeling of empowerment and encourage the exercise of greater initiative. For example, in order to increase room revenue one front office manager may prefer to follow a policy of concentrating on high tariff business with a lower occupancy rate, while another manager may opt for lower tariffs but obtain a consistently high occupancy rate. Depending on the particular environmental situation both methods could ultimately lead to the same result of achieving a specified total room revenue, which might not have been the case if the managers had been told the way in which they had to go about it.

Potential criticisms and limitations of MBO

- An effective system of MBO requires the full commitment and active support of top management, good superior–subordinate relationships and genuine participation by staff. It is also important to maintain the impetus of the system but without generating an excessive amount of paperwork or forms which lead to a bureaucratic approach.

- Objectives which are more difficult to specify and measure in precise terms may be neglected at the expense of an emphasis on objectives which are more easily set and monitored. A system of MBO may also be more difficult to apply where objectives are subject to continual and rapid change.

- MBO should not be applied simply as a pressure device by which superiors apply increasingly demanding targets which subordinates are expected to achieve. Placing too much emphasis on results can have an adverse affect on behaviour and performance. For example, a waiter striving to meet the objective of increased wine sales may feel obliged to use high-pressure sales techniques, even though this leads to loss of job satisfaction and may also offend some customers.[25]

- The system of MBO is usually associated with a sophisticated performance appraisal scheme and rating scales. This can give rise to a number of common problems, for example lack of comparability in performance standards or excessive emphasis on short-term achievements.[26] MBO-based appraisal schemes should not be regarded as a substitute for the successful management of people.

- Under-achievement might be the result of external environmental factors outside the control of the subordinate or the superior. It is important therefore to distinguish clearly between mere excuses and genuine reasons for the failure to obtain a satisfactory level of performance. It is also necessary to have a quick and effective procedure for the review and any necessary restatement of objectives and targets.

Applications within the hospitality industry

Despite these criticisms and limitations, the system of MBO has been adopted in a wide range of organisational settings, in the public as well as the private sector. However, despite the many potential benefits the introduction of MBO into hospitality organisations appears to have made only slow progress.

In keeping with the author's own views, Wood offers the following reasoning for this situation:

As far as the hospitality industry is concerned, the ad hoc *nature of management and the unpredictability of demand, when combined with high levels of labour instability, can mean that the human and financial cost of introducing MbO is, from managements' point of view, simply not worth it. Further, there is evidence to suggest that management styles in the hospitality industry are in the main disinclined to be participative. Instead, managers see themselves as the major source of authority. Moreover, the nature of demand for hospitality services means that unit managers tend to focus primarily on short and medium term objectives rather than on the long term. Similarly, the absence of a highly developed personnel function and personnel procedures means that implementation of MbO on a systematic basis in hospitality organisations would present administrative problems and costs of dubious benefit the organisation as a whole.*[27]

Boella, however, suggests that MBO is an approach to management which, if operated effectively, influences all levels and activities of an organisation. Although in concept it is typical of a democratic style of management, in practice it is often introduced by other types of managers.

Where MBO concepts have been used in hotels and catering to set standards, generally speaking it is found that the performance standards of operative staff are 'guest centred', that is they are concerned with identifying standards of service to the guest. The performance standards of heads of departments, on the other hand, are 'profit centred', that is, they identify the cost criteria for producing the services to the guest. Heads of departments are, however, directly responsible for ensuring that the operational performance standards are met by departmental staff, so their performance standards may incorporate quality management standards as well as the 'profit centred' standards.[28]

Attention to performance of the work group

MBO normally focuses attention on the performance of individual members of staff. In many situations, however, it is team effort and effective group working, rather than individual performance, which are important. This is especially so in many hospitality operations which tend to divide naturally into group-based work activities. Greater attention could be given therefore to agreement on objectives and targets for the members of a work group. This will help foster unity of effort and supportive relationships among group members.

Personality profile of hospitality managers

As we discussed in Chapter 2, many comments are made about the particular features of the hospitality industry and it is often assumed that because of its 'unique' nature the requirements of its managers are somehow different from those of other managers. As an example of the continual debate on the special nature of the industry, a number of studies have focused attention on the personality characteristics of hospitality managers. But to what extent are these studies likely to help in their education and development?

Shaner suggests that because of the unique demands of the hospitality industry the personal values and behaviour of its managers differ from those of managers in other industries. The most important values perceived by hospitality managers are honesty, responsibility and capability.[29] However, while it is difficult to argue against such values, they are of a very general nature and tell us little about the attributes required of a successful manager. Shaner also suggests that obedience and cheerfulness were considered to be of least importance compared with other values possessed by non-hospitality managers.

Based on a sample of 28 hotel general managers of the same UK hotel chain, Worsfold found that compared with general management norms, hotel managers were more assertive, venturesome and imaginative. They also placed more emphasis on people skills and group working.[30]

Particular form of behaviour

Another survey, by Stone, involved 140 UK general managers, 71 employed by hotel groups and 69 independent owner/managers.[31] From the survey Stone suggests that hotel managers display a particular form of behaviour and identifies a number of factors which distinguish them from non-hotel managers. Compared with other managers, hotel managers are:

- more calm, realistic and stable;
- more assertive, competitive and stubborn;
- more cheerful, active and enthusiastic;
- socially bolder and more spontaneous;
- more realistic, independent and cynical;
- harder to fool, more deliberate and concerned with self;
- more concerned with practical matters and detail.

It should not be assumed, however, that such personality characteristics are necessarily the most appropriate or will result in improved organisational performance. The existing managerial style may have consequences in terms of staff morale, development and retention.[32]

Stone also found that hotel managers have a lower scholastic and mental capacity. This dimension, however, is one of the most problematic. And while the finding *may* be representative of present managers, it does not necessarily apply to hotel managers of the future.

The idea of looking at personality characteristics as an indicator of effective performance is not new. For example, an early approach to the study of leadership was an attempt by a number of writers to identify the common personality characteristics of 'good' or 'successful' leaders.[33] However, extensive research into this area has revealed little to explain the nature of leadership or to help in the training of future leaders. Investigations have identified lists of traits which tend to be overlapping or contradictory and with little significant correlation (this approach is discussed more fully in Chapter 9).

The attributes of a hospitality manager

Rather than attempting to identify any particular, or unique, set of personality characteristics of the hospitality manager, a more constructive approach is to concentrate attention on the general attributes required of the successful manager.[34]

In order to carry out the process of management and execution of work the manager requires a combination of technical competence, social and human skills, and conceptual ability (Figure 5.4). Although a simplistic approach it does provide a useful and pragmatic framework within which to examine the attributes of the successful hospitality manager.

- *Technical competence* relates to the application of specific knowledge, methods and skills to discrete tasks, the actual 'doing' of work and day-to-day operations concerned with the actual provision of services.
- *Social and human skills* refer to interpersonal relationships in working with other people, team-work, and direction and leadership of staff to achieve coordinated effort and high levels of performance.
- *Conceptual ability* is required in order to view the complexities of the operations of the organisation as a whole, including external environmental influences. It also involves strategic planning and decision-making skills.

Figure 5.4:
The combination
of the attributes
of a manager

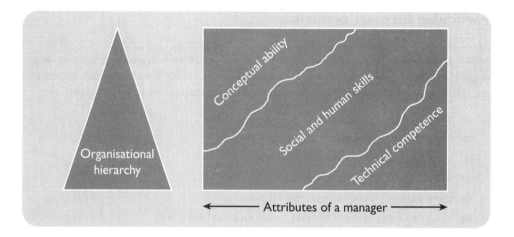

The multi-unit manager

In the case of the multi-unit manager, Goss-Turner suggests that the role itself is one of implementation of standards which requires a broader range of management skills, such as marketing and HRM, in order to support unit management. Traditional sector-based technical skills become less significant, and general managerial abilities more important. Positions higher up the organisation will require additional and enhanced skills in the area of strategic formulation and corporate decision-making, and there is potential for a serious mismatch between the necessary skills at multi-unit management level and management roles immediately higher in the organisation structure.[35]

Appropriate balance

Attempting to secure the most appropriate balance among these desirable attributes presents a constant discussion on the design and content of educational and training programmes for managers in the hospitality industry.

As the manager advances up the organisational hierarchy we would usually expect greater emphasis to be placed on conceptual ability and proportionally less on technical ability. Accordingly, the balance between technical competence and conceptual ability should be determined by the potential managers' expected level of entry into the industry and the likely pattern of their future career progression.

The nature of the industry does make particular demands upon its managers. In hotel operations, for example, managers are still often expected to have training and proficiency in craft skills and to display a high level of technical expertise as well as more general managerial ability.[36] It might be, therefore, that the requirement of perceived technical competence is greater than in other industries. This demand for technical expertise is understandable and may be in keeping with the present nature of the industry. But it must not be at the expense of general management education and development.

According to a HCTC report 30 per cent of managers still have no formal qualifications.[37] In the particular areas of human resource/personnel management an investigation by Maher found that only a minority of head office staff held a professional personnel qualification. The investigation did, however, indicate an apparently increasing awareness of the importance of recruiting quality staff and a growing demand for high educational qualifications for managerial positions.[38] Technical expertise alone is not enough; it must be more than balanced by managerial competence. No amount of practical training or experience will, by itself, however, produce good managers if they do not possess the required social and human skills.

See also the discussion on management development in Chapter 10.

Hard and soft skills of management

It is increasingly common to distinguish between 'hard' skills and 'soft' skills.[39] Hard skills are the technical skills required to undertake work and to accomplish jobs. Soft skills concern interpersonal relationships with other people and team-building. (Hard and soft skills can be related to the idea of group task and group building and maintenance roles discussed in Chapter 8.) Green refers to the importance of the ability to conceptualise how to manage other people. The managerial activity operates along a continuum of hard skills and soft skills. Examples at the extremities of the continuum would be the hard skills of conducting serious disciplinary matters or fighting your corner in a debate about allocation of budgets; and the soft skills of counselling or a member of staff looking for support, advice and empathy. Effective managers need the sensitivity and ability to move along the continuum, and to adjust their attitude and approach as each occasion demands.[40]

Social and human skills

Social and human skills reflect the ability to get along with other people and are, therefore, important attributes at all stages and levels of management, and in the development of staff. The ability to make the best use of people is a distinctive feature of management. Drucker, for example, makes the point that:

> The function that distinguishes the manager above all others is the function no one but the manager can perform. The one contribution a manager is uniquely expected to make is to give others vision and ability to perform.[41]

The importance of people as a major resource of the hospitality industry is also well recognised.

> The only resources within an organisation capable of transformation are human resources. Money and materials are depleted. Meals are consumed, beds are slept in. Equipment is subject to wear and tear; it can be used well or badly, but can never perform more efficiently than it was originally designed to do. Humans only can grow and develop. Therefore, it is this resource in industry which is both the most complex to deal with and the most rewarding.[42]

The hospitality industry is very much a 'people-industry'. Many members of the workforce have direct contact with the customer and people are an essential ingredient of effective operations: they are part of the finished product that the customer is paying for. Customer satisfaction is likely to be affected as much by the attitudes and behaviour of staff as by the standard of accommodation, food and beverages, and other services provided. This emphasises the importance of the effective management of human resources. Interpersonal skills are an especially important feature of hospitality management.[43]

People a common factor

Jones makes the point that the principal factor that underpins his assertion that services and managing services are different is the role of people.[44] This may be true, but at the same time it also illustrates that people are a common factor in any form of work organisation. The perceived role of people within the hospitality industry serves to emphasise the importance of the social and human skills of its managers.

Managers achieve results through the efforts of other people. An understanding of the pervasive influences which determine the behaviour of people within the work organisation should therefore form a central focus of the education and development of managers.

Theory and practice are not inseparable. For example, using accumulated knowledge of management theory, Mullins and Aldrich have constructed an integrated model of managerial behaviour and development which applies as much to the hospitality industry as to any other business organisation.[45]

The effective management of people

Whatever the debate on the personality characteristics or attributes of an effective hospitality manager, one central requirement is abundantly clear – competence in dealing with people. The one essential ingredient of any successful manager is the ability to manage people effectively. Popular books on managerial behaviour appear to take a positive view of human nature, and support an approach which gives encouragement for people to work willingly and to perform to the best of their ability.[46] However, as many of us will have witnessed for ourselves, an understanding, people-centred approach to management seems often to be lacking in practice.

The culture of management is important. For example, Freemantle suggests that a festering deficiency in management culture is that managers are not really concerned about people until they become a problem. According to Freemantle, the perception of 'people as costs' leads to relatively little weight being given to people management and leadership skills when appointing managers. Many companies tend to appoint technical specialists to managerial positions, neglecting the vital task of managing people.[47]

Despite the particular importance of people within the hospitality industry it does not have a good reputation for adopting a caring and positive approach to the management of people.

> As an industry looking after people, we seem to make an absolute dog's breakfast of caring for employees.[48]
>
> Management in the hospitality industry pays considerable lip service to the notion that human resources constitute a major organisational asset . . . Although the contribution and importance of human resource decisions are often acknowledged abstractedly (i.e. 'our people are our most important asset'), the day-to-day decisions of line and top management often belie this sentiment.[49]

Autocratic style of hospitality managers

Despite the lessons to be learnt from studies such as those by McGregor, Blake and Mouton, and Likert, many hospitality managers still appear to adopt a more autocratic, task-orientated approach.

Using a similar set to Likert's four systems of management, White asked staff to identify the preferred style they would most like to work for – from the autocratic manager, the persuasive manager, the consultative manager or the participative manager.[50]

In manufacturing industries the most preferred style of management was consultative. However, in the hotel study the majority of responses were split between those preferring either the autocratic style or the consultative style of management.

White also asked the respondents to indicate the perceived style of their own manager. In manufacturing industries respondents identified their managers as having a variety of styles. In the hotel study, however, the majority of respondents perceived their manager as adopting an autocratic style. This can influence staff retention. White suggests that although older, long-standing staff may be happy with an autocratic style, this may lead to high levels of turnover among younger staff. He advocates a change from the prevailing autocratic style to a more consultative style.

However, it seems doubtful whether much change has in fact taken place. For example, Wood maintains that: 'there is evidence to suggest that management styles in the hospitality industry are in the main disinclined to be participative'.[51]

But why do many hotel managers adopt a task-orientated, autocratic style of management? We can consider five main possible reasons.

An overriding concern for short-term results

There is a widely held view in the industry that every activity should be related directly to profitability. For example, Umbreit makes the point that:

> Traditionally, the hotel industry has had a strong operational orientation with concern primarily focussed on short-term results. Hotel managers have been evaluated on profitability measures and control of expenses.[52]

From their studies of managers in a wide range of hospitality organisations, Hales and Nightingale comment that: 'Senior/head office staff expectations of unit managers seem to be predominantly focused on tasks, rather than activities, upon what unit managers should achieve rather than what they should do.'[53]

Profitability and control of expenses, and attention to tasks, are clearly important aspects of effective management. But attention to results in these areas should be matched with an equal concern for the proper treatment and well-being of staff.

A high concern for front-line operations

Hospitality operations combine a wide range of activities, many of which are provided simultaneously. Services are provided direct to the guests who are on the premises. A high degree of coordination is required, often measured over very short timescales. Managers have a high concern, therefore, with defining and organising group interactions towards the achievement of goals and objectives.

The need to maintain high standards could also, in part, explain why managers often display high levels of task-orientated behaviour. For example, Worsfold points out that in the hospitality industry it is necessary:

> to maintain high standards (some of which are legally enforceable) in a highly variable environment with a transient product. In order to maintain these standards, it is necessary to establish rules and procedures to which staff adhere.[54]

Traditional management practices

Managers tend to rely on traditional and outdated practices, and show too much concern with perceived differences between the hospitality and other industries. This results in a blinkered approach, isolating managers from the applications of more general management theories and practices. Examples are the slow progress in recognition of the potential contribution of the concepts of management by objectives (referred to above) and developments in human resource management. For example, Wood refers to the absence of a highly developed personnel function and personnel procedures within the hospitality industry which has a track record of conditioned indifference to personnel administration and excessive bureaucracy, and which, particularly in human resource areas, is resisted by managers at all levels.[55]

This might also, perhaps, be one reason why there is still some apparent reluctance from certain (but not all) hospitality managers to welcome management degree course students, regarding them as too 'academic', and possibly also as a threat to their own positions. By contrast there is often less apparent resistance to the employment of diploma course students who are seen as more 'practically' orientated.[56,57]

Failure to manage through people

A task-orientated approach may be seen as easier. People are not by nature passive, they have minds of their own and all differ as individuals. Human behaviour is capricious and scientific methods cannot be applied with reliability. People bring their own feelings and attitudes towards their duties and responsibilities. You will recall that Venison makes the point that a Theory Y style of management is not a 'soft' approach but is in fact more difficult to achieve, although potentially more successful.[58]

Too many managers appear to opt for the 'easy' approach and attempt to manage through achievement of the task, the organisational hierarchy, and systems and procedures, rather than to manage *with and through people*. Managers need to broaden their sense of people-perception and to understand the feelings of staff, and their needs and expectations as human beings. The development of human and social skills is a priority.

Increasing recognition of Investors in People standard should help to reduce problems related to the management of people and improve a hospitality organisation's performance through its people.[59]

A vicious circle

Many hospitality managers will claim that shortages of suitable staff, the nature of the working conditions, and high staff turnover demand a task-orientated approach to management. But, because management adopt such an approach this may well be, at least in part, the *underlying cause* of the staffing problems to which they claim they are reacting.

For example, we can recall that Likert found an authoritarian system of management may yield high productivity in the *short term*, but it is a participative-group system that will lead to long-term improvement in staff turnover, high productivity and improved organisational performance. We can also recall that White suggests that an autocratic style of management may lead to high levels of turnover among younger staff. We can conclude that a high level of turnover, especially among younger staff, may well be the *result* of an autocratic style of management.

High staff turnover should not, therefore, be excused as an inherent, characteristic feature of the industry. The attitude of management should be to see this as a problem area – a problem in terms of cost, time, staff morale and possible effects on the standard of service provided. Managers should be prepared to adopt a more participative style of management and to develop supportive relationships with subordinates. Managers should also be ready to learn from experiences in other industries, to review their procedures and practices, and, for example, to give greater attention to human resource planning, recruitment and selection, and induction and training.

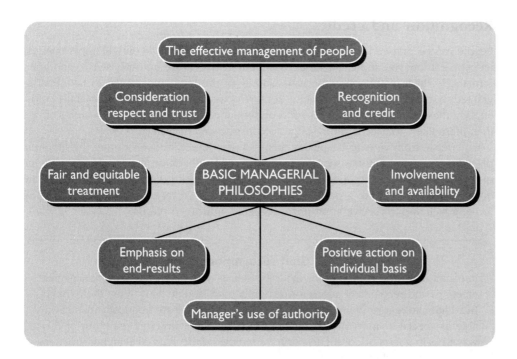

Basic managerial philosophies

A positive policy of investment in people and an interpersonal relationship approach to management is, in the longer term, worth the effort. It is important that managers have a highly developed sense of 'people perception' and understand the feelings of staff, and their needs and expectations. It is people who are being managed and people should be considered in human terms. A genuine concern for staff and their welfare goes a long way in enhancing organisational performance and effectiveness. In the belief of the author there are a number of basic, underlying philosophies which are likely to make for the successful management of people *and* lead to improved work performance (Figure 5.5).

Consideration, respect and trust

People generally respond according to the way they are treated.[60] If you give a little you will invariably get a lot back. Make people feel important and give them a sense of personal worth. The majority of staff will respond constructively if treated with consideration and respect, and as responsible individuals who wish to serve the organisation well. 'If people feel trusted they will make extraordinary efforts to show the trust to be warranted.'[61]

From their research of outstandingly successful American companies, Peters and Waterman make the following comment on the fundamental lesson of achieving productivity through people.

> *Treat people as adults. Treat them as partners; treat them with dignity; treat them with respect. Treat them – not capital spending and automation – as the primary source of productivity gains.*[62]

Recognition and credit

People can be praised on to success. Give full recognition and credit when it is due and let people know you appreciate them. Too often managers are unresponsive to good performance, which may happen the vast majority of the time, and appear to take this for granted; but they are quick to criticise the few occasions when performance falls below expectations. Positive feedback on good performance is a strong motivator, *and* staff are then more likely to accept and respond to constructive criticism.

Experience from visits to hospitality management degree students during their training placement year has emphasised the importance of feedback on their performance. One of the most common enquiries is the desire for more information on how well they are doing. If staff are to take a pride in their work they need to know when they are performing well and to receive appropriate recognition for their efforts.

Staff recognition

Recognition of the contributions made by staff is always discussed at management meetings and recommendations for recognition are sought actively by the partners. In addition to regular planned team events, bottles of wine are frequently made available as special 'thank-you's' to any members of staff who have gone out of their way to help guests or colleagues, or have handled difficult or challenging situations with initiative and enthusiasm.

THE SEAVIEW HOTEL AND RESTAURANT

If You Catch Someone Doing Something Right, Let Us Know!

Employee Name: _____

Date: _____

(Brief Description On Back)

BEST WESTERN HOTEL, USA

Involvement and availability

Involve yourself with the work of the staff, and make sure you fully understand the difficulties and distastes of their duties and responsibilities. Ensure an open flow of communications, and encourage participation and feedback. Take an active interest in the work of staff but without excessive supervision or inhibiting their freedom of action. Wherever possible be available to staff as a priority, rather than to administration, and remember the importance of giving time to listen to the feelings and problems of staff. It is important to remember what Fletcher reminds us: 'Hearing is not listening. Listening is not a passive activity. It is hard work. It demands attention and concentration.'[63]

Fair and equitable treatment

Treat people fairly but according to merit. Ensure justice in treatment, equitable systems of motivation and rewards, clear personnel policies and procedures, and full observance of all laws and codes of conduct relating to employment. People expect certain outcomes in exchange for certain contributions or inputs. A feeling of inequality causes tension and motivates the person to indulge in certain forms of behaviour in order to remove or to reduce the perceived inequity. Equity theory of motivation is discussed in Chapter 7.

Positive action on an individual basis

Treat members of staff as individuals. Deal with individual situations on an individual basis and avoid the 'blanket' approach. For example, it has come to the manager's attention that a couple of members of staff on the same shift have been late in arriving for work. The manager's reaction is to send a circular to *all* members of the department reminding them of the need for, and importance of, good timekeeping. This may appear to be an easy way out to the manager. But what is likely to be the reaction of staff in the department?

The two members of staff concerned might shield behind the generality of the circular and even persuade themselves that it does not apply particularly to them. They might even choose to believe that the manager must be referring to staff on a different shift, and take little notice of the circular. In contrast, the majority of staff in the department who do have a good record of timekeeping might well be annoyed or upset by the circular.

There could, for example, be some staff who, despite pressing personal difficulties, have taken great pride in their work and made special efforts to maintain an excellent record of time-keeping – quite possibly without any previous positive recognition from management. Again, it would be understandable if the reaction of these staff was one of resentment and disillusionment, with a possible adverse effect on their future attitude to work. The manager has more to lose than to gain from adopting a 'blanket' approach to a particular problem and from failing to take selective, positive action on an individual basis.

Emphasis on end-results

Good time-keeping can be an important part of the job and especially in a service industry such as hospitality. However, if 'always being there' is not an absolute requirement per se for effective performance, what is to be gained by insisting on rigid times of attendance? The increasing movement to flexible working patters are placing growing attention on what staff actually achieve rather than just time spent at work. The important criteria are the level and quality of service and performance. Even where 'being there' is an essential requirement of the job, managers should place emphasis on end-results, and levels of actual performance and achievement, rather than just hours in attendance or compliance with detailed instructions, rules or regulations.

The manager's use of authority

Some might argue that these philosophies are too idealistic and that, given the harsh realities of the hospitality industry, managers need to adopt a more dominant stance. But it is not suggested that managers should in any way give up the right to manage: it is a question of *how* they manage and how they use their authority.

An interesting example is provided by the West German hotelier, Klaus Kobjoll, whose hotel has a 92 per cent occupancy and a long waiting list of applicants to join an already highly motivated workforce.

> *modern times require a basic shift in the management/employee relationship. There are three types of authority: the God-given sort of Louis XIV which many company presidents assume – but it means nothing to the guy on the shopfloor: authority gained through the exercise of professional skills: and finally authority by 'human sympathy' where you show that you care as much for employees privately as you do professionally. That's the best and highest form of authority . . . If a hotel owner says his staff are working poorly, it's him that needs to change his style.*[64]

A caring attitude towards staff

Managers need to adopt a positive attitude towards staff and to develop a spirit of mutual cooperation. Staff should feel that they are working with the manager rather than for the manager.

As an overriding principle on which to guide managerial behaviour, it is difficult to argue against putting people first and a philosophy based on the Golden Rule of life – **manage others as you would like to be managed yourself**. Venison draws a striking comparison between the hotel industry and the retail industry,[65] and an interesting and enlightened example of a people approach to management based on the Golden Rule is that of Mary Kay Cosmetics in America. Other enlightened examples of a caring attitude towards staff are provided by Marks & Spencer and the Body Shop.[66]

Good management is not easy

No one should pretend that good management is easy. But is it really asking too much for managers to treat members of staff with courtesy and consideration? And why should this in any way detract from the managers' ability to fulfil their duties and responsibilities effectively? Provided managers are prepared to make the effort, and *have full confidence in their own abilities*, they are likely to gain much from adopting a caring approach to their staff and treating them with dignity.

Such an approach requires positive and cooperative action from both hospitality managers and staff. But it is up to management to take the initiative. If certain members of staff do not cooperate or fail to respond in a constructive way, then management should take appropriate action. Managers must be flexible and prepared, if necessary, to use their judgement in adopting different styles of behaviour in particular situations or towards particular individuals or groups.

The human cost of poor management

The style of managerial behaviour has an obvious and direct effect on the well-being of staff, and on their levels of work performance. Managers decide the manner in which work duties and responsibilities are to be carried out. Different styles of management may be appropriate to managing different people in different circumstances. A more autocratic style of management may not *necessarily* be a bad thing in particular individual situations.

However, an unpleasant working environment and poor manager–subordinate relationships can cause tension and stress. Increasing attention is being given to the number of health problems that are classified as stress-related and affected by working conditions. It is important to remember both the effects on organisational performance and the potentially high human cost of inappropriate managerial behaviour.

Summary

- People are the central focus of management. The nature of the manager–subordinate relationship is crucial to effective hospitality operations and to both staff and customer satisfaction. The behaviour that managers display towards subordinate staff is conditioned by predispositions about human nature and work. One means of evaluating different styles of management is in terms of concern for production and concern for people.

- A key aspect of effective management is visibility. The approach of 'management by walking about' is a feature of hospitality management. The nature of the manager–subordinate relationship can be viewed in terms of a four-fold model of management systems and a profile of organisational characteristics. A participative-group system of management practices based on involvement and supportive relationships is more likely to lead to long-term improvements in performance and organisational decisions.

- Effective team management is especially important within the hospitality industry. One major participative approach is management by objectives (MBO). MBO is particularly suited to service operations and properly installed offers a number of potential benefits. There are, however, potential criticisms and limitations of MBO and attention should be given to the performance of work groups.

- A number of studies have focused on the personality characteristics of hospitality managers. However, a more constructive approach is to concentrate on the general attributes required of the successful manager. Technical expertise must be balanced with managerial education and competence. Managers need ability in both 'hard' and 'soft' skills. Interpersonal skills are especially important in the hospitality industry. People are a common factor and a priority is the development of human and social skills.

- The one essential ingredient of any successful manager is the ability to manage people effectively. However, an understanding people-centred approach seems often to be lacking in the hospitality industry. Attention should be given to basic managerial philosophies and to a positive policy of investing in people. The style of managerial behaviour affects the well-being of staff and their levels of performance. In the longer term an interpersonal relationship approach to management is worth the effort.

Review and discussion questions

1. Discuss how the manager–subordinate relationship can be influenced by the manager's assumptions about human nature and the behaviour of people at work.

2. Explain the Manageral/Leadership Grid as a means of comparing managerial styles. What is the importance of team management in the hospitality industry?

3. How might the nature of the manager–subordinate relationship be explained in terms of a four-fold model of management systems? Explain what you understand by the principle of supportive relationships.

4. What are the potential benefits and criticisms/limitations of management by objectives (MBO)? Assess critically the applications of MBO to service operations and the hospitality industry.

5. It is often claimed that, because of the nature of the hospitality industry, the requirements of its managers are somehow different from those of other managers. Discuss critically the validity of this claim and suggest how you would analyse the qualities of a successful manager.

6. Suggest why it is that many hotel managers appear to adopt a task-orientated, autocratic style of management.

7. Debate critically the suggestion that there are a number of basic, underlying philosophies which are likely to make for the successful management of people and lead to improved organisational performance.

8. Give your views on the manager's right to manage and the use of authority. Why is it important to distinguish between the 'intent' and the 'implementation' of management decisions and actions?

Assignment I

(i) From your own experience, explain fully a situation which you believe demonstrates an effective and/or an ineffective way of dealing with subordinate staff. Comment critically on the behaviour, actions and decisions of the manager or supervisor concerned.

(ii) Explain to what extent you can relate this situation to the application of theories and/or principles of managerial behaviour.

(iii) Meet in groups of four to six to share and discuss your observations. Make notes of your colleagues' perceptions of the situation and ways in which they support, or differ from, your own observations.

(iv) Prepare a summary of your discussions to share with other groups in the class.

Assignment 2

Using Likert's short-form profile of organisational characteristics (see Figure 5.2, p. 147), investigate a hospitality organisation of your choice.

(i) Circle what you believe to be the most accurate answer for each of the 18 questions. Where possible, give brief supporting reasons for your answers and make clear any necessary assumptions.

(ii) Summarise the pattern of your answers and the extent to which this suggests a clear indication towards one particular model of management system.

(iii) If possible, try to repeat this investigation for a different hospitality organisation.

(iv) Explain the conclusions you draw from your investigation(s).

(v) Compare your results with those of your colleagues. To what extent do you feel the investigations support the view that the most efficient organisations adopt Systems 3 or 4 management?

Case study: Who are the managers now? The changing nature of management in Park Taverns

Notes: (i) For the usual reasons of confidentiality, the identity of the company has been concealed through the invention of this name. It should also be noted that the figures presented later in the paper do not represent the actual figures of the real organisation; other than the name change and these alterations, however, what follows is a true record and reflection of what has been happening in this UK public house retailing organisation. (ii) The author wishes to acknowledge the contribution made to this case study by Gordon Steven.

Introduction

In response to some major changes in the outer contexts of Park Taverns, and to certain very stretching longer-term financial targets set by the plc to which it reports, an extensive change programme was initiated in the organisation, one of the UK's larger public-house owning companies. This case examines the origins, contexts and nature of these changes, and then focuses on the ways in which the nature and process of management is being transformed as both a constituent element and an unintended consequence of the change programme.

Park Taverns is a division of a much larger leisure retailing company, and operates public houses and restaurants throughout the UK (other divisions include Breweries; Wines and Spirits; and Hotels). Taverns originated in 1989, through the splitting up of the brewing and public house retailing interests of the plc. The latter is one of the UK's largest hospitality companies, employing over 100,000 people worldwide. It is not possible, of course, to entirely divorce what has been happening in the Taverns business from events and changes in the rest of the plc, for there are a number of interdependencies between the divisions, for example between Taverns and Hotels, Wines and Spirits, Brewers, and the plc. The latter, of course, takes a close interest in the performance of its constituent divisions, through, for example, setting and agreeing objectives and targets which the divisions are expected to achieve over a given time period.

▷

Who are the managers now? The changing nature of management in Park Taverns continued

Park Taverns makes a major contribution to the plc's profits (having generated at least 35 per cent of total profits for a number of years), employs approximately thirty thousand people, and has around 2,500 managed and 1,250 leased hostelries. The figures for previous years are as follows:

Table 1:
Hostelry numbers, 1990–96

Year	Number of hostelries in total
1990	7330
1991	5800
1992	4350
1993	4270
1994	4220
1995	4165
1996	4110

Until recently, the hostelries were organised into eight regions, each region in turn being split into a number of areas. A variety of specialist services were provided for the hostelries by the head office and/or the regional offices, examples include Acquisitions (for new hostelries or restaurants), Marketing, Construction, Surveying, Personnel and Training, IT and Finance. A Managing Director headed up each of the Regions and there was a strong regional identity, one which had been nurtured by the company over a number of years through means such as having different and distinct trading names for each region. Territories and resources were jealously guarded, risk aversion was the predominant ingredient of decision-making, and accountability was thinly spread. The organisation culture was predominantly conservative, slow to change and had an emphasis upon management control and accountability.

The predominant cultural orientation in the company (and this typified the sector at the time) can be typified as follows: (i) 'Hostelry managers are not to be trusted, therefore they must be controlled'; (ii) 'The hostelry is supply driven – the "shop window" for a range of ales and lagers'; (iii) 'Individual outlet performance is the key consideration'. More specifically, the organisation structure was hierarchically based; business expertise was based upon function; managers acted predominantly as supervisors and the Board as a scorekeeper, senior management's priority being control over operations; staff values were essentially defensive; and a VIP was a manager.

On the basis of this brief overview of Park Taverns' structure and culture, let us now look at the ways in which the outer contexts of its operations have been changing in recent years.

Changing external contexts

Four key elements of the changing nature of the external contexts of Park Taverns' operations can be identified, as follows.

Changes in consumer preferences Examples here include the impact of the health-food and drink lobby, and the shift away from the 'on trade' (buying drink and food in hostelries) to the 'off trade' (people buying all or most of their wine, spirits and beer from supermarkets or off-licences for consumption at home).

Economic recession in the late 1980s and early 1990s As a result of economic recession many consumers had less discretionary spending power, therefore the lower prices to be found in some parts of the off trade (such as supermarkets) and through beer and spirits imports, became more appealing.

The changing nature of competition   Mergers and alliances have been forged between brewing and retailing groups; foreign brewing companies entered the UK market in a major way for the first time; and many hostelries have been regenerated by smaller, independent companies which have focussed upon service, customer choice, the offering of a variety of real ales, and a return to the basics of a 'good local'.

Legislative changes   As a result of the UK government's 'Beer Orders' of 1989, a ceiling has been placed upon the number of hostelries which can be owned by a brewing group, where those hostelries were tied in terms of supply to that particular group. For Park Taverns, this meant that it had to sell off over 40 per cent of its hostelries during the period 1990–92, in order to comply with the Orders (this in turn meant that the support structure was too large for the new estate; corporate employee numbers were reduced by 23 per cent). Although it is now below its ceiling, there is a strict legal limit on the number of hostelries it can open without simultaneously closing others (in other words, without going above its legally allowed maximum).

Genesis of the change programme

In 1992 the plc set Taverns some extremely challenging targets, which were to be achieved by 1997/8 (1992 base measures):

 (i) out-perform the on-trade by 7 per cent;

 (ii) increase net profit per £ taken from 12p to 22p;

 (iii) increase average volume by 16 per cent per hostelry;

 (iv) open one new pub every eight working days and sell or lease at least one pub every other day;

 (v) increase the return on the book value of the hostelries from 8 per cent to 15 per cent.

   This could simply not be achieved by cost-cutting or any other traditional response (such as developing new brands – these are more or less instantly copiable by other pub-owning groups), and it was decided that the company had to 'start all over again'. This is where BPR (Business Process Redesign, or Business Process Reengineering) came in (Hammer and Champy, 1993; Davenport, 1993). At this time BPR was a new concept to the company, but senior managers pretty quickly came to understand what it involved, and what it might deliver, assisted by a management consultancy company. The view emerged that BPR could help the company to deliver the 'quantum leap' in performance which was required, as it involves 'The fundamental rethinking and radical redesign of business processes to achieve dramatic improvements in critical, contemporary measures of performance such as cost, quality, service and speed . . . more succinctly it is starting over' (Hammer and Champy, 1993). As a result of workshops and simulations facilitated by the consultants, three core processes were identified for the whole organisation: operate pubs, develop pubs, and manage cash.

   While BPR was therefore seen as having an important role to play in the organisational change programme upon which the company was embarking, it was nevertheless only one element in a continuous series of strategic changes which had been introduced since 1989. Other change initiatives included the splitting of Taverns into a separate division from Brewers in 1989; major property disposals in 1991; Total Quality Management (TQM) adoption, and infrastructure changes in 1993; new reward structures in 1994; and the introduction of a new IT System (PTS). The latter involves a fully ▷

Who are the managers now? The changing nature of management in Park Taverns continued

integrated electronic point of sale system in the pub, with checkout pads and touch screens, and with dispense monitoring – all linked into a back office PC, and, via this, the wider business. This means that at any time, in any place, in every office, managers and staff can tell what is being sold in the pubs, at what price, to whom, at what time, who sold it, etc.

An indication of the way in which thinking about change was developing in the company at the time can be gleaned from a discussion document produced by a member of the Change Management Team in 1993. Some of the key organisational and cultural issues were identified as follows:

One of the problems with organisations is that they keep trying to recreate themselves. Innovation and fuelling innovation processes for new products are not especially easy cohabitees with existing organisational design, bureaucracy and specialist functions. Are we taking the path of least resistance right now via the functional or divisional chimneys we are in and we love to be in? We need to consider the issue of cross-disciplinary conversations, structures and purposes, and also we need to consider the issue of innovating in a lot less time than we are at the moment.

The following observation in a BPR journal was quoted approvingly in the paper: 'Where do most change programmes go wrong? They: Overlay new processes onto old organisational structures; introduce functionally based management teams; redefine new jobs without changing old values; go soft on change' (CSC Index: 1994).

Two options for the new organisation were tried out as pilots during 1993, one in each of two of the eight regions of the company which existed at the time. In early 1994 a leading member of the Change Team expressed the following view, based upon an analysis of what had been achieved by the pilots:

It is our contention that neither or both of these strategic goals (profit, and return on market value of the hostelry assets, as required by the plc) is capable of being delivered in the delineated time scale (i.e. by 1997/8) by (the two options) without other organisational interventions. At they stand they are simply not radical enough in terms of 'setting the people free' or in terms of removing the burden of 'overhead shackle' to deliver the plc profit requirements. To do nothing is not an option; the need to develop radical alternatives becomes a key results area.

A 'critical mass' of hostelry numbers was identified, below which it was felt that the company would not be able to achieve the profit goal. 'Therefore (it was argued in a company paper) in hotels or pub retailing markets, competitive advantage can only come from our people doing things better, or for less, than our competitors . . . Laboratory finding after Laboratory finding in the BPR series of studies concluded that team working and team rewards were essential elements in the delivery of substantially improved performance'. Four structural redesigns based upon BPR principles were then considered in detail. After much debate, both within and between the Change team and top management, the most radical option was chosen – 'most radical' in the sense of entailing the greatest degree of change from the structure and mode of operating in place at the time. It was described as follows in an internal company paper:

This really is the 'small is beautiful' case. Our thinking is rooted in the creation of new pub companies, each run by an Operations Director, and each being responsible for 90–110 outlets. They will be loosely based on geographical boundaries, and a key element is the ability of these companies to organise themselves as they see fit to respond to their customers' needs.

▷

Certain 'mandatory' requirements were to be imposed upon the operating companies, such as they must:

 (i) use only PTS and other Park Taverns/plc systems

 (ii) comply with 'manage cash' requirements

 (iii) bid for scarce capital and other resources

 (iv) comply with minimum plc standards on terms and conditions of employment

 (v) support higher-level management development initiatives.

The Operations Director (OD) role was to be 'no more or less than the Central Banker and the developer of general management talent . . . they will have to accept that some of this new generation will make mistakes. The OD role is to ensure that the "Young Turks" learn from their mistakes and that they continue to take controlled risks. The OD role is really about the creation of that Enterprise Culture' (internal document). The two keys to the success of the reorganisation were seen as: will it achieve the required level of profit by 1997/8, and 'does it change the culture from that of a "control orientation" to that of a "customer orientation"?'

Reorientation and restructuring

The new organisation was aimed at 'delivering a quantum leap in hostelry performance through increased turnover'. The key elements were:

1. Pubs grouped in teams of six or seven licensed house managers (LHMs) by type of trade, with a Retail Manager (RM) running three teams

2. Team rewards and recognition

3. LHMs given more autonomy

4. The RM role was now centred on business development (rather than controlling the LHMs, as before)

5. IT in all outlets.

As noted earlier, three core business processes were identified as the central organising principle for the redesigned company: manage cash, manage pubs and develop pubs. In order to illustrate what this has meant in practice, let us look at some of their key elements and underlying principles:

- cross-functional and interdisciplinary teams;
- appropriate measurement systems for the core process, e.g. measuring performance for team rewards;
- the sharing of best practice;
- a critical evaluation of performance: constructive rather than destructive;
- 'getting close to the customer' through, for example, using data to develop new projects or products;
- the recruitment and retention of 'the very best people';
- a series of trial and error innovations, developed through close contact with customers and other team members;
- 'small is beautiful';
- dissemination and acceptance across the company that innovation is the key to growth; that it is a core process and not an event; and is an ongoing project, sustained by continuous debate within the company. ▷

Who are the managers now? The changing nature of management in Park Taverns continued

The new organisation structure at the local level was as follows:

An important role in the new regime, and one which was seen as being particularly crucial to the 'develop pubs' core process, is that of Retail Manager. The extract below from the job description for this new job illustrates the orientation and mode of operation which was favoured.

Job description: Retail Manager

Job objective   To develop an environment of trust, creativity, teamwork and support within the management teams in order to maximise the turnover, cash flow and profit of each outlet. To ensure that the necessary return is achieved through individual outlet and team business plans.

Key accountabilities   In conjunction with the LHM and the team, develop and implement individual and team plans to ensure that all opportunities are identified and actioned appropriately . . .

Managerial competencies   Managing people: achieves high performance through others, using coaching techniques to involve and develop teams and individuals. Actively listens, facilitates action, provides advice and feedback to improve performance . . .

Motivating   Motivates others through personal drive, energy and commitment to achieve results. Consults and negotiates in order to achieve targets with individuals and teams . . .

Team player   Acts as a team member, allowing team decision making, encouraging and demonstrating team behaviours, such as supporting, listening, challenging . . .

Business development   Maximises profits through personal and team incentives, assessing risks and taking action; encouraging and using creative thinking and innovation to generate increased business.

Having outlined and discussed the origins, contexts (internal and external), and nature of Park Taverns' major change programme, the paper now concludes by offering a brief analysis of their implications (both intended and unintended) for the (changing) nature and process of management.

Discussion

What, then, are the implications of the restructuring and reorientation for the nature of the managerial role at the level of the hostelry and immediately above, and, indeed, is it meaningful now to talk about 'managers' in the usual senses in which that term is understood?

To begin to address the above questions, it is necessary first of all to ask 'What do we mean by "manager"?' Hales, who has devoted a good deal of attention to this matter, has observed that:

Few modern phenomena so patently pervasive and systematically scrutinised as 'management' have been so beset by ambiguity, confusion and, at times, obfuscation. In its English usage the term 'management' denotes, inter alia*: an organisational function, an organisational stratum, an occupational group, an organisational process, an interpersonal process and an intrapersonal process (self-management), each with their own associated body of knowledge and set of skills. The term is employed as both noun and verb, descriptively and normatively, approvingly and pejoratively (1993: 1).*

Following a review of earlier research which points to and elaborates upon these complexities, Hales concludes 'Overall, therefore, the commonalities of content and form in managerial work reflect the separation and problematic character of management. Variations in managerial work reflect the dispersion of management functions across a diversity of managerial jobs . . . management entails taking responsibility for a work process, from which flow the processes of planning/decision-making, allocation, motivation, coordination and control . . . Consequently, management is the inherently problematic process of managing others, whether workers or other managers' (1993: 15). This conceptualisation could come across as overly rational-linear; useful 'correctives' can be found in the research and writings of, *inter alia*, Watson (1994), Alvesson and Willmott (1996) and Mangham (1986).

Is, then, the nature and process of management in Park Taverns being transformed as a result of the change programme? On the basis of the above review of some key changes at the levels of LHM and RM, we can now take up Hales' point about management quintessentially involving the taking of responsibility for work processes, and therefore implying decision-making and the allocation of resources relating to, and the motivation, coordination and control (etc.) over, the work of other people (managers and non-managers alike). In particular, we want to know whether LHMs have, net, gained or lost more control, autonomy and responsibility (or, indeed, stayed about the same), and, correspondingly, where RMs now stand. It was noted earlier that a central tenet of the 'old' managerial culture was that 'Hostelry managers are not to be trusted, therefore they must be controlled'. Has this view changed, or, at least, is change beginning to occur here?

A detailed response to this question would entail, among other things, a dissection of the concepts of control and autonomy into their constituent elements; for example: autonomy in what sense(s)?, and from whom – more senior managers or the organisation more generally? Clearly, control and autonomy are closely interrelated, and the view could be taken that the more control a LHM has, the greater the degree of autonomy s/he also has within the organisation (or is it the other way around?). At the same time, all managers within the company (LHM and above) might be seen as gaining more control and autonomy simultaneously, it is just that the *nature* of control and autonomy has changed across the organisation. On the other hand, a zero-sum perspective would see the gaining by LHMs of more control/autonomy as resulting from other staff in the company losing some of theirs. Thus, for example, if one focusses upon the control relationship between the LHM and the RM, then if the LHM gains more control/autonomy, the RM must lose some control. The discussion which follows is based upon our observations, questionnaire returns and interviews with a sample of LHMs and RMs across the UK. We first put the argument for LHMs having less, or, at best, no more control/autonomy after the changes had taken place:

▷

Who are the managers now? The changing nature of management in Park Taverns continued

Argument 1: the status quo has been maintained

1. A managerial hierarchy and structure of control is still in place, albeit with a somewhat different 'texture' from before. The key strategic decisions are still taken at the apex of Park Taverns, with operating decisions being taken at the local company level by the Operations Director. Consultation takes place much as before (i.e. their equivalent in the old regime) with RMs, and instructions are handed down through the hierarchy to LHMs.

2. The PTS allows RMs and senior managers to oversee and monitor what is happening in the pubs (e.g. which products are being sold, at what price, when, and by whom) in even greater detail than before, and on a real time basis. This is, of course, an example of how IT can be used for surveillance and control purposes (see, for example, Sewell and Wilkinson, 1992).

3. Competition within the sector is just as intense as ever, if anything it is even *more* intense, unpredictable and unstable. In a company of this size in particular, this acts as a constraint upon the degree of risk decision makers are prepared to take in attempting to alter the status quo, given that the organisation has a long history of profitability, sales growth and return on capital.

On the other hand, there are a number of arguments which would support the proposition that LHMs *have* been 'set free' by the new organisational arrangements (gaining, *inter alia*, more autonomy and control over hostelry operations), and thus supporting a view that the nature of management and managing in the company has changed in a significant way:

Argument 2: the nature of management has significantly changed

1. Taking point 3 above, but turning it around, one could equally well argue that the changing nature of the competition and the toughness of the targets set by the plc, have led to a freeing up of the control structure, manifested for example in LHMs now being encouraged to use their initiative to come up with new ideas and being given the autonomy and flexibility to experiment, in a 'no blame' culture. The requirement now is for a company which displays 'fleet-footedness', and is innovative and responsive to customers; this quality has hitherto been in short supply in such bureaucratic and control-focussed organisations.

2. Public houses have always been 'mini-businesses' in their own right (including managed houses, albeit not to the same extent as tenancies and free houses), therefore the argument that they were and are subject to a strong degree of control from the centre and the tier of management above has been overdrawn. What has happened is that as a result of the change and restructuring programme, this autonomy has been recognised, encouraged and extended.

3. A main objective in reorientating the organisation around the new pub operating companies has precisely been to decentralise and devolve control, with, for example, RMs now acting as 'coaches' and 'facilitators' rather than monitors and controllers.

4. In the new regime it is easier to reject aspects of the company's past mode of operating. An example of this was provided during an interview with a LHM: he pointed out how a LHM could now (using the hostelry IT – it should be noted – thus showing how the IT does not necessarily have to be used exclusively for one main purpose, i.e. control; see Preece, 1995) compare what had been gained from a particular promotion with what was spent on it, and then come to a decision about its effectiveness, and whether to do something different next time. A business case for a new/improved promotion could then be put forward to, and discussed with, the RM, in the ▷

expectation that it would be supported if the case had been well-made. It is worth noting that in this LHM's view, this could be particularly liberating for new hostelry managers, as 'many older hands did their own thing anyway' (see 2 above).

5. Our findings show that team-working is giving LHMs the support and confidence to try out new ideas, either within the group itself or the individual hostelry. It is sometimes acting as a 'launch-pad' to innovation, and as a means for trying out new ideas/concepts.

We do not feel able at this point in time, so relatively soon after the implementation of the change programme, to come to a definitive conclusion about the 'net' result of the above 'pushes and pulls' for the status quo vs. change in the nature of the managerial role at the company. We conclude that, at least for the two managerial positions of LHM and RM at Park Taverns, the nature and future development of the managerial role is relatively 'open', to an extent which would probably not have been anticipated just a few years ago. Our data indicates, however, that the process of management, as an activity which involves the exercise of discretion and control, is seen increasingly by many actors in this company as by no means the exclusive preserve of certain roles within the middle and higher echelons of the organisation.

References

Alvesson, M. and Willmott, H. (1996) *Making Sense of Management: A Critical Introduction*, Sage, London.

CSC Index (1994) *State of Reengineering Report: North America and Europe*, CSC Index: Cambridge, MA.

Davenport, T. (1993) *Process Innovation: Re-engineering Work through Information Technology*, Harvard University Press, Boston, MA.

Hales, C. (1993) *Managing through Organisation: The Management Process, Forms of Organisation and the Work of Managers*, Routledge, London and New York.

Hammer, M. and Champy, J. (1993) *Reengineering the Corporation. A Manifesto for Business Revolution*, Nicholas Brealey, London.

Mangham, I. (1986) *Power and Performance in Organizations*, Blackwell, Oxford.

Preece, D. (1995) *Organizations and Technical Change: Strategy, Objectives and Involvement*, Routledge, London and New York.

Preece, D., Steven, G. and Steven, V. (1996) 'The End of Organized Management in (Park Taverns)', paper presented to Tenth Annual Conference of the Association of Industrial Relations Academics of Australia and New Zealand, University of Western Australia, Perth, February, 1996.

Preece, D., Steven, G. and Steven, V. (1998) *Work, Change and Competition*, Routledge, London.

Sewell, G. and Wilkinson, B. (1992) '"Someone to Watch Over Me": Surveillance, Discipline and the Just-in-Time Labour Process', *Sociology*, 26, 2, 271–91.

Watson, T. (1994) *In Search of Management: Culture, Chaos and Control in Managerial Work*, Routledge, London and New York.

Source: The copyright of this case study rests with the author's colleague David Preece, University of Portsmouth. The case is reprinted with permission.

TASKS

(i) **How would you describe the management style which typified Park Taverns before the change programme?**

(ii) **What sort of management style is evolving now?**

(iii) **What were seen to be the main impediments to the creation of a more innovative and responsive organisation?**

(iv) **Why is the nature of management/managing problematic in the new organisation?**

Notes and references

1. Mullins L J, 'Management and Managerial Behaviour', *International Journal of Hospitality Management*, vol. 4, no. 1, 1985, p. 39.
2. Waterman R, *The Frontiers of Excellence*, Nicholas Brearley (1994).
3. Klein S, 'Customer Care Needs Staff Care', *Proceedings of The International Association of Hotel Management Schools Symposium*, Leeds Polytechnic, November 1988.
4. McGregor D, *The Human Side of Enterprise*, Penguin (1987).
5. Venison P, *Managing Hotels,* Heinemann (1983), p. 56.
6. Blake R R and McCanse A A, *Leadership Dilemmas – Grid Solutions*, Gulf Publishing Company (1991).
7. Jones P J and Lockwood A, *The Management of Hotel Operations*, Cassell (1989).
8. Newborough G, 'People vs production', *Manager, The British Journal of Administrative Management*, May/June 1999, pp. 13–14.
9. See, for example, Sieff M (Lord Sieff of Brimpton), *Management the Marks & Spencer Way*, Fontana Collins (1991).
10. See, for example, Coates J, 'It is Legitimate to be Unavailable', *Industrial and Commercial Training*, vol. 22, no. 5, 1990, pp. 8–11.
11. For a Fuller account of MBWA, see: Peters T J and Austin N K, *A Passion for Excellence*, William Collins (1985).
12. See, for example, Wood R C, *Organizational Behaviour for Hospitality Management*, Butterworth-Heinemann (1994).
13. Venison P, *Managing Hotels*, Heinemann (1983), p. 32.
14. Waterman R, *The Frontiers of Excellence*, Nicholas Brealey (1994).
15. Lockwood A, Baker M and Ghillyer A, (eds) *Quality Management in Hospitality*, Cassell (1996).
16. Wood R C, *Working in Hotels and Catering*, 2nd edn, International Thomson Business Press (1997).
17. Lee-Ross D, 'Two Styles of Hotel Manager, Two Styles of Worker', *International Journal of Contemporary Hospitality Management*, vol. 5, no. 4, 1993, pp. 20–24.
18. Likert R, *New Patterns of Management*, McGraw-Hill (1961).
19. Likert R and Likert J G, *New Ways of Managing Conflict*, McGraw-Hill (1976).
20. Likert R, *The Human Organisation,* McGraw-Hill (1967), p. 138.
21. Drucker P F, *The Practice of Management*, Heinemann Professional (1989).
22. See, for example, Humble J W, *Management By Objectives*, Management Publications Ltd for The British Institute of Management (1972).
23. For example, see Medlik S, *The Business of Hotels,* 3rd edn, Butterworth-Heinemann (1994).
24. Jones P J and Lockwood A, *The Management of Hotel Operations*, Cassell (1989).
25. Mill R C, *Managing for Productivity in the Hospitality Industry*, Van Nostrand Reinhold (1989).
26. Kane J S and Freeman K A, 'MBO and Performance Appraisal', *Personnel*, vol. 63, no. 12, December 1986, pp. 26–36.
27. Wood R C, *Organizational Behaviour for Hospitality Management*, Butterworth-Heinemann (1994), p. 107.
28. Boella M J, *Human Resource Management in The Hospitality Industry*, 6th edn, Stanley Thornes (1996), pp. 55–56.
29. Shaner M C, 'The Nature of Hospitality Managers', *Cornell HRA Quarterly*, November 1978, pp. 65–70.

30. Worsfold P, 'A Personality Profile of the Hotel Manager', *International Journal of Hospitality Management*, vol. 8, no. 1, 1989, pp. 51–62.

31. Stone G, 'Personality and Effective Hospitality Management', *Proceedings of The International Association of Hotel Management Schools Symposium*, Leeds Polytechnic, November 1988.

32. Guerrier Y and Lockwood A, 'Developing Hotel Managers – A Reappraisal', *International Journal of Hospitality Management,* vol. 8, no. 2, 1989, pp. 82–89.

33. See, for example, Mullins L J, *Management and Organisational Behaviour*, 5th edn, Financial Times Pitman Publishing (1999).

34. Mullins L J and Davies I, 'What Makes for an Effective Hotel Manager?', *International Journal of Contemporary Hospitality Management*, vol. 3, no. 1, 1991, pp. 22–25.

35. Goss-Turner S, 'The Role of the Multi-unit Manager in Branded Hospitality Chains', *Human Resource Management Journal*, vol. 9, no. 4, 1999, pp. 39–57.

36. For a discussion on operational and business skills see Guerrier Y, *Organizational Behaviour in Hotels and Restaurants: An International Perspective*, Wiley (1999).

37. *Meeting Competence needs in the Hotel and Catering Industry Now and in the Future*, HCTC Research Report, September 1992.

38. Maher A, 'Accounting for Human Resources in UK Hotels', *Proceedings of CHME Research Conference*, Manchester Metropolitan University, April 1993.

39. See, for example, Handy C, *The Empty Raincoat*, Hutchinson (1994).

40. Green J, 'When was your Management Style last Applauded?', *Chartered Secretary*, December 1998, pp. 28–29.

41. Drucker P F, *People and Performance*, Heinemann (1977), p. 59.

42. Mercer K, 'Psychology at Work in the Hotel and Catering Industry', *HCIMA Review*, 4, 1978, p. 212.

43. See, for example, Clark M, *Interpersonal Skills for Hospitality Management*, Chapman & Hall (1995).

44. Jones P (ed.), *Management in Service Industries,* Pitman (1989).

45. Mullins L J and Aldrich P, 'An Integrated Model of Management and Managerial Development', *Journal of Management Development*, vol. 7, no. 3, 1988, pp. 29–39.

46. See, for example, Blanchard K and Johnson S, *The One Minute Manager*, Willow Books (1983).

47. Freemantle D, 'The People Factor', *Management Today*, December 1985, pp. 68–71.

48. Gunn B, 'Are Educationalists and Employers in Harmony on Hotel Management Training?', *Master Innholders' Forum*, London, June 1990. Reported in *Caterer & Hotelkeeper*, 14 June 1990, p. 14.

49. Maher A, 'Accounting for Human Resources in UK Hotels', *Proceedings of CHME Research Conference*, Manchester Metropolitan University, April 1993.

50. White M, 'Management Styles in Hotels', *HCIMA Journal*, October 1973, pp. 9–11.

51. Wood R C, *Organizational Behaviour for Hospitality Management*, Butterworth-Heinemann (1994), p. 107.

52. Umbreit W T, 'Developing Behaviorally-Anchored Scales for Evaluating Job Performance of Hotel Managers', *International Journal of Hospitality Management*, vol. 5, no. 2, 1986, p. 56.

53. Hales C and Nightingale M, 'What are unit managers supposed to do? A contingent methodology for investigating managerial role requirements', *International Journal of Hospitality Management*, vol. 5, no. 1, 1986, p. 9.

54. Worsfold P, 'Leadership and Managerial Effectiveness in the Hospitality Industry', *International Journal of Hospitality Management*, vol. 8, no. 2, 1989, p. 152.

55. Wood R C, *Organizational Behaviour for Hospitality Management*, Butterworth-Heinemann (1994).

56. A view supported by the industrial placement officers for Hospitality Management degree students at University of Portsmouth Business School.

57. See also Robinson S, 'The Learning Curve', *Inside Hotels*, April/May 1992, pp. 40–45.

58. Venison P, *Managing Hotels*, Heinemann (1983).

59. *Building Capability for the Twenty-First Century*, Investors in People, UK (1999).

60. See, for example, Freemantle D, 'The People Factor', *Management Today*, December 1985, pp. 68–71.

61. Martin P and Nicholls J, *Creating a Committed Workforce*, Institute of Personnel Management (1987), p. 97.

62. Peters T J and Waterman R H, *In Search of Excellence,* Harper & Row (1982), p. 238.

63. Fletcher W, 'Good Listener, Better Manager', *Management Today*, January 2000, p. 30.

64. Tarpey D, 'Handling With Care', *Caterer & Hotelkeeper*, 12 July 1990, p. 52.

65. Venison P, *Managing Hotels,* Heinemann (1983).

66. See Mullins L J, *Management and Organisational Behaviour*, 5th edn, Financial Times Pitman Publishing (1999).

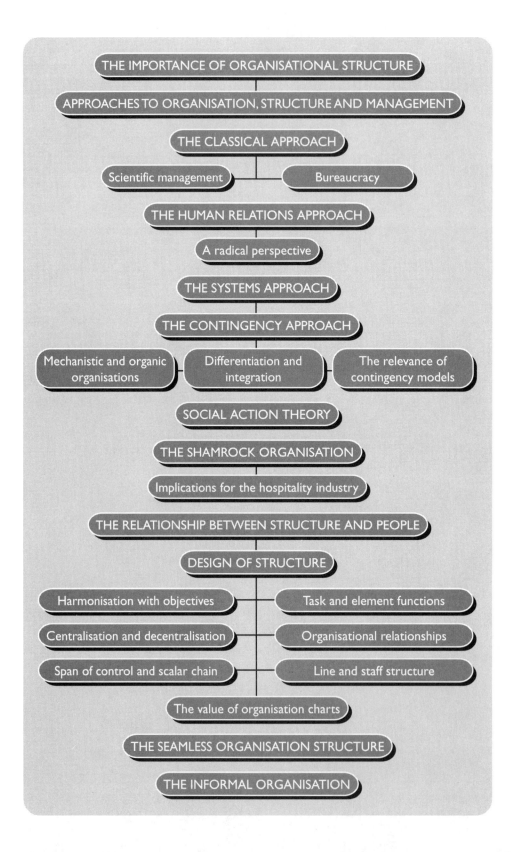

Chapter six

Organisational processes and structure

Introduction

It is by means of structure that the work of the hospitality organisation is carried out. Structure provides the framework for the organisation's pattern of management. It affects economic performance and the behaviour of staff. The development of organisation theory has highlighted the importance of structural design and the management of human resources.

The importance of organisational structure

The application of the process of management and the execution of work take place within the structure of the hospitality establishment. Structure is the pattern of relationships among positions in the establishment and among members of the staff. Structure creates a framework of order and command through which the work activities are planned, organised, directed and controlled.

It is structure, therefore, that gives shape to the establishment, and provides the basis for organisational processes and the execution of work. The purpose of structure is to define:

- the division of work;
- tasks and responsibilities;
- work roles and relationships; and
- channels of communication.

In the very small establishment there are likely to be fewer problems with structure. The distribution of tasks, the definition of authority and responsibility, and relationships among members of staff can be built on a personal and informal basis. But all establishments, of whatever type or size, require some form of structure by which people's interactions

Framework of the business

There is no organisation chart. People work in teams (as illustrated) that have to work co-operatively and flexibly to provide a seamless service to the customer. This is controlled by log books that are used to record issues, comments, faults, suggestions and instructions that ensure continuity of service across shift boundaries. These are the **Office Book, Manager's Book**, **Telephone Message Book** and diaries for **Bedroom Reservations**, **Restaurants**, **Conferences** and **Functions**. They are contributed to by all staff and are read every day by the partners, team leaders and staff coming on shift. They are referred to frequently at team meetings and are the source for many process improvement initiatives.

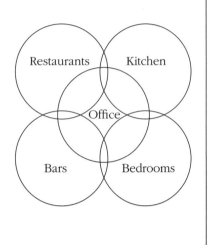

THE SEAVIEW HOTEL AND RESTAURANT

and efforts are channelled and coordinated. With larger establishments there is a greater need for a carefully designed and purposeful form of structure.

An outline of typical key activities and division of work is given in Figure 6.1.

Structure and effective performance

In order to achieve its goals and objectives the work of the establishment has to be divided among its members. The resulting structure should be that which is most appropriate to the objectives of the establishment. Structure is necessary for the effective performance of key activities and to support the efforts of staff. It provides accountability for areas of work undertaken by groups and individual members of staff. Structure therefore involves the organisation of human assets.[1]

The correct design of structure is a major determinant of effective organisational performance. Drucker, for example, makes the point that:

> *Good organisation structure does not by itself produce good performance. But a poor organisation structure makes good performance impossible, no matter how good individual managers may be. To improve organisation structure . . . will therefore always improve performance.*[2]

There is also a need for the continual review of structure to ensure that it is the most appropriate form for the particular establishment, and in keeping with its change and development. The quality of structure will affect the grouping of functions, the allocation of responsibilities, decision-making, coordination, control and reward. These are all fundamental requirements for the continued operation of an organisation.[3]

Structure will affect not only economic efficiency and performance, but also the morale and job satisfaction of the staff. Managers need to consider how structural design and methods of work organisation influence the behaviour and performance of members of the establishment. Structure is also a major component of an effective corporate strategy.[4]

Figure 6.1: Typical key activities and division of work for a 100-bedroom four-star hotel

Approaches to organisation, structure and management

Organisation structure, the process of management and the behaviour of people at work are inextricably linked. Underlying the development of management theory and practice are contrasting ideas on structural design and attitudes towards people. Identification of major trends in the study of organisations and management will help to provide a perspective on concepts and ideas discussed in subsequent chapters.

Much has been written about different approaches to improving the effectiveness of work organisations. It is usual, therefore, to categorise the work and ideas of writers into various 'approaches' based on their views of structure and management. This provides a framework in which to direct study and focus attention.

It is important, however, to emphasise that no single approach provides all the answers. It is the comparative study of different approaches which yields benefits for the manager. The skill of organisational design lies in taking from the different approaches those ideas which suit best the particular situation and requirements.

Categorisation of approaches

There are many different ways of attempting to categorise these various approaches. For example, Gullen and Rhodes refer to the traditional, empirical, human relations, decision theory and formalism approaches.[5] On the other hand, Keiser identifies the classical scientific, classical organisation, human relations, management science, contingency and Japanese approaches.[6]

Whatever the broad classification of main approaches it is possible to identify a number of possible cross-groupings and sub-groupings. Some of these sub-groupings might be seen as mutually exclusive while others might be viewed as sub-divisions of broader approaches.[7]

In order to provide a convenient framework as a basis for our discussion we will use a broad four-fold categorisation of:

- the classical approach – including scientific management and bureaucracy;
- the human relations approach – including the structuralists;
- the systems approach; and
- the contingency approach (Figure 6.2).

Figure 6.2: Main approaches to organisation, structure and management

The classical approach

The classical approach is associated with work carried out initially in the early part of this century. Classical writers placed emphasis on purpose and structure, and on the technical requirements of the organisation. Identification of general objectives would lead to clarification of purposes and responsibilities at all levels of the organisation, and to the most effective structure.

Attention is focused on the division of work, reporting relationships, the clear definition of duties and responsibilities, and maintaining specialisation and coordination. The emphasis is on structure based upon a hierarchy of management and formal organisational relationships.

Principles of organisation

The classical writers were concerned with improving the process of management and organisation structure as a means of increasing efficiency. Emphasis was placed on the importance of a common set of principles for the design of a logical structure. Most classical writers had their own set of principles but probably the leading authority was Urwick, who specified ten principles of organisation.[8]

1. *The principle of the objective*:
   'Every organisation and every part of the organisation must be an expression of the purpose of the undertaking concerned, or it is meaningless and therefore redundant.'

2. *The principle of specialisation*:
   'The activities of every member of any organised group should be confined, as far as possible, to the performance of a single function.'

3. *The principle of coordination*:
   'The purpose of organising per se, as distinguished from the purpose of the undertaking, is to facilitate coordination and unity of effort.'

4. *The principle of authority*:
   'In every organised group the supreme authority must rest somewhere. There should be a clear line of authority to every individual in the group.'

5. *The principle of responsibility*:
   'The responsibility of the superior for the acts of the subordinate is absolute.'

6. *The principle of definition*:
   'The content of each position, both the duties involved, the authority and responsibility contemplated and the relationships with other persons should be clearly defined in writing and published to all concerned.'

7. *The principle of correspondence*:
   'In every position, the responsibility and the authority should correspond.'

8. *The principle of span of control*:
   'No person should supervise more than five, or at the most, six direct subordinates whose work interlocks.'

9. *The principle of balance*:
   'It is essential that the various units of an organisation should be kept in balance.'

10. *The principle of continuity*:
    'Re-organisation is a continuous process: in every undertaking specific provision should be made for it.'

The definition of responsibilities

Another major contributor to the classical approach, Brech, attempts to provide a practical approach to organisation structure based on tried general principles as opposed to concentrating on specific cases or complex generalisations.[9] Brech emphasises the importance of formal relationships, written definition of responsibilities and the value of job descriptions as an aid to effective structure and delegation. His work builds on the ideas of earlier writers and therefore provides a comprehensive view of the classical approach.

Relevance and applications

The classical writers have been criticised generally for not taking sufficient account of personality factors, and of creating an organisation structure in which people can exercise only limited control over their work environment. Research studies have also expressed doubts about the effectiveness of the classical approach when applied in practice.[10]

However, although the work of the classical writers is sometimes regarded as an out-of-date approach, it does focus attention on important factors in the study of organisational design.[11] Good structure is necessary for efficiency and an essential factor in improving performance.

The idea of common sets of principles has been subject to much criticism. Simon, for example, states that:

Organisational design is not unlike architectural design. It involves creating large, complex systems having multiple goals. It is illusory to suppose that good designs can be created by using so-called 'principles' of classical organisation theory.[12]

Many of the principles are expressed as bland statements in non-operational terms and give little basis for specific managerial action. Nevertheless, the principles are still relevant and they do provide general guidelines on the design and structuring of organisations. It is also of interest to note that, despite the criticisms, many of the more recent writings on the subject appear to be based on the original work of the classical writers.

The basic concepts can be of value to the hospitality manager if modified to suit the demands of the particular situation. The application of these principles needs to take account of:

- the particular situational variables of the establishment; and
- the psychological and social factors relating to the people who work within the structure.

Two major 'sub-groupings' of the classical approach of particular importance for organisational design and structure are:

- scientific management; and
- bureaucracy.

Scientific management

Scientific management places emphasis on obtaining increased productivity from individual workers through the technical structuring of the work organisation. The major contributor to this approach was F. W. Taylor (1856–1917), who believed that in the same way that there is a best machine for each job, so there is a best working method by which people should undertake their jobs.[13]

Taylor was concerned with finding more efficient methods and procedures for the co-ordination and control of work. He also believed in the rational-economic needs concept of motivation. The provision of monetary incentives was the primary motivator for higher levels of output. Workers would be motivated by obtaining the highest possible wages through working in the most efficient and productive way.

Principles of scientific management

Scientific management was based on the principles of:

- the scientific selection, training and development of workers;
- the clear division of work and responsibilities between management and workers; and
- close management control over the actual processes of work.

Taylor considered that all work processes could be analysed into discrete tasks and that by scientific methods it was possible to find the 'one best way' to perform each task. Each job was broken down into component parts, each part timed, and the parts rearranged into the most efficient method of working.

Criticisms of scientific management

Scientific management is often referred to as a machine theory model. It adopts an instrumental view of human behaviour together with the application of specialisation and standard procedures of work. Workers were viewed less as isolated individuals and more as units of production to be handled in much the same way as machines. The scientific study of work can lead to jobs becoming repetitive, boring and requiring little skill.

The ideas behind scientific management have been largely discredited by subsequent management writers. There has been strong criticism of scientific management as representing close management control over workers. By removing decisions about how their work is carried out, by division of labour, and by dictating precise stages and methods for every aspect of work performance, management could gain control of the actual process of work. The rationalisation of production processes and division of labour tends to result in the de-skilling of work, and this may be a main strategy of management.[14]

The question of de-skilling would appear to have particular significance in hotel and catering where in recent years there have been many examples of the de-skilling of work.[15] (See also the discussion on the shamrock organisation later in this chapter.)

Relevance to the hospitality industry

Despite the criticisms, the underlying approach of scientific management still has some relevance to the hospitality industry. Taylor and his followers introduced the concept of a systematic approach to management. They have left to modern management the legacy of practices such as job analysis, systematic selection and training, work study, payment by results, production control and management by exception. The adoption of such practices has a significant effect on hospitality management.

Managers need to find the most efficient and productive methods of work. In particular, the efficiency of 'production' areas, such as food preparation and service and housekeeping is likely to benefit from a clear division of work and responsibilities, prescribed methods of working and labour-saving approaches.

Standard recipes and performance standard manuals including photographs of finished dish presentations are widely used in the industry. With chain hotels in particular, it is common to have a prescribed standard layout for each room with training based on procedure manuals and the one best way. Staff are expected to clean a given number of rooms per shift with financial incentives for additional rooms. What is important, however, is the context and manner in which such practices are put into effect and whether there is any scope for personal initiative.

Bureaucracy

A common form of structure, especially in large-scale establishments, is bureaucracy, though today the term has common connotations of rigidity and red tape. However, in the study of organisation and management it is important that the term is seen not *necessarily* in a deprecative sense but as applying to certain structural features of formal organisation.

The German sociologist, Max Weber, showed particular concern for what he called 'bureaucratic structures'. He argued that the decisive reason for the growth of bureaucratic organisation was its purely technical superiority over any other form of organisation.[16] Although Weber did not actually define bureaucracy, he did attempt to identify the main characteristics of this type of organisation.

Main features of bureaucracy

Bureaucracy is characterised by:

- clear role definitions of duties and responsibilities;
- division of labour and a high level of specialisation;
- a hierarchical structure of authority;
- uniformity of decisions;
- an elaborate system of rules, procedures and regulations;
- employment based on technical qualifications and formally attested merit;
- impartiality in undertaking duties and responsibilities.

Four main features of bureaucracy are summarised by Stewart as: specialisation, hierarchy of authority, a system of rules, and impersonality.[17]

- *Specialisation* applies more to the job than to the person undertaking the job. This makes for continuity, as the job usually continues if the present job holder leaves.
- *Hierarchy of authority* makes for a sharp distinction between management and workers. Within the management ranks there are clearly defined levels of authority.
- *A system of rules* aims to provide for an efficient and impersonal operation. The system of rules is generally stable although some rules may be changed or modified over time. Knowledge of the rules is a requisite of holding a job in a bureaucracy.
- *Impersonality* means that allocation of privileges and the exercise of authority is in accordance with the laid-down system of rules. In more highly developed bureaucracies there may be carefully defined procedures for appealing against certain types

of decisions. According to Stewart, the characteristic of impersonality is the feature of bureaucracy which most distinguishes it from other types of organisation. A bureaucracy should not only be impersonal but it should be seen to be impersonal.

Criticisms of bureaucracy

These features provide an accurate account of how many organisations actually do function. However, bureaucratic structures have a number of potential disadvantages and are subject to severe criticisms, including the following.

- The over-emphasis on rules and procedures. Record-keeping and paperwork may become more important in their own right rather than as a means to an end.
- Members may develop a dependence upon bureaucratic status, symbols and rules.
- Initiative may be stifled and there is lack of flexibility or adaption to changing circumstances.
- Hierarchical position and responsibilities in the organisation can lead to officious bureaucratic behaviour.
- Impersonal relationships can lead to stereotyped behaviour and a lack of responsiveness to individual situations or problems.

Among the strongest critics of bureaucratic organisation, and the demands it makes on the worker, is Argyris. He claims that the formal, bureaucratic organisation restricts the pyschological growth of the individual. It causes feelings of failure, frustration and conflict. Argyris argues that the organisation should provide a more 'authentic' relationship with its members and provide:

- a significant degree of individual responsibility and self-control;
- commitment to the goals of the organisation;
- productiveness and work; and
- an opportunity for individuals to apply their full abilities.[18]

Hotels as bureaucracies

The growth of bureaucracy has come about through the increasing size and complexity of modern work organisations and the associated demand for effective operations. Greater emphasis has been placed on the careful design of structure, and the definition of individual duties and responsibilities. Greater specialisation and expertise, and applications of technical knowledge, have highlighted the need for laid-down procedures.

As a result, many hotels, especially large-scale ones, reflect – at least in part – similar characteristics to a bureaucratic form of organisation. This view is supported by Lockwood and Jones:

On looking at organisation structures within hotels, we find an emphasis on a mechanistic or bureaucratic format, such as the classical kitchen brigade. This structure is based on tradition, with a breakdown of the operations into specialist occupational areas. It is also influenced by the need for a formal framework within which the uncertainty and instability of the guest input can be handled – all staff know their respective roles and positions and therefore the basis of their reactions to customers' requests.[19]

There appears therefore to be a particular dilemma for management between the underlying characteristics of bureaucracy and the inherent nature of the hospitality industry. The concept of personal service delivery requires a flexible approach and responsiveness to individual requirements and problems of guests. This demands that staff should have a broad definition of their duties and responsibilities and the opportunity to use their initiative and inventiveness.

In practice, however, few organisations fit neatly into any particular model of organisational design and structure. Most are a hybrid and will lie somewhere on a continuum between bureaucracy and more organic forms of structure. The hotel organisation in particular seems unlikely to fit fully into the bureaucratic model of structure.[20]

Much of the criticism of bureaucracy is undoubtedly valid, but much also appears to be unfair comment. In any case, many staff working in the hotel industry are generally conservative by nature. They feel more comfortable working within a rigid structure and 'knowing where they stand'. The main point, however, is that whatever the validity of the criticisms it is difficult to envisage how modern large-scale hotels could function effectively without exhibiting at least some of the features of a bureaucratic structure.

The human relations approach

The main emphasis of the classical approach was on structure and the formal organisation as the basis for achieving high levels of work performance. But during the 1920s greater attention began to be given to the social factors at work and to the behaviour of people in the organisation – that is, to human relations. Whereas the classical approach adopted more of a managerial perspective, the human relations approach strove for a greater understanding of people's psychological and social needs at work as well as improving the process of management. It is usually regarded as the first major approach to organisation and management to show concern for industrial sociology. The major impetus to the human relations approach came with the famous Hawthorne studies at the Western Electric Company in America (1924–1932).

There were four main phases to the Hawthorne studies: the illumination experiment, the relay assembly test room, the interviewing programme and the bank wiring observation room.

The illumination experiment

This investigation was conducted to test the belief that improvements in physical working conditions, such as the intensity of lighting, would improve productivity. The results of the tests were inconclusive as production varied with no apparent relationship to the level of lighting, but actually increased when conditions were made worse. Production also increased in the control group although the lighting remained unchanged. Clearly other factors influenced the level of production and this prompted a series of further experiments.

The relay assembly test room

This experiment involved six women workers who assembled telephone relays by hand. The work was boring and repetitive. The researchers selected two assemblers who were friends with each other, and they chose three other assemblers and a layout operator. The six workers were moved to a room by themselves but with the same general environmental conditions as the main assembly area. The workers were subjected to a series of planned and controlled changes such as hours of work, rest pauses, and refreshment breaks. During the experiment the observer adopted a friendly manner, consulting with the workers, keeping them informed and listening to their complaints. Following all but one of the changes there was a continuous rise in the level of production. Also, sickness and absenteeism dropped, and morale appeared to improve. The researchers formed the conclusion that the main reasons were small group working, the extra attention given to workers, and the apparent interest in them shown by management.

The interviewing programme

In an attempt to find out more about the workers' feelings towards their supervisors and conditions of work, a large interviewing programme was introduced. Initially the interviewers approached their tasks using a set of prepared questions related mainly to how workers felt about their jobs. However, this method produced only limited information, so the style of interviewing was changed to be more non-directive and open-ended. Workers were free to talk about any aspect of their work. Everything was confidential, no identification was given and no personal details were revealed to management.

The interviewers set out to be friendly and sympathetic. They adopted an impartial, non-judgemental approach and did not take sides or offer opinions. If necessary they would explain company policy and details of, for example, benefit schemes but they concentrated on listening. Using this approach the interviewers found out far more about the workers' true feelings towards the company, working conditions, supervision and management, group relations and matters outside work.

Many workers appeared to welcome the opportunity to have someone who would listen to their feelings and problems, and to whom they could 'let off steam' in a friendly atmosphere. The interviewing programme was significant in giving an impetus to present-day personnel management and the use of counselling interviews. It also highlights the importance of managers actively listening to the workers.[21] Given the nature of the hospitality industry and the importance of good employee relations, the lessons learnt from the interviewing programme have particular significance for the manager.

The bank wiring observation room

This experiment involved the observation of a group of 14 men working in the bank wiring observation room. It was noted that the men formed their own informal organisation with sub-groups and cliques, and with natural leaders emerging with the consent of members. The group developed its own pattern of informal social relations with 'norms' of what constituted 'acceptable' behaviour together with a system of sanctions against those members who did not conform with the group norms. Group pressures on individual workers restricted the level of work achieved despite financial incentive schemes offered by management. The importance of informal working practices and group 'norms' is discussed further in Chapter 8.

Evaluation of the human relations approach

The Hawthorne studies have been subject to criticism and to a number of different interpretations.[22] But, however the results are regarded, the studies have important implications for organisational structure. They generated new ideas on social interaction, output restrictions and individuals within work groups. As Nailon, for example, points out: 'Most managers have experienced antagonism when any suggestion is made for the composition of groups to be changed.'[23]

The human relations approach marked a change in emphasis away from the precision of scientific management and led to ideas on increasing productivity by humanising the work organisation. The classical approach sought to increase production through means of formal structure and rationalisation of the work organisation. With the human relations approach, recognition was given to the importance of the informal organisation which will always be present within the formal structure. Workers were seen as individuals and members of a social group, with their behaviour and attitudes as the key to effectiveness.[24]

Neo-human relations

The results of the Hawthorne studies and the subsequent attention given to social organisation gave rise in the 1950s and 1960s to a group of writers who are usually categorised under the heading of neo-human relations. The major focus of concern was the personal adjustment of the individual within the structure of the work organisation, the effects of group relationships and leadership styles. Writers under this heading include Maslow, Argyris, Herzberg, McGregor and Likert. The works of these writers are examined in more detail in subsequent chapters.

A radical perspective

Sometimes the work of Weber is associated with the ideas of writers such as Karl Marx under the sub-heading of the structuralist approach, which is a synthesis of the classical (or formal) school and the human relations (or informal) school.[25] A major line of thought was that the earlier approaches were incomplete. The structuralist approach provides a radical perspective of social and organisational behaviour. Greater attention should be given to the relationships between the formal and informal aspects of the organisation, and the study of conflict between the needs of the individual and the organisation, and between workers and management. (See also the discussion on conflict and the radical perspective in Chapter 12.)

The systems approach

The classical approach emphasised the formal structure as a major mechanism in optimising organisational performance. The human relations approach emphasised the social needs of people at work and the importance of the informal organisation. The systems approach attempts to reconcile these two earlier approaches. Attention is focused on the total work organisation and the interrelationships of structure and behaviour. The systems approach views the organisation within its broader external environment and with multiple channels of interaction.

The systems approach draws attention to the importance of the socio-technical system. This directs attention to viewing the organisation as a whole and the relationships between technical and social variables. Changes in one part, technical or social, will affect other parts and thus the whole organisation as a system. An analysis of the hotel as an open system was discussed in Chapter 2.

The contingency approach

The contingency approach, which can be viewed as an extension of the systems approach, highlights possible means of differentiating between alternative forms of organisation structure and systems of management. There is no one optimum state. The structure of the organisation and its 'success' are dependent upon a range of situational factors.

The contingency approach takes the view that there are a large number of variables or situational factors which influence organisational design and performance. There is therefore no one best, universal structure. The most appropriate structure is dependent upon the contingencies of the situation for each individual hotel. It is these situational factors which account for variations in the structure of different hotels.

Although contingency models have not involved the hospitality industry directly, their relevance and potential applications should be readily apparent. Managers can use these models to compare and contrast the structure and functioning of their own hotel, and to take from them those ideas which suit best their particular requirements.

An 'if–then' relationship

Contingency models can be seen as a form of 'if–then' matrix relationship.[26] If certain situational factors exist, then certain variables in organisational structure and systems of management are most appropriate. A simplified illustration of contingency relationships is given in Figure 6.3.

Situational variables may be identified in a number of different ways. Some obvious bases for comparison are the type and nature of the establishment, the range and standard of services and facilities offered, and the nature of the customers and characteristics of

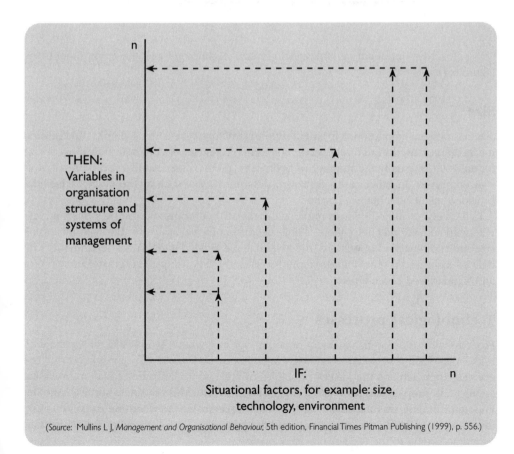

Figure 6.3:
A simplified illustration of the 'if–then' contingency relationship

(*Source:* Mullins L J, *Management and Organisational Behaviour*, 5th edition, Financial Times Pitman Publishing (1999), p. 556.)

Figure 6.4:
The contingency approach – main influences on organisation and management

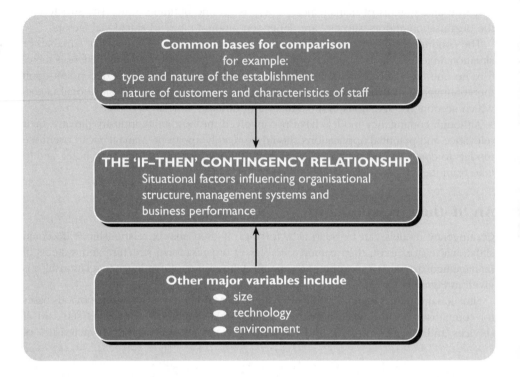

the staff. Other important variables include size, technology and the environment (see Figure 6.4).

Size

Size has obvious implications for the design of structure. Size is not a simple variable, and it can be measured in different ways. For example, the most common indication of size for an hotel is usually the number of bedrooms, perhaps associated with the number of staff employed. In other cases, however, different factors such as the range of facilities provided might be a better indicator.

In the very small hotel, for example with only six bedrooms and run by a husband and wife with some family help, there is little need for a formal structure. But with increasing size and complexity of operations, the hotel may be divided into distinct departments with defined tasks and responsibilities, more formalised relationships, and greater use of rules and standardised procedures.

Technological processes

From a major study of management organisations in England, Woodward draws attention to the relationships between technology, organisation structure and business success.[27] The classical approach and the idea of principles of organisation appeared to fail in providing a direct and simple basis for relating organisation structure and business success. Another important finding was the nature of the actual relationship between the three key 'task' functions of development, production and marketing. The most critical of these functions varied according to the type of production system.

Patterns of organisation were found to be related more to similarity of objectives and the technology of production. Among the organisational characteristics showing a direct relationship to technology were the ratio of managers to total staff, the shape of the structure, the span of control and the number of levels of authority. One might consider how the nature of the 'production technology' process accounts for differences in the patterns of structure and systems of management of different hospitality organisations – between for example a fast-food burger chain, a large hotel concentrating on conference and leisure facilities, a public house attracting largely family customers, a small country club hotel, a very expensive up-market restaurant.

Environment influences

Two important studies have focused on the effects of uncertainty and a changing environment on the organisation, and its management and structure. These are:

- Burns and Stalker – mechanistic and organic organisations; and
- Lawrence and Lorsch – differentiation and integration.

Mechanistic and organic organisations

Burns and Stalker investigated the relationship between the pattern of structure, the nature of the external environment and economic performance.[28] They identified two ideal types of organisation at opposite extremes of a continuum – the 'mechanistic' organisation and the 'organic' organisation. These represented the polar extremes of the form which organisations could take when adapted to technical and commercial change. In practice, most organisations are likely to be a mix of both mechanistic and organic structures.

The mechanistic organisation

The mechanistic organisation resembles a bureaucracy and has a rigid, hierarchical structure. It is characterised by closely defined duties, responsibilities and technical method, the specialisation of tasks, knowledge centred at the top of the hierarchy, instructions from superiors and vertical interaction between superior and subordinates.

The mechanistic organisation is unable to deal adequately with rapid change. It is therefore more appropriate for stable environmental conditions. An example might be a traditional, high-class and expensive hotel operating along classical lines and with an established reputation and type of customer.

The organic organisation

The organic organisation is more flexible and has a fluid structure. It is characterised by a network structure of control and authority, lateral communications based on information and advice, the contribution of special knowledge and expertise throughout the organisation, the continual redefinition of tasks, and commitment to the common task of the organisation.

The organic organisation is required when new problems and unforeseen circumstances arise constantly. It is therefore more appropriate for uncertainty and changing environmental conditions. An example could be a holiday or tourist hotel with an unpredictable

Figure 6.5: Characteristics of mechanistic and organic organisations

Mechanistic		Organic
High, many and sharp differentiations	SPECIALISATION	Low, no hard boundaries, relatively few different jobs
High, methods spelled out	STANDARDISATION	Low, individuals decide own methods
Means	ORIENTATION OF MEMBERS	Goals
By superior	CONFLICT RESOLUTION	Interaction
Hierarchical based on implied contractual relation	PATTERN OF AUTHORITY CONTROL AND COMMUNICATION	Wide net based upon common commitment
At top of organisation	LOCUS OF SUPERIOR COMPETENCE	Wherever there is skill and competence
Vertical	INTERACTION	Lateral
Directions, orders	COMMUNICATION CONTENT	Advice, information
To organisation	LOYALTY	To project and group
From organisational position	PRESTIGE	From personal contribution

(*Source:* © Joseph A. Litterer, 1973 reprinted with permission of the author, Litterer, Joseph A. *The Analysis of Organizations*, 2nd edn, John Wiley & Sons (1973), p. 339.)

demand and many different types of customer. Another example could be a country club hotel specialising in a range of different functions, such as wedding receptions and corporate sports days, which require the erection of marquees and provision of other facilities according to particular requirements.

A summary of the main characteristics of mechanistic and organic systems is provided by Litterer (Figure 6.5) and this provides a helpful basis for reviewing the structure and management of a particular hospitality organisation.

Differentiation and integration

Lawrence and Lorsch undertook a study of a number of firms, including two in the consumer food industry, and analysed the structure of organisation in terms of 'differentiation' and 'integration'.[29] They attempted to extend the work of Burns and Stalker and examined not only the overall structure, but also the way in which specific departments were organised to meet different aspects of the external environment.

Differentiation

Differentiation refers to differences among departments of the organisation in terms of their goals, timespans, interpersonal relations and formality of structure. It was recognised that different departments could have their own distinctive forms of structure according to the nature of their tasks, the different demands of the environment and the different levels of uncertainty.

Integration

Integration refers not to the minimising of differences between departments but to the degree of coordination and cooperation between different departments and attempts to achieve unity of effort. The mechanisms to achieve integration include: policies, rules and procedures; teamwork and mutual cooperation; formal lateral relations, committees and project teams; and assigned 'integrators' or liaison officers.

Demands of the environment

Lawrence and Lorsch suggest that the extent of differentiation and integration in effective organisations will vary according to the demands of the environment. In an unstable and dynamic environment the more effective organisation would be highly differentiated and highly integrated. This study would seem to have particular relevance to the hotel industry because of the different orientations and demands among departments such as the kitchen, front office, conference and banqueting, security and maintenance.

The relevance of contingency models

Contingency models of organisation draw attention to the situation factors which account for variations in structural design. They are more concerned with differences among organisations than with similarities. The contingency approach tends to assume, however, that organisational performance is dependent upon the extent to which the structure of the organisation matches prevailing contingencies.

As with other approaches to organisation and management, contingency theory has been subject to a number of criticisms.[30] It does run the risk of concluding that 'it all depends on everything' and there is the danger of over-emphasis on differences between organisations and the exclusion of similarities. There must be a balance.

Greater understanding of organisation and structure

Despite the criticisms and limitations, contingency theory has provided a further insight into our understanding of relationships among factors influencing the structure, management and operations of organisations. It can help our thinking about how hotels should be organised.

Based on the distinction between mechanistic and organic organisations, Shamir suggests that hotels tend to resolve the conflict between the demands for bureaucracy and hospitality service by the mixture of informal, organic systems of control and a lateral pattern of communication which lies behind the facade of a formal, mechanistic structure. Apart from those managers who have responsibility for coordinating the work of a number of different departments, most large hotels appear to lack formal integrating mechanisms at the organisational level.[31]

Contingency models draw attention to the importance of different structures for different organisations and for different activities of the organisation. Nailon, for example, feels that most theories have helped to provide a greater understanding of the catering industry and that: 'choosing the appropriate form of organisation will prevent the problems created by inappropriate structures'.[32]

Social action theory

Social action represents a contribution from sociologists to the study of organisations. Social action writers attempt to view the organisation from the standpoint of individual members (actors) who will each have their own goals, and interpretation of their work situation in terms of the satisfaction sought and the meaning that work has for them. Social action looks to the individual's own definition of the situation as a basis for explaining behaviour. Conflict of interests is seen as normal behaviour and part of organisational life.

Action theory of hotel and catering

A particular theory of human behaviour from an 'action approach' to hotel and catering is presented by Bowey.[33] She suggests that it would be possible to take the best parts of systems theory and contingency theory and combine them into a theory that would model empirical behaviour and also facilitate the analysis of large numbers of people in organisations.

Bowey gives four basic concepts taken from systems theory and redefined in accordance with an action approach.

- *Role* – this is needed for the analysis of behaviour in organisations. It explains the similar action of different people in similar situations within the organisation, and the expectations held by other people.
- *Relationships* – this is needed to explain the pattern of interaction among people and the behaviours displayed towards one another.
- *Structure* – the relationship among members of an organisation give rise to patterns of action which can be identified as a 'transitory social structure'. The social factors and non-social factors such as payment systems, methods of production and physical layout, together form the behavioural structure.
- *Process* – human behaviour can be analysed in terms of processes, defined as 'continuous interdependent sequences of actions'. The concept of process is necessary to account for the manner in which organisations exhibit changes in structure.

Bowey goes on to illustrate her theory by cases studies of five different types of organisations, all in the restaurant industry.

The shamrock organisation

One particular approach to structural design which appears to have interesting applications for the hospitality industry is Handy's concept of the 'shamrock' organisation.[34] The three leaves to each stem of the shamrock are symbolic of the organisation which is seen as made up of three distinct groups of people who are managed, organised and paid differently, and who have different expectations: the professional core, the contractual fringe and the flexible labour force (see Figure 6.6).

- *The professional core* comprises qualified professionals, technicians and managers essential to the existence and effective performance of the organisation. Collectively these people own the knowledge which distinguishes the organisation. The

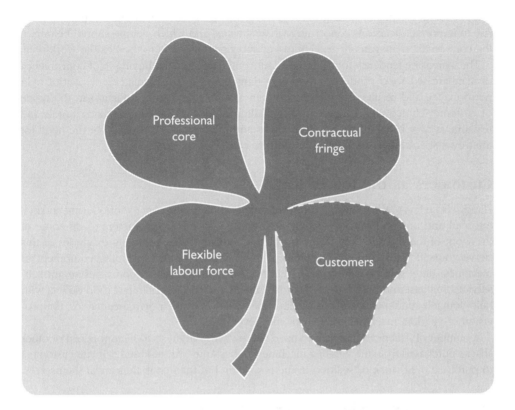

professional core are expensive and the tendency has been for organisations to restructure in order to reduce their numbers.

● *The contractual fringe* comprises those people, or other organisations, outside of the organisation who provide specialist services and undertake all non-essential work which can be done by somebody else, and in theory are able to do it better for less. It is wise for the shamrock organisation to put boring and repetitive work out to contract, specifying the results expected and then paying the fee.

● *The flexible labour force* represents all those part-time and temporary workers which are the fastest growing group in the pattern of employment. It provides for flexibility in human resourcing. People are brought in as occasional extra part-time labour or temporary staff as changing work situations demand.

● *Customers* sometimes referred to as the fourth leaf in that many more organisations now provide facilities for customers to 'serve themselves'.

According to Handy, organisations now have three significant workforces each with a different kind of commitment to the organisation and a different set of expectations, and each workforce needs to be managed in different ways.

Implications for the hospitality industry

Economic pressures, rapid developments in information technology and the need for review of structural design have highlighted the significance of these different groups. Organisations have reduced the size of their workforce, especially full-time staff, and have flatter structures with fewer levels of authority. The concept of the shamrock organisation can encourage hospitality managers to question the operation of their organisations. It gives rise to important decisions concerning what activities and which people should belong to the core, to the management and control of subcontracting and to the flexible workforce.

The increasing tendency to make use of subcontracting and the buying-in of convenience or standardised food products raises important questions of management control over performance and results. Contracting out can arguably lead to a reduction in the range of customer choice and the potential de-skilling of jobs. For example, many hotels and restaurants now buy in their pastry products and as a result no longer have the need for their own specialist pastry chef as part of the core.

Customers as the fourth leaf?

Handy also refers to the growing practice of saving labour in the core by introducing another, informal and unpaid, form of subcontracting – that of getting customers to do some of the work of the organisation. In the hospitality industry there are many examples of this 'serve yourself' philosophy. Examples are the provision of shoe cleaning equipment or machines, hotel guests making their own tea and coffee in their rooms, restaurant self-service breakfast and buffet meals, standard meals and beverages in fast-food outlets with help-yourself condiments and customers expected to clear their own meal tables, the provision of vending machines for snacks and beverages.

A number of American motels also have microwaves for guests to heat popcorn or other snacks purchased from the vending machines. Other American restaurants invite customers to purchase their steak or seafood in the restaurant but then cook their meal themselves.

Managing the flexible labour force

The increase in the flexible labour force is particularly noticeable with the growth of service industries. As discussed in Chapter 2, services are created and consumed simultaneously. Unlike manufacturing, services are time-perishable and cannot be stored. The flexible labour force has increasingly been used as a cheaper and more convenient means of dealing with the peaks and troughs of demands, and as a means of adjusting the level of service to match changing customer requirements.

Although casual and part-time staff are unlikely to have the same degree of commitment or ambition as the core it is important that they are taken seriously and regarded as a valuable part of the organisation. The flexible workforce should be treated with respect, given fair and equitable treatment, adequate training and status, and decent pay and conditions. If casual and part-time staff are to respond in a positive way and provide a high standard of service then they have to be managed in a considerate and effective manner.

The relationship between structure and people

Whatever the overall shape of the organisation, its effectiveness will be influenced both by sound structural design and by the individuals filling the various positions within the structure. The views of the human relations writers remind us of the importance of the human element in the design of structure. Managers need to consider how structural design and methods of work organisation influence the behaviour and performance of staff.

The functions of the formal structure, and the activities and defined relationships within it, exist independently of the members of staff who carry out the work. Personalities, however, are an important aspect of the working environment. The actual operation of the establishment and success in meeting its objectives will be dependent upon the behaviour of people who work within the structure, and who give shape and personality to the framework. 'Organisational structure is but a simplification of complex patterns of human behaviour'.[35]

Lord Forte has drawn attention to the importance of the human element in structure:

> *the human aspect in a business is vital: you can keep drawing squares and lines, but within these squares you must have people and they must be deeply involved with the business. If this does not happen, then the lines and squares and the diagrams mean nothing.*[36]

Maintaining the socio-technical system

In Chapter 2 we referred to the importance of the relationships between technical efficiency and social considerations. Structure must be designed, therefore, to maintain the effectiveness of the socio-technical system and of the establishment as a whole. Attention must be given to the interactions between both the structural and technological requirements, and human factors and the needs and demands of people.

Design of structure

In the final analysis, however, there is an underlying need to establish a framework of order and command by which the activities of the establishment are accomplished successfully. This demands that attention be given to certain basic considerations in the design of structure (Figure 6.7).

Harmonisation with objectives

Structure must harmonise with the goals and objectives of the establishment. Only when the objectives have been clearly stated and agreed can alternative forms of structure be analysed and compared. A clear definition of goals and objectives provides a basis for the division of work and grouping of activities into sub-units. The objectives for these sub-units must be related to the overall strategy of the hotel in order that an appropriate pattern of organisation structure is established.

For example, Schaffer emphasises the importance of lodging organisations continuously engaging in the process of matching their competitive strategies and organisation structures to changes in the environment. In order to achieve effective performance, strategy must be adjusted to suit the environment. Organisation structure and processes must then be created that properly support that strategy.[37]

Task and element functions

In her study of the management organisation of firms in the United Kingdom, Woodward distinguishes between 'task' functions and 'element' functions.[38] Task functions are those basic activities which are related to the actual completion of the 'productive' process, and directed towards specific and definable end-results. These are the essential functions that the organisation must perform and involve: developing the product/facility/service, providing the product/facility/service, marketing it, and financing the organisation.

Figure 6.7:
Basic
considerations
in the design
of structure

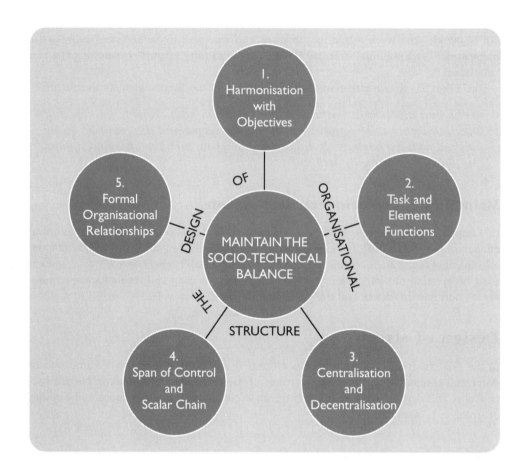

Element functions are those activities which are not directed towards specific and definable ends but are supportive of the task functions and form an intrinsic part of the management process. These include, for example, planning, management services, administrative support, quality control and maintenance.

Structure based on task functions

Within the formal structure, duties and responsibilities have to be divided among members and different jobs related to each other. The difference between task and element functions forms the basis for the division of work and has important implications for organisation.

> *Organisation is a function of purpose and the complexity of the hotel business arises because it is concerned with several distinct products, services and facilities, which are offered in various combinations.*[39]

Structure should therefore be centred around the key activities which relate directly to the products, services and facilities offered by the establishment. These task functions are likely to relate to such activities as front office and reception, food and beverage, accommodation, conferences and banqueting, marketing or sales, and other direct customer facilities or services, for example leisure facilities or laundry and valeting. Support services are likely to include, for example, accounting, security, works and maintenance, and administration.

Need to distinguish task and element functions

Failure to distinguish between task and element functions can lead to confusion and difficult-ies in relationships among members. Woodward comments on the bad relationships between management accountants and other managers. The accountants tended to assume respons-ibility for end results that were not properly theirs. They saw their role as a controlling and sanctioning one, rather than as a servicing and supportive one. Activities concerned with raising funds for the business, keeping accounts and determination of financial policy are task functions. But management accounting is an element function. Relationships seemed better when the two functions were organisationally separate.

The personnel function

The personnel function is generally identified as one of the element functions of an organisation. But in the hospitality industry the importance of staff contact to customer satisfaction means that personnel can be seen as associated closely with a task function (see Chapter 10).

Centralisation and decentralisation

The division of work and grouping together of activities raises the question of the extent of centralisation or decentralisation. This arises at two levels:

- the authority of individual managers within a chain or group, for example the extent of authority for local purchasing, or to recruit or dismiss staff; and
- specific delegation to sub-units, departments or sections within the individual establishment, for example a central kitchen, or decentralisation of some of the food preparation.

The underlying issue is the measure of devolved autonomy, independence and freedom of action enjoyed by the hospitality manager or by the individual sub-units.

Advantages and disadvantages

The general advantages claimed for centralisation usually include identification of a cor-porate image (discussed in Chapter 3), better decision-making, easier implementation of a common policy for the chain/group or the hotel as a whole, improved coordination and control, economies of scale and reduction in overhead costs, and use of specialisation, including better facilities and equipment.

There are, however, a number of arguments against centralisation. It creates a more bur-eaucratic structure and may result in a longer chain of command. The decision-making process may be cumbersome when needing to be cleared through top, and perhaps distant, management. Too much centralisation can stifle initiative and the sense of responsibility.

In addition, there are positive arguments in favour of decentralisation. It enables deci-sions to be made closer to the operational level of work and according to immediate needs. Support services are more likely to be effective if provided closer to the activities they serve. Decentralisation provides greater opportunities for management training and devel-opment. Also, it usually has a positive effect on the motivation and morale of staff.

The extent of centralisation or decentralisation should be considered in terms of the size and nature of the establishment, geographical location and particular circumstances, and the quality of staff. It is a question of balance and managerial choice. The growth of international hospitality organisations has drawn particular attention to the question of the extent and manner of decentralisation and empowerment related to design of structure and management control.[40]

Span of control and scalar chain

Two of the most specific, and related, principles of good organisational design are: (a) the span of control; and (b) the scalar chain. The span of control arises in line authority and refers to the number of subordinates who report *directly* to a given manager or supervisor. It does not refer to the total number of subordinate operating staff. Hence the term 'span of responsibility' or 'span of supervision' is sometimes preferred.

Limits to span of control

The classical writers placed emphasis on the span of control but tended to suggest that this should be limited to a definite figure. Graicunas emphasised that the number of subordinates who can effectively be supervised is based on the total number of direct and cross relationships.[41] He developed a mathematical formula for the span of control:

$$R = n\left(\frac{2^n}{2} + n - 1\right)$$

where n = number of subordinates and R = number of interrelationships.

With five subordinates the total number of interrelationships requiring the attention of the manager is 100; with six subordinates the number of interrelationships is 222.

Importance of span of control

If the span of control is too narrow it increases the number of levels of authority. A narrow span of control can result in too close a level of supervision and failure to make best use of potential managerial talent. But with too wide a span of control it becomes difficult to supervise subordinates effectively. Sub-groups or cliques and informal leaders may evolve. A wide span of control places more demands on the manager with less time to carry out all activities properly. It may also limit opportunities for promotion.

In discussing the span of control, Venison comments that:

> *The hotel general manager has an impossible task to perform because it is generally beyond the behavioural range of most human beings and the sufferer has been the hotel guest – since guest contact and, to a large degree, staff contact have often been lost in the process.*[42]

This observation illustrates the importance of good organisation structure including attention to span of control.

Practical considerations

In practice, however, it is not feasible to lay down a single, ideal, span of control: there are many situational variables which influence the limit of how many subordinates one person can control successfully. These include the nature of the establishment and facilities/services offered, standardisation of methods and procedures, the ability of the manager, the quality, training and motivation of subordinates, communication and control systems, geographical or physical location, and length of the scalar chain.

The scalar chain

The 'scalar chain' refers to the number of different levels in the structure, the chain of hierarchical command. The scalar chain establishes the vertical graduation of authority and responsibility, and the framework for superior–subordinate relationships. The very act of creating structure introduces the concept of the scalar chain.

All members of staff must know their position within the structure. A clear line of authority and responsibility is necessary for the effective operation of the organisation. It is generally accepted, however, that there should be as few levels as possible. Too long a scalar chain can have an adverse effect on morale, decision-making and communications.

Need for balance

There is a general movement towards flatter organisation structures. However, if efforts are made to reduce the number of levels, this may bring about an increase in the span of control. The design of structure therefore necessitates maintaining a balance between span of control and scalar chain. It is the combination of span of control and scalar chain which determines the overall pyramid shape of the organisation and whether the hierarchical structure is 'flat' or 'tall'. (See Figure 6.8.)

Figure 6.8: Effects of span of control and scalar chain

SPAN OF CONTROL = 7

49 POSITIONS   NUMBER OF LEVELS = 3

SPAN OF CONTROL = 3

49 POSITIONS   NUMBER OF LEVELS = 4

Organisational relationships

Within the structure the defined pattern of duties and responsibilities creates certain formal organisational relationships between individual members. These *individual* relationships establish the nature of the superior–subordinate hierarchy, flows of authority and responsibility, and patterns of role relationships.

Line relationships

Managers who have responsibility for the primary objectives or essential activities, for example front office, accommodation, food and beverage, are usually known as 'line' managers. Line managers have authority and responsibility for the activities of their own department. Line relationships are the most simple and direct form of structure. There is a direct vertical relationship between superiors and subordinates, and each subordinate reports to only one person. Authority flows down through the structure from, for example, the general manager to departmental (line) managers, section supervisors and other staff. Each level of the hierarchy has authority over the level below it.

Staff relationships

As establishments develop in size and work becomes more complex, the range of activities and functions undertaken increases. The line structure may then be supplemented by specialists who provide a common advisory function, horizontally, throughout all departments. Such specialist advisory functions are often known as 'staff'. They should serve to support the primary activities and work of the line managers. Staff functions include, for example, personnel, management accounting, marketing, maintenance and administration.

People in a 'staff' relationship have little or no direct authority over employees in other departments: this is the responsibility of the line manager. However, as the role and responsibilities of the staff positions would have been established by top management, line managers might be expected to accept the specialist advice which is given. Staff managers may also be assigned a specific responsibility which gives direct authority over other workers, for example if the personnel manager is appointed as health and safety officer for the establishment as a whole. And within their own group there is still a line relationship between functional specialists and their own subordinates and superior.

Line and staff structure

When staff positions are created they have to be integrated into the managerial structure. A 'line and staff' structure attempts to make full use of specialists while maintaining the concept of line authority (Figure 6.9). But this form of structure can present potential difficulties, and friction often occurs between line and staff managers. A major source of difficulty is often to persuade line managers to accept, and to act upon, the advice and recommendations which are offered.

Line managers may feel that staff managers have an easier and less demanding job because they have no direct responsibility for providing facilities or services to the customer. Staff managers are often criticised for unnecessary interference in the work of the line manager, and for attempting to impose their views and advice. Line managers are often

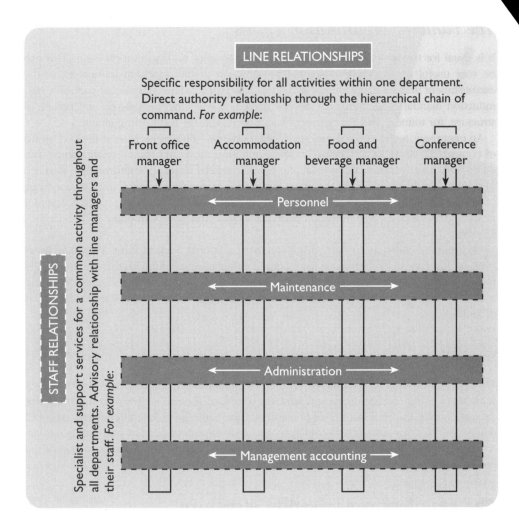

Rep
of lin
structu

criticised for resisting the attempts of staff managers to provide assistance and coordination, and for making unnecessary demands for departmental independence. Staff managers may also feel that their own difficulties and work problems are not appreciated fully by the line manager.

Need for effective cooperation

It is not always easy to distinguish clearly between what is directly essential to the operation of the establishment, and what might be regarded only as a support function. The distinction between a line manager and a staff manager is not absolute. The important thing is that both line and staff recognise fully the purpose and role of the other. To be successful, line and staff need to work together and establish effective cooperation. The more staff managers can demonstrate the practical benefits of their specialist advice to line managers, the more such advice is likely to be heeded – and actively sought in the future.

of structure

205

Figure 6.9:
resentation
and staff
presentation

e of organisation charts

he structure to be depicted in the form of an organisation chart. This can
in providing a pictorial presentation of the structural framework of the
d its main area of activities. It is helpful, for example, as part of a staff
The chart may also be used as a basis for the analysis and review of
ng and management succession, and for formulating changes.

chart may show, at a given moment in time, how work is divided, spans
, the levels of authority, lines of communication, and formal relationships. But
charts vary greatly. Some are intended to give a minimal amount of information, perhaps
for example only an outline of the management structure of the hotel. Others give a range
of additional detail – for example, all main positions in the structure, names of senior
post holders, and a broad indication of the duties and responsibilities of the various
sections.

Organisation charts are usually displayed in a traditional, vertical form. They can, however, be displayed in other ways, for example either horizontally with the details reading
from left to right,[43] or concentrically with top management at the centre. Some charts add
a rider, for example: 'The chart indicates lines of communication and not necessarily lines
of authority.'

Limitations

There are a number of limitations with most organisation charts. They depict only a
static view of the establishment and what the structure should be. They do not show, for
example, comparative authority of positions on the same level, lateral contacts, personal
delegation from superior to subordinates, or relationships between line and staff positions.
A chart does not show the informal structure, how an organisation actually works, or the
behaviour of people.

The seamless organisation structure

Chacko suggests that although the pyramid has been the framework of organisational structure for a very long time this structure does not support front-line workers as well as it
controls them. As hospitality customers become more seasoned, well-travelled and quality
conscious, a hotel's organisation structure must facilitate the implementation of strategies
designed to provide higher levels of service quality. The need is for the development of
a seamless hotel organisation. The structure is designed to be circular, flat and dynamic:
circular, so that all boundaries of the hotel, where employees serve customers are equally
accessible; *flat*, to reduce the number of hierarchical levels within the hotel; and *dynamic*
to create the flexibility to serve the changing needs of guests. In this seamless design there
will be no departments, as exist currently, only two job categories. The first is named Guest
Service and the second is Internal Service.

Guest Service employees take care of all guest needs in the hotel and must be trained
to be truly multi-skilled and prepared to work in cross-functional teams. The first and
most important skill is the ability to satisfy each guest's unique needs. Internal Service,
traditionally called staff functions, comprises certain specialised skills, apart from guest
service, necessary for the effective functioning of the hotel. Employees have the primary

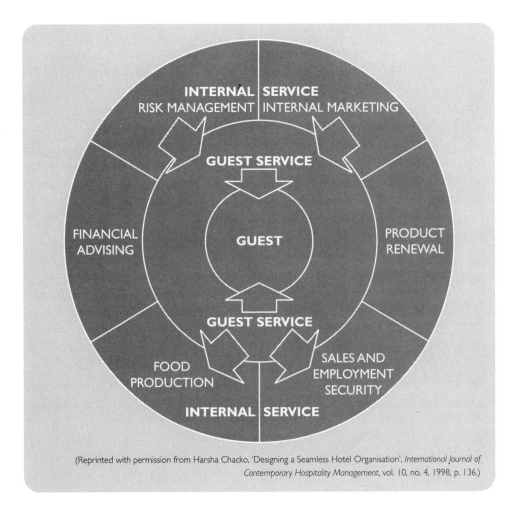

Figure 6.10:
The seamless
hotel
organisation

(Reprinted with permission from Harsha Chacko, 'Designing a Seamless Hotel Organisation', *International Journal of Contemporary Hospitality Management*, vol. 10, no. 4, 1998, p. 136.)

responsibility of supporting guest service employees. These are traditionally called staff functions but in the new organisation the purpose of each group will be redefined as: internal marketing (human resource management); financial advising (accounting); risk management (security); product renewal (housekeeping and maintenance); sales and employment security (sales and marketing); and food production (if necessary).[44] (Figure 6.10.)

The informal organisation

The formal organisation is deliberately planned and created. It is hierarchically structured with the division of tasks, and defined relationships of authority and responsibilities. An organisation chart, for example, gives a representation of the formal structure. Within the formal structure an informal organisation will always be present. People will modify the formal organisation, methods of operations and actual working practices. What happens in practice will vary from the formal structure. See for example Figure 6.11.

The hospitality establishment is not only a work organisation, it is also a social organisation. Members of staff will establish their own social groupings and relationships,

Figure 6.11: How the organisation looks should be compared with how it actually works

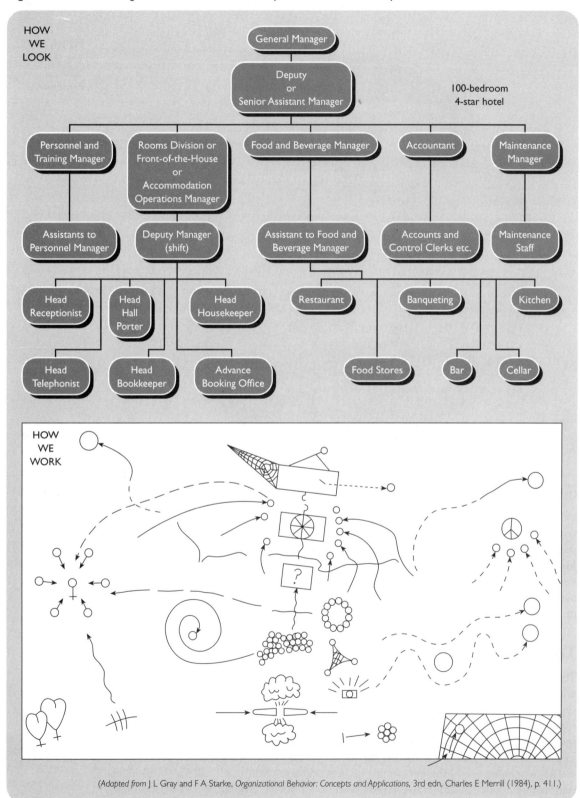

(Adapted from J L Gray and F A Starke, *Organizational Behavior: Concepts and Applications*, 3rd edn, Charles E Merrill (1984), p. 411.)

irrespective of those defined within the formal structure. The informal organisation arises from the interactions of people, their psychological and social needs, and the development of groups with their own relationships and norms of behaviour. The informal organisation is flexible and loosely structured. Relationships may be left undefined. Membership is spontaneous and with varying degrees of involvement.[45]

The style of management, the personality of members and the informal organisation will influence the operation of the establishment and actual working arrangements. What happens in practice may differ from the formal structure. According to Stewart there is a reciprocal relationship between people and the organisation.

> *People modify the working of the formal organisation, but their behaviour is also influenced by it. The method of work organisation can determine how people relate to one another, which may affect both their productivity and morale. Managers, therefore, need to be conscious of the ways in which methods of work organisation may influence people's attitudes and action.*[46]

Importance of the informal organisation

The informal organisation can serve a number of important functions.

- The satisfaction of members' social needs at work, and a sense of personal identity and belonging.

- A means of motivation, for example through status, social interaction, variety in routine or tedious jobs, and informal methods of work.

- Additional channels of communication. For example, through the 'grapevine' information of importance to members is communicated directly and quickly.

- A feeling of stability and security. Through informal 'norms' of behaviour a form of control is exercised over members.

- A means of highlighting deficiencies or weaknesses in the formal organisation, for example areas of responsibilities not covered in job descriptions, or outdated systems and procedures. The informal organisation may also be used when formal procedures would not be appropriate to deal with an unusual or unforeseen situation.

The informal organisation, therefore, has an important influence on the behaviour of people. It affects morale, motivation, job satisfaction and work performance. The informal organisation can provide members with greater opportunity to use their initiative and creativity in both personal and organisational development. People will view the hospitality organisation through the values and attitudes of their colleagues.

An illustration of the formal and informal organisation is given in Figure 6.12. (The importance and nature of informal groups is discussed in more detail in Chapter 8.)

Managing through the informal organisation

It is necessary for managers to recognise the existence, and importance, of the informal organisation. They should attempt to manage through the informal organisation and where appropriate use it to their advantage. Attempting to ignore the existence of the informal organisation is likely to lead only to frustration and potential conflict.

Figure 6.12: The formal and informal organisation

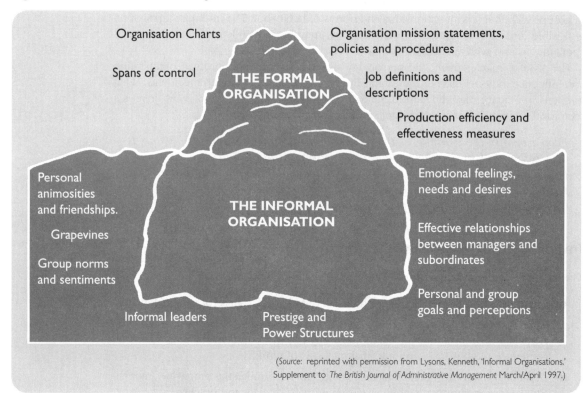

Organisation Charts

Spans of control

THE FORMAL ORGANISATION

Organisation mission statements, policies and procedures

Job definitions and descriptions

Production efficiency and effectiveness measures

Personal animosities and friendships.

Grapevines

Group norms and sentiments

THE INFORMAL ORGANISATION

Emotional feelings, needs and desires

Effective relationships between managers and subordinates

Personal and group goals and perceptions

Informal leaders

Prestige and Power Structures

(*Source:* reprinted with permission from Lysons, Kenneth, 'Informal Organisations.' Supplement to *The British Journal of Administrative Management* March/April 1997.)

Summary

- Structure provides the basis for organisational processes and the execution of work. The structure of the organisation will affect both economic performance, and the morale and job satisfaction of staff. Underlying the development of management theory are contrasting ideas on organisation and structural design.

- The classical approach places emphasis on purpose, technical structure and hierarchy of management, and includes scientific management and bureaucracy. The human relations approach gives attention to social factors and human behaviour at work including the informal organisation. The systems approach attempts to integrate these two earlier approaches and views the organisation with multiple channels of interaction.

- The contingency approach highlights variations in structure and management, and the influence of situational variables. One particular approach to structural design is the concept of the shamrock organisation. This draws attention to the constitution of the professional core, and to the management and control of subcontracting and the flexible labour force. ▷

- It is important to remember the human element and to consider how structural design can influence the behaviour and performance of staff. Attention must be given to maintaining the socio-technical system and to the interactions between structure and technological requirements, and to the needs and demands of people.

- In order to establish a system of order and command it is also important to give attention to certain basic considerations in the design of structure: harmonisation with objectives, task and element functions, centralisation and decentralisation, the span of control and scalar chain, and formal organisational relationships. The formal structure of the organisation will also be modified by the informal structure.

Review and discussion questions

1. What is the importance of organisation structure? How does structure relate to the effective performance of hospitality operations?

2. Contrast approaches to improving organisational performance based on attention to technical and structural features, with those based on concern for psychological and social factors.

3. Explain your understanding of scientific management. Assess critically the relevance of scientific management for the hospitality industry today.

4. Despite the criticisms of bureaucracy, it is difficult to envisage how modern large-scale establishments could function effectively without exhibiting at least some of the features of a bureaucratic structure. Discuss critically the validity of this contention.

5. What are the main conclusions that can be drawn from the human relations approach to organisation, structure and management? Evaluate the practical applications of the human relations approach to the hospitality industry.

6. Explain what is meant by contingency models of organisation. Contrast mechanistic and organic systems of management practice and structure, and suggest ways in which a hospitality organisation of your choice tends towards one type of system or the other.

7. Explain, with supporting practical examples, the main factors to be considered in the design of organisation structure. Assess the implications for the hospitality industry of the shamrock organisation.

8. Discuss critically the contention that a logical structure of organisation is better for efficiency and morale than a structure allowed to develop around personalities.

Assignment

Investigate a hospitality organisation of your choice and obtain, or prepare, a chart depicting the structural design of the organisation.

(i) Comment critically on:
- the relationships between task and element functions;
- the extent of centralisation and decentralisation;
- span of control and scalar chain; and
- formal organisational relationships.

(ii) Applying your knowledge of contingency models, comment on the apparent effectiveness of the structure of the organisation and/or particular departments of the organisation.

(iii) Identify and explain what you believe to be good and poor examples of structural design.

(iv) Explain, with supporting reasons, the changes you would recommend to the organisation structure. Where appropriate, prepare a revised organisation chart.

(v) Give practical examples of the influence and importance of the *informal* organisation.

Case study: Hazel Wood Court

1.1 Introduction
Hazel Wood Court was built in 1958, when its owners claimed that it was one of the first motels to be opened in Britain. The motel is situated in south-east England on the outskirts of a large seaport and within easy reach of a major trunk road and the motorway system. It lies about five miles north of a busy cross-Channel ferry service terminal and is also within four miles of an expanding industrial estate. Hazel Wood Court stands on the site of a ruined sixteenth-century inn, where the original tavern known as the King's Retreat still remains, and is still in everyday use as a public bar. The bar is very popular because of its authentic period character which is derived from a large open fireplace, wooden settees, and low ceilings supported by thick oak beams. Such is its attraction that the local people who use the bar still refer to it as The Retreat nearly 30 years after it started trading under the name of Hazel Wood Court.

1.2 Other facilities
As well as the popular King's Retreat public bar, the motel's other facilities include 51 bedrooms, a conference suite with seating for 40 delegates, a restaurant capable of serving up to 160 covers, and an attractive cocktail bar with seating for 55 persons. Hazel Wood Court is surrounded by extensive, well-kept gardens on three sides and there is a large free car park at the rear of the motel.

The motel is AA and RAC appointed with a three-star classification.

1.3 Accommodation
Only 25 bedrooms were included in the original design of the motel, but as the reputation of the Hazel Wood Court grew this total was increased to 40 rooms in 1968, and a new wing was built in 1976. The 51 bedrooms include 31 twin-bedded, 12 double, and eight rooms with three beds in each which can be converted into 'quads' if required.

▷

All the rooms have private bathrooms, colour television, radio and tea- and coffee-making facilities. It should be noted that despite the company's attempts to 'standardise' the accommodation units, the management has had to contend with numerous complaints, mainly from regular customers, since soon after the final extension was completed in 1976. The substance of most of these complaints is that the tariff charges do not reflect the allegedly different standards of accommodation provided by the motel.

1.4 Sources of revenue
Revenue is obtained from the following main sources:

(a) *Local business trade* – uses the restaurant to entertain guests for lunch and dinner, makes frequent use of the conference suite, and provides a steady flow of reservations for overnight accommodation.

(b) *Tour operators* – accommodation is also provided for various tour operators, on a dinner, room and breakfast basis, and several groups of 30–60 people (mainly American, Dutch, Australian and German) arrive at the motel each week during the summer season.

(c) *Visiting business trade* – close proximity to the motorway system makes the motel an ideal stopping-off point for visiting business people, and 'regulars' stay at the motel at least one night every week, booking accommodation many months in advance.

(d) *Casual trade* – because of the easy access to a cross-Channel ferry terminal there is a regular demand during the high season for overnight visitors travelling to and from the continent. Special arrangements are made for the service of early breakfasts for these visitors if required.

(e) *Wedding receptions/functions* – a steady trade has been developed mostly at weekends.

(f) *Bar trade* – the cocktail bar provides steady revenue from resident guests and diners in the restaurant, in contrast to the King's Retreat which derives most of its sales from the local inhabitants and chance trade. Snack-bar meals are a popular feature.

1.5 Fluctuations in trade
Apart from a general seasonal fall in demand for the motel's services outside the June–September period, there are also weekly fluctuations in demand which result in services being well utilised from Monday through to Friday morning throughout the rest of the year. Various attempts have been made to increase trade in the motel on Friday and Saturday nights, and on Sundays during the off-season period. Sustained local advertising has created a heavy demand for dinner on Saturday evenings and luncheon on Sundays.

Sunday nights, however, continue to be regarded as what are known in the trade as 'dead nights'. Despite these difficulties an annual guest occupancy of between 70 and 75 per cent is generally achieved in Hazel Wood Court and none of these fluctuations affects trade in the King's Retreat.

1.6 Group structure
The Hazel Wood Court is owned by a large group of companies. The group's interests are split into different divisions which are controlled by numerous subsidiary companies, most of which are also based in London. The relationship between hotels and motels like Hazel Wood Court and the parent company is shown in Figure 6.13.

The subsidiary company has its own board of directors and is run by a managing director, who is directly responsible to the board of directors of the parent company. The subsidiary company consists of hotels and motels throughout Britain which are divided into four areas. The general manager of a hotel/motel in any one of these areas is responsible to the catering adviser for all food and beverage operations and to a district manager for the overall profitability of the hotel. ▷

Hazel Wood Court continued

Figure 6.13:
Group structure

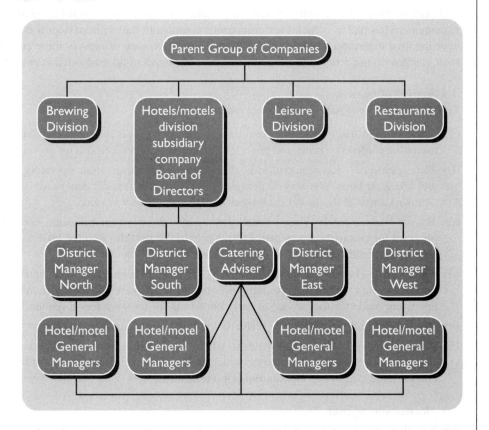

Communication between the hotel/motel general manager and these district executives is normally confined to one visit per month in the case of the catering adviser, and to one visit per week from the district manager.

1.7 Hazel Wood Court organisational structure
The staff at the Hazel Wood Court consists of 50 full- or part-time personnel, all of whom are ultimately responsible to the motel general manager, as shown in Figure 6.14.

2.1 A new general manager is appointed
Mid-way through 198_ Mr Jack Cox, who had been general manager of Hazel Wood, was promoted to the position of catering adviser for all the hotels and motels operating under the subsidiary company's banner. Numerous applications were received when Mr Cox's position was advertised in the trade press and the board eventually decided to appoint Mr Pat Squires as the new general manager of the motel from August onwards.

Mr Squires possessed nearly 32 years' experience in the hotel and catering industry, including six years as an officer of field rank in the Army Catering Corps. He had previously been general manager of a small chain of three motels in south-west England, but had decided to accept what was on paper a less demanding position at the Hazel Wood Court, after his doctor had advised him to reduce his workload.

Figure 6.14: Organisation structure of Hazel Wood Court

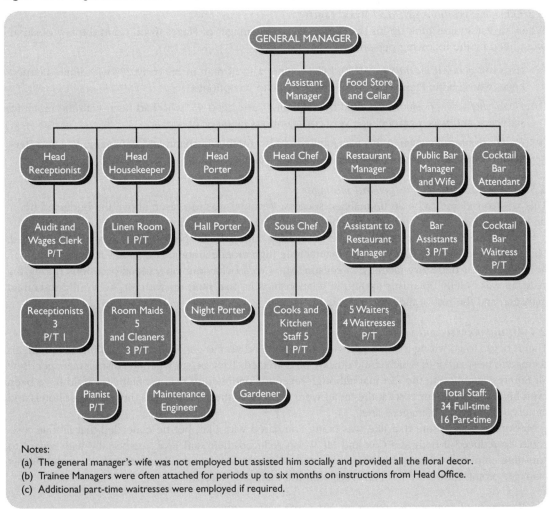

Notes:
(a) The general manager's wife was not employed but assisted him socially and provided all the floral decor.
(b) Trainee Managers were often attached for periods up to six months on instructions from Head Office.
(c) Additional part-time waitresses were employed if required.

Mr Squires was appointed by the managing director of the subsidiary company who informed him that, as general manager, he would be jointly responsible to the newly appointed catering adviser for food and beverage operations and to the District Manager for the overall profitability of the motel.

Mr Squires' remuneration included a substantial salary, plus a 5% commission on net profitability, which would be progressively reduced to 2% as net profits increased beyond agreed targets. Accommodation for Mr Squires and his family would also be provided above the King's Retreat public bar.

The managing director forewarned Mr Squires that the restaurant manager, Mr Ray Welsh, and head housekeeper, Mrs Brenda Cox, might find it difficult to adjust to his appointment, as both employees were inclined to be temperamental and had enjoyed considerable privileges under the previous general manager. The managing director added that Mrs Brenda Cox was, in fact, the wife of Mr Jack Cox, the newly appointed catering adviser. He urged Mr Squires to do what he could to develop a new team spirit, but stressed that if this proved to be impossible, disciplinary action was not to be taken against either employee without his prior permission.

Hazel Wood Court continued

2.2 Other key positions at Hazel Wood Court
When Mr Pat Squires took up his position as general manager of Hazel Wood Court the key positions were filled by the following personnel:

(a) *Assistant general manager* – Mr Ted Gascoigne, a local man in his early 20s with limited experience, whose wife, Frances, was employed as head receptionist.

(b) *Head chef* – this position was held by Mr John Drury, aged 45, who had been with the motel for six years, and was regarded as a very conscientious member of staff.

(c) *Public bar management* – this was jointly held by another husband and wife team, Lee and Beryl Marks, who had only recently taken up the appointment.

2.3 Mr Squires' first year as general manager
This was considered to be an unqualified success. Revenue was increased above the budgeted figure on both accommodation and food and beverage sales by over 15 per cent.

Several ways of increasing revenue over weekends during the off-peak season were also introduced. Mr Squires worked particularly hard at maintaining high morale amongst the motel staff and, although he had found it necessary tactfully to censure Mrs Cox's behaviour on various occasions during the year, he was quietly optimistic about the relationships he had built up with Mr Welsh, the restaurant manager, and the rest of the staff at the motel.

2.4 An unhappy second year
Things began to go wrong for Mr Squires during his second year as general manager. At first the problems seemed to be small ones which could quickly be corrected. They began when the district manager drew Mr Squires' attention to the fact that although revenue continued to rise, profitability could have been even higher if the labour costs at the motel were reduced to the same level as those at other hotels and motels in the district manager's area.

Mr Squires was unsure that like was being compared with like, but he conceded that labour costs could be reduced if both Mrs Cox and Mr Welsh reduced their staff levels, especially with regard to part-time employees. Mr Squires was requested to submit a report on the situation which the district manager promised to raise in confidence with the managing director.

2.5 Summary of confidential report on Mrs Cox's performance
Attention was drawn to the following problems:

(a) Mrs Cox had always taken every Saturday and Sunday off since she joined the company, and was never available to supervise her staff during weekends.

(b) Her department had always been overstaffed by at least two operatives.

(c) Overtime was offered to her staff on an indiscriminate basis and often when double-time rates had to be paid.

(d) She was inefficient in checking rooms and this had resulted in guests complaining on several occasions about the standard of cleanliness, etc.

(e) She ordered cleaning materials and other cleaning equipment without prior approval and authorisation from the manager.

In conclusion, Mr Squires expressed the view that, had he not been specifically advised by the managing director to retain Mrs Cox's services, it would not have been necessary to write a report ▷

on her performance as she would have been replaced soon after his appointment because of her general inefficiency.

2.6 Summary of confidential report on Mr Welsh's performance
With regard to the restaurant manager, Mr Squires stated that in his opinion Mr Welsh had recently adopted an arrogant approach to the management, his own staff and visitors alike.

Other main problems were as follows:

(a) Mr Welsh, having been employed at the motel since it had opened, was apparently of the opinion that he could run his department as he wished, irrespective of demand. The restaurant was overstaffed at most times; however, when staff were needed at peak periods they were not all available.

(b) Mr Welsh's unfavourable attitude to guests, other than regular well-liked customers, was becoming more obvious and in some cases it had brought complaints from diners about some of his remarks which appeared to be bordering on the offensive.

Mr Squires was fully prepared to resolve these difficulties with Mr Welsh, but was of the opinion that he could no longer entirely count on his loyalty.

2.7 Bar problems
Bar and stocktaking was carried out at agreed intervals of approximately six weeks by a firm from London which had been appointed by the parent company. Normally this took place on a Monday afternoon with two representatives commencing work at 2 pm and finishing at approximately 5 pm. They obtained all the sales figures and 'goods inwards' information from the weekly returns sent to Head Office by the motel. Their results were received approximately two to three weeks after each stock-take. The cocktail bar and wine cellar produced excellent figures, indicating that they were being run in accordance with good commercial practice.

The public bar results caused Mr Squires considerable concern because deficiencies occurred on the cellar reconciliation figures, and the external stocktakers concluded that these shortages mainly concerned the public bar.

It was decided that all goods were delivered to the main cellar, and that each bar requisitioned from the food and beverage manager, who issued the items daily. These requisitions were then aggregated over the stocktaking period and were added to the stocks for each bar. For total cellar stocks to be reconciled, the opening cellar stock with all the purchases added, less the total of all the requisitions, etc., had to equal the closing stock of each item in the cellar, and it was these discrepancies, amounting to nearly 3 per cent of turnover, which were serious and could never be explained adequately by either the bar manager or his wife.

As the refrigerated cold room, which housed all the beers, was within the cellar compound, there had to be access for deliveries, maintenance, cleaning of the pipes and the replacement of kegs, etc.

The bar manager therefore had a set of keys for this purpose, but not to the section housing the spirits, liqueurs, aperitifs, etc., which were stored in a separate cage in the main cellar. Mr Squires and his assistant manager shared the view that the entrance to the main cellar was too easily accessible, being located behind the service counter of the public bar.

Between them they devised a tactful system of monitoring staff movements, and were disturbed to notice that Mr Welsh, the restaurant manager, who was on very friendly terms with Mr Marks and his wife, made regular visits to this part of the motel outside normal working hours. Mr Squires reported his concern to both the district manager and the catering adviser as, even though the case against Mr Welsh was purely circumstantial and far from proven, they should be aware of the situation in case corrective action eventually had to be taken.

▷

Hazel Wood Court continued

2.8 The response of the district manager

After discussing Mr Squires' complaints with the Managing Director, the district manager informed him that two courses of action would be taken:

(a) Mrs Cox would be interviewed by the district manager in the presence of Mr Squires and, unless she provided a satisfactory explanation for her behaviour, would receive a verbal disciplinary warning from the company.

(b) No action would be taken against Mr Welsh for the time being, but stocktaking in the public bar and cellar would be carried out at more regular intervals, possibly unannounced.

3.1 Disciplinary proceedings against the head housekeeper

The district manager kept his word, and Mrs Cox was requested to attend disciplinary proceedings in the presence of Mr Squires. The meeting was well conducted by the district manager, who kept proceedings at a low key, raised each complaint calmly, allowed Mrs Cox the opportunity to defend herself, and remained impartial throughout. Mrs Cox was denied the opportunity to turn the meeting into an angry debate and ended up by admitting responsibility for all of the criticisms raised against her by Mr Squires.

The meeting closed with the district manager quietly insisting that a change of attitude was called for from Mrs Cox, who should communicate more frequently and in a more cooperative way with Mr Squires in the future; she should also introduce a more effective system of supervision to cover weekend work.

3.2 Additional public bar and main cellar stocktake by external auditors

Within three weeks of the previous stocktake a further audit was carried out by the same two representatives. The surprise element of the check was lost when the firm telephoned the public bar manager on the day before to enquire if an afternoon visit would be acceptable. The stocktake was completed in under two hours and the senior auditor advised Mr Squires that no significant discrepancy had been discovered. Mr Squires enquired how it was possible to carry out a detailed audit of this proportion in such a short time and draw such conclusions, but his question was received in embarrassed silence.

He later communicated his dissatisfaction to the district manager at Head Office, but was informed that the additional audit had been accepted by the board and the complaints against Mr Welsh would be dropped and the matter closed. By persisting, Mr Squires did receive a begrudging acceptance from the outside firm of stocktakers that he or his assistant should be present at all audits in the future.

3.3 Complaints from the catering adviser

During the months that followed the catering adviser, who had previously been satisfied with the improvements that Mr Squires had introduced, began complaining about unacceptable profit margins on the food sales at the motel.

Normal procedure was for the catering adviser to call once a month for a meeting with Mr Squires, but he suddenly began appearing every week at unconventional hours. An unpleasant situation occurred when he arrived at the motel at 7 o'clock one Saturday evening and remonstrated with Mr Squires because he was not on duty. The explanation that Mr Squires had only shortly left the motel for a rest after officiating at a large wedding reception all afternoon, leaving his assistant on duty, was not accepted. Mr Cox insisted that as Saturday evenings were extremely busy he should have been there personally to see that everything was progressing satisfactorily.

He also broadened his criticism of Mr Squires for complaining to Head Office about the newly introduced 'Country Style' menu, before this experiment had been given a fair chance to prove itself. Mr Squires denied this allegation by pointing out that in the past Hazel Wood Court had ▷

enjoyed a very good reputation for its à la carte menu. He had tried to enhance this reputation during his time as the manager. The 'Country Style' menu experiment, which entailed prepacked frozen foods being despatched from London for re-processing and serving to the motel's clientele, had not been successful. The meals were reasonably priced, but the choice was extremely limited and every regular customer had complained about this change in policy. All Mr Squires had done was to pass these complaints on to the district manager in the usual way. The catering adviser again refused to accept this explanation and left the motel in an angry mood.

3.4 The restaurant manager's response

Relations between the restaurant manager and the general manager deteriorated thereafter and Mr Squires formed the opinion that Mr Welsh took every opportunity to 'fan the flames' of the growing conflict between the motel manager and the catering adviser.

Matters came to a head between Christmas and the New Year when the motel advertised a Christmas luncheon at a fixed charge, to which Mr Welsh added a 10 per cent service charge while Mr Squires was indisposed with flu. This caused numerous complaints and Mr Squires had to rise from his sick bed to calm the situation and authorise the necessary refunds.

During the following week when Mr Squires had recovered and was entertaining some prominent members of the local business community to dinner, a *flambé* dish was ordered by several guests, but this was presented so far below the accepted standard by the restaurant manager that Mr Squires' party suffered considerable embarrassment.

3.5 Mr Squires decides to resign

Mr Squires informed his wife soon afterwards that he had decided to seek another position. His wife was relieved as she had never settled in the limited accommodation provided, and she was of the opinion that a flat above a public bar was no place to raise a teenage daughter.

Quite fortunately, Mr Squires met an old army colleague at a hotel and catering exhibition in London a few weeks later, who was now employed as chief catering officer for a large county council in the Midlands. A vacancy as catering consultant had arisen at the county's largest teacher training college, and Mr Squires was urged to apply.

Mr Squires' application and interviews were successful and he was offered the appointment, subject to a satisfactory medical which took another two months to arrange.

Although Mr Squires was in sound health, he decided not to hand in his notice until after the medical. Somehow word of this intended move leaked out, and about 10 days later he was surprised by an unexpected visit from the district manager, who mentioned that word had been received that Mr Squires wished to leave, and a decision had been taken by the managing director that he should depart in four weeks' time. Mr Squires responded by pointing out that he was entitled to four weeks' holiday by the company which he would take and leave at the end of that week. He left with a letter from the district manager confirming that he had been given four weeks' notice 'because of staff re-organisation'.

The following week Mr Squires signed on as unemployed and received benefit for three weeks before this was stopped by the Department of Employment because his former employers had stated that he had resigned from his position. Mr Squires produced the letter stating that he had been asked to leave and was able to obtain unemployment benefit for a further five weeks until he could take up his new appointment.

Postscript

Mr Squires is still employed in a catering consultancy role by a Higher Education Institution in the Midlands and he has since taken on more responsibility.

Hazel Wood Court continued

He was replaced at Hazel Wood Court by a young graduate who, before taking up his appointment, telephoned Mr Squires at home to ask his advice about running the motel. As a consequence the new manager insisted that the head housekeeper should be transferred or dismissed before he would accept the appointment, and that he would also be given a free hand to make any decision he felt was necessary regarding the running of the restaurant and public bar. These requests were granted.

The head housekeeper decided to resign to concentrate more on her home life, during the week before the new manager arrived, and the restaurant manager took an early retirement a few months later. Shortly after these changes, the parent company were taken over by an international organisation and both the district manager and the catering adviser left the company.

Source: McEwan T and Mullins L J, *Horae*, Portsmouth Business School,
Hotel and Catering Research Unit Review vol. 1, no. 1, Summer 1989, pp. 3–13.

TASKS

(i) **Identify clearly the main issues of organisation and management raised in this case study.**

(ii) **Suggest how the situation at Hazel Wood Court could be improved.**

Notes and references

1. See, for example, Boella M J, *Human Resource Management in the Hospitality Industry*, 6th edn, Stanley Thornes (1996).
2. Drucker P F, *The Practice of Management*, Pan Books (1968), p. 273.
3. Child J, *Organisation: A Guide to Problems and Practice*, 2nd edn, Harper & Row (1984).
4. Schaffer J D, 'Structure and Strategy: Two Sides of Success', in Rutherford D G (ed.), *Hotel Management and Operations*, Van Nostrand Reinhold (1990).
5. Gullen H V and Rhodes G E, *Management in the Hotel and Catering Industry*, Batsford (1983).
6. Keiser J R, *Principles and Practices of Management in the Hospitality Industry*, 2nd edn, Van Nostrand Reinhold (1989).
7. For a detailed account, see Mullins L J, *Management and Organisational Behaviour*, 5th edn, Financial Times Pitman Publishing (1999).
8. Urwick L, *The Elements of Administration*, 2nd edn, Pitman (1974).
9. Brech E F L, *Organisation: The Framework of Management*, 2nd edn, Longman (1965).
10. Woodward J, *Industrial Organization: Theory and Practice*, 2nd edn, Oxford University Press (1980).
11. See, for example: 'Managing in the 21st Century', *Manager, The Institute of Administrative Management*, January/Februay 2000, pp. 8–10.
12. Simon H A, *Administrative Behavior*, 3rd edn, Free Press (1976), p. xxii.
13. Taylor F W, *Scientific Management*, Harper & Row (1947).
14. See, for example, Gospel H F and Littler C R (eds), *Managerial Strategies and Industrial Relations*, Heinemann (1983).
15. For an interesting debate on de-skilling and work flexibility, see Wood R C, *Working in Hotels and Catering*, 2nd edn, International Thomson Business Press (1997).
16. Weber M, *The Theory of Social and Economic Organization*, Collier Macmillan (1964).

17. Stewart R, *The Reality of Management*, 2nd edn, Pan Books (1986).
18. Argyris C, *Integrating the Individual and the Organization*, Wiley (1964).
19. Lockwood A and Jones P, *People and the Hotel and Catering Industry*, Holt, Rhinehart & Winston (1984), p. 173.
20. Shamir B, 'Between Bureaucracy and Hospitality: Some Organisational Characteristics of Hotels', *Journal of Management Studies*, vol. 15, no. 3, October 1978, pp. 285–307.
21. See, for example, Fletcher W, 'Good Listener, Better Manager', *Management Today*, January 2000, p. 30.
22. See, for example, Rose M, *Industrial Behaviour*, 2nd edn, Penguin (1988).
23. Nailon P, 'A Theory of Organisation in the Catering Industry', *HCIMA Journal*, vol. 61, 1977, p. 7.
24. Torrington D, Weightman J and Johns K, *Effective Management: People and Organisation*, Prentice-Hall (1989).
25. See, for example, Etzioni A, *Modern Organizations*, Prentice-Hall (1964).
26. See, for example, Luthans F, *Organizational Behavior*, 5th edn, McGraw-Hill (1989).
27. Woodward J, *Industrial Organization: Theory and Practice*, 2nd edn, Oxford University Press (1980).
28. Burns T and Stalker G M, The *Management of Innovation*, Tavistock (1966).
29. Lawrence P R and Lorsch J W, *Organization and Environment*, Irwin (1969).
30. See, for example, Child J, *Organization: A Guide to Problems and Practice*, 2nd edn, Harper & Row (1984).
31. Shamir B, 'Between Bureaucracy and Hospitality: Some Organizational Characteristics of Hotels', *Journal of Management Studies*, vol. 15, no. 3, October 1978, pp. 285–307.
32. Nailon P, 'A Theory of Organisation in the Catering Industry', *HCIMA Journal*, vol. 61, 1977, p. 9.
33. Bowey A M, *The Sociology of Organisations*, Hodder & Stoughton (1976).
34. Handy C B, The *Age of Unreason*, Business Books (1989).
35. Meyer M W, *Theory of Organizational Structure*, Bobbs–Merrill (1977), p. 44.
36. Forte, Charles (Lord), *Forte: The Autobiography of Charles Forte*, Sidgwick & Jackson (1986), p. 122.
37. Schaffer J D, 'Structure and Strategy: Two Sides of Success', in Rutherford D G (ed.), *Hotel Management and Operations*, Van Nostrand Reinhold (1990).
38. Woodward J, *Industrial Organization: Theory and Practice*, 2nd edn, Oxford University Press (1980).
39. Medlik S, *The Business of Hotels*, 2nd edn, Heinemann (1989), p. 74.
40. See, for example, Goss-Turner S, 'Human Resource Management', in Jones P and Pizam A (eds), *The International Hospitality Industry: Organizational and Operational Issues*, Pitman (1993), pp. 152–164.
41. Graicunas V A, 'Relationships in Organisation', in *Papers on the Science of Administration*, University of Columbia (1937).
42. Venison P, *Managing Hotels*, Heinemann (1983), p. 33.
43. For an example, see Medlik S, *The Business of Hotels*, 3rd edn, Butterworth-Heinemann (1994), p. 81.
44. Chacko H E, 'Designing a Seamless Hotel Organization', *International Jorurnal of Contemporary Hospitality Management*, vol, 10, no. 4, 1998, pp. 133–138.
45. For a detailed account of the informal organisation, see: Gray J L and Starke F A, *Organizational Behavior: Concepts and Applications*, 4th edn, Charles E Merrill (1988).
46. Stewart R, *The Reality of Management*, 2nd edn, Pan Books (1986), p. 127.

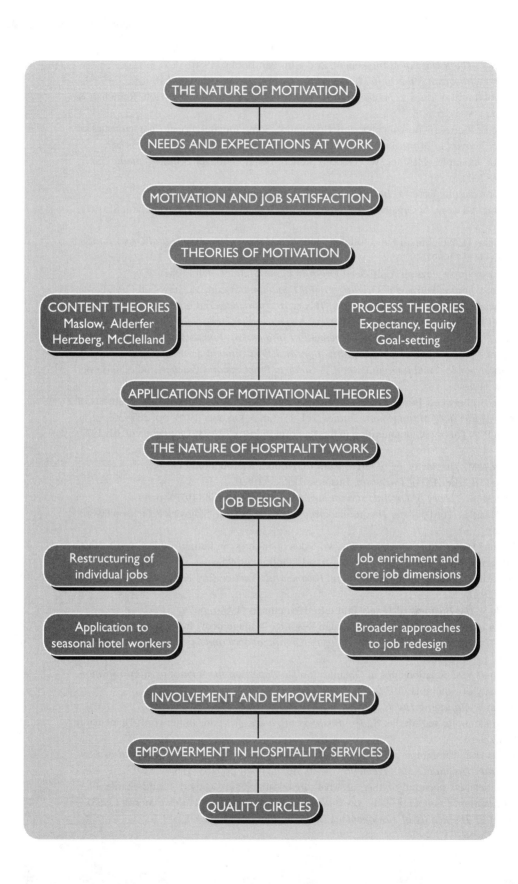

THE NATURE OF MOTIVATION

NEEDS AND EXPECTATIONS AT WORK

MOTIVATION AND JOB SATISFACTION

THEORIES OF MOTIVATION

CONTENT THEORIES
Maslow, Alderfer
Herzberg, McClelland

PROCESS THEORIES
Expectancy, Equity
Goal-setting

APPLICATIONS OF MOTIVATIONAL THEORIES

THE NATURE OF HOSPITALITY WORK

JOB DESIGN

Restructuring of
individual jobs

Job enrichment and
core job dimensions

Application to
seasonal hotel workers

Broader approaches
to job redesign

INVOLVEMENT AND EMPOWERMENT

EMPOWERMENT IN HOSPITALITY SERVICES

QUALITY CIRCLES

Chapter seven

Motivation, job satisfaction and performance

Introduction

The nature of the people–organisation relationship is influenced by what motivates staff to work and the satisfaction they derive from it. Managers achieve results through the efforts and performance of other people. The ability to motivate staff to work willingly and effectively is an essential ingredient of successful management.

The nature of motivation

The effective management of people is influenced by the attitudes which are brought to bear on relationships with staff and to the problems which affect them. Attention should be given to the feelings of staff and to appropriate systems of motivation, job satisfaction and rewards. This is clearly important in any work organisation but especially so in labour-intensive service organisations such as those in the hospitality industry.[1] As Riley, for example, suggests, 'Hotel and catering management has a real investment in motivation because most of its jobs require input where effort and personal character actually matter.'[2]

The study of motivation is concerned with why people behave in a certain way, and with what determines the direction and persistence of their actions. Levels of work performance are determined not only by the ability of staff but also by the strength of their motivation. If staff are to perform to the best of their abilities, attention must also be given to the nature of work motivation and job satisfaction.

The underlying concept of motivation is a driving force within individuals by which they attempt to achieve some goal in order to satisfy a need or expectation. This gives rise to the basic motivational model, illustrated in Figure 7.1.

The opportunity to perform

If the manager is to improve the work of the organisation, attention must be given to the level of motivation of its members. The manager must encourage staff to direct their efforts (their driving force) towards the successful attainment of the goals and objectives of the organisation.

Figure 7.1: The basic motivational model

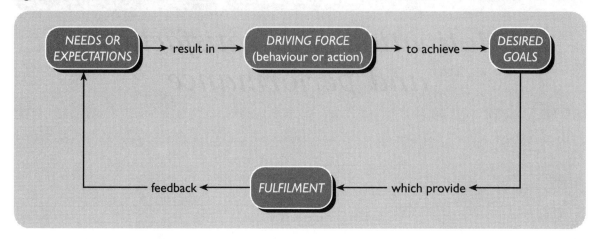

Performance is a function of both ability level and the motivation to use ability.[3]

Performance = function (**ability** × **motivation** to use ability)

You cannot motivate someone to do something that they do not have the ability to do. This emphasises the importance of training to motivation (see Chapter 10).

The desire to perform well must be encouraged and supported by the opportunity for staff to perform and to realise their full potential. People should be able to experience a sense of achievement and personal growth in a purposeful and meaningful job. Staff are then more likely to feel motivated to perform to the best of their abilities. Motivation is derived from the fulfilment of an individual's needs and expectations.[4]

Needs and expectations at work

People's behaviour and actions are directed towards the satisfaction of certain needs and expectations which form the basis of their motivational driving force. Motivation is a complex subject, it is a very personal thing, it is multifaceted and influenced by many variables. For example, Green suggests over 30 ideas worthy of consideration by managers to positively influence members of their staff.[5]

Individuals have a variety of changing, and often conflicting, needs and expectations at work which they seek to satisfy in a number of different ways. These various needs and expectations can be categorised in various ways. One basic form of categorisation is into the simple division of extrinsic and intrinsic motivation.

- ● *Extrinsic motivation* – relates to 'tangible' rewards such as pay and fringe benefits, subsidised accommodation or meals, job security, promotion, contract of service, the work environment and conditions of work.

- ● *Intrinsic motivation* – relates to 'psychological' rewards and internal feelings such as a sense of personal satisfaction from the job, the opportunity for challenge and achievement, receiving appreciation, positive recognition, and being treated in a caring and considerate manner.

A broad, three-fold framework

Because of the diverse and complex nature of motivation it is helpful to have some initial framework of analysis. The following broad, three-fold framework provides a convenient starting point as a focus on work motivation and job satisfaction.

- *Economic rewards* – such as pay, perks and fringe benefits, material goods, job security and pension rights. The provision of live-in accommodation and meals at work could also be included under this heading.
- *Intrinsic satisfaction* – which is derived from the nature of the work itself and includes an interesting and challenging job, variety, a sense of involvement and achievement, and scope for personal development.
- *Social relationships* – such as the nature of the work environment, comradeship, friendship, group membership, the desire for affiliation, and a feeling of status, support or belonging.

Comparative importance

Motivation, job satisfaction and work performance will be determined by the comparative importance of these sets of needs and expectations, and the extent to which they are fulfilled (Figure 7.2).

Economic rewards are clearly a motivating factor to a greater or lesser extent for all staff. But given the generally low levels of pay for the majority of staff within the hospitality industry, other motivating influences would seem to be of particular significance. But see the discussion on pay as a motivator later in this chapter.

Intrinsic satisfaction will vary from job to job and often between different parts of the same job. Most of us would probably perceive a distinction between the intrinsic satisfaction of the head chef compared with a kitchen porter, or between that of serving in the bar compared with cleaning or porterage. It is difficult to generalise, however. Intrinsic

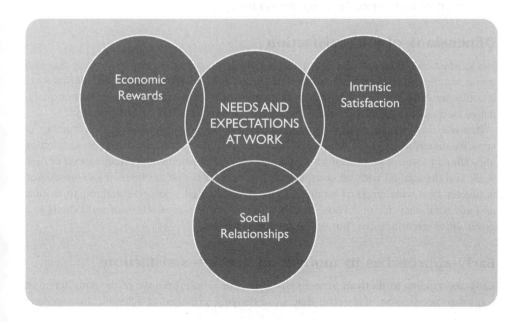

Figure 7.2:
Needs and expectations of people at work

satisfaction is a personal attitude which varies according to the individual and according to particular circumstances.

Social relationships would appear to be an important feature for many staff. The characteristics of the hospitality industry as a service industry, the role of people, interactions with others, and the importance of good teamwork and supportive working relationships can be strong motivators at work.

Combination and balance

Motivation at work is a very personal thing. Each individual will seek to achieve the desired combination and balance of economic rewards, intrinsic satisfaction and social relationships. For some hospitality workers the potential for tips, and subsidised live-in accommodation and meals may be important considerations. For others, a low level of pay, although obviously not welcomed, may be accepted because of the strong motivating influence of an interesting job and rewarding social relationships. The comparative importance of the three sets of needs and expectations are liable to change according to the particular situation in which individuals find themselves.

The motivation to work is also influenced by the 'psychological contract' (discussed in Chapter 3). Although not defined formally, the psychological contract implies a series of mutual expectations and satisfaction of needs between the individual and the organisation. It covers a range of rights, privileges, behaviours, duties and obligations which have an important influence on the behaviour and actions of people at work.

Motivation and job satisfaction

The motivation to work well is usually related to job satisfaction. But the nature of this relationship is not clear. Satisfaction with the job may motivate a person to achieve a high level of performance. The content theories of motivation, in particular, are related more to satisfaction. For example, Herzberg's two-factor theory (discussed below) is essentially a theory of job satisfaction. However, although the level of job satisfaction may well affect the strength of motivation, this is not always the case.

Dimensions of job satisfaction

Job satisfaction is a complex concept and not always easy to measure objectively. Satisfaction is not the same as motivation. Job satisfaction is more of an attitude, an internal state. It could, for example, be associated with a personal feeling of achievement, either quantitative or qualitative. Motivation is a process which may lead to job satisfaction.

It is not clear whether job satisfaction consists of a single dimension or a number of separate dimensions. There does appear to be a positive correlation between satisfaction and different areas of work. But some workers may be satisfied with certain aspects of their work and dissatisfied with other aspects.[6] What is clear is that the level of job satisfaction is affected by a wide range of variables related to individual, social, cultural, organisational and environmental factors. These factors all influence job satisfaction of individuals in a given set of circumstances, but not necessarily in others.

Early approaches to motivation and job satisfaction

Early approaches to motivation were based on the simple premise of the satisfaction of economic needs. You may recall that an underlying principle of scientific management (discussed in Chapter 6) was a belief in the rational-economic concept of motivation. Workers would be motivated primarily by the satisfaction of the highest possible wages. Emphasis was placed on the content of a 'fair day's work' and on optimising the level of workers' productivity. However, the definition of a fair day's work is very subjective and, if individuals work hard to increase their earnings, management might redefine the target for a fair day's work.

A range of different needs

The findings of the Hawthorne experiments and the human relations writers demonstrated that people are motivated to work in order to satisfy a range of different, complex needs; not simply monetary reward. Emphasis was given to the importance of the satisfaction of the psychological and social needs of individuals; group values and norms; and styles of leadership. This in turn gave rise to the work of the neo-human relations writers and to theories of motivation based on the personal adjustment of the individual, and the content and meaning of work.

Theories of motivation

Unfortunately there is no single or simple answer to the question of what motivates people to work well. Motivation is by its nature a complex subject and is influenced by a wide range of individual, social, cultural and situational variables. Motivation also varies over time and according to circumstances. It is often most acute for people at a mid-career position and especially for those who find opportunities for further advancement or promotion are limited.[7]

The complex and variable nature of work motivation has given rise to many competing ideas and theories. *But these theories are not conclusive.* They are all subject to criticism or alternative findings. It is always easy to quote an example which appears to contradict any generalised observation on what motivates people to work well (Figure 7.3).

These theories, however, help to highlight the many motives which influence people's behaviour and performance. Collectively, the different theories provide a framework within which the manager can direct attention to the problem of how best to motivate staff to work willingly and effectively. Anything which aids an understanding of how best to motivate staff must be useful.

> *All managers have a duty to motivate their teams. Motivated people take more pride in their jobs and work better. But many managers don't know how to motivate their staff.*[8]

Motivation in the service sector

Willman refers to the particular difficulties of motivating non-career staff in the service sector. These staff are often female, part-time non-graduates, who work in important customer-contact roles, but who infrequently move up into managerial ranks.

> *Their attachment to the organisation is fleeting, their pay often low, their job content often routine. However, the problem for service businesses is that, frequently, they are all the customer sees. They define the quality of service the organisation can offer. This matters more in businesses where the service itself is the product, than where poor service may be offset by good products . . . The*

Figure 7.3:
Framework for
the study of
motivation at
work

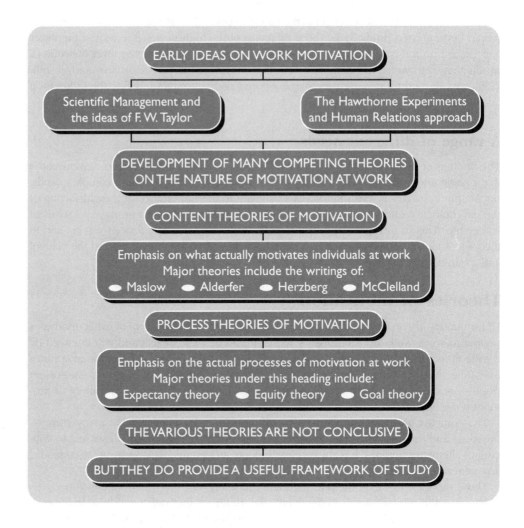

motivation, skills and knowledge of these staff is a key issue for the quality of service offered by an organisation.[9]

Managers can learn from the different theories and approaches to motivation. If a hospitality manager can identify different motivating factors within staff, this is likely to lead to improved attitudes to work, lower turnover and improved customer relations. The manager can judge the relevance of the different theories, how best to draw upon them and how they might successfully be applied in particular work situations. This is part of being an effective manager.

Content and process theories of motivation

Theories of motivation can be divided into two broad approaches – content theories and process theories. Content theories place emphasis on *what motivates* and attempt to explain those specific things which actually motivate the individual at work. These theories are concerned with identification of people's needs and their relative strengths, and the goals they pursue in order to satisfy these needs. Major content theories include:

- Maslow's hierarchy of needs model;
- Alderfer's continuum of needs model (ERG theory);
- Herzberg's two-factor theory; and
- McClelland's theory of achievement motivation.

Process theories place emphasis on the actual *process of motivation* and attempt to identify the relationships among the dynamic variables which make up motivation. These theories are discussed later in this chapter.

Maslow's hierarchy of needs

Maslow's theory of individual development and motivation, originally published in 1943, provides a useful starting point.[10] The basic proposition of Maslow's work is that people are wanting beings; they always desire more, and what they want depends on what they already have. He suggests that human needs are arranged in a series of levels – a hierarchy of importance. At the lowest level are physiological needs, then safety needs, love (or social) needs, esteem needs – to, at the highest level, the need for self-actualisation (Figure 7.4).

The basic premise of Maslow's theory is that once a lower-level need has been satisfied it no longer acts as a strong motivator. The needs of the next highest level in the hierarchy

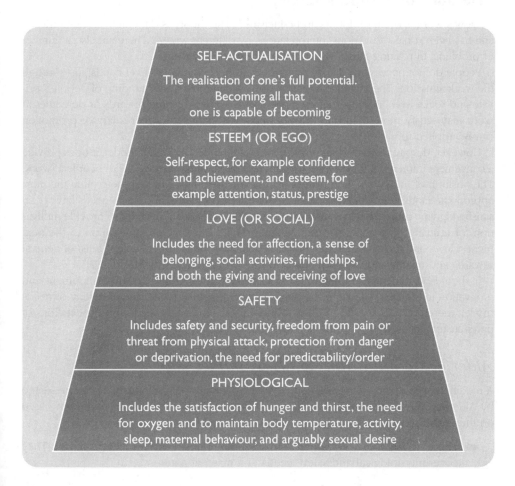

Figure 7.4: Maslow's hierarchy of human needs model

demand satisfaction and become the primary motivating influence. Only the unsatisfied needs motivate a person. Thus Maslow asserts that: '*a satisfied need is no longer a motivator*'.

It is important to note, however, that Maslow points out that a particular need at one level does not necessarily have to be satisfied fully before a subsequent need arises. There is a gradual emergence of a higher-level need as lower-level needs become 'largely' satisfied.

Not necessarily a fixed order

The hierarchy is not necessarily a fixed order and for some people there will be more dominant needs and a reversal of the hierarchy. To some people, for example, self-esteem may seem to be more important than love or social needs. For some innately creative people the desire to satisfy esteem needs or self-actualisation may be the prime motivating influence. This might be true for some chefs, for example.

A (then) HCITB report highlights the image of the job of the chef as very definitely seen as important, skilled and responsible. It is a challenging rather than an easy job. Although it is seen as secure, a number would prefer a more adventurous job rather than security. The most satisfying aspects of its image are that the job is seen as well respected and offering good opportunities for promotion.[11]

Relevance of Maslow's theory

Maslow's work is open to doubts and criticisms.[12] The theory is difficult to test empirically and has been subject to various interpretations by different writers. There are also a number of problems in relating Maslow's theory to the work situation.

People do not necessarily satisfy their needs, especially higher-level needs, just through the work situation. The manager would require a complete understanding of people's private and social lives, not just their behaviour at work. Also, some rewards or outcomes at work may satisfy more than one level of need. For example, higher salary or promotion can be applied to all levels of the hierarchy.[13]

However, despite the rather simplistic nature of the need hierarchy model, it does provide a convenient framework for viewing the different needs and expectations of people at work. The position of individual members of staff in the hierarchy will help determine the most appropriate motivators. For example, if a person's physiological and safety needs have been satisfied, giving more of the same does not provide motivation. In order to provide motivation for a change in behaviour, the manager would need to direct attention to the next highest level and the satisfaction of social needs. Steers and Porter suggest a list of general rewards and organisational factors used to satisfy different needs[14] (Figure 7.5).

It should be remembered that Maslow's theory relates to individual development and motivation in life and not just to the behaviour of people at work. The hierarchy of needs model, therefore, can also be applied to the satisfaction of the needs and expectations of hotel customers as well as to members of staff.[15]

Alderfer's continuum of needs model

A modified need hierarchy model, applied to the organisational setting, has been presented by Alderfer. This model condenses Maslow's five levels of need into a continuum based on three core sets of needs: existence, relatedness and growth (ERG theory).[16]

- ● *Existence needs* are concerned with sustaining human existence and survival. They cover physiological and safety needs of a material nature.

Needs levels	General rewards	Organisational factors
1 Physiological	Food, water, sex, sleep	a Pay b Pleasant working conditions c Cafeteria
2 Safety	Safety, security, stability, protection	a Safe working conditions b Company benefits c Job security
3 Social	Love, affection, belongingness	a Cohesive work group b Friendly supervision c Professional associations
4 Esteem	Self-esteem, self-respect, prestige, status	a Social recognition b Job title c High status job d Feedback from the job itself
5 Self-actualisation	Growth, advancement, creativity	a Challenging job b Opportunities for creativity c Achievement in work d Advancement in the organisation

Figure 7.5: Applying Maslow's need hierarchy

(*Source:* Reproduced with permission from Steers R M and Porter L W, *Motivation and Work Behavior,* 5th edn, McGraw-Hill (1991), p. 35.)

- *Relatedness needs* are concerned with relationships to the social environment. They cover love or belonging, affiliation and meaningful interpersonal relationships of a safety or esteem nature.

- *Growth needs* are concerned with the development of potential. They cover self-esteem and self-actualisation.

A continuum of needs

Alderfer suggests that although individuals normally progress through the different levels of needs, they are more of a continuum than a hierarchy. ERG theory states that an individual may be motivated to satisfy more than one basic set of needs. Individuals may also move down to a lower level need. For example, if an individual is continually frustrated in attempting to satisfy growth needs, then relatedness needs may reassume importance as a motivating influence and become the main focus of the individual's efforts.

The results of Alderfer's work support the idea that lower-level needs decrease in strength as they become satisfied. However, lower-level needs do not have to be satisfied before a higher-level need emerges. The order of the sets of needs and their relative importance varies from individual to individual. Some people will be motivated by a strong desire to satisfy their existence needs, while others will have a high desire for satisfaction of relatedness and/or growth needs.

Flexible strategies of motivation

ERG theory appears to provide for a practical and more flexible approach to motivation. One set of needs does not operate to the exclusion of others. Therefore, if a person's needs at a particular level are blocked, then the manager should focus attention on the satisfaction of other sets of needs. Alternative strategies of motivation may be more appropriate for different departments and for different types of staff. For example, if waiters feel their growth needs are blocked through lack of opportunity for personal development, the manager should attempt to provide increased opportunities to satisfy existence and relatedness needs.

Herzberg's two-factor theory

Herzberg's two-factor theory is essentially a theory of job satisfaction related to motivation at work.[17] The original study consisted of interviews with 203 accountants and engineers in America. They were asked to relate: (i) times when they felt exceptionally 'good' about their present job or a previous job, and (ii) times when they felt exceptionally 'bad' about their job.

From the responses to the interviews Herzberg revealed two distinct sets of factors affecting motivation and work: the two-factor theory of motivation and job satisfaction, or the motivation-hygiene theory (Figure 7.6).

Figure 7.6:
Representation of Herzberg's two-factor theory

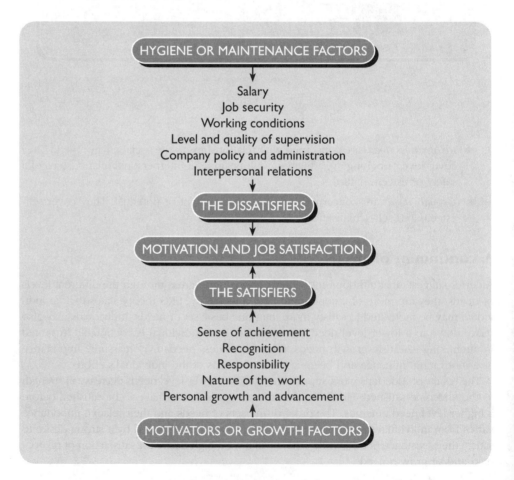

HYGIENE OR MAINTENANCE FACTORS

Salary
Job security
Working conditions
Level and quality of supervision
Company policy and administration
Interpersonal relations

THE DISSATISFIERS

MOTIVATION AND JOB SATISFACTION

THE SATISFIERS

Sense of achievement
Recognition
Responsibility
Nature of the work
Personal growth and advancement

MOTIVATORS OR GROWTH FACTORS

Hygiene factors or dissatisfiers

One set of factors, known as the 'hygiene' (indicating preventative and environmental) or 'maintenance' factors, serve to prevent dissatisfaction. These factors are related to job context and include salary, job security, working conditions, level and quality of supervision, company policy and administration, and interpersonal relations. The hygiene factors are concerned with how people are treated at work.

If the hygiene factors are absent or inadequate they cause dissatisfaction. Proper attention to the hygiene factors will tend to overcome dissatisfaction and bring motivation back to normal – a zero – state. But the hygiene factors do not by themselves create a positive attitude or increase the motivation to work. Accordingly, *the opposite of dissatisfaction is not satisfaction but rather no dissatisfaction.*

Motivating factors or satisfiers

To motivate workers to give of their best and to sustain higher levels of performance, the manager must give attention to a second set of factors – the 'motivators' or 'growth' factors. These factors are related to job content and include a sense of achievement, recognition, responsibility, the nature of the work itself, and personal growth and advancement. The motivating factors are concerned with what people are able to do at work. The strength of the motivators will affect feelings of satisfaction or no satisfaction, but not dissatisfaction.

Herzberg emphasises that both sets of factors are important, but for different reasons. Hygiene factors are not a 'second-class citizen system'. They are as important as the motivators and necessary to avoid unpleasantness at work, and to deny unfair treatment by management. The motivating factors relate to what people are allowed to do at work. They are the variables which actually motivate people.

Applications to guest satisfaction

In addition to its normal application to employee motivation, Herzberg's theory and the importance of hygiene and motivating factors can also be applied to the area of guest satisfaction.[18]

Criticisms and limitations

The two-factor theory is a source of frequent debate and controversy. It is also subject to a number of different interpretations. One general criticism relates to methodology. Describing events which gave rise to good or bad feelings is subjective and likely to influence the results. People are more inclined to attribute satisfying incidents at work, the motivators, as a favourable reflection on their own performance. The dissatisfying incidents are more likely to be attributed to external factors and to other people.

Another general, major area of criticism is the simplistic nature of the theory and the lack of allowance for individual differences. Not all workers are greatly interested in the job content of their work, or with motivators or growth factors. (See the discussion on motivating hourly workers later in this chapter.) Some staff appear content to adopt an 'instrumental' view – that is, work as a means to an end (discussed in Chapter 3). They are motivated almost solely by financial rewards and security rather than by the nature of the work or the satisfaction of social needs.[19] Other staff appear happy to work within a tightly structured framework, with closely defined work tasks and limited autonomy or responsibility.

Continuing relevance of the theory

Despite these criticisms there is still evidence of support for the continuing relevance of Herzberg's theory. For example, although based on a small sample of engineers within a single company in Canada, Phillipchuk concludes that Herzberg's methods still yield useful results. Respondents did not offer any new event factors from the original study although some old factors were absent. Salary and working conditions did not appear at all, and advancement as a satisfier did not appear. The top demotivator was company policy and the top motivator was achievement.[20]

Applications to hospitality staff

It is often claimed that the theory has only limited application to 'manual' workers, or to people with unskilled jobs or whose work is limited in scope. Yet these are the people who often present management with the biggest problem of motivation. For example, in considering the application of Herzberg's work to hospitality staff, MacQueen comments:

> The trouble with Herzberg's motivation-hygiene theory of motivation is that it applies least to the people management most want to motivate – those with monotonous, repetitive, uninteresting jobs.[21]

Hygiene factors are more likely to be significant in the hospitality industry than in other industries. Workers who live in or take meals when on duty are more likely to be concerned with the workplace and the quality of their working conditions. It might also be that some workers have a low expectation of satisfying higher-level needs and therefore place greater emphasis on the hygiene factors.

This view would seem to be supported from a study by Chitiris on the application of Herzberg's theory to workers in the Greek hotel industry. From the results of questionnaire interviews on levels of job satisfaction and the importance of certain job factors, Chitiris found that in general workers were more interested in the hygiene factors than in the motivators.[22]

The importance of job design

Despite doubts concerning the two-factor theory, Herzberg's work has drawn attention to wider issues which may influence motivation and job satisfaction. If managers are to provide positive motivation and improve job satisfaction, then attention must be given to both the hygiene and the motivating factors.

A particular feature of Herzberg's theory is that it drew attention to the importance of job design and the structuring of hospitality jobs. This point is acknowledged by MacQueen.

> The value of Herzberg's approach lies in its emphasis on the need for the re-design of jobs in order to bring the motivators to bear.[23]

We return to the importance of job design later in this chapter.

McClelland's achievement motivation

The need for achievement underlies the higher levels of Maslow's hierarchy and is also one of Herzberg's motivating factors. The importance of achievement is emphasised by McClelland, who has developed a theory of motivation which is rooted in culture.[24] The work of McClelland is based on the concept of four main sets of needs and socially developed motives:

- the need for **affiliation**;
- the need for **power**;
- the need for **achievement**;
- the need for **avoidance**.

People possess all four needs but the relative intensity of these motives varies among individuals and different occupations. Although all four needs are important, McClelland's research had concentrated mainly on how managers can develop the need for achievement in subordinate staff.

Variations among individuals

The extent of achievement motivation varies among individuals. It is dependent upon cultural influences, occupational experiences and the type of organisation in which they work. Some people rate very highly in achievement motivation. They are challenged by opportunities and work hard to achieve a goal. Other people rate very low in achievement motivation. They do not care much and have little urge to achieve.

Characteristics of high achievers

For high achievers money may seem to be important, but it is valued more as symbolising successful goal achievement. Money may serve as a means of giving feedback on performance. People with high achievement motivation seem unlikely to remain long with an organisation that does not pay them well for good performance. For people with low achievement motivation, money may serve more as a direct financial incentive for performance.

Although it is difficult to apply objective measures, McClelland has identified four common characteristics of people with high achievement needs: the preference for personal responsibility, the setting of moderate goals, the desire for specific feedback and innovativeness.

- Personal satisfaction is derived from the accomplishment of the task itself and recognition need not come from other people. They prefer situations in which they can assume *personal responsibility* for solving problems. They like to attain success through their own efforts, rather than by teamwork or by chance factors outside their control.
- They tend to set *moderate achievement goals* with an intermediate level of difficulty, and to take calculated risks. If a task is too difficult or too risky it would reduce the chances of success and of gaining need satisfaction. If the course of action is too easy or too simple, there is little challenge in accomplishing the task and little satisfaction from successful performance,
- They want *clear and unambiguous feedback* on how well they are performing. A knowledge of results within a reasonable time is necessary for self-evaluation. Feedback enables them to determine success or failure in the accomplishment of their goals, and satisfaction from their activities.

- They are *more innovative* and tend always to be moving on to something a little more challenging. There is a constant search for variety and for information to find new ways of doing things.

Development of achievement drive

McClelland has attempted to understand the characteristics of high achievers. He suggests that n-Ach (need for achievement) is not hereditary but results from environmental influences. McClelland has investigated the possibility of training people to develop a greater motivation to achieve and suggests four steps in attempting to develop achievement drive:

- Striving to attain feedback on performance. Reinforcement of success serves to strengthen the desire to achieve higher performance.
- Developing models of achievement by seeking to emulate people who have performed well.
- Attempting to modify their self-image and to see themselves as needing challenges and success.
- Controlling day-dreaming and thinking about themselves in more positive terms.[25]

Applications to the hospitality industry

There are, of course, potential benefits to any business organisation from the efforts and performance of high achievers. But McClelland's theory implies an individualistic approach to the motivation of staff. The hospitality industry, however, is characterised by the need for close cooperation and effective teamwork in order to provide customer satisfaction. The behaviour and performance of work groups is as important as individual motivation. Attempts to satisfy the needs of higher achievers must be matched with the requirements of the industry and this may not be an easy task.

Pay and motivating hourly workers

The content theories of motivation place emphasis on the importance of psychological rewards, and personal growth and achievement. According to Weaver, however, such theories have little meaning for hourly workers in the hotel and restaurant industry.[26] The work of, for example, cooks, dishwashers and waiting or housekeeping staff does not change much among different companies, so such staff feel little attachment to a particular company. Where there is little pleasure in the work itself or the job offers little opportunity for career advancement, personal challenge or growth, hourly workers are working for their pay cheque.

Motivating with money

Weaver proposes a 'Theory M' programme of motivation based on direct cash rewards for above-average productivity. A percentage base is calculated from the average performance of workers on the staff. Workers then receive a percentage of any *increase* in sales or savings to the company generated by their efforts. Although particularly suited to food and beverage operations, Weaver suggests that the programme could be extended to other hotel employees, for example a bonus payment to night-desk staff for selling as many vacant rooms as possible or a wage incentive to housekeeping staff for cleaning an above-average number of rooms in a shift.

Note, however, that on a more general level, a recent survey of human resource managers responding to *Personnel Journal* found that it is often difficult to attract, retain and motivate minimum wage workers on pay alone. The survey uncovered that 62 per cent of respondents had a problem retaining minimum wage workers strictly because of pay. Many employers must provide other incentives, such as bonuses or prizes, on top of pay to keep workers on the job.[27] (Note, also, the study by Simons and Enz on what hotel employees want from work jobs, later in this chapter.)

Process theories of motivation

Process theories attempt to identify relationships among the dynamic variables which make up motivation. They provide a further contribution to our understanding of behaviour and performance at work, and the complex nature of motivation. Process theories are concerned with how behaviour is initiated, directed and sustained. There are a number of different process theories but major approaches under this heading include:

● Expectancy theory
● Equity theory
● Goal theory

The basis of expectancy theory

Expectancy theory provides a dominant framework in which to view motivation at work. The basis of expectancy theory is that people are influenced by the expected results of their actions. Motivation to work well is a function of the relationship between:

(1) effort expended and the perceived likely outcomes; and

(2) the expectations that reward will be related to performance.

There must also be (3) the expectation that rewards (desired outcomes) are available (Figure 7.7).

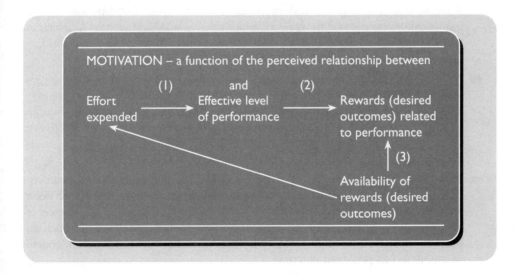

MOTIVATION – a function of the perceived relationship between

(1) and (2)

Effort expended → Effective level of performance → Rewards (desired outcomes) related to performance

(3) ↑

Availability of rewards (desired outcomes)

Figure 7.7:
Expectancy theory: the motivational link

The level of performance depends upon the perceived expectations regarding effort expended and the desired outcome. For example, a sous chef desires higher status and seeks promotion to head chef. This desire will lead to a high level of performance only if the sous chef believes that the opportunity for promotion is available, there is a strong expectation that higher performance will lead to promotion, and that promotion will result in a satisfactory increase in status.

As another example, a personnel assistant, who is unqualified, desires a higher salary but believes this is not possible in the present job. The assistant also believes that promotion would be most unlikely without an examination qualification. In this case there is likely to be a lack of positive motivation to achieve a high level of performance.

In broader terms, however, the generally high levels of staff turnover in the industry may well mean that good performance is perceived as very likely to lead to greater opportunities for rapid promotion.

Effort, performance and rewards

The underlying premise of expectancy theory, therefore, is that motivation is determined by the perceived strength of the link between:

Effort expended – Performance achieved – Rewards obtained

A person's behaviour reflects a conscious choice between the comparative evaluation of alternative behaviour. The choice of behaviour is based on the expectancy of the most favourable consequences. And expectancy is based on the person's **perception** of the situation, irrespective of whether or not this is *de facto* the situation.

Vroom's expectancy theory

Vroom's expectancy model is aimed specifically at the work situation. It is centred on three key variables: valence, instrumentality, and expectancy (VIE theory). On the basis of Vroom's work it is possible to depict a general model of expectancy theory[28] (Figure 7.8).

- *Valence.* This is the feelings that individuals have about specific outcomes. It is a measure of the attractiveness or preference for a particular outcome to the individual. Valence is not the same as value. Valence is *the anticipated satisfaction provided by an outcome.* This may differ from value, which is the actual satisfaction derived by an outcome.

- *Instrumentality.* This is the extent to which performance-related (first-level) outcomes lead to the satisfaction of need-related (second-level) outcomes. Some people may seek to achieve a high level of performance 'for its own sake' and without thought to further expectations. Usually, however, good performance achieves valence because this will be *instrumental* in leading to the satisfaction of second-level outcomes, for example the need for higher wages, promotion or status.

- *Expectancy.* This is the perceived degree of probability that the choice of a particular action will actually lead to the desired outcome. When a person chooses between alternative forms of behaviour which have uncertain outcomes, the choice is affected not only by preference (valence) but also by the probability that such an outcome will be achieved. Expectancy is the relationship between a chosen course of action and its predicted outcome.

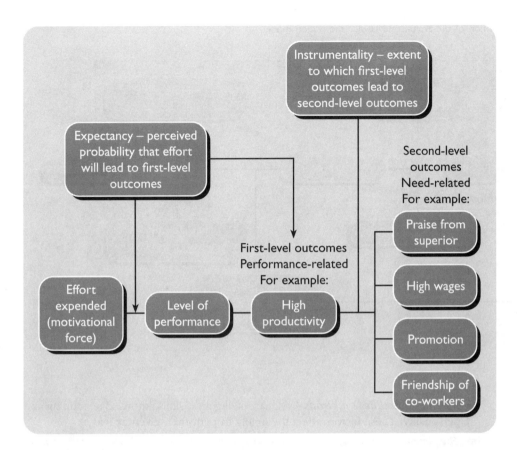

Motivational force

The assumption of expectancy theory is that an individual considers in a rational manner the comparative advantages of alternative choices of action and the likelihood of attaining the desired outcome from that action. It is the combination of valence and expectancy which determine a person's motivation for a given form of behaviour. This is the motivational force. Expressed as an equation, this is:

M (Motivation) = V (valence) × E (expectancy)

If either valence or expectancy is zero, then motivation is zero. There are likely to be a number of different outcomes for a given choice of action. Accordingly the measure of V × E is summed across the total number of possible outcomes to provide a single figure indicating the attractiveness for a particular choice of behaviour.

The Porter and Lawler expectancy model

A development of the VIE theory has been put forward by Porter and Lawler. They present a model which extends beyond motivational force and considers performance as a whole.[29] Porter and Lawler maintain that effort expended (the motivational force) does not lead directly to performance. It is mediated by three sets of intervening variables:

Figure 7.9: Representation of the Porter and Lawler motivation model

- *Individual abilities and traits* – such as intelligence, skills, knowledge, training and personality. These factors affect the ability to perform a given activity.
- *The person's role perceptions* – that is, the way in which individuals view their work and the role they should adopt. This influences the type of effort expended, and the direction and level of action.
- *The nature of intrinsic and extrinsic rewards*, and perceived equitable rewards.

A representation of the Porter and Lawler model is given in Figure 7.9.

Intrinsic and extrinsic rewards

Rewards are desirable outcomes and both intrinsic and extrinsic rewards are important. Intrinsic rewards derive from the individuals themselves and include personal satisfaction, a sense of achievement, a feeling of responsibility and recognition. Extrinsic rewards derive from the organisation and the actions of others, and include salary, working conditions and supervision. The proportion of intrinsic and extrinsic will vary among individuals and different work situations, but there must be a minimum of both. However, Porter and Lawler suggest that intrinsic rewards are more likely to produce job satisfaction related to performance than are extrinsic rewards.

Most people have an implicit perception about the level of rewards, intrinsic and extrinsic, they should receive commensurate with the requirements and demands of the job, and the contribution expected of them. Perceived equitable reward is the level of rewards people feel they should fairly receive for a given standard of performance. The experience of satisfaction derives from actual rewards which meet or exceed the perceived equitable rewards.

Motivation, satisfaction and performance

Porter and Lawler see motivation, satisfaction and performance as separate variables, and attempt to explain the complex relationships among them. The effort, or amount of energy a person exerts on a given activity is associated more with motivation than with performance. It does not relate to how successful a person is in carrying out an activity.

The human relations approach tended to assume that job satisfaction leads to improved performance. In contrast, Porter and Lawler suggest that job satisfaction is an effect rather than a cause of performance. Job satisfaction is more dependent upon performance, than performance is upon job satisfaction.

Practical applications of expectancy theory

There are a number of different versions of expectancy theory and it is not always easy to understand or apply them. There are many variables which affect behaviour at work. A problem can arise in attempting to identify those variables which are most important in particular situations. Expectancy theory applies only to behaviour which is under the voluntary control of the individual. Individuals may have only limited freedom to make choices because of constraints imposed by, for example, policies and procedures, the nature of technology, the organisation structure or role prescriptions.

Complexities of work motivation

Expectancy theory does, however, draw attention to the complexities of work motivation. It provides further information in helping to explain the nature of behaviour in the work situation, and in identifying problems in motivation and performance. Research studies highlight difficulties with some of the concepts involved but do appear to provide general support for the theory.[30]

Porter and Lawler emphasise that the expectancy model is just a model. People rarely sit down and consciously list their expected outcomes, expectancies and valences. But they do consider the likely outcomes of their actions and the attractiveness of various alternatives in deciding what they will do. The expectancy model provides a means of mirroring the process and predicting its outcome.[31]

Attention by management

Expectancy theory indicates that, in order to improve the motivation and performance of staff, the manager should give attention to a number of factors including the following:

- Attempt to establish clear relationships and strong links between effort and performance, and performance and rewards.
- Review appropriateness of rewards in terms of individual performance rather than on a more general basis. Outcomes with a high valence for the individual should be used as an incentive for improved performance.
- Establish clear procedures for the monitoring and evaluation of individual levels of performance.
- Ensure subordinates have the required understanding, knowledge and skills to enable them to achieve a high level of performance.

- Give attention to intervening variables such as company policies, organisational procedures and support facilities which, although not direct motivational factors, may still affect performance.

- Minimise undesirable outcomes which may be perceived to result from a high level of performance, for example accidents, sanctions from co-workers or the imposition of increased targets. Also minimise those undesirable outcomes which result despite a high level of performance, such as a reduction in bonus payments.

Equity theory of motivation

One of the variables identified in the Porter and Lawler expectancy model is perceived equitable rewards. This leads to consideration of another process theory of motivation – equity theory – which adds further to our understanding of the behaviour of people at work. *Equity theory focuses on people's feelings of how fairly they have been treated in comparison with the treatment received by others.* Applied to the work situation, equity theory is usually associated with the work of Adams.[32]

People evaluate their social relationships in the same way as buying or selling an item. Social relationships involve an exchange process. People expect certain outcomes in exchange for certain contributions or inputs. Equity theory is based on this concept of exchange theory. For example, a person may expect promotion as an outcome (and in exchange for) a high level of contribution in helping to achieve an important organisational objective (input).

Comparison of outcomes and inputs

People also compare their own position with that of others. They determine the *perceived* equity of their own position. Feelings about the equity of the exchange are affected by the treatment they receive when compared with what happens to other people. Most exchanges involve a multiple of inputs and outcomes. According to equity theory, people place a weighting on these various inputs and outcomes according to how they perceive their importance.

If the ratio of a person's total outcomes to total inputs equals the perceived ratio of other people's outcomes and inputs, there is equity. But when there is an unequal comparison of ratios the person experiences a sense of inequity. The feeling of inequity might arise when an individual's ratio of outcomes to inputs is either greater than or, more usually, less than that of other people.

Behavioural consequences of inequity

The feeling of inequity causes tension. This motivates the person to take action to restore equity. The magnitude of perceived inequity determines the level of tension, and the level of tension determines the strength of motivation. Adams identifies six broad types of behaviour which arise as a consequence of inequity (Figure 7.10).

- *Changes to inputs* – for example, through the amount or quality of work, timekeeping or absenteeism.

- *Changes to outputs* – for example, attempting to improve pay, working conditions, fringe benefits or perks, status and recognition, without changes to inputs.

- *Cognitive distortion of inputs or outcomes* – for example, the belief about how hard a person is really working, the value of examination qualifications, or what can be achieved with a given level of pay.

Figure 7.10: Representation of Adams's equity theory of motivation

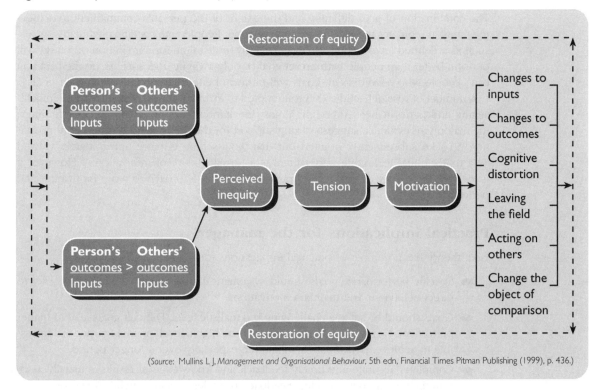

(*Source:* Mullins L J, *Management and Organisational Behaviour*, 5th edn, Financial Times Pitman Publishing (1999), p. 436.)

- *Leaving the field* – for example, through absenteeism, lack of interest or involvement with the work, request for transfer, or resignation from a job or the organisation.

- *Acting on others* – for example, tempting others to increase their inputs or lower their outcomes, or trying to force others to leave the field.

- *Changing the object of comparison* – for example, viewing people with whom comparisons have previously been made as now belonging to a different level in the organisation, and finding a new reference group with whom comparison is made.

Managers need to recognise such forms of behaviour as possible consequences of perceived inequity, and to take appropriate action to reduce tension and restore a sense of equity.

Goal theory

Another theory sometimes considered under the heading of motivation to work is goal theory, or the theory of goal-setting. This theory is based mainly on the work of Locke.[33] **The basic premise of goal theory is that people's goals or intentions play an important part in determining behaviour**. Locke accepts the importance of perceived value, as indicated in expectancy theories of motivation, and suggests that these values give rise to the experience of emotions and desires. People strive to achieve goals in order to satisfy their emotions and desires. Goals guide people's responses and actions. Goals direct work behaviour and performance, and lead to certain consequences or feedback.

Goal-setting and performance

The combination of goal difficulty and the extent of the person's commitment to achieving the goal regulates the level of effort expended. People with specific quantitative goals, such as a defined level of performance, or a given deadline for completion of a task, will perform better than people with no set goal or only a vague goal such as 'do the best you can'. People who have difficult goals will perform better than people with easier goals.

A number of research studies have attempted to examine the relationship between goal-setting and performance. Although, almost inevitably, there are some contrary findings, the majority of evidence suggests strong support for the theory, and its effects on motivation.[34] Locke subsequently pointed out that 'goal-setting is more appropriately viewed as a motivational technique rather than as a formal theory of motivation'.[35] However it is viewed, the theory of goal-setting provides a useful approach to work motivation and performance.

Practical implications for the manager

Goal theory has a number of practical implications for the manager.

- Specific performance goals should systematically be identified and set in order to direct behaviour and maintain motivation.

- Goals should be set at a challenging but realistic level. Difficult goals lead to higher performance. However, if goals are set at too high a level, or are regarded as impossible to achieve, performance will suffer, especially over a longer period.

- Complete, accurate and timely feedback and knowledge of results is usually associated with high performance. Feedback provides a means of checking progress on goal attainment and forms the basis for any revision of goals.

- Goals can be determined either by a superior or by individuals themselves. Goals set by other people are more likely to be accepted when there is participation. Employee participation in the setting of goals may lead to higher performance.[36]

Applications of motivational theories

The application of motivational theories, and a greater understanding of job satisfaction and work performance, has led to increasing interest in job design. Redesigning the nature of the work organisation and the structure of jobs can have a significant effect on the attitudes and satisfaction of staff, and their level of performance.

A major contribution of Herzberg's two-factor theory lies in the emphasis on the redesign of jobs in order to bring the motivators to bear. His belief is that people should have the opportunity to use their talents and abilities, and to exercise more self-control over the job. Inherent in the job should be a learning and growth experience.[37] Expectancy theory suggests that improving the effort–performance–reward link through job design will have a powerful motivating influence on people, especially those who place a high value on intrinsic rewards.

Alienation at work

One common approach to job satisfaction and work performance is in terms of frustration and alienation at work. Alienation refers to the feeling of detachment of individuals from their work roles. Four major dimensions of alienation are powerlessness, meaninglessness, isolation and self-estrangement.[38]

- *Powerlessness* denotes the workers' lack of control over management policy, their immediate work processes or conditions of employment.
- *Meaninglessness* stems from standardisation and the division of labour. It denotes the inability to see the purpose of work done, or to identify with the total process or completed product or service.
- *Isolation* is the feeling of not belonging to an integrated work group or to the social work organisation, or not being guided by group norms of behaviour.
- *Self-estrangement* arises from the failure to see work as an end in itself or as a central life issue. Workers experience a depersonalised detachment and work is seen solely as a means to an end.

In order to help overcome alienation, management should attempt to develop within individuals a feeling of attachment to the organisation and to the work situation. The attachment of individuals and the satisfaction derived from their jobs are influenced by the formal structure, managerial style, and the nature of technology and work organisation.

The impact of information technology can also have a significant influence on the feelings of attachment to the job. Information technology will demand new patterns of work. It can affect the nature and content of individual jobs; the function and structure of work groups; changes in the nature of supervision; the hierarchical structure of jobs and responsibilities; and the nature of the management tasks.

The nature of hospitality work

Unlike many manufacturing or administrative situations, the hospitality industry offers potentially high levels of attachment to the work.[39] As mentioned previously, workers who live in or take meals on duty are especially likely to feel closely involved with their workplace. You may also recall one of the comments from a hotel manager in Assignment 3 of Chapter 2: 'For many live-in workers, it is not a job – it is their life. Everything rolled into one. It is not a job where you clock off and go home on Friday forgetting everything until Monday morning.'

Conflicting opinions

However, there appear to be conflicting opinions as to the nature of work in the hospitality industry. One view is that many jobs are monotonous, basic and routine in nature, performed under difficult working conditions and with added harassment from customers. Job enrichment may be difficult to achieve and in any case many workers do not seem greatly interested.

According to a (then) HCITB report, low status and the servile nature of jobs is a feature of work in the industry. Jobs such as those of cashier, kitchen staff and (surprisingly) receptionists lack variety and job satisfaction. The nature of the working environment deters substantial numbers of job seekers from accepting kitchen jobs.[40]

In contrast, a later HCTC publication suggests an alternative and more positive view, that the industry offers great potential for job satisfaction. Many jobs provide satisfying contact with the customer and allow individual flair and creativity. Staff usually have close and frequent contact with their manager or supervisor, unlike the 'anonymous' nature of some factory or office situations.[41] These positive features should be built upon and developed through the restructuring of work and job design.

Figure 7.11:
Hospitality jobs:
likes and dislikes

Likes:
1. Challenge, direct involvement, autonomy, independence, rewarding work
2. People, the public, and professional contacts
3. Working environment, opportunity for growth and advancement
4. Fast pace, change
5. Benefits, travel, prestige

Dislikes:
1. Long hours, nights and weekend schedule
2. Low pay
3. Stress, demanding supervisors and duties, no personal time, quality of life
4. Routine, no advancement or growth, no import or recognition
5. Company politics, management
6. Labor shortages, poor staff, lack of employee motivation, employees' and co-workers' attitudes

Note: Each list is presented in descending order of frequency.

(Source: reprinted by permission of Elsevier Science Inc. from 'Job Satisfaction: What's Happening to the Young Managers?' by Pavesic D V and Brymer R A, *Cornell Hotel and Restaurant Administration Quarterly,* vol. 30, no. 4, February 1990, p. 95, Copyright 1990 by Cornell University.)

Likes and dislikes about working in the industry

A study of 442 recent graduates from 11 American hospitality management colleges highlighted the importance of job challenge and career advancement as a key factor of job satisfaction.[42] Responses to an open-ended question on what was liked and disliked about working in the hospitality industry were categorised into five groups of likes and six groups of dislikes (Figure 7.11).

The most frequent response on what was liked best about the job or career referred to the challenge and direct involvement in their work. The second most frequent set of liked factors referred to interactions with others and people-related responses. Other attractions related to the nature of the work environment, including opportunities for learning and the physical surroundings, the fast pace of the industry, and for a relatively small group, benefits, travel and prestige. Women were more likely to mention likes relating to people and the public than were men, who were more likely to mention challenges and the work environment.

Positive aspects of the hospitality industry – a personal view

I started working in hotels full time from the age of 17, over the next 10 years I was fortunate to work in a variety of hotels and gain valuable experience. Very few industries offer the same opportunities with regard to career advancement and responsibility as the hospitality industry. From my personal experience by the age of 20, having worked in hotels in Blackpool and Oxford, I applied for my first post as head receptionist in a three-star 120-bedroom hotel. This was my first management

continued

continued

position and the responsibility was enormous, my salary with the benefits was far higher than most people of my age in other industries.

The image is still a conflicting one and many of the benefits of the industry are overlooked. Although research shows that money is not the most important aspect of the job, most would agree that a reasonable wage is essential. What most people fail to realise is that additional benefits are incorporated within the salary.

● Accommodation is often provided for hotel workers either as part of the package, or for a minimum amount of rent.

● Accommodation is often either on the premises or close by, reducing or eliminating the cost of travel to and from work.

● Heating, lighting, water and other amenities are provided free of charge.

● Meals on and off duty are provided for live-in staff.

● Uniforms are often part of the package, saving on the cost of work clothes.

● Use of on site laundry facilities is often available to live in staff.

● The social activities often centre around the live in staff.

Taking all of the above into account means that hotel staff often earn far more than they think, so, although the salaries are low in comparison with other sectors of the industry the benefits are worth a great deal. It is, however, difficult to appreciate these benefits, and they are often taken for granted. So it is up to the employers to make this clear to future employees.

I spent 10 years working and living in hotels, generally in pleasant furnished flats, with no expenses, so my salary was 'pocket money'. It also gave me the opportunity to move within the industry without having the added problem of looking for somewhere to live. It was an invaluable education and one which I enjoyed enormously, it also had great social benefits, and many of the people I worked with over 15 years ago are still great friends.

(*Source*: The author is grateful to Sandra Cartwright for providing this contribution.)

The most disliked factors related to the long hours involved in hotel and food-service work, particularly hours worked at evenings and weekends. Many respondents also referred to not being paid enough for working the odd hours. Other dislikes referred to the stress of the job and the demands of supervisors and their duties, the routine nature of jobs and lack of recognition, especially with lower level jobs, company politics and management, staffing shortages and the nature of the staff. Women were more likely to mention low pay and management politics than men were. But both men and women were equally likely to refer to long hours and low pay as the features most disliked about their jobs.

What hotel employees want from their work

Simons and Enz undertook a study of 278 employees in 12 different hotels in the United States and Canada to learn what employees want from their work.[43] In order to understand how hotel workers might differ from other workers, the hotel employees were asked to rank

Figure 7.12:
Work factors
ranked by
hospitality
and industrial
workers

Work Factor	Hospitality Workers	Industrial Workers
Good wages	1	5
Security	2	4
Opportunity	3	6
Good working conditions	4	7
Interesting work	5	1
Appreciation	6	2
Loyalty to employees	7	8
Feeling of being in on things	8	3
Tactful discipline	9	9
Sympathetic personal help	10	10

(*Source:* reprinted by permission of Elsevier Science, Inc. from 'Motivating Hotel Employees: Beyond the carrot and the stick', by Simons, T and Enz, C A, *Cornell Hotel and Restaurant Administration Quarterly*, vol. 35, February 1995, p. 23. Copyright 1995 by Cornell University.)

Figure 7.13: Work factors ranked by employees in different hotel departments

Work Factor	F&B Servers	Rooms, Front desk	House-keeping	Accounting, Control	Sales, Marketing	Back of House F&B	Human Resources
Good wages	1	1	2	1	2	1	3
Security	3	4	1	4.5	4	5	6
Opportunity	2	2	5	2	1	4	1
Good working conditions	4	5.5	3	4.5	5	2	4
Interesting work	6	5.5	4	3	3	3	2
Appreciation	5	3	6	6	6	6	5
Loyalty to employees	7	7	7	8	8	7	7
Feeling of being in on things	9	8	8	7	7	8	8
Tactful discipline	8	9	9	9	9	9	9
Sympathetic personal help	10	10	10	10	10	10	10

(*Source:* As for Figure 7.12.)

the same 10 job-reward work factors used in an earlier major study of industrial workers by Kovach.[44] Only a single factor was to be ranked in any order.

The responses from the hotel workers showed a marked difference from those described in the earlier studies of workers in manufacturing industries (Figure 7.12). Overall, the three things most wanted by hotel employees were: (1) good wages; (2) job security; and (3) opportunities for advancement and development.

Simons and Enz also found that the job factors were ranked differently by workers in different hotel departments (Figure 7.13) and they suggest that: 'the adept manager should take these differences into account when considering what kinds of incentives and rewards to offer for high performance'.

Job design

To make the best use of people as a valuable resource, attention must be given to the relationship between staff and the nature and content of their jobs. The work organisation and the design of jobs can have a significant effect on the behaviour and performance of staff.

Job design is concerned with the relationship between workers and the nature and content of jobs, and their task functions. It attempts to meet people's personal and social needs at work through the reorganisation or restructuring of work. There are two major, interrelated reasons for attention to job design:

- to enhance the personal satisfaction that people derive from their work; and
- to make the best use of people as a valuable resource and to help overcome obstacles to their effective performance.

There are many broader ways of viewing job design. For example, Boella relates job design to five sets of expectations:

- Employer's expectations;
- Employee's expectations;
- Customer's expectations;
- Colleagues' expectations;
- Society's expectations.[45]

There are then many possible aspects of job design. We can view attention to job design in terms of two broad, related approaches (Figure 7.14):

- the restructuring of individual jobs; and
- broader approaches concerned with the wider organisational context.

Restructuring of individual jobs

Earlier approaches to job design concentrated on the restructuring of individual jobs and the application of three main methods: (i) job rotation, (ii) job enlargement and (iii) job enrichment.

The extent of centralisation/decentralisation (discussed in Chapter 6) can also be seen as a feature of job design.

Job rotation

Although usually included under this heading, job rotation is not strictly job design because neither the nature of the task nor the method of working is restructured. Job rotation involves moving a person from one job or task to another, for example rotating staff from kitchen work to waiting and to reception in order to gain some understanding and experience of the work of other departments. This can benefit the hotel by increasing flexibility in staffing and reducing differences in occupational status.

Job rotation may lead to the acquisition of additional skills and can be applied as a form of training. A planned programme of job rotation is often used, for example, for hospitality

Figure 7.14:
Main aspects
of job design

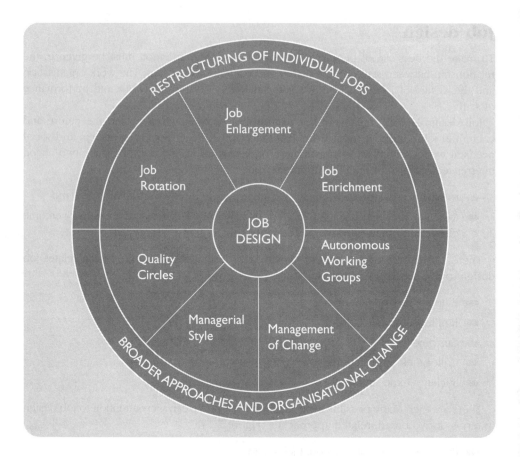

management students on their industrial training placements. There is also growing attention to cross-training as a means of enhancing employees' knowledge of a wider range
of jobs. When business dropped dramatically during the Gulf War, staff at Portsmouth
Holiday Inn accepted a four-day week and learned to undertake new jobs as an alternative to redundancies.

Job rotation should help the person to identify more with the total work of the establishment and with the completed delivery of service. It may add some variety to work and
help remove monotony and boredom. Under normal circumstances, however, job rotation
is often positively resisted by some staff. If the tasks involved are all very similar and
routine, then once the person is familiar with new tasks the work may quickly prove
boring again.

Job enlargement

This involves increasing the scope of the job and the range of tasks that the person is
responsible for carrying out. It is usually achieved by combining a number of related jobs
at the same level. Job enlargement is *horizontal job design*. It makes the job structurally
larger. It lengthens the time-cycle of operations and may give the person greater variety –
for example, allowing commis chefs to undertake a wider range of food preparation. A

group of banquet waiters who each set only part of the placement for each guest could undertake the entire setting for a smaller number of guests.

Job enlargement, however, is not always very popular and may even be resisted by workers. Although it may give the person added variety and a wider range of tasks, it does little to improve intrinsic satisfaction or the development of skills. Workers may see job enlargement as simply increasing the number of routine, boring tasks they have to perform.

Job enrichment

This attempts to enrich the job by incorporating motivating or growth factors such as increased responsibility and involvement, opportunities for personal development and a sense of achievement. Job enrichment involves *vertical job enlargement*. It aims to give the person greater autonomy and authority over the planning, execution and control of their own work. Job enrichment should help provide the person with a more meaningful and challenging job, and focuses attention on intrinsic satisfaction.

Methods of achieving job enrichment can include allowing workers to undertake a full task-cycle or provide a more complete delivery of service, providing opportunities for more direct contact with the customers, giving workers greater freedom over the scheduling and pacing of their own work, reducing the level of direct supervision, and giving workers increased responsibility for the monitoring and control of their own work.[46]

For example, receptionists could be encouraged to monitor guest comment cards, and to handle complaints and develop solutions to problems rather than bringing every concern to management. Room attendants could be given greater autonomy for complying with the checklists and inspection of rooms instead of relying on a supervisor to find mistakes. Holiday Inn, for instance, have introduced a system of self-checking attendants who are responsible for supervision of their own work. Supervisors now check only a sample number of rooms to monitor the overall standard of performance. Kitchen staff could be given greater responsibility for their own budget, including ordering supplies and controlling the costs of wastage and breakages.

Stages of a job

Magurn views every job as consisting of three separate stages:

- planning and organising the job, such as use of people and equipment, standards of quality, quantities needed, and work layout;
- doing the job, such as cooking meals, waiting at tables, serving drinks and cleaning;
- control, such as evaluating what is done, inspecting, measuring and adjusting, and correcting.[47]

Most jobs in the hospitality industry are concerned only with the 'doing' stage. Attention to job design would involve exploring ways in which people could have increased autonomy and responsibility for the planning and organising, and the control stages, of their jobs.

Job enrichment and core job dimensions

A popular and comprehensive model of job enrichment has been developed by Hackman and Oldham.[48] (See Figure 7.15.) The model views job enrichment in terms of increasing

Figure 7.15:
A job
characteristics
model of work
motivation

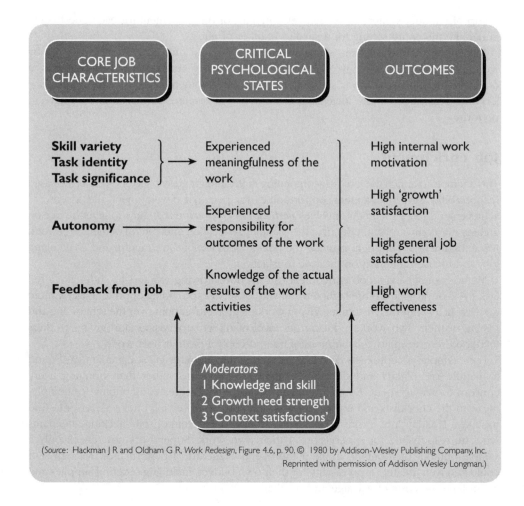

(*Source:* Hackman J R and Oldham G R, *Work Redesign*, Figure 4.6, p. 90. © 1980 by Addison-Wesley Publishing Company, Inc. Reprinted with permission of Addison Wesley Longman.)

five core job dimensions (CJD); skill variety, task identity, task significance, autonomy and feedback. These core job characteristics create three psychological states:

● experienced meaningfulness of the work;

● experienced responsibility for the outcomes of the work;

● knowledge of the actual results of the work activities.

The five core job dimensions can be summarised as follows:

● *Skill variety* – the extent to which a job entails different activities and involves a range of different skills and talents.

● *Task identity* – the extent to which a job involves completion of a whole piece of work with a visible outcome.

● *Task significance* – the extent to which a job has a meaningful impact on other people, either inside or outside the organisation.

● *Autonomy* – the extent to which a job provides freedom, independence and discretion in planning the work and determining how to undertake it.

● *Feedback* – the extent to which work activities result in direct and clear information on the effectiveness of job performance.

Motivating potential score (MPS)

From these five core job dimensions, Hackman and Oldham have developed an equation which gives a single index of a person's job profile. By answering a questionnaire – the Job Diagnostic Survey (JDS) – and by giving a score (between 1 and 7) to each job dimension, the person can calculate an overall measure of job enrichment, called the motivating potential score (MPS). Examples of questions from the JDS are:

● How much variety is there in your job?

● To what extent does your job involve doing a whole and identifiable piece of work?

● In general, how significant or important is your job?

● How much autonomy is there in your job?

● To what extent does doing the job itself provide you with information about your work performance?

$$MPS = \left\{ \frac{\text{Skill variety} + \text{Task identity} + \text{Task significance}}{3} \right\} \times \text{Autonomy} \times \text{Feedback}$$

The first three job dimensions of skill variety, task identity and task significance are averaged, since it is the combination of these dimensions which contributes to experienced meaningfulness of work. The remaining two job dimensions, autonomy and feedback, stand on their own. Since scores for skill variety, task identity and task significance are additive, this means that the absence of one dimension can be partially offset by the presence of the other dimensions. However, if either autonomy or feedback is absent then, because of the multiplicative relationship, the MPS would be zero. The job would offer no potential to motivate the person.

Application to seasonal hotel workers

In an attempt to account for the impact of individual worker differences on job attitudes, Lee-Ross undertook a study of 163 hotel workers using the Hackman and Oldham's job diagnostic survey.[49] The questionnaire consisted of 83 randomly arranged positively and negatively worded questions including questions on hotel residency and work preferences. Lee-Ross suggests that seasonal hotel workers can be divided into four sub-groups depending on whether respondents lived in or out, and whether they *preferred* seasonal or year-round working.

All groups of hotel workers showed a similar pattern of core job dimensions (CJD) scores. In terms of job profiles, seasonal work is low in skill content but workers seemed to identify with their tasks and view them as important.

The seasonal, live-in group (SI) undertake hotel employment but value (hotel-based) non-work factors linked to a desire for relationships and social needs.

The seasonal, live-out group (SO) need employment which provides extra money but does not interfere with family commitments. The year-round, live-out group (YO) have jobs whose characteristics change every six months. During the summer they usually supervise and have jobs which are enriched and enlarged. The year-round, live-in group (YI) express a desire for year-round work but out of necessity work seasonally. In the main they have little background in hotel work.

In descending order SI, YO, and YI groups scored CJDs higher than SO workers, This later group scored skilled variety, task significance, autonomy, job feedback and dealing with others significantly lower than all other groups.

Positive attitude to work

In a subsequent study of a sample of six hotels (with between 35 and 65 bedrooms) in Great Yarmouth, Lee-Ross undertook a further examination of the reliability of the job diagnostic survey among seasonal workers.[50] From an analysis of one hundred and sixty-three questionnaires, Lee-Ross concludes that, in general, reliability scores were compatible with those of Hackman and Oldham. The job diagnostic survey appears to hold just as well for hotel workers as for workers in other industries. In general, hotel workers have a positive attitude to their work but low Growth Need Strength, and its effectiveness alone as a moderator of hotel work attitudes was less than that noted by Hackman and Oldham. Hotel workers were satisfied with their job despite poor working conditions in some cases. This could probably be explained by the opportunities hotels provide for social interactions.

Much of the theory of goal-setting can be related to the system of Management by Objectives (discussed in Chapter 5). MBO is often viewed as an application of goal-setting, although MBO was devised originally before the development of goal-setting theory.

Broader approaches to job design

The restructuring of individual jobs *may* help increase motivation and job satisfaction, and lead to improved work performance. However, strategies of job rotation, job enlargement and job enrichment are only likely to be effective if they are introduced in a planned and systematic manner. Such strategies must be implemented not simply in an effort to economise on staff and increase managerial control but in the genuine belief that staff will respond in a positive manner to the acceptance of greater responsibility in their work.[51]

In the context of technological developments, attention to improved job design has spread from manipulating the tasks of individual jobs and has taken a broader perspective. Emphasis is placed on organisational change and concern for the quality of working life. The focus of attention is on the wider organisational context, the effective use of human resources and development of skills, and the way the organisation functions.

This involves the concept of a socio-technical approach (discussed in Chapter 2) and concern for people systems as well as technical systems. Broader approaches to job design include attention to autonomous work groups, the management of change, and managerial style.

Autonomous work groups

An important development in job design is a form of work organisation based on autonomous (self-regulating) work groups and teamworking. This involves a small group of workers assuming responsibility for the regulation and organisation of their jobs. Specific goals are agreed for the group, but members decide the means by which these goals are to be achieved. Group members have greater freedom and choice, and wider discretion over the planning, execution and control of their own work. The role of the supervisor is that of giving advice and support to the group as well as monitoring the standard and quality of completed work.[52]

As an example, a group of attendants may be allocated their own block of rooms for which they are collectively responsible. Group members decide on the division of work and the manner in which the various tasks are undertaken, and have discretion over when to take breaks. The group control the quality of their own work and are responsible for the standards of performance achieved.

The management of change

The increasing pace of technological and structural change has made it imperative to address the management of change in ways that would ensure the best outcomes for the organisation and its staff. It is understandable that people tend to be resistant to change. But new ideas and innovations should not be perceived as threats to members of staff. When change is being planned it is necessary to think about the work that people will do and the design of their jobs.

Improving job design needs to take account of how people perceive their present tasks, and to involve them closely in changes which affect them and their work. The way in which work is carried out and the technological processes involved should be integrated with the social needs of people at work. Management needs to adopt a clearly defined strategy for the initiation of change, and to take into account the social and human factors. The aim should be to ensure that the quality of working life is enhanced rather than undermined. The management of change is discussed further in Chapter 12.

Managerial style

The potential benefits of improved job design are unlikely to be realised if attention is focused on the content of jobs alone. Equally important is the process by which redesign is carried out and the importance of managerial style. The redesign of jobs to benefit both employees and the hospitality organisation is not an easy task. It is a continuous process that requires skill, imagination and commitment. Central to improving the quality of working life is a participative, open style of management involving members of staff in decisions which affect them, their work and the nature of their jobs.

In a discussion on managerial leadership in the hospitality industry, Keegan argues that the challenge is not so much to change the job but to provide a supportive and participative relationship with employees. The manager should create an environment in which the employee's real needs are satisfied.[53] (This view is discussed in more detail in Chapter 9.)

Managers should attempt to develop an atmosphere of mutual trust with staff and encourage their active participation including involvement in problem-solving. There must be full organisational support, including the availability of information for decision-making. Personnel policies and procedures, for example those relating to pay and benefits, incentive schemes, conditions of employment and consultation, should facilitate and help new concepts of improved job design.

The impact of new technology on working practices in hotels

Porter and Roberts comment that technology is the primary determinant of organisational structure because it suggests the testable hypothesis:

Communication, whatever it is, should be the same at the interpersonal level in different organisational sub-units with similar technologies, and internal organisational communication should differ between units with different technologies.[54]

McEwan tested this hypothesis by categorising all the jobs performed in two hotels into six classifications, according to the access employees had to formal information

continued

continued

channels and the type of technology they used in carrying out their jobs. Strong support for the hypothesis was recorded for employees at both extremes of this job-classification typology. For example housekeeping chambermaids, cleaners and kitchen stewards, who used simple technology and were physically isolated from other employees for long periods in carrying out their jobs, were compared with managers and front-desk staff, who relied heavily on technological aids and interacted constantly with other employees.

New technology was also found to have altered the working conditions of most people employed in the food and beverage departments, particularly kitchen stewards, the modern-day 'plongeurs', whose work was memorably described by Orwell as a job 'which offers no prospects, is intensely exhausting, and at the same time has not a trace of skill or interest'.[55]

This transformation was initially due to the introduction of automatic washing equipment which required kitchen stewards to be retrained so that they could operate the controls, monitor the water level, temperature and steam pressure, and add the correct amounts of detergents at regular intervals.

Several other changes in traditional working practices including the need to sort kitchen utensils into different-coloured plastic containers were necessary so that the correct washing time could be allocated. The sorting of utensils actually reduced the efficiency of the washing machine, if left to a single kitchen steward, and this task was eventually shared by waiters and chefs, who all benefited from the rapid washing and return of equipment to their respective work stations. Kitchen stewards admitted to being more involved in the daily work and social activities in the hotel. For example, one male steward became engaged to a receptionist and another female steward and her fiancé chef were subsequently given transfers to the same company hotel in another town. One unexpected outcome involved two Portuguese stewards, who could speak no English, despite being employed in the same hotel for over five years, but who each had married English-speaking Philippino waitresses.

Finally, the need to use different concentrations of detergent in the automatic washing machine also resulted in the creation of a new role of stewards' supervisor, who was later given responsibility for ordering all detergents and cleaning materials used in the hotel, a task that was eventually allocated to new management trainees, who were required to carry out these duties for an initial six-month period on being appointed.

Further contact with other staff was maintained by giving these supervisors responsibility for issuing tokens, which permitted staff to obtain free food from the 'automat' in their canteen.

Conversely, the later introduction of microwave ovens and portion-control meals in the hotel kitchens caused resentment among chefs, particularly at one of the Scottish hotels, where changes in the preparation of meals were regarded as a de-skilling activity that lowered their status and resulted in staff dissatisfaction and labour turnover. On the other hand, room-service staff, who worked alone or in pairs in isolated areas of other company hotels, welcomed these changes because the use of this technology raised their status, widened the range of their activities, and made them less dependent on kitchen chefs, etc., who had previously been regarded as rather unhelpful.

Source: McEwan T, *A Replicated Study of Communication Networks, Job Retention and Labour Turnover in Two British Hotels*, Unpublished doctoral thesis, Cranfield Institute of Technology, Cranfield, 1988.

Involvement and empowerment

Increasing business competitiveness demands that hospitality organisations have to offer the best quality products and services to meet the demands of the customers. This requires that organisations develop and harness the talents and commitments of all their employees. In order to improve business performance managers will need to relinquish close control in favour of greater empowerment of employees. The general movement towards downsizing and delayering, together with developments in social democracy and recognition of the efficient use of human resources for organisational success, have highlighted the increasing importance attached to employee involvement and empowerment.

Empowerment permits members of staff to undertake duties and accept responsibilities which were previously the prerogative of management. The concept of empowerment is therefore associated with the process of delegation (discussed in Chapter 11) and with autonomous work groups, mentioned above.

Empowerment in hospitality services

According to Jones and Davies evidence suggests that empowerment will become a significant factor in how hotel and food service firms are managed. From a study of attitudes to empowerment by general managers of four-star hotels in the UK, Jones and Davies were encouraged by the response rate to their investigations. The level of interest displayed suggests a great deal of interest over the issue of empowerment in the hotel industry.[56]

From a discussion of the benefits and problems of empowerment and a review of its operation in a number of companies, Pickard concludes that empowerment does appear to be having an effect on the way people work. As an example, Pickard describes improved job satisfaction and the changing attitudes of staff arising from the introduction of empowerment in Harvester restaurants. Within a framework handed down from head office, staff work in teams which are responsible for making their own decisions on the running of individual restaurants.[57]

Managerial meanings and initiatives

Lashley argues that interest in employee empowerment in hospitality operations has been associated chiefly with interest in gaining competitive advantage through service quality and the paramount importance which is placed on the performance of front-line staff.[58]

By employing and adapting terms used in the wider literature on empowerment, Lashley suggests it is possible to summarise four managerial initiatives and meanings which claim to be empowering:

- *Empowerment through participation* – for example, the delegation for decision-making which in a traditional organisation would be the domain of management.
- *Empowerment through involvement* – for example, when management concern is to gain from employees' experiences, ideas and suggestions.
- *Empowerment through commitment* – for example, through greater commitment to the organisation's goals and through improvement in employees' job satisfaction.
- *Empowerment through delayering* – for example through reducing the number of tiers of management in the organisation structure.

Empowerment takes a variety of forms. Managers frequently have different intentions and organisations differ in the degree of discretion with which they can empower employees. Lashley concludes therefore that the success of a particular initiative will be judged ultimately by the extent to which the empowered employees feel personally effective, able to determine outcomes and have a degree of control over significant aspects of their working life.

Managerial perceptions of empowerment

Based on a further cluster of research projects into employee participation in services, Lashley concludes that although, on face value, empowerment has much to offer organisations' operating services, employees will react more quickly to customer needs and to rectify complaints, take personal pride in successful service encounters, and feel pride and concern for the customer experience. However, account needs to be taken of different definitions and meanings used by managers; and different perceptions of business problems and motives for introducing empowerment.

The term 'empowerment' is used to describe a wide variety of practice in service delivery. There is considerable overlap between employee empowerment, employee participation, employee involvement and even employee commitment, yet these terms are often used interchangeably. Ultimately, the success of a particular initiative will be dependent in the first instance on the empowered being given the authority and freedom to make decisions which they themselves consider to be valuable, significant and important. Whatever the intentions of managers, the effects of empowerment will be mediated by the feelings and experiences of the supposedly empowered. Hence any consideration of the various forms which empowerment takes must be sensitive to the potential tensions between managerial meanings and employees experiences.[59]

Empowerment and organisational change

According to Erstad, among the many fashionable management terms, empowerment refers to a change strategy with the objective of improving both the individual's and the organisation's ability to act. In the service sector, and more specifically the hotel industry, empowerment is often seen as a way to gain competitive advantage but the true potential is broader. From the context of articles specialising in this area, Erstad concludes that empowerment is a complex process. In order to be successful it requires a clear vision, a learning environment both for management and employees, and participation and implementation tools and techniques. In order to achieve a truly entrepreneurial culture the hospitality industry can learn many lessons from research and experience in other business sectors.[60]

Quality circles

Although perhaps not strictly job design, a particular feature which is associated with part of the wider organisational context, and which can be seen as a form of involvement and empowerment, is the concept of quality circles. A quality circle is a group of people within an organisation who meet together on a regular basis to identify, analyse and solve problems relating to quality, productivity or other aspects of day-to-day working arrangements using problem-solving techniques. Quality circles are compatible, therefore, with the quality of working life and effective use of human resources in that they provide an opportunity for people at work to become more involved in matters which affect the jobs they do.

Underlying principles

The concept of quality circle groups is based on a number of underlying principles including the following.

- Membership is voluntary.
- The group usually numbers between five and ten members, normally from the same work station or concerned with similar work.
- The group selects the problems to be tackled and the methods of operation.
- The leader of the circle is usually the immediate supervisor but can be decided within the group.
- The group recommends solutions to management and where possible has authority to implement agreed solutions.
- Members receive training in the understanding of group processes, communication and problem-solving skills, and quality-control techniques.

The effective implementation of quality circles relies on the trust and goodwill of all sides. It requires full commitment and active support from top management and line managers. It also requires a participative style of managerial behaviour, full consultation with staff and the delegation of decision-making. Quality circles should not be seen as just another instrument of management. There must be a realistic time perspective for the effective operation of the group, coupled with the continuous monitoring and review of results.[61]

Potential benefits

Quality circles offer a number of potential benefits. They place emphasis on a problem-solving approach and provide for the direct participation of employees in work-related decisions which concern them. Supervisors can gain greater confidence and assume the role of communicators. Quality circles can lead to increased motivation and job satisfaction for members. They can help bring about a more positive attitude to work. In appropriate applications, quality circles can be part of a broad, long-term strategy for organisational change aimed at improving economic performance and the quality of working life.

Quality circles do work and are used successfully by a number of British organisations. However, quality circles do not always succeed, and there may be opposition from top management, line managers or trade unions. Quality circles may also fail because of insufficient preparation or lack of positive support from management.[62]

Summary

- Managers achieve results through the efforts of other people and attention must be given to systems of motivation, job satisfaction and rewards. Individuals have a variety of changing and often conflicting needs and expectations at work. These can be viewed within a broad three-fold heading of economic rewards, intrinsic satisfaction and social relationships.

- The complex and variable nature of work motivation has given rise to many competing ideas and theories. These different theories are not conclusive but help to highlight the many motives which influence people's behaviour and performance. They enable the manager to direct attention to how best to motivate staff to work willingly and effectively.

- Content theories attempt to explain those specific things which actually motivate people at work and include the work of Maslow, Alderfer, Herzberg and McClelland. Process theories attempt to identify the relationships among the dynamic variables which make up motivation and include expectancy theories, equity theory and goal theory.

- The motivation to work well is usually related to job satisfaction but the nature of the relationship is not clear. There appear to be conflicting opinions about the nature of jobs and work in the hospitality industry. A key factor of job satisfaction appears to be the importance of challenges, autonomy and direct involvement in work. Other important factors are good wages, job security, and opportunities for advancement and development.

- The restructuring of individual jobs and strategies of job rotation, job enlargement and job enrichment need to be planned and implemented in a positive manner. A popular and comprehensive model of job enrichment has been developed by Hackman and Oldham. The focus of improved job design has now taken a broader organisational approach and includes attention to autonomous work groups, management of change, managerial style, involvement and empowerment, and quality circles.

Review and discussion questions

1. How would you attempt to explain the basic nature of work motivation? Discuss the relationship between motivation and job satisfaction.

2. Distinguish between content and process theories of motivation. Why is the study of different theories of motivation important for the hospitality manager?

3. Critically assess the practical value of Maslow's hierarchy of needs model to improving the motivation of staff in the hospitality industry.

4. Discuss critically the contention that the main factors affecting motivation and job satisfaction are high wages and good working conditions.

5. Explain your understanding of expectancy theories of motivation. What are the practical applications of expectancy theory?

6. Suggest situations when each of the following theories might have particular significance for the hospitality manager: (i) achievement motivation; (ii) equity theory; (iii) goal theory.

7. What are the major reasons for increasing attention to improved job design? Given the nature of hospitality work, discuss critically the likely value of the restructuring of individual jobs.

8. Explain what is meant by broader approaches to job design. Suggest, with supporting examples, how these approaches might be applied within the hospitality industry.

Assignment 1

Referring to Maslow's hierarchy of needs model and Figure 7.5 (page 231), give your own specific examples of general rewards and organisational factors to satisfy different needs.

In small groups, discuss with colleagues the importance and significance of these rewards and factors in terms of how they influenced your motivation to work.

Assignment 2

(i) Interview at least three people with different jobs in any aspect of the hospitality industry. Identify as clearly as possible, together with reasons and supporting examples:
   - those aspects of the job which the person feels to be of particular importance and/or significance;
   - what aspects of the job the person likes most and those aspects disliked the most; and
   - what motivates each person to work well and perform to the best of his or her ability.

(ii) Select a particular department within a hospitality organisation and investigate specific causes of job dissatisfaction. Suggest how these particular problems of dissatisfaction could be tackled in a positive and practical way.

(iii) Explain what conclusions you draw from your observations and the extent to which you can relate your findings to different theories/studies of motivation and job satisfaction.

Assignment 3

You are the newly appointed general manager of ABC Hotel. At interview you were informed that there is serious concern about the generally poor level of work performance, that morale is low and that there is a disturbingly high level of staff turnover.

(i)   Explain fully the likely actions you would take to help overcome the present situation.

(ii) Indicate clearly the priorities you would have in mind.

(iii) Make clear any necessary, reasonable assumptions.

(iv) Explain how you might draw upon those theories/studies of motivation and job satisfaction you consider to be relevant.

Case study: Happy Hotels – flexible working or stretching a point?

Happy Holdings plc operate some 10 four-star hotels in the UK under the trade name of Happy Hotels. Additionally, within the portfolio there is also a budget chain marketed as Happy Traveller, aimed at the two- to three-star market.

Both brands operate in very different ways. Happy Hotels are traditionally managed with relatively strong demarcation lines between food and beverage, front of house and administration. Seniority is indicated by the uniform and type of name badge worn – for example, operative level staff wear a basic uniform and have a name badge engraved with their christian, or first, name; supervisory staff are given a jacket and their surname is added to their name badge. These tokens of seniority are much prized and jealously guarded, as is the perceived expertise of each job holder – gained after, in some cases, several years of specialised college and industrial training.

Conversely, Happy Traveller is managed very differently. The food and beverage operation is franchised to a national brewery chain and, to promote flexibility, the remaining staff are employed as general assistants who work as required in all other areas of the hotel.

Both operations worked effectively until Jeff Broadfield, a young and ambitious graduate, was promoted from manager of a Happy Traveller to general manager of a Happy Hotel. The hotel he left was two years old, sited on a motorway interchange and very profitable, enjoying 90 per cent occupancy rates. The hotel he inherited was 10 years old, in need of a major refurbishment and suffering financially as a result of economic recession. Occupancy levels had dropped and staff were demotivated; Broadfield was under pressure both to prove himself worthy of the promotion and to restore the ailing fortunes of his new property.

His immediate action was to introduce a method of job evaluation into the hotel in an attempt to identify similar jobs in order to establish similar flexible working arrangements to those at the Happy Traveller. He felt that not only would this flexibility improve efficiency levels but that the resulting job rotation would increase job satisfaction and thus morale among the staff.

Constrained by finances, the job evaluation which was implemented was of a somewhat basic approach. With the aid of the personnel officer, Broadfield himself classified jobs according to skill level and the amount of training required to reach competence, the lowest level rather unfortunately being classified as 'straight off the street', implying that little or no skill was needed and training minimal to bring the job holder to full competence.

▷

Accompanying this flexible approach was to be a change in staff uniforms; since they would be working at a variety of jobs during the working day, all staff would wear broadly the same uniform. In an attempt to promote democracy and engender feelings of equality, name badges would be changed to christian, or first, names only.

Having planned the strategy for implementing these changes, Broadfield then communicated this in a memo to head office. Unfortunately, at this stage, events overtook him: his memo was mistakenly left in the photocopier where it was discovered by a member of the maintenance team – easily the most militant and vociferous in the hotel. Events further conspired against Broadfield: the discovery of the memo coincided with his absence from the hotel on a training course. Mayhem ensued when the memo 'found' its way onto the staff canteen notice board, and irate husbands telephoning to demand why their spouses had been classified as 'straight off the street' were met with a blank wall of silence.

On his return, Broadfield was met with a deputation of staff demanding to know what was happening. He decided to call a general staff meeting to explain to the staff the reasoning behind his proposals. However, the meeting fell short of total success; his urge to communicate his ideas to staff, particularly the concept of job rotation to improve motivation, individual skills and morale, fell on stony ground.

Nevertheless, the new scheme was introduced the following week. Accounts department staff were deputed to train on bed-making, Broadfield's secretary was sent to the kitchen, the second chef was told to train as a waiter. A disgruntled maintenance engineer was heard to comment, as he cleared the potwash machine, 'So much for *my* training – I spent four years serving my apprenticeship, 30 years as a craftsman carpenter and I'm now washing pots. What can I do about it – who would want me at my age with few jobs about anyway? All this talk about job rotation, new skills and motivation is a load of rubbish – the only place he's motivated me is over a barrel and there isn't a thing that I can do about it.'

Source: The copyright of this case study rests with the author's colleague Karen Meudell, University of Portsmouth. The case is reprinted with permission.

Notes and references

1. Mullins L J, 'Management and Managerial Behaviour', *The International Journal of Hospitality Management*, vol. 4, no. 1, 1985, pp. 39–41.

2. Riley M, *Human Resource Management in The Hospitality and Tourism Industry*, 2nd edn, Butterworth-Heinemann, (1996), p. 44.

3. See, for example, Vroom V H and Deci E L (eds), *Management and Motivation*, Penguin (1970).

4. See, for example, Rudolph P A and Kleiner B H, 'The Art of Motivating Employees', *Journal of Managerial Psychology*, vol. 4, no. 5, 1989, pp. i–iv.

5. Green J R, 'Has Motivation Anything to do With You?', *Administrator*, October 1994, pp. 29–30.

6. Ellis P, *The Image of Hotel and Catering Work*, HCITB Research Report (1981).

7. Hunt J W, *Managing People at Work; A Manager's Guide to Behaviour in Organizations*, 3rd edn, McGraw-Hill (1992).

8. British Institute of Management, *Management News*, no. 64, February 1990, p. 6.

9. Willman I, 'Human Resource Management in the Service Sector', in Jones P (ed.), *Management in Service Industries*, Pitman (1989), p. 217.

10. Maslow A H, 'A Theory of Human Motivation', *Psychological Review*, vol. 50, no. 4, July 1943, pp. 370–396, and Maslow A H, *Motivation and Personality*, 3rd edn, Harper & Row (1987).

11. Ellis P, *The Image of Hotel and Catering Work*, HCITB Research Report (1981).

12. See, for example, Hornsey T and Dann D, *Manpower Management in the Hotel and Catering Industry*, Batsford (1984), and Mullins L J, *Management and Organisational Behaviour*, 5th edn, Financial Times Pitman Publishing (1999).

13. For example, see Robertson I T, Smith M and Cooper D, *Motivation: Strategies, Theory and Practice*, 2nd edn, Institute of Personnel and Development (1992).

14. Steers R M and Porter L W, *Motivation and Work Behavior*, 5th edn, McGraw-Hill (1991).

15. For a more detailed account of Maslow's model applied to guest behaviour, see Venison P, *Managing Hotels*, Heinemann (1983).

16. Alderfer C P, *Existence, Relatedness and Growth*, Collier Macmillan (1972).

17. Herzberg F, Mausner B and Synderman B B, *The Motivation to Work*, 2nd edn, Chapman & Hall (1959).

18. Balmer S and Baum T, 'Applying Herzberg's Hygiene Factors to the Changing Accommodation Environment', *International Journal of Contemporary Hospitality Management*, vol. 5, no. 2, 1993, pp. 32–35.

19. See, for example, Goldthorpe J H *et al.*, *The Affluent Worker: Industrial Attitudes and Behaviour*, Cambridge University Press (1968).

20. Phillipchuk J, 'An Inquiry Into The Continuing Relevance of Herzberg's Motivation Theory', *Engineering Management Journal*, vol. 8, no. 1, March 1996, pp. 15–20.

21. MacQueen N, 'What Happened to Herzberg: Is Motivation Theory Out of Date?' *Hospitality*, no. 29, May 1982, p. 16.

22. Chitiris L, 'Herzberg's Proposals and Their Applicability to The Hotel Industry', *Hospitality Education and Research Journal*, vol. 12, 1988, pp. 67–79.

23. MacQueen N, 'What Happened to Herzberg: Is Motivation Theory Out of Date?' *Hospitality*, no. 29, May 1982, p. 16.

24. McClelland D C, *The Achieving Society*, Van Nostrand Reinhold (1961) (also published by Irvington, 1976), and *Human Motivation*, Cambridge University Press (1988).

25. McClelland D C, 'Business Drive and National Achievement', *Harvard Business Review*, vol. 40, July–August 1962, pp. 99–112.

26. Weaver T, 'Theory M: Motivating with Money', *Cornell HRA Quarterly*, vol. 29, no. 3, November 1988, pp. 40–45.

27. 'What You Thought: Motivating Minimum-Wage Workers', *Personnel Journal*, vol. 75, no. 3, March 1996, p. 16.

28. Vroom V H, *Work and Motivation*, Wiley (1964) (also published by Krieger, 1982).

29. Porter L W and Lawler E E, *Managerial Attitudes and Performance*, Irwin (1968).

30. See, for example, Graen G, 'Instrumentality Theory of Work Motivation', *Journal of Applied Psychology Monograph*, vol. 53, no. 2, 1969, part 2.

31. Porter L W, Lawler E E and Hackman J R, *Behavior in Organizations*, McGraw-Hill (1975).

32. Adams J S, 'Injustice in Social Exchange', abridged in Steers R M and Porter L W, *Motivation and Work Behaviour*, 2nd edn, McGraw-Hill (1979), pp. 107–124.

33. Locke E A, 'Towards a Theory of Task Motivation and Incentives', *Organizational Behavior and Human Performance*, vol. 3, 1968, pp. 157–189.

34. For examples, see: (i) Latham G P and Yukl G A, 'A Review of the Research on the Applications of Goal Setting in Organizations', *Academy of Management Journal*, vol. 18, 1975, pp. 824–845; (ii) Latham G P and Locke E A, 'Goal Setting: A Motivational Technique that Works', *Organisational Dynamics*, Autumn 1979, pp. 28–80.

35. Locke E A, 'Personal Attitudes and Motivation', *Annual Review of Psychology*, vol. 26, 1975, pp. 457–480.

36. For a summary of research supporting these conclusions, see: Miner J B, *Theories of Organizational Behavior*, Holt, Rinehart & Winston (1980).

37. Herzberg F, 'One More Time: How do you Motivate Employees?', *Harvard Business Review*, vol. 46, 1968, pp. 3–62.

38. Blauner R, *Alienation and Freedom*, University of Chicago Press (1964).

39. See, for example, Riley M, *Human Resource Management: A guide to personnel practice in the hotel and catering industry*, Butterworth-Heinemann (1991).

40. Ellis P, *The Image of Hotel and Catering Work*, HCITB Research Report (1981).

41. *Employee Relations for the Hotel and Catering Industry*, 7th edn, HCTC (1990).

42. Pavesic D V and Brymer R A, 'Job Satisfaction: 'What's Happening to the Young Managers?' *Cornell HRA Quarterly*, vol. 30, no. 4, February 1990, pp. 90–96.

43. Simons T and Enz C A, 'Motivating Hotel Employees: Beyond the carrot and the stick', *Cornell HRA Quarterly*, February 1995, pp. 20–27.

44. Kovach K, 'What Motivates Employees? Workers and Supervisors Give Different Answers', *Business Horizons*, September–October 1987, pp. 58–65.

45. Boella M J, *Human Resource Management in the Hospitality Industry*, 6th edn, Stanley Thornes, (1996), p. 45.

46. See, for example, Mill R C, *Managing for Productivity in the Hospitality Industry*, Van Nostrand Reinhold (1989).

47. Magurn J P, *A Manual of Staff Management in the Hotel and Catering Industry*, Heinemann (1983).

48. Hackman J R and Oldham G R, *Work Design*, Addison-Wesley (1980).

49. Lee-Ross D, 'Attitudes and Work Motivation of Subgroups of Seasonal Hotel Workers', *The Services Industries Journal*, vol. 15, no. 3, July 1995, pp. 295–313.

50. Lee-Ross D, 'The Reliability and Rationale of Hackman and Oldham's Job Diagnostic Survey and Job Characteristics Model among Seasonal Hotel Workers', *International Journal of Hospitality Management*, vol. 17, 1998, pp. 391–406.

51. See, for example, Hales C, 'Quality of Working Life: job redesign and participation in a service industry: a rose by any other name?', *The Service Industries Journal*, vol. 7, no. 3, 1987, pp. 253–273.

52. See, for example, Grayson D, *Self-Regulating Work Groups*, Work Research Unit, Occasional Paper no. 46, HMSO (July 1990).

53. Keegan B M, 'Leadership in the Hospitality Industry', in Cassee E and Reuland R (eds), *The Management of Hospitality*, Pergamon (1983).

54. Porter L W and Roberts K H, *Communication in Organizations*, Penguin (1977), p. 97.

55. Orwell G, *Down and Out in Paris and London*, Penguin (1933), p. 69.

56. Jones P and Davies A, 'Empowerment: A study of general managers of four-star hotel properties in the UK', *International Journal of Hospitality Management*, vol. 10, no. 3, 1991, pp. 211–217.

57. Pickard J, 'The Real Meaning of Empowerment', *Personnel Management*, vol. 25, no. 11, November 1993, pp. 28–33.

58. Lashley C, 'Towards an Understanding of Employee Empowerment in Hospitality Services', *International Journal of Contemporary Hospitality Management*, vol. 7, no. 1, 1995, pp. 27–32.

59. Lashley C, 'Employee Empowerment in Services: A Framework for Analysis', *Personnel Review*, vol. 28, no. 3, 1999, pp. 169–191.

60. Erstad M, 'Empowerment and Organizational Change', *International Journal of Contemporary Hospitality Management*, vol. 9, no. 7, 1997, pp. 325–333.

61. See, for example, Simmons P and Teare R, 'Evolving a Total Quality Culture', *International Journal of Contemporary Hospitality Management*, vol. 5, no. 3, 1993, pp. v–viii.

62. For a more detailed account of quality circles, see Mullins L J, *Management and Organisational Behavior*, 5th edn, Financial Times Pitman Publishing (1999).

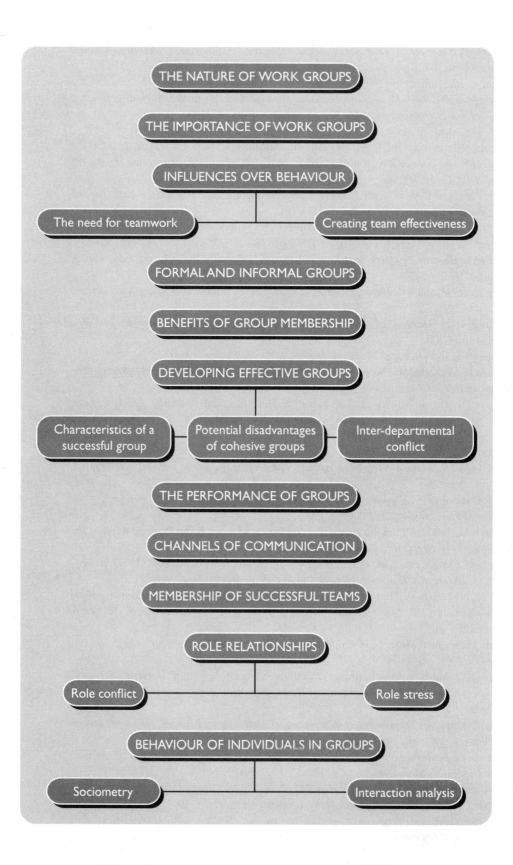

Chapter eight

Group behaviour and performance

Introduction

Groups are an essential feature of the structure of any hospitality organisation. Individuals seldom work in isolation from others and almost all staff in the hospitality industry will be a member of one or more groups. If performance is to be successful, the activities of staff require coordination through the operation of groups and effective teamwork.

The nature of work groups

The structure of the hospitality organisation is made up of groups of people. Members of a group must cooperate together in order that activities are carried out. Groups are a major influence over behaviour and the work pattern of the organisation. The manager must use groups in order to achieve a high standard of work and improve the effectiveness of hospitality operations. This requires an understanding of the functioning and processes of groups, and their influence on the behaviour and performance of people at work.

What is a group?

Most people will readily understand what constitutes a group although there appears to be no single, accepted definition. The central feature of a group is that its members regard themselves as belonging to the group. One way of defining a work group is a collection of people who share most if not all of the following characteristics:

- a definable membership;
- group consciousness;
- a sense of shared purpose;
- interdependence;
- interaction; and
- ability to act in a unitary manner.[1]

It is important to consider both the structure and processes of the group, and its effects on the behaviour of individual members. Another useful definition of the group, in psychological terms, is any number of people who:

(i) interact with one another;

(ii) are psychologically aware of one another; and

(iii) perceive themselves to be a group.[2]

The importance of work groups

The large majority of activities and processes in the work situation require at least some degree of group, as well as individual, effort.[3] This is an important point to emphasise. Recall that the classical approach to organisation and management tended to ignore the importance of groups and the social factors at work. Scientific management, for example, popularised the concept of the 'rabble hypothesis'. This assumed that people carried out their work, and could be motivated, as solitary individuals unaffected by others.

The human relations approach, however, drew attention to the work organisation as a social organisation. Recognition was given to the power of group membership over individual behaviour and work performance. Emphasis was placed on the importance of the informal organisation, and the influence of groups on social satisfaction and work performance.

The socio-technical approach

The systems approach also gave recognition to the importance of groups. The concept of the organisation as a socio-technical system is concerned with the interactions between psychological and social factors, as well as the structural and technical requirements of the organisation. The importance of the socio-technical system was illustrated by the introduction of technological change and new methods of working in the coalmining industry.[4]

Small self-selecting groups of miners worked together as independent teams on one part of the coalface. The increasing use of mechanisation and the introduction of shift-working enabled coal to be extracted on a 'longwall' method. This was, technically, a more efficient and economic system. However, the new method of working disrupted the integration of the groups and brought about changes in the social relationships of the miners. As a result there was a lack of cooperation between and within shifts, an increase in absenteeism, scapegoating and signs of social stress.

The 'longwall' method was socially disruptive to the work groups and did not prove as economically efficient as it could have done with the new technology. The result was a 'composite' method of working with more responsibility taken by the team as a whole, shifts carrying out composite tasks and the reintroduction of multi-skilled roles. The composite method proved to be both more rewarding socially for the miners and also a more efficient method of working.

Influences over behaviour

Groups, therefore, are a characteristic feature of all social situations. The working of groups and the influence they exert over their membership is a major feature of human behaviour and group processes. People in groups influence each other in many ways, and groups develop their own hierarchies and leaders. Group pressures to conform with 'norms' and social conventions can have a significant influence over the behaviour of individual members and their work performance.

You may recall that one experiment of the Hawthorne studies (discussed in Chapter 6) was the observation of a group of 14 men working in the bank wiring room. It was noted that the men formed their own informal organisation with sub-groups and cliques, and with natural leaders emerging with the consent of members. They would often help each other with the work and, contrary to management instructions, members would often exchange jobs.

Group values and norms of behaviour

The group developed its own pattern of informal social relations, and codes and practices ('norms') of what constituted 'proper' group behaviour:

- *not to be a 'rate buster'* – not to produce at too high a rate of output compared with other members or to exceed the production restriction of the group;
- *not to be a 'chiseller'* – not to shirk production or to produce at too low a rate of output compared with other members of the group;
- *not to be a 'squealer'* – not to say anything to the supervisor or management which might be harmful to other members of the group;
- *not to be 'officious'* – people with authority over members of the group, for example inspectors, should not take advantage of their seniority or maintain a social distance from the group.

Despite a financial incentive scheme where workers could receive more money for the more units they produced, the group decided on 6,000 units a day as a fair level of output. This was well below the level they were capable of producing but group pressure was stronger than financial incentives offered by management.

It was also company policy that the supervisor should report daily on each man's output. However, the workers preferred to do their own reporting. On some days the men would actually produce more than reported in order to 'build up' extra units for days when they produced less than reported. In order to remain in favour with the group the supervisor did nothing to stop this practice.

System of sanctions

If individual members did not conform to these norms of behaviour the group had its own system of sanctions. These included ostracising members, sarcasm and verbal abuse, damaging completed work, hiding tools, and playing tricks on inspectors. Threats of physical violence were also made. The group developed a system of 'binging' which involved striking someone a fairly hard blow on the upper part of the arm. The process of binging also became a recognised method of controlling conflict within the group.

Overlapping group structure

Groups are formed as a consequence of the structure of the organisation and arrangements for the division of work. They help shape the activities and work pattern of the organisation, and the attitudes of members to their jobs. The formation and operation of work groups, and the behaviour of their members, has important significance for the manager and the effective performance of activities and operations.

Likert, for example, has developed a theory of organisation based on work groups. In his discussion of group processes and organisational performance he concludes that:

Figure 8.1:
Representation
of Likert's
overlapping
group structures

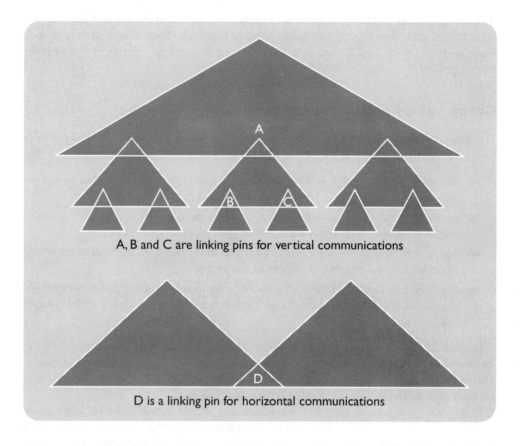

A, B and C are linking pins for vertical communications

D is a linking pin for horizontal communications

Group forces are important not only in influencing the behavior of individual work groups with regard to productivity, waste, absence and the like, they also affect the behavior of entire organisations.[5]

Part of the criteria for System 4 participative group management (discussed in Chapter 4) is the use of overlapping group structures. Likert suggests that the organisation functions best when members act, not as individuals, but as members of highly effective work groups. He proposes a structure based on overlapping group membership with a 'linking pin' process. The superior of one group is a subordinate member of, and the linking pin with, the next authority-level group.

A structure of vertical overlapping groups helps to develop a committed team approach and improve the flow of communications, coordination and decision-making. Members of one group could also serve as linking pins between different groups on the same level. This provides improved horizontal communications and coordination (Figure 8.1).

The need for teamwork

Work is a group-based activity and especially so in hospitality operations. How people behave and perform as a member of a group is as important as their behaviour or performance as individuals. If the hotel, for example, is to operate effectively it requires good teamwork.[6] Simmons and Teare draw attention to the emphasis on teamwork at every level of Scott's Hotels and to the importance of group working, quality improvement teams and action teams as part of a total quality management approach to improved quality and performance.[7]

Not only must members of a group work well as a team but each group must also work well with other groups. It is important to reduce conflict between different groups, and especially between front-of-house staff such as receptionists, and back-of-house staff such as housekeepers.[8]

Groups and teams

Whereas all teams are by definition a group it does not necessarily follow that all groups are teams. A team, therefore, involves something extra such as high levels of morale and group cohesiveness, mutual trust and goodwill among members, and commitment to group goals and objectives.[9]

> All new staff on joining are given an induction pack the very first sentence of which is:
>
> ### 'The hotel is a team of people, not a collection of individuals'
>
> This epitomises The Seaview's approach to the recruitment, management and development of its staff as an integrated team that works hard to present a united, competent service capability to its customers.
>
> Each team leader and the partners have clearly defined understandings of the aims, priorities and working systems and procedures within each area of the hotel. These are regularly communicated to their entire team, with each department involved in the recruitment, training and appraisal of their own staff. All team leaders have received management training.
>
> **THE SEAVIEW HOTEL AND RESTAURANT**

It is not easy, however, to distinguish clearly between a 'group' and a 'team'. Riley, for example, offers the following observation:

> *Managers like to talk of teams and teamwork but these words are both difficult to define, let alone achieve. Giving a set of individuals a group task to do won't of itself, form them into groups. Putting on a coloured shirt and running onto a field with others similarly attired won't make them a team! Yet teamwork can be seen and felt – it is a tangible thing. The real problem is that we organise people into groups, call them teams, but don't look to see if they are actually behaving like groups or teams. The words 'group' and 'team' tend to be used coterminously, but one expression is central to both concepts and that is 'common identity'.*[10]

Harmonious working relationships and good teamwork help make for a high level of both staff morale and customer satisfaction. An example of the importance placed on teamwork is the extract from the introductory pages of Foxhills' staff induction manual.

The importance of teamwork

What is teamwork?

When a group of people communicate well and clearly, work closely together and help each other with instruction and/or actual labour during work, teamwork is achieved. This means HELPING your colleagues WHENEVER and WHEREVER they need it.

Why is teamwork important?

Teamwork makes everyone's job easier and makes the department a better place to work in. It also allows and promotes friendship and caring. When you help another colleague get their job done, you are helping yourself. If the customer is served by a person with a confident attitude everyone benefits. This means the co-operation of all staff is essential. It is very obvious that the waiting and barstaff are contributing to customer service and satisfaction. There are others who will ensure a customer is comfortable and happy. The kitchen staff doing their job well is of the highest import-ance. There are good food waiters and waitresses but you cannot be good without a good product. Think about it!

> THE NUMBER ONE RULE IS TO COMMUNICATE CLEARLY AND
> EFFECTIVELY WITH YOUR COLLEAGUES

If you expect and receive instructions and help, return the favour. Before you know it everyone is not only doing their job well, but also helping others and working as part of the team.

Remember to tell people you appreciate what they are doing for you. Thank each person that helps you do your job. We all play a role in customer satisfaction.

Watch your attitude – no one wants to work with a grump or worse, if you are down you spread it around and nobody needs that.

Teamwork at Foxhills is essential to everyone's morale. Try it. Help out a fellow employee and watch it come back to you in the form of appreciation. Teamwork means helping each other and solving problems together. It is mutual respect and open communications on all levels, employee to employee, employee to manager, manager to manager.

> TEAM WORK IS WORK
> BUT IT IS WORTH IT.

Source: Extract from staff induction manual, Foxhills Golf and Country Club; reproduced with permission.

Creating team effectiveness

The importance of people's ability to work together in the hospitality industry and the many potential benefits from successful team-building are emphasised by Berger and Vanger.

> *A successful team-building effort will improve your employees' productivity. They will be better able to handle complex operations; they will respond more quickly to new situations; they will be more motivated and will make better decisions.*[11]

Berger and Vanger suggest six main steps in the team-building cycle.

● *Identify the problem you wish to solve and define the objective for team-building.* An example would be to encourage a competent team to work together even more successfully or to assemble a new team for a special project. It is important to secure the willingness and commitment of staff to the team-building process.

● *Gather information about the problem.* This can be achieved through: (i) an open 'clear the air' meeting to discuss grievances; (ii) conducting a survey to establish the conflicts and difficulties the group might face; or (iii) bringing in an outside consultant.

● *Communication with group members.* Sufficient time should be allowed so that the discussion can focus on each item in turn and be free-ranging. The group leader should participate and encourage group members to join the discussion, and to elaborate their views on each topic.

● *Plan for change.* Group members should be able to work together and establish plans for eliminating blockages to the operation's effectiveness. Each member must be willing to compromise. The team should establish group objectives, the decision-making process and strategies for overcoming conflict.

● *Implement the plans.* The team should continue to function according to the guidelines it has established for itself. Other members of staff who have not been involved in the team-building sessions should be kept fully informed and involved in the plans.

● *Evaluate the group's ability as a team.* One way of measuring success is for the group to establish its own charter of procedures and to survey team members to find out how well the charter is being adhered to. Negative feedback should be addressed to the group as a whole and balanced with complimentary remarks. Reassurance and appreciation should be given when overall performance is acceptable.

Berger and Vanger claim that one of the greatest blocks to teamwork is a failure of communications. If members of staff feel isolated, they avoid talking with each other. This can result in a number of individuals, each operating according to their own concept of customer service. Such an attitude means that functioning as a team is extremely difficult and it makes for an erratic service to customers.

From a study of three TGI Friday's restaurants, Gardner and Wood found that team-building was the result of practical measures, especially the careful selection of employees, and identified six key features which contributed to the achievement of teamwork:

● careful selection of employees;

● substantial training;

● regular formal meetings of service personnel;

● a small number of explicit articulated rules of behaviour and procedure;

● emphasis on relationships with customers;

● clear and open systems of performance rewards in addition to formal remuneration.[12]

Happy teams at Heineken

Included in a study of top European companies and 'making teamwork work', Heller refers to the happy teams at Heineken. As part of the cultural strength of Heineken is a realisation that the best culture for an organisation is a strong team culture, and that people who have to work together as a team must also think together as a team, the team-thinking at Heineken demonstrates 'the power of decentralised team management'. The essence of teamworking is that all members are responsible for the results of the team – but this principle in no way absolves leadership in cases of disaster.[13] (Leadership is discussed in Chapter 9.)

Formal and informal groups

Groups are deliberately planned and created by management as part of organisational design. An organisation chart, for example, gives a representation of the formal structure of the hotel. But groups also arise from social processes and the informal organisation, which was discussed in Chapter 6. The informal organisation arises from the interactions of people working within the hospitality organisation and the development of groups with their own relationships and norms of behaviour, irrespective of those defined within the formal structure. This leads to a major distinction between formal groups and informal groups.

Formal groups

Formal groups are concerned with the achievement of specific organisational objectives and with the *coordination of work activities*. They are created by management with established rules, relationships and norms of behaviour. The nature of the tasks to be undertaken is a predominant feature of the formal group. People are brought together on the basis of defined roles within the structure of the establishment. Formal groups tend to be relatively permanent although there may be changes in actual membership. However, temporary formal groups may also be established by management, for example to undertake a specific task such as preparations for a special banquet.

Informal groups

Within the formal structure there will always be an informal structure. The formal structure, and system of role relationships, rules and procedures, will be augmented by interpretation and development at the informal level. Informal groups are based more on personal relationships and agreement of group members than on defined role relationships. They serve to satisfy psychological and social needs which are not necessarily related to the tasks to be undertaken.[14]

Informal groups may arise from the same horizontal level, but they also arise vertically or diagonally. The membership of informal groups therefore cuts across the formal structure. They may comprise individuals from different parts of the establishment and/or from different levels. An informal group could also be the same as the formal group or it might comprise a part only of the formal group (Figure 8.2).

Characteristics of informal groups

Informal groups develop their own characteristics. They may have their own culture, status values and symbols, and their own system of communications through the 'grapevine'. Informal groups are also agents of social satisfaction and control. As a result there is often strong resistance to changes which threaten the status quo, or the environment or working practices of the group.[15]

Figure 8.2: Possible examples of informal groups within the formal structure

It is possible for the leader of an informal group to be the same person as the formal leader appointed officially by management. It is more usual, however, for the group to have its own informal leader who exercises authority by the consent of the members themselves. The informal leader may be chosen as the person who reflects the attitudes and values of the members, helps to resolve conflict, leads the group in satisfying its goals, or liaises with management or other people outside the group.

You may recall the discussion on the importance of cultural influences in Chapter 3. A multi-cultural work environment may lead to the emergence of informal groups and cliques based on common nationality, religion or shared ethnic values, and with their own leaders and spokespersons. Such informal groups are not necessarily harmful to the operations of the establishment but it is important that the manager emphasises the need for effective cooperation and teamwork.

The formal and informal roles of hotel security staff

Security staff are normally responsible to the hotel general manager for ensuring that company property and the personal belongings of guests and staff are protected. They are also required to intervene when problems arise with guests who do not pay their accounts and, if any disorder occurs, they are expected to apprehend the troublesome guest(s) or visitor(s) and escort them quietly off the hotel premises, if need be with police assistance. Additional duties include responsibility for the health and safety of all persons in the hotel, especially guests and hotel employees. Most security staff are retired male police officers, or have gained experience in the military police service, and they normally work shifts to ensure that continuous surveillance is maintained.

As might be expected, security staff tend to keep a low profile and the typical guest would not normally be able to distinguish them from other departmental managers, since they usually wear the same company dress, and their section is normally regarded as an administrative department in the hotel's organisational structure. They have an office of their own, however, for occasions when guests and staff have to be interviewed in private. Otherwise, many of their activities are carried out in the reception area, where the hotel safe is often located along with other automatic security and safety monitoring equipment.

Other more discreet tasks undertaken by security staff, rarely discussed with other managers at departmental meetings, depend on the location of the hotel.

For example, some of the major concerns of security teams in London hotels include the prevention of fraudulent activities or drug trafficking by guests, car thefts, and ensuring that prostitutes, known as 'Toms', do not loiter in the public areas and solicit guests before they retire for the night. Electronic locks are fitted on the bedroom doors in most London hotels and movements in and out of rooms can be monitored on a control panel located in the reception area. Whenever soliciting is observed, security staff inform the guest by telephone that the room-charge will be raised from a single- to a double-room rate unless an immediate inspection is allowed, and the interloper is almost always intercepted on leaving and 'warned off' from entering the hotel again under threat of police action.

These problems rarely occur in suburban hotels where the chief security officer usually acts as a duty manager and often interviews all new employees at the start

continued

continued

of their induction period. It is also common for security officers to 'clear' any new employee confidentially through contacts with former police colleagues. Housekeeping and laundry staff are also encouraged to report unusual guest behaviour directly to the security officer and employees who cooperate are usually nominated for an 'Employee of the Month' cash award. Despite their lack of technical skills in the running of hotels, security staff enjoy considerable informal power which is not always used impartially. For example, the dismissals or resignations of several managers were provoked by 'whispering campaigns' instigated by security staff and members of their informal cliques in two different hotels.

Source: McEwan T, *A Replicated Study of Communication Networks,*
Job Retention and Labour Turnover in Two British Hotels,
Unpublished doctoral thesis, Cranfield Institute of Technology, Cranfield, 1988.

Benefits of group membership

Individuals have varying expectations of the benefits from group membership (formal and/or informal) relating to both social processes and work performance.

- Groups provide companionship and a source of mutual understanding and support from colleagues. This can help in solving work problems or mitigating against stressful or demanding working conditions.

- Membership of the group can provide the individual with a sense of belonging. The group provides a feeling of identity, and the chance to acquire role recognition and status within the group.

- The group provides guidelines on generally acceptable behaviour. It helps to clarify ambiguous situations such as, for example, the extent to which official rules and regulations are expected to be adhered to in practice. Group allegiance can serve as a means of determining norms of behaviour, such as in the bank wiring room mentioned above.

- The combined efforts of members of a group can have a synergistic effect. The collective knowledge and expertise of members can help in problem-solving and in the performance of complex or difficult tasks.

- Groups may encourage the modification of formal working arrangements to become more to the liking of members, for example by sharing or rotating unpopular tasks. Group membership can provide opportunities for initiative and creativity.

- The group may provide mutual support and protection for its members, for example by collaborating to safeguard their interests from outside pressures or threats.

Morale and work performance

Groups are therefore a potential source of motivation and job satisfaction, and also a major determinant of effective organisational performance. Membership of a cohesive group can be a rewarding experience for the individual and can contribute to the promotion of morale. Members of a high-morale group are more likely to think of themselves as a group and to work together effectively.

Lysons suggests four main reasons why people form **informal** groups:

- the perpetuation of the informal group culture;
- the maintenance of a communication system;
- the implementation of social control; and
- the provision of interest and fun in work life.[16]

Developing effective groups

Cooperation among members is likely to be greater in a united, cohesive group. The manager's main concern is that members of a work group cooperate in order to achieve the results expected of them. The work of a hospitality organisation entails a wide range of operations, many of which are undertaken simultaneously, and depend upon a high degree of coordination and team-work. This calls for good working relationships among staff and effective group activities.[17]

In order to develop the effectiveness of work groups, the manager will be concerned with those factors that contribute to group cohesiveness, or that may cause frustration or disruption to the operation and performance of the group. The manager needs to consider, therefore, both the needs of individual members of the group, and the promotion of a high level of group identity and cohesion.

Many factors contribute to group cohesiveness and performance.[18] These can be summarised under four broad headings: membership, work environment, organisational, and group development and maturity (Figure 8.3).

Figure 8.3:
Factors
contributing
to group
cohesiveness
and performance

Membership of the group

- *Size of the group* – It is difficult to put a figure on the ideal size of a work group and much will depend upon other variables. But it seems to be generally accepted that cohesiveness becomes more difficult to achieve when a group exceeds 10–12 members. Berger and Vanger, for example, suggest that team-building is most successful in groups of six to ten people.[19] As a group increases in size, problems arise with communications and coordination. Large groups are more difficult to handle and require a higher level of supervision. Absenteeism also tends to be higher in larger groups. When a group becomes too large, it may split into smaller units and friction may develop between sub-groups.

- *Compatibility of the members* – The more homogeneous the members of a group in terms of, for example, shared backgrounds, interests, attitudes and values, the easier it is to promote cohesiveness. Differences between individual members such as personality and skills can serve to complement each other and help make for a cohesive group. However, such differences may also be the cause of disruption and conflict.

- *Permanence of membership* – Group spirit and relationships take time to develop. Cohesiveness is more likely to be achieved when members of a group are together for a reasonable length of time and changes occur only slowly. A frequent turnover of members is likely to have an adverse effect on morale and social satisfaction, and on the cohesiveness of the group.

The work environment

- *The nature of the task* – Where individuals are involved in similar work, share a common task or face the same problems, this may assist cohesiveness. The nature of the task may serve to bring people together. An example could be receptionists working in a large and busy international hotel.

- *Physical setting and communications* – Where members of a group work in the same location or in close physical proximity to each other, this will often help cohesiveness. The more easily members can communicate freely with each other, the greater the likelihood of group cohesion. Members of the maintenance staff working on their own in different parts of a hotel may experience a lack of group identity. However, isolation from other workers may also tend to build cohesiveness. This may apply, for example, to a smaller number of workers on the night rota.

- *Technology and the manner in which work is carried out* – Where the nature of the work process involves a craft- or skill-based 'technology' there is a higher likelihood of cohesiveness. For example, in a small, high-class hotel particularly noted for the standard of its cuisine, members of the kitchen brigade need to interact and work closely with each other for effective performance. (You could compare this, for instance, with the mass production technology of fast-food chain stores.)

Organisational

- *Managerial style* – The activities of groups cannot be separated from management and the process of leadership. The style of leadership adopted will influence the relationship between the group and management, and is a major determinant of group cohesiveness. In general terms, cohesiveness will be affected by the manner in which the manager gives guidance, encouragement and support to the group, provides opportunities for participation, attempts to resolve difficulties and conflicts, and adopts a Theory Y approach.

● *Success and positive motivation* – The more successful the group, the more cohesive it is likely to be: and cohesive groups are more likely to be successful. Success is usually a strong and positive motivational influence on the level of work performance. Success or reward as a positive motivator can be perceived by group members in a number of ways, for example, the satisfactory completion of a difficult task through cooperative action, recognition and praise from management, a feeling of high status or esteem, high wage payments from a group-based bonus scheme.

● *Personnel policies and procedures* – Attention should be given to the effects that systems of appraisal, transfers, promotion and discipline, and opportunities for training and personal development, have on members of the group. Harmony within the group is more likely to be achieved if personnel policies and procedures are perceived to be equitable, and all members receive what they believe is fair treatment by management.

● *External threat* – Cohesiveness may be enhanced by members cooperating with one another when faced with a common external threat, for example the introduction of new technology or changes in their method of work, or the appointment of a new supervisor. Even if the threat is subsequently removed, the group may still continue to have a greater degree of cohesion than before the threat arose. Conflict between groups will also tend to increase the cohesiveness of each group and the boundaries of the groups become drawn more closely.

Group development and maturity

Cohesiveness is also affected by the manner in which groups progress through the various stages of development and maturity. Tuckman, for example, identifies four main successive stages of group development and relationships: forming, storming, norming and performing.[20]

● *Stage 1: Forming* – The initial formation of the group. This involves the bringing together of a number of individuals and the tentative identification of the purpose of the group, its composition and terms of reference. Consideration is given to the hierarchical structure of the group, pattern of leadership, individual roles and responsibilities, and codes of conduct. At this stage there is likely to be considerably anxiety as members attempt to create an impression, to test each other and to establish their personal identity within the group.

● *Stage 2: Storming* – As members of the group get to know each other better, they will put forward their views more openly and forcefully. Disagreements will be expressed and challenges offered on the nature of the task and the arrangements made during the forming stage. The storming stage is important because, if it is successful, there will be discussions on reforming the working and operation of the group, and agreement on more meaningful structures and procedures.

● *Stage 3: Norming* – As conflict and hostility start to be controlled, members of the group will establish guidelines and standards, and develop their own norms of acceptable behaviour. The norming stage is important in establishing the need for members to cooperate together in order to plan, agree standards of performance and fulfil the purpose of the group.

● *Stage 4: Performing* – When the group has progressed successfully through the earlier three stages it will have created structure and cohesiveness to work effectively as a team. At this stage the group can concentrate on the attainment of its purpose, and performance of the common task is likely to be at its most effective.

> *These main stages of forming, storming, norming and performing are at the basis of effective team-building.*[21]

Characteristics of a successful group

Bass and Ryterband also identify four distinct stages in effective group development:

● mutual acceptance and membership;
● communication and decision-making;
● motivation and productivity; and
● control and organisation.[22]

Another writer suggests that new groups go through the following stages:

● the polite stage;
● the why are we here, what are we doing? stage;
● which dominant will emerge? – the power stage;
● the constructive stage, when sharing beings; and
● the unity stage – which often takes weeks, eating together and talking together.[23]

The characteristics of a successful work group are not always easy to isolate clearly. The underlying feature is a spirit of cooperation in which members work well together as a united team, and with harmonious and supportive relationships. This may be evidenced when members of a group exhibit:

● a belief in shared objectives;
● a sense of commitment to the group;
● acceptance of group values and norms;
● a feeling of mutual trust and dependency;
● full participation by all members and decision-making by consensus;
● a free flow of information and communications;
● the open expression of feelings and disagreements; and
● the resolution of conflict by the members themselves.[24]

Potential disadvantages of cohesive groups

In order to develop effective working groups the manager should give attention to those factors which influence the creation of group identity and cohesiveness. But strong, cohesive groups also present potential disadvantages for management. Cohesive groups do not necessarily produce a higher level of output. Performance varies with the extent to which the group accepts or rejects the goals of the organisation. The level of output is likely to respond to a standard acceptable as a norm by the group.[25] It may be remembered, for example, that in the bank wiring room experiment group norms and pressures on individual members led to unofficial working methods, and restrictions on the level of output. But cohesive groups may result in greater interaction, lower turnover and absenteeism, and after higher output.[26]

It is important, therefore, that the manager attempts to influence the group during the norming stage when members are establishing guidelines and standards and their own norms of acceptable behaviour. Once a group has become fully developed, created cohesiveness and established its own culture, it is more difficult for the manager to change successfully the attitudes and behaviour of the group.[27]

Inter-group conflict

Strong, cohesive groups may develop a critical or even hostile attitude towards people outside the group or members of other groups. This can be the case, for example, when group cohesiveness is based on common status, social background, qualifications or technical expertise. Strong, cohesive groups might cause difficulties for the socialisation and effective assimilation of new members of staff and add to the induction crisis and high staff turnover. For example, Bowey reports a case of high staff turnover among waitresses in a restaurant where in order to protect their own interests the established waiting staff adopted an unpleasant demeanour to new members of staff.[28]

Group cohesiveness may result in a lack of cooperation with other groups. Resentment and inter-group conflict may arise, to the detriment of the organisation as a whole. A classic example is Whyte's study of the American restaurant industry and the social interactions between two groups of workers – the chefs and the waiting staff.[29] The chefs, who regarded themselves to be of high status and generally recognised as such by the staff, resented being 'told' what to do by the waitresses, who were generally regarded to be of lower status. As a result arguments resulted, disrupting performance. The conflict in status was resolved by the introduction of an ordering process by which the chefs received customers' orders without the appearance of taking instructions from the 'lower-status' waitresses.

In order to help prevent, or overcome, unconstructive inter-group conflict, the manager should attempt to stimulate a high level of communication and interaction between the groups, and to maintain harmony. Where appropriate, rotation of members among different groups should be encouraged.

However, inter-group rivalry may sometimes be encouraged as a means of helping to build stronger within-group cohesiveness.[30] The idea is that a competitive element may help to promote unity within a group. But inter-group rivalry and competition need to be carefully handled by the manager. Groups should not normally be put in a situation where they have to compete for resources, status or approval.[31] The manager should attempt to avoid the development of 'win–lose' situations. Emphasis should be placed on broader objectives of the organisation which are over and above the issues at conflict and which, if they are to be achieved, require effective cooperation of the competing groups.

Inter-departmental conflict

Dann and Hornsey draw attention to the prevalence of inter-departmental conflict as a distinctive feature of hotel operations. They suggest four main reasons which, either in isolation or collectively, may heighten inter-departmental conflicts:

- interdependence and the relationships between departments;
- the hotel environment and the framework within which activities occur;
- rewards and the nature of the total payment package;
- status and stigma, and the perceptions of workers within the industry.[32]

Interdependence

Interdependence arises from the nature of work flows in the industry, and the require-ment for close and often immediate cooperation between two or more departments, for example the kitchen and the restaurant. A fundamental conflict may arise between the desire for autonomy and independence, and the necessity for interdependence and reliance on other people. If one department feels that the other has acted unfairly or not reciprocated a favour, there is potential for conflict. An important reason for inter-departmental conflict is goal differentiations, for example between the chef's concern for quality and that of the service staff for speed.

Social environment

The social environment of the hotel industry has a number of distinctive features which are potential sources of conflict. Departments which have direct contact with the customers adapt their attitudes and work behaviour to the situation, and this emphasises differences from other departments. The speed of operations and need for quick decisions put stress and pressure on staff. The industry is typified by authoritarian leadership styles and formal patterns of organisation. There are often strong territorial perspectives about the place of work, for example in the kitchen or the front office desk.

Reward structure

The structure of the reward system can cause perceived inequity and result in conflict between departments. The presence of tips can lead to a distorted view of differentials in earnings, and different attitudes towards the customers and management. The perceived opportun-ities for fiddles can also be a source of conflict between departments. Another source of conflict is perceived inequity in the allocation of scarce resources to different departments.

Perceived status or stigma

Rigid organisational hierarchies have resulted in a highly differentiated and established status system in the industry. This is based on the perception of different positions and job titles. For example, receptionists see themselves as a high-status group whilst other positions such as kitchen porters carry a distinct stigma. The status system is established by tradition and myth, and reinforced through group pressure. Perceived differences in status can also arise between different nationalities or between men and women. (You may recall the discussion on sex stereotyping and gender in Chapter 3.)

The performance of groups

We have seen the importance of groups to the working life of the hospitality industry, and of creating effective team-work. But is group performance better than individual performance? It is difficult to draw any firm conclusions. An example is the process of decision-making. Certain groups may be concerned more specifically with decision-making, such as a management team, but all groups must make some decisions. Group decision-making can be costly, time-consuming and possibly frustrating for members but it would appear to offer a number of advantages.

- Groups bring together a range of complementary knowledge, skills and experience.
- Interaction among members can have a 'snowball' effect, and provide an impetus for further thoughts and ideas in the minds of others.
- Group discussion leads to the evaluation and revision of possible decisions.
- Provided full participation has been facilitated, decisions will have the acceptance of all, or most, members. They are then more likely to be committed to decisions made, and to their implementation.

Given these advantages, one might expect a higher standard of decision-making to result from group discussion. However, there is the danger of compromise and decisions being made in line with the 'highest common view'. There is also the phenomenon of the so-called 'risky-shift', and the concept of 'groupthink'.

The 'risky-shift' phenomenon

This suggests that instead of the group taking fewer risks and making safer or more conservative decisions, the reverse is often the case. There is a tendency for groups to make more risky decisions than would be taken by members of the group as individuals.[33]

It is perhaps understandable that members of a group do not feel the same sense of responsibility for decisions of the group or their possible outcomes. This seems to be summed up in the belief that: 'a decision which is everyone's is the responsibility of no one'. Other possible explanations for the risk-shift phenomenon include:

- people who are inclined to be more adventurous and take more risks may be more influential in group discussions;
- the group may generate a greater range of possible solutions including those that carry greater risk; and
- risk-taking may be perceived as a desirable cultural characteristic which is more likely to be expressed in a social situation such as group discussion.

Groups do, however, appear to work well in the evaluation of ideas. They are more effective than individuals for problem-solving tasks requiring a range of knowledge and expertise. Research evidence appears to support the view that, compared with individuals, groups produce more solutions, and better solutions, to problems.[34]

Groupthink

The effectiveness of group behaviour and performance can be adversely affected by the idea of 'groupthink'. From an examination of some well-known government policy-making groups, Janis concluded that decisions can be characterised by groupthink which he defines as: 'a deterioration of mental efficiency, reality testing, and moral judgement that results from in-group pressures'. The idea of groupthink is not, however, limited to government policy-making groups but it is a generalised feature and can be apparent in any organisational situation where groups are relied upon to make important decisions.[35]

Janis identifies a number of specific symptoms of groupthink, including the following:

- There is *an illusion of invulnerability* with excessive optimism and risk-taking.
- *Pressures on individual members to conform and reach consensus* mean that minority or unpopular ideas may be suppressed. Members who oppose the group are stereotyped as evil, weak or stupid.
- The search for group consensus can result in *collective rationalisation* by members to discount warnings and there is an illusion of unanimity. There is self-censorship of any deviation from group norms or apparent group consensus.
- An unquestioned belief in the *inherent morality of the group* which leads members to be convinced of the logical correctness of what it is doing and to ignore ethical or moral consequences of decisions.

The effects of groupthink often occur in committees and working parties with a drifting along towards decisions which may be inappropriate or which are not questioned fully.[36]

Brainstorming

One method of attempting to evoke full group discussion and to generate possible solutions to problems is through a 'brainstorming' approach.[37] Brainstorming is based on the assumption that creative thinking is achieved best by encouraging the natural inclinations of group members and the free association of ideas. The quantity of ideas will lead to quality of ideas. A brainstorming approach involves the group adopting a 'free-wheeling' attitude and generating as many ideas as possible. The more wild or apparently far-fetched the ideas, the better.

There are a number of basic procedures for a brainstorming approach.

- Emphasis is placed initially on the quantity of ideas generated, and not the quality of ideas.
- No matter how wild or fanciful they may appear, no individual ideas are criticised or rejected at this stage.
- Members are encouraged to elaborate or build on the ideas of others and to bounce suggestions off one another.
- There is no evaluation of any particular idea or suggestion until all possibilities have been generated.

Channels of communication

The level of interaction among members of a group is influenced by the structuring of channels of communication. Laboratory research by Bavelas[38] and subsequent studies by other researchers such as Leavitt[39] have resulted in the design of a series of communication networks.

There are five main types of communication networks: wheel, circle, all-channel, Y and chains (see Figure 8.4).

- The **wheel**, also sometimes known as the star, is the most centralised network. This network is most efficient for simple tasks. Problems are solved more quickly with fewer mistakes and with fewer information flows. The link person is at the centre of the network and acts as the focus of activities and information flows, and the

Figure 8.4:
Communication
networks in
small groups

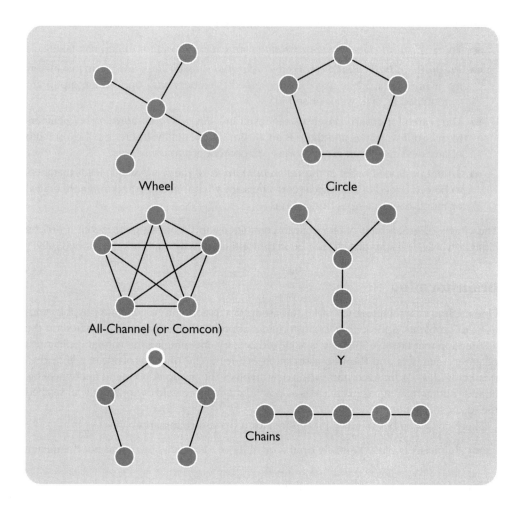

coordinator of group tasks. The central person is perceived as leader of the group
and experiences a high level of satisfaction. However, for members on the periphery,
the wheel is the least satisfying network.

● The **circle** is a more decentralised network. Overall it is less efficient. The group
is unorganised, with low leadership predictability. Performance tends to be slow
and erratic. However, the circle is quicker than the wheel in solving complex problems, and also copes with change or new tasks more efficiently. The circle network
is most satisfying for all the members. Decision-making is likely to involve some
degree of participation.

● The **all-channel network** involves full discussion and participation. This network
appears to work best where a high level of interaction is required among all members of the group in order to solve complex problems. Leadership predictability is
very low. There is a fairly high level of satisfaction for members. The all-channel
network may not stand up well under pressure, in which case it will either disinteg-
rate or reform into a wheel network.

● A **Y** or **chain network** might be appropriate for more simple problem-solving tasks,
requiring little interaction among members of the group. These networks are more

centralised, with information flows along a predetermined channel. Leadership predictability is high to moderate. There is a low to moderate level of satisfaction for members.

Implications for managers

Findings from these studies indicate that the greater the amount of interconnectedness of the network, the higher the general level of satisfaction of members in the group. Groups allowed to establish their own communication networks, and who did so with the minimum of links, took less time to solve their tasks. Those groups who did not minimise the number of links in their network took more time to solve the tasks.

From a review of studies in communication networks, Shaw confirmed that simple tasks were consistently undertaken most efficiently in more centralised networks such as the wheel. More complex tasks were performed more efficiently by decentralised networks such as the circle or the all-channel.[40]

Despite the artificiality of these communication network studies, they do have certain implications for managers who can observe the patterns of communication adopted by different groups in different situations, and also note how communication networks change over time. A knowledge of the findings may be applied to influence the patterns of communication in work groups and how they relate to the performance of the group. Problems which require a high level of interaction among members of the group may not be handled efficiently if there are inadequate channels of communication or sharing of information. The choice of a particular communication network may involve trade-offs between the performance of the work group and the satisfaction of its members.

Membership of successful teams

What factors should be considered in deciding the membership of a management team? Based on years of research and empirical study, Belbin concludes that the most consistently successful teams comprise a range of roles undertaken by various members.[41] The constitution of the team itself is an important variable in its success. Teams composed entirely of clever people, or of people with similar personalities, display a number of negative results and lack creativity.

Key team roles

Belbin describes 'team role' as a pattern of behaviour characteristic of the way in which one team member interacts with another where performance serves to facilitate the progress of the team as a whole. There are eight useful types of contribution:

- Company worker (CW)
- Shaper (SH)
- Resource investigator (Rl)
- Team worker (TW)
- Chairman (CH)
- Plant (PL)
- Monitor–evaluator (ME)
- Completer–finisher (CF)

An explanation of these team roles is given in Figure 8.5. The eight types of people identified are useful team members and form a comprehensive list. These are the key team roles and the primary characters for successful teams. Creative teams require a balance of all these roles and comprise members who have characteristics complementary to one

Figure 8.5: Useful people to have in a team

Type	Symbol	Typical features	Positive qualities	Allowable weaknesses
Company worker	CW	Conservative, dutiful, predictable.	Organising ability, practical common sense, hard-working, self-discipline.	Lack of flexibility, unresponsiveness to unproven ideas.
Chairman	CH	Calm, self-confident controlled.	A capacity for treating and welcoming all potential contributors on their merits and without prejudice. A strong sense of objectives.	No more than ordinary in terms of intellect or creative ability.
Shaper	SH	Highly strung, outgoing, dynamic.	Drive and a readiness to challenge inertia, ineffectiveness, complacency or self-deception.	Proneness to provocation, irritation and impatience.
Plant	PL	Individualistic, serious-minded, unorthodox.	Genius, imagination, intellect, knowledge.	Up in the clouds, inclined to disregard practical details or protocol.
Resource investigator	RI	Extroverted, enthusiastic, curious, communicative.	A capacity for contacting people and exploring anything new. An ability to respond to challenge.	Liable to lose interest once the initial fascination has passed.
Monitor – evaluator	ME	Sober, unemotional, prudent.	Judgement, discretion, hard-headedness.	Lacks inspiration or the ability to motivate others.
Team worker	TW	Socially orientated, rather mild, sensitive.	An ability to respond to people and to situations, and to promote team spirit.	Indecisiveness at moments of crisis.
Completer – finisher	CF	Painstaking, orderly, conscientious, anxious.	A capacity for follow-through.	A tendency to worry about small things. A reluctance to 'let go'.

(*Source:* reprinted, with permission, from Belbin R M, *Management Teams: Why They Succeed or Fail*, Butterworth-Heinemann (1981), p. 78.)

another. Belbin claims that good examples of the eight types would prove adequate for any challenge, although not all eight types are necessarily needed. Other members may be welcome for their personal qualities, for example a sense of humour, but experience suggests there is no other team role that it would be useful to add.

Back-up team roles and functional roles

The most consistently successful teams were 'mixed' with a balance of team roles. The role that a person undertakes in a group is not fixed and may change according to circumstances. Individuals may have a 'back-up team role' with which they have some affinity other than their primary team role. If certain roles were missing, members would call upon their back-up roles. Team roles differ from what Belbin calls 'functional roles'. These are the roles that members of a team perform in terms of the specifically technical demands placed upon them. Team members are typically chosen for functional roles on the basis of experience and not personal characteristics or aptitudes.

Revised list of nine team roles

In a follow-up publication Belbin discusses the continued evolution of team roles which now differ in a few respects from those identified in earlier research.[42] Two roles are renamed, largely for reasons of acceptability: 'coordinator' replaces chairman, and 'implementer' replaces company worker. The most significant change is the addition of a ninth role, that of 'specialist'. This role was added because of the significance of the importance of a given form of professional expertise in much project work and its recurring importance as an issue in career development. A description of the evolved nine team roles is given in Figure 8.6.

A Summary outline of effective workgroups is given in Figure 8.7.

Constructing the perfect team

Referring to the research of Belbin, White writes of a team in the proper sense of the word as something about the way they work as a group that adds up to a sum greater than the individual parts – a collective spirit, a managerial alchemy that makes them such a force. If business people are happy to accept that group effort is always better than individuals working in isolation, the research of Belbin may help in constructing the perfect team. White suggests that, in the end, it is all about trust. The dream team is probably out there, sitting opposite you or just around the corner; all you have to do is fit them into Belbin's nine defined roles.[43]

Role relationships

In order that the organisation can achieve its goals and objectives, the work of individual members must be linked into coherent patterns of activities and relationships. This is achieved through the role structure. *A 'role' is the expected pattern of behaviours associated with members occupying a particular position within the organisation structure.* (The formal organisational relationships discussed in Chapter 6 can also be seen as types of role relationships.)

The concept of 'role' is important to the functioning of groups, and for an understanding of group processes and behaviour. It is through role differentiation that the structure

Figure 8.6:
Revised list of
nine team roles

Roles and descriptions – team-role contribution	Allowable weaknesses
Plant: Creative, imaginative, unorthodox. Solves difficult problems.	Ignores details. Too pre-occupied to communicate effectively.
Resources investigator: Extrovert, enthusiastic, communicative. Explores opportunities. Develops contacts.	Overoptimistic. Loses interest once initial enthusiasm has passed.
Co-ordinator: Mature, confident, a good chairperson. Clarifies goals, promotes decision-making, delegates well.	Can be seen as manipulative. Delegates personal work.
Shaper: Challenging, dynamic, thrives on pressure. Has the drive and courage to overcome obstacles.	Can provoke others. Hurts people's feelings.
Monitor evaluator: Sober, strategic and discerning. Sees all options. Judges accurately.	Lacks drive and ability to inspire others. Overly critical.
Teamworker: Co-operative, mild, perceptive and diplomatic. Listens, builds, averts friction, calms the waters.	Indecisive in crunch situations. Can be easily influenced.
Implementer: Disciplined, reliable, conservative and efficient. Turns ideas into practical actions.	Somewhat inflexible. Slow to respond to new possibilities.
Completer: Painstaking, conscientious, anxious. Searches out errors and omissions. Delivers on time.	Inclined to worry unduly. Reluctant to delegate. Can be a nit-picker.
Specialist: Single-minded, self-starting, dedicated. Provides knowledge and skills in rare supply.	Contributes on only a narrow front. Dwells on technicalities. Overlooks the 'big picture'.

Strength of contribution in any one of the roles is commonly associated with particular weaknesses. These are called allowable weaknesses. Executives are seldom strong in all nine team roles.

(*Source:* reprinted, with permission, from Belbin R M, *Team Roles at Work*, Butterworth-Heinemann (1933), p. 23.)

Figure 8.7: Summary outline of effective workgroups

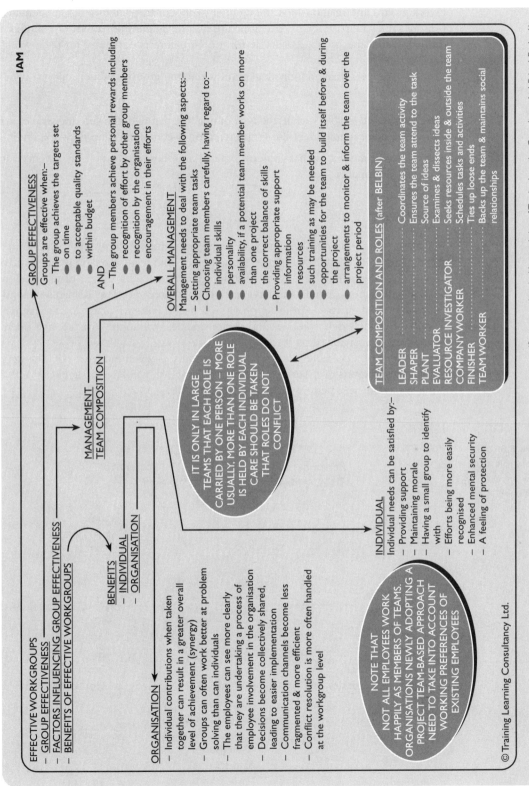

(*Source:* reprinted with permission of Traning Learning Consultancy Ltd. Bristol, England.)

of work groups and relationships among their members are established. The identification of distinct roles helps to clarify the structure and to define the pattern of complex relationships within the group. A suitable form of structure is necessary for team-work and cooperation.

The role, or roles, that an individual plays within the group is influenced by a combination of:

● *situational factors*, such as the type of unit, the nature of the task, the style of leadership, other members of the group, pattern of communication network; and

● *personal factors*, such as values, beliefs, attitudes, motivation, experience, ability and personality.

A role set

In addition to the role relationships with members of their own group – superior, peers, subordinates – individuals will have a number of role-related relationships with other people. This is a person's 'role set'. A role set comprises the range of associations or contacts with whom individuals have meaningful interactions in connection with the performance of their role. A role set provides a useful basis for analysing the nature of a person's job, and associated duties and responsibilities, within the structure and operation of the hospitality organisation.[44]

An example of a possible role set for a receptionist is given in Figure 8.8. The range of different expectations of these associations and contacts will have a significant influence on the behaviour and performance of the receptionist.

Figure 8.8:
Possible role
set for a
receptionist

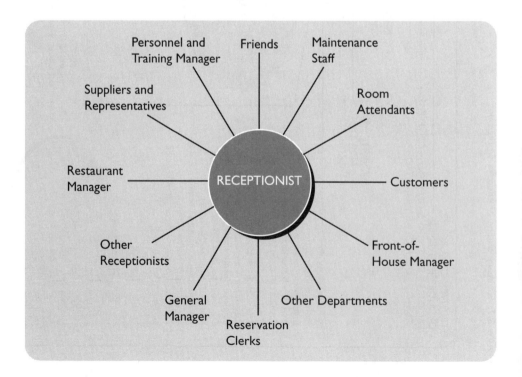

Role expectations

The role that a person plays in one work group may be quite different from the role that person plays in other work groups. However, everyone within a group is expected to behave in a particular manner and to fulfil certain role expectations. These role expectations may be established formally, or be informal, or they may be self-established.

- *Formal role expectations* indicate what the person is expected to do, and the duties and obligations. Formal role prescriptions provide guidelines for expected behaviour. Examples are a written contract of employment, rules and regulations, policy decisions or standards, compliance with legal requirements, job descriptions or directives from superiors.

- *Informal role expectations* are not prescribed formally but nevertheless are expected patterns of behaviour. These informal role expectations may be imposed by the group itself. Examples include general conduct, mutual support to co-members, attitudes towards superiors, means of communication, dress and appearance. Members may not always be consciously aware of these informal expectations, yet they still serve as important determinants of behaviour. Under this heading could be included the psychological contract, discussed in Chapter 3.

- *Self-established role expectations* arise when members have formal expectations which are specified loosely or only in very general terms. This allows members to determine their own role expectations and patterns of behaviour. Opportunities for self-established roles are more likely in senior positions, for example the general manager or senior departmental managers. They may also arise within certain professional or technical groups or where there is a demand for creativity or artistic flair, for example the head chef.

Role conflict

Patterns of behaviour result from both the role and the personality. The concept of role focuses attention on aspects of behaviour existing independently of an individual's personality. A personality clash arises from incompatibility between two or more people as individuals, even though their roles may be defined clearly and understood fully. Role conflict, however, arises from inadequate or inappropriate role definition. A classic example is the conflict in status between chefs and waiting staff. (See Whyte's study above and below.)

In practice, the manner in which a person actually behaves may not be consistent with their expected pattern of behaviour. This inconsistency may be a result of role conflict. As a generic term, role conflict may include role incompatibility, role ambiguity, role overload and role underload. These are all areas associated with the creation of role expectations (Figure 8.9).

Role incompatibility

This occurs when a person faces a situation in which simultaneous different or contradictory expectations create inconsistency. Compliance with one set of expectations makes it difficult or impossible to comply with other expectations. The two incompatible sets of expectations are in conflict. A typical example concerns the person 'in the middle', such as the supervisor or section head who faces opposing expectations from subordinates and from senior management. For example, the subordinates may expect a relaxed, Theory Y

Figure 8.9:
Role
relationships and
role conflicts

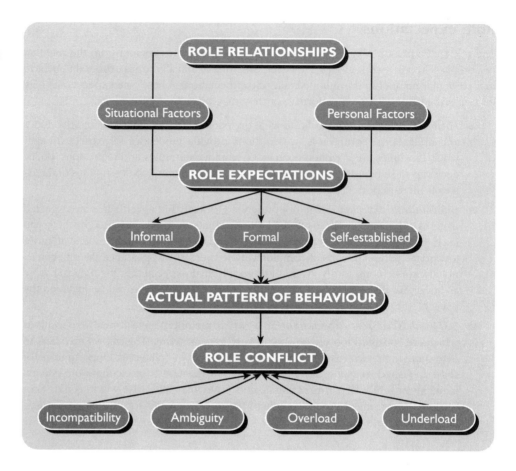

approach and good working relationships, but management may expect the supervisor to adopt a more directive, Theory X approach with emphasis on achieving maximum output.

Role incompatibility may also be used to describe situations in which the person is expected to fulfil a role for which they are not suited.[45] This may arise when the values, attitudes, personality, skills or interests of the person do not equate with the demands of the role. An obvious example is a person with an introverted personality occupying a role that demands frequent dealings with people. Role incompatibility may also arise when a person accepts promotion without taking account of the different expectations of the new position. Revised working practices may result in changes to the nature and expectations of a person's role, for example from the introduction of computers or the appointment of a new manager.

Role ambiguity

This occurs when there is lack of clarity as to the precise requirements of the role and the person is unsure what to do. The person's own perception of the role may differ from the expectations of others. The person is uncertain about the expected pattern of behaviour. This implies that insufficient information is available for adequate performance of the role. The characteristic nature of service industries, discussed in Chapter 2, gives rise to a high potential for ambiguity. Role ambiguity may result from a lack of formally prescribed expectations and often arises at times of constant change. Uncertainty may relate to such matters as the range of duties and responsibilities, the method of performing tasks, standards of work, or the evaluation and appraisal of performance.

Common examples of role ambiguity concern management trainees who may be uncertain as to how much authority they are expected to exercise over other members of staff. Management degree students on their industrial placement training may suffer from role ambiguity. It may be unclear to what extent they are expected to be involved in practical working experience at the operator level, or in gaining exposure to supervisory responsibilities. Another example could be a person appointed to a newly created position, perhaps because of the expansion or reorganisation of the establishment. The person may be uncertain about the exact nature of the new job or the authority and responsibility it involves.

Role overload

This is where a person faces too many separate roles or too great a variety of expectations. The person is unable to meet satisfactorily all expectations and some must be neglected to satisfy others. This leads to a conflict of priorities. Role overload can be distinguished from work overload. Role overload is seen in terms of the total role set and implies that the person has too many separate roles to handle at the same time. Where there are too many expectations of a single role, i.e. it is a problem of quantity rather than variety, this is work overload.[46]

An example of role overload for a hotel assistant manager is given by Lockwood and Jones. The manager is already responsible for personnel and training, but is now asked to act as duty manager, and in addition become health and safety officer, security officer and to chair the staff social committee.[47]

Role underload

This can arise when the prescribed role expectations fall short of the person's own perception of their role. The person may feel the role is not demanding enough or that it lacks variety, responsibility or challenge. It is possible, however, that the person could still suffer from work overload. Role underload may arise, for example, from the initial effects of delegation or from the appointment of an over-qualified member of staff. It may also arise from examples mentioned above such as the cases of management trainees, students on their industrial training, or members of staff appointed to a new position.

Role stress

Role conflict can result in role stress. Although work may be a source of satisfaction it is also increasingly a potential source of stress. Given the nature of service industries discussed in Chapter 2, stress is arguably a prevailing feature of hospitality organisations. According to Wood, for example:

> *In the hospitality industry unpredictability (of demand, of employees) is a major source of stress, but the high levels of responsibility that many managers bear can also be significant in stress causation, particularly as a sense of isolation may be experienced because of a unit's independence from other units and the larger organisation.*[48]

Although a certain amount of stress may arguably be a good thing and helps to promote a high level of performance, it is also potentially very harmful. Stress is a source of tension, frustration and dissatisfaction. It can lead to difficulties in communication and interpersonal relationships. Research evidence points to the consequences of role conflict leading to lower job satisfaction, and an adverse effect on the level of individual performance.[49,50]

An example of role stress is Whyte's study of chefs and waiting staff discussed above. One reason was the constant conflict between the demands of the customers to be served quickly and pressure from the chefs who were unable to produce the food in time. The waitresses were caught between two incompatible expectations and pulled both ways. As a result, a number of waitresses found the job very stressful and they often cried.

Reducing role stress

There is increasing evidence concerning stress-related illnesses and social problems, for example marriage breakdowns, which can have stress as a contributory factor. And decreasing efficiency resulting from work stress is extremely costly to organisations.[51] It is therefore important that managers make every effort to minimise the causes of stress. There are a number of ways in which management might attempt to avoid or reduce role conflict and the possibilities of role stress:

- increased clarity and specification of prescribed role expectations, for example through job descriptions;

- improved recruitment, selection and induction, the careful matching of abilities, motivations, personalities and interests to the demands of particular roles;

- a systematic approach to job training and retraining, staff development and career progression plans;

- review of organisation structure, for example the creation of new roles, assimilation of existing roles or reallocation of tasks and responsibilities;

- attention to group structures and group cohesiveness, and overcoming inter-group conflict, the possible use of autonomous working groups;

- changes in management systems and leadership style, for example a move towards System 4 management, the use of MBO, increased delegation, improved communications;

- advance notice and explanations of what is likely to happen, for example plans for a major refurbishment of the establishment, an unexpectedly large number of customers arriving together, preparations for a special banquet or conference;

- programme of medical examinations and health screening which may give early indications of potential stress-related problems.

Behaviour of individuals in groups

In order to understand and to influence the functioning and operation of groups, it is necessary to study patterns of interaction, and the parts played by individual members. For example, Green questions the characteristics that should be shown by the smooth running team. It should be obvious that it is unified, self-organised and self-supporting. Although team members should be recognised as individuals, each with a personality, likes and dislikes, and changing wants and needs, team members should feel a sense of belonging and should all pull in the same direction.[52] Two methods of analysing the behaviour of individuals in group situations are sociometry and interaction process analysis.

Sociometry

Sociometry is a method of obtaining and analysing data about social interactions and communication patterns among individuals. In the group situation, a common basis of sociometry, as proposed by Moreno, is 'buddy rating' or peer rating as a means of indicating feelings of acceptance or rejection among members.[53] Each member of the group is asked to nominate or to rate, privately, other members in terms of some given context or characteristic, for example how influential or how likeable. Questions may relate to either a work situation or a social situation. Choices may be limited to a given number and sometimes individuals may be asked to rank their choices.

Sociograms

Data derived from sociometry may be displayed by graphic means in the form of a sociogram. This is a diagrammatic representation which depicts the choices, preferences, likes or dislikes, and interactions among individual members of a group. Usually, positive choices only are recorded. The sociogram can also be used to display the structure of the group and to record the observed frequency and/or duration of contacts among members.

Figure 8.10 shows a simple illustration of a sociogram for a group of 15 members with single, positive choices only.

- G and M are popular (the stars) and chosen most often.
- M is the link between two overlapping cliques, KML and MNO.
- H and P are unpopular (isolated) and chosen least.
- JKMO is a chain.
- ABCD is a sub-group and separated from the rest of the members.

It should be noted, however, that there are several methods of compiling/drawing sociograms and a number of potential criticisms and limitations with the contribution of Moreno. Problems also arise over how to draw the sociogram and how to interpret the roles of individual members: the drawing of a sociogram is a highly arbitrary and time-consuming task.[54]

Figure 8.10: A simple sociogram illustrating interaction among 15 members of a group

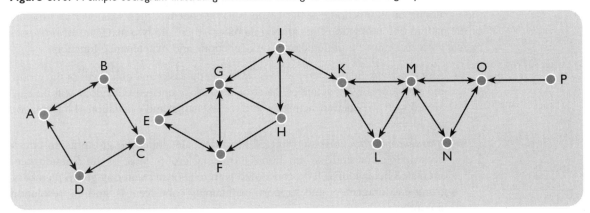

Figure 8.11:
Example of a 'tabulated' sociogram

	WORK RELATED PROBLEM			PERSONAL PROBLEM	
Second Choice	First Choice		First Choice	Second Choice
		A					
		B			||
|||			C	||		
			D	||	
		E			
		F				
			G	||	
|||||	||	H	||	
		J			
	||	K			
||||	|||||||	L		||
			M				
		N				
			O			
14	**14**		**14**	**14**

Members' choices could also be shown in tabular form. For example, Figure 8.11 shows first and second choices (positive choices only) for a seminar group of final-year degree students. Members were asked to indicate in confidence, those from their group whom they would most prefer to talk to about: (i) a major work-related problem; and (ii) a difficult personal problem.

Interaction analysis

In addition to occupying a position within the structure of the group, each member may fulfil a distinctive role as part of the operations and processes of the group. The basic assumption behind interaction analysis is that behaviour in small groups may be analysed from the viewpoint of its function.[55] If the group is to be effective, then whatever its structure or the pattern of interrelationships among members, there are two main sets of processes or functions that must be undertaken – task functions and maintenance functions.

● *Task functions* are directed towards achieving the tasks and objectives of the group, and problem-solving activities. Most of the task-orientated behaviour will be concerned with 'production' activities, and the exchange and evaluation of information and ideas.

● *Maintenance functions* are directed towards maintaining the group as an effective working unit and the emotional life of the group. Most of the maintenance-orientated behaviour will be concerned with relationships among group members, giving encouragement and support, maintaining cohesiveness, and the resolution of conflict.

The appropriate combination and balance of task-orientated behaviour and maintenance-orientated behaviour is essential to the success and continuity of the group.

Classification of member roles

In addition to the fulfilment of task or maintenance functions, members of a group may say or do something to satisfy a personal need or goal. The display of behaviour in this way is termed *self-orientated (or individual) behaviour*. This gives three main types of functional behaviour which can be exhibited by members of a group: task-orientated, maintenance-orientated and self-orientated.

A popular system for the classification of member roles under these three broad headings is that devised originally by Benne and Sheats and summarised as follows.[56]

- *Group task roles* – These assume that the task of the group is to select, define and solve common problems. Any of the roles may be performed by the various members or the group leader. Examples include initiator, information seeker, opinion giver, coordinator, elaborator, evaluator–critic and recorder.

- *Group building and maintenance roles* – The analysis of member-functions is orientated towards activities which build group-centred attitudes or maintain group-centred behaviour. Contributions may involve a number of roles, and members or the leader may perform each of these roles. Examples include encourager, harmoniser, compromiser, gate-keeper, standard setter, observer and commentator.

- *Individual roles* – These are directed towards the satisfaction of personal needs. Their purpose is not related to either group task or to the group functioning. Examples include aggressor, blocker, recognition-seeker, play actor, dominator.

Analysis of behaviour

A number of different frameworks have been designed for observers to analyse patterns of behaviour of group members. Observers chart members' behaviour on specially designed forms. These forms may be used to focus on single individuals or to record the total small-group interactions. The interaction process can become complex, especially if non-verbal behaviour is included, and headings of the observation sheet are not necessarily exclusive. It is important, therefore, to keep the framework simple, and easy to understand and to complete.[57] An example of the 10-point observation sheet used by the author is given in Figure 8.12.

The system of categorisation may distinguish between different forms of behaviour in terms of the functions they serve. Completed observation forms can be used as a basis for discussing individual contributions or the group performance related to the strength/weaknesses of different functional behaviours. Different frameworks use varying categories for studying behaviour in groups. Observation sheets can be designed to suit the particular requirements of the group situation and the nature of the activity involved.

Figure 8.12:
Observation
sheet for
behaviour
in groups

Nature of group						
Nature of activity						
Date Name of observer(s)						

Initial arrangement of group

```
              C     D
         B                    E
    A                    F
```

Names of group members
(or reference letters)

	A	B	C	D	E	F
Taking initiative – e.g. attempted leadership, seeking suggestions, offering directions						
Brainstorming – e.g. offering ideas or suggestions, however valid						
Offering positive ideas – e.g. making helpful suggestions, attempting to problem-solve						
Drawing in others – e.g. encouraging contributions, seeking ideas and opinions						
Being responsive to others – e.g. giving encouragement and support, building on ideas						
Harmonising – e.g. acting as peacemaker, calming things down, compromising						
Challenging – e.g. seeking justification, showing disagreement in *constructive way*						
Being obstructive – e.g. criticising, putting others down, blocking contributions						
Clarifying/summarising – e.g. linking ideas, checking progress, clarifying objectives/proposals						
Performing group roles – e.g. spokesperson, recorder, time keeper, humourist						
Other comments						

(*Source*: Mullins L J, *Management and Organisational Behaviour*, 5th edn, Financial Times Pitman Publishing (1999) p. 498.)

Summary

- Groups are a characteristic feature of all work organisations and social situations. They have a major influence on individual behaviour and performance. Work is a group-based activity especially in the hospitality industry. Harmonious working relationships and good team-work help make for a high level of staff morale and customer satisfaction.

- There are two major types of groups at work: formal, which are deliberately planned and created by management; and informal, which are based on personal relationships and serve to satisfy psychological and social needs. Individuals have varying expectations of the benefits from group membership relating to both work performance and social processes.

- Cooperation among members is likely to be greater in a strong, cohesive group. Many factors contribute to group cohesiveness and performance and can be summarised under the main headings of membership, work environment, organisational, and group development and maturity. There are, however, potential disadvantages from strong, cohesive groups.

- Group performance and the standard of decision-making can be influenced by the 'risky-shift' phenomenon and the concept of 'groupthink'. Consistently successful teams comprise a range of roles undertaken by various members. The concept of role is important to an understanding of group functioning. The manager should make every effort to minimise role conflict and role stress.

- Two methods of analysing the behaviour of individuals in group situations are sociometry and interaction analysis. The basic assumption of interaction analysis is the examination of behaviour from the viewpoint of its function. The success and continuity of a group is dependent upon the appropriate combination of task functions and maintenance functions.

Review and discussion questions

1. Why is an understanding of the functioning and operation of work groups important for the hospitality manager?

2. Distinguish between formal and informal groups. From your own experience give practical examples of the influence of group values and norms.

3. What actions would you, as a hospitality manager, take in order to create successful team-building? Explain the likely characteristics of an effective work group.

4. As a manager explain what action you would take in order to develop effective group relationships and performance among members of your staff.

5. Explain why strong, cohesive groups may present potential disadvantages for management. Where possible, support your answer with practical examples. ▷

Review and discussion questions continued

6. Assess critically those factors which are likely to influence the performance of groups compared with individual performance. Give practical examples by reference to a work group to which you belong.

7. Explain fully the importance of the concept of 'role' to an understanding of group processes and behaviour. Distinguish between role conflict and a personality clash. As manager, what actions would you take to reduce the possibilities of role stress?

8. Discuss how you would attempt to analyse the parts played by, and the behaviour of, individual members in group situations.

Assignment 1

(i) Construct a diagram to show fully your own role-set within a work situation.

(ii) Think of any work group(s) to which you belong, or have recently belonged. Identify clearly and give examples of your:
   ● formal role expectations;
   ● informal role expectations; and
   ● self-established role expectations.

(iii) Give a detailed account of a work situation in which you have experienced role conflict. Explain what form(s) this conflict took and how you attempted to overcome or reduce the conflict.

Assignment 2

Observe a small group at work.

(i) Explain the extent to which the group progressed through the stages of: forming, storming, norming and performing.

(ii) Provide examples of group values or norms which constituted 'proper' behaviour of group members.

(iii) Attempt to construct a simple sociogram to display the structure of the group, and the frequency and duration of contacts among members.

(iv) Summarise the extent to which the behaviour of each individual member could be classified under:
   ● group task roles;
   ● group building and maintenance roles; and
   ● individual roles.

(v) Explain the conclusions you draw from your observation.

Assignment 3

A self-perception inventory

This inventory was developed from a number of earlier versions which had been designed to give Henley members a simple means of assessing their best team roles.

DIRECTIONS: For each section distribute a total of 10 points among the sentences which you think best describe your behaviour. These points may be distributed among several sentences: in extreme cases they might be spread among all the sentences or 10 points may be given to a single sentence. Enter the points in Table 1.

SECTION	ITEM a	b	c	d	e	f	g	h
I								
II								
III								
IV								
V								
VI								
VII								

Table 1: Points table for self-perception inventory

I. What I believe I can contribute to a team:
   (a) I think I can quickly see and take advantage of new opportunities.
   (b) I can work well with a very wide range of people.
   (c) Producing ideas is one of my natural assets.
   (d) My ability rests in being able to draw people out whenever I detect they have something of value to contribute to group objectives.
   (e) My capacity to follow through has much to do with my personal effectiveness.
   (f) I am ready to face temporary unpopularity if it leads to worthwhile results in the end.
   (g) I can usually sense what is realistic and likely to work.
   (h) I can offer a reasoned case for alternative courses of action without introducing bias or prejudice.

II. If I have a possible shortcoming in teamwork, it could be that:
   (a) I am not at ease unless meetings are well structured and controlled and generally well conducted.
   (b) I am inclined to be too generous towards others who have a valid viewpoint that has not been given a proper airing.
   (c) I have a tendency to talk too much once the group gets on to new ideas.
   (d) My objective outlook makes it difficult for me to join in readily and enthusiastically with colleagues.
   (e) I am sometimes seen as forceful and authoritarian if there is a need to get something done. ▷

   (f) I find it difficult to lead from the front, perhaps because I am over-responsive to group atmosphere.
   (g) I am apt to get too caught up in ideas that occur to me and so lose track of what is happening.
   (h) My colleagues tend to see me as worrying unnecessarily over detail and the possibility that things may go wrong.

III. When involved in a project with other people:
   (a) I have an aptitude for influencing people without pressurising them.
   (b) My general vigilance prevents careless mistakes and omissions being made.
   (c) I am ready to press for action to make sure that the meeting does not waste time or lose sight of the main objective.
   (d) I can be counted on to contribute something original.
   (e) I am always ready to back a good suggestion in the common interest.
   (f) I am keen to look for the latest in new ideas and developments.
   (g) I believe my capacity for judgement can help to bring about the right decisions.
   (h) I can be relied upon to see that all essential work is organised.

IV. My characteristic approach to group work is that:
   (a) I have a quiet interest in getting to know colleagues better.
   (b) I am not reluctant to challenge the views of others or to hold a minority view myself.
   (c) I can usually find a line of argument to refute unsound propositions.
   (d) I think I have a talent for making things work once a plan has to be put into operation.
   (e) I have a tendency to avoid the obvious and to come out with the unexpected.
   (f) I bring a touch of perfection to any job I undertake.
   (g) I am ready to make use of contacts outside the group itself.
   (h) While I am interested in all views I have no hesitation in making up my mind once a decision has to be made.

V. I gain satisfaction in a job because:
   (a) I enjoy analysing situations and weighing up all the possible choices.
   (b) I am interested in finding practical solutions to problems.
   (c) I like to feel I am fostering good working relationships.
   (d) I can have a strong influence on decisions.
   (e) I can meet people who may have something new to offer.
   (f) I can get people to agree on a necessary course of action.
   (g) I feel in my element where I can give a task my full attention.
   (h) I like to find a field that stretches my imagination.

VI. If I am suddenly given a difficult task with limited time and unfamiliar people:
   (a) I would feel like retiring to a corner to devise a way out of the impasse before developing a line.
   (b) I would be ready to work with the person who showed the most positive approach.
   (c) I would find some way of reducing the size of the task by establishing what different individuals might best contribute.
   (d) My natural sense of urgency would help to ensure that we did not fall behind schedule.
   (e) I believe I would keep cool and maintain my capacity to think straight.
   (f) I would retain a steadiness of purpose in spite of the pressures.
   (g) I would be prepared to take a positive lead if I felt the group was making no progress.
   (h) I would open up discussions with a view to stimulating new thoughts and getting something moving.

▷

VII. With reference to the problems to which I am subject in working in groups:
   (a) I am apt to show my impatience with those who are obstructing progress.
   (b) Others may criticise me for being too analytical and insufficiently intuitive.
   (c) My desire to ensure that work is properly done can hold up proceedings.
   (d) I tend to get bored rather easily and rely on one or two stimulating members to spark me off.
   (e) I find it difficult to get started unless the goals are clear.
   (f) I am sometimes poor at explaining and clarifying complex points that occur to me.
   (g) I am conscious of demanding from others the things I cannot do myself.
   (h) I hesitate to get my points across when I run up against real opposition.

To interpret the self-perception inventory you should look at the Analysis sheet at the back of the book.

Source: Reprinted with permission from Belbin R M, *Management Teams: Why They Succeed or Fail*, Butterworth-Heinemann (1981), pp. 153–156.

Case study: When the last guest has gone to bed

Up-market hotels, especially in London, take pride in offering round-the-clock service to guests who may arrive from overseas on international flights at all hours, so a skeleton staff of up to 12 people is employed on the night shift from 11 pm to 7 am. They work in reception, telephone, room-service and security sections and there are also several night cleaners and kitchen stewards. All staff are responsible to a night manager. After the last of the guests has gone to bed, the manager's main task is to supervise the 'night audit'. This entails checking the bar, restaurant and room-service receipts against actual payments, and allocating the balances to guest accounts, which are prepared in advance of the rush to 'check out' which starts at about 7:30 am the next day.

Depending on the room occupancy and day of the week, this audit once took 5–6 hours when it was done manually, but it is completed nowadays in less than half that time using a computer/laser printer.

From about 2 am onwards, a deep hush descends on the hotel as the taped music is turned off, the lifts no longer descend to the basement car park, the sliding front doors are locked, even the water stops rippling in the swimming pool, and the lights are dimmed in the foyer. Shortly after this, the night staff begin to gather in ones and twos and settle themselves on sofas and armchairs in the main lounge. What follows comes as a complete surprise when witnessed for the first time. A transistor radio appears from nowhere and music is turned on at low volume. Coffee, sandwiches, cold meats, pastries, and beer, crockery and glasses, are brought in on trays by two beaming night porters. Soon everyone has arrived for a late-night meal. No one discusses the work that has been completed. Porters' jackets and receptionists blazers are removed as the night shift relaxes and the talk is about sport and TV programmes.

With one exception, they are all males and the one woman is also the only English person present. She is a night-telephonist, middle-aged, fluent in four languages, and a retired Foreign Office civil servant, who reads Proust while she waits for international calls. She has taken the job 'because I am middle-aged, a spinster with a limp, and sometimes get fed up with my own company'. The remaining 11 male employees are from eight different countries and include an Indian–Jewish security officer who works permanent nights 'because I love driving in the opposite direction to the heavy traffic at rush hours', and a Sri Lankan night manager who describes how he enjoys 'the authority of ▷

When the last guest has gone to bed continued

being in charge, because nobody will let me run a hotel in Britain during the daytime, will they?' All 12 of them have worked in the hotel for two to eight years and none wishes to work on days again.

Not only is it clear that job status and authority are acknowledged, but never stated, but it also emerges that these after-midnight 'feasts' occur every night after their work has been completed. The informal gatherings last until about 5 am, when the daytime doorman and the morning papers arrive and the hotel gradually returns to its more familiar, bustling, formal routines and procedures.

Source: McEwan, T, *A Replicated Study of Communication Networks,*
Job Retention and Labour Turnover in Two British Hotels, Unpublished
doctoral thesis, Cranfield Institute of Technology, Cranfield (1988), pp. 175–176.

TASKS

(i) **Do you think the night manager was exaggerating when saying that 'nobody will let me run a hotel in Britain during the daytime, will they'?**

(ii) **If you were a senior manager would you stop the after-midnight 'feasts' taking place in the hotel? If so why? If not, why not?**

Notes and references

1. Adair I, *Effective Teambuilding*, Gower (1986).
2. Schein E H, *Organizational Psychology*, 3rd edn, Prentice-Hall (1988), p. 145.
3. See, for example, Riley M, *Human Resource Management: in the Hospitality and Tourism Industry*, 2nd edn, Butterworth-Heinemann (1996).
4. Trist E L *et al.*, *Organizational Choice*, Tavistock Publications (1963).
5. Likert R, *New Patterns of Management*, McGraw-Hill (1961), p. 38.
6. See, for example, Venison P, *Managing Hotels*, Heinemann (1983).
7. Simmons P and Teare R, 'Evolving a Total Quality Culture', *International Journal of Contemporary Hospitality Management*, vol. 5, no. 3, 1993, pp. v–viii.
8. Jones P and Lockwood A, *The Management of Hotel Operations*, Cassell (1989).
9. See, for example, Drummond K E, *Human Resource Management for the Hospitality Industry*, Van Nostrand Reinhold (1990).
10. Riley M, *Human Resource Management in the Hospitality and Tourism Industry*, 2nd edn, Butterworth-Heinemann (1996), p. 60.
11. Berger F and Vanger R, 'Building Your Hospitality Team', *Cornell HRA Quarterly*, February 1986, pp. 83–84.
12. Gardner K and Wood R C, 'Theatricality in Food Service Work', *International Journal of Hospitality Management*, vol. 10, no. 3, 1991, pp. 267–278.
13. Heller R, *In Search of European Excellence*, HarperCollins Business (1997).
14. See, for example, Gullen H V and Rhodes G E, *Management in the Hotel and Catering Industry*, Batsford (1983).
15. See, for example, Keiser J R, *Principles and Practices of Management in the Hospitality Industry*, 2nd edn, Van Nostrand Reinhold (1989).
16. Lysons K, 'Organisational Analysis', supplement to *The British Journal of Administrative Management*, no. 18, March/April 1997.

17. Mullins L J, 'Management and Managerial Behaviour', *The International Journal of Hospitality Management*, vol. 4, no. 1, 1985, pp. 39–41.

18. See, for example, Atkinson P E, 'Developing Cohesive Working Groups', *Hospitality*, no. 29, May 1983, pp. 19–23.

19. Berger F and Vanger R, 'Building Your Hospitality Team', *Cornell HRA Quarterly*, February 1986, pp. 82–89.

20. Tuckman B W, 'Development Sequence in Small Groups', *Psychological Bulletin*, vol. 63, 1965, pp. 384–399.

21. See, for example, Adair, *Effective Teambuilding*, Gower (1986).

22. Bass B M and Ryterband E C, *Organisational Psychology*, 2nd edn, Allyn & Bacon (1979).

23. Green J, 'Are your Teams and Groups at Work Successful?', *Administrator*, December 1993, p. 12.

24. See also Jones P and Lockwood A, *The Management of Hotel Operations*, Cassell (1989).

25. Seashore S E, *Group Cohesiveness in the Industrial Work Group*, Institute for Social Research, University of Michigan (1954).

26. Argyle M, *The Social Psychology of Work*, 2nd edn, Penguin (1986).

27. See, for example, Allcorn S, 'Understanding Groups at Work', *Personnel*, vol. 66, no. 8, August 1989, pp. 28–36.

28. Bowey A, *The Sociology of Organizations*, Hodder & Stoughton (1976).

29. Whyte W F, *Human Relations in the Restaurant Industry*, McGraw-Hill (1948).

30. Staw B M, 'Organisational Psychology and the Pursuit of the Happy/Productive Worker', *California Management Review*, vol. 28, no. 4, Summer 1986, pp. 40–53.

31. Schein E H, *Organizational Psychology*, 3rd edn, Prentice-Hall (1988).

32. Dann D and Hornsey T, 'Towards a Theory of Interdepartmental Conflict in Hotels', *The International Journal of Hospitality Management*, vol. 5, no. 1, 1986, pp. 23–28.

33. See, for example, Kogan N and Wallach M A, 'Risk-taking as a Function of the Situation, the Person and the Group', in Newcomb T M (ed.), *New Directions in Psychology III*, Holt, Rinehart and Winston (1967).

34. Shaw M E, *Group Dynamics*, McGraw-Hill (1976).

35. Janis J L, *Groupthink*, 2nd edn, Houghton Mifflin (1982).

36. See, for example, Leane C R, 'A Partial Test of Janis' Groupthink Model', *Journal of Management*, vol. 11, no. 1, 1985, pp. 5–17.

37. Osborn A F, *Applied Imagination*, rev'd edn, Scribner (1957).

38. Bavelas A, 'Communication Patterns in Task-Oriented Groups', in Lasswell H N and Lerner D (eds) *The Policy Sciences*, Stanford University Press (1951).

39. Leavitt H J, *Managerial Psychology*, 4th edn, University of Chicago Press (1978).

40. Shaw M E, 'Communication Networks', in Berkowitz L (ed.), *Advances in Experimental Social Psychology*, vol. 1, Academic Press (1964).

41. Belbin R M, *Management Teams: Why They Succeed or Fail*, Heinemann (1981).

42. Belbin R M, *Team Roles at Work*, Butterworth-Heinemann (1993).

43. White J, 'Teaming with Talent', *Management Today*, September 1999, pp. 57–61.

44. For an example of a role-set for a unit manager, see Hales C and Nightingale M, 'What Are Unit Managers Supposed to Do?' *The International Journal of Hospitality Management*, vol. 5, no. 1, 1986, pp. 3–11.

45. Jones P and Lockwood A, *The Management of Hotel Operations*, Cassell (1989).

46. See, for example, Handy C B, *Understanding Organizations*, 4th edn, Penguin (1993).

47. Lockwood A and Jones P, *People and the Hotel and Catering Industry*, Holt, Rinehart & Winston (1984).

48. Wood R C, *Organizational Behavior for Hospitality Management*, Butterworth-Heinemann (1994), p. 78.

49. Filley A C and House R J, *Managerial Process and Organizational Behavior*, Scott Foresman (1969).

50. *Are Managers Under Stress? A Survey of Management Morale*, The Institute of Management, September 1996.

51. Hall K and Savery L K, 'Stress Management', *Management Decision*, vol. 25, no. 6, 1987, pp. 29–35.

52. Green J, 'Team Building in Practice', *Chartered Secretary*, November 1997, pp. 34–37.

53. Moreno J L, *Who Shall Survive?*, Beacon House (1953).

54. Rogers E M and Kincaid D L, *Communication Networks: Towards a New Paradigm for Research*, The Free Press (1981), p. 92,

55. Bales R F, *Personality and Interpersonal Behavior*, Holt, Rinehart & Winston (1970).

56. Benne K D and Sheats P, 'Functional Roles of Group Members', *Journal of Social Issues*, vol. 4, 1948, pp. 41–49.

57. For a more detailed account of frameworks for behavioural analysis and their use, see Mullins L J, *Management and Organisational Behaviour*, 5th edn, Financial Times Pitman Publishing (1999).

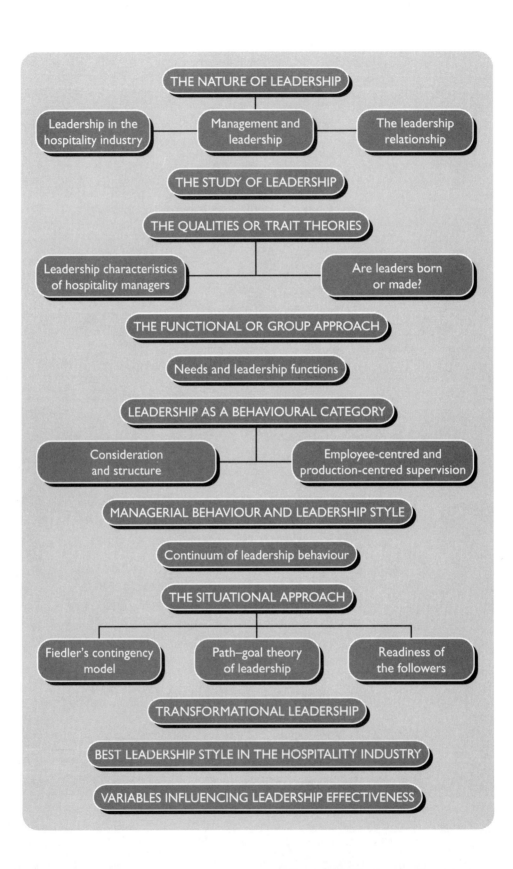

THE NATURE OF LEADERSHIP

Leadership in the hospitality industry — Management and leadership — The leadership relationship

THE STUDY OF LEADERSHIP

THE QUALITIES OR TRAIT THEORIES

Leadership characteristics of hospitality managers — Are leaders born or made?

THE FUNCTIONAL OR GROUP APPROACH

Needs and leadership functions

LEADERSHIP AS A BEHAVIOURAL CATEGORY

Consideration and structure — Employee-centred and production-centred supervision

MANAGERIAL BEHAVIOUR AND LEADERSHIP STYLE

Continuum of leadership behaviour

THE SITUATIONAL APPROACH

Fiedler's contingency model — Path–goal theory of leadership — Readiness of the followers

TRANSFORMATIONAL LEADERSHIP

BEST LEADERSHIP STYLE IN THE HOSPITALITY INDUSTRY

VARIABLES INFLUENCING LEADERSHIP EFFECTIVENESS

Chapter nine

Managerial leadership

Introduction

An essential part of management is coordinating and directing the efforts of members of staff. A major influence on effective performance in the hospitality industry is the nature of the manager–subordinate relationship. This entails the process of leadership and the choice of an appropriate style of managerial behaviour.

The nature of leadership

It is difficult to generalise about leadership. It is a complex and discursive subject area, and there are many ways of looking at leadership and the interpretations of its meaning. Leadership may be exercised as an attribute of position or because of personal knowledge or wisdom. It may be based on a feature of personality or it can be seen as a behavioural category. Leadership may also be viewed in terms of the role of the leaders and their ability to achieve effective performance from others. Essentially, however, we can see leadership as a *relationship through which one person influences the behaviour and actions of other people.* Leadership is a dynamic process and not limited to influences over people in a subordinate position. The leader–follower relationship is reciprocal, and effective leadership is a two-way process.

The effective management of people

The organisation is made up of groups of people. Leadership is closely associated with the activities of groups and effective team building. For example, Lord Sieff maintains that:

> *Leadership is the moral and intellectual ability to visualise and work for what is best for the company and its employees . . . The most vital thing the leader does is to create team spirit around him and near him, not in a schoolboy sense, but in realistic terms of mature adults . . . To be effective leadership has to be seen, and is best seen in action.*[1]

Leadership is therefore a central feature of the effective management of people. It is related to motivation, interpersonal behaviour and patterns of communication.[2] It is leadership which gives direction and guidance to the efforts created by motivation. The manager's style of leadership also affects employee job satisfaction and performance.[3] Leadership is important in attempting to reduce employee dissatisfaction.[4] And effective leadership is never more sought after than in times of change and uncertainty.[5]

Leadership in the hospitality industry

From a survey of managers in the hospitality industry which asked how leadership should be, it was described as: 'the ability to stimulate people to understand for themselves what they should do and be motivated to do it'.[6] However, despite the obvious importance of leadership and effective team-work the subject has received scant attention as a topic of research in the hospitality industry.[7]

From a study of leadership research in the hospitality industry, Pittaway *et al.* refer to the importance of effective leadership for all hospitality organisations as increasing demands are made to improve their performance, anticipate change and develop new structures. The labour-intensive nature of the industry also emphasises the importance of leadership skills. Although the nature of leadership is a dominant area of study in organisation and management, 'leadership' remains an ambiguous word that is difficult to define with any degree of precision. Pittaway *et al.* found only a few studies of research into leadership in the hospitality industry and suggest that a conceptual understanding of leadership is needed to help to improve the application of leadership research.[8]

Management and leadership

Sometimes management and leadership are seen as synonymous, but there is a difference. Whereas effective management involves leadership, it does not follow that every leader is necessarily a manager. You may recall from our discussion in Chapter 4 that the primary concern of managers is the achievement of organisational objectives through the use of systems and procedures. Management relates to people working within a hierarchy, and with prescribed positions and roles within the formal structure of the organisation. Hollingsworth for example, poses the question: 'How many managers consider themselves, first and foremost, to be leaders, thereby relegating "manager" simply to their job title? Not many I think'.[9]

The changing nature of business organisations including downsizing, flatter structures and greater attention to the efficient use of human resources have combined to place growing importance on leadership and an environment of coaching, teamwork and empowerment.[10] However, despite all the attention to, and writing about leadership, Taffinder suggests that although we know quite a lot about management, we do not know as much about leadership.[11]

The leadership process

The emphasis of the leadership process, however, is on interpersonal behaviour in a broader context. It is often associated with the willing and enthusiastic behaviour of followers. A leader often has sufficient influence to bring about long-term changes in people's attitudes and to make change more acceptable. Leadership therefore can be seen primarily as an inspirational process.[12] It does not necessarily take place only within the hierarchical structure. Many people operate as leaders without their role being formally established or defined.

Managers are more concerned with the 'hard' Ss of strategy, structure and systems. Leaders have an inherent inclination for utilisation of the 'soft' Ss of style, staff, skills and shared goals.[13] Managers also tend to adopt impersonal or passive attitudes towards goals. They maintain a low level of emotional involvement in their relationships with other people. Leaders adopt a more personal and active attitude towards goals. They have empathy with other people and give attention to what events and actions mean.[14]

Leadership skills and the management of people

Despite the differences, there is a close relationship between management and leadership, and it is not easy to separate them as distinct activities. For example, a Theory X or Theory Y style of managerial behaviour will have a significant influence on the nature of leadership. Many methods of management training can also be used as a means of measuring leadership style. For example, the Leadership Grid (discussed in Chapter 5) was until recently known as the Managerial Grid.

Being an effective manager involves the successful management of people. Chris Bonnington, for example, suggests that the same basic skills of leadership which enabled his successful expedition to climb Everest can be learned and practised in business. There is a similarity between the leadership skills required on Everest and the same skills required by team leaders in management.[15]

To be an effective manager it is necessary to exercise the role of leadership. You may recall, for example, that one of the interpersonal roles of a manager identified by Mintzberg (discussed in Chapter 4) is that of leader. The leader role permeates all activities of a manager and includes a responsibility for the motivation and guidance of subordinate staff.[16] Leadership is therefore a part of managerial behaviour, although it is a special attribute which can be distinguished from other elements of management.

The leadership relationship

A leader may be imposed, or formally appointed or elected. The leader exercises authority as an attribute of position or because of a stated position within the hierarchical structure of the organisation. Leadership, however, is more than just adherence to a formal role prescription or a superior–subordinate relationship.

> *Remember that you can be appointed a manager but you are not a leader until your appointment is ratified in the hearts and minds of those who work for you.*[17]

A leader may also be chosen informally, or emerge through the wishes of the group or the demands of the situation.[18] Leadership may be exercised because of accepted knowledge, wisdom or expertise, or by reputation (sapiential authority). It may also be based on the personal qualities, or charisma, of the leader and the manner in which authority is exercised. This view of leadership gives rise to the debate over 'born' or 'natural' leaders.

Leadership is therefore a dynamic form of behaviour. McGregor, for example, suggests that leadership is not a property of the individual but a complex relationship among a number of variables. The leadership relationship is affected by:

- the characteristics of the leader;
- the attitude, needs and other personal characteristics of the followers;
- the nature of the organisation, such as its purpose, structure and tasks to be performed; and
- the social, economic and political environment.[19]

Leadership power and influence

The nature of the leadership relationship can arise in a number of different ways. Leadership influence will be dependent upon the type of 'power' that the leader can exercise over other people. The exercise of power is a social process which helps to explain how different people are able to influence the behaviour and actions of others.

French and Raven have identified five main sources of power upon which the influence of the leader is based.[20] It is important to note that these sources of power are based on the **perception** of the influence of the leader, whether it is real or not. The leader may exercise different types of power in particular circumstances and at different times. We can consider these in terms of the work situation of the hospitality organisation.

- *Reward power* is based on the perception that the leader has the ability and resources to obtain rewards for those who comply with directives, for example pay, promotion, allocation of tasks, responsibilities and hours of work, granting of privileges, praise, recognition.

- *Coercive power* is based on fear and the perception that the leader has the ability to bring about punishment or undesirable outcomes for those who do not comply with directives. This is in effect the opposite of reward power. Examples include withholding pay rises, promotion or privileges, allocating undesirable duties or responsibilities, withdrawal of friendship or support, formal reprimands or possibly dismissal.

- *Legitimate power* is based on the perception that the leader has a right to exercise influence because of role or position. Legitimate power is based on formal authority, for example that of managers and supervisors within the hierarchical structure. The leader's influence arises from 'position' power and not from the nature of personal relationships.

- *Referent power* is based on a feeling of identification with the leader. Influence over others arises because of the perceived reputation, personal characteristics or 'charisma' of the leader. For example, a particular member of staff may not be in a position to influence rewards or punishments but may still exercise power through commanding respect or esteem.

- *Expert power* is based on the perception of the leader as someone who is competent and who has some special knowledge or expertise in a given area. Expert power is based on credibility and is usually limited to narrow, well-defined areas of activity or specialisms, for example the technical expertise of the head chef or catering manager, or the professional knowledge of the accountant or personnel manager.

The five sources of power are interrelated. The use of one type of power, for example coercive, may affect the ability to use another type, for example referent power.

The study of leadership

Because of its complex and variable nature there are many ways of analysing leadership. It is helpful therefore to have some framework in which to approach further study of the subject area (Figure 9.1). We can examine leadership in terms of:

- the qualities or trait theories;
- the functional or group approach;

Figure 9.1:
A framework
for the study
of leadership

QUALITIES OR TRAITS APPROACH

Assumes leaders are born and not made. Leadership consists
of certain inherited characteristics or personality traits.
Focuses attention on the person in the job and not on the job itself.

THE FUNCTIONAL OR GROUP APPROACH

Attention is focused on the functions and responsibilities of leadership,
what the leader actually does and the nature of the group.
Assumes leadership skills can be learned and developed.

LEADERSHIP AS A BEHAVIOURAL CATEGORY

The kinds of behaviour of people in leadership positions and the
influence on group performance. Draws attention to range of
possible managerial behaviour and importance of leadership style.

STYLES OF LEADERSHIP

The way in which the functions of leadership are carried out and the
behaviour adopted by managers towards subordinate staff.
Concerned with the effects of leadership on those being led.

THE SITUATIONAL APPROACH AND CONTINGENCY MODELS

The importance of the situation. Interactions between the variables
involved in the leadership situation and patterns of behaviour.
Belief that there is no single style of leadership appropriate to all situations.

TRANSFORMATIONAL LEADERSHIP

Leadership as a process of engendering motivation and
commitment, creating a vision for the organisation,
and appealing to the higher ideals and values of followers.

- leadership as a behavioural category;
- styles of leadership;
- the situational approach and contingency models; and
- transactional or transformational leadership.

The qualities or trait theories

The qualities (or trait) approach is based on the belief that leadership consists of certain inherited characteristics, or personality traits, which distinguish leaders from their followers. This is the so called 'Great Person' theory of leadership and leads to the suggestion that leaders are born and not made. Drucker, for example (writing originally in 1955), makes the point that:

> leadership is of utmost importance. Indeed there is no substitute for it. But leadership cannot be created or promoted. It cannot be taught or learned.[21]

The qualities approach focuses attention on the man or woman in the job and not on the job itself. It suggests that people with certain personality traits or characteristics would be successful leaders whatever the situation. Attention is given to the selection of leaders rather than to the training for leadership.

Limitations

Despite many research studies, attempts to find common personality, physical or mental characteristics of 'good' or 'successful' leaders have met with little success.[22] Investigations have identified lists of traits which tend to be overlapping, contradictory or with little correlation for most features. The lists of possible traits tend to be very long and there is not always agreement on the most important. It is noticeable, however, that such characteristics as individuality or originality usually feature in these lists of traits. This suggests that there is little in common between specific personality traits of different leaders.

There is, in any case, bound to be some subjective judgement in agreeing who is regarded as a good or successful leader. Even if it were possible to identify an agreed list of more specific qualities this would provide little explanation of the nature of leadership. It would do little to help in the training and development of future managers.

Early developments in the hospitality industry

In the early development of the hospitality industry many organisations were based upon the family unit and leadership was closely associated with ownership. Attempts to maintain the dynasty were based on the acceptance of a natural leader with the 'right' of leadership passing down to departmental levels.[23] However, as hospitality organisations have grown in size and complexity increasing attention has been given to the need for a more broadly based approach to the appointment and development of leaders.

Leadership characteristics of hospitality managers

Attempting to find a common list of those characteristics which make for an effective leader is likely to encounter the same limitations as the qualities approach. Based on the perceptions of a group of catering students who were asked about effective leaders they had encountered, Jacob presents a 'simplistic' profile of a good leader as a person who: has a positive manner; is respected and liked; knows the job; is a proven problem solver; is a communicator; is a persuader; is dedicated to the job; has drive, enthusiasm and initiative; has confidence in own ability; gives praise when due; motivates others to act; does not hold grudges; listens; relaxes under stress; has the strength of character to admit weaknesses; and has the ability to empathise.[24]

Writing in the *Cornell HRA*, Walker however suggests that excellent leadership is not just a matter of talent. The real key to leadership involves developing appropriate personality characteristics and the talents of other members of the organisation.[25]

Proven managers have generally developed an intuitive ability to evaluate the leadership potential of others. The objective of screening for managerial potential is to locate the individuals whose past experience and temperament show a pattern typical of successful leaders. Walker identifies the following as some of the most important indicators of the appropriate temperament for leadership.

- *Self-control* – potential leaders should be above-average in their ability to exercise self-control as this ability will be most frequently called upon.

- *Sense of values* – the greatest leaders are those who downplay materialistic values and status symbols, and instead respect the intangible, spiritual side of life.

- *Drive* – a strong drive is an advantage in any assignment and a 'doer' is preferred to the person who procrastinates.

- *Moodiness* – the manager should not be prone to inconsistency in personality but be optimistic, cheerful and generally capable of maintaining morale and team spirit.

- *Sensitivity* – people who are sensitive themselves are generally sensitive to others and have a high potential for managerial success.

- *Defence of ideas* – successful managers must be willing and able to support and defend their own ideas while remaining receptive to the ideas of others.

- *Self-awareness* – everyone needs a certain amount of appreciation from others but the person needing less recognition for *individual* contribution is generally more successful as a manager.

- *Balance* – the best managers seem to have the ability to defend their ideas and a low degree of self-consciousness, coupled with a high degree of sensitivity to other people.

Are leaders born or made?

Despite the limitations of the qualities or traits approach, there is still a frequent debate about whether leaders are born or made, or whether leadership is an art or a science. The important point, however, is that these should not be viewed as mutually exclusive alternatives. Even if there are certain inborn qualities which make for a good leader, these natural talents need encouragement and further development. Even if leadership is an art, it still requires knowledge and application of special skills or techniques.

> *Now the big question is whether you are born with charisma or whether you can develop it. I believe you can develop elements of it. For example, you can take courses to improve your speaking skills. You can learn to stage events that send powerful messages. You can learn to think more critically about the status quo and its shortcomings. You can do more on a daily basis to motivate your team. What you simply cannot learn is how to be passionate about what you do. You have to discover that for yourself, and passion is a big part of what drives a charismatic leader. It is also what motivates and inspires those who work for the charismatic leader.*[26]

There is, then, still some interest in the qualities or trait approach but increasing attention has been directed to other approaches to leadership. The focus now is more on what the leader does and how the functions of leadership are carried out.

The importance of the situation

A variety of people with different personalities and from varying backgrounds have emerged as effective leaders in different situations. The person who becomes the leader is regarded as most appropriately qualified, who knows best what to do and who is seen as the most suitable leader in the particular set of circumstances. This gives rise to the influence of situational factors in analysing the nature of leadership. The importance of situational factors is discussed later in this chapter.

The functional or group approach

This approach is based on the process and content of leadership. Attention is focused on the functions and responsibilities of leadership, what the leader actually does and the nature of the group. Leadership is always present in any group engaged in a task. Greater attention can be given to the successful training of leaders by concentrating on those functions which lead to effective performance by the work group.

The functional approach believes that the skills of leadership can be learned, developed and perfected. In contrast to the view of Drucker (referred to above), Kotter, for example, makes the point that successful companies do not wait for leaders to come along.

They actively seek out people with leadership potential and expose them to career experiences designed to develop that potential. Indeed, with careful selection, nurturing and encouragement, dozens of people can play important leadership roles in a business organisation.[27]

The functions and responsibilities of leadership

In order to help understand the process of leadership it is necessary to analyse the role of the leader. The functions and responsibilities of leadership require varying emphasis in different situations according to the nature of the group. It is possible, however, to identify a range of general functions which are served by the leadership position. For example, Krech provides a useful summary of 14 functions.[28]

- *The leader as executive* – coordinating group activities and overseeing the execution of policies.
- *The leader as planner* – deciding the ways and means by which the group achieves its objectives.
- *The leader as policy-maker* – establishing group goals, objectives and policies.
- *The leader as expert* – acting as a source of readily available information and skills, although there will be some reliance on technical expertise and advice from other members of the group.
- *The leader as external representative* – acting as official spokesperson for the group, representative of the group and the channel for communications.
- *The leader as controller of internal relations* – determining specific aspects of the group structure and functioning.
- *The leader as purveyor of rewards and punishment* – controlling group members by the use of reward power and coercive power.
- *The leader as arbitrator and mediator* – controlling interpersonal conflict among members of the group.

- *The leader as exemplar* – acting as a model of behaviour for members of the group and setting an example of what is expected.
- *The leader as symbol of the group* – enhancing the group unit by providing a cognitive focus and establishing the group as a distinct entity.
- *The leader as substitute for individual responsibility* – relieving individual members from the necessity of, and responsibility for, personal decisions.
- *The leader as ideologist* – serving as the source of beliefs, values and standards of behaviour for individual members of the group.
- *The leader as father figure* – serving as focus for the positive emotional feelings of individual members, and the object for identification and transference.
- *The leader as scapegoat* – serving as a target for aggression and hostility of the group, and accepting blame in the case of failure.

These 14 functions help illustrate the range of roles and responsibilities that the leader might be expected to fulfil. Leadership resides in the functions and not a particular person and can be shared among members of the group. When a member fulfils a particular activity which is accepted by members as relevant to the needs of the group, then this could become a leadership function.

Needs and leadership functions

A major contribution to the functional approach to leadership is the work of John Adair, and his ideas on action-centred leadership and the 'three circles' model.[29] The effectiveness of the leader is dependent upon meeting three key functions, or areas of need, within the work group:

- the need to *achieve the common task*;
- the need for *building and maintaining the team*; and
- the need for *developing the individual*.

These areas of need are symbolised by three overlapping circles in Figure 9.2.

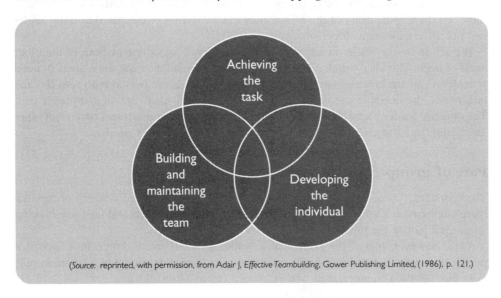

Figure 9.2: The core responsibility of the leader

(*Source:* reprinted, with permission, from Adair J, *Effective Teambuilding*, Gower Publishing Limited, (1986), p. 121.)

Task functions involve:

- achieving the objectives of the group;
- defining group tasks and planning the work;
- allocation of resources;
- organisation of duties and responsibilities;
- controlling quality, checking performance and reviewing progress.

Team functions involve:

- maintaining morale and building team spirit;
- maintaining the cohesiveness of the group as a working unit;
- setting standards and maintaining discipline;
- establishing systems of communication within the group;
- training the group and appointment of sub-leaders.

Individual functions involve:

- meeting the needs of individual members of the group;
- attending to personal problems;
- giving praise and status;
- reconciling conflicts between group needs and individual needs;
- training the individual.

The responsibilities of the leader

The elements of task, team and individual constitute the core responsibility of the leader. In order to achieve effectiveness and satisfaction, all three kinds of needs present in every group must be met to some extent. When the necessary functions are missing, group progress is slow and uneven. A function is what you do, as opposed to a quality or trait. To fulfil the three circles of responsibility certain key functions have to be performed. Although these are the responsibility of the leader, they can be shared or delegated and the leader will not undertake them all personally.

The action by the leader in any one area of need will affect one or both of the other areas of need. The ideal position is where complete integration of the three areas of need is achieved. In any work group the most effective leader is the person who sees that the task needs, the needs of the group, and those of the individual, are all adequately met. The effective leader elicits the contribution of members of the group and draws out other leadership from the group to satisfy the three interrelated areas of need.

Part of group functions and activities

The characteristics of the hospitality industry and the nature of the delivery of services place emphasis on a leadership style which should result in managers and supervisors being an integral part of the functions and activities of work groups.

Adair, however, makes the point that a leader is not there to dominate a group of people or simply to coordinate functions. The leader strengthens unity of a common purpose through the complementary and enhanced efforts of individuals.

McGregor, attitudes towards people	Theory X	Theory Y
Blake and McCanse, Leadership Grid	Concern for production	Concern for people
Group interaction analysis	Task functions	Maintenance functions
Ohio State leadership study	Initiating structure	Consideration
University of Michigan study	Production-centred supervision	Employee-centred supervision

In industry, as in every other sphere where free and able people need to co-operate, effective leadership is founded upon respect and trust, not fear and submission. Respect and trust help to inspire whole-hearted commitment in a team; fear and submission merely produce compliance. Leadership involves focusing the efforts of a group towards a common goal and enabling them to work together as a team. A leader should be directive in a democratic way.[30]

Leadership as a behavioural category

This approach draws attention to the kinds of behaviour of people in leadership positions and to the influence of leadership style on group performance. There are many types of actual leadership behaviour and their effectiveness depends upon the variables in any particular situation. However, there does appear to be general agreement on two major dimensions of leadership which can also be related to studies discussed in previous chapters (Figure 9.3).

Two major research studies on behavioural categories of leadership are those relating to:

● consideration and structure; and

● employee-centred and production-centred supervision.

Consideration and structure

Results of a study undertaken at Ohio State University indicated two major dimensions of leadership behaviour – 'consideration' and 'initiating structure'.[31]

● *Consideration* reflects the extent to which the leader establishes trust, mutual respect and rapport with the group, and shows concern, warmth, support and consideration for subordinates. This dimension is associated with two-way communication, participation and a human relations approach to leadership.

● *Structure* reflects the extent to which the leader defines and structures group interactions towards attainment of formal goals, and organises group activities. This dimension is associated with efforts to achieve organisational goals and objectives.

Figure 9.4:
The Ohio State quadrants of leadership behaviour

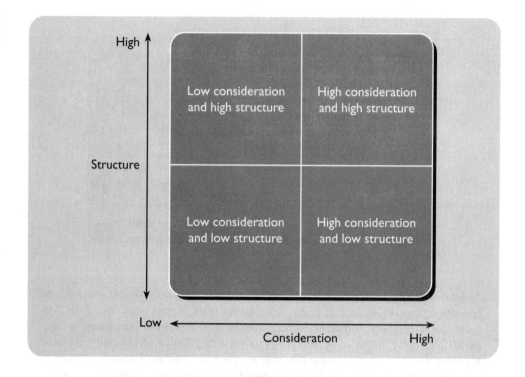

Separate behavioural categories

The two dimensions were found to be uncorrelated and separate behavioural categories. This gives rise to the development of four quadrants which illustrate the different combinations of consideration and structure (Figure 9.4). Some balance is needed between consideration and structure in order to satisfy both individual needs and formal goals. Although much depends upon situational factors, a high consideration and high structure category of behaviour appears to be generally more effective in terms of member satisfaction and group performance.

Consideration and structure can be related to the two major sets of group processes, task functions and maintenance functions, discussed in Chapter 8. Consideration can be seen to be the same as the maintenance function of building and maintaining the group as a cohesive working unit. Structure can be seen to be the same as the task function of accomplishing specific tasks of the group and achieving goals.

Leadership style of hotel general managers

Using the dimensions of consideration and initiating structure, Worsfold studied the leadership style of 31 general managers of a major UK hotel group.[32] The managers obtained a relatively high mean score for both dimensions. This indicates good interpersonal relationships with subordinates and an active role in directing group activities through planning and trying out new ideas.

Worsfold refers to the image of the hotel and catering industry as being people-orientated with a need to maintain good interpersonal relations. This suggests the need for high scores on consideration. But it is also necessary to maintain high standards, and to establish rules and procedures to which staff adhere. This suggests the need for effective hotel managers to demonstrate high levels of initiating structure.

Employee-centred and production-centred supervision

Another major research study relating to leadership behaviour was conducted at the University of Michigan. Effective supervision (measured along dimensions of group morale, productivity and cost reduction) appeared to display four common characteristics:

- delegation of authority and avoidance of close supervision;
- an interest and concern in subordinates as individuals;
- participative problem-solving; and
- high standards of performance.

The need for balance

The findings were summarised by Likert, who used the terms *employee-centred* and *production-centred supervision*.[33] (See the discussion on supervision and supportive relationships in Chapter 11.) These terms are similar to the dimensions of consideration and structure. The first three supervisory characteristics listed relate to consideration; the fourth characteristic exemplifies structure. And, like consideration and structure, employee-centred and production-centred supervision need to be balanced. Employee-centred supervisors who also recognise production as one of their main responsibilities tend to achieve the best results.

The importance of leadership style

Both the Ohio State University study and the University of Michigan study give support to the idea that there is no single behavioural category which is superior. These studies have drawn attention to the range of possible managerial behaviour, and the importance of leadership style. This provides another heading under which to analyse the nature of leadership.

Managerial behaviour and leadership style

It has become increasingly clear that managers can no longer rely solely on the use of their position in the hierarchical structure as a means of exercising the functions of leadership. In order to get the best results from subordinates, the manager must also have regard for the need to encourage high morale, a spirit of involvement and cooperation, and a willingness to work.[34]

This gives rise to the importance of appropriate forms of managerial behaviour and leadership style for effective human resource management. Boella, for example makes the point that:

> *The 'style' of management is therefore of vital importance in an organisation because this determines to a large extent whether employees obtain satisfaction from their jobs and whether managers will achieve their business objectives.*[35]

Leadership style is the way in which the functions of leadership are carried out, the way in which the manager typically behaves towards subordinate staff and members of the group.

There are many possible ways of describing the behaviour adopted by managers towards subordinate staff, for example dictatorial, unitary, bureaucratic, benevolent, supportive, charismatic, consultative, participative and abdicatorial. And there are therefore a number of possible classifications of leadership styles.

The focus of power

A broad, three-fold heading, based on the focus of power, is: authoritarian (or autocratic); democratic; and laissez-faire.

- *Authoritarian style* is based on the manager as the focus of power, and the issuing of orders and instructions. All interactions within the group move towards the manager. The manager alone exercises decision-making and authority for determining policy, procedures, work tasks and relationships, and control of rewards and punishments.

- *Democratic style* is based on the manager as part of a team. The focus of power is more with the group as a whole. There is greater interaction and the leadership function is shared with members of the group. Members have a greater say in decision-making, determination of policy and the implementation of systems and procedures.

- *Laissez-faire style* is based on the focus of power being passed to the group and allowing members freedom of action. There is often confusion over the meaning of this form of behaviour. For example, according to Boella the laissez-faire type of manager: 'abdicates responsibility – leaving his or her staff to face the problems that are rightly more the manager's. The staff are left to face complaints from customers without the authority to rectify or overcome causes of disruption.'[36] This may be a popular view but it is really more a non-style of leadership, or an 'abdicator'. The definition of laissez-faire as meaning 'freedom from interference' or 'let people do as they think fit' arguably gives rise to a 'genuine' style of leadership whereby the manager observes that members of the group are working well on their own. The manager consciously makes a decision not to interfere but to monitor their progress and to be readily available if help is needed. This is to be contrasted with the manager who could not care, does not wish to get involved and leaves the group to face problems which rightly belong with the manager.

Leadership related to decision-making

An alternative classification is suggested by Magurn. He categorises the manner adopted by managers towards staff leadership in terms of four main approaches related to decision-making: autocratic, persuasive, consultative and participative.[37]

- Managers make a decision and issue instructions, and expect it to be carried out without question – an **autocratic** approach.

- Managers make a decision and expect compliance – a **persuasive** approach.

- Managers make decisions but put ideas forward for discussion and take account of staff views – a **consultative** approach.

- Managers bring staff into a problem and accept the view of the majority as the basis of the decision – a **participative** approach.

Solo leader and team leader

Belbin distinguishes between two broad contrasting or diverging styles of leadership in industry: the solo leader and the team leader.[38] The solo leader enjoys free range, and rules as if absolutely. The leader takes no risks with other people, adopts a directive approach, prefers specific tasks and goals, expects compliance and acts as a model for others to follow. In times of crisis or urgency the talented solo leaders have been effective in overcoming departmental barriers and obstacles, and implementing decisions quickly. However, when the solo leaders fail, they are discarded.

By contrast, the team leader declines to rule as if absolutely and deliberately limits his or her role. The leader creates a sense of mission, expresses greater respect for and trust in subordinates, recognises the skills and strengths of others, and is more inclined to delegate. Belbin suggests that solo leadership is familiar to most people because part of crowd psychology is to seek to be led and to have faith in the leader. However, increasing uncertainty and continuous change together with societal pressure for the sharing of power has led to increasing attention to team leadership.

Attention to styles of leadership

The development of behavioural science has drawn attention to the processes of interpersonal behaviour in the work situation and to the effects of leadership on those being led. The attention given to leadership style is based on the assumption that subordinates are more likely to work willingly and effectively for managers who adopt a certain style of leadership than for those managers who adopt alternative styles.

Attention to the manager's style of leadership has come about because of a greater understanding of individual motivation, and the needs and expectations of people at work. It has also been influenced by broader standards of education and training, changes in the value system of society, pressure for a greater social responsibility towards employees, and the concept of the quality of working life. These have all combined to create resistance against purely dictatorial styles of leadership. For example, the demands for organisational change and creating an empowerment culture require employees who are self-managed and leadership existing not only at the top of the hospitality organisation.[39]

Continuum of leadership behaviour

A popular model of leadership style is that presented by Tannenbaum and Schmidt, (Figure 9.5).[40] They suggest a continuum of possible behaviour available to the manager and along which various styles of leadership may be placed. The continuum presents a range of actions related to the degree of authority used by the manager and to the area of freedom available to subordinates. At one extreme is boss-centred (authoritarian) leadership and at the other extreme is subordinate-centred (democratic) leadership. These extreme forms of leadership behaviour can be related to McGregor's Theory X and Theory Y suppositions.

Four main styles of leadership

Neither extreme of the continuum is absolute as there is always some limitation on the use of authority or the area of freedom. Moving along the continuum, the manager may be characterised according to the degree of control that is maintained over subordinates. This approach leads to the identification of four main styles of leadership – tells, sells, consults, joins.

Figure 9.5: Continuum of leadership behaviour

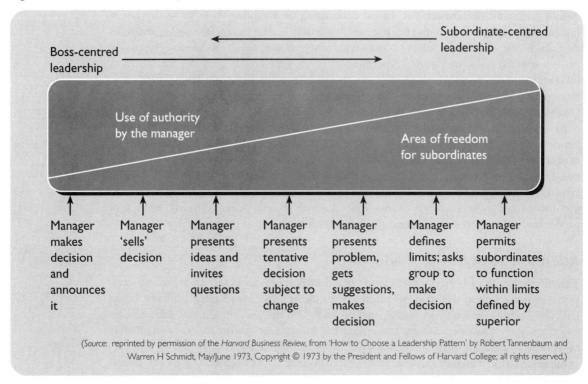

Boss-centred leadership

Subordinate-centred leadership

Use of authority by the manager

Area of freedom for subordinates

| Manager makes decision and announces it | Manager 'sells' decision | Manager presents ideas and invites questions | Manager presents tentative decision subject to change | Manager presents problem, gets suggestions, makes decision | Manager defines limits; asks group to make decision | Manager permits subordinates to function within limits defined by superior |

- *Tells* – the manager identifies a problem, chooses a decision and announces this to subordinates, and expects them to implement it without an opportunity for participation.

- *Sells* – the manager still chooses a decision but recognises the possibility of some resistance from those faced with the decision and attempts to persuade subordinates to accept it.

- *Consults* – the manager identifies the problem but does not choose a decision until the problem is presented to the group, and the manager has listened to the advice and solutions suggested by subordinates.

- *Joins* – the manager defines the problem and the limits within which the decision must be chosen and then passes to the group, with the manager as a member, the right to make decisions.

Forces influencing the type of leadership

Tannenbaum and Schmidt suggest that there are three factors, or forces, of particular importance in deciding which types of leadership are practical and desirable. These are: forces in the manager, forces in the subordinates and forces in the situation.

- *Forces in the manager* – managers' behaviour will be influenced by their own personalities, backgrounds, knowledge and experiences. These internal forces include: value systems, confidence in subordinates, leadership inclinations, and feelings of security in uncertain situations.

- *Forces in the subordinate* – subordinates are influenced by many personality variables and individual sets of expectations about relationships with the manager. Characteristics of the subordinates include the need for independence and readiness to accept responsibility, identification with the goals of the organisation, interest in, and perceived importance of, the problem, knowledge and experience, extent of learning to share in decision-making.
- *Forces in the situation* – managers' behaviour will be influenced by the general situation and environmental pressures. Characteristics of the situation include the type and nature of organisation, group effectiveness, the nature of the problem, pressure of time.

Successful leaders are keenly aware of those forces which are most relevant to their behaviour at a particular time. They are able to behave appropriately in terms of their understanding of themselves, the individuals and the group, the organisation, and environmental influences. Successful managers are both perceptive and flexible.

The situational approach

The continuum of leadership behaviour draws attention to forces in the situation as one of the variables influencing the nature of managerial behaviour. The situational approach, however, concentrates on the importance of the situation as the dominant feature in considering the characteristics of leadership. Despite the more recent interest in this approach, it is interesting to note that the idea of the manager applying the law of the situation was put forward over 50 years ago.

The law of the situation

This idea was propounded by Mary Parker Follet, who considered the way orders should be given in the manager–subordinate relationship. The problem is to avoid the two extremes of (i) too much bossism in giving orders; and (ii) practically no orders given. Follett's solution was what she called the 'depersonalising of orders and obeying the law of the situation'.

> *My solution is to depersonalise the giving of orders, to unite all concerned in a study of the situation, to discover the law of the situation and obey that. Until we do this I do not think we shall have the most successful business administration . . . This is, ideally, what should take place between any head and subordinates. One person should not give orders to another person but both should agree to take their orders from the situation. If orders are simply part of the situation, the question of someone giving and someone receiving does not come up. Both accept the orders given by the situation.*[41]

Contingency theories of leadership

More recent studies under the situational approach focus on the interactions between the variables involved in a leadership situation and patterns of leadership behaviour. This gives rise to the study of leadership-contingency theories. Contingency theories are based on the belief that there is no single style of leadership appropriate to all situations. Also, depending upon the nature of the situation, different individuals within the group may fulfil the functions of leadership.

Three major contingency models of particular relevance to the hospitality manager are those which relate to:

- the favourability of the leadership situation;
- path–goal theory; and
- the 'readiness' (or maturity) of followers.

Fiedler's contingency model

A major leader-situation model is that developed by Fiedler in his contingency theory of leadership effectiveness.[42] In order to measure the attitudes and effectiveness of the leader, Fiedler developed a 'least preferred co-worker' (LPC) scale. The LPC score is determined by the ratings given by leaders about the person with whom they could work least well. The questionnaire contains up to 20 bipolar items. Each item on the scale is given a single ranking of between one and eight points (Figure 9.6).

Interpretation of the LPC score

The more a leader is generally 'lenient' in rating the least preferred co-worker, the higher the LPC score, and the more critical the rating, the lower the LPC score. Interpretation of the LPC score appears to be that:

- a high-rating leader derives most satisfaction from interpersonal relationships and is motivated to act in a supportive considerate manner when relationships with subordinates need to be improved;
- a leader with a low LPC score derives most satisfaction from performance of the task and achieving objectives – establishing good relationships with subordinates is a secondary motivation.

Favourability of the situation

The relationship between the LPC score and leadership behaviour is dependent upon the favourability of the situation. This is the extent to which the situation gives a leader control over subordinates. There are three major variables which determine the favourability of the situation and which affect the leader's role and influence.

- *Leader–member relations* – the degree to which the leader is trusted and liked by group members, the willingness of members to follow the leader's guidance.
- *The task structure* – the degree to which the task is clearly defined for the group, the extent to which the task can be carried out by detailed instructions or standard procedures.
- *Position power* – the power of the leader by virtue of position in the organisation, the degree to which the leader can exercise authority to influence, for example rewards and punishments, promotions and demotions.

Group–task situations and leadership style

From these three variables, Fiedler constructs eight combinations of group–task situations through which to relate favourability and leadership style. The variables are weighted and assume leader–member relations as the most important, with task structure next and then

Figure 9.6:
Least preferred
co-worker
(LPC) scale

Pleasant	:_:_:_:_ :_:_:_:_	Unpleasant
	8 7 6 5 4 3 2 1	
Friendly	:_:_:_:_ :_:_:_:_	Unfriendly
	8 7 6 5 4 3 2 1	
Rejecting	:_:_:_:_ :_:_:_:_	Accepting
	1 2 3 4 5 6 7 8	
Helpful	:_:_:_:_ :_:_:_:_	Frustrating
	8 7 6 5 4 3 2 1	
Unenthusiastic	:_:_:_:_ :_:_:_:_	Enthusiastic
	1 2 3 4 5 6 7 8	
Tense	:_:_:_:_ :_:_:_:_	Relaxed
	1 2 3 4 5 6 7 8	
Distant	:_:_:_:_ :_:_:_:_	Close
	1 2 3 4 5 6 7 8	
Cold	:_:_:_:_ :_:_:_:_	Warm
	1 2 3 4 5 6 7 8	
Cooperative	:_:_:_:_ :_:_:_:_	Uncooperative
	8 7 6 5 4 3 2 1	
Supportive	:_:_:_:_ :_:_:_:_	Hostile
	8 7 6 5 4 3 2 1	
Boring	:_:_:_:_ :_:_:_:_	Interesting
	1 2 3 4 5 6 7 8	
Quarrelsome	:_:_:_:_ :_:_:_:_	Harmonious
	1 2 3 4 5 6 7 8	
Self-assured	:_:_:_:_ :_:_:_:_	Hesitant
	8 7 6 5 4 3 2 1	
Efficient	:_:_:_:_ :_:_:_:_	Inefficient
	8 7 6 5 4 3 2 1	
Gloomy	:_:_:_:_ :_:_:_:_	Cheerful
	1 2 3 4 5 6 7 8	
Open	:_:_:_:_ :_:_:_:_	Guarded
	8 7 6 5 4 3 2 1	

(*Source:* reprinted with permission of Professor F E Fiedler.)

position power. As the favourability of the leadership situation varies, the leadership style varies (Figure 9.7).

When the situation is:

(i) very favourable, with good leader–member relations, structured task and strong position power; or

(ii) very unfavourable, with poor leader–member relations, unstructured task and weak position power;

then a **task-orientated leader** (low LPC score) with a directive, controlling style will be more effective.

Figure 9.7: Correlations between leader's LPC scores and group effectiveness–leadership style. The appropriateness of a leadership style for maximising group performance is dependent upon the three variables in the leadership situation.

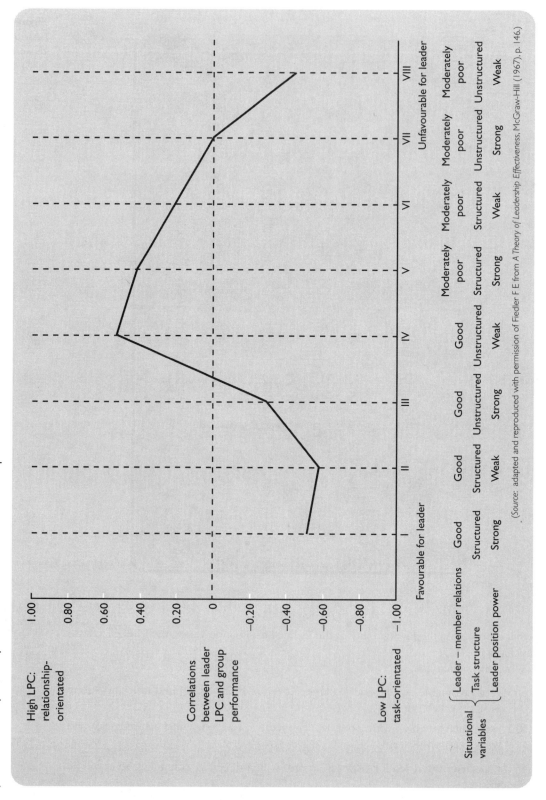

(*Source:* adapted and reproduced with permission of Fiedler F E from *A Theory of Leadership Effectiveness*, McGraw-Hill (1967), p. 146.)

When the situation is:

(iii) moderately favourable and the variables are mixed;

then an **interpersonal-orientated leader** (high LPC score) with a participative approach will be more effective.

Applications to the hospitality industry

Although there appears to be some uncertainty about the interpretation of the LPC scale, and Fiedler's work may at first appear somewhat complex, it does provide a further dimension to the study of leadership. Consideration is given to the importance of organisational variables which affect leadership effectiveness.

As discussed previously, the nature of the hospitality industry does make particular demands upon its managers. The nature of managerial behaviour and style of leadership is a significant factor in both staff and customer satisfaction.

> *The industry provides the manager, in most situations, with a multiplicity of tasks and very complex interrelationships between staff and customers. Together with this the nature of demand in hotels is highly fluctuating. These factors mean that the hotel manager must be highly adaptable to prevailing circumstances.*[43]

Fiedler's contingency model draws attention to the importance of situational variables and leadership style, and matching changes in the leader-member relations, task structure and position power to the characteristics of the leader. The model would therefore appear to have particular significance for the hospitality manager.

Path–goal theory of leadership

The importance of the path–goal theory for the hospitality manager is that it attempts to explain the influence of leadership behaviour on the performance and job satisfaction of subordinates. The model is based on the expectancy theory of motivation (discussed in Chapter 7). The main work in this field has been undertaken by House[44] and House and Dessler.[45]

The theory suggests that the performance of subordinates is affected by the extent to which the manager satisfies their expectations. Subordinates will see leadership behaviour as a motivating influence to the extent that it means:

(i) satisfaction of their needs is dependent upon effective performance; and

(ii) the necessary direction, guidance, training and support, which would otherwise be lacking, is provided.

Four main styles of leadership

The path–goal approach identifies four main types of leadership behaviour.[46]

- *Directive leadership* involves letting subordinates know exactly what is expected of them and giving specific directions. Subordinates are expected to follow rules and regulations. This type of behaviour is similar to 'initiating structure'.

- *Supportive leadership* involves a friendly and approachable manner, and displaying concern for the needs and welfare of subordinates. This type of behaviour is similar to 'consideration'.

Figure 9.8: Representation of the path–goal theory of leadership

- *Participative leadership* involves consulting with subordinates, and the evaluation of their opinions and suggestions before the manager makes the decision.
- *Achievement-orientated leadership* involves setting challenging goals for subordinates, seeking improvement in their performance and showing confidence in their ability to perform well.

Situational factors

According to path–goal theory, the effect of leadership behaviour is determined by two main situational factors: the personality characteristics of subordinates; and the nature of the task (Figure 9.8).

- *The personality characteristics of subordinates* determine how they will react to the manager's behaviour and the extent to which they perceive such behaviour as an immediate or potential source of need satisfaction.
- *The nature of the task* relates to the extent that it is routine and structured, or non-routine and unstructured.

These situational factors determine the subordinates' perceptions and motivation, which in turn lead to improved goal clarity, performance and job satisfaction. The situational factors also influence the subordinates' preferences for a particular style of managerial behaviour. For example, when a task is highly structured, the goals are readily apparent and subordinates are confident, then a directive style of leadership may not be welcomed. However, when a task is highly unstructured, the nature of the goals is not clear and subordinates lack experience, then a more directive style of leadership may be welcomed.

Motivational leadership

Different types of behaviour can be practised by the same person at different times in varying situations. By using one of the four styles of leadership the manager attempts to influence subordinates' perceptions and motivation, and smooth the path to their goals. Effective leadership is based on both the willingness of the manager to help subordinates, and the needs of subordinates for help. Leadership behaviour will be motivational to the extent that it provides necessary direction, guidance and support, helps clarify path–goal relationships and removes any obstacles which hinder the attainment of goals.

Readiness of the followers

A major variable in the style of leadership adopted by the hospitality manager is the nature of subordinate staff. This leads to consideration of another important contingency model – the situational leadership model presented by Hersey and Blanchard.[47] The model is based on the 'readiness' level of the people the leader is attempting to influence. Readiness (formerly called 'maturity') is the extent to which followers have the ability and willingness to accomplish a specific task. It is not a characteristic of the individual, but how ready the individual is to perform a particular task.

A continuum of four levels

Readiness (R) is divided into a continuum of four levels: R1 (low), R2 and R3 (moderate), and R4 (high).

- *R1 – low follower readiness.* This refers to followers who are both unable and unwilling, and who lack commitment and motivation, or who are unable and insecure.
- *R2 – low to moderate follower readiness.* This refers to followers who are unable but willing, and who lack ability but are motivated to make an effort, or who are unable but confident.
- *R3 – moderate to high follower readiness.* This refers to followers who are able but unwilling, and who have the ability to perform but are unwilling to apply their ability, or who are able but insecure.
- *R4 – high follower readiness.* This refers to followers who are both able and willing, and who have the ability and commitment to perform, or who are able and confident.

For each of the four levels of readiness, the appropriate style of leadership is a combination of task behaviour and relationship behaviour (Figure 9.9).

- *Task behaviour* is the extent to which the leader provides directions for the actions of followers, sets goals for them, and defines their roles and how to undertake them.
- *Relationship behaviour* is the extent to which the leader engages in two-way communications with followers, listens to them, and provides support and encouragement.

Four leadership styles

The combination of task behaviour and relationship behaviour produces four leadership styles (S): telling, selling, participating and delegating.

- *S1 – telling.* This emphasises high amounts of guidance (task behaviour) but limited supportive (relationship) behaviour. This style is most appropriate for low follower readiness (R1).
- *S2 – selling.* This emphasises high amounts of both directive (task) and relationship behaviour. This style is most appropriate for low to moderate follower readiness (R2).
- *S3 – participating.* This emphasises a high amount of two-way communication and supportive (relationship) behaviour but low amounts of guidance (task behaviour). This style is most appropriate for moderate to high follower readiness (R3).

Figure 9.9:
Situational
leadership model

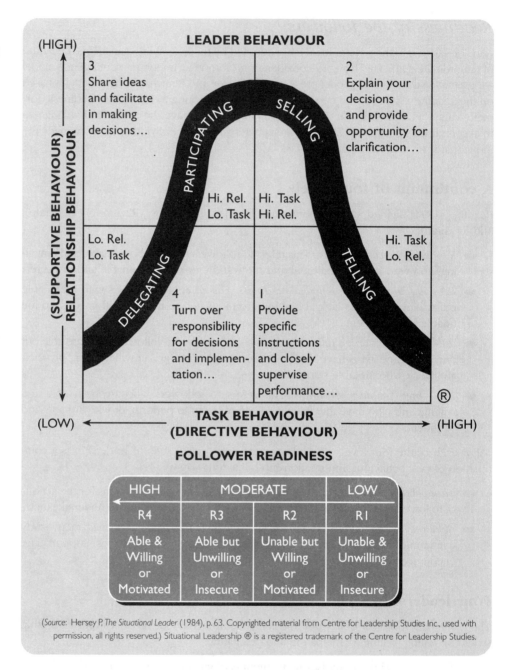

(*Source:* Hersey P, *The Situational Leader* (1984), p. 63. Copyrighted material from Centre for Leadership Studies Inc., used with permission, all rights reserved.) Situational Leadership ® is a registered trademark of the Centre for Leadership Studies.

● *S4 – delegating.* This emphasises little direction or support with low levels of task and relationship behaviour. This style is most appropriate for high follower readiness (R4).

Flexible leadership behaviour

According to Hersey and Blanchard, the key to using situational leadership is that any leader behaviour may be more or less effective depending on the readiness of the followers whom the leader is attempting to influence. An important contribution for the hospitality manager is therefore the need for a flexible style of leadership behaviour. It is important to treat subordinates differently according to their 'readiness' (or maturity), and to treat the same subordinate differently according to changes in the situation.

The model also draws attention to the importance of developing the ability, confidence and commitment of subordinates. The manager should help subordinates to develop in readiness to the extent that they are able and willing. This development should take place by adjusting leadership behaviour through the four styles of telling, selling, participating and delegating.

Transformational leadership

In recent years, increasing business competition and the need for the most efficient use of human resources has resulted in writers on management focusing attention on how leaders revitalise or transform organisations. Based on the work of Burns, this has given rise to a distinction between two fundamental forms of leadership: transactional and transformational.[48]

- *Transactional leadership* is based on legitimate authority within the bureaucratic structure of the organisation. The emphasis is on clarification of goals and objectives, work tasks and outcomes, and organisational rewards and punishments. Transactional leadership appeals to the self-interest of followers and an exchange process of: 'I will give you this, if you do that.'

- *Transformational leadership* is a process of engendering higher levels of motivation and commitment among followers. The emphasis is on generating a vision for the organisation and the leader's ability to appeal to higher ideals and values of followers, and creating a feeling of justice, loyalty and trust.

Some writers see transformational leadership as the same thing as charismatic or inspirational leadership. For example, according to Kreitner and Kinicki: 'Charismatic leadership can produce significant organisational change and results because it "transforms" employees to pursue organisational goals in lieu of self-interests.'[49] However, Hunt suggests that while charismatic leaders can have a tremendous effect on members of an organisation there is no guarantee that this will be positive. What really matters is the nature of outputs and that the leadership mobilises power to change social systems and reform organisations.[50]

Components of transformational leadership

According to Bass, the transformational leader motivates followers to do more than originally expected and the extent of transformation is measured in terms of the leader's effects on followers. Bass proposed a theory of transformational leadership which argues that the leader transforms and motivates followers by: (1) generating greater awareness of the importance of the purpose of the organisation and task outcomes; (2) inducing them to transcend their own self-interests for the sake of the organisation or team; and (3) activating their higher-order needs.[51]

Transformational leadership comprises of four basic components:

- *idealised influence* – the charisma of the leader and the respect and admiration of the followers;

- *inspirational motivation* – the behaviour of the leader which provides meaning and challenge to the work of the followers;

- *intellectual stimulation* – leaders who solicit new and novel approaches for the performance of work and creative problem solutions from followers; and

- *individualised consideration* – leaders who listen and give special concern to the growth and developmental needs of followers.[52]

Transformational leadership in the hospitality industry

A number of recent articles have drawn attention to the increasing complexity of, and dramatic changes that have occurred within, the hospitality industry, and to the importance and benefits of transformational leadership.[53] From their study of 291 managers in 47 US lodging properties, Tracey and Hinkin conclude that:

> It is unlikely that the hospitality industry will become any more stable or less complex in future. As such, transformational leadership, exemplified by the ability to create and communicate a vision and adapt the organisation to a rapidly changing environment, may be the most crucial type of leadership in the years to come.[54]

Best leadership style in the hospitality industry

We have seen that different individuals may fulfil the leadership functions and that there are many alternative styles of leadership. And contingency models demonstrate the importance of situational variables. Different types of leadership may also be most appropriate at different stages in the development of a business organisation.[55] Clearly, there is no simple answer to what is the best style of leadership.

Studies on leadership in the hospitality industry appear to yield conflicting results. For example, using Fiedler's contingency model, Nebel and Stearns conducted a survey of first-line supervisors in the American hotel and restaurant industry. Their findings indicate that a task-orientated style of management leadership would be most effective.[56]

In contrast, however, is the survey by Keegan of managers in the hotel and restaurant industry. The managers identified effective leadership neither as being autocratic or dictatorial, nor as creating followers out of fear or patronising dedication. Rather, they were aware of the need for, and the trend towards, a more human relations style of leadership. Changing social values have increased the demands of employees for a 'good' job and it is the style of managerial leadership which contributes most to their satisfaction and motivation.

Keegan presents a strongly argued case for the adoption of a more supportive, behavioural approach to managerial leadership and draws the following conclusion.

> The challenge for us is not so much to change the job, but to provide the managerial leadership that would create an environment in which the employee's real needs are satisfied. Such a leadership is characterised as being personal, supportive and participative, and is firmly based on a solid relationship between the manager and employees. This managerial leadership should be an integral part of the hospitality environment, a behavioural model as it were, of how best to behave with people in general whether they be guests or employees. Such a leadership style is in many ways in direct opposition to the leadership traditionally associated with our industry. We must change and change dramatically, so let our goal be then to develop this new leadership for our industry.[57]

Leadership research in the hospitality industry

In their discussion of an understanding of leadership theory and application of leadership research to the hospitality industry, Pittaway *et al.* refer to the assumption that if leadership were dependent on the situation, different types of technology, organisation and industry segment would influence the type of leadership behaviour required. Differences may occur between the hospitality industry and other industries, and between segments of the industry. As a starting point for research, Pittaway *et al.* present a situational leadership model identifying the key variables which are considered to influence the leadership process in the hospitality industry.[58] (See Figure 9.10.)

Figure 9.10: Situational leadership model

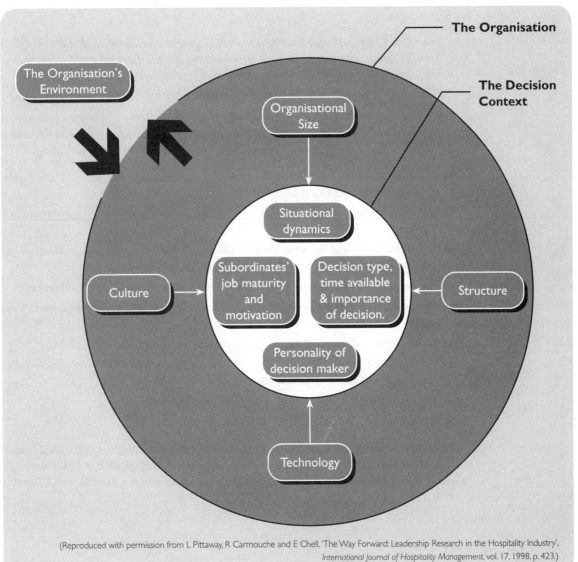

(Reproduced with permission from L Pittaway, R Carmouche and E Chell, 'The Way Forward: Leadership Research in the Hospitality Industry', *International Journal of Hospitality Management*, vol. 17, 1998, p. 423.)

Variables influencing leadership effectiveness

Many research studies tend to indicate that democratic styles of leadership are more likely to produce effective performance from work groups. A human relations, people-orientated approach is more likely to lead to job satisfaction and group cohesiveness. However, it is not always the case that democratic styles of leadership are best. There are occasions when an autocratic style of leadership is more likely to be effective,

We saw in Chapter 6 that despite the particular importance of people within the hospitality industry it does not have a good reputation for adopting a caring and positive approach to staff. Within business organisations generally there is a movement away from managers relying solely on their positional power within a hierarchical structure of authority and a greater emphasis on more participative styles of leadership. However, investigations by Croney,[59] as reported in Wood, into the analysis of management and leadership in four hotel groups found:

> a commitment at corporate level to a management/leadership style that employed communication, consultation and involvement on the part of employees, but participation was generally seen as being management-led, i.e. 'top down' with managers taking any initiatives and setting the boundaries of tolerance.[60]

There is no one 'best' style of leadership which will result in the maintenance of morale among group members and high work performance. There are many variables which underlie the effectiveness of managerial leadership in the hospitality industry, including:

- the type and nature of the establishment, its goals and objectives, and the organisational culture and climate;
- the characteristics of the manager, personality, attitudes, abilities, value system and personal credibility;
- the characteristics of the subordinates, their needs and expectations, motivation and commitment, and their knowledge, confidence and experience;
- the basis of the leadership relationship and the type of power and influence;
- the relationships between the manager and the group, and among members of the group;
- the type of problem and nature of the manager's decisions;
- the nature of the tasks to be achieved, the extent to which they are structured or routine, the technology and work organisation;
- the organisation structure and systems of management;
- the nature and influence of the external environment.

The most effective form of leadership behaviour is therefore a product of the total leadership situation. Education and training in management need to emphasise not only the interpersonal skills of leadership but also the importance of adopting a flexible and adaptable approach.

Managerial leadership – a personal perspective

Many of those who work within hospitality, and therefore know the industry, comment upon the quality of service (and the attitude of those they see working) when they themselves are customers of a hospitality outlet. The comments generally centre on the attitudes of people working together and the treatment of staff by managers.

What is this problem that so many managers appear to have with the treatment of their staff? Quality of service and managerial leadership are inextricably linked in an industry where people – be they guests, customers or staff – and their treatment are paramount to organisational performance and success.

The hospitality industry is a people industry. This is what attracted me to the industry. I like people and I enjoy making people feel welcome, at home and valued. The industry works hard to project this welcoming message to its customers, and all forward-looking organisations, in their own way, tell customers how they can ease their burdens. They offer positive and life-enhancing, relaxing experiences based upon levels of service and attention to the details, which make life so special. Each tries to out-do its nearest competitor in terms of facilities and guest comforts – gyms, beauty salons, IT, conference facilities, baby-sitting services, play areas, etc., solely to say we care about our customers' needs and meet them at all times.

The problem with the image of this 'caring' industry is the horror stories that both employees and customers can tell of situations where staff have been maltreated, or instances of management actions or decisions that destroyed a pleasant atmosphere.

Recently I had a discussion with students who had been on their industrial placement and also held jobs within the industry. One of the salient comments was that managers in a variety of different scenarios did not appear to have any training or skills in the effective management of people. Too many individual managers treated staff very poorly. There was little or no regard for personal issues or even for systems and policies which previously had worked well but were now abandoned either by the individual or, more seriously, by a policy decision of the organisation. Both on an individual manager and organisational level, teamwork and leadership skills were often poor to non-existent.

There are a number of basic underlying factors which relate to people management. First, the hospitality industry has always attracted people at all levels of the social scale. It is considered an easy option by many and the practical nature of the work is also appealing to a section of the population who enjoy 'doing' rather than the outcomes of more academic pursuits.

The hospitality industry is seen as one where employment is easy – service staff are always required and the transient nature of staff almost an accepted characteristic of the trade. People move from job to job within a town or an area, a country or various countries, something that attracts many students to hospitality courses.

In recent years and partly in line with government-led trends, organisations large and small have tried to keep their staff by offering company benefits and additional training as an incentive to staff to stay and develop. This does work, but why does the transience nature of the business remain? Is there a link between transience and staff handling?

continued

continued

Hospitality is not known as a high-paying industry at an operative or even supervisory level. Certain managers can be very well paid but also many are very badly paid. Financial benefits as a whole are few. Accommodation for staff may be provided but it is often basic to poor in standard. The conditions of the job involve unsocial hours with few opportunities to socialise out of the working colleague circle. Food is often of a low standard with staff being offered leftovers from the main restaurant. Larger organisations may offer greater benefits but they make up a relatively small percentage of hospitality employers. Most hospitality employees work for medium to small organisations, run on low overheads.

That being the case, it seems clear that all members of an organisation's staff should support their fellow employees and use all their self-awareness, people management and managerial skills to create a working environment, which is happy, successful and profitable for the organisation. This does happen, but not always, and apparently not often enough.

The following scenarios heard through a variety of people in many walks of the industry are legion. They serve to illustrate general patterns and types of managerial behaviour.

1. The new broom. Often a young manager comes to an outlet and immediately begins to make changes which are not announced previously or are communicated badly. Staff become upset and anxious and begin to leave. The drift may start very quickly or start slowly and build in momentum. Sometimes this is for the good, if things have been badly run and changes have to be made, but the failure is that the effect on staff is not calculated. A variation on this scenario is where a manager has been moved by the organisation from one outlet to another. Whether or not there is a reputation to precede that person, the damage that can be done will be the same.

2. The weak manager who can be bullied by certain members of staff and or will not challenge problems or bad working practices. This is usually in the name of ensuring a happy environment but staff will become resentful. If someone is perceived to be a manager, then people want that person to manage.

3. The manager whose *raison d'être* is ensuring profitability. The profit and loss sheet is this person's Bible and new practices will be introduced or systems will be abandoned if he or she feels that profit margins are being affected. This type of manager is uninterested in the staff as a whole and on an individual level, seeing them as truly an 'economic resource' to be exploited at will. Again staff react badly to this form of management. They feel that they do not know where they stand and that any personal touches or influences they bring to the situation are unappreciated and ignored.

continued

continued

4. The manager who wishes to stamp his or her authority on the staff (most often, again, new staff) by disciplining at the first opportunity a subordinate to 'show them who's boss'. This sad ploy is all too often used as a management tool. Initially, it may appear to work for the manager and problems may seemingly remain few: but more likely the manager loses credibility in the eyes of staff who would have worked happily and well anyway without this unnecessary show of strength.

All these scenarios can be transferred to the organisational level and can be seen in all types of industry. Why the problem is exacerbated in the hospitality industry is that our staff work in an industry that is completely people-focused – at least, 'customer'-focused. They are expected to treat those whom they serve with respect and grace, but they are highly aware that their employers do not have the same feelings towards them.

The sad fact is, however, that the loss of staff in these scenarios is put down to a variety of 'personnel'-based excuses – the old staff not being able to take change or, 'well, it is expected that people move on in this industry'.

So we have a set of problems which stem from poor team-building and leadership, but their cause goes undetected because the results – staff dissatisfaction and staff turnover – are blamed on the industry rather than on bad management practices.

Considering the comment 'Did these managers have any training in the skills of people management, and if so what happened?', various thoughts come to mind:

- Does profit have to affect the way staff are treated?
- Do staffing limitations and the busy environments typical of the hospitality industry mean that good leadership and team-building techniques are ignored or abandoned?
- In training people to be leaders and team-builder, should self-confidence and trust be highlighted to a greater degree than theoretical learning?
- Should both managers and organisations be more aware of the psychology of leadership and team-building in terms of motivation?

If we continue to blame poor terms and conditions of employment – which appear to be an accepted part of the hospitality industry – for the transient nature of a disinterested staff, we overlook a far greater evil. Unless managers exhibit confidence and ability in successful team-building and readership skills at a practical level, the industry is unlikely ever to solve labour shortages or improve the motivation of staff.

Source: The author is grateful to Nigel Maggs-Oosterhagen, Department of Catering and Hospitality Studies, Highbury College, Portsmouth, for providing this contribution.

Summary

- There are many ways of looking at leadership. Essentially it is a relationship through which one person influences other people, and is closely associated with the activities of groups. The labour-intensive nature of the hospitality industry emphasises the importance of leadership skills. To be an effective manager it is necessary to exercise the role of leadership. The leadership relationship is dependent upon the perceived power which the leader can exercise over other people.

- Because of its complex and variable nature there are many ways of analysing leadership. The qualities or trait approach is based on the belief that leadership consists of certain inherited characteristics or personality traits. The functional approach focuses attention on the work group, and functions and responsibilities of leadership.

- Increasing attention has been given to leadership as a behavioural category and the importance of leadership style. Two main dimensions of leadership behaviour are consideration and structure. There are many possible classifications of styles of leadership. One approach is based on the focus of power or the degree of authority used by the manager.

- The situational approach draws attention to variables influencing the nature of managerial leadership. This gives rise to the study of leadership-contingency models. Major models of particular relevance to the hospitality manager are those which relate to the favourability of the leadership situation, path–goal theory, and the readiness of followers. Contingency models demonstrate the importance of situational variables.

- Transformational leadership is a process which creates a vision for the organisation, and appeals to higher ideals and values of followers. Many research studies suggest the advantages of a participative approach but this is not always apparent. There is no one 'best' style of leadership and there are many variables which underlie the effectiveness of managerial leadership in the hospitality industry.

Review and discussion questions

1. Explain the meaning and nature of leadership. How would you attempt to distinguish leadership from management?

2. What is meant by the leadership relationship? Give practical examples of the different sources of leadership power and influence within the hospitality industry.

3. Critically assess the relevance of the qualities or trait theories of leadership. Suggest what you believe to be the most important characteristics of an effective leader in the work situation.

4. Explain your understanding of the functional approach to leadership. Discuss the main areas of need which constitute the core responsibility of the leader. ▷

5. Explain the meaning and importance of leadership style. Suggest ways in which leadership styles can be classified. Why do think greater attention is being given to more participative styles of managerial leadership?

6. Discuss critically the practical value of contingency models of leadership. What are the main factors which are likely to influence the most appropriate form of managerial leadership in the hospitality industry?

7. Contrast transactional and transformational forms of leadership. Discuss critically the relevance and applications of transformational leadership within the hospitality industry.

8. Why do you think it is that studies on leadership in the hospitality industry appear to yield conflicting results? Justify what you think is the best style of leadership.

Assignment 1

Assume you are a departmental manager in a hospitality organisation of your choice.

(i) Using the Tannenbaum and Schmidt continuum, identify your *preferred* style of leadership. Explain fully the rationale for your preference.

(ii) Detail fully, and preferably from actual experience, an example of a particular situation when you believe a different form of managerial leadership is likely to be most effective.

Assignment 2

Three months ago you were appointed head housekeeper at ABC Hotel. A member of your staff, several years older than yourself and with five years' service, and who you understand was very popular with colleagues has in recent weeks had a poor record of punctuality and sickness absence, and often a below-expected standard of work. Despite speaking about it informally and attempts to find out what might be the cause, the member of staff has been reluctant to say anything. Other members of the group have been covering for their colleague but now the strain is showing and morale is beginning to suffer. The general manager has expressed concern at the situation. You are given clear instructions as 'leader of the group' to sort out the problem as quickly as possible. If not, action will have to be taken at a higher level.

Explain fully and with supporting reasons the actions you would propose to take.

Assignment 3

The following items (see Figure 9.11) describe aspects of leadership behaviour. Respond to each item according to the way you would most likely act if you were the leader of a work group. Circle whether

Figure 9.11: Leadership questionnaire

A	F	O	S	N	1.	I would most likely act as the spokesperson of the group.
A	F	O	S	N	2.	I would encourage overtime work.
A	F	O	S	N	3.	I would allow members complete freedom in their work.
A	F	O	S	N	4.	I would encourage the use of uniform procedures.
A	F	O	S	N	5.	I would permit the members to use their own judgement in solving problems.
A	F	O	S	N	6.	I would stress being ahead of competing groups.
A	F	O	S	N	7.	I would speak as a representative of the group.
A	F	O	S	N	8.	I would needle members for greater effort.
A	F	O	S	N	9.	I would try out my ideas in the group.
A	F	O	S	N	10.	I would let the members do their work the way they think best.
A	F	O	S	N	11.	I would be working hard for a promotion.
A	F	O	S	N	12.	I would tolerate postponement and uncertainty.
A	F	O	S	N	13.	I would speak for the group if there were visitors present.
A	F	O	S	N	14.	I would keep the work moving at a rapid pace.
A	F	O	S	N	15.	I would turn the members loose on a job and let them go to it.
A	F	O	S	N	16.	I would settle conflicts when they occur in the group.
A	F	O	S	N	17.	I would get swamped by details.
A	F	O	S	N	18.	I would represent the group at outside meetings.
A	F	O	S	N	19.	I would be reluctant to allow the members any freedom of action.
A	F	O	S	N	20.	I would decide what should be done and how it should be done.
A	F	O	S	N	21.	I would push for increased production.
A	F	O	S	N	22.	I would let some members have authority which I could keep.
A	F	O	S	N	23.	Things would usually turn out as I had predicted.
A	F	O	S	N	24.	I would allow the group a high degree of initiative.
A	F	O	S	N	25.	I would assign group members to particular tasks.
A	F	O	S	N	26.	I would be willing to make changes.
A	F	O	S	N	27.	I would ask the members to work harder.
A	F	O	S	N	28.	I would trust the group members to exercise good judgement.
A	F	O	S	N	29.	I would schedule the work to be done.
A	F	O	S	N	30.	I would refuse to explain my actions.
A	F	O	S	N	31.	I would persuade others that my ideas are to their advantage.
A	F	O	S	N	32.	I would permit the group to set its own pace.
A	F	O	S	N	33.	I would urge the group to beat its previous record.
A	F	O	S	N	34.	I would act without consulting the group.
A	F	O	S	N	35.	I would ask that group members follow standard rules and regulations.

T... P...

you would most likely behave in the described way: always (A); frequently (F); occasionally (O); seldom (S); or never (N).

Scoring

1. Circle the item number for items 8, 12, 17, 18, 19, 30, 34 and 35.

2. Write the number 1 in front of a *circled item number* if you responded S (seldom) or N (never) to that item.

3. Also write a number 1 in front of *item numbers not circled* if you responded A (always) or F (frequently).

4. Circle the number 1 which you have written in front of the following items: 3, 5, 8, 10, 15, 18, 19, 22, 24, 26, 28, 30, 32, 34 and 35.

5. Count the circle number 1s. This is your score for concern for people. Record the score in the blank following the letter P at the end of the questionnaire.

6. Count the uncircled number 1s. This is your score for concern for task. Record this number in the blank following the letter T.

Source: Reprinted from Pfeiffer J W and Jones J E (eds), *A Handbook of Structured Experiences for Human Relations Training*, vol. 1, San Diego, Pfeiffer (1974). Used with permission. The T–P Leadership Questionnaire was adapted from Sergiovanni, Metzcus and Burden's revision of the 'Leadership Behavior Description Questionnaire', *American Educational Research Journal*, vol. 6, no. 1. Copyright by the American Educational Research Association and reprinted by permission of the publisher.

To determine your style of leadership, look at the Interpretation Sheet at the back of the book.

Case study: The Promenade Hotel

The Promenade Hotel was developed from a Georgian mansion into a 117 bedroomed hotel in the 1930s. It sits on the promenade of a south coast resort, where it holds an imposing position. Since that time it has seen many ups and downs. In recent years it has been taken over by a small hotel group specialising in resort type hotels at the three-star level.

The Manager, Peter Crane, has been at the hotel for two years – his first General Manager position. He and his wife live in a pleasant purpose-built flat within the building. Jill Crane began her career as a Receptionist at a hotel in Bournemouth. She and Peter began dating when Peter was a Duty Manager at the same hotel. When they married, eight years ago, Jill was a Head Receptionist and decided that she would not work as she felt it might lead to conflicts of interests if she and Peter worked in the same establishment. Now in their early thirties, they enjoy running a large, prestigious hotel on the front.

The Deputy Manager is Duncan Williams. He joined the hotel eighteen months ago. He has known Jill Crane from their college days together. Duncan also knew the Cranes because he worked in Bournemouth, although at a different hotel when they were there.

The Restaurant/Duty Manager is Jamie Lloyd. He joined the staff three months ago. Jamie comes from a family of Hoteliers on the Isle of Wight and this job is a promotion for him, being a Restaurant Supervisor at a five-star hotel in Buckinghamshire.

The whole complement of staff numbers twenty-five full- and part-timers. Few of the staff have been with the hotel very long. When the hotel was taken over by its present owners many of the old-timers took the opportunity to retire, as they were unsure of what to expect from the new situation.

The general atmosphere of the hotel is good. The arrival of the Cranes was greeted with interest. Peter's reputation was as a switched-on chap who knew his stuff. This reputation has puzzled

The Promenade Hotel continued

the staff, as he appears quite ineffectual. He is perfectly pleasant for most of the time but has a fierce temper, which is displayed at the oddest times. The staff have begun to ignore him somewhat. He often passes responsibility on to Duncan, leaving him with decision to be made while he concentrates on the paperwork.

Duncan is a strange man. A good-looking chap in his late twenties, he is always well turned out and good with guests. To the staff, though, he is known as 'the Fish'. This nickname has been bestowed upon him, as he is a very cold man. He shows little emotion and is quite happy to be unpleasant to staff in order to get his way. This has made most of the staff very wary of him; they don't like his sharp tongue and they don't feel valued by him. The consensus is that he enjoys being unpleasant. This would certainly appear to be true. In conversation Duncan will say that he is there to be the Deputy Manager and not to be liked by the staff. He doesn't actually care what people say about him – in fact it appears to amuse him. A few of the staff find it stimulating to try to get into his less-acerbic books but they are in a minority and even they are tiring of his constant cold demeanour.

Jamie's first months have been a complete eye opener; a larger hotel with more room has been a dream of his to work in. He is in his mid-twenties and this is his second job since gaining an HND in Hotel, Catering and Institutional Management. Jamie's parents run a fifty-bed hotel on the Isle of Wight that was run by Jamie's grandparents before that. He has served at table and prepared rooms for use since he was a boy.

The Promenade came at an ideal time for Jamie. Since he went to college he had been working at the same mainland hotel where he had worked his way through all the departments and he was fed up with the place. He was ready for a change but wanted to keep his interests in F&B alive while progressing his career. The job at the Promenade was exactly right for him.

It is part of Jamie's plan to take over the family's hotel eventually, but he is in no hurry to push his parents out so he wants to get as much experience as he can in order to open a small establishment of his own. He is not sure what form this place will take but he is keen to get his ideas off the ground.

Jamie has become popular with the staff in the short time that he has been at the hotel. He is always cheerful and acknowledges all the staff of the hotel both at work and outside work. He obviously enjoys what he does and is always happy to help a member of staff achieve the task in hand. The Restaurant has eighty covers and the staff is made up of three full-time staff who cover the whole day from breakfast to dinner with ten part-timers who spread their time throughout the day. Many of these staff are students at the local college who need to earn money and wish to gain as much experience as they can. They like Jamie because he encourages their project work and helps them with problems when he can.

In the time that Jamie has been with the hotel, Jill Crane's standing has fallen in the eyes of the Reception staff. They have always found Jill to be aloof; although she is happy to give them instructions about what to do and what instructions they need to leave for her husband when she is going out. She has, in fact, become something of a laughing stock with them and when she comes towards the desk they take it in turns to serve her and enjoy talking about the experience during their breaks.

The staff overall appear to be on the move. The Head Housekeeper was the first to leave and the Reservations Manager has recently announced his departure. In an unusual meeting of the senior staff of Peter, Duncan and Jamie the problem has been discussed. Peter is concerned that the trend may spread. Business has been all right over the past eight months but not as good as he was expecting and the Area Manager questioned the figures Peter presented at his last meeting with him.

Duncan feels that there is nothing to worry about. He feels that the staff are malleable and that there is nothing to be concerned about. Jamie is quite nervous of this meeting. It is his first meeting of this sort at the Promenade. He finds Duncan quite an intimidating man and tends to agree with ▷

the staff that Peter is pleasant but ineffectual. Jamie actually feels that there are some pretty big problems on the horizon. The word in the staff room is that every one is fed up with working there. Picking the bones out of the usual mixture of scare talk, Jamie has discovered that the Head Housekeeper has moved to another large hotel in the next resort and is busy encouraging the best of the housekeeping staff to join her.

The Restaurant team is about to undertake some changes as many of the students are going on placement and they need to train new staff fairly quickly to deal with the start of the season.

There was also an incident a month ago when a management student from another college asked to leave because she was not getting the training promised and Peter paid her off using the petty cash out of the safe. The student took the money but told Peter within ear-shot of the kitchens that she thought he was an idiot and the sooner he realised what a mess the hotel was in, the sooner things might improve. This has been the talk of the hotel staff since then and the Cranes' name now holds little respect.

The receptionists are beginning to get a little irked by Jill's antics and their gossip about her is now being passed on to regular guests.

TASKS

(i) **Explain the managerial leadership styles in operation in this case.**

(ii) **Do you think that these leadership styles will ultimately help or hinder the problems the hotel is experiencing?**

(iii) **Suggest what steps might be taken to help to improve the situation.**

Source: The copyright of this case study rests with the author's colleague, Nigel Maggs-Oosterhagen, Highbury College, Portsmouth. The case is reprinted with permission.

Notes and references

1. Sieff M (Lord Sieff of Brimpton), *Management the Marks and Spencer Way*, Fontana Collins (1991) p. 133.
2. Tack A, *Motivational Leadership*, Gower (1984).
3. See, for example, Mill R C, *Managing for Productivity in the Hospitality Industry*, Van Nostrand Reinhold (1989).
4. Crow S M and Hartman S J, 'Can't Get No Satisfaction', *Leadership and Organization Development Journal*, vol. 16, no. 4, 1995, pp. 34–38.
5. Hooper A and Potter J, 'Take it from the Top', *People Management*, 19 August 1999, pp. 46–49.
6. Keegan B M, 'Leadership in the Hospitality Industry' in Cassee E and Reuland R (eds), *The Management of Hospitality*, Pergamon (1983), p. 78.
7. Worsfold P, 'Leadership and Managerial Effectiveness in the Hospitality Industry', *International Journal of Hospitality Management*, vol. 8, no. 2, 1989, pp. 145–155.
8. Pittaway L, Carmouche R and Chell E, 'The Way Forward: Leadership Research in the Hospitality Industry', *International Journal of Hospitality Management*, vol. 17, 1998, pp. 407–426.
9. Hollingsworth M J, 'Leadership: Purpose and Values', *Manager, The British Journal of Administrative Management*, January/February 1999, p. 22.
10. See, for example, Gretton I, 'Taking the Lead in Leadership', *Professional Manager*, January 1995, pp. 20–22.

11. Taffinder P, *The New Leaders: Achieving corporate transformation through dynamic leadership*, Kogan Page (1995).

12. Hunt J W, *Managing People at Work*, 2nd edn, McGraw-Hill (1986).

13. Watson C M, 'Leadership, Management and the Seven Keys', *Business Horizons*, March–April 1983, pp. 8–13.

14. Zaleznik A, 'Managers and Leaders: Are They Different?', *Harvard Business Review*, May–June 1977, pp. 67–78.

15. Bonnington C, 'Leading to the Top: The Successful Management of People', *Office and Information Management International*, September 1988, pp. 8–9.

16. Mintzberg H, *The Nature of Managerial Work*, Harper & Row (1973).

17. Adair J, *Effective Teambuilding*, Gower (1986), p. 123.

18. For an example, see Riley M, *Human Resource Management in The Hospitality and Tourism Industry*, 2nd edn, Butterworth-Heinemann (1996).

19. McGregor D, *The Human Side of Enterprise*, Penguin (1987), p. 182.

20. French J R P and Raven B, 'The Basis of Social Power', in Cartwright D and Zander A F (eds), *Group Dynamics: Research and Theory*, 3rd edn, Harper & Row (1968).

21. Drucker P F, *The Practice of Management*, Pan Books (1968), p. 194.

22. See, for example, Jennings E E, 'The Anatomy of Leadership', *Management of Personnel Quarterly*, vol. 1, no. 1, Autumn 1961, pp. 2–9.

23. Hornsey T and Dann D, *Manpower Management in the Hotel and Catering Industry*, Batsford (1984).

24. Jacob J, 'Towards a Simplistic Theory of Leadership', *Hospitality*, June 1980, pp. 40–41.

25. Walker R G, 'Wellsprings of Managerial Leadership', *Cornell HRA Quarterly*, vol. 27, no. 2, August 1986, pp. 14–16.

26. Conger J, 'Charisma and How to Grow It', *Management Today*, December 1999, p. 81.

27. Kotter J P, 'What Leaders Really Do', *Harvard Business Review*, May–June 1990, p. 103.

28. Krech D, Crutchfield R S and Ballachey E L, *Individual in Society*, McGraw-Hill (1962).

29. Adair J, *The Skills of Leadership*, Gower (1984).

30. Adair J, *Effective Teambuilding*, Gower (1986), p. 116.

31. Fleishman E A and Bass A R, *Studies in Personnel and Industrial Psychology*, 3rd edn, Dorsey (1974).

32. Worsfold P, 'Leadership and Managerial Effectiveness in the Hospitality Industry', *International Journal of Hospitality Management*, vol. 8, no. 2, 1989, pp. 145–155.

33. Likert R, *New Patterns of Management*, McGraw-Hill (1961).

34. See, for example, Van der Wagen L and Davies C, *Supervision and Leadership in Tourism and Hospitality*, Cassell (1999).

35. Boella M J, *Human Resource Management in the Hospitality Industry*, 6th edn, Stanley Thornes (1996), p. 40.

36. *Ibid.*

37. Magurn J P, *A Manual of Staff Management in the Hotel and Catering Industry*, Heinemann (1983).

38. Belbin R M, *Team Roles at Work*, Butterworth-Heinemann (1993).

39. Erstad M, 'Empowerment and Organizational Change', *International Journal of Contemporary Hospitality Management*, vol. 9, no. 7, 1997, pp. 325–333.

40. Tannenbaum R and Schmidt W H, 'How to Choose a Leadership Pattern', *Harvard Business Review*, May–June 1973, pp. 162–180.

41. Follett M P, 'The Giving of Orders', in Pugh D S (ed.), *Organization Theory*, Penguin (1971), pp. 154–155.

42. Fiedler F E, *A Theory of Leadership Effectiveness*, McGraw-Hill (1967).

43. Hornsey T and Dann D, *Manpower Management in the Hotel and Catering Industry*, Batsford (1984), p. 108.

44. House R J, 'A Path-Goal Theory of Leadership Effectiveness', *Administrative Science Quarterly*, vol. 16, September 1971, pp. 321–338.

45. House R I and Dessler G, 'The Path–Goal Theory of Leadership', in Hunt J G and Larson L L (eds), *Contingency Approaches to Leadership*, Southern Illinois University Press (1974).

46. House R I and Mitchell T R, 'Path–Goal Theory of Leadership', *Journal of Contemporary Business*, vol. 3, Autumn 1974, pp. 81–97.

47. Hersey P and Blanchard K, *Management of Organizational Behavior*, 6th edn, Prentice-Hall (1993).

48. Burns J M, *Leadership*, Harper & Row (1978).

49. Kreitner R and Kinicki A, *Organizational Behavior*, 3rd edn, Irwin (1995), p. 441.

50. Hunt J W, *Managing People at Work*, 3rd edn, McGraw-Hill (1992), p. 255.

51. Bass B M, *Leadership and Performance Beyond Expectations*, Free Press (1985).

52. Bass B M and Avolio B J, *Improving Organizational Effectiveness Through Transformational Leadership*, Sage Publications (1994).

53. See, for example, Hinkin T R and Tracey J B, 'Transformational Leadership in the Hospitality Industry', *Hospitality Research Journal*, vol. 18, no. 1, 1994, pp. 49–63.

54. Tracey J B and Hinkin T R, 'How Transformational Leaders Lead in The Hospitality Industry', *International Journal of Hospitality Management*, vol. 15, no. 2, 1996, p. 174.

55. See, for example, Clarke C and Pratt S, 'Leadership's Four-Part Progress', *Management Today*, March 1985, pp. 84–86.

56. Nebel E C and Stearns K, 'Leadership in the Hospitality Industry', *Cornell HRA Quarterly*, vol. 18, no. 3, November 1977, pp. 69–76.

57. Keegan B M, 'Leadership in the Hospitality Industry', in Cassee E and Reuland R (eds), *The Management of Hospitality*, Pergamon (1983), pp. 69–93.

58. Pittaway L, Carmouche R and Chell E, 'The Way Forward: Leadership Research in the Hospitality Industry', *International Journal of Hospitality Management*, vol. 17, 1998, pp. 407–426.

59. Croney P, 'An Investigation Into The Management of Labour in The Hospitality Industry', MA Thesis, University of Warwick, 1988.

60. Wood R C, *Organizational Behaviour for Hospitality Management*, Butterworth–Heinemann (1994), p. 126.

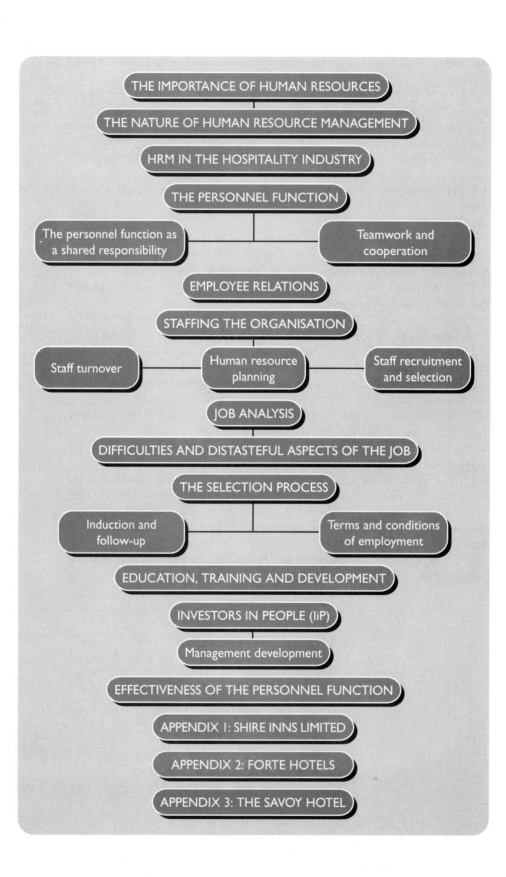

THE IMPORTANCE OF HUMAN RESOURCES

THE NATURE OF HUMAN RESOURCE MANAGEMENT

HRM IN THE HOSPITALITY INDUSTRY

THE PERSONNEL FUNCTION

The personnel function as a shared responsibility

Teamwork and cooperation

EMPLOYEE RELATIONS

STAFFING THE ORGANISATION

Staff turnover

Human resource planning

Staff recruitment and selection

JOB ANALYSIS

DIFFICULTIES AND DISTASTEFUL ASPECTS OF THE JOB

THE SELECTION PROCESS

Induction and follow-up

Terms and conditions of employment

EDUCATION, TRAINING AND DEVELOPMENT

INVESTORS IN PEOPLE (IiP)

Management development

EFFECTIVENESS OF THE PERSONNEL FUNCTION

APPENDIX 1: SHIRE INNS LIMITED

APPENDIX 2: FORTE HOTELS

APPENDIX 3: THE SAVOY HOTEL

Chapter ten

The personnel/HRM function

Introduction

Whatever the structure of a hospitality organisation or the nature of its activities, an essential part of the process of management is the effective use of human resources. Proper attention to the personnel/HRM function will help to improve the efficiency of the workforce and the level of organisational performance.

The importance of human resources

Hospitality is a major industry in this country and throughout the world. A report of the Hotel and Catering Training Company (HCTC) indicates that the industry employs nearly 10 per cent (in excess of 2.4 million) of the UK total working population.[1] The industry is also forecast to continue to grow until beyond the year 2004.[2] World-wide, the number of jobs in the hospitality and tourism industry is estimated to be 365 million by the year 2006.[3]

The industry is service-orientated and labour-intensive; and its pattern of staffing is characterised by such features as mobility, seasonal and part-time work, a high proportion of unskilled, part-time and casual staff, a high labour turnover, and many trade unions but low trade union membership.

It is therefore particularly important that the industry attracts and retains staff with the right skills and attitudes to meet satisfactorily the demands of the customer. There must be effective management of human resources – there must be an effective personnel function.

The human element

The human element plays a major part in the overall success of any organisation, but especially so in a service industry such as hospitality. Many members of the workforce are in direct contact with the customer and are seen as being involved in achieving the objectives of the organisation. The quality of service offered is dependent not only upon the skills but also upon the attitudes of the staff. Both are essential if the demands of the customer are to be met satisfactorily. This places particular importance on the personnel function. This may appear to be an obvious statement. But it is worth emphasising that it is debatable how much time, care and attention is actually given to the personnel function and to the effective management of people within the hospitality industry.[4]

Personnel as a task function?

You will recall that in Chapter 6 we made the distinction between task functions – those basic activities directed towards specific and definable end results – and element functions – those activities that are supportive of the task functions. In the majority of organisations the personnel function does not normally have any direct accountability for the performance of a specific end-task. Personnel is generally identified therefore as an element or support function.

However, it is arguable to what extent this applies strictly in the hospitality industry. The people employed are more than just a means to an end, more than just inputs to a finished product. People are, at least in part, an end in themselves. They are part of the finished product for which the customer is paying. For example, the customer in the restaurant is buying not only food and beverage and the skills of the chef, but also the service and attention of the waiting staff. Should either of these give a service less than is required of them, then this will lead to customer dissatisfaction.[5]

The importance of staff contact to customer satisfaction means that personnel can be seen as closely associated with a task function. Customer satisfaction is likely to be affected as much by the courtesy, helpfulness and personal qualities of the staff as by the standard of food and beverage, accommodation or other facilities of the organisation.

The nature of human resource management

The increasing emphasis on effective employee relations, and the importance of securing the involvement of staff and their commitment to the aims of the organisation, has led to the increasing use of the term 'human resources' to replace 'personnel'. There is, however, no clear distinction between personnel management and human resource management (HRM). For example, Guest suggests three ways in which human resource management has been used to distinguish it from traditional personnel management:

(i) simply to re-title personnel management to capture the new fashion;

(ii) to re-conceptualise and reorganise personnel roles, and the work of personnel departments; and

(iii) as distinctively different and offering a new approach for management.[6]

Guest goes on to describe some broad stereotypes which could be used to highlight the differences. Compared with personnel management, human resource management is concerned more with a long-term rather than a short-term perspective, with the psychological contract based on commitment rather than compliance, with self-control rather than external controls, with a unitarist rather than a pluralist perspective, with an organic rather than a bureaucratic structure, with integration with line management rather than specialist or professional roles, and with maximum utilisation rather than cost-minimisation.

HRM and personnel management

Torrington and Hall distinguish between personnel management as 'workforce-centred' directed mainly at the organisation's employees, and human resource management as 'resource-centred' directed mainly at management needs for human resources to be provided and deployed. However, they see the nature and degree of difference between personnel management and human resource management as remaining 'largely matters of opinion rather than fact, and the similarities are much greater than the differences'.[7]

A detailed analysis by Storey identifies 27 points of difference between personnel and IR, and HRM categorised under four main headings of: beliefs and assumptions; strategic aspects; line management; and key levers.[8] From a critical analysis of human resource management, Legge suggests that: 'The differences between the normative models of personnel and human resource management are more than those of meaning and emphasis than substance – but nonetheless "real" for that.'[9]

It can be argued that HRM is the elevation of personnel management to a more strategic level. It is not easy, however, to distinguish clearly HRM from personnel management.

According to Cuming, for example, some argue that human resource management is just a new term for what most good personnel managers have already been practising. The extent to which personnel management has moved into another historical phase of human resource management is debatable.[10]

HRM in the hospitality industry

According to Willman, human resource management in the service sector is concerned with:

> *mechanisms through which the organisation attracts candidates for employment, selects them, introduces them to the organisation's structure and culture, motivates them to perform a given set of tasks, pays them for this and seeks to identify their potential for future development. It is then concerned with systems of promotion, manpower planning, succession planning, and coping with labour turnover of one form or another.*[11]

As part of research on the extent to which hotel companies account for human resource management, Maher questioned senior human resource managers on the perceived difference between the HR specialist and the personnel specialist. Reactions to the question were mixed and ranged from antagonism to enthusiasm for the ideas embodied in HRM.[12] Maher also found that although the HRM function had become more important in the past few years, this was seen to be because of the need to reduce costs in that area rather than as increasing recognition of the importance of the HRM function or its significance within the overall business strategy of the organisation.

Policies and practices of HRM

From a survey of 241 UK hotel and restaurant establishments, Price found the broad picture of personnel practice in the commercial sector of the hospitality industry and the more focused picture within hotels and restaurants to be poor, and far removed from an ideal-type personnel or HRM model. The development of sound personnel practice was to a degree dependent on how well proprietors and managers were informed about legal obligations and recommended personnel practices. Many of the larger establishments were part of a chain with extensive head office personnel support. There was a strong correlation between the size of an establishment and the extent to which it conformed to employment legislation and appropriate personnel policies and procedures.[13]

A study by Kelliher and Johnson also suggested that personnel management in the hospitality industry has suffered a poor image, particularly in small hotels where it was often marginalised and well down the order of priorities.[14] In the ten years since the original study, in larger hotels the personnel function has expanded and improved but with little evidence of a significant move to a model of HRM.[15]

Goldsmith *et al.* believe that effective management of personnel or human resources is as much a matter of policy as the day-to-day matters of people management and seek to chart a path between the demands of good personnel practice and many of the aspirations of the HRM approach.

> *We are persuaded of many of the benefits of the human resource management approach, which, theoretically at least, links the welfarism of traditional personnel administration to strategic consideration of the value of labour in the organization.*[16]

Baum *et al.* refer to the increasing global competition and globalisation of products and consumer expectations within tourism and hospitality which will increasingly depend on the human factor and the ability to deliver quality products and services. Integrating policy development with HRM is a central strategic and operational concern at local, regional and national levels.[17]

HRM and service quality

Lashley argues that the management of human resources in service organisations is likely to be influenced by the nature of the service being delivered. Styles in the management of human resources relate implicitly to the extent of employee involvement and participation, and the manner and form of empowerment to employees. Techniques used to recruit, select, train, appraise, reward, supervise and design the jobs of service employees have to be compatible with the service being offered to customers. Lashley suggests that there is likely to be an ideal match between styles in the service offer and styles in the management of employees.[18]

From a review of literature, Worsfold found that for the most part this directs attention to the poor uptake of HRM in the majority of hotels, although this does not appear significantly different from other small service and manufacturing companies. The literature has established that HRM can be of benefit to improving company performance, and a rather tenuous link between HRM and performance can be established via commitment and service quality.

Worsfold concludes that there is clearly need for additional research relating to the hospitality industry, which should seek to examine the links between HRM and service quality, service behaviour and profitability. He also suggests that, in the case of small hotels, we may need to abandon the search for formal HRM approaches and attempt to establish whether 'caring management' can provide the concern for employee well-being which appears to be linked to service quality.[19]

The psychological contract and the management of people

It is not easy to distinguish clearly human resource management from personnel management. And however HRM is perceived or described, it does not follow that it will necessarily lead to a higher level of organisational performance than would be achieved with a traditional personnel management approach. Human resources are clearly the most important asset of any organisation and need to be managed; however, attention must also be given to the importance of the psychological contract (discussed in Chapter 3).

The changing nature of organisations has placed an increasing emphasis on the import-ance of effective HRM, including the psychological contract within the employment relationship. For example, McBain maintains that HRM plays a key role in ensuring the promotion of business success and managing change. This involves paying attention to the psychological contract and the establishment of expectations and obligations with all groups of employees within the organisation.[20]

However, whether one is talking about personnel management or human resource man-agement, it is important to remind ourselves that, unlike physical resources, people are not owned by the organisation. People are individuals who bring their own perceptions, feelings and attitudes towards the organisation, systems and styles of management, their duties and responsibilities, and the conditions under which they are working. **What really matters is the effective management of people.**

The personnel function

The hospitality industry is made up of units which vary greatly in size and type. Smaller establishments may not justify a specialist personnel manager or a separate personnel depart-ment. *But it is still necessary to have an effective personnel* **function**, whether it be the responsibility of, for example, the owner or the general manager or shared among heads of departments.

Even the smallest establishments will have the need, for example, to recruit and train staff, to motivate and reward them, and to comply with the law relating to employment. The personnel function must still be carried out even if a unit is too small to justify, or chooses not to establish, a separate personnel department.

The importance of the personnel function has been emphasised by, among others, Rocco Forte.

> *In a service industry the most important ingredient in the product is people. The quality of our people determines the quality of the service we give to cus-tomers and thus our success in the market-place. Not surprisingly, almost every discussion we have in the company starts or finishes with personnel matters. We recognise that we can only continue to exist by attracting, training and motivating good people. Doing that successfully means having a caring and efficient personnel function to assist line managers in what is one of their primary responsibilities.*[21]

A similar sentiment has been expressed, for example, by Venison. 'A personnel func-tion in an hotel is required beyond any doubt. Whether that function takes up the full-time employment of one or more people, thus rendering it a service department, or whether it is the part-time responsibility of a particular member of management depends upon the size of the hotel. Irrespective of hotel size, however, and notwithstanding the style of the hotel manager, the need for the function always exists.'[22]

Personnel management specialist

In the larger establishments where more time is taken up with problems of organisation and personnel, there is greater need for a specialist to whom is delegated specific respons-ibilities for personnel matters. A specialised personnel manager would be expected to advise top management on the implementation of clearly defined policies which permit consist-ent personnel practices.

There are no hard and fast rules on what size of establishment justifies a separate personnel department. The number of staff is clearly a significant but not the only consideration. In addition to the type and nature of the organisation, there are a number of other important factors which emphasise the importance of the personnel function. These include, for example,

● increasing business competitiveness, and greater demands for high standards of service quality and delivery;

● the increasing level of government involvement in employment legislation;

● pressures for a greater social responsibility towards employees through for example, schemes of worker participation, including European Union proposals on employee involvement;

● high staffing costs;

● developments in the applications of behavioural science;

● the role of industrial tribunals and ACAS; and

● the possible growth of trade unions in the industry.

These factors all combine to suggest the increasing need for a personnel management specialist.

The role of top management

The overall objective of the personnel function is to create an environment in which staff work willingly and effectively. Management should attempt to maintain a level of morale and commitment of all members of staff in order to secure the optimum operational performance. The effective management of people is influenced by the part played by top management and the attitudes which they bring to bear on relationships with staff. Personnel policies are a reflection on the overall style of management.[23] Policies should emanate from the top of the hospitality organisation. They should be defined clearly and communicated through managers and supervisors to staff at all levels.

Underlying philosophies

The formulation of personnel policies, and the implementation of HRM practices and procedures, should be based on underlying philosophies of managerial behaviour and employee relationships.

Such philosophies should embrace:

● respect for the individual;

● the recognition of people's needs and expectations at work;

● justice in treatment and equitable reward systems;

● stability of employment;

● good working environment and conditions of service;

● opportunities for personal development and career progression;

● democratic functioning of the organisation;

● full observance of all laws and codes of conduct relating to employment.

The range of the personnel function

The range and scope of the personnel function are wide. This is illustrated by the definition of personnel management given by the Institute of Personnel and Development.

> *Personnel management is that part of management concerned with people at work and with their relationships within an enterprise. Its aim is to bring together and develop into an active organisation the men and women who make up an enterprise and, having regard for the well-being of the individual and of working groups, to enable them to make their best contribution to its success. Personnel management is also concerned with the human and social implications of change in internal organisation and methods of working, and of economic and social changes in the community.*[24]

Personnel activities may be considered within the framework of the following broad headings:

- human resource planning;
- organisation design and patterns of work;
- recruitment and selection;
- pay and employment conditions;
- education, training and development;
- employee relations and welfare services.

The personnel function as a shared responsibility

The Institute of Personnel and Development's definition draws attention to personnel management as part of the responsibility of all managers and supervisors. Getting work done through the efforts of other people is an integral part of any managerial activity. The personnel function is part of the generality of management.[25]

For example, when the head chef ensures that the kitchen brigade are clean and that standards of hygiene are observed, this is carrying out a personnel function. If the accommodation manager reprimands a room attendant for lateness, this is carrying out a personnel function. And if the front of house manager trains a receptionist in receiving advance reservations, this is carrying out a personnel function.

We saw above that Rocco Forte has emphasised the importance of a caring and efficient personnel function to assist line managers in what is one of their primary responsibilities. The nature of business with many separate units of differing size, location and mix of skills means of necessity the personnel function is decentralised and prime responsibility has to be with line management.

> *However, even if we had a choice, I believe we would elect to put the prime responsibility for personnel on line management rather than on specialists. The nature of our work calls for active participation by management in day to day operations and they need to have a very close relationship and understanding with their staff. Equally, staff need to know that line management has the authority and responsibility for taking actions which vitally affect them in their work and in their working environment. The link therefore must be a direct one.*[26]

Functional relationship

The role of the personnel manager is to implement personnel policies throughout all departments of the organisation, to provide specialist knowledge and services for the line managers, and to support them in the performance of their work. The personnel manager should operate in terms of a 'functional' relationship with the line managers. It should not be the job of the personnel manager to manage other staff, other than any direct subordinates.

Whatever the organisation of the personnel function, a personnel manager operates through a form of delegated authority. The degree of authority given to the personnel manager is dependent upon the philosophy and attitudes of top management, the role the position is intended to perform, and the formal relationships with other managers. The personnel manager has no direct control over staff in other departments except where a specific responsibility is delegated directly by top management, for example for health and safety matters. In all other respects the personnel manager's responsibility with other managers and their staff should be indirect – that is, as a specialist adviser.

Specialist expertise and advice

However, although the line managers are specialists in their own areas of work, they are not necessarily specialists in personnel matters. In the same way that line managers may need help and guidance on legal and accounting matters, so they may need help and specialist advice on personnel management. It is the personnel manager who has the professional expertise and specialist knowledge of personnel work. Line managers might be expected, therefore, to heed and to act upon the advice which is given. The personnel manager is responsible for the interpretation and implementation of personnel policies and procedures, and sees the overall effect throughout the establishment, as a whole. It is important to keep a balance between departments, and to maintain equitable treatment for all staff and a sense of fair play.

Teamwork and cooperation

If the personnel function is to be effective, there has to be good teamwork and cooperation and consultation between line managers and the personnel manager. This is made easier when top management, who retain ultimate responsibility for the personnel function, take an active part in fostering goodwill and cooperation between departments.

Top management should agree clear terms of reference for the personnel manager within a framework of sound and clear personnel policies. Within this framework the personnel function can be seen as operating at two levels: the organisational level and the departmental level (Figure 10.1).

The organisational level

At the organisational level the detailed involvement of the work activities of several departments, available time and the need for specialisation suggest that the personnel manager has a prominent role to play. The personnel manager is the main executor of personnel policies and is concerned mainly with broader aspects which affect all members of staff and the organisation as a whole.

This could include such activities as human resource planning, procedures for recruitment and selection, induction and training, health and safety, welfare, employee relations,

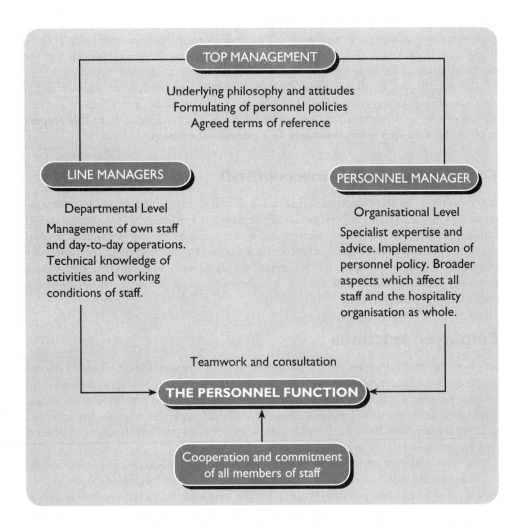

Figure 10.1:
The personnel
function –
a shared
responsibility

compliance with employment legislation, dealings with trade unions or staff representatives, maintaining statistics and records, and liaison with outside bodies such as HCTC, HCIMA, employers' associations or ACAS. The personnel manager should act in consultation with, and taking advice from, line managers.

The departmental level

At the departmental level the line managers might assume a prominent role for day-to-day personnel matters. They would be concerned, at least in the first instance, with the operational aspects of personnel activities within their own department, for example minor disciplinary matters, poor time-keeping, unsatisfactory work performance, calling in stand-by staff, safety, on-the-job training, allocation of duties and rota schedules, communication of information, and the welfare of, and grievances from, staff. The personnel manager would be expected to act as adviser, and if necessary as arbitrator.

It is the line managers who have the technical expertise, together with a detailed knowledge of the activities of their department and the working conditions of staff. They have the responsibility for the management of their own staff.

Line managers have both the right and the duty to be concerned with the efficiency of their own department and the well-being of their staff. Line managers are on hand to observe directly the behaviour and performance of staff. For example, the restaurant manager (or the head waiter) is in the restaurant; the chef is in the kitchen. They will actually see, and be directly affected by, the lateness of staff, unsatisfactory work, insufficient training, staff unrest or poor planning of work duties and responsibilities. It is therefore the line managers who have the immediate responsibility for personnel management. **In this respect it could be said that every manager is a personnel manager.**

Commitment of all members of staff

It is clear then that the personnel function is a shared responsibility among top management, line managers and supervisors, and the personnel manager. But if the personnel function is to be implemented successfully it also requires the cooperation and commitment of all members of staff, whatever their duties or positions within the hospitality organisation. The personnel function cannot be housed within one discrete department or be the sole responsibility of selected members of staff. It permeates all levels of the organisation and all phases of its operations.

Employee relations

However the responsibilities for the personnel function are shared and whatever the respective roles of the personnel manager and line managers, the personnel function can be effective only if it is based on sound personnel policies. Good employee relations are fostered by good personnel policies. Broadly defined, employee relations is concerned with the relationships between the policies and practices of the organisation and its staff, and the behaviour of work groups.

The traditional view of industrial relations has often been associated in particular with the activities of trade unions and their officials, and collective bargaining. Trade unions may be seen as existing primarily to promote the best interests of their members and to improve the quality of working life and the general standard of living. According to Lucas, 'Industrial relations is the more traditional, and still most widely used, term for discussing issues in the employment relationship, although employee relations is becoming more widely used.'[27]

Good management–staff relationships are not limited, however, to trade unions and employment legislation. They also entail broader informal and social relationships, and the importance of the role of management.[28]

According to an HCTC booklet, employee relations embraces:

all the factors in the relationships between employers, staff and other individuals and institutions involved in the employment process.[29]

To understand any employee relations situation it is necessary to take account of the institutions and parties involved, and their ideologies and motives.

Employee relations policy

Having well-defined and agreed policies is increasingly seen as important in establishing effective employee relations. Cuming, for example, makes the following point.

Accepting that human resources are the most important that an organisation has, and that their effective management is essential, the principle underlying HRM is that success is most likely to be achieved if personnel policies and practices clearly and positively contribute to the achievement of corporate objectives and strategic plans.[30]

The HCTC booklet provides a 25-point checklist which covers many of those matters about which it is useful for an employer to have a considered policy (Figure 10.2). It is important that the employer's policies and procedures are kept up to date, successfully communicated, and understood properly by all staff.[31]

Legal and behavioural dimensions

Effective employee relations embrace not only legal dimensions but also behavioural dimensions.[32] Legal dimensions regulate the relationship between employers and employees, provide individual rights for employees and strengthen the position of trade unions. The legal dimensions embody observance of employment legislation, the formal contract of employment and codes of practice.

The observance of legal rules and regulations is a necessary part of effective employee relations but does not by itself make for a harmonious environment at work. Behavioural dimensions embodies recognition of the individual, the social responsibilities of management, the psychological contract (discussed in Chapter 3) and style of managerial behaviour. Social responsibilities extend beyond terms and conditions of employment and give recognition to the social and human needs of people at work.

The importance of listening

Whatever procedures are used, an important part of good employee relations is managers listening to the feelings and problems of the staff.[33] You may recall that in Chapter 6 we discussed the contribution of the interviewing programme of the Hawthorne studies to the development of a human relations approach to organisation and management. Many workers appeared to welcome the opportunity to have someone who would listen to their feelings and problems, and to whom they could 'let off steam' in a friendly atmosphere.

The interviewing programme highlighted the importance of counselling interviews and of managers actively listening to the staff. Given the nature of the hospitality industry and the importance of good employee relations, the lessons learnt from the interviewing programme have particular significance for the manager.

Staffing the organisation

Whatever the type, size or structure of the hospitality establishment it has to be staffed with people of the right quality. The effectiveness of any organisation will inevitably depend very largely upon the staff it employs and on good management–staff relationships. Larger establishments may perhaps have a designated personnel manager, but this does not detract from the concern of every manager for the maintenance of good staff relations and the management of their own staff. It is only right and sensible, therefore, that managers and supervisors have at least some say in the appointment of their own staff or those staff whose work they have to supervise.

Figure 10.2: Checklist for an employee relationship policy

DEVELOPING AN EMPLOYEE RELATIONS POLICY

Recruitment

1 What steps have you taken to produce an 'Equal Opportunity' employment policy statement?

2 Do you select on merit – regardless of sex or race?

3 Do you know that the Commission for Racial Equality and the Equal Opportunities Commission can help by giving examples of equal opportunity policies and advice on how to monitor their use?

Pay and other benefits

4 Do you plan your pay policy?

5 Do you *plan* to be a 'low' or a 'high' payer?

6 Do you know what benefits your competitors offer?

7 Is your pay structure planned and understood, or based on 'grace and favour'?

8 Do you understand and comply with current wages council orders and with the provisions of the Equal Pay Act?

Staff representation

9 What is your declared approach to staff representation?

10 Do you, where appropriate, recognise and negotiate with a trade union?

11 Do you make adequate facilities available for the representatives of your staff?

12 If you do not recognise a trade union, do your staff have adequate opportunities to represent their views?

Communication and consultation

People are often so busy that they can easily be unaware of what other working groups are doing or what problems there may be

13 What do you do to find out about these problems and to help resolve them?

14 How do you consult staff on changes that will affect them and how do you gain commitment to new policies?

Staff development and training

15 What initiatives have you taken to develop and train your staff, especially young people?

16 Do you have a policy about promotion from within the organisation and do you seek to develop staff by an effective appraisal scheme?

17 Do you select staff for training and development on the basis of merit and their needs – regardless of sex or race?

Disciplinary matters and grievances

18 Do you have adequate, readily understood procedures that are available for all to see?

19 How are these communicated?

Retirement

20 At what age do you normally retire staff?

21 How do you decide who is to retire and who can stay?

22 Are your staff aware of the policy and are they clear on whether you have a defined age of retirement?

Redundancy or lay off

23 In what circumstances will staff be made redundant or laid off?

24 What system of notification, consultation and selection will be used? (Remember that you are obliged to consult the relevant recognised trade union if one exists, and that race and sex discrimination legislation also applies to decisions about redundancy selection)

25 Are alternatives, such as work sharing or short time, built into your procedures?

Finally

Considering your employment policies in general – have they been discussed with your staff?

Even if they do not belong to a trade union, it is preferable to discuss and agree on such matters with staff or their representatives, before making rules.

(*Source:* reprinted, with permission, from *Employee Relations for the Hotel and Catering Industry*, 7th edn, Hotel and Catering Training Company (1990), pp. 24–26.)

Within an organisational context, the prerequisites of an effective system for staffing include:

- the clarification of aims and objectives;
- the design of an effective organisation structure through which work is carried out, and to support the efforts of staff; and
- a system of human resource planning as the framework within which personnel policies and a systematic approach to recruitment and selection are planned and implemented.

The overall aim must be to select the best available staff in the first place, to train and develop them, and to retain them for a reasonable period of time.

Core and peripheral staff

Staffing of an organisation can be viewed in terms of 'core' and 'peripheral' employees, and the nature of flexible working.[34] **Core** denotes permanent, full-time employees. They undertake key activities of the organisation and are expected to be functionally flexible. Career prospects and job security are high. Peripheral denotes numerically flexible employees with fairly easy jobs, limited career opportunities and less job security. The peripheral groups surround the core employees and insulate them from the effects of changes in demand.

From a study of ten major hotel groups in the UK, Guerrier and Lockwood identify three categories of core employees and two categories of peripheral employees.[35]

- *Company core staff* have potential access to career prospects throughout the range of units within the company and consist largely of management or trainee management staff, but not usually departmental heads.
- *Unit core staff* have access to career opportunities within a single hotel, but not within the wider company, and consist of departmental heads, supervisors, certain skilled operatives and some hotel trainees.
- *Operative core* consist of staff such as receptionists, skilled kitchen staff, waiting staff and chambermaids.
- *Peripheral group 1*, by whom numerical flexibility is achieved through high turnover rate, includes highly mobile skilled kitchen and waiting staff, and students or foreign workers in the UK for a limited period.
- *Peripheral group 2* consists of part-time and casual staff, and staff who are on call, for example chambermaids.

Staff turnover

In the hospitality industry staff turnover is generally acknowledged to be high, especially in comparison with other industries. There is an average staff turnover rate of 43 per cent and high levels of skills shortages.[36] Much of the turnover is movement within the industry. Although hotels and guesthouses had the highest total turnover rate, less than half went outside the industry. But this does not alter the frequency with which staff have to be replaced or the need for retraining in particular working methods and practices. Staff turnover is highest in the first few months of employment. Such turnover – the 'induction crisis' – is particularly disruptive and costly.

The costs of high staff turnover

A high level of staff turnover is likely to have an adverse effect on the morale, motivation and job satisfaction of staff, and on the level of organisational performance and customer satisfaction. It also has a disruptive effect on the use of managerial time. The costs of high staff turnover are emphasised by the HCTC.

> *The costs of recruiting and engaging a new member of staff are considerable – not only the direct costs like advertising, agency fees, paper-work, interview time, but the many hidden or indirect costs. For example the expenses incurred in training and supervising new entrants, as well as those they are replacing, overtime that may have been paid during staff shortages, an increase in wastage and losses while new staff settle in, customer irritation and low staff morale if staff turnover is high.*[37]

Reducing staff turnover

So what can be done to help overcome a high level of staff turnover, reduce costs and make more effective use of managerial time? You may recall the discussion in Chapter 4 when it was argued that high staff turnover should not be excused as an inherent, characteristic feature of the industry. The starting point, therefore, is recognition of high staff turnover as a problem area that demands management action.[38]

There is a continuing debate on the causes, true costs and other effects of high staff turnover within the hospitality industry and how best to overcome the problem. Riley, for example, suggests that it would be particularly helpful for research to focus on the relationship between organisational commitment and job satisfaction, and the intention to leave.[39]

Properly designed and conducted, exit interviews may also be a powerful management tool to help in analysing and reducing staff turnover.[40]

Attention to recruitment and selection practice

Bonn and Forbringer refer to the challenge of a major personnel shortage facing the American hospitality industry and the need to give attention to methods of attracting and retaining staff. There are no easy solutions and the complexity of staff turnover demands a systemic approach for the assessment and diagnosis of the nature of the problem, and the causes and consequences for each organisation.

A strategic orientation will assist organisations in determining what solutions may be appropriate in a particular situation. The organisation can theoretically influence turnover by various intervention processes including placement and orientation, job design, leadership and supervision, job performance, and training and development. Central to all these processes is the critical activity of recruitment and selection practices.[41] (Staff recruitment and selection is discussed below.)

Human resource planning

Human resources are the main asset of the work organisation, especially in the hospitality industry. The high level of staff turnover, the need for trained and experienced staff, and the need for management development draw attention to the importance of effective human resource planning. It is understandable, therefore, that in recent years greater re-cognition has been given to the importance of planning human resources as well as other economic resources. Human resource planning (HR planning) was previously described as manpower planning and has been defined as 'a strategy for the acquisition, utilisation, improvement and retention of an enterprise's human resources'.[42]

A survey of steps taken to overcome staffing problems in 92 organisations concludes that greater priority will need to be given to planning and human resource management as the availability of people and skills becomes more critical. Employers will have to con-tinue to identify the skills needed to achieve business objectives and to restructure to make best use of the skills available. In addition they will need to devise human resource policies aimed at maintaining competitiveness in the labour market and to meeting employees' aspirations.[43]

The importance of human resource planning has been emphasised by the Hotels and Catering EDC. The industry 'produces' a service provided by people in face-to-face rela-tionships with the customer. HR planning should be adopted to ensure that employment policies form an integral part of general company policy. The type of planning advocated is one which stresses the way in which action and policy should be brought together.[44]

A broad approach to HR planning

HR planning should not be viewed in isolation but as an integral part of the broader process of strategic planning (discussed in Chapter 2) and linked to the development of the organ-isation as a whole. It should take account of external environmental factors, for example demographic changes, patterns of employment such as part-time, female or older workers, developments in the educational system, the level of competition, government initiatives on employment and training or employment legislation, and developments in information technology and automation.

It will be necessary to clarify the extent and scope of the HR plan, the target date and the length of the forecast period, the departments, types of occupations and skills for which forecasts are to be made, and the amount of information and detail required. Management will need to determine the desired staffing levels for the various operational activities, for example, the number of cleaning staff to the number of rooms, or the number of waiting staff to the number of covers in the restaurant.

Main stages in HR planning

Whatever the nature and scope of the HR plan, it is possible to identify four main stages (Figure 10.3):

(i) an analysis of present staffing resources;

(ii) an estimation of likely changes by the target date – this determines the supply forecast;

(iii) a forecast of staffing requirements for the target date – this determines the demand forecast; and

(iv) measures to ensure the required staffing resources are available as and when required.

The reconciliation of supply and demand is the basis of the HR plan and a personnel management action programme.

Figure 10.3:
Outline of main
stages in human
resource
planning

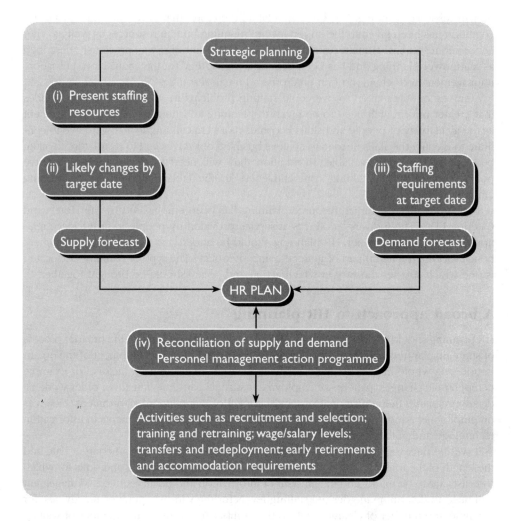

HR supply forecast

In order to determine an accurate supply forecast it is necessary to have an effective staffing inventory and system of personnel records including details of occupational structure and staff turnover. It is important that the record system is kept up to date, including new training, experience, skills or qualifications acquired by staff. The record system should be able to indicate readily both more basic details, such as the age distribution of managerial staff, and more specific details, such as those members of staff able to converse in a foreign language.[45]

The supply forecast must also take account of changes, additions and losses, incremental improvements in staff experience and training, and current programmes of management development.

Potential benefits

The use of HR planning offers many potential benefits. An effective HR plan will provide:

- links between objectives and organisation structure, and clarification of personnel policies;

- information on staffing requirements for forward planning at both the strategic level, for example a major extension to a hotel, and at the day-to-day operational level;

- indication of trends and likely changes in staffing resources in order to anticipate potential future difficulties while there is still a choice of action;

- a trigger for the development of effective personnel strategies and procedures, and a personnel management action programme for such activities as recruitment and selection, training and retraining, wage/salary levels, management development, transfers and redeployment, early retirements, and accommodation requirements.

HR planning involves considerable uncertainty and mistakes are bound to occur. Forward planning is particularly difficult in the hospitality industry, which is susceptible to changes in the external environment and consumer tastes, and seasonal patterns of demands. But HR planning is therefore even more important. Coupled with good communications and meaningful participation, effective HR planning will help to alleviate effects which are potentially harmful to members of staff or to organisational performance.

The underlying concepts of HR planning are basically straightforward. Although there are a number of sophisticated quantitative techniques and computer programs available, these should be applied only when really necessary and most probably only in the larger units.[46] HR planning can take a number of different forms in different organisations. In smaller establishments, for example, it can be undertaken at a more basic level. The important point is the recognition of the need for an effective system of HR planning appropriate to the demands and requirements of the particular hospitality organisation.

Staff recruitment and selection

The nature of the hospitality industry and its pattern of staffing are such that most managers are likely to be faced frequently with the need to recruit and select staff.

The need is for effective methods and procedures of recruitment and selection.

> *People are the primary factor in sustaining competitive advantage. To ensure that businesses within the hospitality sector are able to attract the 'best' in their marketplace, adequate recruitment strategies need to be reviewed and regularly updated.*[47]

The important message for managers is:

- recognise the importance of a planned and systematic approach to recruitment and selection;

- assess the effectiveness of present policies and design new procedures as necessary; and

- review the methods, skills and techniques of staff selection.

A planned and systematic approach

It is possible to identify five basic stages in a planned and systematic approach to recruitment and selection.

- *Stage 1: The need to know about the job to be filled* – Is the job really necessary, or can it be covered adequately by reorganising or reallocating other jobs? If the job is necessary, what does it entail? What are the duties and responsibilities attached to the job?

- *Stage 2: The need to know about the type of person to do the job* – What qualities and attributes are required for a person to perform the job effectively?
- *Stage 3: The need to know the likely means of attracting suitable applicants* – Is it necessary to recruit outside? If so where are suitable applicants most likely to be found? Which are the best sources of labour and methods of recruitment?
- *Stage 4: The need to know how best to assess the candidates' likely suitability for the job* – How best should information be collected about the candidates? How should the selection process be planned? What are the most appropriate methods of selection?
- *Stage 5: The need for induction and follow-up* – How best should the socialisation process be undertaken? How should new members of staff be introduced to the policies, procedures and working practices?

Degree and application

In the smaller hospitality establishments an elaborate selection procedure may be neither readily practicable nor appropriate, but there is still the need for a planned and systematic approach (Figure 10.4). This provides a framework and set of principles which should underlie all recruitment and selection. Between the larger and the smaller establishment there is the difference only of degree and application.

Underlying considerations

Whatever the procedures for the selection of staff there are three fundamental considerations which should underlie recruitment policy.

- Recruitment and selection should not be considered in isolation, i.e. simply finding someone to do a particular job, but in the context of the overall HR plan and personnel management action programme. It may be necessary to consider, for example, the potential for training and future promotion, and adaptability to possible future changes in working practices.
- There is a need to consider not just technical competence and the ability to perform certain tasks, but also sociability. In the hospitality industry it is especially important to consider how new members of staff are likely to fit into the social structure and membership of work groups.
- Recruitment must comply fully with all legal requirements relating to employment and follow recommended codes of practice. It is important to ensure justice and fair treatment to all applicants, and the exercise of 'social' responsibilities, for example the employment of registered disabled people and ethnic minorities. Note, for example, the following section.

Enhancing the recruitment and selection effort

In their discussion of interventions to manage staff turnover (discussed above) Bonn and Forbringer draw attention to the critical activity of recruitment and selection. Approaches that organisations in the American hospitality and other service industries have adopted to enhance the recruitment and selection effort include the following:

- referrals of applicants by family or friends who are given a monetary or other reward if a referred applicant is subsequently hired. An additional reward may also be given if the applicant remains with the organisation for a stated time;

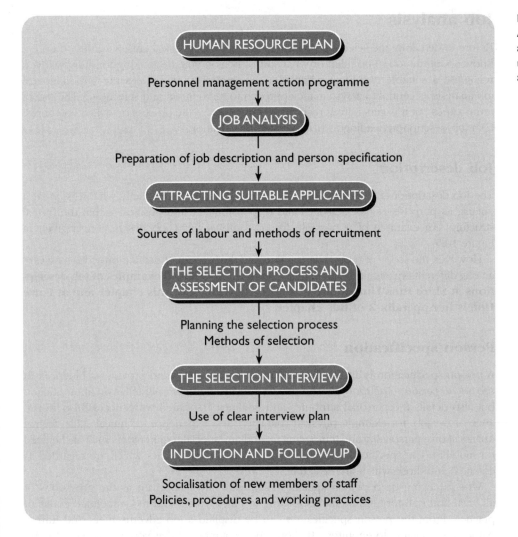

Figure 10.4: A systematic approach to recruitment and selection

- developing tactics to attract the hiring of minorities, the elderly and handicapped;
- attention to effective selection procedures including identification of the critical activities and duties of a job, and the required skills, knowledge and abilities, realistic job previews, biodata items, personality questionnaires and skills related tests;
- retention programmes such as monetary incentives including profit sharing, share ownership and suggestion schemes, educational incentives where staff can earn cash or credit for educational purposes, and parental leave and childcare programmes.[48]

Williams and Hunter suggest that it often makes sense for hotel companies to attract and develop management personnel from the ranks of supervisory staff already working in the organisation. However, their survey of supervisory personnel in large hotels in Toronto suggests that although many supervisors may be predisposed to a management career with their present organisation, they frequently are hesitant about making such a move. There is a need for greater cooperative action between hotel company management and supervisory employees.[49]

Job analysis

Before undertaking the selection process managers should ask themselves: 'If you do not know about the job to be filled or what sort of person you are looking for, how will you recognise a suitable candidate when you see one?' This underlines the importance of job analysis as central to a systematic approach to recruitment and selection.[50] The use of terms varies but it is generally agreed that 'job analysis' is the process by which you derive (i) a job description, leading to (ii) a person specification.

Job description

The job description explains the total requirements of the job: exactly what it is, what it entails, its purpose, duties, activities and responsibilities, and position within the formal structure. An example of a possible list of contents for a job description is given in Figure 10.5.

However, the scope of the job description and the amount of detail it provides may vary among different organisations and different types of job. **Detailed examples of job descriptions at Shire Inns Limited are given in Appendix 1 of this chapter and at Forte Hotels in Appendix 2 of this chapter.**

Person specification

A person specification is an extension of the job description and provides a blueprint of *the 'ideal' person to do that job.* The person specification not only tells you about the job but also details the personal attributes and qualities associated with successful perform-ance of the job, for example physical characteristics, experience, technical skills, formal qualifications, personality and temperament, and any special requirements such as the need for mobility. The specification could indicate those characteristics which are regarded as essential and those which are desirable.

When drawing up a person specification regard must be given to the provisions of all legal and statutory requirements relating to employment and recommended codes of practice. From the person specification can be distilled a job advertisement and further particulars available to enquirers. It should be remembered that you are unlikely to find the perfect or absolutely ideal candidate. The person specification should therefore be prepared in a practical manner and it should not unduly restrict the need for flexibility.

Difficulties and distasteful aspects of the job

The process of job analysis is even more meaningful if it includes considerations of the difficulties and distasteful aspects of the job. These may often go together but this is not necessarily the case.

Difficulties are those aspects of the job which are regarded as particularly demanding or hard to perform competently. Examples might be the bar manager dealing with drunken or unruly guests, waiting staff serving a large number of unexpected customers arriving together, a washer-up scrubbing heavy copper pans, a receptionist dealing with complaints or awkward guests, section heads operating within restricted budget limits.

Distasteful aspects of the job are those which are regarded as particularly tedious or unpleasant. Examples might be the waiting staff polishing silver before each service, a

Figure 10.5:
Possible list of contents for a job description

Job title (whether a new or replacement appointment)

Department/section and location

Wage/salary range

Duties and responsibilities – including ad hoc or occasional requirements.
It may be appropriate here to give precise and detailed information or it may only be necessary to set out the general scope and level of the job. Details may be quantified wherever possible. For example, an average of, or perhaps a minimum or maximum of: meals produced each day, rooms to be cleaned, covers per service, bills prepared each week for departing guests.

Duties and responsibilities can also be broken down into approximate percentage of time likely (or expected) to be devoted to each main activity over the average of, say, a week or a month, for example: % organisation of daily servicing and cleaning of guests' rooms, % training of kitchen staff, or % opening and distribution of incoming mail.

Specific limitations on authority
For example, not to authorise cash purchases above £X per item without prior approval of General Manager; not to accept payment by cheque for bills exceeding £X without authorisation of Head Receptionist.

Responsible to – that is, the job title of immediate superior.
(This superior would normally expect to be involved in the selection, induction and training programme for the new member of staff.)

Responsible for – that is, the number and job titles of direct subordinates.

Specific functional contacts – main lateral communications and working relationships with staff in other departments/sections.

Signature of head of department/section

Date job description prepared

(Source: Mullins L J, 'Job Analysis – Know the Job and the Person to do It', International Journal of Hospitality Management, vol. 4, no. 4, 1985, p. 181.)

commis chef preparing the same vegetable day after day for a standard menu, the kitchen porter emptying swill bins, cleaning staff changing soiled bed linen, restaurant staff unblocking the toilet.

It should be recognised, however, that for some people certain perceived 'difficulties' may be an attractive feature of the job. They may enjoy what is seen as the challenge or responsibility that the difficulties of the job present. Also for some people the 'easier' aspects of the job may be disliked and seen with distaste, for example because of the lack of variety or challenge, or because they prefer to be kept active.

Full knowledge of what the job entails

Although it may be tempting to do so, there is little to be gained from concealing the perceived difficulties or distastes of a job. This is short-sighted. If staff are appointed without full knowledge of what the job actually entails they are likely to join the number who leave within the first three months. This only adds to the 'induction crisis' and means starting the recruitment and selection process all over again. Even if staff do stay there is likely to be loss of goodwill, possible mistrust of management, and an adverse effect on their attitude, job satisfaction and work performance.

The selection process

The manner in which the selection process is planned and conducted is doubly important. It should of course be efficient in its own right to ensure that every effort is made to reach the 'best' decision. Equally important, however, is that for most candidates the selection process is the first point of contact with the establishment. Candidates will tend to judge the organisation as a whole by the manner in which the selection process is conducted, looking upon this as an indication of how it manages itself and its staff. *The other side of the selection process is the candidates' acceptance of you and your establishment.*

Methods of selection

There are a variety of methods which can be used in staff selection. These include peer rating, in-tray exercises, selection tests and personality questionnaires, group exercises assessment centres, graphology and individual (one-to-one), panel or board interviews.[51]

The design of the selection process is a matter of choice within each individual unit. It should be designed to meet specific requirements and matched to available facilities, both personal and physical. The choice, combination and application of methods should be appropriate to the nature and type of establishment, the position, tasks and responsibilities of the vacant position and the number of candidates.

The selection interview

Although often criticised, the interview is usually the central and indispensable element of the selection process. The interview involves an interaction of personalities and perception of other people. It is important, therefore, to bear in mind the possibility of perceptual distortions and errors, such as the 'halo effect' and stereotyping, which we discussed in Chapter 3.

Candidates tend to copy the mannerisms and postures of the interviewer. A seating arrangement which is comfortable and informal helps candidates to be more at ease and reduces the element of confrontation. Candidates should be encouraged to do most of the talking and asked questions that will encourage them to describe experiences and develop ideas.

The interviewer should probe the candidates and ask meaningful, searching and practical questions. Skilled interviewers will know how to change their interview style and form of questions according to the behaviour of candidates and the extent of their social skills. Interviewers should listen carefully, observe how candidates respond to a question, and be responsive to both verbal and non-verbal cues and body language.

The type of questions asked influences the candidate's reply. By using the right form of question your are better able to control the interview and the candidate's behaviour. In most cases a successful interview will contain a balance of open questions, direct closed questions and reflective remarks or questions. Interviewers should avoid the temptation to suggest possible answers to their own questions. Interviewers should at all times show respect for and consideration of candidates, be honest and behave ethically. Interview questions should observe equal opportunities principles and avoid any bias or unfair discrimination.

Interview on the move

The traditional face-to-face interview can be augmented by taking candidates round the organisation and conducting a two-way interview 'on the move'. This enables candidates to gain a fuller appreciation of the job, equipment and methods, and working conditions. It gives candidates an opportunity to meet some of the staff and to see them at work, and to ask further questions. An additional advantage of the interview on the move is that the selector is able to observe what are likely to be more natural responses of the candidates to actual situations.

The interview plan

In order to make a fair and objective assessment of candidates you must know what information is needed and how best to collect this from the interview. A clear interview plan is necessary. But whatever plan is used, by the end of the interview all points should have been covered adequately. The important thing is that some suitable plan is used. Many organisations have their own interview plan/checklist. The plan should be appropriate to the desired characteristics of the candidates and specific interview checklists may be drawn up for particular appointments. Each of the headings in the interview plan can be related to the requirements of the job, and to the essential and desirable characteristics looked for in candidates.

The more information interviewers have about the job, the more they know about which questions to ask and the more structured the interview the more effective it is likely to be.[52] Candidates should be encouraged to do most of the talking and to describe experiences and develop ideas. However, it is important that interviewers avoid simply going through a list. Information should be assembled not necessarily in any fixed order but under each heading of the plan as it is encountered during the interview discussion. At the end of the interview all points on the plan should have been covered adequately.

Figure 10.6 gives an example of notes on interviewing from a company's personnel manual. For reasons of confidentiality the detailed assessment sheet is omitted.

Induction and follow-up

We have seen that staff turnover is particularly high during the first three months of employment – the induction crisis. We have also referred to the high costs of recruiting and engaging new members of staff. This draws attention to the importance of an effective induction programme. Induction involves the introduction and socialisation of a new member of staff to the culture of the organisation, to its policies, procedures and working practices, and to other members of staff.

The first impressions of the organisation and its managers are seldom forgotten. New members of staff face an unfamiliar working environment and have to make a number of personal adjustments. A warm welcome, initial introductions, and a properly planned and conducted induction programme will do much to reassure members, and aid their motivation and attitudes to work performance. Induction is a key factor in the longer-term retention of staff.

Figure 10.6:
Interviewing

INTERVIEWING

Interviewing is the most widely used assessment technique. It looks easy and everyone is inclined to believe they are good at it.

On the following page is a sheet designed to assist you in noting, from the application form, and then during the interview, brief notes that should be useful. You should note, prior to the interview, any issues from the application form, that you wish to raise.

KEY NOTES

- 'A stitch in time saves nine', i.e., a well planned, thorough interview can save the time and expense of a bad recruitment decision.
- Plan the times of your interview to ensure that you can concentrate on the relevant areas.
- Mix the content of 'task' and 'process' issues. The more senior the role, the more important the 'process element'.
- Never reject other applicants until written acceptance of the job has been received.
- Pass on other good candidate's information to Head Office for circulation with the rest of the Group.

Interview Plan:

Company Information: Hotels in group
                                       Specific Hotel
                                       H.O.

Candidate's CV

Position Available

Rate of pay and Benefits

Questions

Next Stage

(*Source:* reproduced with permission)

The induction training programme

Induction is viewed best as a natural extension of the recruitment and selection process, starting at the interview and covering the first few months at work. The induction programme should be designed to help new members of staff to familiarise themselves with their new environment, to settle easily into their new jobs and to establish good working relationships with other members of staff.

Given the cosmopolitan nature of the hospitality industry, a particular feature of the selection process is the recognition of different cultural and ethnic values, discussed in Chapter 3. Induction training should make clear the nature of a multi-cultural working environment, and the need for integration and for people to work together harmoniously.

It is important to remember that people cannot fully absorb a large amount of information at one time, particularly in what is likely to be a strange and initially uncomfortable environment. The induction programme should therefore be planned carefully and staggered over a reasonable period of time. Video presentations can form a useful part of induction training.[53] But whatever the nature of the programme, if induction is to be effective it requires reinforcement and regular review and follow-up sessions. It will also involve the active cooperation of managers, supervisors and colleagues.

Design of the induction programme

The design and content of the induction programme is a matter of choice for each individual unit and its particular circumstances. Different members of staff will require different forms of induction depending upon, for example, their knowledge and previous experience, and the type and level of their new job. Nevertheless, it is important that some suitable form of induction is carried out for all new staff including managerial appointments.

A comprehensive induction training programme could include such information as the following:

- the nature of the establishment, its facilities and services, and type of guests or customers;
- requirements of the job and to whom responsible, and any subordinate staff;
- main terms and conditions of employment including circumstances which could lead to dismissal, and disciplinary and grievance procedures;
- introductions to working colleagues, and the work and functions of other relevant departments;
- the organisation and management structures including responsibilities for the personnel function;
- the physical layout of the establishment and the use of equipment;
- any special policies or procedures, and any house rules such as no eating or drinking, or no-smoking areas;
- fire, health and safety regulations;
- trade union membership, staff representations, consultation and communications, suggestion schemes;
- social and welfare facilities;
- opportunities for training and personal development.

Staff induction manuals

It is helpful to provide a Staff Induction Manual or Employee's Guide which sets out and elaborates the above information. The manual could be used to incorporate checklists and a personal log book, and also to include any additional information useful to members of staff. (Details of the Employee's Guide for The Savoy are given in Appendix 3 of this chapter.)

Recruitment and induction

When recruiting employees the hotel has a clear list of the personal attributes required. Top priority is attitude and a genuine desire to please. Previous experience is not imperative and can be quickly compensated for by good training and supportive leadership, which are both supplied liberally. Consequently the hotel has an incredibly low staff turnover. Many staff started their service as seasonal part-timers who proved their value, liked what they saw and took on full-time contracts when leaving school or college. Potential recruits are interviewed initially by the department requiring them and then by the partners.

On joining, all new staff are given professional induction by a trained team leader and take delivery of a comprehensive induction pack, which includes:

- List of the hotel's key policies and rules of contact
- Health and Safety policies and instructions, including care of hazardous substances
- Hotel Disciplinary Procedure
- Guidance on facilities for the disabled
- Contract of Employment
- Training Event & Benchmark feedback form
- Appraisal form
- Modern Apprenticeship/NVQ Programme record
- Hotel training record
- Use of staff changing rooms
- Rules for staff accommodation and meals at the hotel
- Set of comprehensive job descriptions with detailed checklists and duties

THE SEAVIEW HOTEL AND RESTAURANT

Terms and conditions of employment

For most of the twentieth century the terms and conditions of those working in the hospitality industry were regulated by Wages Council Orders which set minimum rates of pay, holiday entitlements and conditions relating to shift work arrangements. After the Wages Councils were abolished in 1992 employers generally had considerable freedom to determine the pay and other terms of their workers' employment.

However, two recent changes in employment law have reinstated the core terms of employment as: pay, hours and holidays, subject to statutory control.

The Minimum Wage Act 1998

The first is the Minimum Wage Act, 1998. Under this piece of legislation the United Kingdom (UK) has, for the first time, statutorily enforceable minimum pay rates for all workers who are 18 or more years of age. The Act's provisions apply to *all workers*, and so include casual staff working in the hospitality industry. Employers may make a lawful deduction from wages where accommodation is provided for their staff.

Working Time Regulations

The second important piece of employment law is the Working Time Regulations introduced to meet the UK's obligations under its membership of the European Union. Like the minimum wage provisions, the Regulations apply to all workers and not just those to employed under a contract of employment. Their details are complex but the principal provisions are:

- a limit on weekly working time to 48 hours (averaged over a 17-week reference period)
- a limit on night workers' normal working time of eight hours (again averaged over a 17-week period)
- a minimum daily rest period of 11 hours in addition to a day off each week
- a minimum rest break of 20 minutes after six hours' work
- an entitlement to four weeks' paid annual leave (which can include payment for bank or public holidays).

The Regulations, however, allow employees, individually, to agree to work more than the average of 48 hours provided that they do not suffer any detriment if they refuse. The parts of the Regulations dealing with daily and weekly rest periods do not apply where a worker works 'split shifts', for example waiting staff serving breakfast and dinner in a restaurant, nor if shift changes make it impossible for the rest periods to be taken. In such cases the employer must allow the workers affected to take a similar period of rest within a reasonable time.

Impact on operations and profitability

When these legislative changes were proposed it was thought that they would have a serious impact on the operations and profitability of many firms. However, a study by Adam-Smith et al.[54] found that this was generally not the case. Many employers found that flexibility in the Working Time Regulations – for example, the provision for workers to agree to work longer than 48 hours per week – provided considerable scope for them to maintain their previous working arrangements. Similarly, the rate at which the minimum wage has been set has had little impact except in very small firms. They do note, however, that of all the measures, the entitlement to four weeks' paid holiday has had some effect on many businesses.

Education, training and development

Staff are a crucial but expensive resource and it is important to optimise their contribution to improving effective organisational performance. A significant factor in the image of the hospitality industry, in the performance and retention of employees and in levels of productivity is the extent and quality of staff education, training and development.

The ultimate purpose of training is to help the industry improve its operational effectiveness and its economic and competitive performance, including the ability to cope with future challenges. Closer links between Britain and other members of the European Union further emphasise the importance of vocational education and training. And training is clearly an important feature of international hospitality management.

Training needs within the industry

In the most comprehensive examination of training ever undertaken, the HCTC Research Report of 1995 shows clearly that all is not well in the hospitality industry.[55] The report claims that the hospitality industry does not take training seriously yet points out that the benefits of doing so are clear. It tells a story of under-investment in the skills of the industry's workforce. The report goes on to set out a number of recommendations for future action to stimulate skills development in the hospitality industry. Overarching all of them is the need to increase awareness of the benefits of training, which is especially weak among smaller employers, and the need to promote training for *all* staff – full- or part-time; permanent or casual; management or supervisory; craft or operative; male or female; people with special needs; and ethnic minorities – throughout their working lives.

The importance of training

Training is necessary to ensure an adequate supply of staff who are technically and socially competent, and capable of career progression. The objective of training is to enhance knowledge and skills, and to develop attitudes. A central and indispensable part of the training provision is related to task and on-the-job performance and the delivery of service.

Training also forms a basis for both individual development and management succession including, for example, the acceptance and practice of delegation and empowerment, problem-solving and decision-making, teamworking and responsibility for quality standards.[56] Training for change is also vital for the long-term survival of an organisation. Increasing emphasis is being placed on both the need for continuous training to support change and on training as a vital investment for the future.[57]

It is widely accepted that training can lead to many potential benefits for both individuals and the organisation. Training is potentially one of the most important motivators. It is a key element in the ability, morale, job satisfaction and commitment of staff, and in improved delivery of service and customer relationships, and economic performance. However, despite an apparent recognition of the importance of training there seems doubt as to what actually happens in practice, and the extent to which the industry or employers evaluate the scope, relevance or effectiveness of its education and training programmes.[58]

McDonald's – five stars

Each new employee at McDonald's, whether full- or part-time, is given five or ten months respectively to be fully trained – that is to have gained five stars. Each of the five stars corresponds to a different part of the training, for example grill area training, front counter training, hygiene, etc. Each star is made up of between three or four modules and in order to pass a module two observations have to be passed at 90 per cent or above. The observations known as OCL's (observation checklists) serve two purposes. The first to gain the initial training stars and the second as ongoing training. After every six months each hourly paid employee has a performance review. A 60 per cent weighting is given to the OCLs that have been passed in that period. Pay in McDonald's is related to performance, so obviously the higher

continued

continued

percentages that are given in OCLs lead to a higher pay rise. A bonus of 15p per hour is given to employees who pass all five stars. On the whole, employees of McDonald's appear to be quite interested in gaining the five stars, especially with the prospect of the pay rise at the end.

One major problem with this scheme is that the OCLs have to be completed by managers and senior crew members whose main role within McDonald's is to manage people, to cook food and to keep the stores clean. If a store is very busy the first thing that has to be given up is the completion of OCLs – that is, the initial and ongoing training. The management of each restaurant is assessed by how many completed modules each employee has attained through a training audit that is completed by an area administrator on behalf of McDonald's Head Office.

An integral part of business strategy

In order to pursue a positive policy of investing in people it is necessary to demonstrate a continuous commitment to education, training and development as an integral part of business strategy.[59] There has to be active support from top management and throughout all levels of the organisation. There is also a need to evaluate both the costs and benefits of the training programme.[60] Attention should be given to the maintenance of training standards. Training should be real, operational and rewarding.

Employees should receive positive recognition for good training achievements, for example through increased job satisfaction, higher wages or greater opportunities for career advancement. Successful training requires the cooperation of line managers, adequate finance and resources, time, skilled staff and a supporting appraisal system. In order to secure the full benefits of successful training there must therefore be a planned and systematic approach to the effective management of training.[61]

Investors in People (IiP)

Investors in People is a standard for the training and development of people within an organisation. The standard was seen as coming originally from business as there was a need to recognise the importance of people as a strategic response. In response, the IiP Standard was launched in 1991 as the national standard of good practice for the training and development of people. In 1993 Investors in People UK (a private company limited by guarantee) was established to take ownership of the Standard, protect its integrity, and ensure its successful promotion and development. The company is led by a board of business people from across the country, representing large and small firms from a variety of industrial sectors.

The IiP initiative provides a national framework in order to maintain and increase the UK's competitive position in world markets through its increased commitment to developing a more highly skilled and flexible workforce.[62] It seeks to reward organisations that achieve the prescribed training standards which allows them to display the IiP kitemark logo. The IiP Standard provides a framework for improving business performance and competitiveness through a planned approach to setting and communicating business objectives and developing people to meet these objectives. The standard is held for three years after which time organisations must apply for reassessment to retain it.

Four key principles

The standard is a cyclical process based on four key principles:

- a public commitment from the top to invest in and develop people in order to achieve business goals;
- planning how individuals and teams are to be developed to achieve these goals;
- taking relevant action to meet training and development needs throughout people's employment; and
- evaluating the outcomes of training and development for individuals and the organisation as a basis for continuous improvement.

The focus is not on training and development per se, but is purposefully aligned to business strategy so that training is directed more to the needs of the business. IiP is investing in the members of the workforce, developing them and helping them to achieve not only their own personal goals but the goals and objectives of the organisation. Investors in People is recognised as one of the most successful quality awards ever introduced. It can be viewed as part of a wider quality management process with natural progression to total quality management (TQM).

IiP and service quality

From a study of case histories of hospitality organisations, Lockwood et al. comment: that every one of the case studies demonstrates the importance placed on training by organisations committed to service quality.

> *Most of the case study companies have found that IiP complements their strategies. This is not surprising. IiP sets out to develop in the firm's employees the abilities they need to achieve the company's business goals. In service industries particularly the employees' performance can make a critical contribution to the customers' expectations of the product. Consequently, training can change significantly the customers' perception of value for money.*[63]

Queens Moat Houses Hotels

In the early 1990s Queens Moat Houses Hotels (QMH) had yet to develop its branding and was lagging behind other hotel companies in the field of customer care. A sustained training initiative involving over 8000 employees has transformed the performance of the group – and been the key to successful Investor in People (IiP) recognition for 38 of its 44 hotels. Nearly 800 employees are now working towards an NVQ.

The strategy aimed to use training to improve customer service and so boost business performance. The underlying aim of the programme was to increase customer loyalty by prioritising customers' service needs. This meant aiming to make every stay at a Moat House Hotel memorable and individual. Translated into practical terms, this involved focusing on every area of customer contact, from personal greeting to prompt message handling and quality of service in the hotels' restaurants.

continued

---

continued

The starting point for the design of the training was a survey which covered 5000 customers and every single employee. The results were analysed and used as the basis for 'Rainbow' – an initiative to deliver training in seven key areas, each of which was given its own colour. At the same time a new role of Customer Host was created, with each representative wearing a distinctive rainbow-coloured waistcoat. A regular programme of independent audits, including mystery customer assessments, ran parallel to Rainbow and provided managers with a snapshot of progress and areas where more training was needed.

Starting from what hotel management admits was very much a 'zero baseline' meant that winning the support and commitment of general and departmental managers was a vital element in the training process. They were to be responsible for implementing the initiative and carrying out ongoing training. To support managers, new *service champions* were created, with responsibility for training staff, as well as evaluating progress towards the new Rainbow Service Standards.

Once the new training resource pack had been created and specific training had been given to the service champions, the training was launched on an individual hotel basis. Each hotel manager was given the autonomy to target and tailor the training so as to achieve individual targets. Human resources director Pat Perridge adds:

> One year after the training was launched, 55% of the hotels in the group were scoring over 80% in the regular audits – a dramatic improvement on the 4% score before the training started. The hope-for improvement in business performance has been achieved and productivity has increased by around 10%.

> (Reproduced with permission of Patrick Perridge, Human Resources Director, Queens Moat Houses UK Ltd.)

Management development

The quality of management is one of the most important factors in the effectiveness of any organisation including those in the hospitality industry. Management succession planning is necessary to ensure that a sufficient supply of appropriately qualified and capable men and women are available to meet the present and future needs of the organisation. Managers need an appropriate balance of technical, social and conceptual knowledge and skills (discussed in Chapter 5). An essential component of an effective training programme therefore is management development.

Management development is an organisational concept and should take place within the framework of a clear policy related to the nature, objectives and requirements of the organisation as a whole including the effective management of people. Managers need to be equipped to deal with the critical issues and requirements facing the particular organisation and the demands of specific managerial jobs. Linked to succession planning and management development should be a programme of planned career progression supported by a performance review system.

Mullins and Aldrich have constructed an integrated model of managerial behaviour and development[64] which applies as much to the hospitality industry as to any other business organisation.[65] However, despite the obvious importance of effective management for the hospitality industry, it is not clear how much attention is really given to management education and development. For example, Wood casts doubt about the quality and standards of hotel and catering management education, and the level of professionalisation and qualifications of its managers.[66] In order to achieve improved organisational performance the industry must ensure the development of both present and future management. There is a continual need for effective managerial development.

Training and development of the multi-unit manager

From an examination of the role and responsibilities of the multi-unit manager in branded hospitality chains, Goss-Turner draws attention to the importance of their training and development, including a greater depth in matters such as recruitment and selection, and performance appraisal. Changes in organisation development in recent years including a reduction in central support offices and the devolution of HRM activities to line management has placed increasing importance on general managerial abilities. In the longer term this trend must affect career development and long-term achievement. Companies will need to review their human resources policies with regard to their organisation development stage, their expansion strategies, and their future succession plans.[67]

Effectiveness of the personnel function

However the personnel function is organised, proper attention to the establishment of good personnel policies, including employee relations and training, will help to improve the efficiency of the workforce and standards of service to customers. Greater use should be made of specialist personnel managers, the involvement of line managers and modern methods of personnel management.

Attention to human resource management

Greater attention to human resource management and the personnel function will of course cost money. Unfortunately the industry has a reputation for short-term cost-consciousness and the widely held view that every activity should be seen as making a direct working contribution to profitability.

The ultimate measure of the effectiveness of the personnel function is the contribution it makes to the objectives of the organisation and to improved organisational performance. But achievement in the area of personnel management is difficult to measure and it is not easy to establish satisfactory methods of assessment. There is also the more general problem of assessing managerial work where the end-product results from the efforts of other people.[68]

Cost is obviously a major consideration but should not be viewed in isolation. Not every activity can be identified clearly as making a direct contribution to profitability. A balance must be kept between more easily identified financial costs of the personnel function and less readily apparent but very important long-term benefits which also make a positive contribution to the effectiveness of hospitality operations.

Contribution of the personnel function

The contributions from an effective personnel function are not always readily apparent nor are they easy to identify. Over a period of time, however, some quantified measures should provide management with an indication of its effectiveness. Possible examples include labour costs, staff turnover and stability index, complaints from customers, absenteeism/timekeeping, breakages, scrap or waste, accidents at work, promotions and staff development, discipline and grievance procedures, and dismissals.

The nature of human resource management will determine both business efficiency and the performance of individual members. Account must be taken of intangible benefits such as improved morale, job satisfaction and staff development. The attitudes, behaviour and performance of staff, and thus the performance of the hospitality organisation, will be influenced by sound personnel policies and an effective personnel function.

Summary

- The human element plays a major part in customer satisfaction and in the overall success of the organisation and this is especially important in the hospitality industry. This places particular emphasis on human resource management. Whether or not there is a separate personnel department it is still important to give proper attention to the personnel function. Personnel policies are a reflection of the overall style of management.

- The implementation of personnel policies practices should be based on underlying philosophies of managerial behaviour and employee relationships. The personnel function is a shared responsibility among top management, line managers and supervisors, and the personnel manager. Sound personnel policies and practices help foster good employee relations. What really matters is the effective management of people.

- The high level of staff turnover in the industry should be recognised as a problem area which demands management attention. It is important to attract and retain staff with the right skills and abilities to satisfy the demands of the customer. An effective system of human resource planning provides the trigger for an effective management action programme.

- Most managers are likely to be faced with the frequent need to recruit and select staff. This requires a planned and systematic approach including recognition of underlying considerations. Careful attention should be given to the process of job analysis, to the planning and conduct of the selection process, and to an effective induction programme.

- A key factor in the image of the hospitality industry, staff retention and level of productivity is training including managerial development. Education, training and development should be an integral part of the business strategy of the organisation. Greater attention to the personnel function will cost money but must be balanced against the long-term benefits to improved organisational effectiveness.

Appendix 1(A): Shire Inns Limited

JOB DESCRIPTION POLICY & PROCEDURE

Shire Inns believes that each individual understands exactly what is expected of them in their job. A job description is an outline of the main duties that are undertaken to help understand the contribution that can be made to the success of the company.

The job description is used for the following purposes:

● To assist recruitment. A prospective employee will receive a copy of a job description, and the person responsible for recruiting will use the job description to assess the suitability of any individual.

● To discuss performance. The job description forms an important part of the appraisal process. It is the job description that is the statement of what is expected, and the individual will be measured against those statements.

Job descriptions are written by taking into account the particular needs of the business, and the role that the person will fulfil, in achieving the overall goals of the company, the hotel and the department.

The people responsible for compiling the job description are Heads of Department and Management, at hotel level, along with the company's Personnel Department.

Job descriptions are kept in the Job Description Manual, at the hotel.

Job descriptions will be reviewed annually in February. The company's Personnel Department will facilitate the review. Any amendments can, therefore, be incorporated into the business planning process for the next financial year.

This introduction to job descriptions should be attached to the front of every job description that is issued and is incorporated in all staff handbooks.

Appendix 1(B): Shire Inns Limited

JOB DESCRIPTION

Job title: Receptionist
Responsible to: Head Receptionist

Overall job scope and purpose

To uphold the core values of Shire Inns . . .

To provide an efficient and courteous service to guests, whilst maintaining the company standards of control and procedures outlined in this job description and in the company's Reception manual.

Main responsibilities

(a) Reservations, checking in and out of Guests.

(b) Provision of Hotel and general information.

(c) Reconciliation of Guest and Hotel accounts.

(d) Cash and credit account handling.

(e) To provide a customer-focused service.

Personal requirements

1. To conform to all of the Rules and Regulations outlined in the Staff Handbook and Staff Contract, in addition to those outlined by the Hotel General Manager.

2. To represent the Company and the Hotel in a loyal, professional and knowledgeable manner at all times.

3. To demonstrate knowledge of the Company's Health & Safety Procedure and Fire Procedure.

4. Not to engage in other paid (or otherwise) work outside of the Company without the written permission of the Company Personnel & Training Manager.

Duties

(a) Reservations, checking in and out of Guests

1. To accurately accept reservations, subject to availability, incoming via telephone, fax, telex, face to face, letter.

2. To be conversant with, and able to use, all above equipment safely and effectively.

3. To sell-up reservations and executive rooms/suites.

4. To enter reservations, amendments and cancellations accurately into the computer system.

5. To check Guests in speedily, accurately and hospitably.

6. To use Guest's name whenever and wherever possible.

7. To ensure complete accuracy of bills being raised and paid by Guests.

(b) Provision of Hotel and general information

1. To represent the Hotel, at all times, in a professional and knowledgeable manner.

2. To be fully conversant with:
   - Current Room Tariff – Midweek
   - Current Room Tariff – Weekend
   - Current Conference Tariffs
   - Hotel facilities and times of opening
   - Sister Hotels, locations and details

3. To be aware of the responses expected from questions prompted by the reading of the Guest Service Information folder.

4. To be knowledgeable of who to contact at all times for information which you, personally, are unable to answer.

(c) Reconciliation of Guest and Hotel accounts

1. To receive, check and post to accounts all relevant charges.

2. To produce and be knowledgeable of scales of charges for billing purposes.

3. To deal politely with account queries.

(d) Cash and credit account handling

1. To be responsible for the security and safekeeping of the Front Desk cash float.

2. To accurately administer all incoming monies, cheques and credit card transactions.

3. To maintain adequate change supplies, whilst minimising sums of cash held in the Front Desk drawers.

4. To receive, be responsible for, whilst on duty and balance at the end of each shift, the Front Desk float against the computer system.

5. To be responsible for the accurate completion of associated paperwork and documentation.

(Reference and date)

Appendix 1(C): Shire Inns Limited

JOB DESCRIPTION

Job title: Restaurant Supervisor
Responsible to: General Manager Duty Manager

Overall job scope and purpose

To uphold the core values of Shire Inns . . .

- To supervise Restaurant/Bar staff in the preparation of their areas for service.
- To provide guests with a warm welcome and to serve food and liquor in an efficient, effective and well-mannered way. Advising guests, as and when required, regarding Menu content, Wine List and complementary wines, etc.
- To train and review standards achieved to ensure consistent delivery of product in all service areas.
- To ensure that the Restaurant and Bar areas are always kept to a high standard of cleanliness in accordance with the Hygiene Regulations.

Main responsibilities

(a) To demonstrate your responsibility, to other members of staff, by setting a good example via the relevant task and process skills.

(b) To ensure that tasks performed in the department are done in accordance with the Product Plan.

(c) To be able to deal with cash, credit facilities, equipment, deliveries etc.

(d) To demonstrate the qualities of someone in a supervisory position, e.g., motivation, organisation, delegation.

(e) To realise the importance of your position in the eyes of the guests and other members of staff and conduct yourself accordingly.

(f) To develop, by liaison with other departments, the importance of teamwork.

(g) To be aware of how each department works and of their special requirements, e.g., licensing laws, requisitions for wine.

Personal requirements

1. To conform to the Rules and Regulations outlined in the Staff Handbook and Staff Contract, in addition to those established by your Hotel General Manager.

2. To represent the Company and the Hotel in a loyal, professional and knowledge-able manner at all times.

3. To demonstrate knowledge of the Company's Health & Safety Procedure and Fire Procedure.

4. Not to engage in other paid (or otherwise) work outside of the Company without the written permission of the Company Personnel & Training Manager.

Duties

(a) Supervision of the department.

Preparation: laying tables, vacuuming carpets, sweeping floors, polishing cutlery, preparing condiments and garnishes, setting out cheese boards, preparing coffee.

Serving: familiarisation with Menu. The serving of drinks as well as food. Making up bills, taking payment and giving change.

Clearing away for next service.

(b) Inform Duty Manager of any shortages and liaise with Duty Manager regarding any departmental problems.

(c) Ensure that standards are being maintained in terms of both staff appearance and conduct.

(d) Responsibility for ensuring that all meals and drinks are charged for at the correct tariff and that Kitchen and Reception receive the relevant 'Checks and Bills'.

(e) Responsibility for the paying-in of any cash transactions handled.

(f) Deal with customer complaints efficiently and effectively.

(g) To organise linen returns and receipts.

(h) Ensure that all areas are secure at the end of each shift.

(i) To organise duty rotas in relation to staff hours of work and cleaning duties taking the amount of business into consideration.

(j) Demonstrate skills in dealing with staff problems that may arise and knowing the correct procedure for grievances.

(k) To attend courses as required by your General Manager, e.g.

Hygiene Training
Hospitality Training
Fire Training
Cellar Management Course
Craft Trainer Award CTA

(Reference and date)

Appendix 1(D): Shire Inns Limited

JOB DESCRIPTION

Job title: Hotel Controller
Reporting to: Hotel General Manager

Overall job scope

To uphold the core values of Shire Inns . . .

The support, monitoring and control of hotel administration procedures as established by:

- Company Administration PPP's (Plans, Policies and Procedures).
- Hotel General Manager.

Main responsibilities

(a) Docket Control

(b) Invoice Control

(c) Monitoring of Shire Inns internal sales procedures.

(d) Central Sales Ledger back-up information/queries.

(e) Hotel Administration/Audit checks.

(f) General Administrative Duties.

Personal requirements

(a) To conform to all the personal requirements outlined in the Senior Staff Handbook and Senior Staff Contract.

(b) To represent the Company and the Hotel in a loyal, professional and knowledgeable manner at all times.

(c) To demonstrate knowledge of the Company's Health & Safety Procedure and Fire Procedure.

(d) Not to engage in other paid (or otherwise) work outside of the Company without the written permission of the Director: Human Resources.

Main duties

(a) Docket control

1. Implementing and up-keep of numerical Docket Control System.

2. Reconciliation with appropriate 'back-up' documentation.

3. Audit spot checks, ensuring all manual Restaurant/Bar/Function Dockets are all correctly invoiced.

(b) Invoice control

1. Preparation of Food and Non-Food Invoice Sheets and subsequent presentation to Hotel General Manager for authorisation.
2. Ensure prompt dispatch, i.e. Monday of relevant invoicing.

(c) Cash control

1. Monitor Master Cashiers over/under Bankings dealing with returned cheques and supplying relevant customer information via Transax – address, etc.
2. Petty Cash completion – Monday morning posted to H.O.
3. Weekly collection and paying-in of Payphone (including Staff House Payphone), Squash and Snooker monies – ensuring relevant paperwork is completed.
4. Checking of foreign cash and sterling cash reimbursement.

(d) Monitoring of Shire Inns internal sales procedures

1. Hotel Sales Reconciliation: correcting UR100/S.O.B. imbalances, highlighting any missing code links and posting errors. Correcting stats as necessary.

(e) Central Sales Ledger back-up information/queries

1. Ensuring Shire Inns Internal Allowance Sheets are completed correctly by Reception, signed by General Manager and forwarded to Head Office on a weekly basis.
2. Ensure that Sales Ledger backup is checked daily to Function Sheets and that all backup documentation is enclosed for posting/TNT. Assisting with Sales Ledger queries.

(f) Hotel administration/audit checks

1. The Hotel Suspense Account daily reconciliation – keeping transactions/balance to a minimum.
2. Trade Sheet Balancing: review of completed Trade Sheet, highlighting errors along with monitoring of cash discrepancies.
3. Conduct 'spot checks' for till reconciliations including Food & Beverage and Leisure outlets, together with Leisure Club stocks, as directed by the Hotel General Manager.
4. Month End Reports to Head Office complete and on time.

(g) General administrative duties

1. In discussion with the General Manager and the Company Accountant, to regularly review the Job Description.
2. Agreed additional duties will be incorporated into this Job Description.
3. To agree administrative duties – currently undertaken by either Hotel Management and Reception personnel – which will enable departmental time to be released for guest care.
4. Any other general duties that may be required from time-to-time as requested by the Accounts Department.

(Reference and date)

The author is grateful to Ctris Kelsall, Personnel & Training Manager, Solent Hotel, Hampshire and to Janet Richardson, Human Resources Director, Shire Inns for providing these examples.

Appendix 2(A): Forte Hotels

JOB DESCRIPTION

Job descriptions are standard throughout Forte. If a job description is tailored to a specific hotel a TASK LIST detailing specific 'Tasks' and 'Standards of Performance Expected' is added.

Appendix 2(B): Forte Hotels

JOB DESCRIPTION

1. Job title: Commis Chef

2. Reports to: Chef de Partie

3. Prime function: Through the consistent delivery of the highest standards of product and service; a passionate approach to exceeding our customers' expectations and as a champion of our vision and values, promote a professional and positive image to all of our guests and contribute to the hotels targets.

4. Key performance areas:
- Maintain work environment
- Customer service
- Prepare, maintain and clean areas for food preparation
- Prepare and cook dishes
- Receive, handle and store food deliveries
- Effective working relationships
- Personal development

4.1 Maintain work environment
The function of the Commis Chef in this area is being performed competently when:

- A safe and secure environment for customers, staff and visitors is maintained
- In the event of a fire alarm activation the statutory procedures are adhered to
- The highest standards of personal health and hygiene are maintained at all times
- All equipment is operated in line with the trained instructions
- Equipment is maintained in a clean working condition
- Personal organisation and that of the work area is maintained to assist work flow
- Hygiene is maintained and promoted in food preparation in accordance with Company Policy and Statutory requirements.

4.2 Customer service
The function of the Commis Chef in this area is being performed competently when:

- Products and services are explained to the customer at all appropriate times
- Information on customer problems is gathered in order to propose and deliver solutions

- Prompt responses is given to the service needs of customers
- Service reliability is improved through obtaining customer feedback and working with colleagues
- A positive personal image is presented to the customer at all times
- The needs of the customer are kept in balance with those of the organisation
- Feelings expressed by the customer are responded to appropriately
- Methods of communication are adapted to meet the needs of the customer
- All visitors are received and offered assistance in an appropriate manner
- Service is maintained when systems go wrong.

4.3 Prepare, maintain and clean areas for food preparation
The function of the Commis Chef in this area is being performed competently when:

- Food preparation areas are cleaned prior to use, maintained in a hygienic condition during service and cleaned down afterwards
- Food preparation equipment and utensils are cleaned and stored in accordance with Hotel standards
- Assistance is given in the maintenance of food display areas
- Cleaning equipment and materials are handled and stored in line with trained COSSH instructions
- Waste is promptly removed from the food preparation area and disposed of appropriately.

4.4 Prepare and cook dishes
The function of the Commis Chef in this area is being performed competently when:

- Knives are handled and stored in a safe manner according to trained instructions
- Food preparation is carried out in a hygienic manner with attention paid to the Critical Control Points of Food Safety
- Raw and High Risk foods are prepared separately
- Food items are maintained at a safe temperature through the cooking process in line with current food hygiene legislation
- All ingredients are checked for the correct type and quality required
- All dishes within area of responsibility are prepared, cooked and presented to the correct Menu Specification with regard to quality and quantity
- Problems with food quality are identified and reported promptly to the appropriate person
- All food not for immediate consumption is stored in the correct manner at a safe temperature according to current food hygiene legislation
- Random temperature checks are made on hot and cold food displayed for service.

4.5 Receive, handle and store food deliveries
The function of the Commis Chef in this area is being performed competently when:

- Receiving and storage areas are prepared ready for delivery
- Food items are checked for quality, expiry date and temperature

- Random temperature checks are made of chilled and frozen goods delivered
- All food items are handled with care to avoid damage
- Delivery packaging is removed and disposed of appropriately
- Storage areas are kept secure from unauthorised access
- All food items are stored under the correct conditions according to food type
- Stock rotation and date coding procedures are followed
- Storage areas are maintained with regard to temperature, ventilation and cleanliness
- Temperature checks are made twice daily on fridges and freezers and the results recorded
- Problems identified with storage areas are reported promptly to the appropriate person.

4.6 Effective working relationships
The function of the Commis Chef in this area is being performed competently when:

- Effective working relationships are created and maintained with colleagues and managers
- New colleagues are assisted in becoming familiar with the workplace
- Colleagues are supported in the performance of their work.

4.7 Personal development
The function of the Commis Chef in this area is being performed competently when:

- Self-development needs are identified and agreed within a Personal Development Plan arising from a 6-monthly appraisal
- Personal Development Plans are reviewed through regular Job Chats and future appraisals
- Commitment is displayed to training through attendance as required
- An up-to-date personal log book is maintained to record all training received.

I confirm that I have read and agreed this job description.

Signed: .... *(Job Holder)*

Print Name: ....

Date: ....

Signed: .... *(Dept. Manager)*

Print Name: ....

Date: ....

Appendix 2(C): Forte Hotels

JOB DESCRIPTION

1. Job title: Team Manager *(Catering/Rooms)*

2. Reports to: Operations Manager *(Catering/Rooms)*

3. Prime function: To maximise profit through the consistent delivery of the highest standards of product and service, the optimisation of sales and the effective performance of the team.

4. Key performance areas:
- Customer service
- Statutory management
- Profit focus
- Planning
- Operations management
- Performance management
- Personal effectiveness

4.1 Customer service
The function of the Team Manager in this area is being performed competently when:

- A positive personal image is presented to the customer and interaction is developed
- A climate and environment are fostered that delight customers
- The needs and feelings of the customer are anticipated and responded to appropriately and kept in balance with the needs of the organisation
- Feedback from customers is actively solicited
- Problems affecting the customers are identified and interpreted and solutions agreed and implemented
- Systems, procedures and practice for the maintenance of quality and customer service standards are monitored, maintained, evaluated and enhanced
- Improvement targets are met relating to formal measurement criteria.

4.2 Statutory management
The function of the Team Manager in this area is being performed competently when:

- Procedures and legal requirements pertaining to safety, hygiene and security are adhered to within own area of responsibility
- The health and safety of employees and members of the public are monitored and maintained
- In the event of a fire alarm activation the statutory procedures are adhered to
- The highest standards of personal health and hygiene are maintained at all times
- Personal organisation and that of the work area are maintained to assist workflow
- Equipment and supply needs are identified and defects in equipment reported in line with Hotel procedures
- All work is carried out in an organised and efficient manner in line with appropriate organisational and legal requirements
- Energy efficiency is promoted and improvement identified to support the Hotel Green Policy
- Team members are trained in safe working practices and their legal responsibilities
- Appropriate records are maintained in accordance with Company and legal requirements.

4.3 Profit focus
The function of the Team Manager in this area is being performed competently when:

- Information is obtained to assist sales forecasting
- Contributions are made to the efficient planning and implementation of sales activities
- Pricing policy, promotions and discounts are recommended and implemented
- Selling opportunities are identified and generated
- Recommendations are made for the development and marketing of products and services
- Expenditure is monitored and controlled within budget
- Team members are trained in upselling techniques and cost efficiency
- Business performance targets are met.

4.4 Planning
The function of the Team Manager in this area is being performed competently when:

- The requirement for manpower and material resources is identified and planned within budget
- Contribution is made to the setting of departmental objectives in relation to the business strategy
- Objectives for teams and individuals are agreed and updated
- Action plans are agreed, implemented within deadlines, reviewed and updated
- Teams are consulted to assist in problem resolution and identification of improvements
- Contribution is made to management discussions to solve problems, identify improvements and make decisions.

4.5 Operations management
The function of the Team Manager in this area is being performed competently when:

- Services and operation are maintained to satisfy qualitative and quantitative standards of performance
- The necessary conditions are created and maintained for productive work
- Work is organised to achieve daily requirements
- Team members are empowered to work with minimal supervision
- Manpower and material resources are effectively used, monitored and controlled balancing both budgetary requirements and customer needs
- Effective cash handling and accounting procedures are implemented and adhered to, and remedial action is taken to address related problems
- Hands-on support is given to colleagues in the performance of their work as and when required
- Oral and written communication is carried out in a manner, and at a level and pace, likely to promote understanding, effective performance and harmonious working relationships

- Productive working relationships are established, maintained and enhanced at all levels and interpersonal conflict is identified and minimised
- The recruitment and selection of new employees is carried out effectively in accordance with company procedures and best practices and in line with wage budgets and manpower plans
- Information is recorded, stored and retrieved as necessary to statutory standards
- Changes to improve operational efficiency are implemented and evaluated
- There is a quick and decisive response to resolve immediate and short-term problems
- Duty/Senior Management responsibility is undertaken and carried out effectively when required.

4.6 Performance management

The function of the Team Manager in this area is being performed competently when:

- Training is focused on the delivery of operational standards of performance and customer service
- Training needs of the department and individual are identified in relation to departmental objective and business plans
- Training is planned to meet the identified needs
- Group and individual training is carried out to the Hotel and department standards
- The team is developed through planned activities to enhance morale and commitment
- Motivation is sustained through recognition, reward and incentives
- Training and development programmes are evaluated against departmental objectives
- Contribution is made to the improvement of development processes
- Feedback is given to individuals through the appraisal process and personal development plans set and actioned accordingly
- Individuals and teams are coached in and given feedback on the daily performance of duties
- Team members are encouraged to think and share ideas
- Disciplinary and grievance procedures are implemented in conjunction with the Personnel Department
- Improvement targets are met relating to relevant formal measurement tools such as labour turnover and employee attitude survey.

4.7 Personal effectiveness

The function of the Team Manager in this area is being performed competently when:

- Self-development needs are identified and agreed within a personal development plan and commitment made to its implementation
- Personal work planning is monitored and evaluated to enhance performance
- Initiative is taken to pursue opportunities for self-development and business improvement through experimentation and by seeking exposure to new challenges and experiences

- Issues are confronted assertively
- The commitment of others is secured through persuasion
- Previous experience, knowledge and best practices are applied effectively
- Focus, energy and tenacity are demonstrated in the pursuit of results
- There is a decisive response to change and a readiness to challenge tradition
- Standards are achieved with minimal intervention from Line Manager.

I confirm that I have read and agreed this job description.

Signed: .... *(Job Holder)*

Print Name: ....

Date: ....

Signed: .... *(Dept. Manager)*

Print Name: ....

Date: ....

The author is grateful to Andrea McIntyre, Human Resources Officer, The Compleat Angler, and to Marie Pollock, Regional Human Resources Manager, for providing these examples.

Appendix 3: The Savoy Hotel

STAFF HANDBOOK

The staff handbook opens with the following introduction.

Welcome to The Savoy. *I am delighted you have joined our team, not only as an employee but also as a custodian, to ensure preservation of the standards which make* The Savoy *the most famous hotel in the world.*

The Savoy was founded on family tradition and has always been concerned with the training and development of its staff. It is for this reason that The Savoy *has become a cornerstone of our profession and is affectionately known at the 'University of the Industry'. Its reputation for elegance, excellence and efficient service inspires many to begin and further their careers here, and we are relying on you to continue this tradition.*

I trust that you will enjoy your time with us and appreciate the great social panorama of events and people you will witness. The Savoy *has participated in history for the past one hundred years – from the first radio broadcast to the first private cable television – always aided by a staff dedicated to maintaining the tradition of the highest standards.*

General Manager

This is followed by a comprehensive list of contents including information on the following:

- personnel office, personal appearance, company identity cards, lockers and personal property, smoking, staff entrance;

- pay, income tax, national insurance, attendance recording, change of address, security;

- meals, accommodation, staff restaurant, additional hours, absence from work, company sick pay, statutory sick pay, annual holidays;

- termination of employment, company pension schemes, confidential information, disciplinary rules and procedures;

- training and development, health and safety, hygiene, fires and bombs;

- living-in staff, hotel facilities, gambling and private trading, energy conservation;

- accident procedure and first aid, reporting accidents, safety checking, fire alarm procedure;

- employee of the month award, staff social activities, staff introductory bonus;

- The Savoy – background information, company history.

(Reproduced by permission of Tim Gates, Human Resources Director, The Savoy Hotel)

Review and discussion questions

1. Explain the importance of effective human resource management within the hospitality industry. How would you distinguish between personnel management and human resource management?

2. Discuss the nature of the personnel function as a shared responsibility. What are the justifications for personnel management specialists? To what extent do you accept the suggestion that every manager is a personnel manager?

3. Explain the importance of an effective employee relations policy. Suggest main headings for those matters about which it is useful for an employer to have a considered policy of employee relations.

4. Give your own reasons to explain the generally high levels of staff turnover in the hospitality industry. What are the costs involved? What actions would you recommend be taken to help reduce the level of staff turnover?

5. Explain the importance and main stages of human resource planning. Discuss fully the potential benefits of human resource planning.

6. Give your views on the fundamental considerations which should underlie the recruitment and selection of staff. Outline the basic stages in a planned and systematic approach to staff recruitment and selection. In your experience, to what extent are these basic steps followed within the hospitality industry?

7. Give main headings for a possible list of contents for: (i) a job description; and (ii) a person specification. Provide your own examples of possible difficulties and distastes of hospitality jobs.

8. Suggest what measures might be applied to help evaluate the effectiveness and contribution of the personnel function within the hospitality industry.

Assume that a vacancy has arisen for a new senior or supervisory position of your choice in a large hospitality organisation.

  (i) State clearly the nature of this new position and prepare a detailed job description and person specification. Include what you believe to be the likely difficulties and distastes of the job.

 (ii) Explain how you would plan and conduct the selection process, and the methods of selection that would be most appropriate for this particular appointment.

(iii) Design a suitable induction programme specifying the duration, timing and contents of the programme, including the departments and persons involved.

Case study 1: All change at Crown and Sceptre

Susan Kennedy has recently been appointed to head the new human resources function of the Crown and Sceptre Hotels Limited group. Until recently comprising just the one hotel, Crown and Sceptre have now added a further five properties to the company which employs a total of 650 full-, part-time and casual staff. All hotels in the group are in the three-star market with between 100 and 170 bedrooms, and situated within a 30-mile radius of each other. The original Crown and Sceptre has taken over the role of head office.

Prior to the takeover, all the separate hotels had very much their own individual culture and style of operations, and there is clearly some resistance to belonging to a larger grouping. General managers appear reluctant to 'toe the corporate line', particularly if they perceive this to devalue their ability to make decisions over such matters as, for example, staffing levels and salary reviews.

The organisation of the personnel function appears to be somewhat haphazard. Kennedy herself reports to the chief accountant who, in turn, reports to the managing director. The personnel department consists of a recruitment and training officer, a personnel administration clerk and a secretary shared with the chief accountant. None of the other hotels in the group has any full-time personnel staff. Matters relating to this area are usually handled by the assistant manager and general manager's secretary, with wages being administered by each individual accounts office.

The chief accountant has, on a number of occasions, expressed concern about the organisation of the personnel function throughout the group and feels there is an urgent need for attention to such matters as standardisation, policy-making and strategic planning. The managing director, however, is wary about how the general managers will react to any suggested changes and is unsure of the scope or extent of centralisation/decentralisation which is desirable.

A main concern of the chief accountant is to determine which human resource functions should be accorded priority over the next year and during the next five years. However, the managing director seems more interested in ensuring that all staff within the enlarged group identify with corporate aims and objectives, and how they can best be inculcated into the culture of the new organisation.

Kennedy herself believes that the management of human resources is equally haphazard and considers there is a clear need for improvement, including urgent attention to modern personnel procedures and practices.

Source: This case study has been prepared jointly with, and from original material provided by, the author's colleague Karen Meudell, University of Portsmouth.

TASK

As the 'personnel specialist' Kennedy has now been asked by the managing director to put forward a detailed set of specific recommendations.

Case study 2: Devolution of the HRM function

A large research project was carried out to conduct an analysis of the human resource management function within selected UK hotel companies with particular reference to the devolution of the function. Fifteen hotel companies with more than 10 hotels in the UK (some of them with international operations) were surveyed. The survey was followed by semi-structured interviews with senior HRM Directors from these companies.

There has been much discussion and evidence of the changes that have taken place within the HRM function in the hotel industry within the last few years, due mainly to recessionary pressures. The question of whether HRM contributes to the overall business success was being asked in many hotel companies. The time came to cut overheads and maximise profits; in many cases the first casualty of this process was the training budget and the 'welfare', 'non-profit' side of the business.

Many hotel companies claimed to respond to this situation by devolving tasks formerly undertaken by personnel and training managers to line managers. Formerly, it had been traditional to have a personnel and training manager in an hotel with more than 50 staff. The business demands of the hotel industry have necessitated a rethink of the role of the HRM function.

The initial aim when embarking on this research was to test the effects of devolving the personnel and training functions in selected UK hotel companies; by investigating the trend of devolution, identifying how widespread it was within the industry; evaluating the effect on hotel performance.

Researching the literature and initiating discussions at the early phase of the research, however, indicated that there was confusion over the term 'devolution', and it appeared that there was considerable variation on the theme. This lack of synergy and relevant literature forced a rethink of the initial hypothesis, and it appeared to be essential to produce an effective analysis of current practice within the HRM function in the hotel industry.

Findings

One of the main conclusions that can be derived from the literature review and the subsequent survey is that it is very difficult to arrive at a model of HRM practices within the hotel industry. There are many factors which influence the process of HRM; the culture of the company together with resource considerations appear to play a part in determining how the HRM function operates within each hotel company. Anomalies exist between what the human resource directors say is company standard and what is practised by the personnel professionals in their day-to-day work.

Upon analysis, the perception of what the term 'devolution' means has many variations and it appears that companies say they have devolved without really understanding what real devolution means. This was highlighted when the HRM practitioners' definition of devolution was compared to the textbook definition. The whole area of devolved decision-making authority seems, in most cases, not to accompany the devolved responsibility as the previously agreed textbook definition says it should.

Each company has devised a system to meet its own individual needs. This is not to say that it is wrong, as meeting the company needs and contribution to overall company success is seen as a prime responsibility of HRM, but it does seem to add to the confusion and lack of understanding that exists about devolution in industry as a whole.

In the majority of hotel companies, the core elements of HRM such as recruitment, grievance handling, disciplinary procedures, appraisals and training were all managed in different ways and with differing levels of authority. One of the major considerations of this is that there is no uniform HRM operating system which could become an industry standard.

▷

Devolution of the HRM function continued

Another consequence of what is happening is a lack of training in HRM practice. This is highlighted in one company which expects assistant managers to perform the personnel and training function, but offer no training in employment law or any other aspect of the function.

The lack of monetary reward and recognition for taking on devolved HRM responsibilities has not motivated line management to accept the 'people issues' of their departments as part of their legitimate job. Role overload, ambiguity and conflict was seen by line management as a real problem. This is a consequence which the hotel industry must take seriously as the recession fades and business improves. The role ambiguity of being a task-orientated business manager or a more socially-orientated manager of people, must be addressed. Otherwise it is the task-orientated business manager that will take precedence.

The findings and results of this research project have pointed the way towards a need to clarify the purpose and role of the HRM function in hotels. A lot of jargon, terminology and concepts seem to abound without any clear understanding of what they mean and how they contribute to overall company performance. The issues that need to be addressed are the need to clarify the concept of HRM and the establishment of a benchmark of common practice.

Devolution looks like a trend that is going to stay, so getting it right must be an objective for the future. The results highlight the need for the hotel industry to change its attitude and culture from the short-term view that exists at present.

Brief

The researcher attended a Council for Hospitality Management Education (CHME) conference when she heard the General Manager of a 200-bedroomed five-star hotel state, 'I have asked my Personnel Manager to talk herself out of a job in two years' time.'

Source: This case study has been prepared by the author's colleague, Kate Giannopoulou, South Bank University.

TASK

Taking into account the findings of the above research, discuss the implications of preparing for this HRM role to be devolved to line management.

Notes and references

1. *Catering and Hospitality Industry – Key Facts and Figures*, HCTC, 1994.
2. *Training: who needs it? Research Report 1995: Executive Summary*, HCTC, 1995.
3. *British Hospitality: Trends and Statistics*, British Hospitality Association (1998).
4. See, for example, Maher A, 'Accounting for Human Resources in UK Hotels', *Proceedings of CHME Research Conference*, Manchester Metropolitan University, April 1993.
5. Mullins L J, 'The Personnel Function', *HCIMA Journal*, no. 94, October 1979, pp. 22–25.
6. Guest D E, 'Human Resource Management and Industrial Relations', *Journal of Management Studies*, vol. 24, no. 5, September 1987, pp. 503–521.
7. Torrington D and Hall L, *Personnel Management: A New Approach*, 2nd edn, Prentice-Hall (1991), pp. 15–16.
8. Storey J, *Developments in the Management of Human Resources: An Analytical Review*, Blackwell (1992).
9. Legge K, *Human Resource Management: Rhetorics and Realities*, Macmillan (1995), p. 74.

10. Cuming M W, *The Theory and Practice of Personnel Management*, 7th edn, Butterworth Heinemann (1993).

11. Willman P, 'Human Resource Management in the Service Sector', in Jones P (ed.), *Management in Service Industries*, Pitman (1989), p. 210.

12. Maher A, 'Accounting for Human Resources in UK Hotels', *Proceedings of CHME Research Conference*, Manchester Metropolitan University, April 1993.

13. Price L, 'Poor Personnel Practice in the Hotel and Catering Industry: Does it Matter?', *Human Resource Management Journal*, vol. 4, no. 4, 1994, pp. 44–62.

14. Kelliher C and Johnson K, 'Personnel Management in Hotels – Some Empirical Observations', *International Journal of Hospitality Management*, vol. 6, no. 2, 1987, pp. 103–108.

15. Kelliher C and Johnson K, 'Personnel Management in Hotels – An Update: A move to Human Resource Management?', *Progress in Tourism and Hospitality Research*, vol. 3, 1997, pp. 321–331.

16. Goldsmith A, Nickson D, Sloan D and Wood R C, *Human Resource Management for Hospitality Services*, International Thomson Business Press (1997), p. 11.

17. Baum T, Amoah V and Spivack S, 'Policy Dimensions of Human Resource Management in the Tourism and Hospitality Services', *International Journal of Contemporary Hospitality Management*, vol. 9, no. 5/6, 1997, pp. 221–229.

18. Lashley C, 'Matching the Management of Human Resources to Service Operations', *International Journal of Contemporary Hospitality Management*, vol. 10, no. 1, 1998, pp. 24–33.

19. Worsfold P, 'HRM, Performance, Commitment and Service Quality in the Hotel Industry', *International Journal of Contemporary Hospitality Management*, vol. 11, no. 7, 1999, pp. 340–348.

20. McBain R, 'The Role of Human Resource Management and the Psychological Contract', *Manager Update*, vol. 8, no. 4, Summer 1997, pp. 22–31.

21. Forte R, 'How I See the Personnel Function', *Personnel Management*, August 1982, p. 32.

22. Venison P, *Managing Hotels*, Heinemann (1983), p. 111.

23. Boella M J, *Human Resource Management in the Hotel and Catering Industry*, 6th edn, Stanley Thornes (1996).

24. Information and Advisory Services, Institute of Personnel and Development.

25. Mullins L J, 'The Personnel Function – A Shared Responsibility', *Administrator*, vol. 5, no. 5, May 1985, pp. 14–16.

26. Forte R, 'How I See the Personnel Function', *Personnel Management*, August 1982, p. 32.

27. Lucas R, *Managing Employee Relations in the Hotel and Catering Industry*, Cassell (1995), p. 8.

28. For a more detailed discussion see, for example, Rollinson D, *Understanding Employee Relations: A Behavioural Approach*, Addison Wesley (1993).

29. *Employee Relations for the Hotel and Catering Industry*, 7th edn, HCTC, 1990, p. 9.

30. Cuming M W, *The Theory and Practice of Personnel Management*, 7th edn, Butterworth-Heinemann (1993), p. 9.

31. *Employee Relations for the Hotel and Catering Industry*, 7th edn, HCTC, 1990.

32. For a fuller account see: Mullins L J, *Management and Organisational Behaviour*, 5th edn, Financial Times Pitman Publishing (1999).

33. See, for example, Fletcher W, 'Good Listener, Better Manager', *Management Today*, January 2000, p. 30.

34. Atkinson J, *Flexibility, Uncertainty and Manpower Management*, Institute of Manpower Studies, 1985.

35. Guerrier Y and Lockwood A, 'Core and Peripheral Employees in Hotel Operations', *Personnel Review*, vol. 18, no. 1, 1989, pp. 9–15.

36. 'Managing Diversity: An Age Diverse Workforce', *Management Brief No. 6*, HCIMA, October 1999.

37. *Employee Relations for the Hotel and Catering Industry*, 7th edn, HCTC, 1990, p. 43.

38. See, for example, Wasmuth W J and Davis S W, 'Managing Employee Turnover', *Cornell HRA Quarterly*, February 1983, vol. 23, no. 4, pp. 15–22, and 'Strategies for Managing Employee Turnover', *Cornell HRA Quarterly*, August 1983, vol. 24, no. 2, pp. 65–75.

39. Riley M, 'Labour Turnover: Time to Change the Paradigm?' *International Journal of Contemporary Hospitality Management*, vol. 5, no. 4, 1993, pp. i–iii.

40. See for example: Mok C and Luk Y, 'Exit Interviews in Hotels: Making them a more powerful management tool', *International Journal of Hospitality Management*, vol. 14, no. 2, 1995, pp. 187–194.

41. Bonn M A and Forbringer L R, 'Reducing Turnover in the Hospitality Industry: An Overview of Recruitment, Selection and Retention', *International Journal of Hospitality Management*, vol. 11, no. 1, 1992, pp. 47–63.

42. Department of Employment, *Company Manpower Planning*, HMSO (1974).

43. *Manpower Planning Survey Report*, Williamm Mercer Fraser Ltd, August 1989.

44. *Employment Policy and Industrial Relations in the Hotels and Catering Industry*, Hotels and Catering EDC (1977).

45. For further details of HR planning, records and statistics, see, for example, Boella M J, *Human Resource Management in the Hospitality Industry*, 6th edn, Stanley Thornes (1996).

46. See, for example, 'A Computer System for Payroll Control – the challenge for suppliers', *The Hospitality Yearbook 1995*, HCIMA, pp. 94–95.

47. 'Managing Diversity: An Age Diverse Workforce', *Management Brief No. 6*, HCIMA, October 1999.

48. Bonn M A and Forbringer L R, 'Reducing Turnover in the Hospitality Industry: An Overview of Recruitment, Selection and Retention', *International Journal of Hospitality Management*, vol. 11, no. 1, 1992, pp. 47–63.

49. Williams P W and Hunter M, 'Supervisory Hotel Employee Perceptions of Management Careers and Professional Development Requirements', *International Journal of Hospitality Management*, vol. 11, no. 4, 1992, pp. 347–358.

50. Mullins L J, 'Job Analysis – Know the Job and the Person to Do It', *International Journal of Hospitality Management*, vol. 4, no. 4, 1985, pp. 181–183.

51. For an explanation of different methods of selection, see Mullins L J, *Management and Organisational Behaviour*, 5th edn, Financial Times Pitman Publishing (1999).

52. See, for example, Simons T, 'Interviewing Job Applicants – How to get beyond first impressions', *Cornell HRA Quarterly*, December 1995, pp. 21–27.

53. For example, at The Waldorf two videos are shown. One introduces new employees into the company and shows information on its outlets. Another video gives information on The Waldorf Hotel.

54. Adam-Smith D, Goss D and Bairstow S, 'Coming to Terms with New Labour's Laws', *Employment Relations Review*, Issue 12, February 2000.

55. *Training: who needs it? Research Report 1995: Executive Summary*, HCTC (1995).

56. See, for example, Hubrecht J and Teare R, 'A Strategy for Partnership in Total Quality Service', *International Journal of Contemporary Hospitality Management*, vol. 5, no. 3, 1993, pp. i–iv.

57. See, for example, 'Change and Innovation in Education and Training', *The Hospitality Yearbook 1995*, HCIMA, pp. 37–48.

58. Robinson S, 'The Learning Curse', *Inside Hotels*, April/May 1992, pp. 40–45.

59. See, for example, Haywood K M, 'Effective Training: Toward a Strategic Approach', *Cornell HRA Quarterly*, vol. 33, no. 6, December 1992, pp. 43–52.

60. See, for example, Clements C J and Josiam B M, 'Training: Quantifying the Financial Benefits', *International Journal of Contemporary Hospitality Management*, vol. 7, no. 1, 1995, pp. 10–15.

61. Mullins L J, 'Successful Training – A Planned and Systematic Approach', *Administrator*, July 1991, pp. 4–5.

62. *The Investors in People Standard*, Investors in People UK (1995).

63. Lockwood A, Baker M and Ghillyer A (eds), *Quality Management in Hospitality*, Cassell (1996), pp. 160–161.

64. Mullins L J and Aldrich P, 'An Integrated Model of Management and Managerial Development', *Journal of Management Development*, vol. 7, no. 3, 1988, pp. 29–39.

65. Mullins L J, 'Managerial Behaviour and Development in the Hospitality Industry', *Proceedings of The International Association of Hotel Management Schools Symposium*, Leeds Polytechnic, November 1988.

66. Wood R C, *Working in Hotels and Catering*, 2nd edn, International Thomson Business Press (1997).

67. Goss-Turner S, 'The Role of the Multi-unit Manager in Branded Hospitality Chains', *Human Resource Management Journal*, vol. 9, no. 4, 1999, pp. 39–57.

68. See, for example, Tyson S and Fell A, *Evaluating the Personnel Function*, 2nd edn, Stanley Thornes (1992).

DELEGATION, SUPERVISION AND CONTROL

AUTHORITY, RESPONSIBILITY AND ACCOUNTABILITY

THE PRACTICE OF DELEGATION

Improved use of human resources

Difficulties and problems with delegation

THE NEED FOR MANAGEMENT CONTROL

Improvement in performance

Main stages in control systems

PERFORMANCE APPRAISAL

THE REGULATION OF BEHAVIOUR

QUALITY ASSURANCE IN THE HOSPITALITY INDUSTRY

THE MEASUREMENT OF SERVICE QUALITY

SUPERVISION AND SUPPORTIVE RELATIONSHIPS

THE EXERCISE OF CONTROL

A behavioural approach to management control

Implementation of a behavioural approach

FINANCIAL AND ACCOUNTING CONTROLS

APPENDIX: SWALLOW HOTELS-PERFORMANCE APPRAISAL

Chapter eleven

The execution of work

Introduction

In order for the hospitality organisation to function effectively the activities of members of staff need to be channelled and guided towards the achievement of corporate goals and objectives. The process of management is concerned with the utilisation of human resources, arrangements for the carrying out of organisational processes, and the execution of work.

Delegation, supervision and control

We saw in Chapter 4 that successful management involves getting work done through the efforts of other people. This entails the distribution of duties, authority and responsibilities throughout the organisation structure, and an attempt to influence the behaviour and performance of subordinate staff. The execution of work involves the processes of delegation, supervision and control. Delegation is a necessary function of management. If you are doing it yourself then you are not managing.[1]

Delegation is an essential feature of organisational effectiveness, and is related to managerial style and leadership. Delegation can be seen as taking place both at the organisational or structural level, and at the individual or personal level.

The organisational level

The structure of the establishment (as depicted in an organisation chart, for example) is itself a result of delegation. If there is no delegation, there is no structure. As establishments grow in size the extent of delegation increases. At the organisational level delegation involves consideration of the division of work, centralisation/decentralisation and departmentalisation. Decentralisation may be federal or functional.[2] Federal decentralisation is the establishment of autonomous units operating in their own market with self-control and with the main responsibility of contributing profit to the parent body. Functional decentralisation is based on individual processes or products.

Departments or sections may be established on the basis of the task or element functions. The extent of decentralisation and divisionalisation provides the basic structural pattern of the organisation. The nature of organisation structure has already been discussed in Chapter 6. Here we are concerned with delegation at the individual or personal level.

Delegation at the individual level

Within the structure of the organisation the various activities that have to be undertaken must be distributed among individual members of the workforce. It is possible to have delegation upwards, for example when a manager takes over from a subordinate who is experiencing difficulty in performing a particular task, or who has an exceptionally high work load, or when a manager temporarily undertakes the work of a subordinate who is absent through holiday or sickness. It is also possible to have delegation laterally to another manager on the same level. But, usually, delegation is interpreted as a movement down the organisation.

Delegation is not just the issuing and following of orders or the carrying out of specified tasks in accordance with detailed instructions. It is not just the arbitrary shedding of work. Delegation is an essential feature of organisational effectiveness. It is related to other concepts such as managerial style and leadership. **Within the formal hierarchical structure of the organisation, delegation creates a special manager–subordinate relationship.**

Authority, responsibility and accountability

The whole basis of delegation is founded on the concepts of authority, responsibility and accountability (ultimate responsibility) (see Figure 11.1).

Authority

Authority is the right to take actions or make decisions that the manager would otherwise have taken or made. Authority legitimises the exercise of power within the structure and policies of the organisation. It enables subordinates to issue valid instructions for others to follow. Delegated duties are sometimes delegated further down the structure.

Riley, for example, discusses the relationship between power and authority:

Figure 11.1:
The basis of
delegation

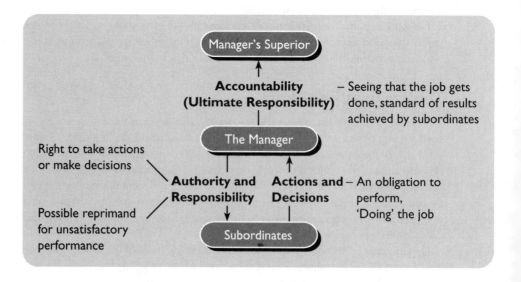

Clearly, if power is seen to be constantly misused, or blatantly unfair, then subordinates will begin to question the authority of the user of power. The less legitimate your authority is, the more you may need to use power, which only undermines your authority still more. It is a cycle which is all too easy to get into.[3]

(Leadership power and influence was discussed in Chapter 9.)

Responsibility

Responsibility involves an obligation by the subordinate to perform certain duties or make certain decisions, and having to accept possible reprimands from the manager for unsatisfactory performance. However, the acceptance of responsibility should give rise not only to negative sanctions but also to positive rewards.

But effective delegation is not abdication of responsibility. The manager is still responsible for ensuring that the work gets done and is performed to a satisfactory standard. The manager is in turn accountable to a superior for the actions and decisions of subordinates.

Accountability

Accountability is interpreted as meaning ultimate responsibility. Managers have to accept ultimate responsibility for the control of their staff, for the performance of duties allocated to their department/section within the structure of the organisation, and for the standard of results achieved. The manager is in turn responsible to higher management. *This ultimate responsibility cannot be delegated.*

The concept of accountability means that effective delegation involves a 'dual responsibility'.

Delegation means the conferring of a specified authority by a higher authority. In its essence it involves a dual responsibility. The one to whom authority is delegated becomes responsible to the superior for doing the job, but the superior remains responsible for getting the job done. This principle of delegation is the centre of all processes in formal organisation.[4]

In order to help clarify the nature of 'dual responsibility' in delegation it might be better expressed as: The subordinate is *responsible* to the manager for doing the job, while the manager is responsible for seeing that the job gets done. The manager is *accountable* to a superior for the actions of subordinates (Figure 11.1). If a manager delegates some task to a subordinate member of staff who does a bad job then the manager must accept ultimate responsibility (accountability) for the actions of the subordinate.

You may be able to pass over most of your job to another person but you can't pass over the responsibility for checking it. You cannot delegate accountability.[5]

The manager should accept the 'blame' as the person obligated to the superior for the performance of the department/section, and accountable to see that the task was completed satisfactorily. It is then up to the manager to sort out things in their own department, to counsel members of staff and to review the system of delegation.

Delegation of authority and responsibility

Although accountability can be delegated, effective delegation must still embrace both authority and responsibility. It is not practical to delegate one without the other. Authority and responsibility are at the basis of the manager–subordinate relationship and recognised as 'rules' or principles of good management. Responsibility is a corollary of authority. Wherever authority is exercised, responsibility arises. Sanctions are needed to encourage useful actions and to discourage others.[6]

For example, if the general manager gives the food and beverage manager authority to purchase certain items up to a given value without prior reference, then the food and beverage manager should be held responsible for the expenditure which is incurred. To exercise authority without accepting responsibility gives rise to the possible abuse of delegation. It can lead to complacency and a misplaced sense of security.

Equally, responsibility must be supported by the authority to take action and make decisions within the limits of that responsibility. To hold subordinates responsible for areas of performance over which they have no authority to influence is another abuse of delegation.

> *If people do not have sufficient power or authority to enable them to give the necessary instructions, order the required goods, or hire the necessary staff, then delegation has not been properly carried out and inefficiency will be the result.*[7]

Responsibility should be sufficient to give the subordinate freedom of action within agreed terms of reference and to avoid excessive supervision. Part of the manager's job is the development of subordinates. A sense of responsibility will help in the performance of their tasks and in dealing with customers.

Parity with accountability

The delegation of authority and responsibility must, however, be kept in parity with accountability. The manager retains ultimate responsibility for the behaviour of staff and for actions taken and decisions made by subordinates. The manager remains accountable to a superior for the total operations of the department/section.

The manager must be on the lookout for subordinates who are more concerned with personal empire-building than meeting stated objectives of the establishment. The manager must prevent a strong personality exceeding the limits of formal delegation. In short, the manager must remain in control. This calls for a planned and systematic approach to the practice of delegation. But such an approach is easier said than done, and few actually achieve it.

The practice of delegation

In order to achieve an effective system of delegation it is necessary that:

- subordinates know exactly what is expected of them, what has to be achieved, the boundaries within which they have freedom of action, and how far they can exercise independent decision-making; and
- the manager remains accountable for the actions and decisions of subordinates.

Delegation therefore creates a special form of manager–subordinate relationship. It involves the manager examining four basic questions: what opportunities are there for staff to learn and develop; what tasks could be performed better by subordinate staff; how should the increased tasks and responsibilities be implemented; and what form of monitoring control system would be the most appropriate?

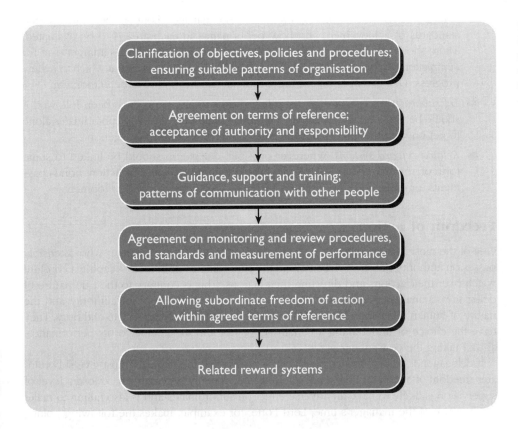

Figure 11.2:
Main stages in
a planned and
systematic
approach to
delegation

A planned and systematic approach

Setting up a successful system of delegation requires a planned and systematic approach involving five main stages (Figure 11.2).

- *Clarification of policies and procedures.* In order to provide a framework for the exercise of authority and acceptance of responsibility there must be clearly established policies and procedures. Managers must be clear about the opportunities and limitations of their own jobs. There should be a clear chain of command with effective communications and coordination between the various levels of authority within the organisation structure.

- *Agreement on terms of reference.* Those areas of activities which are to be delegated to subordinates should be identified clearly. Wherever possible, emphasis should be placed on the achievement of end results rather than a set of detailed instructions. It is important to make sure that the subordinates accept both the extent of, and any restrictions on, the exercise of authority, and the responsibility delegated to them.

- *Briefing, guidance and training.* Once subordinates have accepted the delegation, they should be properly briefed, and given guidance and any necessary training. They should be advised where, and to whom, they can go for further advice or help. The manager should make clear to other staff the nature and extent of delegation, and obtain their cooperation. Delegation may well involve subordinates having dealings with staff in other departments or sections, in which case the manager should also communicate with the other managers.

● *An effective review and monitoring system.* The manager should make clear expected standards of achievement and how performance in each area is to be evaluated. There should be agreement on time limits for delegation (such as a target date for completion of a task, or a specified time period), and check points at which to review progress. Delegation is not an irrevocable act and can always be withdrawn.

● *Let subordinates get on with the job.* If the previous stages have been followed it should be possible, within the agreed terms of reference, to leave subordinates alone to get on with the job. This is the true nature of successful delegation.

● *Related reward systems.* Wherever possible, delegation should be linked to some form of 'reward' system such as for example improved job satisfaction, bonus payments, or enhanced opportunities for promotion or personal development.

Freedom of action

One of the most frustrating aspects of so-called delegation is the manager who ostensibly passes on authority but stays close behind the subordinates' shoulders, keeping a constant watch over their actions and directing their actions. This is contrary to the true nature of delegation. Managers need to be aware of the 'acceptance theory' of authority and the nature of human behaviour. It is subordinates who control the response to authority. They have the choice of undertaking a certain act or not and the manner of its performance, and of taking the consequences.[8]

If delegation is to be effective, therefore, it means that the manager must give subordinates freedom of action and must not interfere unless really necessary. Too close a level of supervision is likely to have an adverse effect on subordinates and is also failing to make the best use of the manager's time. Lord Forte, for example, makes the following point.

> *I delegate wherever possible and I try to give the person to whom I delegate complete authority, with the responsibility the delegation brings. I try not to interfere. Only a very conceited man feels that he is the only one who can do a job properly. Thus the very conceited man remains very limited in his field of activity. If he is always interfering with people, he is limiting his time to do other things.[9]*

Improved use of human resources

Properly handled, delegation is a powerful and effective instrument of management. It offers many potential advantages to the organisation, to the manager and to subordinates. The main feature underlying successful delegation is that it should lead to the optimum use of human resources and improved organisational performance. Studies of successful organisations lend support to the advantages to be gained from effective delegation.[10] Also managers who delegate effectively may be seen as rewarding talent and this helps to build a team of prominent subordinates.[11]

Best use of manager's time

Delegation leaves the manager free to make profitable use of time and to concentrate on the more important tasks and to spend more time in managing and less in doing. This should lead to a more even flow of work, a reduction in bottlenecks and improve the process of communication. It should make the manager more accessible for both customers and staff. Time is one of the most valuable but limited resources and it is important that the manager utilises time to the maximum advantage.

Improved strength of the workforce

As organisations become more complex and have to face increasing environmental change there is a greater need for staff with high levels of specialist expertise. Delegation can help encourage the development and utilisation of knowledge, interest and skills. It enables specific aspects of management to be brought within the province of specialist members of staff. This should help enhance the quality of decision-making.

Delegation focuses attention on higher-level needs. It can be seen as a form of participation and can lead to improved morale by increasing motivation and job satisfaction. Delegation can provide subordinates with greater scope for action and opportunities to develop their aptitudes and abilities, and increase their commitment to the goals of the organisation.[12] Delegation should lead to an improvement in the strength of the workforce.

A means of training and development

Delegation provides a valuable means of training and testing the subordinate's suitability for promotion. It can be used as a means of assessing the likely performance of the subordinate at a higher level in the organisation structure and with enhanced authority and responsibility. If managers have trained, competent subordinates capable of taking their place this will not only aid organisational progress but should enhance their own prospects for further advancement. Delegation can help to avoid the 'Peter Principle', that is, 'In a hierarchy employees tend to rise to their level of incompetence.'[13]

Sound economics

Successful delegation benefits both the manager and subordinate and enables them both to play their respective roles in the effective operation of the hospitality organisation. Activities should be undertaken at the lowest level compatible with efficiency and customer satisfaction. It is a question of opportunity cost. If activities are undertaken at a higher level than necessary, they are being undertaken at greater cost than necessary. Successful delegation is therefore a matter of sound economics as well as good organisation.

Difficulties and problems with delegation

Despite the many potential benefits of delegation, managers often fail to delegate successfully. There are a number of difficulties and problem areas which affect the amount of delegation and its effectiveness. Delegation is influenced by the manager's perception of subordinate staff. It is also influenced by the subordinates' perception of the manager's reasons for delegation.

The extent or otherwise of delegation is also influenced by the nature of the organisation, the design of structure and by management systems and procedures. For example, Wood suggests that the heavy responsibility that hospitality organisations place 'on the role of managers in integrating various sub-systems within a unit' is why 'so many hotel and catering general managers have a poor reputation for delegation'.[14]

Delegation: a social skill

Delegation is not easy. It involves behavioural as well as organisational considerations. Successful delegation is a social skill. Where managers lack this skill, two extreme forms of behaviour can result. At one extreme there is the almost total lack of *real* delegation. Subordinates are only permitted to operate within closely defined and often routine areas of activity with detailed supervision. Staff are treated as if they are incapable of thinking for themselves and given little or no opportunity to exercise initiative or responsibility, or to experience a learning situation.

At the other extreme there can be an excessive zeal for so-called 'delegation' but delegation which is often more like just 'passing the buck'. A manager may leave subordinates to their own resources, often with minimal guidance or training, and expect them to take the consequences for their own actions or decisions. And somehow, such managers seem often not to be around when difficult situations arise. The nature of the hospitality business does place particular demands upon staff who, partly through necessity, are often thrown into the deep end. But this should not be an excuse for the manager's abdication of responsibility.

Either of these two forms of behaviour can also be frustrating and potentially stressful for staff, and unlikely to lead to improved performance. Poor delegation is a potential source of health problems, work stress and role conflict. Work stress is often caused by the failure to delegate properly and by a hierarchical structure which does not permit sufficient autonomy.[15] The downsizing of organisations, reduction in staffing levels and increased business competitiveness have placed greater pressures on managers. This can lead to enforced or inadequate systems of delegation resulting in work stress.

Dependence upon other people

Delegation entails reliance on other people. The manager must know what to delegate, when and to whom. This involves confidence and trust – both in subordinates and in the manager's own performance and system of delegation.

> *Lack of trust is probably one of the greatest time and resource wasters in the workplace. Managers who do not trust their employees are probably wasting hours every week checking up on them at every turn and failing to utilise the resources at their disposal.*[16]

But learning to put trust in other people is one of the most difficult lessons for many managers, and some never learn it. **Managers who claim that opportunities for delegation are limited by the nature of staffing in the hospitality industry should heed the words of Stewart.**

> *Managers must learn to accept their dependence upon people. A key part of being a good manager is managing that dependence. Managers who say they cannot delegate because they have poor subordinates may genuinely be unfortunate in the calibre of the subordinates that they have inherited or been given. More often this view is a criticism of themselves: a criticism either of their unwillingness to delegate when they could and should do so, or a criticism of their selection, training and development of their subordinates.*[17]

In allowing freedom of action to subordinates within agreed terms of reference, managers must accept that subordinates may undertake delegated activities in a different manner from themselves. This involves the acceptance theory of authority mentioned above.

Courage – and support for subordinates

Delegation is also a matter of courage. Managers may be reluctant to delegate for fear that subordinates will not perform the job as well as they can – the 'I can do it better myself' syndrome. Mistakes will inevitably occur and the subordinate will need to be supported by the manager and protected against unwarranted criticism. Giving subordinates delegated authority and responsibility should also give them 'the right to be wrong'.[18] Managers should protect and support subordinate staff and accept personally any reprimand for unsatisfactory performance.

The acceptance of ultimate responsibility is at the basis of the true nature of delegation. This philosophy is evidenced by the following two comments, the first from Lord Forte, the second from the West German hotelier Klaus Kobjoll.

> *'I am so sorry I have made a mistake.' 'No, you have not made a mistake,'* I replied. *'We have made a mistake.'*[19]

> *My role is that of delegator. Each person is fully responsible for their own section and they are allowed to make mistakes and learn from them. Nobody will yell at them here.*[20]

The second comment also highlights the educational aspect of the manager's job. The manager should view mistakes as part of the subordinate's training and an opportunity for further development. When mistakes do occur it is up to managers to counsel members of staff concerned and to review the effectiveness of their system of delegation. 'Even if mistakes occur, good managers are judged as much by their ability to manage them as by their successes.'[21]

Confidence in their own abilities

Some managers show a reluctance to delegate for fear that the subordinate will do too good a job and show the manager in a bad light. It is important that managers have full confidence in their own abilities, but they should of course remember that managing is not a solo activity. The task of management is to get work done through the efforts of other people. If a subordinate performs particularly well, this reflects favourably on the ability of the manager.

The manager needs to make full use of the technical expertise and specialist knowledge of subordinates. Failure to delegate successfully to a competent or more knowledgeable subordinate may mean that the subordinate emerges as an informal leader. This could have possible adverse consequences for the manager, and for the organisation.

The need for management control

Hospitality operations involve a wide range of operations, many of which are provided simultaneously, and services may be provided direct to the customers on the premises. Some sectors of the industry such as hotels may be a 24-hour, 7-day a week business. Managers cannot be expected to be present at all times, or to be able to carry out all the duties which require their personal attention, as well as dealing with all the day-to-day activities.

The effective execution of work and achievement of customer satisfaction will therefore necessitate delegation of the distribution of activities and tasks to other people, and the

Figure 11.3:
The balance
between
delegation
and control

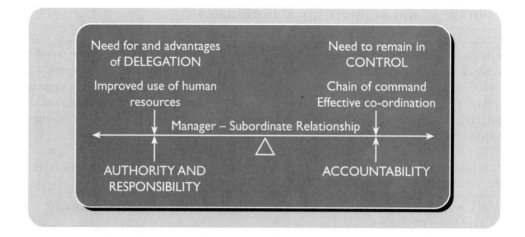

issuing of instructions and advice. This involves the direction of staff and the checking and review of their performance. It involves the process of management control.

A question of balance

The concept of ultimate responsibility gives rise to the need for effective management control. Managers must exercise control over the actions and decisions of subordinates, and be kept informed of the relevance and quality of their work. Managers need to monitor the behaviour and actions of staff in order to ensure they maintain a satisfactory standard of performance. The manager will need to keep open the lines of delegation and to have an upward flow of communication.

> *The essence of the delegation problem lies in the trust–control dilemma. The dilemma is that in any one managerial situation, the sum of trust + control is always constant. The trust is the trust that the subordinate feels that the manager has in him. The control is the control that the manager has over the work of the subordinate.*[22]

Control is therefore an integral part of a system of delegation. It is necessary to ensure the effective co-ordination of activities and to maintain the chain of command. But control should not be so close as to inhibit the effective operation or benefits of delegation. It is a question of securing the right balance (Figure 11.3).

The meaning and interpretation of control

The term 'control' often has an emotive connotation and is interpreted in a negative manner to suggest direction or command by the giving of orders. Staff may be suspicious of control systems and see them as emphasising punishment, an indication of authoritarian management, and a means of exerting pressure and maintaining discipline.

But this is too narrow an interpretation. There is far more to control than simply a means of restricting behaviour or the exercise of authority over others. **Control is not only a function of the formal organisation and a hierarchical structure of authority. It is also a function of interpersonal influence.** Control is a general concept which is applied to both individual behaviour and effective organisational performance.

Different approaches to management control

Different approaches to organisation and management, as discussed in Chapter 4, have illustrated contrasting approaches to the nature of management control. The **classical approach** places emphasis on the technical requirements of the organisation and tends to support a high level of control as necessary for efficiency. It may be recalled, for example, that a criticism of scientific management is the high level of management control over workers and the actual process of work.

Those writers who place emphasis on a **human relations approach** and the social needs of individuals see a high level of control as self-defeating. It produces a negative response, increases internal conflict and results only in short-term improvement in performance.[23] Control should not be seen therefore only in the sense that it suggests close and constant supervision or as a constraint on freedom of action by the individual.

In terms of the **systems approach**, control relates to both the measurement of organisational effectiveness, and to the inputs and series of activities by which inputs are transformed into outputs. Control emphasises the interrelationships among the different sub-systems of the establishment. The **contingency approach** views management control as an organisational variable. The most appropriate methods of control will depend upon the contingencies of particular situations.

Improvement in performance

Control can be interpreted in different ways. It is far-reaching and can be manifested in a number of different forms. Control systems can be concerned with general results, specific actions or day-to-day operational activities, with an evaluation of overall performance of the establishment as a whole or with particular parts of it.

Whatever the different forms of management control, the underlying feature is checking and reviewing progress towards the attainment of stated objectives. The whole purpose of management control is the improvement in performance. Lord Forte, for example, makes the following point:

> *we have an intensive system of controls. The word is often misinterpreted. I do not mean controls in the sense of cutting down on quality, but of setting standards and seeing that the operation conforms.*[24]

Control can be seen to operate at both the individual and at the organisational level (Figure 11.4).

The individual level

At the individual level members of staff want to know what is expected of them, and if they are performing well and in the right areas. Control is a basis for training needs, the motivation to achieve standards and for the development of individuals. Whenever a person inquires 'I would like to know how well I am doing', this can be seen in effect as asking for control. An effective control system places emphasis on the exchange of information, and feedback on actual results against planned targets.[25]

The concept of ultimate responsibility gives rise to the need for effective management control. Managers must exercise control over the actions and decisions of subordinates and be kept informed of the relevance and quality of their work. Managers need to monitor the behaviour and actions of staff in order to ensure they maintain a satisfactory standard of performance.

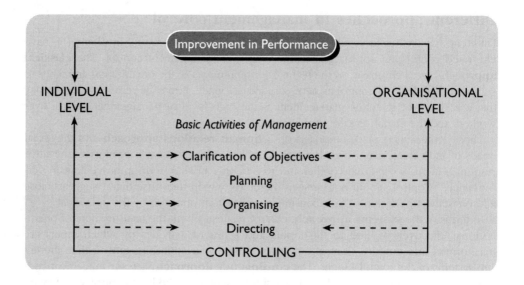

The organisational level

At the organisational level control completes the cycle of managerial activities. It involves reviewing the planning and organisation of the work of the establishment, and guiding and regulating the activities of staff. Management control is concerned with organisational effectiveness and determining whether the objectives of the establishment are being achieved.

The purpose of organisational control is to prevent impropriety, to monitor the use of resources, to check up on the progress of work and provide feedback on the success or failure of operations. Control is an inherent characteristic of the work situation and an important feature of the people–organisation relationship.

Within a service industry such as hospitality the demand for quality assurance places particular emphasis on the importance of effective control procedures.

> *Control is also an important management function, no less important in the delivery of quality than in other aspects of management activity. Indeed, to the extent that the essence of quality is consistency, must of the delivery of quality is a matter of good control.*[26]

Main stages in control systems

Whatever the nature of control there are five essential stages in the design of a management control system (Figure 11.5):

1. Planning what is desired.
2. Establishing standards of performance.
3. Monitoring actual performance.
4. Comparing actual results against planned targets.
5. Rectifying and taking any corrective action.

Clear objectives and targets

Planning provides the framework against which the process of control takes place. It is important that staff understand their duties and responsibilities, and know exactly what is required of them. Objectives and targets should be stated clearly in order to establish defined standards of performance against which the level of achievement can be determined. This requires realistic means of measurement, which wherever possible should be stated in quantitative terms.

The importance of feedback

There must be some system of feedback and reporting of information in order to monitor progress and review results. The information should be accurate, relevant, timely and easily understood by all concerned. It should be in a form which enables management to compare actual performance against planned targets, and which highlights any deviations. This information should be fed back to the staff concerned to let them know how well they are doing.

If it is to be effective, feedback should identify probable causes of any deviations and provide the basis for decisions on taking any corrective action. This might involve consideration of what can or should be done to improve the level of actual performance, revisions to the original objectives and targets, or adjustments to the standards of performance or the operation of the control system itself. Feedback and review should be a continual part of a management control system.

Performance appraisal

One method of attempting to monitor, control and improve the activities of staff and the operations of hospitality organisations is through a system of performance appraisal. A formalised and systematic appraisal scheme can enable a regular assessment of individuals' performance, highlight potential, and identify training and development needs. An effective appraisal scheme can help improve the future performance of staff, and form the basis of financial rewards and planned career progression.

Performance appraisal in the hospitality industry

According to Boella, 'Each time a supervisor praises, counsels or disciplines a subordinate some form of performance appraisal has almost certainly taken place.'[27] However, from a review of literature by Lucas there appears to be doubt as to the extent of, or importance attached to, formal performance appraisal within the hospitality industry, and appraisal can mean different things to different people. Nevertheless, 'performance appraisal is a more common practice in hotels and catering than elsewhere, particularly in relation to determining pay'.[28]

360° feedback and upward appraisal

Increasing attention is being given to broader and more flexible forms of appraisal with greater emphasis on meaningful feedback. The idea of 360° feedback involves appraisal and feedback from different groups within the organisation – peers and subordinates as well as bosses, and possibly internal and external customers. The idea is to provide a broader appraisal covering good working relationships, team-work, leadership, decision-making and quality of service provided.[29] An upward review system involves subordinates' appraisal of managers. This can help to judge, among other things, managers' ability to accept constructive criticism.

> Regular 360° appraisals are conducted with all employees by the partners and team leaders. A standard appraisal form is used and covers achievement in key job areas, performance against key attributes, adequacy and accuracy of job descriptions, training requirements and areas of improvement. Any issues are noted and acted upon wherever possible. All problem areas are discussed with team leaders so that, even if immediate action is not possible, everyone is aware of the difficulty and can compensate for it. Employees are given their own personnel files containing all their appraisal forms and short- and long-term training certificates (NVQs, etc.), so they can see how they are progressing and how any difficulties are being overcome.
>
> Both partners are appraised too – by The Seaview's staff. Each partner is appraised at a meeting of the management team facilitated by a trained appraiser. In the weeks immediately prior to the appraisal session team leaders seek views on the partners from their own staff at departmental meetings and these are reviewed at the partners' appraisal meetings.
>
> **THE SEAVIEW HOTEL AND RESTAURANT**

Uses of, and difficulties with, performance appraisal

An effective system of performance appraisal requires:

- careful preparation by both the appraiser and the appraisee;
- a well-planned and clearly stood procedure including design of the appraisal form;

- conducting the appraisal interview and discussion including plans for future performance;
- conclusion of the discussion and summary of key points; and
- review and follow-up.[30]

(As an example, details of the staff performance appraisal procedure for Swallow Hotels are given in the Appendix to this chapter.)

Appraisors must make every effort to maintain objectivity. When evaluating performance it is important to avoid perceptual distortions and errors (for example the 'halo effect' discussed in Chapter 3).[31]

Umbreit, Eder and McConnell suggest that performance appraisals have several uses, including that of a management tool, and can be used to stimulate the productivity of managers, supervisors and staff. Employees and management staff change jobs quickly and in large numbers, and hospitality operators especially need a valid method of appraising staff performance.[32]

However, Umbreit *et al.* point out that the major difficulty with most performance appraisal systems is that the judgements involved are frequently subjective, relating primarily to personality traits or to observations that cannot be verified. They suggest that any appraisal system should satisfy ten standards relating to both content requirements and to process requirements.

Content requirements

(i) Performance standards must be based on an analysis of job requirements.

(ii) Evaluation should be based on specific dimensions of job performance, and not on single 'global measures'.

(iii) Performance standards should be objective and observable.

(iv) Ratings should be documented.

(v) The validity of individual raters' ratings should be assessed.

Process requirements

(i) Performance standards should be communicated to and understood by the employee.

(ii) Specific instructions for evaluators should be put in writing.

(iii) More than one evaluator should be used whenever possible.

(iv) The evaluator should review the appraisal results with the employee.

(v) The employee should have a formal appeal procedure.

The regulation of behaviour

By their very nature, control systems are concerned with the behaviour of people, and imply regulation and loss of individual freedom. People may be suspicious of control systems and see them as emphasising punishment and an indication of authoritarian management. Some writers support this view and even appear to suggest that organisational controls amount to exploitation of employees.[33]

Under certain conditions, however, people may actually desire control. For example, Lawler gives three reasons why employees might want to be subject to a control system:

- to give feedback on performance;
- to provide some degree of structure to tasks, and definitions of how the tasks are to be carried out, and how performance will be measured; and
- where reward systems, for example pay, are based on performance.[34]

Ambivalence towards control

Most people, however, show an ambivalence towards organisational control. While they recognise the need for, and usefulness of, control systems they may not wish to have them applied to their own performance. It is important therefore not to ignore the behavioural implications. While the need for some suitable form of control is always present, the extent and manner of control is variable. Control systems can have positive as well as negative effects. They can be designed and implemented in a constructive and rewarding way.

> *Although they do not readily admit it, most people probably prefer some degree of control over their lives because it gives them some stability and contributes to their general welfare and safety. Nevertheless, the negative connotation of control still exists and is amplified by the ways in which controls have been traditionally set, implemented, and used in formal organisations.*[35]

Quality assurance in the hospitality industry

One significant aspect of management control systems of particular importance within the hospitality industry is that of quality assurance processes. In Chapter 2 we saw that profit can be seen as the incentive for the organisation to carry out its activities effectively. In order to continue in business the organisation needs to maintain growth and development, and a steady and continuous level of profitability. The successful hospitality organisation should therefore, as a matter of policy, be constantly seeking opportunities to improve the quality of its products, services and processes.

Attention to quality assurance can be seen to arise from a combination of:

- the natural outcome of good business and the need to provide high quality goods and services in order to ensure survival, competitiveness and economic success;
- the labour-intensive nature and staffing characteristics of the industry;
- the desire to achieve and display some 'tangible' measure of quality through British Standards Institution (BSI) or International Organisation for Standardisation (ISO) certification and designation;
- the need to satisfy an absolute requirement, for example a legal liability such as that established by the Food Safety Act 1990;
- part of the exercise of the broader social responsibilities of management.

Effective systems of quality assurance

The increasing expectations of customers together with the impact of European Union direct-ives have emphasised the importance of the hospitality industry ensuring that adequate attention is given to the planning and implementation of quality assurance systems and the review of existing practices and procedures.[36] Quality control including retrospective inspection is a necessary part of preventative systems and an important element of the quality management process.[37] However, an effective system of quality assurance involves

more than just 'after the event' activities. It is concerned with demands for increased productivity, reduced costs and improved standard of the end products and services to the
consumer.[38]

The need for a systematic approach

Lockwood *et al.* comment on the difficulty of managing quality in hospitality operations.
This is complicated by the complex blend of production and service elements that need
to be managed over the short cycle of operations. Although there is an obvious need for
a systematic and all-encompassing approach, only a few hospitality operations have risen
to the challenge. The need for a systematic approach to quality management is evident.
To be effective, quality assurance must involve the development of a proactive operating
philosophy and approach, including the motivation and involvement of people across departmental barriers. From case studies of a number of hospitality organisations, Lockwood
et al. conclude that 'managing quality into an organisation, and keeping it there, is no
different, and not separate, from management of the organisation as a whole'.[39]

Quality assurance therefore relates to the entire process of management and is an integral
part of the clarification of objectives and policy, planning (including design), organising,
directing and guiding, and controlling performance. As an all-embracing concept quality
assurance is increasingly encompassed as part of the development of a Total Quality
Management (TQM) culture.[40] (TQM is discussed in Chapter 12.)

The measurement of service quality

Effective control systems are necessary in order to ensure that the required levels and standards of performance are maintained. In a service industry, control systems should relate
to the quality of activities and processes that create customer satisfaction. One common
measure is the guest questionnaire or comments card, a typical example of which is given
in Figure 11.6.

However, Johnston suggests that a single measure of service quality would need to establish the degree of conformity to overall expectations and follow-up activities would need
to be used to pinpoint problems and complaints. 'A single measure would ask the questions: did the service meet your expectations, or was it worse or better than expected?'[41]
More comprehensive sets of measures would be based on the analysis of critical points
and activities of the operations of the establishment.

Intangible nature of services

The characteristics of services mean that it is often difficult to establish specific indicators
of effective performance. The intangible nature of services coupled with the individual
demands of customers means that the actual delivery of services may differ widely.
Benefits derived from services are associated with feelings and emotions. The quality of
service in a hospitality organisation is usually identified both with its general culture and
ambience, and with the disposition and attitudes of staff.

It is possible, however, to establish more specific measures of organisational effectiveness. You may recall that in Chapter 2 we considered the hotel as an open system and
identified a number of possible measures of achievement. These measures could include,
for example, returned customers, occupancy rates, recommendations such as 'star' ratings,
cash flow and accounting ratios.

Figure 11.6: An example of a guest questionnaire

COMMENT CARD

Dear Guest

Welcome to   Hotel. We do hope that you will have an enjoyable stay with us, and that means that we must ensure that every facet of our hotel meets your expectations. We therefore ask your assistance in completing the Comment Card.

If the hotel staff are unable to rectify any problems which you may experience, please contact the General Manager who will be pleased to assist you.

Thank you for choosing   Hotel.

Date of:
arrival:

Number
of nights:

	Excellent	Good	Unsatisfactory
ARRIVAL			
Reception	☐	☐	☐
Porters	☐	☐	☐
BEDROOMS			
Appearance	☐	☐	☐
Comfort	☐	☐	☐
Quality of service	☐	☐	☐
RESTAURANT			
Breakfast			
Quality of Service	☐	☐	☐
Quality of Food	☐	☐	☐
Snack lunches			
Quality of Service	☐	☐	☐
Quality of Food	☐	☐	☐
Afternoon tea			
Quality of Service	☐	☐	☐
Quality of Food	☐	☐	☐
Dinner			
Quality of Service	☐	☐	☐
Quality of Food	☐	☐	☐

	Excellent	Good	Unsatisfactory
BAR			
Quality of Service	☐	☐	☐
Appearance	☐	☐	☐
LEISURE FACILITIES			
Swimming Pool	☐	☐	☐
Appearance	☐	☐	☐
Cleanliness	☐	☐	☐
Comfort	☐	☐	☐
GOLF			
Condition of Course	☐	☐	☐
GOLFSHOP			
Appearance	☐	☐	☐
Quality of Service	☐	☐	☐

GENERAL

How did you consider the overall facilities to be?   Excellent ☐   Good ☐   Unsatisfactory ☐

Have you ever stayed at before?   Yes ☐   No ☐

If not how did you select the hotel (i.e. recommended, guide book, advert etc)

Do you intend to visit us again?   Yes ☐   No ☐

YOUR COMMENTS

We would welcome any further comments or suggestions you may wish to make regarding our facilities and overall standards of service.

Name:

Address:

When you have completed our comment card, please seal using the gummed edge on the right and return it to us at the Freepost address on the reverse.

Service procedures and service conviviality

According to Martin, quality service is a complex concept and in the case of restaurants, for example, each exact definition of 'quality' service is unique as each restaurant seeks to fulfill slightly different customer needs. However, regardless of the type of service offered, service quality is always a combination of two major factors – service *procedures* and service *conviviality*.

Procedural service dimensions measure the technical systems involved in getting products and service to the customer, and comprise seven major components: flow of service, timeliness, accommodation, anticipation, communication, customer feedback and supervision. **Convivial** dimensions of service reflect the server's ability to relate to customers as people, to establish rapport and to recognise their needs as human beings. Martin suggests nine notable components of conviviality: attitude, body language, tone of voice, tact, naming names, attentiveness, guidance, suggestive selling and problem-solving.[42]

The management of total design

Drawing from the experiences of manufacturing industries, Hollins and Hollins emphasise the importance of managing the design and implementation of new service products. The concept of total design involves market research, production, accounting and selling, and also the people side, including the structure and operation of teams and their training. Specific aspects of service design include attention to queuing and the incorporation of modern technology.[43]

Quality function deployment

According to Jeong and Oh, hospitality has witnessed increasing competition for high service quality and customer satisfaction, and research has become significant in the industry. They suggest it would be desirable that a systematic, structured framework, Quality Function Deployment (QFD), becomes available to assist management in developing successful strategies for the deployment of service functions as well as service innovations. QFD can be viewed as part of a Total Quality Management process and provides structured guidelines for redesigning services as well as developing new products. It is used to intertwine customer needs, service design/management requirements, target design goals, and competitive product/service evaluations.[44]

Supervision and supportive relationships

Securing the right balance between delegation, individual freedom of action and control requires the correct level of supervision. A fundamental concept of participative management is the principle of supportive relationships, which we discussed in Chapter 5. Managers should have high performance aspirations for themselves and for every member of staff. A supportive relationship requires group decision-making and an employee-centred style of supervision.

In order to achieve a high level of performance it is necessary to create a manager–subordinate relationship which is supportive and intended to enhance self-esteem and ego. Subordinates should feel a sense of personal worth and importance, and maintain their sense of significance and dignity.

Employee-centred or job-centred supervision

Likert provides a contrast between employee-centred and job-centred styles of supervision and orientation towards staff. A job-centred approach to supervision is illustrated by the following point of view.

> *This interest-in-people approach is all right, but it's a luxury. I've got to keep pressure on for production, and when I get production up, then I can afford to take time to show an interest in my employees and their problems.*

An employee-centred approach to supervision is illustrated by this contrasting point of view.

> *One way in which we accomplish a high level of production is by letting people do the job the way they want to so long as they accomplish the objectives. I believe in letting them take time out from the monotony. Make them feel that they are something special, not just the run of the mill . . . If you keep employees from feeling hounded, they are apt to pull out the necessary effort to get the work done in the required time.*
>
> *If people know their jobs I believe in letting them make decisions. I believe in delegating decision-making. Of course, if there's anything that affects the whole division, then the two assistant managers, the three section heads and sometimes the assistant section heads come in and we discuss it. I don't believe in saying that this is the way it's going to be. After all, once supervision and management are in agreement there won't be any trouble selling the staff the idea. My job is dealing with human beings rather than with the work.*[45]

Likert also provides a list of 12 questions to test the extent of supportive relationships and whether a superior's behaviour is favourable (Figure 11.7).

Supportive relationships and control

The relevance of Likert's list of questions on supportive relationships, linked with the importance of maintaining control, is emphasised by Venison.

> *In my experience almost every one of those questions could be asked of any hotel employee in almost any environment and at almost any level in the organisation and if the answers were negative the hotel would not be functioning as well as it could. The creation of a supportive environment should not be confused with the abdication of control or the removal of discipline. In no way is it suggested that management should absolve itself from these things. In fact discipline is exceptionally important in achieving high standards but discipline invariably means confrontation and confrontation can be coped with within a supportive environment because people can call a spade a spade without fear of being misunderstood.*[46]

The exercise of control

The exercise of control is an expression of management systems and style. Under traditional assumptions of organisation and management, control is viewed as an essential feature of formal organisation and a hierarchical structure of authority. Controls will be based on the use of routine procedures and the exercise of rules and regulations in an attempt

Figure 11.7:
Principle of
Supportive
Relationships
Questionnaire

1. How much confidence and trust do you feel your superior has in you? How much do you have in him?

2. To what extent does your boss convey to you a feeling of confidence that you can do your job successfully? Does he expect the 'impossible' and fully believe you can and will do it?

3. To what extent is he interested in helping you to achieve and maintain a good income?

4. To what extent does your superior try to understand your problems and do something about them?

5. How much is your superior really interested in helping you with your personal and family problems?

6. How much help do you get from your superior in doing your work?
   a. How much is he interested in training you and helping you learn better ways of doing your work?
   b. How much does he help you solve your problems constructively – not tell you the answer but help you think through your problems?
   c. To what extent does he see that you get the supplies, budget, equipment, etc., you need to do your job well?

7. To what extent is he interested in helping you get the training which will assist you in being promoted?

8. To what extent does your superior try to keep you informed about matters related to your job?

9. How fully does your superior share information with you about the company, its financial condition, earnings, etc., or keep such information to himself/herself?

10. Does your superior ask your opinion when a problem comes up which involves your work? Does he value your ideas and seek them and endeavour to use them?

11. Is he friendly and easily approached?

12. To what extent is your superior generous in the credit and recognition given to others for the accomplishments and contributions rather than seeking to claim all the credit himself?

(*Source:* Likert R., *The Human Organisation: Its Management and Value*, McGraw-Hill (1967), pp. 48–49, with permission of McGraw-Hill, Inc.)

to create consistency and predictability in behaviour. This form of control is in keeping with a bureaucratic form of structure.

Another view of control is based on behavioural assumptions. Control is seen as a feature of interpersonal influence and takes place within a network structure of interaction and communications. Control is a function of the common commitment to the objectives of the organisation. This view of control is more in keeping with the human relations approach and the belief that the exercise of a high level of control is self-defeating.

Assumptions about behaviour

Control systems are invariably viewed with a certain amount of suspicion, and possible resentment, by members of staff. Often, control over behaviour is perceived as a threat to the need satisfaction of the individual. Even when control systems are well designed and operated there is often strong resistance and attempts at non-compliance from those members of staff affected by them. Therefore, if control systems are to be successful in leading to improved quality and performance, they require attention to the style of management and to the factors which influence human behaviour.

The style of managerial leadership is a function of the manager's attitudes towards people, and assumptions about human nature and behaviour – for example, McGregor's Theory X and Theory Y.[47] The Theory X manager believes that people have an inherent dislike of work, wish to avoid responsibility, and must be coerced and directed, and threatened with punishment in order to achieve results. Such a manager is likely, therefore, to be interested in only limited schemes of delegation with clearly defined limits, and the exercise of close control and authority over members of staff.

By contrast, Theory Y is based on the principle of the integration of individual and organisational goals. People can learn to accept and to seek responsibility for their own actions, and will exercise self-direction and self-control in the service of objectives to which they are committed. The Theory Y manager is more likely to be interested in wider schemes of delegation based on consultation and participation with subordinates, and with responsibility willingly accepted out of personal commitment to the aims and tasks of the establishment.

A behavioural approach to management control

In the hospitality industry people are part of the finished product that the customer is paying for. Customer satisfaction is likely to be affected as much by the courtesy, helpfulness and efficiency of the staff as by the standard of food and beverage and accommodation.[48] As we saw in Chapter 10, the successful management of human resources is therefore an important feature of the hospitality industry. The organisational and staffing characteristics of the industry might suggest the need for the exercise of a high level of management control over the behaviour and performance of staff. This, however, is not necessarily the best approach.

If control systems are to be accepted by members of staff, attention must be given to behavioural factors. The basis of a behavioural approach is founded not just on the provision of control systems but also on the meaningfulness and importance of work, and securing the motivation and commitment of staff.

People like to take pride in their work. The hospitality industry is fortunate in this respect as emphasis is usually placed on the standard of quality, rather than the quantity, of its products and services. There should be a built-in incentive for staff to produce high-quality work, for example in the preparation of food or the cleanliness of rooms. If staff derive a sense of personal satisfaction from performing a competent job there should be little need for a high level of supervision.[49]

Control systems provide an interface between human behaviour and the process of management. We have seen that underlying all control systems is the attempt to influence the behaviour of people.

> *The broad objective of the control function is to effectively employ all the resources committed to an organisation's operations. However, the fact that non-human resources depend on human effort for their utilisation makes control, in the final analysis, the regulation of human performance.*[50]

The control of service activities

The nature of the service industry (discussed in Chapter 2), for example the direct inter-action between employees and customers, the personal nature of activities, intangibility and the heterogeneous nature of customers, means that it is difficult to establish objective standards of effective performance. As a result managers may be tempted to revert to the exercise of control in terms of a feature of formal organisation and authority, as discussed above.

As Riley, for example, comments:

> *In conditions where standards are subjective, managers always try to overcome this subjectivity by standardisation, checklists and other aids which make what is required more specific. In other words, they try to improve formal methods of control. The problem is that these can never be totally successful. What the hotel and catering manager has to realise is that the effective weapons are personal. Example and vigilance with the objective of achieving a shared value with the employees as to what constitutes 'good' in the various circumstances of the operation are effective controls. It is a trust relationship. This relationship between the nature of a job and how management can control it, leads to an important issue for the industry – control versus personal service.*[51]

The effectiveness of management control systems will therefore depend upon both their design and operation, and the attitudes of staff and the way they respond to them. Control often provokes an emotional response from those affected by it. The activities of a man-agement control system raise important considerations of the human factors and of the management of people.

Implementation of a behavioural approach

There are a number of ways in which the manager can attempt to implement a behavioural approach to control.

- *Participation.* The more that staff cooperate and participate in the setting up of control procedures, the more likely they are to accept them. If staff are involved in the decision-making process there is greater encouragement to exercise self-control over their level of performance.

- *Understanding.* Staff should understand the purpose and nature of the control systems. If staff understand and accept the reasons for control, this will help make for improved manager–subordinate relationships.

- *Motivation.* Lack of positive motivation can lead to frustrated behaviour and poor job performance, and result in a higher level of control. Recognition for a satisfactory level of attainment coupled with a suitable reward system, as integral parts of control, can do much to motivate staff and encourage good results. No amount of management control will prove effective unless employees are positively motivated to achieve a high level of performance.

- *Organisation structure*. Features of organisational design will influence the nature and operation of control systems. A 'mechanistic' structure is more likely to be characterised by directions and orders, formal rules and regulations. But with an 'organic' structure there is greater emphasis on a network system of control, communications and authority.

- *Groups and informal organisation*. The operations of groups and the informal organisation influence the functioning of control systems. Informal group 'norms' and peer pressure can be one of the most powerful forms of control. Membership of a harmonious and effective work group can lead to improved motivation and job satisfaction. Socialisation can create a feeling of commitment to the group and reduce the need for formal management control.

- *Management systems*. The character of control processes is one of the organisational variables identified in Likert's four-fold model of management systems: System 1 (benevolent authoritative), System 2 (exploitative authoritative), System 3 (consultative) and System 4 (participative group).[52] With System 1, review and control functions are concentrated with top management and exercised through the hierarchical structure. With System 4, concern for the control function is shared widely throughout the organisation, the formal and informal organisations share the same goals, and there is an emphasis on self-guidance and problem-solving.

Long-term improvement in performance

Likert's findings would appear to have particular relevance to the hospitality industry. In Systems 1 and 2 organisations, high performance goals by superiors coupled with high-pressure supervision using tight budgets and controls yield high productivity *initially* because of compliance based on fear. However, because of unfavourable attitudes, poor communications, lack of cooperative motivation and restriction of output, *the long-term result is high absence and turnover, and low productivity and earnings*. The nearer the behavioural characteristics of an organisation approach to System 4, the more likely it is that this will lead to a long-term improvement in performance.

Maintaining freedom of action

Providing members of staff with a genuine sense of empowerment, for example through membership of autonomous project teams and quality circles and as part of a total quality management philosophy, is an important aspect of a behavioural approach to management control.[53] The more that staff feel they are sharing in a common responsibility for improving service delivery to the customers and are empowered to take corrective action when necessary, the more likely they are to develop a commitment to the quality and performance of hospitality operations.

Modern methods of management can assist the maintenance of management control without reducing the individual's freedom of action. Procedures such as management by exception, staff appraisal and management by objectives can help to maintain control without inhibiting the growth of delegation. A system of Management by Objectives (discussed

Figure 11.8: MBO and management control

Activities in management by objectives	Management control system
Agree what you expect from me	Planning what is desired Specification of objectives and targets
Give me an opportunity to perform	Establishing defined standards of performance
Let me know how I'm getting on	Monitoring and reviewing actual performance Control information and feedback
Give me guidance where I need it	Comparing actual performance against planned targets What can be done to improve performance?
Reward me according to my contribution	Recognition of achievement Motivation for further improvement in performance
Control, review and adjustment	Taking corrective action

(*Source:* adapted from Humble J, *Management by Objectives*, Management Publications Ltd (1972), p. 46.)

in Chapter 5) may allow staff to accept greater responsibility and to make a higher level of personal contribution.

Management by objectives as a control system

Participation is an inherent feature of an effective system of management by objectives (MBO). There is an assumption that most people will direct and control themselves willingly if they share in the setting of their objectives. MBO can therefore be applied as a modern and effective method of control (Figure 11.8).[54] It can be used in a positive and constructive manner to provide a control system related to performance appraisal and career progression.

Financial and accounting controls

Financial and accounting systems are frequently thought of as the major part of management control systems and especially in the hospitality industry.[55] And the reasons for this are easy to understand.

- The stewardship of financial resources and the need to demonstrate value for money is of vital concern to the organisation. Control systems are often geared to highlighting the easily identifiable performance of sales, costs and profits.

- Organisational aims, objectives and targets are often expressed in financial terms and measured in terms of profitability. Results are measured and reported in financial terms.

- Money is quantifiable and a precise unit of measurement. It is easily understood, and is often used as a common denominator and as a basis for comparison.

- Financial limits are easy to apply as a measure of control or limit to authority, and are easy to relate to. We have seen, for example, that control is a necessary part of delegation. A manager might delegate to a subordinate the authority to incur expenditure on certain items up to a given financial limit.

It is understandable, therefore, that so much attention is given to financial and accounting systems of control. Managers rely on an accurate information system as a basis for control and this information is often expressed in financial terms. Management accounting tools such as budgets, ratio analysis and standard costing provide helpful information for control of the operations of the various departments and activities of the hotel. As Venison, for example, emphasises:

> the production of correct and up-to-date accounts is absolutely vital to the success of any hotel venture . . . As an hotel manager . . . you have a primary duty to ensure that somebody is effectively handling the accounts function.[56]

Attention to behavioural factors

There is of course nothing wrong with the use of financial or accounting systems of control. The important point is the manner in which such controls are applied and their effects on the behaviour of staff. Consideration must be given to the behavioural factors and the motivation for staff to improve their performance.[57]

Accounting control systems such as internal audit, management by exception and budgetary control tend to operate in a negative way and to report only on the unfavourable performance, or on variances which may have adverse consequences. As a result there is no specific recognition from management and only a limited sense of achievement for favourable performance. There is little, if any, positive motivation. Budgetary control may be perceived as a means of exerting pressure on staff and can also be seen as imposing restriction on individual freedom of action.[58]

As with other forms of control, financial and accounting systems have positive as well as negative effects. If control systems are to be successful in leading to improved performance, they should be designed and implemented in a constructive and rewarding way. To do this, they must take account of the individual, social and organisational factors which determine people's patterns of behaviour.

Concern for the whole process of management

We have commented previously that the focus of effort in the hospitality industry has traditionally been directed narrowly to profitability and short-term cost-consciousness. However, management control embraces far more than just financial or accounting considerations. It should be concerned with the whole process of management: with the extent to which the aims and objectives of the hospitality organisation are being achieved and with improvement in performance.

Control includes consideration of such factors as quality, judgement, customer satisfaction, social responsibilities, and the human factor and the effective management of people. Regrettably, however, it appears that the industry has given little attention to evaluating the contribution and worth of its human resources or to accounting for the value of its employees.[59]

Summary

- For the hospitality organisation to function effectively there must be processes of delegation, supervision and control. Delegation embraces both authority and responsibility but managers retain accountability (ultimate responsibility) for the actions and decisions of subordinates. Delegation creates a special manager–subordinate relationship. Properly handled delegation is a powerful instrument of management and should lead to improved use of human resources.

- There are, however, a number of potential difficulties and problem areas. Delegation entails reliance on other people. The concept of ultimate responsibility gives rise to the need for effective systems of management control which must be kept in balance with delegation. The whole purpose of control is improvement in individual and organisational performance.

- Control is far reaching and can take a number of different forms. One method of attempting to control and improve the activities of staff is through a system of performance appraisal. A significant aspect of management control in the hospitality industry is that of quality assurance and to the products, services and processes that create customer satisfaction.

- By their very nature, control systems are concerned with the behaviour of people. The exercise of control is an expression of management systems and style. Securing the right balance between delegation, freedom of action and management control requires the correct level of supervision and supportive relationships. Attention must be given to behavioural factors.

- Financial and accounting systems are an important aspect of management control but such systems need to be designed in a constructive and rewarding way. However, management control embraces far more than just financial or accounting considerations. It should be concerned with the whole process of management including accounting for the value of employees.

Appendix: Swallow Hotels – performance appraisal

Introduction

These Guidance Notes aim to provide information on the performance appraisal process when using the staff performance appraisal documentation.

Purpose of performance appraisal

The appraisal meeting provides the opportunity for the manager and job holder to summarise performance for the period under review. The process of reviewing performance and action planning should be ongoing and not confined to the annual appraisal meeting.

The key objectives of the performance appraisal scheme are to help the appraisee (job holder):

- review performance in relation to the achievement of objectives set at the last appraisal;
- identify and review characteristics which directly affect performance;
- establish personal performance objectives which are linked to the Company's business objectives;
- establish assistance needed to achieve objectives and/or improve performance;
- increase their level of motivation.

Important considerations

- Comments on performance and progress should be made as part of a normal day-to-day working relationship, not saved up for the annual appraisal.
- Achievement of actual results must be assessed, not the appraisee's personal characteristics.
- The purpose of assessing past performance is not to apportion blame but to achieve an improvement in future performance.
- Action required and any training identified to assist with the achievement of performance objectives and personal development plans must be established jointly.

The appraisal meeting

The appraisal process

- Details of stages; responsibility; and timescales

Venue

- Ensure that the meeting takes place in a quiet room with no disturbances.

Welcome

- Welcome and put the appraisee at ease.
- Explain the purpose and scope of the performance appraisal.
- Check the details on the front of the appraisal form, i.e. name, job title, start date, etc.

Review of appraisal preparation form

- Review and discuss part 1 of the appraisal form which should have been completed prior to the meeting.

Review objectives

- Review achievement of objectives set at last appraisal (refer to appraisal form completed at last appraisal; comments by the appraisee and appraiser should have been made prior to the appraisal meeting).

Performance characteristics

- Discuss the performance characteristics which are appropriate to the appraisee. Complete with comments and examples.

Career development

- Discuss career development (refer to question 5 on the appraisal preparation form).
- *Note*: Not everybody will want career development. This should be noted on the appraisal form and the appraisee should be assured that it is perfectly acceptable not to want career growth; however, personal development is to be encouraged.

Future objectives

- Agree objectives with standards of performance and timescales for the next appraisal period.

    (A performance objective is a statement of a desired result or condition to be achieved by a specified time and in accordance with quantitative and/or qualitative standards. The ultimate purpose is to improve the organisational effectiveness and individual performance.)

    Performance objectives should be:

    S Specific and clearly linked to the hotel/department's objectives and business plan
    M Measurable with clearly defined standards
    A Achievable and realistic
    R Results orientated – a description of what is to be achieved
    T Time bound, e.g. start by . . . ; finish by . . . ; reviewed on . . .

- Limit performance objectives to cover areas of highest priority. The maximum number of performance objectives should be 6–8.
- Write performance objectives in a clear and concise manner – avoid jargon and technical language.

    Objectives can be:

    Quantifiable, for example:
    - number achieved
    - number processed
    - sales volumes
    - share of market
    - percent utilisation

    Non-quantifiable, for example:
    - quality of proposals
    - type of recommendation
    - quality for ideas generated
    - type of change implemented
    - degree of customer satisfaction
    - performance against specific criteria
    - quality of service

    Refer to examples of how to write performance objectives and standards.

Training and Development

- Agree training and development needs. This may include projects, reading assignments, visits, coaching, distance learning, off job courses etc.

Overall performance

- Agree an overall assessment of the appraisee's performance for the complete review period. When completing this section consider:
  - how well the objectives / targets were achieved;
  - how well the appraisee performed in relation to others;
  - the overall performance of the department or function.
- Each definition allows for variations in describing the actual level of performance. Therefore, an individual who is judged to have performed at a higher level than **good** but who has not been outstanding in every aspect can be marked in the second of the **outstanding** boxes.

Appraising manager's comments

- After the appraisal summarise the appraisee's review period and note any other comments or information relevant to the appraisee's job, performance and/or development.
- Sign and date the appraisal form.

Appraisee's comments

- Return the full appraisal form to the appraisee to complete:
  - the appraisee comments section with comments relating to his/her appraisal, job, performance and/or development;
  - signature and dating of the appraisal form;
  - and return to appraiser.

Completed appraisal form

- Issue a copy of the completed appraisal form to the appraisee.
- Appraiser to retain a copy of future objectives and training needs.
- Forward completed appraisal documentation to the Personnel Department.

Interim reviews

For annual objectives to be achieved successfully, it is necessary to review progress at least twice a year. This will help ensure:

- better motivation of the job holder as he/she will have the opportunity to discuss progress and any problems on a regular basis;
- review of the job holder's objective achievement;
- the opportunity for discussion if job holder's objectives change during the year.

Timing of performance appraisals

New employees

- The timing of a new employee's appraisal should relate to their start date with the Company.

● Objectives should be agreed towards the end of the new employee's trial period. Their first annual appraisal should then take place approximately one year after their objectives were agreed. Interim reviews should take place.

Existing employees

Existing employees should be appraised on an annual basis.

Appraisal skills training

To assist with the appraisal meeting and completion of documentation all appraisers should attend the Company appraisal skills training course.

Appraisal preparation form: Part 1

1. What aspects of your job do you feel have gone particularly well and why?

Appraiser comment:

_____

2. What aspects of your job do you feel have not gone so well?

Appraiser comment:

_____

3. What action can be taken to help and who by?

Appraiser comment:

_____

4. What skills do you have that are not fully utilised in the job?

Appraiser comment:

_____

5. What are your future aims and how would you like to see your career developing with the company?

Appraiser comment:

_____

6. What other areas would you like to discuss at the interview?

Appraiser comment:

_____

7. What personal goals would you like to achieve over the next 6 to 12 months?

Appraiser comment:

_____

Appraisal preparation form: Part 2

1. Performance characteristics

The following performance characteristics are relevant to the position of the job holder. The appraiser will write comments against each characteristic on the performance of the job holder.

N.B. Not all characteristics will be appropriate in every situation.

Characteristics	*Comments with examples*
Customer/guest relations	
Job/product knowledge	
Quality of work	
Communication skills	
Teamwork and attitude to colleagues	
Attitude to work	
Willingness to learn	
Timekeeping/absenteeism	
Other (specify)	

2. Employee career development plan

(a) What skills are not being fully utilised in the job holder's current position?	
(b) How could the job holder's career be developed in the next 1–2 years based upon the current appraisal and overall view of performance?	
(c) What has the job holder said about career interests or expectations?	

3. Action required

(a) Future objectives

Objective	Standard of performance	Target date

(b) Training and development (short/medium/long term)

Training/action	By whom	Purpose	Approximate time frame

4. Overall performance

Rate the job holder's overall performance according to the definitions below, based on their performance for the complete review period.

Outstanding
- ❑ A performance which is consistently outstanding in all key aspects, and which exceed every requirement
- ❑ A performance consistently above required standards, but with a lack of achievement in one non-key area

Good
- ❑ A highly acceptable performance and outstanding in one or two aspects.
- ❑ A good and highly acceptable performance in all areas
- ❑ A good performance, but with one or two relatively minor aspects/tasks below expectations

Satisfactory
- ❑ An acceptable performance which is up to expectations in most areas, but not in others

Unsatisfactory
- ❑ A poor performance requiring resolute improvement
- ❑ The requirements of the position have not been met and improvement has not been forthcoming. Serious consideration should be given to the job holder's ability to carry out his/her responsibilities and he/she should be made aware of this.

5. Appraising manager's comments

Signature: .... Date: ....

6. Appraisee's comments

Signature: .... Date: ....

(*Note:* There is a separate set of guidance notes for Management Performance.) *The author is grateful to Marilyn Harding-Brown, Human Resources Director, Swallow Hotels, for providing this information.*

Review and discussion questions

1. Explain fully the meaning of delegation at both the organisational level and the individual level. Distinguish clearly between the concepts of authority, responsibility and accountability. What is meant by the nature of dual responsibility in effective delegation?

2. Suggest ways in which delegation, if properly handled, should lead to the optimum use of the human resources of the hospitality organisation.

3. What is meant by the acceptance theory of authority and the nature of human behaviour? Why do you think it is that many managers often fail to delegate successfully?

4. Detail the need for management control in the hospitality industry. As a departmental manager, how would you attempt to achieve the full benefits of delegation while still maintaining effective control of subordinate staff?

5. Explain the importance of quality assurance processes within the hospitality industry. Discuss the particular difficulties of the measurement of service quality.

6. Distinguish between employee-centred and job-centred styles of supervision. Discuss the importance of supportive relationships and control.

7. Control systems provide an interface between human behaviour and the process of management. Explain fully how you, as a manager, would attempt to implement a behavioural approach to control.

8. Discuss critically the extent to which you believe attention should be given to financial and accounting systems of control in a hospitality organisation of your choice.

Assignment 1

Assess critically the effectiveness of a process of delegation. Arrange to interview a manager and subordinate staff in a hospitality organisation of your choice. Give details of the nature of delegation involved and the circumstances under which it arose.

(i) Note the extent to which the five main stages in a planned and systematic approach appear to be followed.

(ii) Explain in particular: the nature of the briefing, guidance and training given, and the time limits, check points and performance standards established.

(iii) Enquire of (a) the manager and (b) the member(s) of staff concerned, the benefits each gained from the delegation, and any difficulties or problems involved.

(iv) Explain ways in which you believe the process of delegation appears to be successful or not. Where appropriate suggest ways in which the process of delegation could be made more effective.

(v) Where possible, compare and contrast your findings with your own experiences of delegation.

Assignment 2

From your own experience of a hospitality organisation, answer carefully and fully the 12 questions in Likert's Principle of Supportive Relationships Questionnaire. (Refer back to Figure 11.7, page 425.)

(i) Assess to what extent the principle of supportive relationships is applied well and the behaviour of the superior is favourable. Relate actual examples.

(ii) Highlight negative answers which suggest that the organisation is not functioning as well as it could. Explain fully the actual or likely consequences of these negative answers.

(iii) Summarise the results of the questionnaire, and share and discuss your answers with colleagues. What overall conclusions do you reach concerning the nature of supportive relationships in the hospitality industry?

Case study: Too hot to handle

When offered promotion to manager of the three-star Abbotts Oak hotel, Pat Morgan's reactions had been a mixture of pleasure and surprise, tempered with concern about the added responsibilities of the position. Two months after Morgan's promotion, Peter Carlton was appointed head chef at the Abbotts Oak by the joint owner, Mary Parker. Shortly after taking up his appointment Parker informed Carlton that he was expected to improve the performance of the kitchen in whatever manner he thought appropriate.

At first there were no signs of any problems and as far as Morgan was aware Carlton appeared to confirm his reputation for being very competent and hardworking. Within a matter of weeks, however, the manager started to hear rumblings of discontent among members of staff. A receptionist ▷

had mentioned to Morgan that Carlton was surly and had an offensive manner. But no one had complained formally to Morgan and customers appeared to be very pleased with the standard of the meals.

A couple of weeks passed and then the manager overheard two members of the kitchen staff talking about Carlton. They said that he worked very hard, certainly knew his job and was obviously a very good chef. But they were moaning about his disgusting behaviour, that he was swearing all the time and rude to everyone. Then, ten days later, another receptionist complained to the manager that Carlton was uncooperative, foulmouthed and very quickly showed signs of temper.

Morgan listened carefully and then replied that trade in the restaurant was increasing and customers seemed very pleased. The manager continued: 'We are always told that good chefs tend to have a temperamental nature so I suppose we have to make some allowances. But leave it with me and I will look into things.'

Matters reached a head two weeks later, however, when Morgan felt compelled to reprimand Carlton for disparaging remarks to a waitress who had clearly been distressed. 'Now look here, we just cannot tolerate this obnoxious behaviour of yours,' said Morgan. During the subsequent exchange Carlton became very abusive and agitated, and then threw a tin of biscuits in the direction of Morgan. Carlton refused to apologise and suggested that Morgan should pay more attention to problems nearer home. Morgan retaliated angrily: 'I won't have any of your excuses. Are you going to apologise today, or are you going to leave tomorrow?'

'If that's how you feel, I'm off. You know what you can do with your job,' replied Carlton who turned sharply and hurried out of the kitchen.

After a brief pause Morgan hurried after Carlton and caught up with him walking in the direction of the car park. 'You know that if you don't work your notice you won't be entitled to any pay.' Carlton did not stop and said nothing; but grunted, and gave a wry smile.

The following day a clearly displeased Mary Parker called Morgan to her office. She reminded Morgan that Carlton had come with glowing references and that it had been necessary to offer him a high salary plus bonuses in order to secure his appointment.

Parker continued: 'You know that it is hotel policy to ask customers if they had enjoyed their meal. Since Carlton has been here there have been virtually no complaints and . . .'

'So you are saying that the ends justify the means and that customer satisfaction is more important than good staff relationships,' interrupted Morgan.

'I am saying that acceptance of responsibility involves an obligation to achieve a satisfactory level of performance,' replied Parker.

'That may be,' responded Morgan, 'but who determines the standards and the manner in which results are achieved? And what about the effects on other members of staff? Anyway, who is in charge of the kitchen, me or Carlton?'

Parker responded tersely: 'I am the one in charge here, although you know that I leave the routine management and matters of staffing to you. As I hadn't heard anything to the contrary, I naturally assumed everything was running satisfactorily. But now I suppose I must intervene. And what on earth made you threaten to withhold Carlton's pay?'

'It wasn't like that,' replied Morgan, 'and don't forget that the second chef is about to leave on a postponed holiday.'

'Look, until I decide what needs to be done I expect you as manager to sort out this silly personality clash and to . . .'

'So what are you telling me?' interjected Morgan.

'That I have reinstated Carlton,' replied Parker.

'And what about my position? How does that make me look?' queried Morgan.

'You are still the manager here, but I have always believed that the more confident and assured a manager the easier to exercise authority and the less to fear competition from competent subordinates. The balance between successful delegation and effective control is a fine line, and . . .'

'I see,' said Morgan sharply, then left without another word while Parker was still talking.

Ten minutes later Morgan returned and without knocking entered the owner's office. The manager placed a letter of resignation on the desk in front of a disturbed-looking Mary Parker and said: 'Either he goes or I do,' and stormed out.

TASKS

(i) **Analyse the various issues and problems which are raised by this case.**

(ii) **Explain fully the actions you would recommend should be taken in order to help resolve these issues and problems.**

Notes and references

1. Scott M, *More Time, Less Stress*, Random House (1998).
2. Drucker P F, *The Practice of Management*, Heinemann Professional (1989).
3. Riley M, *Human Resource Management in the Hospitality and Tourism Industry*, 2nd edn, Butterworth-Heinemann (1996), p. 73.
4. Mooney J D, *The Principles of Organization*, rev'd edn, Harper & Row (1947), p. 17.
5. Gracie S, 'Delegate don't Abdicate', *Management Today*, March 1999, p. 93.
6. Gray I, *Henri Fayol's General and Industrial Management*, Pitman (1988).
7. Gullen H V and Rhodes G E, *Management in the Hotel and Catering Industry*, Batsford (1983), p. 49.
8. Newstrom J W and Davis K, *Organizational Behavior: Human Behavior at Work*, 9th edn, McGraw-Hill (1993).
9. Forte, Charles (Lord), *Forte: The Autobiography of Charles Forte*, Sidgwick & Jackson (1986), p. 125.
10. For example, Peters T J and Austin N, *A Passion for Excellence: The Leadership Difference*, Random House (1985); and Waterman R H, *The Frontiers of Excellence*, Nicholas Brealey (1994).
11. Kanter R M, *The Change Masters*, Routledge (1988).
12. See, for example, Vinton D, 'Delegation for Employee Development', *Training and Development Journal,* vol. 41, no. 1, January 1987, pp. 65–67.
13. Peter L J and Hull R, *The Peter Principle*, Pan Books (1970), p. 22.
14. Wood R C, *Organizational Behaviour for Hospitality Management*, Butterworth-Heinemann (1994), p. 45.
15. Hall K and Savery L K, 'Stress Management', *Management Decision*, vol. 25, no. 6, 1987, pp. 29–35.
16. Mann S, 'Give a Little Gain a Lot', *Professional Manager*, March 1999, p. 32.
17. Stewart R, *The Reality of Management*, 2nd edn, Pan Books (1986), p. 190.
18. Kourdi J, *Successful Delegation In a Week*, Institute of Management and Hodder & Stoughton (1998).

19. Forte, Charles (Lord), *Forte: The Autobiography of Charles Forte*, Sidgwick & Jackson (1986), p. 124.

20. Tarpey D, 'Handling With Care', *Caterer and Hotelkeeper*, vol. 12, July 1990, pp. 52–53.

21. Gracie S, 'Delegate don't Abdicate', *Management Today*, March 1999, p. 94.

22. Handy C B, *Understanding Organizations*, 4th edn, Penguin (1993), p. 283.

23. See, for example, Blake R R, and Mouton J S, *The Managerial Grid III*, Gulf Publishing Company (1985).

24. Forte, Charles (Lord), *Forte: The Autobiography of Charles Forte*, Sidgwick & Jackson (1986), p. 190.

25. Mullins L and Banks G, 'How Well am I Doing?', *Euhofa Journal*, International Association of Directors of Hotel Schools, Switzerland, no. 18, June 1986.

26. Lockwood A, Baker M and Ghillyer A (eds), *Quality Management in Hospitality*, Cassell (1996), p. 158.

27. Boella M J, *Human Resource Management in the Hospitality Industry*, 6th edn, Stanley Thornes (1996), p. 107.

28. Lucas R, *Managing Employee Relations in the Hotel and Catering Industry*, Cassell (1995), p. 162.

29. See, for example, Crainer S, 'Feedback to the Future', *Management Today*, June 1997, pp. 90–92.

30. See, for example, Mill R C, *Managing for Productivity in the Hospitality Industry*, Van Nostrand Reinhold (1989).

31. For a more detailed account of performance appraisal, see Mullins L J, *Management and Organisational Behaviour*, 5th edn, Financial Times Pitman Publishing (1999).

32. Umbreit W T, Eder R W and McConnell J P, 'Performance Appraisals: Making Them Fair and Making Them Work', in Rutherford D G (ed.), *Hotel Management and Operations*, Van Nostrand Reinhold (1990), pp. 299–310.

33. See, for example, Salaman G, *Class and the Corporation*, Fontana (1981).

34. Lawler E E, 'Control Systems in Organisations', in Dunnette M D (ed.), *Handbook of Industrial and Organizational Psychology*, Rand McNally (1976).

35. Luthans F, *Organizational Behavior*, 5th edn, McGraw-Hill (1989), p. 547.

36. See, for example, East J, *Managing Quality in The Catering Industry*, Croner (1993).

37. Johns N, 'Quality Management in the Hospitality Industry: Part 2. Applications, Systems and Techniques', *International Journal of Contemporary Hospitality Management*, vol. 4, no. 4, 1992, pp. 3–7.

38. Hayman K G, 'Total Quality Management and Quality Assurance within the Food and Hospitality Service Industries', *The Manager: Journal of The Institute of Commercial Management*, March 1992, pp. 10–11.

39. Lockwood A, Baker M and Ghillyer A (eds), *Quality Management in Hospitality*, Cassell (1996).

40. See, for example, Simmons P and Teare R, 'Evolving a Total Quality Culture', *International Journal of Contemporary Hospitality Management*, vol. 5, no. 3, 1993, pp. v–viii.

41. Johnston R, 'Operations Management Issues', in Jones P (ed.), *Management in Service Industries*, Pitman (1989), p. 201.

42. Martin W B, 'Defining What Quality Service Is For You', *Cornell HRA Quarterly*, vol. 26, no. 4, February 1986, pp. 32–38.

43. Hollins G and Hollins B, *Total Design: Managing Tile Design Process in the Service Sector*, Pitman (1991).

44. Jeong M and Oh H, 'Quality Function deployment: An extended framework for service quality and customer satisfaction in the hospitality industry', *International Journal of Hospitality Management*, vol. 17, 1998, pp. 375–390.

45. Likert R, *New Patterns of Management*, McGraw-Hill (1961), pp. 7–8.

46. Venison P, *Managing Hotels*, Heinemann (1983), p. 64.

47. McGregor D, *The Human Side of Enterprise*, Penguin (1987).

48. Mullins L J, 'The Personnel Function', *HCIMA Journal*, vol. 94, October 1979, pp. 22–25.

49. See, for example, Keiser J R, *Principles and Practices of Management in the Hospitality Industry*, 2nd edn, Van Nostrand Reinhold (1989).

50. Reeser C and Loper M, *Management: The Key to Organizational Effectiveness*, Scott Foresman (1978), p. 437.

51. Riley M, *Human Resource Management in the Hospitality and Tourism Industry*, 2nd edn, Butterworth-Heinemann (1996), p. 42.

52. Likert R and Likert J G, *New Ways of Managing Conflict*, McGraw-Hill (1976).

53. See, for example, Johns N, 'Quality Management in the Hospitality Industry', *International Journal of Contemporary Hospitality Management: Part 3. Recent Developments*, vol. 5, no. 1, 1993, pp. 10–15.

54. Humble J W, *Management by Objectives*, Management Publications Ltd (1972).

55. See, for example, Medlik S, *The Business of Hotels*, 3rd edn, Butterworth-Heinemann (1994).

56. Venison P, *Managing Hotels*, Heinemann (1983), p. 107.

57. Mullins L J, 'Behavioural Implications of Management Accounting', *Management Accounting*, vol. 59, no. 1, January 1981, pp. 36–39.

58. See, for example, Prior P, 'Communicating: An Enthusiast's View', *Accountancy*, vol. 95, no. 1089, May 1984, p. 69.

59. Maher A, 'Accounting for Human Resources in UK Hotels', *Proceedings of CHME Research Conference*, Manchester Metropolitan University, April 1993.

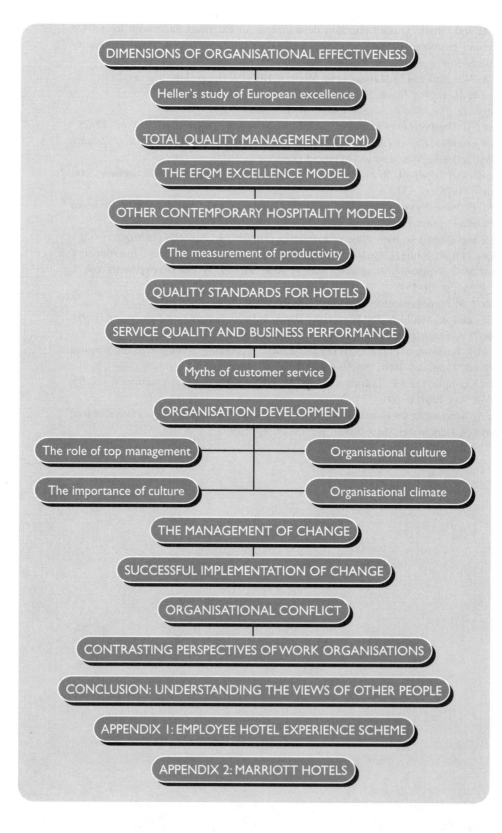

Chapter twelve

Improving organisational performance

Introduction

The hospitality organisation is not only a work organisation, it is also a complex social system and the sum of many interrelated variables. In order to achieve improved performance it is necessary to understand the nature of organisational effectiveness and those factors which influence the successful management of people.

Dimensions of organisational effectiveness

This book has been concerned with interactions among the structure and operation of hospitality organisations, the role of management and the behaviour of people at work. The central theme has been improved organisational performance through the effective management of people (human resources).

Organisations need to be **efficient** in doing the right things with the optimum ratio of outputs to inputs and the use of their resources. But they also need to be **effective** in doing the right things and in their outputs related to a specific purpose, objective or task. **Performance** should be related to such factors as increasing profitability, improved service delivery or obtaining the best results in important areas of organisational activities. Organisations must also ensure that they meet satisfactorily or exceed the demands and requirements of customers, and are **adaptable** to specific requirements, changes in the external environment and demands of the situation.[1]

Organisational performance is affected, then, by a multiplicity of individual, group, task, technological, structural, managerial and environmental variables. Handy, for example, identifies over 60 factors that impinge on any one organisational situation and which illustrate the complicated nature of the study of organisational effectiveness.[2]

Attributes for successful performance

In their study of 62 American companies (including service companies) with outstandingly successful performance, Peters and Waterman identify eight basic attributes of excellence which appear to account for success.[3]

- *A bias for action* – action-orientated and a bias for getting things done.
- *Close to the customer* – listening and learning from the people they serve, and providing quality, service and reliability.
- *Autonomy and entrepreneurship* – innovation and risk-taking as an expected way of doing things.
- *Productivity through people* – treating members of staff as the source of quality and productivity.
- *Hands-on, value driven* – having well-defined, basic philosophies and top management keeping in touch with the 'front lines'.
- *Stick to the knitting* – in most cases, staying close to what you know and can do well.
- *Simple form, lean staff* – simple structural forms and systems, and few top-level staff.
- *Simultaneous loose-tight properties* – operational decentralisation but strong centralised control over the few, important core values.

The 7-S framework

From their research, Peters and Waterman suggest that any intelligent approach to organising needs to encompass at least seven, interdependent variables (the McKinsey 7-S Framework):

- strategy;
- structure;
- staff;
- (management) style;
- systems (and procedures);
- (corporate) strengths or skills;
- shared values (i.e. culture).

Framework for organisational analysis

Although many of the original 'excellent' organisations have since fallen from grace, it should be remembered that the formulas for their success did appear appropriate in the 1980s and the study highlighted the importance of culture and organisational renewal. Important lessons can always be learned and the 7-S model continues to provide a helpful framework as a basis for organisational analysis.

Heller's study of European excellence

In his study of companies and managers who are seeking to create the European future, Heller identifies ten key strategies with which Europe's revolutionaries have set off in search of their own brand of excellence.

1. Developing leadership – without losing control or direction.
2. Driving radical change – in the entire corporate system, not just in its parts.
3. Reshaping culture – to achieve long-term success.

4. Dividing to rule – winning the rewards of smallness while staying or growing large.

5. Exploiting the 'organisation' – by new approaches to central direction.

6. Keeping the competitive edge – in a world where the old ways of winning no longer work.

7. Achieving constant renewal – stopping success from sowing the seeds of decay.

8. Managing the motivators – so that people can motivate themselves.

9. Making team-working work – the new, indispensable skill.

10. Achieving total management quality – by managing everything much better.[4]

Heller suggests that on each of the ten vital renaissance strategies, examples of effective, progressive top managements abound to enlighten and encourage.

Total quality management (TQM)

One particular feature of organisational performance and effectiveness is attention to quality, and this is especially important in a service industry and in hospitality organisations. The successful hospitality organisation should as a matter of policy be constantly seeking opportunities to improve the quality of its products, services and processes. The organisation must also couple quality with a required level of productivity. Such a philosophy is increasingly encompassed as part of a total quality management (TQM) culture.

The key elements of TQM include *a total process* involving all operations and management units in the organisation and led from the top and *the customer as king* with every strategy, process and action directly related to satisfying customers, needs.[5] However, according to James, TQM initiatives will not succeed unless rooted in a supportive Quality of Working Life culture which creates a fear-free organisation in which employee involvement is pursued vigorously. It is necessary to generate a high degree of reciprocal commitment between the needs and developments of the individual, and the goals and development of the organisation.[6]

Quality assurance and human resource management

There are numerous definitions of TQM which are generally expressed in terms of a way of life for an organisation as a whole, commitment to total customer satisfaction through a continuous process of improvement, and the contribution and involvement of people. TQM emphasises the importance of people as the key to quality and the satisfaction of customers' needs.[7] Staff should be properly trained and in a position to take action about quality defects as they notice them. This involves the convergence of quality assurance and human resource management.

TQM therefore requires the creation of a corporate identity, a total organisational approach, and the participation and commitment of staff at all levels, starting with the active support and involvement of top management. It also involves a strategic focus on training for total quality. As an example, Scott's Hotels training programme for quality was based on the managing director's conceptual model of TQM[8] (see Figure 12.1).

TQM involves an increased level of empowerment and providing staff with greater authority and responsibility for self-checking, decision-making and problem-solving. (Recall, for example the discussion on quality circles in Chapter 7.) The introduction of TQM can therefore add to the pressures for a restructuring of the organisation and the move towards flatter hierarchies with the removal of a layer of managers/supervisors.

Figure 12.1: Conceptual model of TQM

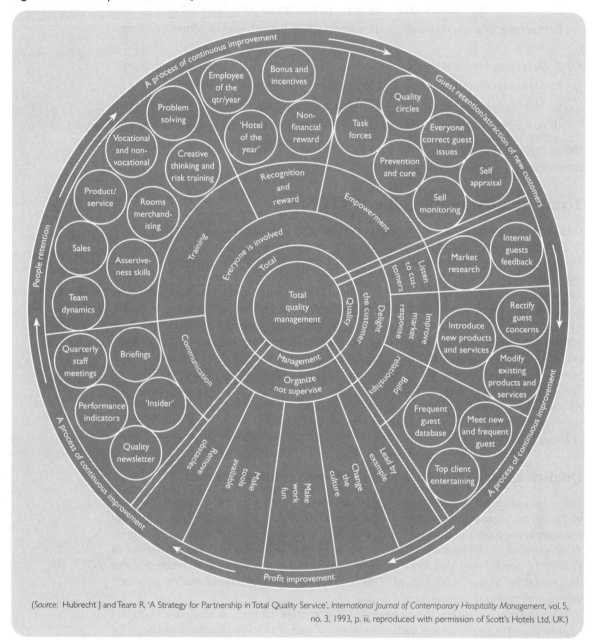

(*Source:* Hubrecht J and Teare R, 'A Strategy for Partnership in Total Quality Service', *International Journal of Contemporary Hospitality Management*, vol. 5, no. 3, 1993, p. iii, reproduced with permission of Scott's Hotels Ltd, UK.)

Benchmarking

As part of TQM standards, a process of benchmarking may be adopted. This is intended to measure an organisation's effectiveness compared to similar enterprises, and to provide a basis against which service and performance can be evaluated. Benchmarking may be both 'competitive', involving a comparison of products, service provision and delivery against competitors; and 'internal', involving an audit of activities and service within the group/ organisation, and a review of whether these could be performed more efficiently or effect- ively. For smaller hotels (three-star or below) the Department of National Heritage provide a do-it-yourself benchmarking set which provides a quick and simple way of review- ing their establishment and identifying possible areas of weakness.[9]

Benchmarking

All aspects of the hotel's processes and performance are frequently reviewed against national trends, competitive offerings in the neighbourhood and further afield. All staff are invited to 'walk the customers' shoes' by experiencing out of season the hotel's restaurant/bedrooms in order to assess the quality and service they themselves provide. They are also provided with vouchers enabling them to make visits to other quality establishments both locally and nationally, particularly those demonstrating the finest examples of best practice (for example, chefs take young trainees to top West End hotels and restaurants). These experiences plus any comments and sug- gestions are recorded on feedback forms, and presented at management and team meetings for the benefit of all.

THE SEAVIEW HOTEL AND RESTAURANT

Employee Hotel Experience Scheme

Shire Inns Limited operates a scheme to encourage employees of the company to experi- ence the products and services of the group. Employees are also expected to meet and talk with colleagues during their visit. The purpose of the scheme is for employees to gain an additional understanding of Guests' requirements by undertaking this customer experience whilst maintaining and improving teamwork and communications around the group.

Full details of the scheme are given in Appendix 1 to this chapter.

Difficulties in implementation

According to Partlow, 'The primary focus of TQM is not so much on quality as it is on the customer who defines that quality. In other words, TQM is concerned with quality because quality is the customer's concern.' From an examination of TQM practices in American hotels, Partlow suggests that TQM definitely pays off in terms of specific improvement meas- ures, for example, cost savings, increased food and beverage sales and reduced staff turnover as well as intangible benefits. However, making the move from a traditional management philosophy to a total quality management (TQM) culture demands much from an organ- isation. Implementing a TQM culture is an involved and demanding process especially in the HRM function.[10]

From a case study of a five-star hotel, Baldacchino argues that in spite of the enthus- iasm of top management, the successful execution of a TQM philosophy may prove extremely difficult and could result in a case of old wine in new bottles with labour– management relationships stubbornly locked in a traditional 'personnel', antagonistic orientation.[11]

The application of TQM

In looking at the application of TQM in manufacturing and service organisations, Macdonald claims that the customer of both is now much more aware of quality and has higher expectations than in the past. However, service organisations are different and it is necessary to consider the internal contrasts between products and services (discussed in Chapter 2). There is a real need for quality improvement in the service sector but successful implementation of the TQM process requires a full understanding of the generic factors which characterise service organisations. The tools of TQM have to be implemented in their own unique way.[12]

In her discussion of the essence of TQM and its application in the hospitality industry, Bo suggests that despite the divergence of views on what constitutes TQM, there are a number of basic principles in the various definitions:

(1) Customer satisfaction; (2) Commitment and leadership of top management; (3) Planning and organisation; (4) Education and training; (5) Involvement; (6) Teamwork; (7) Using tools and techniques; (8) Measurement and feedback; (9) Culture change; and (10) Continuous improvement.[13]

A full account of this discussion is given in the accompanying website for this book.

The EFQM excellence model

Total quality is the goal for many organisations, but it has been difficult until relatively recently to find a universally acceptable definition of what this actually means. The European Foundation for Quality Management (EFQM) Excellence Model[14] builds on the experience of previous models and was adopted by the British Quality Foundation in 1992 as the basis for both self-assessment and for the UK Quality Award for Business Excellence, launched in 1994. Oakland provides the following description:

> *The EFQM Excellence Model recognises that processes are the means by which a company or organisation harnesses and releases the talents of its people to produce results performance. Moreover, improvement in the performance can only be achieved by improving the processes by involving the people.*[15]

The 'Model' is based on the concept that an organisation will achieve better results by involving all the people in the organisation in the continuous improvement of their processes; it provides a focus for integrating all contributors to the organisation's performance. It is a practical tool that facilitates measurement of where an organisation is on the path to excellence, helping them to understand where there are gaps and stimulating solutions. The 'Model' is designed to be non-prescriptive but is there to provide guidelines. Organisations are able to benchmark themselves against others both within and outside their sectors. (See Figure 12.2.)

The basic assumption of the 'Model' is that excellent results to Performance, Customers, People and Society (the Results) are achieved through Leadership driving Policy and Strategy, People, Partnership and Resources, and Processes (The Enablers). Innovation and Learning are key to improving enablers that, in turn, improve results.

Figure 12.2: The Business Excellence Model/EFQM Excellence Model

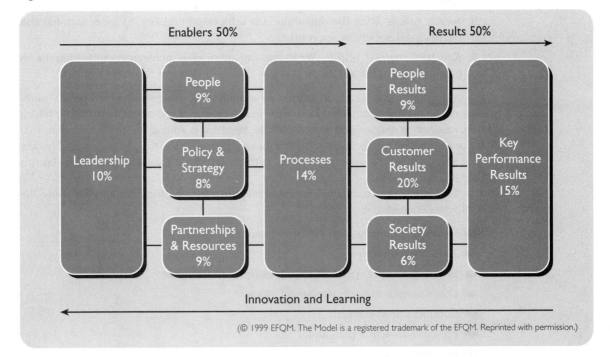

(© 1999 EFQM. The Model is a registered trademark of the EFQM. Reprinted with permission.)

Nine criteria of the Model

Each of the nine criteria featured in the 'Model' are described by the British Quality Foundation as follows:

1. *Leadership.* How leaders develop and facilitate the achievement of the mission and vision, develop values for long-term success and implement these via appropriate actions and behaviours, and are personally involved in ensuring that the organisation's management system is developed and implemented.

2. *People.* How the organisation manages, develops and releases the knowledge and full potential of its people at an individual, team-based and organisation-wide level, and plans these activities in order to support its policy and strategy and the effective operation of its processes.

3. *Policy and strategy.* How the organisation implements its mission and vision via a clear stakeholder-focused strategy, supported by relevant policies, plans, objectives, targets and processes.

4. *Partnerships and resources.* How the organisation plans and manages its external partnerships and internal resources in order to support its policy and strategy and the effective operation of its processes.

5. *Processes.* How the organisation designs, manages and improves its processes in order to support its policy and strategy and fully satisfy, and generate increasing value for, its customers and other stakeholders.

6. *People results.* What the organisation is achieving in relation to its people.

7. *Customer results.* What the organisation is achieving in relation to its external customers.

8. *Society results.* What the organisation is achieving in relation to local, national and international society as appropriate.

9. *Key performance results.* What the organisation is achieving in relation to its planned performance.

Each of the above criteria are supported by a number of sub-criteria which pose a number of questions that should be considered in the course of self-assessment during which an organisation is encouraged to consider the results it is aiming for, the approaches that have been put in place, the deployment of these approaches and the assessment and review of the approaches. This system, which is at the heart of the Excellence Model, is known as the RADAR approach.

The British Quality Foundation recommends the following methodology for using the EFQM Excellence Model:

- Develop commitment to self-assessment
- Plan self-assessment
- Establish teams to perform self-assessment and educate
- Communicate the self-assessment plans
- Conduct self-assessment
- Establish an action plan and
- Implement the action plan.

In the context of this text, it is interesting to note the finding of the 'X Factor' report on the Model in 1999.

> *What is crystal clear is that the management of people, including HR strategy, competencies, training, conditions and benefits and recognition and reward, is the fulcrum of achieving excellence in business and results.*[16]

Other contemporary hospitality models

Other major contemporary hospitality models include:

- Shaping Your Team for Success
- Excellence Through People and
- Hospitality Assured.

'Shaping Your Team for Success'

Developed by the Hotel and Catering International Management Association and Investors in People UK in partnership with Training and Enterprise Councils, Scottish Enterprise and the Northern Ireland Training and Employment Agency, this approach aims to help small to medium-sized businesses within the industry to achieve Investors in People standard. (Recall the discussion on Investors in People in Chapter 10.)

A pack has been developed for the top person in the organisation to use in working towards the Investors in People standard; it focuses on implementation and assumes that a commitment has already been made to the standard and is designed to reduce the amount of external support required to implement the IiP action plan. The pack includes management guides, a resource portfolio and case studies. The management guides include the following:

- Business Planning – where are we now?
- Business Planning – where do we want to be?
- Effective Communication
- Setting Standards
- Clarifying Jobs and Responsibilities
- Identifying Training and Development Needs
- Planning Training and Development
- Training and Developing Your Staff
- Performance Review and Appraisal
- Keeping Your Staff
- Recruiting Your Staff
- Selecting Talent
- Evaluating the Investment
- Collecting the Evidence and Being Assessed
- Continuous Improvement.

'Excellence Through People'

This initiative was born as a result of the British Hospitality Association's response to a damning Department of National Heritage report in 1996 which listed a litany of complaints about the industry's employment practices – the perceived low wage levels, poor image, long working hours, all leading to high levels of staff turnover – 'The tourism and hospitality labour market faces the threat of a self-perpetuating vicious circle that is harmful to profitability and competitiveness.'

The British Hospitality Association decided that the most effective approach to addressing the problems would be to encourage good employment practices through the words and actions of good employers and thus was born the association's 'Excellence Through People' programme, supported by Sector Challenge set up by the Department of Trade and Industry.

In order to gain a Certificate of Good Employment Practice employers must commit to, and be assessed against, the code to:

- recruit and select with care;
- offer a competitive employment package;
- develop skills and performance;
- communicate effectively; and
- recognise and reward.

In order to gain a Certificate of Best Employment Practice a business has to gain five additional endorsements in recognition of:

- forging links with a local school or college;
- widening access for employment opportunities;

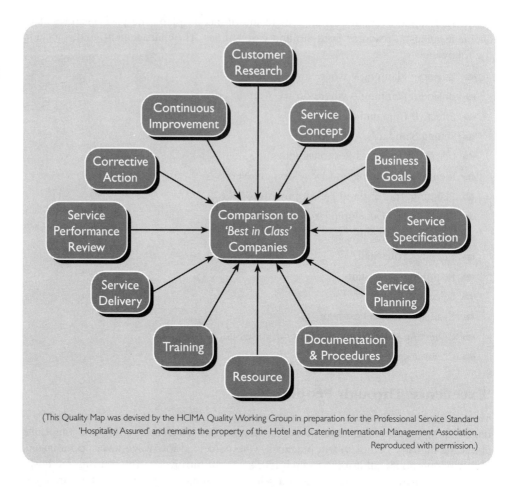

(This Quality Map was devised by the HCIMA Quality Working Group in preparation for the Professional Service Standard 'Hospitality Assured' and remains the property of the Hotel and Catering International Management Association. Reproduced with permission.)

- providing opportunities to gain qualifications;
- taking on a Modern Apprentice; and
- making a formal commitment to achieve Investor in People recognition.

Employers are supported with an initial seminar, video and action pack highlighting good employment practice in the hospitality industry. A self-assessment questionnaire leads to a confidential benchmarking report to be used as a management tool to guide change. The names and addresses of all accredited employers are listed in a BHA publication which is widely circulated to schools, colleges, universities and job centres.

'Hospitality Assured'

Based on international best practice, this standard has been developed by the HCIMA in response to government and industry concerns about low standards of performance in many hospitality operations. 'Hospitality Assured' provides a definitive standard for Service Excellence and identifies 12 steps that any size or type of hospitality business has to address in running its operation effectively if consistent quality of service to meet customers' needs is to be maintained. (See Figure 12.3.)

'Hospitality Assured' offers the following advantages to a business:

- an opportunity to demonstrate to the customer its commitment to service excellence;
- a template for business improvement based on best practice;
- an industry-specific self-assessment diagnostic tool to identify and prioritise action;
- a first step to the achievement of the Investors in People Award;
- the opportunity for accreditation and national recognition; and
- the opportunity to benchmark and work together with like-minded business.

(The author is grateful to his colleague Martin Brunner for providing the above information on the EFQM Excellence Model.)

A fuller discussion on applications within the hospitality industry and related case studies are given in the accompanying website for this book.

The measurement of productivity

Recent reports from the HCTC[17] and from the NEDC[18] have drawn attention to the need for and importance of increasing productivity in the hospitality industry. The characteristic features of service industries (discussed in Chapter 2) include the intangible nature of service delivery and the associated difficulty in the monitoring and measurement of performance. However, despite such difficulties, it is important to attempt some objective measures of productivity.

McLaughlin and Coffey, for example, suggest a classification of available productivity measures including output/input ratios, work measurement, quality and outcome performance, statistical comparisons and mathematical programming techniques.[19] In order to tackle the issue of productivity in service operations, McLaughlin and Coffey suggest that management should:

- specify the reason for investigating productivity;
- analyse the present or proposed service delivery including key specific operational areas;
- be absolutely clear about the service package it wishes to deliver, and specify the characteristics of strategic importance at each process stage and the key decision areas;
- select and investigate the methods of productivity measurement;
- be prepared for all kinds of objections to productivity measures on the basis of quality;
- involve fully the members of staff concerned and secure their acceptance to proposed measures of productivity.

Productivity in the hotel industry

As part of a collaborative research project the HCTC and the Birmingham College of Food are investigating the nature of, and influences on, productivity in hotels, including the importance of training. One of the main aims of the project is to create a comprehensive model which takes into account the factors that impact on productivity in the hotel industry[20] (see Figure 12.4).

Differences in customisation and service mix of operations make it difficult to draw meaningful comparisons between levels of productivity between different units, for example a

Figure 12.4:
A productivity
model for the
hospitality
industry

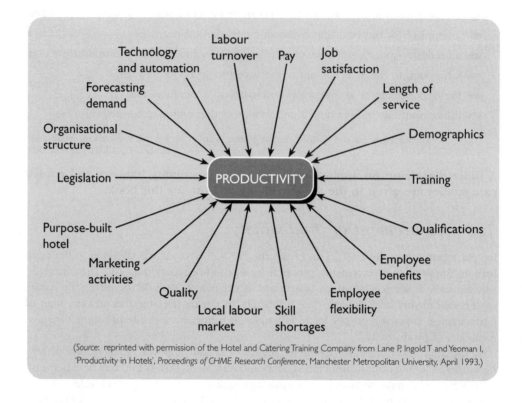

(*Source:* reprinted with permission of the Hotel and Catering Training Company from Lane P, Ingold T and Yeoman I, 'Productivity in Hotels', *Proceedings of CHME Research Conference*, Manchester Metropolitan University, April 1993.)

two-star hotel and a five-star hotel. In attempting to create a productivity model it is also necessary to consider the problems of:

● the interrelationships between variables, for example the cause–effect relationship between job satisfaction and productivity;

● dealing with a large list of factors and investigating the impact of individual factors, such as training, on productivity within a dynamic and constantly changing environment.

Despite these problems the model provides a helpful basis from which to consider the factors which impact upon productivity in the hotel industry.

Quality standards for hotels

The three main accreditation agencies – RAC, AA and English Tourist Council – have been working together to provide Harmonised Quality Standards, and have agreed a common set of rating requirements and inspection criteria. The new inspection criteria take the requirements of the guest as their basis. The RAC awards 'stars', the most widely recognised symbol in the world, to classify hotels on a 1 to 5 star rating. To be recognised at all under the new Quality Standards, the awards take into account the level of general cleanliness; the comfort and degree of style and quality of furnishings and decor throughout the establishment; the levels of service and hospitality displayed by owners and staff; the friendliness of the atmosphere; and the quality of the meals. (There is a separate but related scheme for Guest Accommodation – guesthouses, farmhouses, small private hotels, inns, restaurants with rooms, and bed and breakfast properties – which assesses establishments at five levels of quality from one Diamond to five Diamonds.)

> Of course each inspection is unique, with different styles of property serving differing clienteles and a major part of the Inspector's job is to take into account the individuality of each property. But, the bricks and mortar is only the beginning: in a service industry, it is the quality of the staff which makes the difference and that fact is reflected in the new Harmonised Quality Standards.
>
> *Linda Astbury, Manager of Hotel Operations, RAC Hotel Services*[21]

New RAC hospitality awards

To reflect the increasing standards being achieved in the hotel industry, and to complement the new Harmonised Quality Standards, RAC has taken the opportunity to review its range of awards. For hotels, there is the 'Blue Ribbon' presented to those properties that have achieved consistently high grades in all aspects of hotel keeping. As standards continue to rise there is a new award of 'Gold Ribbon' for those hotels that have raised their standards to even higher levels, continually demonstrating their commitment to superlative standards of customer care, service and accommodation. Both Blue and Gold Ribbon awards are made to hotels in all classifications from 1 to 5 stars.

Service quality and business performance

In Chapter 2, we drew attention to the importance of service management and high quality as a growing feature of hospitality organisations. In Chapter 11 we drew attention to the importance of quality assurance and the measurement of service quality for the effective execution of work in the hospitality industry. **As an example, the service quality strategy for Whitbread Hotel Company is outlined in Appendix 2 to this chapter.**

But what is the relationship between service quality and business performance?

Harrington and Akehurst suggest that to date empirical studies have in the main not included analyses of service quality in the hotel industry and relatively few researchers have addressed the proposition that service quality leads to improved performance and competitiveness. From an exploratory study of 250 UK hotel units with a size of over 100 beds, Harrington and Akehurst suggest four implications for management: (1) the results emphasise the need for hotels to develop more effective internal communications relating to quality service for the customer; (2) the requirement for managers to adopt more representative procedures for evaluating service quality at the unit level; (3) the significance for managers of developing and operationalising service strategies at business and unit level; and (4) concern about the low ranking for image in quality terms.

In conclusion, Harrington and Akehurst observe that:

> *whilst a large proportion of respondents acknowledge the importance of developing, promoting and measuring service quality, it would appear that few managers, at the hotel unit level, have systems in place to effect implementation. Indeed, responsibility for implementing service quality initiatives remains for the most part with senior management.*[22]

Managerial perceptions and attitudes

Harrington and Akehurst also draw attention to the need for further research to be carried out to investigate the nature of service quality implementation in UK hotels. The quality concept has attracted increasing interest in the service sector and there is a growing body of literature on the subject. Results from the study suggest a growing awareness within hotels of the need to manage quality in a complex and competitive marketplace. However, the findings also emphasise the importance of distinguishing *awareness* from *actionable policy* and suggest cause for concern in the attitudes shown by middle managers towards their hotel's quality efforts. There is a need to direct attention towards a critical examination of the effectiveness of implemented quality initiatives.[23]

In order to measure service quality implementation practices, Harrington and Akehurst undertook a further survey of 133 general managers in three-star UK hotel organisations. The reported results add emphasis to the need to closely align human resource considerations with overall strategic concerns in the achievement of quality objectives, and the consideration of people management issues in quality implementation. Although managers may subscribe to the notion of human relations dimensions underpinning quality implementation process, this is not necessarily practised in the organisations surveyed. Further research is needed to examine managerial attitudes and opinions to the *actual* practice of quality management in hotel organisations.[24]

Myths of customer service

In an interesting and thought-provoking account on the provision of customer service, Jamison argues the need to maintain a balance in the belief that 'the customer is always right' and suggest ten myths of customer service.[25]

- *Myth 1: 'Give the customers what they want'* – customers are not able to imagine creative solutions to what they want. Profit-making creative solutions must be designed internally and presented properly to customers in order to stimulate a response.

- *Myth 2: 'The customer is always right'* – this is clearly not evident as there are customers who steal or seek to defraud, and people who try to profit from the high profile image of a particular company.

- *Myths 3 and 4: 'Always delight your customers and exceed their expectations'. 'Always provide the best quality service'* – Not every company should seek to provide the best quality service unless it wishes to go out of business. What is appropriate for the prestigious Ritz-Carlton Hotel chain would clearly be inappropriate for a mass caterer such as McDonalds.

- *Myth 5: 'Empower all your staff'* – Causes of poor quality are not always lack of awareness or the wrong attitude among staff but more often the definition of the role they are asked to perform, or the procedures they are expected to follow.

- *Myth 6: 'Reduce the number of complaints'* – It is better to regard complainers, not in a negative vein but as customers trying to help the company perform better. Encouraging customers to complain direct to the company provides the opportunity to turn them into advocates.

- *Myth 7: 'You must introduce a loyalty card'* – Loyalty consists of far more than a loyalty card. Managers need to design a customer care programme that is relevant and specific to their company.

- *Myth 8: 'Good customer service is just smiling at customers and wishing them a nice day'* – Customer service differs from culture to culture. What may work in the United States does not always work here. McDonald's had to apologise because it infuriated the British public by training its staff to wish everyone to 'have a nice day'.

- *Myth 9: 'You must try to please all the people all the time'* – Customers have different service requirements, and it's not possible to provide one bland service offer to them all.

- *Myth 10: 'Much service improvement is operational and tactical'* – There is a strategic dimension to customer care and service should be as different as their products. It is senseless for a 'least cost' supplier (like Travel Lodge) to try to offer the best service in the industry (like Ritz-Carlton).

Organisation development

In recent years the term organisation development (OD) has become popular in management literature as a generic term embracing a wide range of intervention strategies into the social processes of an organisation. OD is concerned with the diagnosis of organisational health and performance and the ability of the organisation to adapt to change.[26] It involves the applications of organisational behaviour. OD adopts a socio-technical approach and in a very general sense is concerned with attempts to improve the overall effectiveness of an organisation. Essentially, it is an applied behavioural science approach to planned change and development of an organisation.[27]

Many interrelated topics

The broad nature of organisation development means that many interrelated topics could be included under this heading or label. Given the importance of people to effective organisation performance (especially in the hospitality industry), topics normally included under the heading of organisation behaviour can also be seen as relevant to the study of OD. Many of the topics discussed in previous chapters as of particular relevance to the hospitality industry, such as for example team-building, empowerment and quality assurance, may be seen as important parts of OD. However, the emphasis of OD is more on the development of the organisation as a whole rather than the actual processes of organisation and management. This chapter provides an introduction to selected topics of OD: the role of top management; organisation culture and climate; the management of change; and organisational conflict.

The role of top management

Effective management is at the heart of organisation development and improved performance. For example, Patching refers to the importance of the relationship between the three levels of: business strategy; management strategy; and organisation and management development strategy.[28] This applies as much to service organisations and the hospitality industry as to any other industry. The role of management is one of the most important factors in the success of any hospitality organisation. At the corporate level top management have a responsibility for determining the direction of the organisation as a whole and for its survival, development and profitability. For example, recalling (from Chapter 2) the words of Kanter: 'Managing means managing an entire context. If you strip out one element and apply one methodology, it won't work.'[29]

In Chapter 4 we discussed the nature of managerial work, and the importance of the role of management as an integrating activity and the cornerstone of organisational effectiveness. Top management have a particular responsibility for determining the objectives and formulation of policy for the hospitality operations as a whole. For example, in Chapter 10 we looked at the role of top management in formulating personnel policies, establishing underlying philosophy and attitudes, and attempting to maintain a level of morale and commitment of all members of staff in order to secure optimum operational performance.

Attention to key features

Top management clearly have an essential part to play in improving organisational performance and the effective management of human resources. They need to give attention to such features as the following.

- Clarification and communication of corporate aims and objectives. The identification of key areas of performance and results including social responsibilities.
- Interactions with and responsiveness to external environmental influences, and the effective management of change.
- Pursuing corporate goals in accordance with an ethical and operational foundation, and recognition of the psychological contract.
- Design of organisation structure which takes account of the socio-technical system and is most suited to organisational processes and the execution of work.
- Organisational strategies and practices, for example relating to human resource planning and the management of staff turnover.
- Welding a coherent and coordinated pattern of work activities, and harnessing the efforts of staff.
- Clear, consistent and equitable policies and procedures, for example relating to the personnel function including training and development.
- A style of managerial behaviour which adopts a positive policy of investment in people.
- Recognition of the needs and expectations of people at work and systems of motivation, job satisfaction and rewards.
- Effective control of those critical activities important to the overall success of the organisation.
- Creating an organisational climate which encourages members of staff to work willingly and effectively.

The process of management

Top management have a particular concern for the community or institutional level and for the work of the organisation as a whole. But it is the role of management *throughout all levels of the organisation* to act as an integrating activity and to coordinate, direct and guide the efforts of members towards the achievement of goals and objectives. The process of management, however, takes place not in a vacuum but within the context of the organisational setting (discussed in Chapter 2). Applications of organisational behaviour and the effective management of human resources are dependent, therefore, not only upon the nature of the hospitality industry, but also upon the characteristic features of the individual organisation – and its organisational culture and climate.

Organisational culture

Although most of us will understand in our own minds what is meant by organisational culture, it is a general concept which is difficult to define or explain precisely. The concept of culture has developed from anthropology. There is no consensus on its meaning or its applications to the analysis of work organisations.[30] Also, there is sometimes confusion over the difference between the interpretation of organisational culture and organisational climate, which is discussed below.

A popular and simple way of defining culture is: 'how things are done around here'. A more detailed definition is:

> *the collection of traditions, values, policies, beliefs, and attitudes that constitute a pervasive context for everything we do and think in an organisation.*[31]

Culture is reinforced through the system of rites and rituals, patterns of communication, the informal organisation, expected patterns of behaviour and perceptions of the psychological contract.

Schein suggests a view of organisational culture based on distinguishing three levels of culture: artifacts and creations; values; and basic underlying assumptions.[32] From a study of five US restaurant companies, Woods sees much of culture as invisible, or at least unspoken, and identifies at least three main levels:

● starting with *the visible or manifest level* – such as slogans, ceremonies, myths, sagas and legends, uniforms, building design;

● a second level not immediately visible to customers is *the strategic level*, such as beliefs about strategic vision, capital market, product market expectations, and internal approaches to management;

● the third level is most deeply submerged and is *the level of deep meaning*, which embraces the values and assumptions with which the organisation operates. Ideally, the values and assumptions espoused by top management will be the same as those held by hourly workers.[33]

. . . apart from its size, McDonald's draws attention for its distinctive – and to outsiders, extremely opaque – culture. Talk to anyone connected with the company, from CEO to franchisee, for any length of time and you'll notice how little they refer to McDonald's by name. Instead they use two words without any apparent need for explanation – 'the System'. Its derivation is innocent enough – a hangover from the company's pre-flotation days in the US when it was known as McDonald's Systems Inc – but the effect is of arrogance, even evangelism. It is not simply the usual 'the way we do things round here' but an entire philosophy developed and refined over 40 years and supported by a 600-page operating manual.

Management Today[34]

Main types of organisation culture

Developing the ideas of Harrison,[35] Handy describes four main types of organisation culture: power culture; role culture; task culture; and person culture.[36]

- *Power culture* depends on a central power source with influence disseminating from the central figure throughout the organisation. A power culture is frequently found in small entrepreneurial organisations. It is based on trust and personal communication with little bureaucracy and few rules or regulations.

- *Role culture* is often stereotyped as bureaucracy and based on logic and rationality. Role culture rests on the strength of strong organisational 'pillars' and the functions of specialists in, for example, purchasing, production and finance. Work is controlled by procedures and rules and coordinated by a small band of senior managers.

- *Task culture* is job-orientated or project-orientated. It is represented by a net. People generally work in teams and task culture seeks to utilise the unifying power of the group. There are few levels of authority, and influence is widely spread and based more on expert power than positional or personal power.

- *Person culture* where the individual is the central focus and any structure exists to serve the individuals within it. Individuals generally work alone, or several may decide it is in their own interests to band together. Management hierarchies and control mechanisms are possible only by mutual consent. This culture is common with professionals.

Influences on the development of culture

The culture and structure of an organisation develop over time and in response to a complex set of factors. We can, however, identify a number of key influences that are likely to play an important role in the development of any organisational culture. These include: history, primary function and technology, goals and objectives, size, location, management and staffing, and the environment.[37]

History

The reason, and manner in which, the organisation was originally formed, its age, and the philosophy and values of its owners and first senior managers will affect culture. A key event in the organisation's history such as a merger or major reorganisation, or a new generation of top management, may bring about a change in culture.

Primary function and technology

The nature of the organisation's 'business' and its primary function have an important influence on its culture, for example the range and quality of products and services provided, the importance of reputation and the type of customers. The primary function of the organisation will determine the nature of the technological processes and methods of undertaking work, which in turn also affect structure and culture. Compare, for example, a traditional, high-class hotel, particularly noted for its cuisine, with a popular mass-production fast-food chain store.

Goals and objectives

Although a business organisation may pursue profitability, this is not by itself a very clear or sufficient criterion for its effective management. For example, to what extent is emphasis placed on long-term survival or growth and development? How much attention is given to avoiding risk and uncertainties? Or how much concern is shown for broader social responsibilities? The organisation must give attention to objectives in all key areas of its operations. The combination of objectives and resultant strategies will influence culture, and may themselves be influenced by changes in culture.

Size

Usually, larger organisations have more formalised structures and cultures. Increased size is likely to result in separate departments and possibly split-site operations. This may cause difficulties in communication and interdepartmental rivalries with the need for effective coordination. A rapid expansion, or decline, in size and rate of growth, and resultant changes in staffing, will influence structure and culture.

Location

Geographical location and the physical characteristics will have a major influence on culture, for example whether the organisation is located in a quiet rural location or a busy city centre. This will influence the types of customers and the staff employed. It can also can affect the nature of services provided, the sense of 'boundary' and distinctive identity, and opportunities for development.

Management and staffing

Top executives can have considerable influence on the nature of culture; consider, for example, the key role played by Lord Forte when Chief Executive of Trusthouse Forte. But all members of staff help to shape the dominant culture of an organisation, irrespective of what senior management feel it should be.

Culture is also determined by the nature of staff employed and the extent to which they accept management philosophy and policies or only pay 'lip service'. Another important influence is the match between corporate culture and employees' perception of the psychological contract.

The environment

In order to be effective, the organisation must be responsive to external environmental influences. For example, if it operates within a dynamic environment, it requires a structure and culture that are sensitive and readily adaptable to change. An organic structure is more likely to respond effectively to new opportunities and challenges, and risks and limitations, presented by the external environment.

**Management responsibility for the culture and
values of an organisation**

All organisations display attributes that relate to their culture and values. This is particularly important in the hospitality industry where the 'environment' is the background against which the product is judged. Although the facilities and physical setting are important components of environment, no amount of investment in these can make up for a shortfall in ambience or 'feel'. To make matters more difficult for those of us who aspire to excellence in hospitality these attributes are highly subjective and notoriously difficult to influence and control. However, because the feel of an

continued

continued

environment is the result of the interaction of people, it is the responsibility of the management. Successful organisations match the skills, attitudes and behaviours of the staff with the needs and expectations of the customers.

Very often a strong culture grows within a company reflecting the attitudes and behaviours of the most senior people. The company culture does not have to be defined in order for its people to 'know it'. New staff either adapt to and become part of the culture or do not fit and usually do not stay. This is particularly true of owner-managed hospitality businesses and was certainly the case at Highgate House Conference Centre. Highgate House had developed over 25 years under the guidance of an exceptionally energetic and talented mother of 9 who was determined that behaviour standards and individual well-being were paramount. The culture ran right through the business, which established a superb reputation as a high-quality 95-bed residential conference centre.

When the management of the business passed to the next generation there was a very real danger that attitudes could change. This risk was increased when the decision was taken to grow the business to more than one centre with the launch in 1998 of The Sundial Group. Because the feel of Highgate House was identified by the customers as a key reason for their repeat business, the senior management decided that it was important to try to pin down the culture and find ways to describe it. They wanted to ensure that the culture continued as far as possible as the company grew. They identified and published four core values, making them part of the marketing image for customers and the behaviour standards for staff. By being open about what behaviours are expected it became very much easier for the management to safeguard them.

The following is an extract from the document that was circulated to customers and staff at the launch of The Sundial Group and forms part of the induction of all staff, also appearing in the Employee Handbook.

● We are committed to creating an environment that genuinely encourages learning and creative thinking, for our clients and for our staff.

● We believe that our people make us the best conference and training services group in the country. Our values are embodied every day in their professionalism, experience, quality and respect for our guests and each other.

● *Professionalism.* The discreet, seamless hospitality that is Sundial's hallmark is ideally suited to our customers' very specialised needs. Successful business meetings, training courses, and smaller conferences benefit greatly from our attention to detail, secure privacy and focus.

● *Experience.* Understanding customers' needs and providing responsive service are the important long-term benefits Sundial gains from attracting and keeping staff with the right skills and positive attitudes. This continuity enables us to draw on a wealth of experience and helps us to earn the confidence of the organisations we work with.

● *Quality.* Our standards are uncompromising with a relentless drive for value for money and continuous improvement appropriate to needs. Our policies are

continued

continued

designed to help our staff learn and develop, encouraging them to use their initiative and provide what's needed, when it's needed. We thrive on feedback and innovation.

- *Respect.* Sundial is a family business. We started the first independent conference centre over 35 years ago. A lot has changed since then, but not our core belief in respect for those around us. 'Treat people as you would like to be treated' is a golden rule everyone can understand and appreciate, and one which we use to put our services and hospitality into context.

These statements form a manifesto and contain commitments that help set the expectations of customers and staff. Equally they give a clear message to staff and especially to managers about how to behave. However, to translate into organisational culture, it is critical that every level of leadership in the business subscribe to and demonstrate these values consistently.

Expanding from a close knit business, where the entrepreneurial owner knew everything that went on and made pretty much every significant decision, to a multi-site group required far-reaching changes in management and responsibility. Committing to values that can be easily described and understood provides a framework against which decisions can be taken. The right answer is always the one which best fits these values.

In order for Sundial Group to live up to this manifesto it became clear that policies and strategies needed to be developed. Our commitment to Professionalism led us to accreditation under Investors in People, ensuring that we link training and development to business objectives. Experience can only be achieved through a positive approach to controlling staff turnover. Quality must be appropriate to need, we are now much more aware of our customers' expectations and competitors' performance. Respect depends on empathy; we have a much better understanding of the attitudes that need to be demonstrated by prospective staff in order for them to succeed with us.

Although it is still early days in the development of The Sundial Group, we can begin to see the effectiveness of our commitments. Our staff turnover levels have remained well below the industry standard, repeat business levels are also remaining very good and profitability shows a marked improvement. UK conference buyers recently voted Highgate House venue of the year and together the three Sundial venues polled in excess of 50 per cent of the vote in a field of 30 nominated top venues.

The achievement of Investors in People provided a valuable external benchmark and our work with The European Quality Model self-assessment process is providing further valuable feedback. However, we operate in a highly competitive marketplace and are not prepared to rest on our laurels; healthy paranoia is a useful driver for continuous improvement!

Source: The author is grateful to Tim Chudley, Managing Director of The Sundial Group for providing this information.

(The Sundial group currently consists of Highgate House in Northamptonshire, Barnett Hill in Surrey, Woodside in Warwickshire and Sundial Options and Solutions, our venue finding service. www.sundialgroup.com)

The importance of culture

Culture can help reduce complexity and uncertainty. It provides a consistency in outlook and values, and makes possible the processes of decision-making, coordination and control.[38] Culture is clearly an important ingredient of effective organisational performance. In their study, Peters and Waterman draw attention to the importance of corporate culture.

> *Without exception, the dominance and coherence of culture proved to be an essential quality of the excellent companies. Moreover, the stronger the culture and the more it was directed to the marketplace, the less need was there for policy manuals, organization charts, or detailed procedures and rules. In these companies, people way down the line know what they are supposed to do in most situations because the handful of guiding values is crystal clear.*[39]

The importance of culture to effective organisational performance still stands and has been reinforced by a recent study by Heller of Europe's top companies. For example, in commenting on Heineken's superiority in world markets, Heller makes the point that it rests in part on its remarkable corporate culture:

> *There is nothing accidental about cultural strengths . . . There is a relationship between an organization's culture and its performance.*[40]

Organisation culture will influence the pride that people have in their jobs and the appropriateness of the manager's methods of motivation. Culture is also a major determinant of organisational performance and effectiveness. In the hospitality industry culture is a vital component in the standards of delivery of service to the customer. It is important therefore to recognise the essential characteristics of service organisations and to develop a culture which encourages group motivation, harmonious working relationships and good team-work.

Influence of national culture

Culture helps to account for variations among organisations and managers, both nationally and internationally. It helps to explain why different groups of people perceive things in their own way and perform things differently from other groups.[41] With greater international competition, an understanding of national culture has become of increasing importance for managers. According to Siddall, for example: 'international business, the issue of culture and the need for better understanding have become major parts of organisational behaviour'.[42] Cultural practices vary widely among different countries and because of our own values may be difficult to understand.

For example, from a study of international hotel companies operating in the People's Republic of China, Mwaura *et al.* conclude that a strong national culture can have major influences on what happens in the workplace and tends to precipitate numerous conflicts.[43]

Culture and ineffectiveness

According to Glover, for example, a properly developed corporate culture can be a management tool for building product quality and staff productivity. If management misunderstands the effects of corporate culture, the quality of products and services in hospitality operations may suffer through a 'cult of ineffectiveness'.[44]

Glover identifies a number of organisational characteristics that commonly give rise to a cult of ineffectiveness.

- *Missing standards* – through lack of agreement on expectations, inconsistent delivery of products and services, lack of measuring and managing quality, and evaluation based on activity not results.

- *Unbalanced accountability* – although financial accounting is highly developed, effective controls over the people area, and accounting procedures for measuring the effectiveness of managers and supervisors, are less precise.

- *Ineffective communications* – ideas and responses from employees are seldom sought, and comments from guests not appreciated. Neither group is considered in management decision-making. Top-down communication, as well as broken or misunderstood communication, engenders a cult of ineffectiveness.

- *Symptoms, not causes* – emphasis is placed on remedies for symptoms, rather than delving for the underlying cause of problems. For example, the rudeness of a waiter may have less to do with the waiter, and more to do with inappropriate selection and training or poor management practices.

- *Lack of recognition* – most managers admit that they rarely let employees know when a job has been done well. Many employees only hear from their manager when there is a problem.

- *Absence of team-work* – many corporate cultures reward competition among employees and may encourage conflict. If employees are rewarded on the basis of individual action, this can thwart the development of teams. Yet the nature of hospitality operations demands effective team-work.

- *Inadequate training* – a common means of training new members of staff is by 'trailing' an experienced employee. This transfers the most important managerial responsibility to a line employee who may not have a clear view of the company's objectives. Also, managers and supervisors are often expected to sink or swim as they are introduced to new responsibilities.

- *Recriminations* – complaints or other problems are often an occasion for blame, finger-pointing and defensiveness rather than being taken as an opportunity to improve operations. Management has a responsibility to limit problems in the first place.

- *The need for effectiveness* – many hospitality managers fail to recognise the difference between effectiveness and efficiency. 'Getting the job done' should include effective delivery of the product or service and result in achieving established standards.

- *Actions of top management* – an organisation is more than the sum of all its operations and departments. It also includes a culture that is shaped by the actions of top management. The informal social organisation affects all levels of the company, and influences its ability to deliver products and services to the customer.

Organisational climate

In addition to arrangements for carrying out organisational processes, management has a responsibility for creating a climate in which people are motivated to work willingly and effectively.

Climate can be said to relate to the prevailing atmosphere surrounding the hospitality organisation, to the level of morale, and to the strength of feelings of belonging, care and goodwill among members.

Organisational climate, however, is another general concept and difficult to define precisely. It is more something which is felt. Climate arises from a combination of forces, some of which are better understood than others. Climate will influence the attitudes which members of the organisation bring to bear on their work performance and personal relationships. The extent to which employees accept the culture of the organisation will have a significant effect on climate.

The perception of employees

Whereas organisational culture describes what the organisation is about, organisational climate is an indication of the employees' feelings and beliefs of what the organisation is about. Climate is based on the **perceptions** of employees towards the quality of the internal working environment.[45] The extent to which employees accept the culture of the organisation will have a significant effect on climate.

Climate also relates to the recognition of the organisation as a social system and the extent to which membership is perceived as a psychologically rewarding experience. It can be seen as the state of mutual trust and understanding among members of the organisation.

Meudell and Gadd contend that the distinction between organisational culture and climate is of particular importance in service industries, not only from the point of view of guest perception of staff but also from the point of view of teamworking:

> *The culture may, for example, encourage a hotel-wide quality circle but it is only a suitable climate which will prevent verbal and, possibly, physical violence when a laundry worker suggests changes in procedures for issuing kitchen whites which could improve efficiency!*[46]

Characteristics of organisational climate

Organisational climate is characterised, therefore, by the nature of the people–organisation relationship and the superior–subordinate relationship. These relationships are determined by interactions among goals and objectives, formal structure, the process of management, styles of leadership and the behaviour of people. A healthy organisational climate might therefore be expected to exhibit such characteristic features as:

- the integration of organisational goals and personal goals;
- the most appropriate organisation structure based on the demands of the socio-technical system;
- democratic functioning of the organisation with full opportunities for participation;
- justice in treatment with equitable personnel and employee relations policies and practices;
- mutual trust, consideration and support among different levels of the organisation;
- the open discussion of conflict with an attempt to avoid confrontation;
- managerial behaviour and styles of leadership appropriate to the particular work situations;
- acceptance of the psychological contract between the individual and the organisation;
- recognition of people's needs and expectations at work, and individual differences and attributes;

- equitable systems of rewards based on positive recognition;
- concern for the quality of working life and job design;
- opportunities for personal development and career progression;
- a sense of identity with, and loyalty to, the organisation and a feeling of being a valued and important member.

The management of organisational climate

If organisational climate is to be improved, then attention should be given to the above features. The climate created by managers will have a significant influence on the motivation and behaviour of employees.

> *Creating the right climate involves a realisation that all management activity, from the design of systems and procedures to the way the manager handles interpersonal interactions with customers and staff, will contribute to the overall atmosphere of the workplace. The manager is a role model that staff will follow.*[47]

The management of organisational climate is therefore an important means of improving productivity and standards of work performance.

In hospitality operations, customer satisfaction relies heavily on group-based activities and the need for different departments to work closely together. It is particularly important, therefore, to develop an organisational climate which encourages good team-work. However, although similar types of organisations may share certain common features, each will have its own distinctive characteristics. Every organisation has its own climate, or internal environment or 'personality'.

Main dimensions of climate

Climate will influence the level of morale and attitudes which members of the organisation bring to bear on their work performance and personal relationships. Although morale is difficult to measure objectively, a carefully designed and conducted description questionnaire (or attitude survey) will help to establish the true feelings of members on factors contributing to organisational climate.

There are many possible survey instruments with which to gauge climate. Different questionnaires vary greatly in the number of items and in the number of categories. Mill, for example, suggests that climate can be described in terms of six main dimensions: clarity, commitment, standards, responsibility, recognition and team-work (Figure 12.5).[48]

If clarity, commitment or standards are low, this suggests the need for a system of management by objectives. This involves the setting of clearly stated objectives and targets, and developing commitment among employees by participation in agreeing standards of performance.

Where responsibility is low, this suggests the need for attention to job redesign and passing on to employees increased autonomy for the planning, organising and control of their jobs.

When recognition is lacking, management should provide positive reinforcement by giving employees rewards and encouragement when they do something right.

If team-work is lacking, then management should attempt to develop a feeling of trust and supportive relationships with employees and among groups of employees.

Mill suggests that management by objectives, job design, positive reinforcement and the establishment of trust form a basis for management action to improve organisational climate.

Figure 12.5: Organisational climate and management action

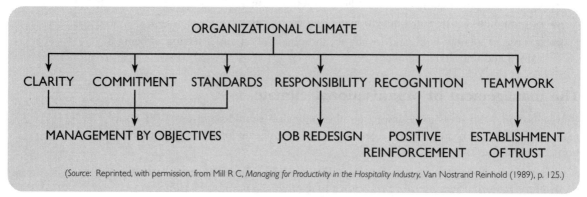

(*Source:* Reprinted, with permission, from Mill R C, *Managing for Productivity in the Hospitality Industry,* Van Nostrand Reinhold (1989), p. 125.)

The management of change

Whatever the nature of its culture, the organisation can only perform effectively through interactions with the broader external environment of which it is part. Factors such as uncertain economic conditions, fierce world competition, the level of governmental intervention, scarcity of natural resources, changing social attitudes and rapid developments in new technology combine to create an increasingly volatile environment.

As the hospitality industry is concerned with both production and service it is particularly susceptible to environmental influences.[49] In order to ensure its survival and future success, the organisation must be readily adaptable, therefore, to the demands placed upon it. A key factor in performance and effectiveness is the successful management of change.

The forces of change

Change is a pervasive influence. We are all subject to continual change in one form or another. It is an inescapable part of both social and organisational life. Change also originates within the organisation itself, for example as part of the natural process of ageing of buildings and equipment, or as skills and abilities become outdated. There are a wide range of forces acting upon organisations which make the need for change inevitable. These forces of change can be summarised under five broad headings: changing technology, the knowledge explosion, rapid product obsolescence, the changing nature of the workforce, and the quality of working life.[50]

- *Changing technology* – for example, advances in computing systems and information technology, and the increasing use of microwave ovens and cook/chill systems. These changes can result in the de-skilling of jobs, especially in the kitchen.

- *Knowledge explosion* – for example the number of people in some form of education, new ideas and methods of working, the number of scientific journals and new books, the increasing number of hospitality management students.

- *Rapid product obsolescence* – changes in consumer preferences together with changing technology have influenced the delivery of many products and services, for example the popularity of convenience foods, an increasing trend away from silver service and towards self-service, reduced personal contact between receptionists and customers.

- *Changing nature of the workforce* – for example, demographic influences and changes in the composition of the workforce, broader educational opportunities, part-time working, changes in family life-cycles, and equal opportunities.

- *Quality of working life* – for example, increased attention to the satisfaction of people's needs and expectations at work, human resource management, job design and work organisation, and styles of managerial behaviour.

Organisations must be responsive to changes in the external environment and changing organisations will affect the nature of managerial work. Stewart, for example, describes how changes in organisations affect the kinds of jobs that managers have to do and the nature of their lives and careers. Older managers now work for very different kinds of organisations from those in which they first became managers. Although hierarchies of authority will continue to exist in large organisations they will be shorter and there will be wider networking. There will be a smaller number of middle managers but with more responsible roles. Managers' jobs are more complex and demanding, and managers' careers are much less predictable.[51]

Managerial resistance to change

Although the organisation has to adapt to its environment, there is often resistance at the managerial level against change.

- Major change often requires large resources which may already be committed to investments in other areas or strategies. Assets such as buildings and furnishings, technology, equipment and people cannot be altered easily.

- Attention is often focused on maintaining stability and predictability, especially in large-scale organisations. The need for formal structures, the division of work and established rules, procedures and methods of work can result in resistance to change.

- Management may feel comfortable operating within the structure, policies and procedures which have been formulated to deal with a range of past or present situations. Managers may set up defences against change and prefer to concentrate on the routine things they perform well.

- Change may also be seen as a threat to the power or influence of management, such as their control over decisions, resources or information. As an example, middle management may be resistant to the introduction of quality circles because the increased empowerment of members is seen as an encroachment on their traditional areas of authority and responsibility.[52]

Individual resistance to change

People are naturally wary of change and, although there may be potential positive outcomes, resistance to change – or the thought of the implications of change – appears to be a common phenomenon. Resistance to change can take many forms and may arise from a combination of factors. It is therefore often difficult to pinpoint the exact cause but some common reasons for individual resistance to change include the following.

Fear of the unknown

Many major changes present a degree of uncertainty, for example the possible effects of new technology or methods of working. A person may resist promotion because of uncertainty over changes in responsibilities or the increased social demands of the higher position. Changes which confront people with the unknown tend to cause anxiety or fear. A proposed change which is likely to break up a cohesive working group or to move an individual to a new work group may be resisted.

Habit

People tend to respond to situations in an established and accustomed manner. Habit may serve as a means of comfort and security, and as a guide for decision-making. Proposed changes to habits, especially if well established and requiring little effort, may well be resisted. If there is a clearly perceived advantage, for example a reduction in working hours without loss of pay, there is likely to be less resistance to the change. However, because of habit, some people may still find it difficult to adjust to the reduced hours of work.

Inconvenience or loss of freedom

If the change is seen as likely to prove inconvenient, make life more difficult, reduce freedom of action or result in increased control, there is likely to be resistance. For example, a manager may resist being moved to another establishment or location, especially if this involves greater travelling or moving house. Staff are likely to resist new working practices which require learning new skills or result in closer management control.

Economic implications

People are likely to resist change which is perceived as reducing either directly or indirectly their pay or other rewards, or requiring an increase in work for the same level of pay. Staff may resist a move to another job, even at the same level of basic pay, if they fear they may receive less overtime payments, gratuities or other perks.

Security in the past

Some people tend to find a sense of security in the past. In times of frustration or difficulty, or when faced with new or unfamiliar ideas or methods, people may reflect on the past and wish to retain old and comfortable ways. There may be a tendency to cling to well-established and well-known procedures as giving a feeling of security.

Threat to status or symbols

Any perceived threat to the status or symbol attached to a job or position is likely to be resisted, for example proposals to remove a private office, reserved car parking space, special uniforms or a private locker.

Selective perception

People tend to have their own, biased view of a particular situation, which fits most comfortably their own perception of reality. This can cause almost a 'built-in' resistance to change. For example, strong trade unionists may have a stereotyped view of management as untrustworthy and therefore oppose any management change, however well-founded might be the intention. Managers may have a particular bias towards a particular theory or practice of organisational behaviour and discard new ideas which they feel to be of no concern or value to them.

Resistance to change in hotel firms

From an in-depth investigation of nine hotels in the UK, Okumus and Hemmington conclude that there are important similarities between hotel firms and manufacturing firms in terms of facing and overcoming barriers and potential resistance to change. They identified main barriers and resistance to change in hotel firms as: financial difficulties; cost of the change; lack of resources; fear of losing the existing customer; time limitation; priority of other businesses; lack of cooperation and skills; fear of insecurity; losing something valuable; and internal politics.

Okumus and Hemmington point out that managers require to understand the nature and forces of change, reasons for resistance and the effective implementation of change. Hotel managers need to adopt multiple strategies to help to overcome potential barriers to change and hotel firms should provide managerial staff with development to help them to cope with complex change situations.[53]

Successful implementation of change

Continual change is inevitable and the effective implementation of change is an increasingly important managerial responsibility. New ideas and innovations should not be perceived as threats by members of staff. One of the most important factors in the successful management of change is the style of managerial behaviour.

> *Never is leadership more sought after than in times of change and uncertainty. Effective change leadership is the key to shifting people's perceptions from seeing change as a threat to seeing it as an exciting challenge.*[54]

In certain situations it may be necessary for management to use compulsion and the hierarchical authority to impose change. This *may* be appropriate, for example, if change is clearly going to be detrimental to staff. It should also be recognised that some people may prefer, and respond better to, an autocratic, directed and controlled style of management. In most cases, however, the introduction of change is more likely to be effective with a participative style of management. If staff are kept fully informed of proposals, are encouraged to adopt a positive attitude and have personal involvement in the implementation of the change, there is a greater likelihood of their acceptance of the change.

Human and social factors of change

Managers must be responsive to change. But activities managed on the basis of technical or economic efficiency alone are unlikely to lead to optimum improvement in performance. The efforts made by management to maintain the balance of the socio-technical system will influence people's attitudes, the behaviour of individuals and groups, and thereby organisational performance and effectiveness. Management must therefore take proper account of the importance of human and social factors of change. This demands that management:

- create an environment of trust and shared commitment, and involve staff fully in decisions and actions which affect them;
- maintain full and open communications, and the genuine participation of all staff concerned, preferably well before the actual introduction of the change;
- emphasise benefits of, and potential opportunities presented by, the change;
- encourage team management and a cooperative spirit among staff;
- give attention to job design, methods of work organisation and the development of cohesive groups;
- provide suitable economic incentive schemes to safeguard potential loss of earnings or job security, and ensure an equitable allocation of any financial savings resulting from the change;

- design a personnel management action programme directed to a review of recruitment and selection, natural wastage of staff, training and re-training, provisions for early retirements, and other strategies to reduce the possible level of redundancies or other harmful effects on staff.[55]

Organisational conflict

Conflict is an inevitable feature of organisational life, and a reality of management and the behaviour of people at work. Within the hospitality industry conflict situations are a common occurrence and manifested largely at the individual, group or unit level rather than on a collective bargaining basis. Organisational conflict is a common theme in discussions on the general nature of working in the industry such as interdepartmental competition,[56] or organisation structure and operation of rules;[57] or related to specific features, for example high staff turnover.[58]

Common definitions of conflict are usually associated with negative features and situations which give rise to inefficiency. Conflict is the harmful side of differences within organisations.[59] The traditional view of conflict is that it is potentially dysfunctional and represents forms of deviant organisational behaviour which should be controlled and changed.

However, it is also arguable that, properly managed, conflict can, at least to a point, have potentially positive outcomes.[60] It can have an energising and vitalising effect within an organisation. Conflict may be seen as a 'constructive force' and in certain circumstances it can be welcomed or even encouraged.

But, clearly conflict situations can give rise to emotional and physical stress and in extreme cases can have very upsetting consequences for some people. Conflict can also have adverse effects on organisational performance and effectiveness. It is important therefore that management make every reasonable effort to avoid the harmful consequences of conflict. An important and central feature of attempts at the resolution of conflict include management strategies related to establishing and maintaining effective employee relations.[61] Improved training and development for empowerment and employee participation may be applied as a change strategy to help employees in the hospitality industry to deal effectively with conflict management and resolution.[62]

The radical (Marxist) approach

The radical approach, which is associated with the ideas of writers such as Karl Marx, challenges the traditional view of conflict. The radical approach views organisations in terms of the disparity in social power and control. Organisational conflict is a feature of the unequal nature of organisational life and is a means of bringing about change.[63] Collective bargaining was not seen as particularly helpful in a system stacked against the workers. Organisational conflict is a natural part of the class struggle between owners and controllers of economic resources and means of production and the workers and wage earners.

According to the radical approach, the design of organisation structure, management systems and the choice and use of technology all form part of the struggle for power and control within the work organisation. Greater attention should be given to relationships between the formal and informal aspects of the organisation and the study of conflict between the needs of the individual and those of the organisation, and between workers and management.

Contrasting perspectives of work organisations

An appreciation of the nature of conflict can help an understanding of social and organisational behaviour, the nature of employee relations and applications of human resource management. Differing views on the explanation and outcomes of conflict can be related to contrasting unitary or pluralistic perspectives of work organisations.

For example, it might be expected that a healthy climate would be reflected by complete harmony in working relationships, and loyalty and common commitment to the goals and objectives of the organisation. This view of work organisations as 'happy families' is a worthwhile and creditable ideal, and as such is implied by many leading management writers.[64] Such a view suggests a unitary perspective of the organisation.

The unitary perspective

With the unitary perspective, the organisation is viewed as a team with a common source of loyalty, one focus of effort and one common leader. There is an image of the organisation as an integrated whole, and with supportive and cooperative structures. Management and workers are viewed as sharing a common interest. Trade unions are seen as an unnecessary evil and restrictive practices are outmoded or caused by troublemakers.

The unitary perspective views authority as vested in management. Where conflict exists it represents a malfunction within the organisation and is attributed to poor communications, personality clashes or the work of agitators. Personnel policies and managerial development can be seen as reflecting a unitary ideology. Developments in human resource management can also arguably be seen as imposing new forms of control and a managerial approach to facilitating organisational goals and the involvement of employees which furthers a unitarist perspective.[65]

The pluralistic perspective

The pluralistic perspective presents an alternative view in which the organisation is viewed in terms of competing sub-groups with their own loyalties, goals and leaders.[66] These competing sub-groups are almost certain to come into conflict. From the pluralistic perspective, conflict is seen as an inherent and accepted feature of work organisations and induced in part by the very structure of the organisation. Conflict can be an agent for evolution, and internal and external change.

Restrictive practices may be seen as a rational response from a group which regards itself as being threatened. Conflict is generated through individuals and groups pursuing their own diverse goals. It is the job of the manager to bring about compromise, and to manage and accommodate the competing interests of different parties. Belief in the principles of a pluralistic perspective can therefore restrict the implementation of a unitary approach to employee relations.

Conclusion: Understanding the views of other people

An important underlying philosophy of this book has been that getting work done through the efforts of other people is an integral part of any effective managerial activity. While neither the unitary nor the pluralist perspective can be seen as 'right' or 'wrong', these contrasting views will influence the nature of employee relations and the management of human resources. The following observation from a Hotel and Catering Training Company publication serves as a salutary comment on which to conclude this book.

Whatever their judgement about these differing views, managers, staff and union representatives need to be aware, in order to operate effectively, that:

- people's actions are determined partly by their ideals and aspirations
- such ideals vary greatly
- we need to understand other people's views as well as our own in forming judgements and making decisions.[67]

Summary

- Organisational effectiveness is influenced by a multiplicity of variables. One particular feature of special importance for successful performance in the hospitality industry is concern for quality. This must be coupled with a required level of productivity. The adoption of a total quality management culture involves the convergence of quality assurance and human resource management. As part of a TQM approach a process of benchmarking may be adopted.

- The EFQM Excellence Model recognises that processes are the means by which a company or organisation harnesses and releases the talents of its people to produce results performance. Other major contemporary hospitality models include: Shaping Your Team for Success; Excellence Through People; and Hospitality Assured. It is important for the hospitality industry to give attention to the measurement of productivity, and to quality standards and business performance.

- Effective management is at the heart of organisation development and improved performance. Applications of human resources management are influenced by the nature of organisational culture and organisation climate. Culture is a major determinant of effective performance and helps to account for variations among organisations and managers both nationally and internationally. Managers have a responsibility for creating a climate in which people work willingly and effectively.

- A key feature in organisational behaviour is the successful management of change and interactions with the external environment. Change is a pervasive influence and an inescapable part of both social and organisational life. Managers need to give attention to the effective implementation of change including proper attention to human and social factors, and to overcoming the barriers and resistance to change.

- Conflict is a reality of management and organisational behaviour. It is a common theme at the individual, group and unit level within the hospitality industry. An explanation of the nature and outcome of conflict can be related to contrasting unitary and pluralistic perspectives of work organisations. However, whatever the judgements about these different perspectives we need to understand other people's views in forming judgements and making decisions.

Appendix 1: Shire Inns Limited Employee Hotel Experience Scheme

Policy

Shire Inns Limited operates a scheme to encourage employees of the company to experience the products and services of the group. We also expect employees to meet and talk with colleagues during their visit.

The purpose of the Scheme is for employees to gain an additional understanding of Guests' requirements by undertaking this customer experience whilst maintaining and improving teamwork and communications around the group.

Qualification

1. Permanent Employees will qualify for the Scheme after the completion of six months' service before the following dates:

    1st April

    1st July

    1st October

    1st January

    It is important to note that:
    Employees can only qualify if they have completed six months' service before these dates. Therefore, entry will only be available four times per year upon these dates.

2. The Assistant Manager responsible for Personnel & Training will issue a letter advising the Employee that they now qualify for this benefit together with a Booking Form.

Entitlement

1. Reservations are subject to availability and are at the absolute discretion of the Management of the Hotel receiving the booking.

2. Reservations may be made up to two weeks prior to the intended dates of the visit.

3. Under the terms of the scheme Employees may not stay at the Hotel at which they are employed. Employees are expected to experience the product of different Hotels.

4. Permanent Employees will be entitled to one × two-night visit per year, which may be taken at any time, subject to availability, with a minimum six-month gap between visits.

5. A visit is for two people (employee and partner, or, friend) for a two-night stay for which the company will pay the current Dinner, Bed and Breakfast (DBB) inclusive package.

6. Employees may be accompanied by their children who will be accommodated on the following terms:
    (a) Children under 16 years will be accommodated, free of charge, subject to availability. This will be offered on either a shared or separate room basis. Meals will be charged as taken.
    (b) Children under 5 years of age will receive a complimentary breakfast.

7. As the purpose of the Scheme is for employees to experience a sister hotel, arrangements should include provision to see the department in which the employee

normally works and to receive an insight into the operaiton of the department in the sister hotel.

Billing

1. Employees are responsible for the payment of all 'extra' accounts prior to departure, e.g.
   - Food charges above the inclusive dinner allowance
   - Children's meals
   - Beverage purchases
   - Leisure services
   - Telephone
   - Executive Room upgrades.

   Please note that:
   The Scheme is to the value of the DBB package. 'Extra' accounts are not subject to the 50% Employee Discount.
   These additional accounts must be paid at the time of departure to the full value.

2. A complete Bill must be raised and signed for by the Employee.

3. Room Sales must be allocated against **House Rooms**.

4. **Costs for Food**, i.e. Dinner and Breakfast Allowances should be clearly marked on the Allowance Sheet.

Administration

1. The General Manager of each hotel will take responsibility for the control of the Scheme.

2. The General Manager will ensure that there is a system in place to ensure that their Staff are aware of Employees taking their Hotel Experience break with them.

3. The Assistant Manager responsible for Personnel & Training will administer the Scheme by:
   (a) advising employees, by letter, of their qualification for the benefit;
   (b) making bookings;
   (c) issuing Staff Questionnaires;
   (d) keeping records, in Personnel Files, as required.

4. The Head of Department will liaise between the Employee requesting a booking, via a completed Booking Form, and the Personnel & Training Manager and vice versa.

   . . .

8. The Head of Department and Employee will meet-up prior to the Employee's visit to complete the pre-visit Questionnaire.

9. The Head of Department and the Employee will meet-up after the Employee's visit to complete the post-visit Review.

10. Management at the 'recipient' Hotel is responsible for making sure that the appropriate 'Colleague' or 'Deputy' is available to meet with the Hotel Experience Guest.

11. The Employee completes the Staff Questionnaire during/after their visit and forwards the completed document to the Human Resources Department at Head Office.

12. Human Resources Department collates the information and prepares a Report for feedback to General Managers.

13. From this Report General Managers are responsible for passing 'core value' information on to their Hotel Champion(s).

Cancellations/Withdrawals

1. If, once a booking has been made, an employee does not take-up their Reservation a member of the Hotel's Management Team will advise the Employee's General Manager who will make appropriate investigations.

2. Employees who fail to represent the company in a proper and professional manner will be excluded from the Scheme at the absolute discretion of the Hotel General Manager.

3. The Scheme is not transferable.

4. The company retains the absolute right to terminate the Scheme, without prior notice, at any time.

As such the Scheme does not form part of the Terms and Conditions of Employment.

CAD
September, 1999

Ref.: ....

Date: ....

Name: ....

Address: ....

Dear: ....

HOTEL EXPERIENCE SCHEME

Congratulations! I am pleased to inform you that as a result of your length of service, with us, you now qualify for a visit to one of our sister hotels under the terms of the above-mentioned Scheme.

Each of our Hotels has a unique style and character and as you will know, if you have already enjoyed a 'break' away with us, a high standard of service and facilities.

The aim of the Scheme is to enable employees to have an opportunity to experience our Hotels from a guest's point-of-view and to understand how our core values operate throughout the whole of the company. We believe that it is important that you experience the products of our company so that you can feel confident when talking to guests about the other Hotels in our group. Also, on your visit, you will be expected to meet and talk to colleagues who work in similar departments to your own to find out about their role and how they do things. This will contribute to teamwork and good communications around the group.

Attached to this letter is a copy of the booking form. Once you have completed this please hand it to your Head of Department who will make the booking on your behalf.

Prior to your visit you will be given a Staff Questionnaire which should be completed during your stay to accurately reflect the service and the quality of the environment you experienced during your visit.

I hope that you will use this opportunity to compare and contrast how a hotel works, especially from a guest's point-of-view and that you enjoy the experience of staying at a Shire Inn for a relaxing two-day break.

Yours sincerely,

(General Manager)
Encs.

Hotel Experience Scheme

BOOKING FORM

Name: ....

Hotel: .... Department: ....

Date of booking: ....

Hotel – at which booking is required: ....

Date of arrival: ....

Date of departure: ....

Number of nights: ....

Accommodation required: ....
(*delete as required*)   Single/Double/Twin/Family room
                                          Smoking/Non-smoking

Name(s) of People for whom Booking is Made
(Adults and Children/Ages)

....

....

....

....

Date on which Booking Confirmed: ....

By: .... (Hotel General Manager)

N.B.

- Reservations may be made up to two weeks prior to the intended dates of the visit.
- Reservations are subject to availability and are at the absolute discretion of the Management of the Hotel receiving the booking.
- Full paying business will always take priority.

Hotel Experience Scheme

STAFF QUESTIONNAIRE

This Scheme allows all employees to experience our Hotels from a guest's point-of-view. In addition it gives you the opportunity to understand how our core values operate throughout the whole of the company.

The main purpose of the Scheme is to let you experience another Hotel allowing you to:

(a) experience our 'products' in Hotels other than the one you currently work in;

(b) meet and talk to colleagues who work in similar departments to your own;

(c) help to give you an improved understanding of our guests' needs as a result of your visit;

(d) talk knowledgeably about our other Hotels to guests in your own hotel;

(e) understand how teamwork operates in different circumstances to benefit both customers and the business.

In order to help us consistently achieve the standards we should be pleased if you would complete and return this document to:

> Human Resources Department,
> Shire Inns Limited,
> Colne Road,
> Reedley,
> BURNLEY.

In order to gain maximum benefit from this Scheme this form can be used to play your visit and review what happened.

Hotel Experience Scheme

DETAILS OF THE VISIT

Hotel: ....

Date: ....

Type of accommodation: ....

Pre-visit meeting with Head of Department or Manager

Why have you chosen this hotel?   . . .

Briefing on hotel structure   . . .

Briefing on hotel operation   . . .

What would you like to see on your visit?   . . .

Who would you like to meet?   . . .

As you know our customers vlaue the difference we make and our attention to our core values helps us to continue to 'make a difference'.

Completing these few brief questions will help us to give feedback to our staff and to assess how well the facilities meet your needs.

Date of Stay: .... Room Number: ....

Was the service you received friendly?

Reception:	Exceptional...	Above Average...	Average...	Below Average...	Unsatisfactory...
Housekeeping:	Exceptional...	Above Average...	Average...	Below Average...	Unsatisfactory...
Restaurant:	Exceptional...	Above Average...	Average...	Below Average...	Unsatisfactory...
Bar/Lounge:	Exceptional...	Above Average...	Average...	Below Average...	Unsatisfactory...
Leisure Club:	Exceptional...	Above Average...	Average...	Below Average...	Unsatisfactory...

Was the service you received efficient?

Reception:	Exceptional...	Above Average...	Average...	Below Average...	Unsatisfactory...
Housekeeping:	Exceptional...	Above Average...	Average...	Below Average...	Unsatisfactory...
Restaurant:	Exceptional...	Above Average...	Average...	Below Average...	Unsatisfactory...
Bar/Lounge:	Exceptional...	Above Average...	Average...	Below Average...	Unsatisfactory...
Leisure Club:	Exceptional...	Above Average...	Average...	Below Average...	Unsatisfactory...

Overall, how would you rate your experience?

Exceptional . . .   Above   Average . . .   Below   Unsatisfactory . . .
                       Average . . .   Average . . .

Under each of the headings let us know of the evidence you found during your visit that support these core values. Please feel free to identify anyone in the Hotel that you visited who was outstanding in any of these areas:

- Passionate about the way they treated customers.

- Proud of their hotel and working hard to uphold our differentiation.

- Respect for each other and worked as a team upholding our family values.

● Approached everything that they did with their future success in mind.

● Had a desire to succeed as an individual.

. . . Making a difference by upholding these core values.

Post-visit Review with Head of Department or Manager.

ARE THERE ANY COMMENTS YOU WOULD LIKE TO MAKE TO HELP US ADD TO YOUR
SATISFACTION ON FUTURE VISITS?

> *Source*: The author is grateful to Chris Kelsall, Personnel & Training Manager, Solent Hotel, Hampshire
> and to Janet Richardson, Human Resources Director, Shire Inns for providing the above information.

Appendix 2: Marriott Hotels

'Britain's Favourite Hotel Company'

SERVICE QUALITY STRATEGY

Background

In August 1995 the Whitbread Hotel Company purchased Scotts Hotels, and simultaneously, acquired the master franchise for the Marriott brand in the UK. This followed a period
of time that had been focused on dramatically improving the service quality and financial
performance of the existing Whitbread Hotels portfolio.

The Marriott acquisition took the number of hotels in the UK to 36 and it was evident
they needed a clear vision to ensure the return on investment requirements were met for
Whitbread plc.

This led to the development of an alignment strategy which aimed to ensure all activities were aligned to the achievement of an overall vision.

This represented an evolution of the TQM strategy that had previously been followed
by Scotts Hotels who owned the hotels prior to the Whitbread Hotel Company.

The Whitbread Hotel Company created a new vision,

> 'By the year 2000 to have clear proof that Marriott Hotels are preferred, above all others,
> by Customers, Investors and Associates. To be Britain's Favourite Hotel Company'

Why change?

The investment made by Whitbread plc, the parent company, required new focus on making a return on the capital that had been employed and external benchmarks indicated
that competitors were outperforming the hotels in terms of profit per room. Whitbread plc
had a desire to ensure all their brands were distinctive in terms of customer service and
were first choice when people wanted to enjoy themselves.

This new vision led to the creation of four new strategies around:

1. Creating customer loyalty. **3.** Operational excellence.

2. Service quality. **4.** Team leadership.

Marriott have a deeply held philosophy that states, 'take care of your associates (employees) and they will take care of the guest'. In view of this the Whitbread Hotel Company
focused on a service quality strategy that would ensure their Marriott Hotels were first choice
for customers and associates.

How?

The Service Quality strategy embraced a number of different activities including the measurement of guest satisfaction but in particular it was aimed at educating associates at all levels about service quality and its practical application throughout the company. The approach used was as follows:

1. Participation by hotel senior management teams in a 5-day 'Service Leadership' programme.

2. Involvement of 3 members of the senior team, to include the General Manager, in a 3-day 'train the trainer' programme to deliver on-property service quality training to all associates.

3. Delivery of 16 hours of 'Spirit to Serve' training to all associates in 4 × 4 hours modules over a 4-month period.

The approach to this training and the implementation of all aspects of the Service Quality strategy was driven by a cross-functional team made up of General Managers and managers from the corporate office who made recommendations to the executive committee about how to deliver this strategy.

This approach was very different to previous attempts at improving service quality as a critical outcome of the programme was the creation of an individual service 'charter' for each hotel that the senior team had developed together and then communicated to all associates via the in-house training.

Where to now?

Three years on the approach has clearly been successful with relevant measures in the Guest Satisfaction Survey indicating associate service and performance has improved and guest loyalty has increased.

However, the overall business performance results had not improved across the board and it was clear the company now needed to help hotel teams take a more holistic view of their business and to manage it in a more autonomous way. As a result all hotel management teams are working with the European Foundation for Quality management (EFQM) Excellence Model to help provide them with a tool for self-assessment and prioritisation as a feed in to a robust, 3-year hotel business plan.

Source: The author is grateful to Jane Neil, Director of Training, Whitbread Hotel Company for providing the above information.

Review and discussion questions

1. Identify clearly examples of main factors which influence the performance and effectiveness of a hospitality organisation of your choice.

2. Critically review the role of top management in your own organisation and the extent to which attention is given to key features of effective human resource management.

3. Explain the key elements of Total Quality Management (TQM), and discuss critically its implementation and applications in the hospitality industry.

4. Give your views on the measurement of productivity in the hospitality industry, and the nature of service quality and business performance. ▷

5. Explain what is meant by organisational culture. How might corporate culture influence the effectiveness of hospitality operations?

6. What do you understand by organisational climate? Discuss with practical examples the main areas in which action could be taken to help improve organisational climate in the hospitality industry.

7. Why do people in organisations tend to resist change? As a manager, explain what actions you would take to help overcome the social and human problems associated with the introduction of technological change.

8. As a senior manager, explain fully the actions you would propose in order to increase the level of productivity in your organisation.

9. Discuss the extent to which you believe conflict is an inherent feature of work organisations. Explain your understanding of the radical approach to organisational conflict.

10. Contrast the unitary and pluralistic perspectives of organisations giving specific examples of their influence on employee relations and human resource management within the hospitality industry.

Assignment

You are the newly appointed human resources manager of a large hospitality organisation. The general manager asks you to address a group of sceptical line managers and supervisors on the practical value of organisational behaviour, and the study of human resource management. Outline clearly the content and manner of presentation of your address.

Case study: Shotley Bridge Hospital catering department

The catering department located at Shotley Bridge Hospital, a District General Hospital located at the edge of the Pennines, has probably much in common with many units around the country. In 1992, the department was closing poorly equipped and geographically remote outstations – a number on severe inclines around the site, reducing staff numbers, and reconfiguring services all whilst trying to maintain service standards.

Although service to patients and staff had never been too much of an issue, the stresses were beginning to show. At a staff meeting, called to examine five possibilities, it was obvious many perceived morale to be low and concerns about the future high.

It was also noted that whilst traditional indications of service efficiency and satisfaction were in place (such as waste, complaints, etc.), these would not be enough if the department was to progress.

The views of yet more future uncertainty were confirmed with the announcement of a merger with Dryburn Hospital some 22 miles away and the certainty of further downsizing. Many

Shotley Bridge Hospital catering department continued

managers and staff would at this point have given up and perhaps the team would have been forgiven for this. However, positive action was in the offing.

All catering staff and managers were called to a meeting where each was invited to comment on the situation and give views on the future. Remarkably, a vision was agreed to involve everyone and to go for quality and provide the finest service. The reasons for this were threefold:

- The remaining services could be consolidated and reconfigured effectively especially by involving staff.
- Training and development could be assessed by all to assist the transition and this meant transferable skills for the future.
- It was good CV material!

The workshop participants decided to pursue what was then BS5750 – not for its own sake but as a stepping stone to Charter Mark and, importantly, recognition by customers and staff that this was a high quality organisation. There were five main actions to achieve this:

1. Achieving BS5750 (ISO9000)
Shotley Bridge Hospital has one of the first NHS catering departments to gain accreditation. The review of the systems and processes led to a number of changes in practice, such as the setting up of personal development files for each member of staff and the collection and actioning of verbal complaints as well as written complaints. The structure of the management review mostly provides a vigorous examination of the processes followed by external audits.

The winning of 'hearts and minds' of the staff in obtaining accreditation was a crucial factor. Presentations were made to staff on the components of BS5750 and every member of staff was seen by the catering manager to explain how going for the award would affect their job and to discuss any concerns. As part of the process, asking the views of the customers of the service was considered paramount.

2. Asking for the views of the external customers
A patient forum was held late 1992, one of the first in the UK to gather the views and suggestions for improvements from patients who had recently spent time in the hospital. The forum proved a big success with over 25 patients turning up to frankly express their views. Facilitators were used from outside the department to facilitate and ask the questions on behalf of the catering staff. The evening finished with a buffet and feedback to the catering manager.

3. Asking for the views of internal customers
A forum was run on behalf of the department by members of the hospital quality department and a representative was invited from each of the wards; in the main they were ward managers. Despite the overwhelming praise for the service, a number of areas of concern were raised by them.

4. Data analysis
From both sets of customers a clear set of issues were raised to be actioned upon, including:

- improve communication between the catering department and the wards;
- improve the description of the food on the menu cards;
- improve the skills of the nursing team in serving food.

5. Asking the views of the catering staff

As part of the examination of quality in the department, two half-day sessions were arranged for all the staff from the departments to share their experiences and give suggestions for improving the service.

By now, the service was nationally recognised for its developments, but a number of proposals for action were implemented to further improve the service to the customer. These included:

- The introduction of a 'named chef' for each ward to improve communication with the department. On a regular basis the chef visits the ward to speak to patients and staff about issues concerning the meals. A photograph of the named chef has been included on the ward staff photograph board.
- Menu cards have been re-written with advice from patients, giving simple and easily understood descriptions of various dishes.
- A major training programme on food handling has been implemented for nursing staff and in NVQ training. This has led to improvements in the awareness and knowledge of staff.
- Clear information has been provided for staff and visitors on how to make a complaint about the service.
- The introduction of a children's menu for the wards, with pictures and diagrams, making it more readable for the target audience.
- Ongoing customer (internal and external) forum.

Conclusion

Customer- and staff-driven improvements were used as part of the Charter Mark application and tested out by the Charter Mark inspecting visit.

During this period, yet again changes in the service were taking place, with another of the hospital's kitchens closing and more staff being made redundant. Despite these changes, improvements in the service took place. As a result of improving the systems and processes, following close consultation with the users of the service and staff, importantly, staff morale still held so that service could continue to develop improvements.

The team has since gone on to play their part in a successful Investor in People award.

The message is clear, *involve staff and listen to your customers*!

Source: The author is grateful to Martin Howe, Nigel Grinstead and Anne Tofts of Healthskills for providing this case study.

TASK

(i) Discuss how the management team at Shotley Bridge Hospital used the quality programme to encourage staff to accept change.

(ii) Using Glover's ideas an organisational culture, discuss characteristics of the Shotley Bridge Hospital catering department that have contributed to a culture of effectiveness.

Notes and references

1. For a fuller discussion see, for example, Baguley P, *Improving Organizational Performance: A Handbook for Managers*, McGraw-Hill (1994).
2. Handy C B, *Understanding Organisations*, 4th edn, Penguin (1993).
3. Peters T J and Waterman R H, *In Search of Excellence*, Harper & Row (1982).
4. Heller R, *In Search of European Excellence*, HarperCollins Business (1997), p. xiv.

5. Pentecost D, 'Quality Management: The Human Factor', *European Participation Monitor*, no. 2, 1991, pp. 8–10.

6. James G, 'Quality of Working Life and Total Quality Management', ACAS, Occasional Paper, no. 50, November 1991.

7. See, for example, Lammermeyr H U, 'Human Relationships – The Key to Total Quality Management', *Total Quality Management*, vol. 12, no. 2, 1991, pp. 175–180.

8. For an account of the application of total quality management in Scott's Hotels Ltd, see Hubrecht J and Teare R, 'A Strategy for Partnership in Total Quality Service', *International Journal of Contemporary Hospitality Management*, vol. 5, no. 3, pp. i–v.

9. DNH, *Tourism: Competing with the Best: Benchmarking for Smaller Hotels*, Department of National Heritage, March 1996.

10. Partlow C G, 'Human Resources Practices of TQM Hotels', *Cornell HRA Quarterly*, October, 1996, pp. 67–77.

11. Baldacchino G, 'Total Quality Management in a Luxury Hotel: A Critique of Practice', *International Journal of Hospitality Management*, vol. 14, no. 1, 1995, pp. 67–78.

12. Macdonald J, 'Service is Different', *The TQM Magazine*, vol. 6, no. 1, 1994, pp. 5–7.

13. Bo, Xiangping, A Personal Report on *The Essence of Total Quality Management (TQM) – Its Application in the Hospitality Industry*, March 2000.

14. I am grateful to my colleague Martin Brunner, for his contribution of The Excellence Model.

15. Oakland J S, *Total Organizational Excellence: Achieving World Class Performance*, Butterworth-Heinemann (1999), p. 99.

16. *Winning Performance Through Business Excellence*, European Centre for Business Excellence (1999), p. 12.

17. *Meeting Competence Needs in the Hotel and Catering Industry: Now and in the Future*, HCTC Research Report, September 1992.

18. *Costs and Manpower Productivity in UK Hotels*, National Economic Development Council, 1992.

19. McLaughlin C P and Coffey S, 'Measuring Productivity in Services', *International Journal of Service Industry Management*, vol. 1, no. 1, 1990, pp. 46–64.

20. Lane P, Ingold T and Yeoman I, 'Productivity in Hotels', *Proceedings of CHME Research Conference*, Manchester Metropolitan University, April 1993.

21. *RAC Inspected Hotels: Great Britain & Ireland 2000*, West One Publishing Ltd (1999), p. 21.

22. Harrington D and Akehurst G, 'Service Quality and Business Performance in the UK Hotel Industry', *International Journal of Hospitality Management*, vol. 15, no. 3, 1996, pp. 283–298.

23. Harrington D and Akehurst G, 'An Exploratory Investigation into Managerial Perceptions of Service Quality in UK Hotels', *Progress in Tourism and Hospitality Research*, vol. 2, John Wiley & Sons (1996), pp. 135–150.

24. Harrington D and Akehurst G, 'An Empirical Study of Service Quality Implementation', *The Services Industries Journal*, vol. 20, no. 2, 2000.

25. Jamison C, 'Top 10 Myths of Customer Service', *Manager: The British Journal of Administrative Management*, July/August 1999, pp. 19–21.

26. For a detailed account of OD see for example: French W L and Bell C H, *Organization Development: Behavioral Science Interventions for Organization Improvement*, 6th edn, Prentice-Hall (1999).

27. See, for example, Mumford E, 'Helping Organizations Through Action Research: The Socio-technical Approach', *Quality of Work Life*, vol. 3, nos 5–6, September–December 1986, pp. 329–44.

28. Patching K, *Management and Organisation Development*, Macmillan (1999).

29. Merriden T, 'The Gurus: Rosabeth Moss Kanter', *Management Today*, February 1997, p. 56.

30. See, for example, Smircich L, 'Concepts of Culture and Organisational Analysis', *Administrative Science Quarterly*, vol. 28, 1963, pp. 339–358.

31. Mclean A and Marshall J, *Intervening in Cultures*, Working Paper, University of Bath (1983).

32. Schein E H, *Organizational Culture and Leadership: A Dynamic View*, Jossey-Bass (1985).

33. Woods R H, 'More Alike Than Different: The Culture of The Restaurant Industry', *Cornell HRA Quarterly*, vol. 30, no. 2, August 1989, pp. 82–97.

34. Hasell N, 'McDonald's Long March', *Management Today*, September 1994, p. 56.

35. Harrison R, 'Understanding Your Organization's Culture', *Harvard Business Review*, vol. 50, May/June 1972, pp. 119–128.

36. Handy C B, *Understanding Organizations*, 4th edn, Penguin (1993).

37. See, for example, Handy C B, *Understanding Organizations*, 4th edn, Penguin (1993); and Mclean A and Marshall J, *Cultures at Work*, Local Government Training Board (October 1988).

38. Gorman L, 'Corporate Culture – Why Managers Should Be Interested', *Leadership and Organization Development Journal*, vol. 8, no. 5, 1987, pp. 3–9.

39. Peters T J and Waterman R H, *In Search of Excellence*, Harper & Row (1982), pp. 75–76.

40. Heller R, *In Search of European Excellence*, HarperCollins Business (1997), p. 229.

41. Potter C C, 'What is Culture: And Can It Be Useful For Organisation Change Agents?', *Leadership and Organization Development Journal*, vol. 10, no. 3, 1989, pp. 17–24.

42. Siddall P, 'Working With Cultural Differences', *Chartered Secretary*, February 1998, p. 30.

43. Muraura G, Sutton J and Roberts D, 'Corparate and National Culture – An Irreconcilable Dilemma for the Hospitality Manager?', *International Journal of Contemporary Hospitality Management*, vol. 10, no. 6, 1998, pp. 212–220.

44. Glover W G, 'The Cult of Ineffectiveness', *Cornell HRA Quarterly*, February 1987, reprinted in Rutherford D G (ed.), *Hotel Management and Operations*, Van Nostrand Reinhold (1990), pp. 29–33.

45. Tagiuri R and Litwin G H (eds), *Organizational Climate*, Graduate School of Business Administration, Harvard University (1968).

46. Meudell K and Gadd K, 'Culture and Climate in Short Life Organizations: Sunny Spells or Thunderstorms?' *International Journal of Contemporary Hospitality Management*, vol. 6, no. 5, 1994, p. 28.

47. Jones P and Lockwood A, *The Management of Hotel Operations*, Cassell (1989), p. 59.

48. Mill R C, *Managing for Productivity in the Hospitality Industry*, Van Nostrand Reinhold (1989).

49. See, for example, Mullins L J, 'The Hotel and the Open Systems Model of Organisational Analysis', *The Service Industries Journal*, vol. 13, no. 1, 1993, pp. 1–16.

50. Hellriegel D, Slocum J W and Woodman R W, *Organizational Behavior*, 6th edn, West Publishing (1992).

51. Stewart R, *Managing Today and Tomorrow*, Macmillan (1991).

52. See for example: Dale B and Barlow E, 'Quality Circles: The View From Within', *Management Decision*, vol. 25, no. 4, 1987, pp. 5–9.

53. Okumus F and Hemmington N, 'Barriers and Resistance to Change in Hotel Firms: An Investigation at Unit Level', *International Journal of Contemporary Hospitality Management*, vol. 10, no. 7, 1998, pp. 283–288.

54. Hooper A and Potter J, 'Take it From the Top', *People Management*, 19 August 1999, p. 46.

55. For a more detailed account, see Mullins L J, 'Information Technology – The Human Factor', *Administrator*, vol. 5, no. 8, September 1985, pp. 6–9.

56. Wood R C, *Working in Hotels and Catering*, 2nd edn, International Thomson Business Press (1997).

57. Carmouche R and Kelly N, *Behavioural Studies in Hospitality Management*, Chapman & Hall (1995).

58. Riley M, *Human Resource Management in the Hospitality and Tourism Industry*, 2nd edn, Butterworth-Heinemann (1996).

59. Handy C B, *Understanding Organizations*, 4th edn, Penguin (1993).

60. See, for example, Townsend R, *Further Up the Organisation*, Coronet Books (1985).

61. See, for example, Lucas R E, *Managing Employee Relations in the Hotel and Catering Industry*, Cassell (1995).

62. Erstad M, 'Empowerment and Organizational Change', *International Journal of Contemporary Hospitality Management*, vol. 9, no. 7, 1997, pp. 325–333.

63. Salaman G, *Class and Corporation*, Fontana (1981).

64. For example, see Drucker P F, *The Practice of Management*, Pan Books (1968).

65. See, for example, Horwitz F M, 'HRM: An Ideological Perspective', *International Journal of Manpower*, vol. 12, no. 6, 1991, pp. 4–9.

66. Fox A, *Industrial Society and Industrial Relations*, HMSO (1966).

67. *Employee Relations for the Hotel and Catering Industry*, 7th edn, HCTC (1990), p. 21.

Chapter 8: Group behaviour and performance

Management teams: A self-perception inventory (Assignment 3)

Interpretation of total scores and further notes

The highest score on team role will indicate how best the respondent can make his or her mark in a management team. The next highest scores can denote back-up team roles towards which the individual should shift if for some reason there is less group need for a primary team role.

The two lowest scores on team role imply possible areas of weakness. But rather than attempting to reform in this area the manager may be better advised to seek a colleague with complementary strengths.

Self-perception inventory analysis sheet

Transpose the scores taken from Table 1 (page 303)*, entering them section by section in Table 2 below. Then add up the points in each column to give a total team role distribution score.

Table 2:
Self-perception inventory analysis sheet

Section	CW		CH		SH		PL		RI		ME		TW		CF	
I	g		d		f		c		a		h		b		e	
II	a		b		e		g		c		d		f		h	
III	h		a		c		d		f		g		e		b	
IV	d		h		b		e		g		c		a		f	
V	b		f		d		h		e		a		c		g	
VI	f		c		g		a		h		e		b		d	
VII	e		g		a		f		d		b		h		c	
TOTAL																

(Source: Belbin R M, *Management Teams: Why They Succeed or Fail*, Butterworth-Heinemann (1981), pp. 156–157.)

Now refer to the details in Figure 8.5 (page 288)*

Chapter 9: Managerial leadership

Leadership questionnaire (Assignment 3)

Interpretation: T-P leadership style profile sheet

To determine your style of leadership, mark your score on the *concern for task dimension* (T) on the left-hand arrow in Figure 9.11A.

Next, move to the right-hand arrow and mark your score on the *concern for people dimension* (P).

Draw a straight line that intersects the P and T scores. **The point at which that line crosses the shared leadership arrow indicates your score on that dimension.**

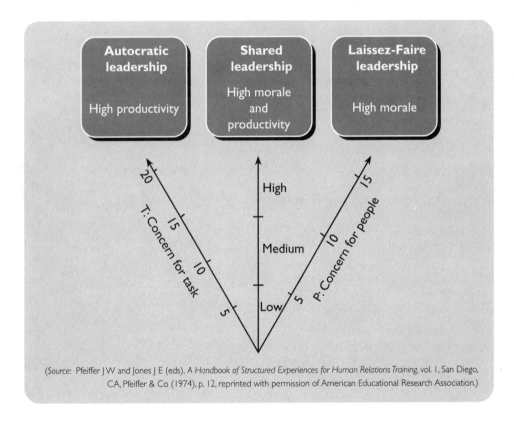

9.11A: Shared leadership results from balancing concern for task and concern for people

(*Source:* Pfeiffer J W and Jones J E (eds), *A Handbook of Structured Experiences for Human Relations Training*, vol. 1, San Diego, CA, Pfeiffer & Co (1974), p. 12, reprinted with permission of American Educational Research Association.)

Index